The Complete Mediterranean For Beginners 2021

1001 Mouth-Watering And Budget-Friendly Recipes Anyone Can Cook

Marta Woods

TABLE OF CONTENTS

INTRODUCTION

The Mediterranean diet is full of never-ending varieties of healthy, fresh, and delicious foods. However, there is more of an emphasis on certain types of foods, nothing is excluded. People who try a Mediterranean diet can relish the dishes they love while also indulging how good the tastiest, freshest foods can be.

The Mediterranean diet pattern, you will come closer to nature as the entire food concept depends on fresh produce. Mealtime, in these lands, is nothing short of a celebration. People, living in these parts have a tradition of eating together. It is time to nurture interpersonal relations as well.

It is the right time to get into the stride and do something that will not only improve your current state but will also gift you a healthy future. After all, there is no more significant wealth than the health of an individual.

Remember, it is safe to presume that the Mediterranean diet will help enhance a person's immune system. A person with a robust immune system will be capable to fight diseases easily. Therefore, your desire of leading a fulfilling, healthy and constructive life will be attained successfully.

The goal was to provide a thorough look at this diet and all the advantages and disadvantages it can bring to your life. As always, when making dietary changes you should consult your physician first to ensure this is a healthy change for you to achieve your goals in regard to your individual health. With the Mediterranean diet, much research has proven it is the most efficient method to lose weight and improve your overall health.

With this book, wanted to provide a detailed look at the Mediterranean lifestyle and exactly what it entails. The more informed you are about this diet and exactly what you should and should not be eating, the greater your chances of success will be!

People love incorporating a Mediterranean diet lifestyle because of how user-friendly it is! There are no counting calories, decreasing your portion sizes, or counting your intake of macronutrients diligently all day. It's about learning what the diet entails and making those choices to fill your pantry and fridge with fresh, healthy ingredients that will promote better health. You will be cutting out the unhealthy things like processed foods, artificial sugars, refined grains, and soda from your diet which is known to cause blood sugar spikes and excess weight gains. Instead, you'll be shopping for ingredients rich in vitamins, minerals, good fats, and antioxidants that will improve your health! With a menu allowing whole grains, fish, seafood, fruit, vegetables, and even a glass of wine a day, the Mediterranean diet allows for such variety that you can't get sick of it!

As long as you do this and stick to the simple rules of a Mediterranean diet, you can attain all the benefits it offers. One of the major benefits of this diet is that it is perfectly sustainable in the long run, not to mention, it is mouth-watering and delicious.

Once you start implementing the various protocols of this diet, you will see a positive change in your overall health. Ensure that you are being patient with yourself and stick to your diet without making any excuses.

Transitioning into the Mediterranean diet is mainly about bracing yourself for a new way of eating, adapting your attitude toward food into one of joyful expectation and appreciation of good meals and good company. It's like a mindset as anything else, so you'll want to make your environment unite so you can quickly adapt to the lifestyle in the Mediterranean way.

BREAKFAST RECIPES

1. Avocado Egg Scramble

Preparation Time: 8 minutes
Cooking Time: 15 minutes
Servings: 4

Ingredients
- 4 eggs, beaten
- 1 white onion, diced
- 1 tablespoon avocado oil
- 1 avocado, finely chopped
- ½ teaspoon chili flakes
- 1 oz Cheddar cheese, shredded
- ½ teaspoon salt
- 1 tablespoon fresh parsley

Directions:
1. Pour avocado oil in the skillet and bring it to boil.
2. Then add diced onion and roast it until it is light brown.
3. Meanwhile, mix up together chili flakes, beaten eggs, and salt.
4. Pour the egg mixture over the cooked onion and cook the mixture for 1 minute over the medium heat.
5. After this, scramble the eggs well with the help of the fork or spatula. Cook the eggs until they are solid but soft.
6. After this, add chopped avocado and shredded cheese.
7. Stir the scramble well and transfer in the serving plates.
8. Sprinkle the meal with fresh parsley.

Nutrition: 236 Calories 20g Fat 8.6g Protein

2. Breakfast Tostadas

Preparation Time: 15 minutes
Cooking Time: 6 minutes
Servings: 6

Ingredients
- ½ white onion, diced
- 1 tomato, chopped
- 1 cucumber, chopped
- 1 tablespoon fresh cilantro, chopped
- ½ jalapeno pepper, chopped
- 1 tablespoon lime juice
- 6 corn tortillas
- 1 tablespoon canola oil
- 2 oz Cheddar cheese, shredded
- ½ cup white beans, canned, drained
- 6 eggs
- ½ teaspoon butter
- ½ teaspoon Sea salt

Directions
1. Make Pico de Galo: in the salad bowl combine together diced white onion, tomato, cucumber, fresh cilantro, and jalapeno pepper.
2. Then add lime juice and a ½ tablespoon of canola oil. Mix up the mixture well. Pico de Galo is cooked.
3. After this, preheat the oven to 390F.
4. Line the tray with baking paper.
5. Arrange the corn tortillas on the baking paper and brush with remaining canola oil from both sides.
6. Bake for 10 minutes.
7. Chill the cooked crunchy tortillas well.
8. Meanwhile, toss the butter in the skillet.
9. Crack the eggs in the melted butter and sprinkle them with sea salt.
10. Fry the eggs for 3-5 minutes over the medium heat.
11. After this, mash the beans until you get puree texture.
12. Spread the bean puree on the corn tortillas.
13. Add fried eggs.
14. Then top the eggs with Pico de Galo and shredded Cheddar cheese.

Nutrition: 246 Calories 11g fat 14g protein

3. Parmesan Omelet

Preparation Time: 5 minutes
Cooking Time: 10 minutes
Servings: 2

Ingredients
- 1 tablespoon cream cheese
- 2 eggs, beaten
- ¼ teaspoon paprika
- ½ teaspoon dried oregano
- ¼ teaspoon dried dill
- 1 oz Parmesan, grated
- 1 teaspoon coconut oil

Directions
1. Mix up together cream cheese with eggs, dried oregano, and dill.
2. Preheat coconut oil in the skillet.
3. Place egg mixture in the skillet and flatten it.
4. Add grated Parmesan and close the lid.
5. Cook omelet for 10 minutes over the low heat.
6. Then transfer the cooked omelet in the serving plate and sprinkle with paprika.

Nutrition: 148 Calories 12g fat 11g protein

4. Menemen

Preparation Time: 6 minutes
Cooking Time: 15 minutes
Servings: 4

Ingredients

- 2 tomatoes, chopped
- 2 eggs, beaten
- 1 bell pepper, chopped
- 1 teaspoon tomato paste
- ¼ cup of water
- 1 teaspoon butter
- ½ white onion, diced
- ½ teaspoon chili flakes
- 1/3 teaspoon sea salt

Directions

1. Melt butter in the pan.
2. Add bell pepper and cook it for 3 minutes over the medium heat. Stir it from time to time.
3. After this, add diced onion and cook it for 2 minutes more.
4. Stir the vegetables and add tomatoes.
5. Cook them for 5 minutes over the medium-low heat.
6. Then add water and tomato paste. Stir well.
7. Add beaten eggs, chili flakes, and sea salt.
8. Stir well and cook Menemen for 4 minutes over the medium-low heat.
9. The cooked meal should be half runny.

Nutrition: 67 Calories 3.4g fat 3.8g protein

5. Watermelon Pizza

Preparation Time: 10 minutes
Cooking Time: 0 minute
Servings: 3
Ingredients

- 9 oz watermelon slice
- 1 tablespoon Pomegranate sauce
- 2 oz Feta cheese, crumbled
- 1 tablespoon fresh cilantro, chopped

Directions

1. Place the watermelon slice in the plate and sprinkle with crumbled Feta cheese.
2. Add fresh cilantro.
3. After this, sprinkle the pizza with Pomegranate juice generously.
4. Cut the pizza into the servings.

Nutrition: 143 Calories 6.2g fat 5.1g protein

6. Ham Muffins

Preparation Time: 10 Minutes
Cooking Time: 15 minutes
Servings: 4
Ingredients

- 3 oz ham, chopped
- 4 eggs, beaten
- 2 tablespoons coconut flour
- ½ teaspoon dried oregano
- ¼ teaspoon dried cilantro

Directions

1. Spray the muffin's molds with cooking spray from inside.
2. In the bowl mix up together beaten eggs, coconut flour, dried oregano, cilantro, and ham.
3. When the liquid is homogenous, pour it in the prepared muffin molds.
4. Bake the muffins for 15 minutes at 360F.
5. Chill the cooked meal well and only after this remove from the molds.

Nutrition: 128 Calories 7.2g fat 10g protein

7. Morning Pizza with Sprouts

Preparation Time: 15 minutes
Cooking Time: 20 minutes
Servings: 6
Ingredients

- ½ cup wheat flour, whole grain
- 2 tablespoons butter, softened
- ¼ teaspoon baking powder
- ¾ teaspoon salt
- 5 oz chicken fillet, boiled
- 2 oz Cheddar cheese, shredded
- 1 teaspoon tomato sauce
- 1 oz bean sprouts

Directions

1. Make the pizza crust: mix up together wheat flour, butter, baking powder, and salt. Knead the soft and non-sticky dough. Add more wheat flour if needed.
2. Leave the dough for 10 minutes to chill.
3. Then place the dough on the baking paper. Cover it with the second baking paper sheet.
4. Roll up the dough with the help of the rolling pin to get the round pizza crust.
5. After this, remove the upper baking paper sheet.
6. Transfer the pizza crust in the tray.
7. Spread the crust with tomato sauce.
8. Then shred the chicken fillet and arrange it over the pizza crust.
9. Add shredded Cheddar cheese.
10. Bake pizza for 20 minutes at 355F.
11. Then top the cooked pizza with bean sprouts.

Nutrition: 157 Calories 8.8g fat 10.5g protein

8. Banana Quinoa

Preparation Time: 10 minutes
Cooking Time: 12 minutes
Servings: 4
Ingredients

- 1 cup quinoa
- 2 cup milk
- 1 teaspoon vanilla extract
- 1 teaspoon honey
- 2 bananas, sliced
- ¼ teaspoon ground cinnamon

Directions

1. Pour milk in the saucepan and add quinoa.

2. Close the lid and cook it over the medium heat for 12 minutes or until quinoa will absorb all liquid.
3. Then chill the quinoa for 10-15 minutes and place in the serving mason jars.
4. Add honey, vanilla extract, and ground cinnamon.
5. Stir well.
6. Top quinoa with banana and stirs it before serving.

Nutrition: 279 Calories 5.3g fat 10.7g protein

9. Avocado Milk Shake

Preparation Time: 10 minutes
Cooking Time: 0 minute
Servings: 2
Ingredients
- 1 avocado, peeled, pitted
- 2 tablespoons of liquid honey
- ½ teaspoon vanilla extract
- ½ cup heavy cream
- 1 cup milk
- 1/3 cup ice cubes

Directions
1. Chop the avocado and put in the food processor.
2. Add liquid honey, vanilla extract, heavy cream, milk, and ice cubes.
3. Blend the mixture until it smooth.
4. Pour the cooked milkshake in the serving glasses.

Nutrition: 291 Calories 22g fat 4.4g protein

10. Egg Casserole with Paprika

Preparation Time: 10 minutes
Cooking Time: 28 minutes
Servings: 4
Ingredients
- 2 eggs, beaten
- 1 red bell pepper, chopped
- 1 chili pepper, chopped
- ½ red onion, diced
- 1 teaspoon canola oil
- ½ teaspoon salt
- 1 teaspoon paprika
- 1 tablespoon fresh cilantro, chopped
- 1 garlic clove, diced
- 1 teaspoon butter, softened
- ¼ teaspoon chili flakes

Directions
1. Brush the casserole mold with canola oil and pour beaten eggs inside.
2. After this, toss the butter in the skillet and melt it over the medium heat.
3. Add chili pepper and red bell pepper.
4. After this, add red onion and cook the vegetables for 7-8 minutes over the medium heat. Stir them from time to time.
5. Transfer the vegetables in the casserole mold.

6. Add salt, paprika, cilantro, diced garlic, and chili flakes. Stir mildly with spatula to get a homogenous mixture.
7. Bake the casserole for 20 minutes at 355F in the oven.
8. Then chill the meal well and cut into servings. Transfer the casserole in the serving plates with the help of the spatula.

Nutrition: 68 Calories 4.5g fat 3.4g protein

11. Cauliflower Fritters

Preparation Time: 10 minutes
Cooking Time: 10 minutes
Servings: 4
Ingredients
- 1 cup cauliflower, shredded
- 1 egg, beaten
- 1 tablespoon wheat flour, whole grain
- 1 oz Parmesan, grated
- ½ teaspoon ground black pepper
- 1 tablespoon canola oil

Directions
1. In the mixing bowl mix up together shredded cauliflower and egg.
2. Add wheat flour, grated Parmesan, and ground black pepper.
3. Stir the mixture with the help of the fork until it is homogenous and smooth.
4. Pour canola oil in the skillet and bring it to boil.
5. Make the fritters from the cauliflower mixture with the help of the fingertips or use spoon and transfer in the hot oil.
6. Roast the fritters for 4 minutes from each side over the medium-low heat.

Nutrition: 167 Calories 12.3g fat 8.8g protein

12. Creamy Oatmeal with Figs

Preparation Time: 10 minutes
Cooking Time: 20 minutes
Servings: 5
Ingredients
- 2 cups oatmeal
- 1 ½ cup milk
- 1 tablespoon butter
- 3 figs, chopped
- 1 tablespoon honey

Directions
1. Pour milk in the saucepan.
2. Add oatmeal and close the lid.
3. Cook the oatmeal for 15 minutes over the medium-low heat.
4. Then add chopped figs and honey.
5. Add butter and mix up the oatmeal well.
6. Cook it for 5 minutes more.
7. Close the lid and let the cooked breakfast rest for 10 minutes before serving.

Nutrition: 222 Calories 6g fat 7.1g protein

13. Baked Oatmeal with Cinnamon

Preparation Time: 10 minutes
Cooking Time: 25 minutes
Servings: 4
Ingredients
- 1 cup oatmeal
- 1/3 cup milk
- 1 pear, chopped
- 1 teaspoon vanilla extract
- 1 tablespoon Splenda
- 1 teaspoon butter
- ½ teaspoon ground cinnamon
- 1 egg, beaten

Directions
1. In the big bowl mix up together oatmeal, milk, egg, vanilla extract, Splenda, and ground cinnamon.
2. Melt butter and add it in the oatmeal mixture.
3. Then add chopped pear and stir it well.
4. Transfer the oatmeal mixture in the casserole mold and flatten gently. Cover it with the foil and secure edges.
5. Bake the oatmeal for 25 minutes at 350F.

Nutrition: 151 Calories 3.9g fat 4.9g protein

14. Almond Chia Porridge

Preparation Time: 10 minutes
Cooking Time: 30 minutes
Servings: 4
Ingredients
- 3 cups organic almond milk
- 1/3 cup chia seeds, dried
- 1 teaspoon vanilla extract
- 1 tablespoon honey
- ¼ teaspoon ground cardamom

Directions
1. Pour almond milk in the saucepan and bring it to boil.
2. Then chill the almond milk to the room temperature (or appx. For 10-15 minutes).
3. Add vanilla extract, honey, and ground cardamom. Stir well.
4. After this, add chia seeds and stir again.
5. Close the lid and let chia seeds soak the liquid for 20-25 minutes.
6. Transfer the cooked porridge into the serving ramekins.

Nutrition: 150 Calories 7.3g fat3.7g protein

15. Cocoa Oatmeal

Preparation Time: 10 minutes
Cooking Time: 15 minutes

Servings: 2
Ingredients
- 1 ½ cup oatmeal
- 1 tablespoon cocoa powder
- ½ cup heavy cream
- ¼ cup of water
- 1 teaspoon vanilla extract
- 1 tablespoon butter
- 2 tablespoons Splenda

Directions
1. Mix up together oatmeal with cocoa powder and Splenda.
2. Transfer the mixture in the saucepan.
3. Add vanilla extract, water, and heavy cream. Stir it gently with the help of the spatula.
4. Close the lid and cook it for 10-15 minutes over the medium-low heat.
5. Remove the cooked cocoa oatmeal from the heat and add butter. Stir it well.

Nutrition: 230 Calories 10.6g fat 4.6g protein

16. Berry Breakfast Smoothie

Preparation Time: 3 minutes
Cooking Time: 0 minute
Serving: 1
Ingredients:
- 1/2 cup vanilla low-fat Greek yogurt
- 1/4 cup low-fat milk
- 1/2 cup blueberries or strawberries
- 6 to 8 ice cubes

Direction:
1. Place the Greek yogurt, milk, and berries in a blender and blend until the berries are liquefied. Mix in ice cubes and blend on high. Serve immediately.

Nutrition: 98 calories10g fats7g protein

17. Mediterranean Omelet

Preparation Time: 7 minutes
Cooking Time: 12 minutes
Serving: 2
Ingredients:
- 2 teaspoons extra-virgin olive oil
- 1 garlic clove
- 1/2 red bell pepper
- 1/2 yellow bell pepper
- 1/4 cup thinly sliced red onion
- 2 tablespoons chopped fresh basil
- 2 tablespoons chopped fresh parsley
- 1/2 teaspoon salt
- 1/2 teaspoon black pepper
- 4 large eggs, beaten

Direction:
1. In a big, heavy skillet, cook 1 teaspoon of the olive oil over medium heat. Add the garlic, peppers, and

onion to the pan and sauté, stirring frequently, for 5 minutes.

2. Add the basil, parsley, salt, and pepper, increase the heat to medium-high, and sauté for 2 minutes. Slide the vegetable mixture onto a plate and return the pan to the heat.
3. Heat the remaining 1 teaspoon olive oil in the same pan and pour in the beaten eggs, tilting the pan to coat evenly. Cook the eggs just until the edges are bubbly and all but the center is dry, 3 to 5 minutes.
4. Either flip the omelet or use a spatula to turn it over.
5. Spoon the vegetable mixture onto one-half of the omelet and use a spatula to fold the empty side over the top. Slide the omelet onto a platter or cutting board.
6. To serve, cut the omelet in half and garnish with fresh parsley.

Nutrition: 197 calories 18g fats 6g protein

18.   Hearty Berry Breakfast Oats

Preparation Time: 11 minutes
Cooking Time: 2 minutes
Serving: 2
Ingredients:
- 11/2 cups whole-grain rolled oats
- 3/4 cup fresh blueberries, raspberries, or blackberries, or a combination
- 2 teaspoons honey
- 2 tablespoons walnut pieces

Direction
1. Prepare the whole-grain oats according to the package directions and divide between 2 deep bowls.
2. In a small microwave-safe bowl, heat the berries and honey for 30 seconds. Top each bowl of oatmeal with the fruit mixture. Sprinkle the walnuts over the fruit and serve hot.

Nutrition: 204 calories 17g fat 4g protein

19.   Garden Scramble

Preparation Time: 9 minutes
Cooking Time: 13 minutes
Serving: 4
Ingredients:
- 1 teaspoon extra-virgin olive oil
- 1/2 cup diced yellow squash
- 1/2 cup diced green bell pepper
- 1/4 cup diced sweet white onion
- 6 cherry tomatoes, halved
- 1 tablespoon chopped fresh basil
- 1 tablespoon chopped fresh parsley
- 1/2 teaspoon salt
- 1/4 teaspoon freshly ground black pepper
- 8 large eggs, beaten

Direction

1. In a large nonstick skillet, cook olive oil over medium heat. Add the squash, pepper, and onion and sauté for 4 minutes.
2. Add the tomatoes, basil, and parsley and season. Sauté for 1 minute, then pour the beaten eggs over the vegetables. Close and reduce the heat to low.
3. Cook for 6 minutes, making sure that the center is no longer runny.
4. To serve, slide the frittata onto a platter and cut into wedges.

Nutrition: 211 calories 17g fats 5g protein

20.   Summer Day Fruit Salad

Preparation Time: 16 minutes
Cooking Time: 0 minute
Serving: 8
Ingredients
- 2 cups cubed honeydew melon
- 2 cups cubed cantaloupe
- 2 cups red seedless grapes
- 1 cup sliced fresh strawberries
- 1 cup fresh blueberries
- Zest and juice of 1 large lime
- 1/2 cup unsweetened toasted coconut flakes
- 1/4 cup honey
- 1/4 teaspoon salt
- 1/2 cup extra-virgin olive oil

Direction:
1. Combine all of the fruits, the lime zest, and the coconut flakes in a large bowl and stir well to blend. Set aside.
2. In a blender, mix lime juice, honey, and salt and blend on low. Once the honey is incorporated, slowly add the olive oil and blend until opaque.
3. Drizzle dressing over the fruit and mix well. Wrap and chill for 4 hours before serving.

Nutrition: 196 calories 16g fats 3g protein

21.   Egg, Pancetta, and Spinach Benedict

Preparation Time: 16 minutes
Cooking Time: 24 minutes
Serving: 2
Ingredients:
- 1/4 cup diced pancetta
- 2 cups baby spinach leaves
- 1/4 teaspoon freshly ground black pepper
- 1/4 teaspoon salt, or to taste
- 2 large eggs
- Extra-virgin olive oil (optional)
- 1 whole-grain English muffin, toasted

Direction
1. In a medium, heavy skillet, brown the pancetta over medium-low heat for about 5 minutes, stirring frequently, until crisp on all sides.

2. Stir in the spinach, pepper, and salt if desired (it may not need any, depending on how salty the pancetta is). Cook, stirring occasionally, for 5 minutes. Transfer the mixture to a medium bowl.
3. Crack the eggs into the same pan (add olive oil if the pan looks dry), and cook until the whites are just opaque, 3 to 4 minutes. Carefully flip the eggs and continue cooking for 30 seconds to 1 minute until done to your preferred degree for over-easy eggs.
4. Situate muffin half on each of 2 plates and top each with half of the spinach mixture and 1 egg, yolk side up. Pierce the yolks just before serving.

Nutrition: 391 calories 21g fats 15g protein

22. **Peach Sunrise Smoothie**

Preparation time: 6 minutes
Cooking Time: 0 minute
Serving: 2
Ingredients:
- 1 large unpeeled peach, pitted and sliced (about 1/2 cup)
- 6 ounces vanilla or peach low-fat Greek yogurt
- 2 tablespoons low-fat milk
- 6 to 8 ice cubes

Direction:
1. Incorporate all ingredients in a blender and blend until thick and creamy. Serve immediately.

Nutrition: 98 calories 16g fats 3g protein

23. **Oat and Fruit Parfait**

Preparation Time: 11 minutes
Cooking Time: 0 minute
Serving: 2
Ingredients:
- 1/2 cup whole-grain rolled oats
- 1/2 cup walnut pieces
- 1 teaspoon honey
- 1 cup sliced fresh strawberries
- 11/2 cups (12 ounces) vanilla low-fat Greek yogurt
- Fresh mint leaves for garnish

Direction:
1. Preheat the oven to 300°F.
2. Spread the oats and walnuts in a single layer on a baking sheet.
3. Toast the oats and nuts just until you begin to smell the nuts, 10 to 12 minutes. Pull out the pan from the oven and set aside.
4. In a small microwave-safe bowl, heat the honey just until warm, about 30 seconds. Add the strawberries and stir to coat.
5. Place 1 tablespoon of the strawberries in the bottom of each of 2 dessert dishes or 8-ounce glasses. Add a portion of yogurt and then a portion

of oats and repeat the layers until the containers are full, ending with the berries. Serve.

Nutrition: 108 calories 10g fats 3g protein

24. **Savory Avocado Spread**

Preparation Time: 17 minutes
Cooking Time: 0 minute
Serving: 4
Ingredient:
- 1 ripe avocado
- 1 teaspoon lemon juice
- 6 boneless sardine filets
- 1/4 cup diced sweet white onion
- 1 stalk celery, diced
- 1/2 teaspoon salt
- 1/4 teaspoon black pepper

Direction
1. In a blender, pulse avocado, lemon juice, and sardine filets
2. Ladle the mixture into a small bowl and stir in the onion, celery, salt, and pepper. Mix well with a fork and serve as desired.

Nutrition: 109 calories 15g fats 6g protein

25. **Cheesy Stuffed Tomatoes**

Preparation Time: 6 minutes
Cooking Time: 22 minutes
Serving: 2
Ingredients:
- 4 large, ripe tomatoes
- 1 tablespoon extra-virgin olive oil
- 2 garlic cloves, minced
- 1/2 cup diced yellow onion
- 1/2-pound cremini mushrooms
- 1 tablespoon chopped fresh basil
- 1 tablespoon chopped fresh oregano
- 1/2 teaspoon salt
- 1/4 teaspoon freshly ground black pepper
- 1 cup shredded part-skim mozzarella cheese
- 1 tablespoon grated Parmesan cheese

Direction
1. Preheat the oven to 375°F. Line a baking sheet with aluminum foil.
2. Cut sliver from the bottom of each tomato so they will stand upright without wobbling. Cut a 1/2-inch slice from the top of each tomato and use a spoon to gently remove most of the pulp, placing it in a medium bowl. Place the tomatoes on the baking sheet.
3. In a skillet, cook olive oil over medium heat. Sauté the garlic, onion, mushrooms, basil, and oregano for 5 minutes, and season with salt and pepper.
4. Transfer the mixture to the bowl and blend well with the tomato pulp. Stir in the mozzarella cheese.

5. Fill each tomato loosely with the mixture, top with Parmesan cheese, and bake until the cheese is bubbly, 15 to 20 minutes. Serve immediately.

Nutrition: 201 calories 19g fats 6g protein

26. Fresh Tomato Pasta Bowl

Preparation Time: 7 minutes
Cooking Time: 26 minutes
Serving: 4

Ingredients:
- 8 ounces whole-grain linguine
- 1 tablespoon extra-virgin olive oil
- 2 garlic cloves, minced
- 1/4 cup chopped yellow onion
- 1 teaspoon chopped fresh oregano
- 1/2 teaspoon salt
- 1/4 teaspoon freshly ground black pepper
- 1 teaspoon tomato paste
- 8 ounces cherry tomatoes, halved
- 1/2 cup grated Parmesan cheese
- 1 tablespoon chopped fresh parsley

Direction
1. Boil water at high heat and cook the linguine according to the package instructions until al dente. Set aside half cup of the pasta water. Do not rinse the pasta.
2. In a large, heavy skillet, heat the olive oil over medium-high heat. Sauté the garlic, onion, and oregano for 5 minutes.
3. Add the salt, pepper, tomato paste, and 1/4 cup of the reserved pasta water. Stir well and cook for 1 minute.
4. Stir in the tomatoes and cooked pasta, tossing everything well to coat. Add more pasta water if needed.
5. To serve, top with Parmesan cheese and parsley.

Nutrition: 391 calories 28g fats 9g protein

27. Garlicky Broiled Sardines

Preparation Time: 6 minutes
Cooking Time: 31 minutes
Serving: 4

Ingredients:
- 4 (3.25-ounce) cans sardines packed in water or olive oil
- 2 tablespoons extra-virgin olive oil
- 4 garlic cloves, minced
- 1/2 teaspoon red pepper flakes
- 1/2 teaspoon salt
- 1/4 teaspoon black pepper

Direction:
1. Preheat the broiler. Line a baking dish with aluminum foil. Lay sardines in a single layer on the foil.

2. Combine the olive oil (if using), garlic, and red pepper flakes in a small bowl and spoon over each sardine. Season with salt and pepper.
3. Broil just until sizzling, 2 to 3 minutes.
4. To serve, place 4 sardines on each plate and top with any remaining garlic mixture that has collected in the baking dish.

Nutrition: 308 calories 17g fats 9g protein

28. Heart-Healthful Trail Mix

Preparation Time: 8 minutes
Cooking Time: 32 minutes
Serving: 12

Ingredients:
- 1 cup raw almonds
- 1 cup walnut halves
- 1 cup pumpkin seeds
- 1 cup dried apricots, cut into thin strips
- 1 cup dried cherries, roughly chopped
- 1 cup golden raisins
- 2 tablespoons extra-virgin olive oil
- 1 teaspoon salt

Direction
1. Preheat the oven to 300°F. Line a baking sheet with aluminum foil.
2. In a large bowl, mix almonds, walnuts, pumpkin seeds, apricots, cherries, and raisins. Pour the olive oil over all and toss well with clean hands. Add salt and toss again to distribute.
3. Fill in the nut mixture onto the baking sheet in a single layer and bake until the fruits begin to brown, about 30 minutes. Chill on the baking sheet to room temperature.
4. Store in a large airtight container or zipper-top plastic bag.

Nutrition: 109 calories 7g fats 1g protein

29. Citrus-Kissed Melon

Preparation Time: 11 minutes
Cooking Time: 0 minute
Serving: 4

Ingredients:
- 2 cups cubed melon
- 2 cups cubed cantaloupe
- 1/2 cup freshly squeezed orange juice
- 1/4 cup freshly squeezed lime juice
- 1 tablespoon orange zest

Direction
1. In a large bowl, incorporate melon cubes. In a bowl, blend the orange juice, lime juice, and orange zest and pour over the fruit.
2. Cover and cool for 4 hours, stirring occasionally. Serve chilled.

Nutrition: 101 calories 11g fats 2g protein

30. Café Cooler

Preparation Time: 16 minutes
Cooking time: 0 minute
Serving: 4
Ingredients:
- Ice cubes
- 2 cups low-fat milk
- 1/2 teaspoon ground cinnamon
- 1/2 teaspoon pure vanilla extract
- 1 cup espresso, cooled to room temperature
- 4 teaspoons sugar (optional)

Direction
1. Fill four tall glasses with ice cubes.
2. In a blender, combine the milk, cinnamon, and vanilla and blend until frothy.
3. Pour the milk over the ice cubes and top each drink with one-quarter of the espresso. If using sugar, stir it into the espresso until it has dissolved. Serve immediately, with chilled teaspoons for stirring.

Nutrition: 93 calories 7g fats 1g protein

31. Spring Caponata with Olives and Pomegranate

Preparation Time: 7 minutes
Cooking Time: 21 minutes
Serving: 4
Ingredients
- 3 ½ oz almonds
- 10 ½ oz olives
- 2oz celery stalk
- 100 ml olive oil
- 2 oz capers
- 1 ½ oz sugar
- 5oz raisins
- 50ml white wine vinegar
- Grenades 1 piece

Directions
1. Boil 1 liter of water with salt in a saucepan and stir in celery chopped into small pieces in it for two minutes. Drain the water, cool the celery so that it does not lose its green color.
2. Pour almonds into a frying pan and put in the oven for five minutes, preheated to 180 degrees.
3. Take out seeds from the olives and chop the flesh roughly.
4. Rinse the salted capers and chop them roughly. Roasted nuts in the oven are also roughly chopped.
5. Heat olive oil in a large saucepan, add sugar, capers, raisins, vinegar, a pinch of black pepper, olives, and simmer over medium heat for five minutes. Then pour celery into a stewpan and simmer for another two to three minutes. When serving, mix with pomegranate seeds and almonds.

Nutrition: 650 Calories 45.8g Fat 8g Protein

32. Smoked Salmon Appetizer with Fresh Cucumber

Preparation Time: 1 0minutes
Cooking Time: 0 minute
Serving: 4
Ingredients
- 2 ½ tbsp sour cream 10%
- 16 slices rye bread
- 3 tbsp Greek yogurt
- Dill to taste
- 16 pieces smoked salmon
- 16 pieces cucumbers

Directions
1. Blend sour cream and yogurt.
2. Put slices of rye bread on the dish (you can cut circles or squares out of them).
3. On each put a mug of cucumber, a little sauce, and a slice of fish. Garnish with dill branches on top.

Nutrition: 225 Calories 9g Fat 24g Protein

33. Cypriot Tomato Salad

Preparation Time: 13 minutes
Cooking Time: 0 minute
Serving: 4
Ingredients
- 4 pieces tomatoes
- 50 ml sesame oil
- 1 tbsp red wine vinegar
- 2 tbsp - dried oregano
- coarse sea salt to taste
- 9 oz feta cheese

Directions
1. Chop the tomatoes into slices and put on a plate.
2. Sprinkle with sesame oil and vinegar, sprinkle with salt and oregano.
3. Cut the cheese and put it on the tomatoes.
4. Allow the dish to stand for 30 minutes so that the tomatoes absorb spices and aromas.

Nutrition: 80 Calories 7g Fat 3g Protein

34. Tangerine and Olive Salad

Preparation Time: 16 minutes
Cooking Time: 0 minute
Serving: 4
Ingredients
- ½ lb. tangerines
- 50 ml extra virgin olive oil
- 3 ½ oz Kalamata olives
- ½ tsp Ground cumin
- 1 tbsp White wine vinegar
- ¼ tsp paprika
- 1/8 tsp Cayenne pepper
- 1-piece Lettuce

- 2 oz Parsley
- Salt to taste
- Ground black pepper to taste

Directions
1. Remove the peel from the tangerines and remove the membranes between the slices (this can be done with a sharp knife, trying to touch the pulp as little as possible, or by hand, if the fruit is easy to peel). Put the naked slices in a wide bowl.
2. Olives (first, they will need to be removed from the seeds) cut in half and add to the tangerines.
3. Beat vinegar, oil, cumin, and paprika with a whisk in a separate bowl until smooth. Add the resulting dressing to a bowl.
4. Wash and dry lettuce with your hands to tear into small flakes and arrange on four plates, put tangerines with olives on top, and sprinkle salad with chopped parsley.

Nutrition: 173 Calories 15.4g Fat 1.4g Protein

35. **Farfalle with Avocado**

Preparation Time: 6 minutes
Cooking Time: 13 minutes
Serving: 4
Ingredients
- 10 ½ oz Farfalle pasta
- 5 oz Champignons
- 1 bunch Radish
- 1-piece Avocado
- 1 oz Parsley
- 6 oz Canned Tuna
- 6 tbsp vegetable broth
- 1 tbsp mustard
- Salt to taste

Directions
1. Cook the pasta.
2. Slice the champignons into thin plates and fry. Cut the radish into 6-8 slices. Cut avocado into slices. Finely chop the parsley.
3. Mix the broth with mustard, salt, and pepper, pour pasta on it.
4. Add tuna (previously draining the liquid), champignons, radishes, avocados, parsley. Mix everything and let it brew for half an hour in a cool place.

Nutrition: 125 Calories 3.2g Fat 7g Protein

36. **Salad of Squid, Apples, and Green Peas**

Preparation Time: 13 minutes
Cooking Time: 4 minutes
Serving: 2
Ingredients
- 7 oz squids
- 2 chicken egg
- ½ apple
- 8 ½ oz canned Green Peas
- Mayonnaise to taste
- Ground black pepper to taste
- Salt to taste
- Lemon juice to taste

Directions
1. Squids boiled in salted water (cook 3 minutes after boiling) cut into strips.
2. Finely chopped boiled eggs and apples.
3. Stir everything. Add peas and pepper. Season to taste with mayonnaise (can be sour cream); add lemon juice if desired.

Nutrition: 303 Calories 7.4g Fat 45g Protein

37. **Three Bean Salad with French Sauce**

Preparation Time: 4 minutes
Cooking Time: 11 minutes
Serving: 4
Ingredients
- 3 ½ oz Green beans
- 7 oz Beans fava
- 11 oz Lima Beans
- 11oz Kidney Beans
- 1 Red onion
- 1 tsp Italian parsley
- 2 tbsp French sauce

Directions
1. Boil slightly salted water in a saucepan. Put in it chopped green beans and fava beans (after defrosting them).
2. Cook for 1 minute, then drain the water. Fill with cold water, cool, and drain again.
3. Finely chop the small onion and parsley. Remove the beans from cans and drain the water.
4. Stir all the ingredients in a bowl, fill with sauce.

Nutrition: 81 Calories 5.5 Fat 0.8g Protein

38. **Sandwich with Tongue, Arugula and Champignons**

Preparation Time: 16 minutes
Cooking Time: 0 minute
Serving: 2
Ingredients
- 1-piece pitta bread
- 1-piece Tomatoes flame
- 1 bunch Arugula
- 5oz Fresh champignons
- 1 tsp Truffle oil
- 2 tbsp Olive Oil
- Dried thyme to taste
- Ground black pepper to taste
- Salt to taste

- 3 ½ oz veal tongue

Direction
1. Chop the tongue into long thin slices and fry in olive oil, salt, pepper, and add thyme to taste.
2. Lightly fry the champignons in olive oil, put in a clean bowl, trying to leave excess oil in a pan. Drizzle with truffle oil to give mushrooms a flavor.
3. Put the arugula, thin slices of tomato, mushrooms, and tongue evenly on the unfolded pita bread.
4. Wrap tightly, if necessary, cut off excess pita bread along the edges. Cut into two and serve.

Nutrition: 200 Calories 13.6g Fat 7.5g Protein

39. Pineapple Raspberry Smoothie

Preparation Time: 20 minutes
Cooking Time: 0 minute
Serving: 4
Ingredients
- 1 ½ lb. pineapple
- 10 ½ oz frozen raspberries
- 300 ml vanilla rice milk
- 3 tbsp buckwheat flakes
- Mint to taste

Direction
1. Chop the piece of pineapple peel and remove the core. Cut into medium pieces.
2. Thaw raspberries overnight on the top shelf of the refrigerator.
3. Take 200 ml of rice milk (in the absence of it, of course, you can replace it with non-fat milk), buckwheat flakes, slices of mandarin and pineapple, and beat at high speed in a blender.
4. Let stand for about 10-15 minutes. During this time, buckwheat flakes will swell.
5. Add another 100 ml of rice drink and punch in the blender again. If the smoothie is still thick, bring the water or rice drink to the desired concentration.
6. Garnish with fresh mint leaves.

Nutrition: 45 Calories 0.3g Fat 8g Protein

40. Morning Cake with Oatmeal, Bananas, and Blueberries

Preparation Time: 18 minutes
Cooking Time: 33 minutes
Serving: 4
Ingredients
- 2 pieces Bananas
- 1 cup Blueberries
- 3 tbsp Honey
- 1oz walnuts
- 1 cup oatmeal
- 200 ml milk
- 1/3 tsp cinnamon
- 1 chicken egg

- 1 tsp vanilla
- 1 tsp powdered sugar

Direction
1. Prep the oven to 375 F. Wrap the bottom dish and sides of the foil
2. Cut the bananas into rings and put them in the prepared dishes. There we add half the blueberries, 1/4 tsp of cinnamon, 1 tbsp of honey, and cover with foil. Bake for 15 minutes
3. Then, in a bowl, mix the oatmeal, half the walnuts, the baking powder for the dough, and the remaining cinnamon; mix everything. In a separate bowl, beat the remaining honey, milk, eggs, and vanilla.
4. Get bananas with blueberries from the oven, sprinkle with an oatmeal mixture. Then evenly pour the mixture from milk. Sprinkle with the remaining blueberries and walnuts.
5. Bake the cake for about 30 minutes. For decoration, sprinkle with powdered sugar. Serve warm.

Nutrition: 83 Calories 2.2g Fat 2.5g Protein

41. Pita Chicken Salad

Preparation Time: 18 minutes
Cooking Time: 4 minutes
Serving: 4
Ingredients
- Olive oil 1 tablespoon
- 1-piece chicken breast
- 2 pieces pita
- Dried basil to taste
- 3 tbsp natural yogurt
- 1 tbsp lemon juice
- 1 clove garlic
- 1 bunch (7 oz) green salad
- 1 tomato
- 2 chives
- 1 cucumber
- Salt to taste
- Ground black pepper to taste

Directions
1. Rub the chicken slices with salt, pepper, and dried basil, fry in a pan until cooked.
2. Put chicken, salad, slices of tomato, cucumber, and onion in half the pits.
3. Mix yogurt with lemon juice and garlic, add to the salad in Pita.

Nutrition 94 Calories 1.8g Fat 6g Protein

42. Salad with Spinach, Tomatoes, and Poached Egg

Preparation Time: 13 minutes
Cooking Time: 5 minutes
Serving: 2
Ingredients

- 3 oz spinach
- 2 tomatoes
- 2 chicken egg
- 2oz Feta cheese
- 2 tsp lemon juice
- 1 tbsp vegetable oil
- 2 tbsp agave syrup
- 1 ½ tsp sour cream 15%
- 1 tbsp dill
- 1 ½ oz Red onion

Directions
1. Pour vegetable oil onto the cling film.
2. Gently break the egg so that the yolk remains intact.
3. Collect the film with the egg in a bag, squeeze out the air, tie and cook for 5 minutes.
4. Mix lemon juice, agave syrup (1 tbsp.) And vegetable oil, let the dressing rest.
5. Cut the tomatoes into a cube and the onion into strips, fill with salt and pepper dressing.
6. Add spinach leaves, mix.
7. Top with feta cheese and poached egg.
8. Mix sour cream with chopped dill and syrup (1 tbsp.).
9. Pour over the salad dressing with the prepared sauce.

Nutrition: 200 Calories 12g Fat 7.5g Protein

43. Potato Scallops with Truffle Oil

Preparation Time: 8 minutes
Cooking Time: 24 minutes
Serving: 1
Ingredients
- 4 oz scallops
- 3 oz potato
- ½ oz Parmesan cheese
- ½ tsp lime zest
- ½ oz butter
- 1 tbsp olive oil
- 1 ½ tsp truffle oil
- 1 tsp arugula
- 2/3 oz cherry Tomatoes
- 1 chive
- ½ tsp thyme
- Sea salt to taste
- Ground black pepper to taste

Directions
1. Fry scallops on both sides in olive oil with thyme. Salt, pepper.
2. Separately, boil the potatoes and rub through a sieve. Add the zest of lime, grated Parmesan cheese, and butter. Salt, pepper.
3. Lightly warm the arugula and cherry tomatoes in olive oil.
4. Put mashed potatoes through the ring on a plate, scallops symmetrically put on it, arugula and cherry

on the scallops, garnish with thyme and onion, pour with truffle oil.

Nutrition: 279 Calories 59.8g Fat 24.5g Protein

44. Mediterranean Pasta with Basil

Preparation Time: 12 minutes
Cooking Time: 19 minutes
Serving: 4
Ingredients
- 2 red bell peppers
- 2 red onions
- 2 chili peppers
- 3 cloves garlic
- 1 tsp brown sugar
- 2 tbsp olive oil
- 2 lb. tomatoes
- 2/3 lb. pasta
- 1 tbsp fresh basil leaves
- 2 tbsp grated Parmesan cheese

Directions
1. Preheat the oven to 390 F degrees. Put pepper, onion, chili, and garlic in a deep pan. Sprinkle with sugar, drizzle with olive oil, and season with salt and ground black pepper to taste.
2. Bake in the oven for 15 minutes, add chopped tomatoes and cook for another 15 minutes.
3. While the vegetables are baking, prepare the pasta following the instructions on the package.
4. Take out the vegetables from the oven and mix the pasta to them. Sprinkle top with parmesan and basil leaves.

Nutrition: 136 Calories 3.2g Fat 4g Protein

45. Pita with Greens, Fried Onions, and Bacon

Preparation Time: 8 minutes
Cooking Time: 3 minutes
Serving: 2
Ingredients
- 2 pitas
- 3 ½ oz bacon
- 1 ½ oz red onion
- 1 bunch green salad
- 3 ½ oz tomatoes
- 2 cloves garlic
- Sea salt to taste
- Ground black pepper to taste
- 2 tbsp vegetable oil
- ½ lemon

Directions
1. Cut onion and tomato into slices, finely chop the garlic.

2. Heat oil and fry the onion and bacon until golden brown.
3. Add garlic, fry for about a minute.
4. Put lettuce leaves on Pita, put tomatoes, fried onions, and bacon on top.
5. Before serving, sprinkle with lemon juice, salt, pepper to taste.

Nutrition: 470 Calories 21g Fat 14.5g Protein

46.   Banana Oats

Preparation Time: 11 minutes
Cooking Time: 0 minute
Serving: 2
Ingredients
- 1 banana, peeled and sliced
- ¾ c. almond milk
- ½ c. cold-brewed coffee
- 2 pitted dates
- 2 tbsps. cocoa powder
- 1 c. rolled oats
- 1 ½ tbsps. chia seeds

Direction
1. Using a blender, add in all ingredients.
2. Process well for 5 minutes and serve.

Nutrition 288 Calories 4.4g Fat 7.7g Protein

47.   Breakfast Sandwich

Preparation Time: 3 minutes
Cooking Time: 20 minutes
Serving: 4
Ingredients
- 4 multigrain sandwich thins
- 4 tsps. olive oil
- 4 eggs
- 1 tbsp. rosemary, fresh
- 2 c. baby spinach leaves, fresh
- 1 tomato, sliced
- 1 tbsp. of feta cheese
- Pinch of kosher salt
- Ground black pepper

Direction
1. Set oven to 375 F/190 C.
2. Brush the thins' sides with 2 tsps. of olive oil and set on a baking sheet.
3. Set in the oven and toast for 5 minutes or until the edges are lightly brown.
4. In a skillet, add in the rest of the olive oil and rosemary to heat over high heat.
5. Break and place whole eggs one at a time into the skillet.
6. Break yolks up with a spatula. Flip the egg and cook on another side until done. Remove eggs from heat.
7. Place toasted sandwich thins on 4 separate plates. Divine spinach among the thins.

8. Top each thin with two tomato slices, cooked egg, and 1 tbsp. of feta cheese.
9. Lightly sprinkle with salt and pepper for flavoring.
10. Place remaining sandwich thin halves over the top and they are ready to serve.

Nutrition 241 Calories 12.2g Fat 13g Protein

48.   Cinnamon Couscous

Preparation Time: 9 minutes
Cooking Time: 8 minutes
Serving: 4
Ingredients
- 3 c. low-fat milk
- 1 c. whole-wheat couscous, uncooked
- 1 cinnamon stick
- ½ chopped apricot, dried
- ¼ c. currants, dried
- 6 tsps. brown sugar
- ¼ tsp. salt
- 4 tsps. melted butter

Direction:
1. Take a large saucepan and combine milk and cinnamon stick and heat over medium.
2. Heat for 3 minutes or until microbubbles forms around edges of the pan. Do not boil.
3. Remove from heat, stir in the couscous, apricots, currants, salt, and 4 tsps. brown sugar.
4. Wrap mixture and allow it to sit for 15 minutes. Remove and throw away the cinnamon stick.
5. Divide couscous among 4 bowls, and top each with 1 tsp. melted butter and ½ tsp. brown sugar. Ready to serve.

Nutrition 306 Calorie 6g Fat 11g Protein

49.   Avocado and Apple Smoothie

Preparation Time: 6 minutes
Cooking Time: 0 minutes
Serving: 2
Ingredients
- 3 c. spinach
- 1 cored green apple, chopped
- 1 pitted avocado, peeled and chopped
- 3 tbsps. chia seeds
- 1 tsp. honey
- 1 frozen banana, peeled
- 2 c. coconut water

Direction
1. Using your blender, add in all the ingredients.
2. Process well for 5 minutes to obtain a smooth consistency and serve in glasses.

Nutrition 208 Calories 10.1g Fat 2.1g Protein

50.   Mini Frittatas

Preparation Time: 9 minutes

Cooking Time: 20 minutes
Serving: 8
Ingredients

- 1 chopped yellow onion
- 1 c. grated parmesan
- 1 chopped yellow bell pepper
- 1 chopped red bell pepper
- 1 chopped zucchini
- Salt and black pepper
- A drizzle of olive oil
- 8 whisked eggs
- 2 tbsps. chopped chives

Direction

1. Set a pan over medium-high heat. Add in oil to warm. Stir in all ingredients except chives and eggs. Sauté for around 5 minutes.
2. Put the eggs on a muffin pan and top by the chives.
3. Set oven to 350 F/176 C. Place the muffin pan into the oven to bake for about 10 minutes.
4. Serve the eggs on a plate with sautéed vegetables.

Nutrition 55 Calories 3g Fat 4.2g Protein

51.   **Sun-Dried Tomatoes Oatmeal**

Preparation Time: 4 minutes
Cooking Time: 20 minutes
Serving: 4
Ingredients

- 3 c. water
- 1 c. almond milk
- 1 tbsp. olive oil
- 1 c. steel-cut oats
- ¼ c. chopped tomatoes, sun-dried
- A pinch of red pepper flakes

Direction

1. Using a pan, add water and milk to mix. Set on medium heat and allow to boil.
2. Set up another pan on medium-high heat. Warm oil and add oats to cook for 2 minutes. Transfer to the first pan plus tomatoes then stir. Let simmer for approximately 20 minutes.
3. Set in serving bowls and top with red pepper flakes. Enjoy.

Nutrition 170 Calories 17.8g Fat 1.5g Protein

52.   **Breakfast Egg on Avocado**

Preparation Time: 9 minutes
Cooking Time: 15 minutes
Serving: 6
Ingredients

- 1 tsp. garlic powder
- ½ tsp. sea salt
- ¼ c. shredded Parmesan cheese
- ¼ tsp. black pepper
- 3 pitted avocados, halved
- 6 eggs

Direction

1. Prep muffin tins and preheat the oven to 350 F/176 C.
2. Split the avocado. To ensure that the egg would fit inside the cavity of the avocado, lightly scrape off 1/3 of the meat.
3. Place avocado on a muffin tin to ensure that it faces with the top-up. Evenly season each avocado with pepper, salt, and garlic powder.
4. Add one egg on each avocado cavity and garnish tops with cheese. Set in your oven to bake until the egg white is set, about 15 minutes. Serve and enjoy.

Nutrition 252 Calories 20g Fat 14g Protein

53.   **Brekky Egg- Potato Hash**

Preparation Time: 8 minutes
Cooking Time: 25 minutes
Serving: 2
Ingredients

- 1 zucchini, diced
- ½ c. chicken broth
- ½ lb. or 220 g cooked chicken
- 1 tbsp. olive oil
- 4 oz. or 113g shrimp
- Salt and black pepper
- 1 diced sweet potato
- 2 eggs
- ¼ tsp. cayenne pepper
- 2 tsps. garlic powder
- 1 c. fresh spinach

Direction

1. In a skillet, add the olive oil.
2. Fry the shrimp, cooked chicken and sweet potato for 2 minutes.
3. Add the cayenne pepper, garlic powder and toss for 4 minutes.
4. Add the zucchini and toss for another 3 minutes.
5. Whisk the eggs in a bowl and add to the skillet.
6. Season using salt and pepper. Cover with the lid.
7. Cook for 1 more minute and mix in the chicken broth.
8. Cover and cook for another 8 minutes on high heat.
9. Add the spinach, toss for 2 more minutes and serve.

Nutrition 198 Calories 0.7g Fat 4g Protein

54.   **Basil and Tomato Soup**

Preparation Time: 7 minutes
Cooking Time: 25 minutes
Serving: 2
Ingredient

- 2 tbsps. vegetable broth
- 1 minced garlic clove
- ½ c. white onion
- 1 chopped celery stalk
- 1 chopped carrot

- 3 c. tomatoes, chopped
- Salt and pepper
- 2 bay leaves
- 1 ½ c. unsweetened almond milk
- 1/3 c. basil leaves

Direction
1. Cook vegetable broth in a large saucepan over medium heat.
2. Add in garlic and onions and cook for 4 minutes.
3. Add in carrots and celery. Cook for 1 more minute.
4. Mix in the tomatoes and bring to a boil. Simmer for 15 minutes.
5. Add the almond milk, basil and bay leaves.
6. Season and serve.

Nutrition 213 Calories 3.9g Fat 6.9g Protein

55. Butternut Squash Hummus

Preparation Time: 16 minutes
Cooking Time: 15 minutes
Serving: 4
Ingredients
- 2 lbs. or 900 g seeded butternut squash, peeled
- 1 tbsp. olive oil
- ¼ c. tahini
- 2 tbsps. lemon juice
- 2 minced cloves garlic
- Salt and pepper

Direction
1. Heat the oven to 300 F/148 C.
2. Coat the butternut squash with olive oil.
3. Set in a baking dish to bake for 15 minutes in the oven.
4. Once the squash is cooked, place in a food processor together with the rest of the ingredients.
5. Pulse until smooth.
6. Serve with carrots and celery sticks
7. For further use of place in individual containers, put a label and store it in the fridge.
8. Allow warming at room temperature before heating in the microwave oven.

Nutrition 115 Calories 5.8g Fat 2.5g Protein

56. Savory Muffins

Preparation time: 9 minutes
Cooking Time: 15 minutes
Serving: 6
Ingredients
- 9 ham slices
- 1/3 c. chopped spinach
- ¼ c. crumbled feta cheese
- ½ c. chopped roasted red peppers
- Salt and black pepper
- 1½ tbsps. basil pesto
- 5 whisked eggs

Direction

1. Grease a muffin tin. Use 1 ½ ham slices to line each of the muffin molds.
2. Except for black pepper, salt, pesto, and eggs, divide the rest of the ingredients into your ham cups.
3. Using a bowl, whisk together the pepper, salt, pesto, and eggs. Pour your pepper mixture on top.
4. Set oven to 400 F/204 C and bake for about 15 minutes.
5. Serve immediately.

Nutrition 109 Calories 6.7g Fat 9.3g Protein

57. Farro Salad

Preparation Time: 7 minutes
Cooking Time: 5 minutes
Serving: 2
Ingredient
- 1 tbsp. olive oil
- Salt and black pepper
- 1 bunch baby spinach, chopped
- 1 pitted avocado, peeled and chopped
- 1 minced garlic clove
- 2 c. cooked farro
- ½ c. cherry tomatoes, cubed

Direction
1. Adjust your heat to medium. Set oil in a pan and heat.
2. Toss in the rest of the ingredients. Cook the mixture for approximately 5 minutes.
3. Set in serving plates and enjoy.

Nutrition 157 Calories 13.7g Fat 3.6g Protein

58. Cranberry and Dates Squares

Preparation Time: 9 minutes
Cooking Time: 30 minutes
Serving: 10
Ingredients
- 12 pitted dates, chopped
- 1 tsp. vanilla extract
- ¼ c. honey
- ½ c. rolled oats
- ¾ c. dried cranberries
- ¼ c. melted almond avocado oil
- 1 c. chopped walnuts, roasted
- ¼ c. pumpkin seeds

Direction
1. Using a bowl, stir in all ingredients to mix.
2. Line a parchment paper on a baking sheet. Press the mixture on the setup.
3. Set in your freezer for about 30 minutes. Slice into 10 squares and enjoy.

Nutrition 263 Calories 13.4g Fat 3.5g Protein

59. Lentils and Cheddar Frittata

Preparation Time: 4 minutes
Cooking Time: 17 minutes
Serving: 4

Ingredients
- 1 chopped red onion
- 2 tbsps. olive oil
- 1 c. boiled sweet potatoes, chopped
- ¾ c. chopped ham
- 4 whisked eggs
- ¾ c. cooked lentils
- 2 tbsps. Greek yogurt
- Salt and black pepper
- ½ c. halved cherry tomatoes,
- ¾ c. grated cheddar cheese

Direction
1. Adjust your heat to medium and set a pan in place. Add in oil to heat. Stir in onion and allow to sauté for about 2 minutes.
2. Except for cheese and eggs, toss in the other ingredients and cook for 3 more minutes.
3. Add in the eggs, top with cheese. Cook for 10 more minutes while covered.
4. Slice the frittata, set in serving bowls and enjoy.

Nutrition 274 Calories 17.36g Fat 11.4g Protein

60. Tuna Sandwich

Preparation Time: 9 minutes
Cooking Time: 5 minutes
Serving: 2

Ingredients
- 6 oz. canned tuna, drained and flaked
- 1 pitted avocado, peeled and mashed
- 4 whole-wheat bread slices
- Pinch salt and black pepper
- 1 tbsp. crumbled feta cheese
- 1 c. baby spinach

Direction
1. Using a bowl, stir in pepper, salt, tuna, and cheese to mix.
2. To the bread slices, apply a spread of the mashed avocado.
3. Equally, divide the tuna mixture and spinach onto 2 of the slices. Top with the remaining 2 slices. Serve.

Nutrition 283 Calories 11.2g Fat 4.5g Protein

61. Mediterranean Pita Breakfast

Preparation Time: 22 minutes
Cooking Time: 3 minutes
Servings: 2

Ingredients:
- 1/4 cup of sweet red pepper
- 1/4 cup of chopped onion
- 1 cup of egg substitute
- 1/8 teaspoon of salt
- 1/8 teaspoon of pepper
- 1 small chopped tomato
- 1/2 cup of fresh torn baby spinach
- 1-1/2 teaspoons of minced fresh basil
- 2 whole size pita breads
- 2 tablespoons of crumbled feta cheese

Directions:
1. Coat with a cooking spray a small size non-stick skillet. Stir in the onion and red pepper for 3 minutes over medium heat.
2. Add your egg substitute and season with salt and pepper. Stir cook until it sets. Mix the torn spinach, chopped tomatoes, and mince basil. Scoop onto the pitas. Top vegetable mixture with your egg mixture.
3. Topped with crumbled feta cheese and serve immediately.

Nutrition 267 Calories 3g Fat 20g Protein

62. Hummus Deviled Egg

Preparation Time: 10 minutes
Cooking Time: 0 minute
Servings: 6

Ingredients:
- 1/4 cup of finely diced cucumber
- 1/4 cup of finely diced tomato
- 2 teaspoons of fresh lemon juice
- 1/8 teaspoon salt
- 6 hard-cooked peeled eggs, sliced half lengthwise
- 1/3 cup of roasted garlic hummus or any hummus flavor
- Chopped fresh parsley (optional)

Directions:
1. Combine the tomato, lemon juice, cucumber and salt together and then gently mix. Scrape out the yolks from the halved eggs and store for later use. Scoop a heaping teaspoon of humus in each half egg. Top with parsley and half-teaspoon tomato-cucumber mixture. Serve immediately

Nutrition 40 Calories 1g Fat 4g Protein

63. Smoked Salmon Scrambled Egg

Preparation Time: 2 minutes
Cooking Time: 8 minutes
Servings: 4

Ingredients:
- 16 ounces egg substitute, cholesterol-free
- 1/8 teaspoon of black pepper
- 2 tablespoons of sliced green onions, keep the tops
- 1 ounce of chilled reduced-fat cream cheese, cut into 1/4-inch cubes
- 2 ounces of flaked smoked salmon

Directions:

1. Cut the chilled cream cheese into ¼-inch cubes then set aside. Whisk the egg substitute and the pepper in a large sized bowl Coat a non-stick skillet with cooking spray over medium heat. Stir in the egg substitute and cook for 5 to 7 minutes or until it starts to set stirring occasionally and scraping bottom of the pan.
2. Fold in the cream cheese, green onions and the salmon. Continue cooking then stir for another 3 minutes or just until the eggs are still moist but cooked.

Nutrition 100 Calories 3g Fats 15g Protein

64. Buckwheat Apple-Raisin Muffin

Preparation Time: 24 minutes
Cooking Time: 20 minutes
Servings: 12
Ingredients:
- 1 cup of all-purpose flour
- 3/4 cup of buckwheat flour
- 2 tablespoons of brown sugar
- 1 1/2 teaspoons of baking powder
- 1/4 teaspoon of baking soda
- 3/4 cup of reduced-fat buttermilk
- 2 tablespoons of olive oil
- 1 large egg
- 1 cup peeled and cored, fresh diced apples
- 1/4 cup of golden raisins

Directions:
1. Prepare the oven at 375 degrees F. Line a 12-cup muffin tin with a non-stick cooking spray or paper cups. Set aside. Incorporate all the dry ingredients in a mixing bowl. Set aside.
2. Beat together the liquid ingredients until smooth. Transfer the liquid mixture over the flour mixture and mix until moistened. Fold in the diced apples and raisins. Fill each muffin cups with about 2/3 full of the mixture. Bake until it turns golden brown. Use the toothpick test. Serve.

Nutrition 117 Calories 1g Fat 3g Protein

65. Pumpkin Bran Muffin

Preparation Time: 20 minutes
Cooking Time: 20 minutes
Servings: 22
Ingredients:
- 3/4 cup of all-purpose flour
- 3/4 cup of whole wheat flour
- 2 tablespoons sugar
- 1 tablespoon of baking powder
- 1/8 teaspoon salt
- 1 teaspoon of pumpkin pie spice
- 2 cups of 100% bran cereal
- 1 1/2 cups of skim milk
- 2 egg whites
- 15 ounces x 1 can pumpkin
- 2 tablespoons of avocado oil

Directions:
1. Preheat the oven to 400 degrees Fahrenheit. Prepare a muffin pan enough for 22 muffins and line with a non-stick cooking spray. Stir together the first four ingredients until combined. Set aside.
2. Using a large mixing bowl, mix together milk and cereal bran and let it stand for 2 minutes or until the cereal softens. Add in the oil, egg whites, and pumpkin in the bran mix and blend well. Fill in the flour mixture and mix well.
3. Divide the batter into equal portions into the muffin pan. Bake for 20 minutes. Pull out the muffins from pan and serve warm or cooled.

Nutrition 70 Calories 3g Fat 3g Protein

66. Buckwheat Buttermilk Pancakes

Preparation Time: 2 minutes
Cooking Time: 18 minutes
Servings: 9
Ingredients:
- 1/2 cup of buckwheat flour
- 1/2 cup of all-purpose flour
- 2 teaspoons of baking powder
- 1 teaspoon of brown sugar
- 2 tablespoons of olive oil
- 2 large eggs
- 1 cup of reduced-fat buttermilk

Directions:
1. Incorporate the first four ingredients in a bowl. Add the oil, buttermilk, and eggs and mix until thoroughly blended.
2. Put griddle over medium heat and spray with non-stick cooking spray. Pour ¼ cup of the batter over the skillet and cook for 1-2 minutes each side or until they turn golden brown. Serve immediately.

Nutrition 108 Calories 3g Fat 4g Protein

67. French Toast with Almonds and Peach Compote

Preparation Time: 10 minutes
Cooking Time: 15 minutes
Servings: 4
Ingredients:
Compote:
- 3 tablespoons of sugar substitute, sucralose-based
- 1/3 cup + 2 tablespoons of water, divided
- 1 1/2 cups of fresh peeled or frozen, thawed and drained sliced peaches
- 2 tablespoons peach fruit spread, no-sugar-added
- 1/4 teaspoon of ground cinnamon

Almond French toast

- 1/4 cup of (skim) fat-free milk
- 3 tablespoons of sugar substitute, sucralose-based
- 2 whole eggs
- 2 egg whites
- 1/2 teaspoon of almond extract
- 1/8 teaspoon salt
- 4 slices of multigrain bread
- 1/3 cup of sliced almonds

Directions:
1. To make the compote, dissolve 3 tablespoons sucralose in 1/3 cup of water in a medium saucepan over high-medium heat. Stir in the peaches and bring to a boil. Reduce the heat to medium and continue to cook uncovered for another 5 minutes or until the peaches softened.
2. Combine remaining water and fruit spread then stir into the peaches in the saucepan. Cook for another minute or until syrup thickens. Pull out from heat and add in the cinnamon. Cover to keep warm.
3. To make the French toast. Combine the milk and sucralose in a large size shallow dish and whisk until it completely dissolves. Whisk in the egg whites, eggs, almond extract and salt. Dip both sides of the bread slices for 3 minutes in the egg mixture or until completely soaked. Sprinkle both sides with sliced almonds and press firmly to adhere.
4. Brush the non-stick skillet with cooking spray and place over medium-high heat. Cook bread slices on griddle for 2 to 3 minutes both sides or until it turns light brown. Serve topped with the peach compote.

Nutrition 277 Calories 7g Fat 12g Protein

68. Mixed Berries Oatmeal with Sweet Vanilla Cream

Preparation Time: 5 minutes
Cooking Time: 5 minutes
Servings: 4
Ingredients:
- 2 cups water
- 1 cup of quick-cooking oats
- 1 tablespoon of sucralose-based sugar substitute
- 1/2 teaspoon of ground cinnamon
- 1/8 teaspoon salt

Cream
- 3/4 cup of fat-free half-and-half
- 3 tablespoons of sucralose-based sugar substitute
- 1/2 teaspoon of vanilla extract
- 1/2 teaspoon of almond extract

Toppings
- 1 1/2 cups of fresh blueberries
- 1/2 cup of fresh or frozen and thawed raspberries

Directions:
1. Boil water in high-heat and stir in the oats. Reduce heat to medium while cooking oats, uncovered for 2 minutes or until thick.

2. Remove from heat and stir in sugar substitute, salt and cinnamon. In a medium size bowl, incorporate all the cream ingredients until well blended. Scoop cooked oatmeal into 4 equal portions and pour the sweet cream over. Top with the berries and serve.

Nutrition 150 Calories 5g Fat 5g Protein

69. Choco-Strawberry Crepe

Preparation Time: 5 minutes
Cooking Time: 10 minutes
Servings: 4
Ingredients:
- 1 cup of wheat all-purpose flour
- 2/3 cup of low-fat (1%) milk
- 2 egg whites
- 1 egg
- 3 tablespoons sugar
- 3 tablespoons of unsweetened cocoa powder
- 1 tablespoon of cooled melted butter
- 1/2 teaspoon salt
- 2 teaspoons of canola oil
- 3 tablespoons of strawberry fruit spread
- 3 1/2 cups of sliced thawed frozen or fresh strawberries
- 1/2 cup of fat-free thawed frozen whipped topping
- Fresh mint leaves (if desired)

Directions:
1. Incorporate the first eight ingredients in a large size bowl until smooth and thoroughly blended.
2. Brush ¼-teaspoon oil on a small size non-stick skillet over medium heat. Pour ¼-cup of the batter onto the center and swirl to coat the pan with batter.
3. Cook for a minute or until crêpe turns dull and the edges dry. Flip on the other side and cook for another half a minute. Repeat process with remaining mixture and oil.
4. Scoop ¼-cup of thawed strawberries at the center of the crepe and toll up to cover filling. Top with 2 tablespoons whipped cream and garnish with mint before serving.

Nutrition 334 Calories 5g Fat 10g Protein

70. No Crust Asparagus-Ham Quiche

Preparation Time: 5 minutes
Cooking Time: 42 minutes
Servings: 6
Ingredients:
- 2 cups 1/2-inched sliced asparagus
- 1 red chopped bell pepper
- 1 cup milk, low-fat (1%)
- 2 tablespoons of wheat all-purpose flour
- 4 egg whites
- 1 egg, whole

- 1 cup cooked chopped deli ham
- 2 tablespoons fresh chopped tarragon or basil
- 1/2 teaspoon of salt (optional)
- 1/4 teaspoon of black pepper
- 1/2 cup Swiss cheese, finely shredded

Directions:
1. Preheat your oven to 350 degrees F. Microwave bell pepper and asparagus in a tablespoon of water on HIGH for 2 minutes. Drain. Whisk flour and milk, and then add egg and egg whites until well combined. Stir in the vegetables and the remaining ingredients except the cheese.
2. Pour in a 9-inch size pie dish and bake for 35 minutes. Sprinkle cheese over the quiche and bake another 5 minutes or until cheese melts. Allow it cool for 5 minutes then cut into 6 wedges to serve.

Nutrition 138 Calories 1g Fat 13g Protein

71. Apple Cheese Scones

Preparation Time: 20 minutes
Cooking Time: 15 minutes
Servings: 10
Ingredients:
- 1 cup of all-purpose flour
- 1 cup whole wheat flour, white
- 3 tablespoons sugar
- 1 1/2 teaspoons of baking powder
- 1/2 teaspoon salt
- 1/2 teaspoon of ground cinnamon
- 1/4 teaspoon of baking soda
- 1 diced Granny Smith apple
- 1/2 cup shredded sharp Cheddar cheese
- 1/3 cup applesauce, natural or unsweetened
- 1/4 cup milk, fat-free (skim)
- 3 tablespoons of melted butter
- 1 egg

Directions:
1. Prepare your oven to 425 degrees F. Ready the baking sheet by lining with parchment paper. Merge all dry ingredients in a bowl and mix. Stir in the cheese and apple. Set aside. Whisk all the wet ingredients together. Pour over the dry mixture until blended and turns like a sticky dough.
2. Work on the dough on a floured surface about 5 times. Pat and then stretch into an 8-inch circle. Slice into 10 diagonal cuts.
3. Place on the baking sheet and spray top with cooking spray. Bake for 15 minutes or until lightly golden. Serve.

Nutrition 169 Calories 2g Fat 5g Protein

72. Bacon and Egg Wrap

Preparation Time: 15 minutes
Cooking Time: 15 minutes
Servings: 4

Ingredients:
- 1 cup egg substitute, cholesterol-free
- 1/4 cup Parmesan cheese, shredded
- 2 slices diced Canadian bacon
- 1/2 teaspoon red hot pepper sauce
- 1/4 teaspoon of black pepper
- 4x7-inch whole wheat tortillas
- 1 cup of baby spinach leaves

Directions:
1. Preheat your oven at 325 degrees F. Combine the first five ingredients to make the filling. Pour the mixture in a 9-inch glass dish sprayed with butter-flavored cooking spray.
2. Bake for 15 minutes or until egg sets. Remove from oven. Place the tortillas for a minute in the oven. Cut baked egg mixture into quarters. Arrange one quarter at the center of each tortillas and top with ¼-cup spinach. Fold tortilla from the bottom to the center and then both sides to the center to enclose. Serve immediately.

Nutrition 195 Calories 3g Fat 15g Protein

73. Orange-Blueberry Muffin

Preparation Time: 10 minutes
Cooking Time: 20 - 25 minutes
Servings: 12
Ingredients:
- 1 3/4 cups of all-purpose flour
- 1/3 cup sugar
- 2 1/2 teaspoons of baking powder
- 1/2 teaspoon of baking soda
- 1/2 teaspoon salt
- 1/2 teaspoon of ground cinnamon
- 3/4 cup milk, fat-free (skim)
- 1/4 cup butter
- 1 egg, large, lightly beaten
- 3 tablespoons thawed orange juice concentrate
- 1 teaspoon vanilla
- 3/4 cup fresh blueberries

Directions:
1. Ready your oven to 400 degrees F. Follow steps 2 to 5 of Buckwheat Apple-Raisin Muffin Fill up the muffin cups ¾-full of the mixture and bake for 20 to 25 minutes. Let it cool 5 minutes and serve warm.

Nutrition 149 Calories 5g Fat 3g Protein

74. Baked Ginger Oatmeal with Pear Topping

Preparation Time: 10 minutes
Cooking Time: 15 minutes
Servings: 2
Ingredients:
- 1 cup of old-fashioned oats

- 3/4 cup milk, fat-free (skim)
- 1 egg white
- 1 1/2 teaspoons grated ginger, fresh or 3/4 teaspoon of ground ginger
- 2 tablespoons brown sugar, divided
- 1/2 ripe diced pear

Directions:
1. Spray 2x6 ounce ramekins with a non-stick cooking spray. Prepare the oven to 350 degrees F. Combine the first four ingredients and a tablespoon of sugar then mix well. Pour evenly between the 2 ramekins. Top with pear slices and the remaining tablespoon of sugar. Bake for 15 minutes. Serve warm.

Nutrition 268 Calories 5g fat 10g Protein

75. Greek Style Veggie Omelet

Preparation Time: 10 minutes
Cooking Time: 20 minutes
Servings: 2
Ingredients:
- 4 large eggs
- 2 tablespoons of fat-free milk
- 1/8 teaspoon salt
- 3 teaspoons of olive oil, divided
- 2 cups baby Portobello, sliced
- 1/4 cup of finely chopped onion
- 1 cup of fresh baby spinach
- 3 tablespoons feta cheese, crumbled
- 2 tablespoons ripe olives, sliced
- Freshly ground pepper

Directions:
1. Whisk together first three ingredients. Stir in 2 tablespoons of oil in a non-stick skillet over medium-high heat. Sauté the onions and mushroom for 5-6 minutes or until golden brown. Mix in the spinach and cook. Remove mixture from pan.
2. Using the same pan, heat over medium-low heat the remaining oil. Pour your egg mixture and as it starts to set, pushed the edges towards the center to let the uncooked mixture flow underneath. When eggs set scoop the veggie mixture on one side. Sprinkle with olives and feta then fold the other side to close. Slice in half and sprinkle with pepper to serve.

Nutrition 271 Calories 2g Fat 18g Protein

76. Summer Smoothie

Preparation Time: 8 minutes
Cooking Time: 0 minute
Servings: 2
Ingredients:
- 1/2 Banana, Peeled
- 2 Cups Strawberries, Halved
- 3 Tablespoons Mint, Chopped
- 1 1/2 Cups Coconut Water

- 1/2 Avocado, Pitted & Peeled
- 1 Date, Chopped
- Ice Cubes as Needed

Directions:
1. Incorporate everything in a blender, and process until smooth. Add ice cubes to thicken, and serve chilled.

Nutrition 360 calories 12g fats 31g protein

77. Ham & Egg Pitas

Preparation Time: 5 minutes
Cooking Time: 15 minutes
Servings: 4
Ingredients:
- 6 Eggs
- 2 Shallots, Chopped
- 1 Teaspoon Olive Oil
- 1/3 Cup Smoked Ham, Chopped
- 1/3 Cup Sweet Green Pepper, Chopped
- 1/4 Cup Brie Cheese
- Sea Salt & Black Pepper to Taste
- 4 Lettuce Leaves
- 2 Pita Breads, Whole Wheat

Directions:
1. Cook olive oil in a pan using medium heat. Add in your shallots and green pepper, letting them cook for five minutes while stirring frequently.
2. Get out a bowl and whip your eggs, sprinkling in your salt and pepper. Make sure your eggs are well beaten. Put the eggs into the pan, and then mix in the ham and cheese. Stir well, and cook until your mixture thickens. Split the pitas in half, and open the pockets. Spread a teaspoon of mustard in each pocket, and add a lettuce leaf in each one. Spread the egg mixture in each one and serve.

Nutrition 610 calories 21g fats 41g protein

78. Breakfast Couscous

Preparation Time: 5 minutes
Cooking Time: 15 minutes
Servings: 4
Ingredients:
- 3 Cups Milk, Low Fat
- 1 Cinnamon Stick
- 1/2 Cup Apricots, Dried & Chopped
- 1/4 Cup Currants, Dried
- 1 Cup Couscous, Uncooked
- Pinch Sea Salt, Fine
- 4 Teaspoons Butter, Melted
- 6 Teaspoons Brown Sugar

Directions:
1. Heat a pan up with milk and cinnamon using medium-high heat. Cook for three minutes before removing the pan from heat.

2. Add in your apricots, couscous, salt, currants, and sugar. Stir well, and then cover. Leave it to the side, and let it sit for fifteen minutes.
3. Throw out the cinnamon stick, and divide between bowls. Sprinkle with brown sugar before serving.

Nutrition 520 calories 28g fats 39g protein

79. **Peach Breakfast Salad**

Preparation Time: 10 minutes
Cooking Time: 0 minute
Servings: 1
Ingredients:
- 1/4 Cup Walnuts, Chopped & Toasted
- 1 Teaspoon Honey, Raw
- 1 Peach, Pitted & Sliced
- 1/2 Cup Cottage Cheese, Nonfat & Room Temperature
- 1 Tablespoon Mint, Fresh & Chopped
- 1 Lemon, Zested

Directions:
1. Situate cottage cheese in a bowl, and top with peach slices and walnuts. Drizzle with honey, and top with mint.
2. Sprinkle on your lemon zest before serving immediately.

Nutrition 280 calories 11g fats 39g protein

80. **Savory Oats**

Preparation Time: 10 minutes
Cooking Time: 10 minutes
Servings: 2
Ingredients:
- 1/2 Cup Steel Cut Oats
- 1 Cup Water
- 1 Tomato, Large & Chopped
- 1 Cucumber, Chopped
- 1 Tablespoon Olive Oil
- Sea Salt & Black Pepper to Taste
- Flat Leaf Parsley, Chopped to Garnish
- Parmesan Cheese, Low Fat & Freshly Grated

Directions:
1. Bring your oats and a cup of water to a boil using a saucepan over high heat. Stir often until your water is completely absorbed, which will take roughly fifteen minutes.
2. Divide between two bowls, and top with tomatoes and cucumber. Drizzle with olive oil and top with parmesan. Garnish with parsley before serving.

Nutrition 408 calories 13g fats 28g protein

81. **Tahini & Apple Toast**

Preparation Time: 15 minutes
Cooking Time: 0 minute
Servings: 1

Ingredients:
- 2 Tablespoons Tahini
- 2 Slices Whole Wheat Bread, Toasted
- 1 Teaspoon Honey, Raw
- 1 Apple, Small, Cored & Sliced Thin

Directions:
1. Start by spreading the tahini over your toast, and then lay your apples over it. drizzle with honey before serving.

Nutrition 366 calories 13g fats 29g protein

82. **Scrambled Basil Eggs**

Preparation Time: 5 minutes
Cooking Time: 10 minutes
Servings: 2
Ingredients:
- 4 Eggs, Large
- 2 Tablespoons Fresh Basil, Chopped Fine
- 2 Tablespoons Gruyere Cheese, Grated
- 1 Tablespoon Cream
- 1 Tablespoon Olive Oil
- 2 Cloves Garlic, Minced
- Sea Salt & Black Pepper to Taste

Directions:
1. Get out a large bowl and beat your basil, cheese, cream and eggs together. Whisk until it's well combined. Get out a large skillet over medium-low heat, and heat your oil. Add in your garlic, cooking for a minute. It should turn golden.
2. Pour the egg mixture into your skillet over the garlic, and then continue to scramble as they cook so they become soft and fluffy. Season it well and serve warm.

Nutrition 360 calories 14g fats 29g protein

83. **Greek Potatoes & Eggs**

Preparation Time: 10 minutes
Cooking Time: 30 minutes
Servings: 2
Ingredients:
- 3 tomatoes, seeded & roughly chopped
- 2 tablespoons basil, fresh & chopped
- 1 clove garlic, minced
- 2 tablespoons + ½ cup olive oil, divided
- sea salt & black pepper to taste
- 3 russet potatoes, large
- 4 eggs, large
- 1 teaspoon oregano, fresh & chopped

Directions:
1. Get the food processor and place your tomatoes in, pureeing them with the skin on.
2. Add your garlic, two tablespoons of oil, salt, pepper and basil. Pulse until it's well combined. Place this mixture in a skillet, cooking while covered for

twenty to twenty-five minutes over low heat. Your sauce should be thickened as well as bubbly.

3. Dice your potatoes into cubes, and then place them in a skillet with a ½ a cup of olive oil in a skillet using medium-low heat.

4. Fry your potatoes until crisp and browned. This should take five minutes, and then cover the skillet, reducing the heat to low. Steam them until your potatoes are done.

5. Stir in the eggs into the tomato sauce, and cook using low heat for six minutes. Your eggs should be set.

6. Remove the potatoes from your pan, and drain using paper towels. Place them in a bowl. Sprinkle in your salt, pepper and oregano, and then serve your eggs with potatoes. Drizzle your sauce over the mixture, and serve warm.

Nutrition 348 calories 12g fats 27g protein

84.   Avocado & Honey Smoothie

Preparation Time: 5 minutes
Cooking Time: 0 minute
Servings: 2
Ingredients:
- 1 1/2 cups soy milk
- 1 avocado, large
- 2 tablespoons honey, raw

Directions:
1. Incorporate all ingredients together and blend until smooth, and serve immediately.

Nutrition 280 calories 19g fats 11g carbohydrates 30g protein

85.   Vegetable Frittata

Preparation Time: 5 minutes
Cooking Time: 10 minutes
Servings: 2
Ingredients:
- 1/2 baby eggplant, peeled & diced
- 1 handful baby spinach leaves
- 1 tablespoon olive oil
- 3 eggs, large
- 1 teaspoon almond milk
- 1-ounce goat cheese, crumbled
- 1/4 small red pepper, chopped
- sea salt & black pepper to taste

Directions:
1. Start by heating the broiler on your oven, and then beat the eggs together with almond milk. Make sure it's well combined, and then get out a nonstick, oven proof skillet. Place it over medium-high heat, and then add in your olive oil.

2. Once your oil is heated, add in your eggs. Spread your spinach over this mixture in an even layer, and top with the rest of your vegetables.

3. Reduce your heat to medium, and sprinkle with salt and pepper. Allow your vegetables and eggs to cook for five minutes. The bottom half of your eggs should be firm, and your vegetables should be tender. Top with goat cheese, and then broil on the middle rack for three to five minutes. Your eggs should be all the way done, and your cheese should be melted. Slice into wedges and serve warm.

Nutrition 340 calories 16g fats 9g carbohydrates 37g protein

86.   Mini Lettuce Wraps

Preparation Time: 15 minutes
Cooking Time: 0 minute
Servings: 4
Ingredients:
- 1 cucumber, diced
- 1 red onion, sliced
- 1-ounce feta cheese, low fat & crumbed
- 1 lemon, juiced
- 1 tomato, diced
- 1 tablespoon olive oil
- 12 small iceberg lettuce leaves
- sea salt & black pepper to taste

Directions:
1. Combine your tomato, onion, feta, and cucumber together in a bowl. Mix your oil and juice, and season with salt and pepper.

2. Fill each leaf with the vegetable mixture, and roll them tightly. Use a toothpick to keep them together to serve.

Nutrition 291 calories 10g fats 9g carbohydrates 27g protein

87.   Curry Apple Couscous

Preparation Time: 20 minutes
Cooking Time: 5 minutes
Servings: 4
Ingredients:
- 2 teaspoons olive oil
- 2 leeks, white parts only, sliced
- 1 apple, diced
- 2 tablespoons curry powder
- 2 cups couscous, cooked & whole wheat
- 1/2 cup pecans, chopped

Directions:
1. Heat your oil in a skillet using medium heat. Add the leeks, and cook until tender, which will take five minutes. Add in your apple, and cook until soft.

2. Add in your curry powder and couscous, and stir well. Remove from heat, and mix in your nuts before serving immediately.

Nutrition 330 calories 12g fats 8g carbohydrates 30g protein

88.   Lamb & Vegetable Bake

Preparation Time: 20 minutes

Cooking Time: 1 hour and 10 minutes
Servings: 8
Ingredients:

- 1/4 cup olive oil
- 1 lb. lean lamb, boneless & chopped into ½ inch pieces
- 2 red potatoes, large, scrubbed & diced
- 1 onion, chopped roughly
- 2 cloves garlic, minced
- 28 ounces diced tomatoes with liquid, canned & no salt
- 2 zucchinis, cut into ½ inch slices
- 1 red bell pepper, seeded & cut into 1-inch cubes
- 2 tablespoons flat leaf parsley, chopped
- 1 tablespoon paprika
- 1 teaspoon thyme
- 1/2 teaspoon cinnamon
- 1/2 cup red wine
- sea salt & black pepper to taste

Directions:

1. Start by turning the oven to 325, and then get out a large stew pot. Place it over medium-high heat to heat your olive oil. Once your oil is hot stir in your lamb, browning the meat. Stir frequently to keep it from running, and then place your lamb in a baking dish.
2. Cook your garlic, onion and potatoes in the skillet until they're tender, which should take five to six minutes more. Place them to the baking dish as well. Pour the zucchini, pepper, and tomatoes in the pan with your herbs and spices. Allow it to simmer for ten minutes more before pouring it into your baking dish.
3. Pour in the wine and pepper sauce. Add in your tomato, and then cover with foil. Bake for an hour. Take the cover off for the last fifteen minutes of baking, and adjust seasoning as needed.

Nutrition 240 calories 14g fats 8g carbohydrates 36g protein

89. Herb Flounder

Preparation Time: 20 minutes
Cooking Time: 1 hour and 5 minutes
Servings: 4
Ingredients:

- 1/2 cup flatleaf parsley, lightly packed
- 1/4 cup olive oil
- 4 cloves garlic, peeled & halved
- 2 tablespoons rosemary, fresh
- 2 tablespoons thyme leaves, fresh
- 2 tablespoons sage, fresh
- 2 tablespoons lemon zest, fresh
- 4 flounder fillets
- sea salt & black pepper to taste

Directions:

1. Ready your oven to 350, and then put all of the ingredients except for the flounder in the processor. Blend until it forms at hick paste.
2. Put your fillets on a baking sheet, and brush them down with the paste. Allow them to chill in the fridge for an hour. Bake for ten minutes. Season and serve warm.

Nutrition 307 calories 11g fats 7g carbohydrates 34g protein

90. Cauliflower Quinoa

Preparation Time: 15 minutes
Cooking Time: 10 minutes
Servings: 4
Ingredients:

- 1 1/2 cups quinoa, cooked
- 3 tablespoons olive oil
- 3 cups cauliflower florets
- 2 spring onions, chopped
- 1 tablespoon red wine vinegar
- sea salt & black pepper to taste
- 1 tablespoon red wine vinegar
- 1 tablespoon chives, chopped
- 1 tablespoon parsley, chopped

Directions:

1. Start by heating up a pan over medium-high heat. Add your oil. Once your oil is hot, add in your spring onions and cook for about two minutes.
2. Add in your quinoa and cauliflower, and then add in the rest of the ingredients. Mix well, and cover. Cook for nine minutes over medium heat, and divide between plates to serve.

Nutrition 290 calories 14g fats 9g carbohydrates 26g protein

91. Mango Pear Smoothie

Preparation Time: 5 minutes
Cooking Time: 0 minute
Servings: 1
Ingredients:

- 2 ice cubes
- ½ cup Greek yogurt, plain
- ½ mango, peeled, pitted & chopped
- 1 cup kale, chopped
- 1 pear, ripe, cored & chopped

Directions:

1. Blend together until thick and smooth. Serve chilled.

Nutrition 350 calories 12g fats 9g carbohydrates 40g protein

92. Spinach Omelet

Preparation Time: 10 minutes
Cooking Time: 20 minutes
Servings: 4
Ingredients:

- 3 tablespoons olive oil
- 1 onion, small & chopped
- 1 clove garlic, minced
- 4 tomatoes, large, cored & chopped
- 1 teaspoon sea salt, fine
- 8 eggs, beaten
- ¼ teaspoon black pepper
- 2 ounces feta cheese, crumbled
- 1 tablespoon flat leaf parsley, fresh & chopped

Directions:

1. Preheat oven to 400 degrees, and pour olive oil in an ovenproof skillet. Place your skillet over high heat, adding in your onions. Cook for five to seven minutes. Your onions should soften.
2. Add your tomatoes, salt, pepper and garlic in. Then simmer for another five minutes, and fill in your beaten eggs. Mix lightly, and cook for three to five minutes. They should set at the bottom. Put the pan in the oven, baking for five minutes more. Remove from the oven, topping with parsley and feta. Serve warm.

Nutrition 280 calories 19g fats 10g carbohydrates 31g protein

93. Almond Pancakes

Preparation Time: 15 minutes
Cooking Time: 15 minutes
Servings: 6
Ingredients:

- 2 cups almond milk, unsweetened & room temperature
- 2 eggs, large & room temperature
- ½ cup coconut oil, melted + more for greasing
- 2 teaspoons honey, raw
- ¼ teaspoon sea salt, fine
- ½ teaspoon baking soda
- 1 ½ cups whole wheat flour
- ½ cup almond flour
- 1 ½ teaspoons baking powder
- ¼ teaspoon cinnamon, ground

Directions:

1. Get out a large bowl and whisk your coconut oil, eggs, almond milk and honey, blending until it's mixed well.
2. Get a medium bowl out and sift together your baking powder, baking soda, almond flour, sea salt, whole wheat flour and cinnamon. Mix well.
3. Mix in your flour mixture to your milk mixture, and whisk well.
4. Get out a large skillet and grease it using your coconut oil before placing it over medium-high heat. Add in your pancake batter in ½ cup measurements.
5. Cook for 3 minutes. The bottom of your pancake should be golden, and bubbles should break the surface. Cook both sides.

6. Wipe clean your skillet, and repeat until all of your batter is used. Make sure to re-grease your skillet, and top with fresh fruit if desired.

Nutrition 205 calories 16g fats 9g carbohydrates 36g protein

94. Quinoa Fruit Salad

Preparation Time: 25 minutes
Cooking Time: 0 minute
Servings: 4
Ingredients:

- 2 tablespoons honey, raw
- 1 cup strawberries, fresh & sliced
- 2 tablespoons lime juice, fresh
- 1 teaspoon basil, fresh & chopped
- 1 cup quinoa, cooked
- 1 mango, peeled, pitted & diced
- 1 cup blackberries, fresh
- 1 peach, pitted & diced
- 2 kiwis, peeled & quartered

Directions:

1. Start by mixing your lime juice, basil and honey together in a small bowl. In a different bowl mix your strawberries, quinoa, blackberries, peach, kiwis and mango. Add in your honey mixture, and toss to coat before serving.

Nutrition 159 calories 12g fats 9g carbohydrates 29g protein

95. Strawberry Rhubarb Smoothie

Preparation Time: 8 minutes
Cooking Time: 0 minute
Servings: 1
Ingredients:

- 1 cup strawberries, fresh & sliced
- 1 rhubarb stalk, chopped
- 2 tablespoons honey, raw
- 3 ice cubes
- 1/8 teaspoon ground cinnamon
- ½ cup Greek yogurt, plain

Directions:

1. Start by getting out a small saucepan and fill it with water. Place it over high heat to bring it to a boil, and then add in your rhubarb.
2. Boil for three minutes before draining and transferring it to a blender.
3. In your blender add in your yogurt, honey, cinnamon and strawberries. Once smooth, stir in your ice. Blend until there are no lumps and it's thick. Enjoy cold.

Nutrition 201 calories 11g fats 9g carbohydrates 39g protein

96. Barley Porridge

Preparation Time: 10 minutes
Cooking Time: 20 minutes

Servings: 4

Ingredients:

- 1 cup wheat berries
- 1 cup barley
- 2 cups almond milk, unsweetened + more for serving
- ½ cup blueberries
- ½ cup pomegranate seeds
- 2 cups water
- ½ cup hazelnuts, toasted & chopped
- ¼ cup honey, raw

Directions:

1. Get out a saucepan and put it over medium-high heat, and then add in your almond milk, water, barley and wheat berries. Let it boil before lowering the heat and allow it to simmer for twenty-five minutes. Stir frequently. Your grains should become tender.
2. Top each serving with blueberries, pomegranate seeds, hazelnuts, a tablespoon of honey and a splash of almond milk.

Nutrition 150 calories 10g fats 9g carbohydrates 29g protein

97. Gingerbread & Pumpkin Smoothie

Preparation Time: 15 minutes
Cooking Time: 50 minutes
Servings: 1

Ingredients:

- 1 cup almond milk, unsweetened
- 2 teaspoons chia seeds
- 1 banana
- ½ cup pumpkin puree, canned
- ¼ teaspoon ginger, ground
- ¼ teaspoon cinnamon, ground
- 1/8 teaspoon nutmeg, ground

Directions:

1. Start by getting out a bowl and mix your chai seeds and almond milk. Allow them to soak for at least an hour, but you can soak them overnight. Transfer them to a blender.
2. Add in your remaining ingredients, and then blend until smooth. Serve chilled.

Nutrition 250 calories 13g fats 7g carbohydrates 26g protein

98. Green Juice

Preparation Time: 5 minutes
Cooking Time: 0 minute
Servings: 1

Ingredients

- 3 cups dark leafy greens
- 1 cucumber
- ¼ cup fresh Italian parsley leaves
- ¼ pineapple, cut into wedges
- ½ green apple
- ½ orange
- ½ lemon
- Pinch grated fresh ginger

Directions

1. Using a juicer, run the greens, cucumber, parsley, pineapple, apple, orange, lemon, and ginger through it, pour into a large cup, and serve.

Nutrition 200 calories 14g fats 6g carbohydrates 27g protein

99. Walnut & Date Smoothie

Preparation Time: 10 minutes
Cooking Time: 0 minute
Servings: 2

Ingredients:

- 4 dates, pitted
- ½ cup milk
- 2 cups Greek yogurt, plain
- 1/2 cup walnuts
- ½ teaspoon cinnamon, ground
- ½ teaspoon vanilla extract, pure
- 2-3 ice cubes

Directions:

1. Blend everything together until smooth, and then serve chilled.

Nutrition 109 calories 11g fats 7g carbohydrates 29g protein

100. Fruit Smoothie

Preparation Time: 5 minutes
Cooking Time: 0 minute
Servings: 2

Ingredients

- 2 cups blueberries
- 2 cups unsweetened almond milk
- 1 cup crushed ice
- ½ teaspoon ground ginger

Directions

1. Put the blueberries, almond milk, ice, and ginger in a blender. Process until smooth.

Nutrition 115 calories 10g fats 5g carbohydrates 27g protein

101. Chocolate Banana Smoothie

Preparation Time: 5 minutes
Cooking Time: 0 minute
Servings: 2

Ingredients

- 2 bananas, peeled
- 1 cup skim milk
- 1 cup crushed ice
- 3 tablespoons unsweetened cocoa powder
- 3 tablespoons honey

Directions

1. In a blender, mix the bananas, almond milk, ice, cocoa powder, and honey. Blend until smooth.

Nutrition 150 calories 18g fats 6g carbohydrates 30g protein

102. Yogurt with Blueberries, Honey, and Mint

Preparation Time: 5 minutes
Cooking Time: 0 minute
Servings: 2
Ingredients
- 2 cups unsweetened nonfat plain Greek yogurt
- 1 cup blueberries
- 3 tablespoons honey
- 2 tablespoons fresh mint leaves, chopped

Directions
1. Apportion the yogurt between 2 small bowls. Top with the blueberries, honey, and mint.

Nutrition 126 calories 12g fats 8g carbohydrates 37g protein

103. Berry and Yogurt Parfait

Preparation Time: 5 minutes
Cooking Time: 0 minute
Servings: 2
Ingredients
- 1 cup raspberries
- 1½ cups unsweetened nonfat plain Greek yogurt
- 1 cup blackberries
- ¼ cup chopped walnuts

Directions
1. In 2 bowls, layer the raspberries, yogurt, and blackberries. Sprinkle with the walnuts.

Nutrition 119 calories 13g fats 7g carbohydrates 28g protein

104. Oatmeal with Berries and Sunflower Seeds

Preparation Time: 5 minutes
Cooking Time: 10 minutes
Servings: 4
Ingredients
- 1¾ cups water
- ½ cup unsweetened almond milk
- Pinch sea salt
- 1 cup old-fashioned oats
- ½ cup blueberries
- ½ cup raspberries
- ¼ cup sunflower seeds

Directions
1. Boil water with almond milk, and sea salt in a medium saucepan over medium-high heat.
2. Stir in the oats. Decrease the heat to medium-low and continue stirring and cook, for 5 minutes. Cover, and let the oatmeal stand for 2 minutes more. Stir and serve topped with the blueberries, raspberries, and sunflower seeds.

Nutrition 106 calories 9g fats 8g carbohydrates 29g protein

105. Almond and Maple Quick Grits

Preparation Time: 5 minutes
Cooking Time: 10 minutes
Servings: 4
Ingredients
- 1½ cups water
- ½ cup unsweetened almond milk
- Pinch sea salt
- ½ cup quick-cooking grits
- ½ teaspoon ground cinnamon
- ¼ cup pure maple syrup
- ¼ cup slivered almonds

Directions
1. Put water, almond milk, and sea salt in a medium saucepan over medium-high heat and wait to boil.
2. Stir continuously with a wooden spoon, slowly add the grits. Continue stirring to prevent lumps and bring the mixture to a slow boil. Reduce the heat to medium-low. Simmer for few minutes, stirring regularly, until the water is completely absorbed.
3. Stir in the cinnamon, syrup, and almonds. Cook for 1 minute more, stirring.

Nutrition 126 calories 10g fats 7g carbohydrates 28g protein

106. Fruity Oats

Preparation Time: 10 minutes
Cooking Time: 10 minutes
Servings: 2
Ingredients
- 1 banana, peeled and sliced
- ¾ c. almond milk
- ½ c. cold-brewed coffee
- 2 pitted dates
- 2 tbsps. cocoa powder
- 1 c. rolled oats
- 1 ½ tbsps. chia seeds

Directions:
1. Using a blender, add in all ingredients. Process well for 5 minutes and serve.

Nutrition 288 Calories 4.4g Fat10g Carbohydrates 5.9g Protein

107. Leafy Sandwich

Preparation Time: 5 minutes
Cooking Time: 20 minutes
Servings: 4
Ingredients
- 4 multigrain sandwich thins
- 4 tsps. olive oil
- 4 eggs
- 1 tbsp. rosemary, fresh
- 2 c. baby spinach leaves, fresh

- 1 tomato, sliced
- 1 tbsp. of feta cheese
- Pinch of kosher salt
- Ground black pepper

Directions:
1. Prepare oven at 375 F/190 C. Brush the thins' sides with 2 tsps. of olive oil and set on a baking sheet. Set in the oven and toast for 5 minutes or until the edges are lightly brown.
2. In a skillet, add in the rest of the olive oil and rosemary to heat over high heat. Break and place whole eggs one at a time into the skillet. The yolk should still be runny, but the egg whites should be set.
3. Break yolks up with a spatula. Flip the egg and cook on another side until done. Remove eggs from heat. Place toasted sandwich thins on 4 separate plates. Divine spinach among the thins.
4. Top each thin with two tomato slices, cooked egg, and 1 tbsp. of feta cheese. Lightly sprinkle with salt and pepper for flavoring. Place remaining sandwich thin halves over the top and they are ready to serve.

Nutrition 241 Calories 12.2g Fat 60.2g Carbohydrates 21g Protein

108. Apricot Couscous

Preparation Time: 10 minutes
Cooking Time: 8 minutes
Servings: 4
Ingredients
- 3 c. low-fat milk
- 1 c. whole-wheat couscous, uncooked
- 1 cinnamon stick
- ½ chopped apricot, dried
- ¼ c. currants, dried
- 6 tsps. brown sugar
- ¼ tsp. salt
- 4 tsps. melted butter

Directions:
1. Take a large saucepan and combine milk and cinnamon stick and heat over medium. Heat for 3 minutes or until microbubbles forms around edges of the pan. Do not boil.
2. Remove from heat, stir in the couscous, apricots, currants, salt, and 4 tsps. brown sugar. Cover the mixture and allow it to sit for 15 minutes. Remove and throw away the cinnamon stick. Divide couscous among 4 bowls, and top each with 1 tsp. melted butter and ½ tsp. brown sugar. Ready to serve.

Nutrition 306 Calories 6g Fat 5g Carbohydrates 9g Protein

109. Guaca-Apple Smoothie

Preparation Time: 5 minutes
Cooking Time: 0 minute

Servings: 2
Ingredients
- 3 c. spinach
- 1 cored green apple, chopped
- 1 pitted avocado, peeled and chopped
- 3 tbsps. chia seeds
- 1 tsp. honey
- 1 frozen banana, peeled
- 2 c. coconut water

Directions:
1. Using your blender, add in all the ingredients. Process well for 5 minutes to obtain a smooth consistency and serve in glasses.

Nutrition 208 Calories 10.1g Fat 6g Carbohydrates 7g Protein

110. Bite-size Frittatas

Preparation Time: 10 minutes
Cooking Time: 20 minutes
Servings: 8
Ingredients
- 1 chopped yellow onion
- 1 c. grated parmesan
- 1 chopped yellow bell pepper
- 1 chopped red bell pepper
- 1 chopped zucchini
- Salt and black pepper
- A drizzle of olive oil
- 8 whisked eggs
- 2 tbsps. chopped chives

Directions:
1. Set a pan over medium-high heat. Add in oil to warm. Stir in all ingredients except chives and eggs. Sauté for around 5 minutes.
2. Put the eggs on a muffin pan and top by the chives. Set oven to 350 F/176 C. Place the muffin pan into the oven to bake for about 10 minutes. Serve the eggs on a plate with sautéed vegetables.

Nutrition 55 Calories 3g Fat 0.7g Carbohydrates 9g Protein

111. Sun-dried Tomatoes Oats

Preparation Time: 10 minutes
Cooking Time: 25 minutes
Servings: 4
Ingredients
- 3 c. water
- 1 c. almond milk
- 1 tbsp. olive oil
- 1 c. steel-cut oats
- ¼ c. chopped tomatoes, sun-dried
- A pinch of red pepper flakes

Directions:
1. Using a pan, add water and milk to mix. Set on medium heat and allow to boil. Set up another pan

on medium-high heat. Warm oil and add oats to cook for 2 minutes.

2. Transfer to the first pan plus tomatoes then stir. Let simmer for approximately 20 minutes. Set in serving bowls and top with red pepper flakes. Enjoy.

Nutrition 170 Calories 17.8g Fat 1.5g Carbohydrates10g Protein

112. **Egg on Avocado**

Preparation Time: 5 minutes
Cooking Time: 15 minutes
Servings: 6
Ingredients

- 1 tsp. garlic powder
- ½ tsp. sea salt
- ¼ c. shredded Parmesan cheese
- ¼ tsp. black pepper
- 3 pitted avocados, halved
- 6 eggs

Directions:

1. Ready the muffin tins and prepare the oven at 350 F/176 C. Split the avocado. To ensure that the egg would fit inside the cavity of the avocado, lightly scrape off 1/3 of the meat.
2. Place avocado on a muffin tin to ensure that it faces with the top-up. Evenly season each avocado with pepper, salt, and garlic powder. Add one egg on each avocado cavity and garnish tops with cheese. Set in your oven to bake until the egg white is set, about 15 minutes. Serve and enjoy.

Nutrition 252 Calories 20g Fat 2g Carbohydrates5g Protein

113. **Egg- Potato Hash**

Preparation Time: 10 minutes
Cooking Time: 25 minutes
Servings: 2
Ingredients

- 1 zucchini, diced
- ½ c. chicken broth
- ½ lb. or 220 g cooked chicken
- 1 tbsp. olive oil
- 4 oz. or 113g shrimp
- Salt and black pepper
- 1 diced sweet potato
- 2 eggs
- ¼ tsp. cayenne pepper
- 2 tsps. garlic powder
- 1 c. fresh spinach

Directions:

1. In a skillet, add the olive oil. Fry the shrimp, cooked chicken and sweet potato for 2 minutes. Add the cayenne pepper, garlic powder and toss for 4 minutes. Add the zucchini and toss for another 3 minutes.

2. Whisk the eggs in a bowl and add to the skillet. Season using salt and pepper. Cover with the lid. Cook for 1 more minute and mix in the chicken broth.
3. Cover and cook for another 8 minutes on high heat. Add the spinach, toss for 2 more minutes and serve.

Nutrition 198 Calories 0.7g Fat 7g Carbohydrates10g Protein

114. **Tomato Basil Soup**

Preparation Time: 10 minutes
Cooking Time: 25 minutes
Servings: 2
Ingredients

- 2 tbsps. vegetable broth
- 1 minced garlic clove
- ½ c. white onion
- 1 chopped celery stalk
- 1 chopped carrot
- 3 c. tomatoes, chopped
- Salt and pepper
- 2 bay leaves
- 1 ½ c. unsweetened almond milk
- 1/3 c. basil leaves

Directions:

1. Cook the vegetable broth in a large saucepan over medium heat. Add in garlic and onions and cook for 4 minutes. Add in carrots and celery. Cook for 1 more minute.
2. Put in the tomatoes and bring to a boil. Simmer for 15 minutes. Add the almond milk, basil and bay leaves. Season it and serve.

Nutrition 213 Calories 3.9g Fat 9g Carbohydrates11g Protein

115. **Butternut Squash Dip**

Preparation Time: 10 minutes
Cooking Time: 15 minutes
Servings: 4
Ingredients

- 2 lbs. or 900 g seeded butternut squash, peeled
- 1 tbsp. olive oil
- ¼ c. tahini
- 2 tbsps. lemon juice
- 2 minced cloves garlic
- Salt and pepper

Directions:

1. Heat the oven to 300 F/148 C. Coat the butternut squash with olive oil. Set in a baking dish to bake for 15 minutes in the oven. When the squash is cooked, incorporate in a food processor together with the rest of the ingredients.
2. Pulse until smooth. Serve with carrots and celery sticks. For further use of place in individual containers, put a label and store it in the fridge.

Allow warming at room temperature before heating in the microwave oven.

Nutrition 115 Calories 5.8g Fat 6.7g Carbohydrates 10g Protein

116. **Ham-Spinach Muffins**

Preparation Time: 10 minutes
Cooking Time: 15 minutes
Servings: 6
Ingredients
- 9 ham slices
- 1/3 c. chopped spinach
- ¼ c. crumbled feta cheese
- ½ c. chopped roasted red peppers
- Salt and black pepper
- 1½ tbsps. basil pesto
- 5 whisked eggs

Directions:
1. Grease a muffin tin. Use 1 ½ ham slices to line each of the muffin molds. Except for black pepper, salt, pesto, and eggs, divide the rest of the ingredients into your ham cups.
2. Using a bowl, whisk together the pepper, salt, pesto, and eggs. Pour your pepper mixture on top. Set oven to 400 F/204 C and bake for about 15 minutes. Serve immediately.

Nutrition 109 Calories 6.7g Fat 1.8g Carbohydrates 9g Protein

117. **Farro-Avocado Salad**

Preparation Time: 10 minutes
Cooking Time: 0 minute
Servings: 2
Ingredients
- 1 tbsp. olive oil
- Salt and black pepper
- 1 bunch baby spinach, chopped
- 1 pitted avocado, peeled and chopped
- 1 minced garlic clove
- 2 c. cooked farro
- ½ c. cherry tomatoes, cubed

Directions:
1. Adjust your heat to medium. Set oil in a pan and heat. Toss in the rest of the ingredients. Cook the mixture for approximately 5 minutes. Set in serving plates and enjoy.

Nutrition 157 Calories 13.7g Fat 5.5g Carbohydrates 6g Protein

118. **Berry Dates Squares**

Preparation Time: 10 minutes
Cooking Time: 20 minutes
Servings: 10
Ingredients

- 12 pitted dates, chopped
- 1 tsp. vanilla extract
- ¼ c. honey
- ½ c. rolled oats
- ¾ c. dried cranberries
- ¼ c. melted almond avocado oil
- 1 c. chopped walnuts, roasted
- ¼ c. pumpkin seeds

Directions:
1. Using a bowl, stir in all ingredients to mix.
2. Line a parchment paper on a baking sheet. Press the mixture on the setup. Set in your freezer for about 30 minutes. Slice into 10 squares and enjoy.

Nutrition 263 Calories 13.4g Fat 14.3g Carbohydrates 7g Protein

119. **Cheesy Lentils Frittata**

Preparation Time: 5 minutes
Cooking Time: 17 minutes
Servings: 4
Ingredients
- 1 chopped red onion
- 2 tbsps. olive oil
- 1 c. boiled sweet potatoes, chopped
- ¾ c. chopped ham
- 4 whisked eggs
- ¾ c. cooked lentils
- 2 tbsps. Greek yogurt
- Salt and black pepper
- ½ c. halved cherry tomatoes,
- ¾ c. grated cheddar cheese

Directions:
1. Adjust your heat to medium and set a pan in place. Add in oil to heat. Stir in onion and allow to sauté for about 2 minutes. Except for cheese and eggs, toss in the other ingredients and cook for 3 more minutes. Add in the eggs, top with cheese. Cook for 10 more minutes while covered.
2. Slice the frittata, set in serving bowls and enjoy.

Nutrition 274 Calories 17.3g Fat 3.5g Carbohydrates 6g Protein

120. **Tuna Spinach Sandwich**

Preparation Time: 5 minutes
Cooking Time: 5 minutes
Servings: 2
Ingredients
- 6 oz. or 170 g canned tuna, drained and flaked
- 1 pitted avocado, peeled and mashed
- 4 whole-wheat bread slices
- Pinch salt and black pepper
- 1 tbsp. crumbled feta cheese
- 1 c. baby spinach

Directions:

1. Using a bowl, stir in pepper, salt, tuna, and cheese to mix. To the bread slices, apply a spread of the mashed avocado.
2. Equally, divide the tuna mixture and spinach onto 2 of the slices. Top with the remaining 2 slices. Serve.

Nutrition 283 Calories 11.2g Fat 3.4g Carbohydrates 8g Protein

121. Denver Fried Omelet

Preparation Time: 10 minutes
Cooking Time: 30 minutes
Servings: 4
Ingredients:
- 2 tablespoons butter
- 1/2 onion, minced meat
- 1/2 green pepper, minced
- 1 cup chopped cooked ham
- 8 eggs
- 1/4 cup of milk
- 1/2 cup grated cheddar cheese and ground black pepper to taste

Directions:
1. Preheat the oven to 200 degrees C (400 degrees F). Grease a round baking dish of 10 inches.
2. Melt the butter over medium heat; cook and stir onion and pepper until soft, about 5 minutes. Stir in the ham and keep cooking until everything is hot for 5 minutes.
3. Whip the eggs and milk in a large bowl. Stir in the mixture of cheddar cheese and ham; Season with salt and black pepper. Pour the mixture in a baking dish. Bake in the oven, about 25 minutes. Serve hot.

Nutrition 345 Calories 26.8g Fat 3.6g Carbohydrates 22.4g Protein

122. Sausage Pan

Preparation Time: 25 minutes
Cooking Time: 1 hour
Servings: 12
Ingredients:
- 1-pound Sage Breakfast Sausage,
- 3 cups grated potatoes, drained and squeezed
- 1/4 cup melted butter,
- 12 oz soft grated Cheddar cheese
- 1/2 cup onion, grated
- 1 (16 oz) small cottage cheese container
- 6 giant eggs

Directions:
1. Set up the oven to 190 ° C. Grease a 9 x 13-inch square oven dish lightly.
2. Place the sausage in a big deep-frying pan. Bake over medium heat until smooth. Drain, crumble, and reserve.
3. Mix the grated potatoes and butter in the prepared baking dish. Cover the bottom and sides of the dish with the mixture. Combine in a bowl sausage,

cheddar, onion, cottage cheese, and eggs. Pour over the potato mixture. Let it bake.
4. Allow cooling for 5 minutes before serving.

Nutrition 355 Calories 26.3g Fat 7.9g Carbohydrates 21.6g Protein

123. Grilled Marinated Shrimp

Preparation Time: 30 minutes
Cooking Time: 1 hour
Servings: 6
Ingredients:
- 1 cup olive oil,
- 1/4 cup chopped fresh parsley
- 1 lemon, juiced,
- 3 cloves of garlic, finely chopped
- 1 tablespoon tomato puree
- 2 teaspoons dried oregano,
- 1 teaspoon salt
- 2 tablespoons hot pepper sauce
- 1 teaspoon ground black pepper,
- 2 pounds of shrimp, peeled and stripped of tails

Directions:
1. Combine olive oil, parsley, lemon juice, hot sauce, garlic, tomato puree, oregano, salt, and black pepper in a bowl. Reserve a small amount to string later. Fill the large, resealable plastic bag with marinade and shrimp. Close and let it chill for 2 hours.
2. Preheat the grill on medium heat. Thread shrimp on skewers, poke once at the tail, and once at the head. Discard the marinade.
3. Lightly oil the grill. Cook the prawns for 5 minutes on each side or until they are opaque, often baste with the reserved marinade.

Nutrition 447 Calories 37.5g Fat 3.7g Carbohydrates 25.3g Protein

124. Sausage Egg Casserole

Preparation Time: 20 minutes
Cooking Time: 1 hour 10 minutes
Servings: 12
Ingredients:
- 3/4-pound finely chopped pork sausage
- 1 tablespoon butter
- 4 green onions, minced meat
- 1/2 pound of fresh mushrooms
- 10 eggs, beaten
- 1 container (16 grams) low-fat cottage cheese
- 1 pound of Monterey Jack Cheese, grated
- 2 cans of a green pepper diced, drained
- 1 cup flour, 1 teaspoon baking powder
- 1/2 teaspoon salt
- 1/3 cup melted butter

Directions:
1. Put sausage in a deep-frying pan. Bake over medium heat until smooth. Drain and set aside.

Melt the butter in a pan, cook and stir the green onions and mushrooms until they are soft.

2. Combine eggs, cottage cheese, Monterey Jack cheese, and peppers in a large bowl. Stir in sausages, green onions, and mushrooms. Cover and spend the night in the fridge.
3. Setup the oven to 175 ° C (350 ° F). Grease a 9 x 13-inch light baking dish.
4. Sift the flour, baking powder, and salt into a bowl. Stir in the melted butter. Incorporate flour mixture into the egg mixture. Pour into the prepared baking dish. Bake until lightly browned. Let stand for 10 minutes before serving.

Nutrition 408 Calories 28.7g Fat 12.4g Carbohydrates 25.2g Protein

125. Baked Omelet Squares

Preparation Time: 15 Minutes
Cooking Time: 30 minutes
Servings: 8
Ingredients:
- 1/4 cup butter
- 1 small onion, minced meat
- 1 1/2 cups grated cheddar cheese
- 1 can of sliced mushrooms
- 1 can slice black olives cooked ham (optional)
- sliced jalapeno peppers (optional)
- 12 eggs, scrambled eggs
- 1/2 cup of milk
- salt and pepper, to taste

Directions:
1. Prepare the oven to 205 ° C (400 ° F). Grease a 9 x 13-inch baking dish.
2. Cook the butter in a frying pan over medium heat and cook the onion until done.
3. Lay out the Cheddar cheese on the bottom of the prepared baking dish. Layer with mushrooms, olives, fried onion, ham, and jalapeno peppers. Stir the eggs in a bowl with milk, salt, and pepper. Pour the egg mixture over the ingredients, but do not mix.
4. Bake in the uncovered and preheated oven, until no more liquid flows in the middle and is light brown above. Allow to cool a little, then cut it into squares and serve.

Nutrition 344 Calories 27.3g Fat 7.2g Carbohydrates 17.9g Protein

126. Hard-Boiled Egg

Preparation Time: 5 minutes
Cooking Time: 15 minutes
Servings: 8
Ingredients:
- 1 tablespoon of salt
- 1/4 cup distilled white vinegar
- 6 cups of water

- 8 eggs

Directions:
1. Place the salt, vinegar, and water in a large saucepan and bring to a boil over high heat. Mix in the eggs simultaneously, and be careful not to split them. Reduce heat and cook over low heat and cook for 14 minutes.
2. Pull out the eggs from the hot water and place them in a container filled with ice water or cold water. Cool completely, approximately 15 minutes.

Nutrition 72 Calories 5g Fat 0.4g Carbohydrates 6.3g Protein

127. Mushrooms with a Soy Sauce Glaze

Preparation Time: 5 minutes
Cooking Time:10 minutes
Servings: 2
Ingredients:
- 2 tablespoons butter
- 1(8 ounces) package sliced white mushrooms
- 2 cloves garlic, minced
- 2 teaspoons soy sauce
- ground black pepper to taste

Directions:
1. Cook the butter in a frying pan over medium heat; stir in the mushrooms; cook and stir until the mushrooms are soft and released about 5 minutes.
2. Stir in the garlic; keep cooking and stir for 1 minute. Pour the soy sauce; cook the mushrooms in the soy sauce until the liquid has evaporated, about 4 minutes.

Nutrition 135 Calories 11.9g Fat 5.4g Carbohydrates 4.2g Protein

128. Pepperoni Eggs

Preparation Time: 10 minutes
Cooking Time: 20 minutes
Servings: 2
Ingredients:
- 1 cup of egg substitute
- 1 egg
- 3 green onions, minced meat
- 8 slices of pepperoni, diced
- 1/2 teaspoon of garlic powder
- 1 teaspoon melted butter
- 1/4 cup grated Romano cheese
- salt and ground black pepper to taste

Directions:
1. Combine the egg substitute, the egg, the green onions, the pepperoni slices, and the garlic powder in a bowl.
2. Cook the butter in a non-stick frying pan over low heat; Add the egg mixture, seal the pan and cook 10

to 15 minutes. Sprinkle Romano's eggs and season with salt and pepper.

Nutrition 266 Calories 16.2g Fat 3.7g Carbohydrates 25.3g Protein

129. Egg Cupcakes

Preparation Time: 15 minutes
Cooking Time: 20 minutes
Servings: 6
Ingredients:
- 1 pack of bacon (12 ounces)
- 6 eggs
- 2 tablespoons of milk
- 1/4 teaspoon salt
- 1/4 teaspoon ground black pepper
- 1 c. Melted butter
- 1/4 teaspoon. Dried parsley
- 1/2 cup ham
- 1/4 cup mozzarella cheese
- 6 slices gouda

Directions:
1. Prepare the oven to 175 ° C (350 ° F). Cook bacon over medium heat, until it starts to brown. Dry the bacon slices with kitchen paper.
2. Situate the slices of bacon in the 6 cups of the non-stick muffin pan. Slice the remaining bacon and put it at the bottom of each cup.
3. Mix eggs, milk, butter, parsley, salt, and pepper. Add in the ham and mozzarella cheese.
4. Fill the cups with the egg mixture; garnish with Gouda cheese.
5. Bake in the preheated oven until Gouda cheese is melted and the eggs are tender about 15 minutes.

Nutrition 310 Calories 22.9g Fat 2.1g Carbohydrates 23.1g Protein

130. Dinosaur Eggs

Preparation Time: 20 minutes
Cooking Time: 15 minutes
Servings: 4
Ingredients:
Mustard sauce:
- 1/4 cup coarse mustard
- 1/4 cup Greek yogurt
- 1 teaspoon garlic powder
- 1 pinch of cayenne pepper

Eggs:
- 2 beaten eggs
- 2 cups of mashed potato flakes
- 4 boiled eggs, peeled
- 1 can (15 oz) HORMEL® Mary Kitchen® minced beef finely chopped can
- 2 liters of vegetable oil for frying

Directions:

1. Combine the old-fashioned mustard, Greek yogurt, garlic powder, and cayenne pepper in a small bowl until smooth.
2. Transfer the 2 beaten eggs in a shallow dish; place the potato flakes in a separate shallow dish.
3. Divide the minced meat into 4 Servings. Form salted beef around each egg until it is completely wrapped.
4. Soak the wrapped eggs in the beaten egg and brush with mashed potatoes until they are covered.
5. Fill the oil in a large saucepan and heat at 190 ° C (375 ° F).
6. Put 2 eggs in the hot oil and bake for 3 to 5 minutes until brown. Remove with a drop of spoon and place on a plate lined with kitchen paper. Repeat this with the remaining 2 eggs.
7. Cut lengthwise and serve with a mustard sauce.

Nutrition 784 Calories 63.2g Fat 34g Carbohydrates 19.9g Protein

131. Dill and Tomato Frittata

Preparation Time: 10 minutes
Cooking Time: 35 minutes
Servings: 6
Ingredients:
- Pepper and salt to taste
- 1 teaspoon red pepper flakes
- 2 garlic cloves, minced
- ½ cup crumbled goat cheese – optional
- 2 tablespoon fresh chives, chopped
- 2 tablespoon fresh dill, chopped
- 4 tomatoes, diced
- 8 eggs, whisked
- 1 teaspoon coconut oil

Directions:
1. Grease a 9-inch round baking pan and preheat oven to 325oF.
2. In a large bowl, mix well all ingredients and pour into prepped pan.
3. Lay into the oven and bake until middle is cooked through around 30-35 minutes.
4. Remove from oven and garnish with more chives and dill.

Nutrition 149 Calories 10.28g Fat 9.93g Carbohydrates 13.26g Protein

132. Paleo Almond Banana Pancakes

Preparation Time: 10 minutes
Cooking Time: 10 minutes
Servings: 3
Ingredients:
- ¼ cup almond flour
- ½ teaspoon ground cinnamon
- 3 eggs

- 1 banana, mashed
- 1 tablespoon almond butter
- 1 teaspoon vanilla extract
- 1 teaspoon olive oil
- Sliced banana to serve

Directions:
1. Whip eggs in a bowl until fluffy. In another bowl, mash the banana using a fork and add to the egg mixture. Add the vanilla, almond butter, cinnamon and almond flour. Mix into a smooth batter. Heat the olive oil in a skillet. Add one spoonful of the batter and fry them on both sides.
2. Keep doing these steps until you are done with all the batter.
3. Add some sliced banana on top before serving.

Nutrition 306 Calories 26g Fat 3.6g Carbohydrates 14.4g Protein

133. Zucchini with Egg

Preparation Time: 5 minutes
Cooking Time: 10 minutes
Servings: 2
Ingredients:
- 1 1/2 tablespoons olive oil
- 2 large zucchinis, cut into large chunks
- salt and ground black pepper to taste
- 2 large eggs
- 1 teaspoon water, or as desired

Directions:
1. Cook the oil in a frying pan over medium heat; sauté zucchini until soft, about 10 minutes. Season the zucchini well.
2. Lash the eggs using a fork in a bowl. Pour in water and beat until everything is well mixed. Pour the eggs over the zucchini; boil and stir until scrambled eggs and no more flowing, about 5 minutes. Season well the zucchini and eggs.

Nutrition 213 Calories 15.7g Fat 11.2g Carbohydrates 10.2g Protein

134. Cheesy Amish Breakfast Casserole

Preparation Time: 10 minutes
Cooking Time: 50 minutes
Servings: 12
Ingredients:
- 1-pound sliced bacon, diced,
- 1 sweet onion, minced meat
- 4 cups grated and frozen potatoes, thawed

- 9 lightly beaten eggs
- 2 cups of grated cheddar cheese
- 1 1/2 cup of cottage cheese
- 1 1/4 cups of grated Swiss cheese

Directions:
1. Prep the oven to 175 ° C (350 ° F). Grease a 9 x 13-inch baking dish.
2. Warm up large frying pan over medium heat; cook and stir the bacon and onion for 10 minutes. Drain. Stir in potatoes, eggs, cheddar cheese, cottage cheese, and Swiss cheese. Fill the mixture into a prepared baking dish.
3. Bake in the oven until the eggs are cooked and the cheese is melted 45 to 50 minutes. Put aside for 10 minutes before serving.

Nutrition 314 Calories 22.8g Fat 12.1g Carbohydrates 21.7g Protein

135. Salad with Roquefort Cheese

Preparation Time: 20 minutes
Cooking Time: 25 minutes
Servings: 6
Ingredients:
- 1 leaf lettuce, torn into bite-sized pieces
- 3 pears - peeled, without a core and cut into pieces
- 5 oz Roquefort cheese, crumbled
- 1/2 cup chopped green onions
- 1 avocado - peeled, seeded and diced
- 1/4 cup white sugar
- 1/2 cup pecan nuts
- 1 1/2 teaspoon white sugar
- 1/3 cup olive oil,
- 3 tablespoons red wine vinegar,
- 1 1/2 teaspoons prepared mustard,
- 1 clove of chopped garlic,
- 1/2 teaspoon ground fresh black pepper

Directions:
1. Incorporate 1/4 cup of sugar with the pecans in a frying pan over medium heat. Continue to stir gently until the sugar has melted with pecans. Carefully situate the nuts to wax paper. Set aside and break into pieces.
2. Combination for vinaigrette oil, vinegar, 1 1/2 teaspoon of sugar, mustard, chopped garlic, salt, and pepper.
3. In a large bowl, mix lettuce, pears, blue cheese, avocado, and green onions. Pour vinaigrette over salad, topped with pecans and serve.

Nutrition 426 Calories 31.6g Fat 33.1g Carbohydrates 8g Protein

136. Roasted Beet Salad with Ricotta Cheese

Preparation Time: 10 minutes
Cooking Time: 1 hour
Serving: 4
Ingredients:
- Red beets (8.8 oz, large, wrapped in foil)
- Yellow beets (8.8 oz, small, wrapped in foil)
- Mesclun (4.3 oz)
- Mustard Vinaigrette (4.4 oz)
- Ricotta cheese (2.1 oz)
- Walnuts (0.1 oz, chopped)

Directions:
1. Bake at 400 F for 1 hour.
2. Set aside the beets lightly. Cut the root and stem ends and pull off the peels.
3. Chop the red beets crosswise into thin slices.
4. Cut the yellow beets vertically into quarters.
5. Arrange the sliced red beets in circles on cold salad plates. Toss the mesclun with half the vinaigrette.
6. Pour in the remaining vinaigrette over the sliced beets.
7. Place small mound of greens in the center of each plate.
8. Lay out the quartered yellow beets around the greens.
9. Drizzle the tops with the crumbled ricotta and walnuts (if using).

Nutrition: 290 Calories 6g Fat 6g Protein

137. Baked Fish with Tomatoes and Mushrooms

Preparation Time: 12 minutes
Cooking Time: 25 minutes
Serving: 4
Ingredients:
- Fish (4, whole and small, 12 oz each)
- Salt (to taste)
- Pepper (to taste)
- Dried thyme (pinch)
- Parsley (4 sprigs)
- Olive oil (as needed)
- Onion (4 oz, small dice)
- Shallots (1 oz, minced)
- Mushrooms (8 oz, chopped)
- Tomato concassed (6.4 oz)
- Dry white wine (3.2 Fl oz)

Directions:
1. Scale and clean the fish but leaves the heads on. Season the fish inside and out with salt and pepper and put a small pinch of thyme and a sprig of parsley in the cavity of each.
2. Use as many baking pans to hold the fish in a single layer. Oil the pans with a little olive oil.
3. Sauté the onions and shallots in a little olive oil about 1 minute. Add the mushrooms and sauté lightly.
4. Place the sautéed vegetables and the tomatoes in the bottoms of the baking pans.
5. Place the fish in the pans. Oil the tops lightly. Pour in the wine.
6. Bake at 400F for 15-20 minutes.
7. Remove the fish and keep them warm.
8. Remove the vegetables from the pans with a slotted spoon and check for seasonings. Serve a spoonful of the vegetables with the fish, placing it under or alongside each fish.
9. Strain, degrease, and reduce the cooking liquid slightly. Just before serving, moisten each portion with 1-2 tbsp of the liquid.

Nutrition: 350 Calories 9g Fat 55g Protein

138. Goat Cheese and Walnut Salad

Preparation Time: 15 minutes
Cooking Time: 10 minutes
Serving: 3
Ingredients:
- Beet (2 oz)
- Arugula (3 oz)
- Bibb lettuce (2 oz)
- Romaine lettuce (9 oz)
- Breadcrumbs (1/4 cup, dry)
- Dried thyme (1/4 tbs)
- Dried basil (1/4 tbs)
- Black pepper (1/3 tsp)
- Fresh goat's milk cheese (6.35 oz, preferably in log shape)
- Walnut pieces (1.1 oz)
- Red wine vinaigrette (2 fl. Oz.)

Directions:
1. Trim, wash, and dry all the salad greens.
2. Tear the greens into small pieces. Toss well.
3. Combine the herbs, pepper, and crumbs.
4. Slice the cheese into 1 oz pieces. In the seasoned crumbs mix, roll the pieces of cheese to coat them
5. Place the cheese on a sheet pan. Bake at the temperate of 425 F for 10 minutes.
6. Simultaneously, toast the walnuts in a dry sauté pan or the oven with the cheese.
7. Toss the greens with the vinaigrette and arrange on

cold plates. Top each plate of greens with 2 pieces of cheese and sprinkle with walnuts.

Nutrition: 460 Calories 40g Fat 17g Protein

139. Grilled Spiced Turkey Burger

Preparation Time: 15 minutes
Cooking Time: 20 minutes
Serving: 3
Ingredients:

- Onion (1.8 oz, chopped fine)
- Extra Virgin Olive Oil (1/3 tbsp)
- Turkey (14.4 oz, ground)
- Salt (1/3 tbsp)
- Curry powder (1/3 tbsp)
- Lemon zest (2/5 tsp, grated)
- Pepper (1/8 tsp)
- Cinnamon (1/8 tsp)
- Coriander (1/4 tsp, ground)
- Cumin (1/8 tsp, ground)
- Cardamom (1/8 tsp, ground)
- Water (1.2 Fl oz)
- Tomato Raisin Chutney (as desired)
- Cilantro leaves (as desired)

Directions:

1. Cook the onions in the oil. Cool completely.
2. Combine the turkey, onions, spices, water, and salt in a bowl. Toss.
3. Divide the mixture into 5 oz portions (or as desired). Form each portion into a thick patty.
4. Broil but do not overcook it.
5. Plate the burgers. Put spoonful of chutney on top of each.

Nutrition: 250 Calories 14g Fat 27g Protein

140. Tomato Tea Party Sandwiches

Preparation Time: 15 minutes
Cooking Time: 0 minute
Serving: 4
Ingredients:

- Whole wheat bread (4 slices)
- Extra virgin olive oil (4 1/3 tbsp)
- Basil (2 1/8 tbsp., minced)
- Tomato slices (4 thick)
- Ricotta cheese (4 oz)
- Dash of pepper

Directions:

1. Toast bread to your preference.
2. Spread 2 tsp. olive oil on each slice of bread. Add the cheese.
3. Top with tomato, then sprinkle with basil and pepper.
4. Serve with lemon water and enjoy it!

Nutrition: 239 Calories 16.4g Fat 6g Protein

141. Veggie Shish Kebabs

Preparation Time: 10 minutes
Cooking Time: 0 minute
Serving: 3
Ingredients:

- Cherry tomatoes (9)
- Mozzarella balls (9 low-fat)
- Basil leaves (9)
- Olive oil (1 tsp.)
- Zucchini (3, sliced)
- Dash of pepper

For Serving:

- Whole Wheat Bread (6 slices)

Directions:

1. Stab 1 cherry tomato, low-fat mozzarella ball, zucchini, and basil leaf onto each skewer.
2. Place skewers on a plate and drizzle with olive oil. Finish with a sprinkle of pepper.
3. Set your bread to toast. Serve 2 bread slices with 3 kebobs.

Nutrition: 349 Calories 5.7g Fat 15g Protein

142. Crispy Falafel

Preparation Time: 20 minutes
Cooking Time: 8 minutes
Serving: 3
Ingredients:

- Chickpeas (1 cup, drained and rinsed)
- Parsley (½ cup, chopped with stems removed)
- Cilantro (1/3 cup, chopped with stems removed)
- Dill (¼ cup, chopped with stems removed)
- Cloves garlic (4, minced)
- Sesame seeds (1 tbsp., toasted)
- Coriander (½ tbsp.)
- Black pepper (½ tbsp.)
- Cumin (½ tbsp.)
- Baking powder (½ tsp.)
- Cayenne (½ tsp.)

Directions:

1. Thoroughly dry your chickpeas with a paper towel.
2. Place the parsley, cilantro, and dill in a food processor.
3. Mix chickpeas, garlic, coriander, black pepper, cumin, baking powder, and cayenne.
4. Place the mixture to an airtight container and chill for about an hour.
5. Take out from the refrigerator and mix the baking powder and sesame seeds.
6. Scoop the mixture into a pan with 3 inches of olive oil over medium heat to create patties. Keep in mind as you create the patties that you are aiming to make 12 with the mixture.
7. Let the falafel patties fry for 1-2 minutes on each side.

8. Once your falafel patties are nicely browned, transfer them to a plate lined with paper towels to finish crisping.
9. Dip, dunk, fill, and enjoy!

Nutrition: 328 Calories 10.8g Fat 24g Protein

143. <u>Onion Fried Eggs</u>

Preparation Time: 15 minutes
Cooking Time: 91 minutes
Serving: 4
Ingredients:
- Eggs (11)
- White mushroom (1 cup)
- Feta cheese (4 oz, crumbled)
- Sun-dried tomatoes (1/2 cup, chopped)
- Onion (2 larges, sliced)
- Garlic clove (2, minced)
- Olive oil (2.5 tbsp.)

Directions:
1. Place a pan with the olive oil over medium-low heat.
2. Once hot, stir onions and mushrooms into the oil.
3. Allow the onion and mushroom mix to cook for about one hour. Stir them every 5-7 minutes to ensure they cook evenly.
4. After the onions have browned, add the sun-dried tomatoes and garlic, and let cook for 2 minutes.
5. Once the sun-dried tomatoes and garlic are fragrant, spread all the ingredients out into an even, thin layer across the pan.
6. Crack the eggs overtop the ingredients already in the pan.
7. Sprinkle your feta cheese and pepper over top of the eggs.
8. Cover the pan with its corresponding lid and let the eggs sit to cook for about 10-12 minutes. Gently shake the pan at 10 minutes to check on the consistency of the egg yolks. Continue cooking until desired level of doneness.
9. Remove pan from heat and divide the mixture between two plates.

Nutrition: 360 Calories 27g Fat 20g Protein

144. <u>Black Bean Cake with Salsa</u>

Preparation Time: 15 minutes
Cooking Time: 18 minutes
Serving: 10
Ingredients:
- Olive oil (1 Fl oz)
- Onion (16 oz,)
- Garlic (2-4 cloves)
- Jalapenos
- Ground cumin (2 tsp)
- Black beans (32 oz.)
- Oregano (1 tsp)
- Salsa cruda (450 ml)

Directions:
1. Cook olive oil in a sauté pan over low heat.
2. Add the garlic and onions, cook until soft. Do not brown.
3. Add the ground cumin and jalapeño. Cook for a few more minutes.
4. Add the oregano and beans. Cook until they are heated through.
5. Situate the mixture in a food processor and blend in a puree.
6. Season well.
7. Divide the mixture into 2 oz portions. Form into small, flat cakes.
8. Brown the cakes lightly on both sides in hot olive oil in a sauté pan.
9. Serve 2 cakes per portion with 1 ½ Fl oz salsa.

Nutrition: 260 Calories 12g Fat 9g Protein

145. <u>Pickled Apple</u>

Preparation Time: 10 minutes
Cooking Time: 20 minutes
Serving: 6
Ingredients:
- Water (1/2 cup)
- Maple syrup (3 ½ oz)
- Cider vinegar (1/2 cup)
- Sachet:
- Peppercorns (3-4)
- Mustard seed (1/4 tsp)
- Coriander seed (1/4 tsp)
- Salt (1/4 tsp)
- Granny smith apple (2,)
- Italian parsley (1 tbsp,)

Directions:
1. Combine the water, maple syrup, vinegar, sachet, and sat in a saucepan. Bring to a boil.
2. Pour the liquid and the sachet over the apples in a nonreactive container.
3. Let it be refrigerated for 3-4 hours or overnight.
4. Drain the apples before serving and toss with the parsley.

Nutrition: 50 Calories 0.1g Fat 0.3g Protein

146. <u>Baked Clams Oreganata</u>

Preparation Time: 30 minutes
Cooking Time: 13 minutes
Serving: 10
Ingredients:
- Cherrystone clams (30)
- Olive oil (2 Fl oz)
- Onions (1 oz, chopped fine)
- Garlic (1 tsp, finely chopped)
- Lemon juice (1 Fl oz)
- Fresh breadcrumbs (10 oz)
- Parsley (1 tbsp, chopped)

- Oregano (3/4 tsp, dried)
- White pepper (1/8 tsp)
- Parmesan cheese (1/3 cup)
- Paprika (as needed)
- Lemon wedges (10)

Directions:
1. Open the clams. Place the juice in a bowl.
2. Take out the clams from the shell. Situate them in a strainer over the bowl of juice. Let them drain 15 minutes in the refrigerator. Save the 30 best half-shells.
3. Cut the clams into small pieces.
4. Cook the oil in a sauté pan. Add the onion and garlic. Sauté about 1 minute, but do not brown.
5. Pour in half of the clam juice, then reduce it over high heat by three-fourths.
6. Remove from the heat and add the crumbs, parsley, lemon juice, white pepper, and oregano. Mix gently to avoid making the crumbs pasty.
7. If necessary, adjust the seasonings.
8. Once the mixture has cooled. Mix in the chopped clams.
9. Place the mixture in the 30 clamshells. Sprinkle with parmesan cheese and (very lightly) with paprika.
10. Place on a sheet pan and refrigerate until needed.
11. For each order, bake 3 clams in a hot oven (450 F) until they are hot and the top brown.
12. Garnish with a lemon wedge.

Nutrition: 180 Calories 8g Fat 10g Protein

147. Tuna Tartare

Preparation Time: 15 minutes
Cooking Time: 0 minute Serving: 8
Ingredients:
- Sashimi quality tuna (26.5 g, well-trimmed)
- Shallots (1 oz, minced)
- Parsley (2 tbsp, chopped)
- Fresh tarragon (2 tbsp, chopped)
- Lime juice (2 tbsp)
- Dijon-style mustard (1 Fl oz)
- Olive oil (2 Fl oz)

Directions:
1. Use a knife to mince the tuna.
2. Mixed the rest of the ingredients with the chopped tuna.
3. Use a ring mold to make a beautifully presented tuna tartare.
4. Season to taste with pepper and salt.

Nutrition 200 Calories 12g Fat 21g Protein

148. Cod Cakes

Preparation Time: 25 minutes
Cooking Time: 30 minutes
Serving: 12
Ingredients:
- Cod (12 oz, cooked)

- Turnips puree (12 oz.)
- Whole eggs (2 ½ oz, beaten)
- Egg yolk (1 yolk, beaten)
- Salt (to taste)
- White pepper (to taste)
- Ground ginger (pinch)

Standard Breading Procedure:
- Whole wheat flour
- Egg wash
- Breadcrumbs
- Tomatoes sauce

Directions:
1. Shred the fish.
2. Combine with the turnips, egg, and egg yolk.
3. Season with salt, pepper, and ground ginger.
4. Divide the mixture into 2 ½ oz portions. Shape the mixture into a ball and then slightly flatten the mixture cakes.
5. Place the mixture through the Standard Breading Procedure.
6. Deep-fry at 350 F until golden brown.
7. Serve 2 cakes per portion. Accompany with tomato sauce.

Nutrition: 280 Calories 6g Fat 23g Protein

149. Grilled Vegetable Kebabs

Preparation Time: 12 minutes
Cooking Time: 13 minutes
Serving: 6
Ingredients:
- Zucchini (6 oz, trimmed)
- Yellow Summer Squash (6 oz, trimmed)
- Bell pepper (6 oz, red or orange, cut into 1 ½ in. squares)
- Onion (12 oz, red, large dice)
- Mushroom caps (12, medium)
- Olive oil (12 Fl oz)
- Garlic (1/2 oz, crushed)
- Rosemary (1 ½ tsp, dried)
- Thyme (1/2 tsp, dried)
- Salt (2 tsp)
- Black pepper (1/2 tsp)

Directions:
1. Cut the zucchini and yellow squash into 12 equal slices each.
2. Arrange the vegetables on 12 bamboo skewers. Give each skewer an equal arrangement of vegetable pieces.
3. Place the skewers in a single layer in a hotel pan.
4. Mix the oil, garlic, herbs, salt, and pepper to make a marinade.
5. Pour the marinade over the vegetables, turning them to coat completely.
6. Marinate 1 hour. Turn the skewers once or twice during margination to ensure the vegetables are coated.

7. Remove the skewers from the marinade and let the excess oil drip off.

Nutrition: 50 Calories 3g Fat 1g Protein

150. Vegetable Fritters

Preparation Time: 15 minutes
Cooking Time: 6 minutes
Serving: 5
Ingredients:
- Egg (3, beaten)
- Milk (8 Fl oz)
- Whole wheat flour (8 oz)
- Baking powder (1 tbsp)
- Salt (½ tsp)
- Maple syrup (1/2 oz)

Vegetables:
- Carrot (12 oz,)
- Baby lima beans (12 oz)
- Asparagus (12 oz)
- Celery (12 oz)
- Turnip (12 oz)
- Eggplant (12 oz)
- Cauliflower (12 oz)
- Zucchini (12 oz)
- Parsnips (12 oz)

Directions:
1. Combine the eggs and milk.
2. Mix the flour, baking powder, salt, and maple syrup. Stir in to the milk and eggs and mix until smooth.
3. Set aside the batter for several hours in a refrigerator.
4. Stir the cold, cooked vegetable into the batter.
5. Drop with a No. 24 scoop into deep fat at 350 F. Toss the content from the scoop carefully in the hot oil. Fry until golden brown.
6. Drain well and serve.

Nutrition: 140 Calories 6g Fat 4g Protein

151. Marinated Feta and Artichokes

Preparation Time: 10 minutes + 4 hours
Cooking Time: 0 minute
Serving: 3
Ingredients:
- 4 ounces traditional Greek feta, cut into ½-inch cubes
- 4 ounces drained artichoke hearts, quartered lengthwise
- 1/3 cup extra-virgin olive oil
- Zest and juice of 1 lemon
- 2 tablespoons roughly chopped fresh rosemary
- 2 tablespoons roughly chopped fresh parsley
- ½ teaspoon black peppercorns

Direction

1. In a glass bowl, combine the feta and artichoke hearts. Add the olive oil, lemon zest and juice, rosemary, parsley, and peppercorns and toss gently to coat, being sure not to crumble the feta.
2. Wrap and cool for 4 hours before serving.

Nutrition: 235 Calories 23g Fat 4g Protein

152. Tuna Croquettes

Preparation Time: 40 minutes
Cooking Time: 25 minutes
Serving: 12
Ingredients:
- 6 tablespoons extra-virgin olive oil, plus 1 to 2 cups
- 5 tablespoons almond flour, plus 1 cup, divided
- 1¼ cups heavy cream
- 1 (4-ounce) can olive oil-packed yellowfin tuna
- 1 tablespoon chopped red onion
- 2 teaspoons minced capers
- ½ teaspoon dried dill
- ¼ teaspoon freshly ground black pepper
- 2 large eggs
- 1 cup panko breadcrumbs

Direction
1. In a huge skillet, heat 6 tablespoons olive oil over medium-low heat. Add 5 tablespoons almond flour and cook, stirring constantly, until a smooth paste forms and the flour browns slightly, 2 to 3 minutes.
2. Adjust the heat to medium-high and gradually stir in the heavy cream, whisking constantly for 5 minutes.
3. Pull out from heat and stir in the tuna, red onion, capers, dill, and pepper.
4. Pour into 8-inch square baking dish that is well coated with olive oil and allow to cool to room temperature. Cover and chill for 4 hours.
5. To form the croquettes, set out three bowls. In one, beat together the eggs. In another, add the remaining almond flour. In the third, add the panko. Line a baking sheet with parchment paper.
6. Place a tablespoon of cold prepared dough into the flour mixture and roll to coat. Shake off excess and, using your hands, roll into an oval.
7. Dip the croquette into the beaten egg, then lightly coat in panko. Set on lined baking sheet and repeat with the remaining dough.
8. In a small saucepan, cook 1 to 2 cups of olive oil over medium-high heat.
9. Once the oil is heated, fry the croquettes 3 or 4 at a time.

Nutrition: 245 Calories 22g Fat 6g Protein

153. Smoked Salmon Crudités

Preparation Time: 10 minutes
Cooking Time: 0 minute
Serving: 4
Ingredients:
- 6 ounces smoked wild salmon

- 2 tablespoons Roasted Garlic Aioli
- 1 tablespoon Dijon mustard
- 1 tablespoon chopped scallions
- 2 teaspoons chopped capers
- ½ teaspoon dried dill
- 4 endive spears or hearts of romaine
- ½ English cucumber

Direction:
1. Cut the smoked salmon. Add the aioli, Dijon, scallions, capers, and dill and mix well.
2. Top endive spears and cucumber rounds with a spoonful of smoked salmon mixture and enjoy chilled.

Nutrition: 92 Calories 5g Fat 9g Protein

154. Citrus-Marinated Olives

Preparation Time: 10 minutes + 4 hours
Cooking Time: 0 minute
Serving: 4
Ingredients:
- 2 cups mixed green olives with pits
- ¼ cup red wine vinegar
- ¼ cup extra-virgin olive oil
- 4 garlic cloves, finely minced
- Zest and juice orange
- 1 teaspoon red pepper flakes
- 2 bay leaves
- ½ teaspoon ground cumin
- ½ teaspoon ground allspice

Direction:
1. In a jar, mix olives, vinegar, oil, garlic, orange zest and juice, red pepper flakes, bay leaves, cumin, and allspice. Cover and chill for 4 hours, tossing again before serving.

Nutrition: 133 Calories 14g Fat 1g Protein

155. Olive Tapenade with Anchovies

Preparation Time: 70 minutes
Cooking Time: 0 minute
Serving: 4
Ingredient:
- 2 cups pitted Kalamata olives
- 2 anchovy fillets
- 2 teaspoons capers
- 1 garlic clove
- 1 cooked egg yolk
- 1 teaspoon Dijon mustard
- ¼ cup extra-virgin olive oil

Direction:
1. Wash olives in cold water and drain well.
2. In a food processor, mix drained olives, anchovies, capers, garlic, egg yolk, and Dijon.

3. Using the food processor running, gradually stream in the olive oil.
4. Wrap and refrigerate at least 1 hour. Serve with Seedy Crackers.

Nutrition: 179 Calories 19g Fat 2g Protein

156. Greek Deviled Eggs

Preparation Time: 45 minutes
Cooking Time: 15 minutes
Serving: 4
Ingredients:
- 4 large hardboiled eggs
- 2 tablespoons Roasted Garlic Aioli
- ½ cup feta cheese
- 8 pitted Kalamata olives
- 2 tablespoons chopped sun-dried tomatoes
- 1 tablespoon minced red onion
- ½ teaspoon dried dill
- ¼ teaspoon black pepper

Direction:
1. Slice the hardboiled eggs in half lengthwise, remove the yolks, and place the yolks in a medium bowl. Reserve the egg white halves and set aside.
2. Smash the yolks well with a fork. Add the aioli, feta, olives, sun-dried tomatoes, onion, dill, and pepper and stir to combine until smooth and creamy.
3. Ladle the filling into each egg white half and chill for 30 minutes, or up to 24 hours, covered.

Nutrition: 147 Calories 11g Fat 9g Protein

157. Manchego Crackers

Preparation Time: 55 minutes
Cooking Time: 15 minutes
Serving: 4
Ingredients:
- 4 tablespoons butter, at room temperature
- 1 cup Manchego cheese
- 1 cup almond flour
- 1 teaspoon salt, divided
- ¼ teaspoon black pepper
- 1 large egg

Direction:
1. Using an electric mixer, scourge butter and shredded cheese.
2. Mix almond flour with ½ teaspoon salt and pepper. Mix almond flour mixture to the cheese, mixing constantly to form a ball.
3. Place onto plastic wrap and roll into a cylinder log about 1½ inches thick. Wrap tightly and cool for at least 1 hour.
4. Preheat the oven to 350°F. Prep two baking sheets with parchment papers.
5. For egg wash, blend egg and remaining ½ teaspoon salt.
6. Slice the refrigerated dough into small rounds,

about ¼ inch thick, and place on the lined baking sheets.

7. Egg wash the tops of the crackers and bake for 15 minutes. Pull out from the oven and place in wire rack.

8. Serve.

Nutrition: 243 Calories 23g Fat 8g Protein

158. Burrata Caprese Stack

Preparation Time: 5 minutes
Cooking Time: 0 minutes
Serving: 4
Ingredients:
- 1 large organic tomato
- ½ teaspoon salt
- ¼ teaspoon black pepper
- 1 (4-ounce) ball burrata cheese
- 8 fresh basil leaves
- 2 tablespoons extra-virgin olive oil
- 1 tablespoon red wine

Direction
1. Slice the tomato into 4 thick slices, removing any tough center core and sprinkle with salt and pepper. Place the tomatoes, seasoned-side up, on a plate.
2. On a separate rimmed plate, slice the burrata into 4 thick slices and place one slice on top of each tomato slice. Top each with one-quarter of the basil and pour any reserved burrata cream from the rimmed plate over top.
3. Sprinkle with olive oil and vinegar.

Nutrition: 153 Calories 13g Fat 7g Protein

159. Zucchini-Ricotta Fritters with Lemon-Garlic Aioli

Preparation Time: 30 minutes
Cooking Time: 25 minutes
Serving: 4
Ingredient:
- 1 large zucchini
- 1 teaspoon salt, divided
- ½ cup whole-milk ricotta cheese
- 2 scallions
- 1 large egg
- 2 garlic cloves
- 2 tablespoons fresh mint (optional)
- 2 teaspoons grated lemon zest
- ¼ teaspoon freshly ground black pepper
- ½ cup almond flour
- 1 teaspoon baking powder
- 8 tablespoons extra-virgin olive oil
- 8 tablespoons Roasted Garlic Aioli

Direction
1. Place the shredded zucchini in a colander or on several layers of paper towels. Sprinkle with ½ teaspoon salt and let sit for 10 minutes. Using

another layer of paper towel, press down on the zucchini to release any excess moisture and pat dry.

2. Incorporate drained zucchini, ricotta, scallions, egg, garlic, mint (if using), lemon zest, remaining ½ teaspoon salt, and pepper and stir well.

3. Blend almond flour and baking powder. Mix in flour mixture into the zucchini mixture and let rest for 10 minutes.

4. In a large skillet, working in four batches, fry the fritters. For each batch of four, heat 2 tablespoons olive oil over medium-high heat. Add 1 heaping tablespoon of zucchini batter per fritter, pressing down with the back of a spoon to form 2- to 3-inch fritters. Cover and let fry 2 minutes before flipping. Fry another 2 to 3 minutes, covered.

5. Repeat for the remaining three batches, using 2 tablespoons of the olive oil for each batch.

6. Serve with aioli.

Nutrition: 448 Calories 42g Fat 8g Protein

160. Salmon-Stuffed Cucumbers

Preparation Time: 10 minutes
Cooking Time: 0 minute
Serving: 4
Ingredients:
- 2 large cucumbers, peeled
- 1 (4-ounce) can red salmon
- 1 medium very ripe avocado
- 1 tablespoon extra-virgin olive oil
- Zest and juice of 1 lime
- 3 tablespoons chopped fresh cilantro
- ½ teaspoon salt
- ¼ teaspoon black pepper

Direction:
1. Slice the cucumber into 1-inch-thick segments and using a spoon, scrape seeds out of center of each segment and stand up on a plate.
2. In a medium bowl, mix salmon, avocado, olive oil, lime zest and juice, cilantro, salt, and pepper.
3. Ladle the salmon mixture into the center of each cucumber segment and serve chilled.

Nutrition: 159 Calories 11g Fat 9g Protein

161. Goat Cheese–Mackerel Pâté

Preparation Time: 10 minutes
Cooking Time: 0 minute
Serving: 4
Ingredients:
- 4 ounces olive oil-packed wild-caught mackerel
- 2 ounces goat cheese
- Zest and juice of 1 lemon
- 2 tablespoons chopped fresh parsley
- 2 tablespoons chopped fresh arugula
- 1 tablespoon extra-virgin olive oil
- 2 teaspoons chopped capers

- 2 teaspoons fresh horseradish (optional)

Direction:
1. In a food processor, blender, or large bowl with immersion blender, combine the mackerel, goat cheese, lemon zest and juice, parsley, arugula, olive oil, capers, and horseradish (if using). Process or blend until smooth and creamy.
2. Serve with crackers, cucumber rounds, endive spears, or celery.

Nutrition: 118 Calories 8g Fat 9g Protein

162. Taste of the Mediterranean Fat Bombs

Preparation Time: 15 minutes + 4 hours
Cooking Time: 0 minute
Serving: 6
Ingredients:
- 1 cup crumbled goat cheese
- 4 tablespoons jarred pesto
- 12 pitted Kalamata olives
- ½ cup finely chopped walnuts
- 1 tablespoon chopped fresh rosemary

Direction:
1. Mix goat cheese, pesto, and olives. Cool for 4 hours to harden.
2. Create the mixture into 6 balls, about ¾-inch diameter. The mixture will be sticky.
3. In a small bowl, place the walnuts and rosemary and roll the goat cheese balls in the nut mixture to coat.

Nutrition 166 Calories 15g Fat 5g Protein

163. Cream of Cauliflower Gazpacho

Preparation Time: 15 minutes
Cooking Time: 25 minutes
Serving: 6
Ingredients:
- 1 cup raw almonds
- ½ teaspoon salt
- ½ cup extra-virgin olive oil
- 1 small white onion
- 1 small head cauliflower
- 2 garlic cloves
- 2 cups chicken stock
- 1 tablespoon red wine vinegar
- ¼ teaspoon freshly ground black pepper

Direction:
1. Boil almonds to the water for 1 minute. Drain in a colander and run under cold water. Pat dry. Discard the skins.
2. Using a food processor, blend together the almonds and salt. With the processor running, drizzle in ½ cup extra-virgin olive oil, scraping down the sides as needed. Set the almond paste aside.

3. In a stockpot, cook remaining 1 tablespoon olive oil over medium-high heat. Sauté onion for 4 minutes. Add the cauliflower florets and sauté for another 3 to 4 minutes. Cook garlic for 1 minute more.
4. Pour in 2 cups stock and bring to a boil. Cover, reduce the heat to medium-low, and simmer the vegetables until tender, 8 to 10 minutes. Pull out from the heat and allow to cool slightly.
5. Blend vinegar and pepper with an immersion blender. With the blender running, add the almond paste and blend until smooth, adding extra stock if the soup is too thick.
6. Cool in refrigerator at least 4 to 6 hours to serve.

Nutrition: 505 Calories 45g Fat 10g Protein

164. Avocado Gazpacho

Preparation Time: 15 minutes
Cooking Time: 0 minute
Serving: 4
Ingredients:
- 2 cups chopped tomatoes
- 2 large ripe avocados
- 1 large cucumber
- 1 medium bell pepper
- 1 cup plain whole-milk Greek yogurt
- ¼ cup extra-virgin olive oil
- ¼ cup chopped fresh cilantro
- ¼ cup chopped scallions
- 2 tablespoons red wine vinegar
- Juice of 2 limes or 1 lemon
- ½ to 1 teaspoon salt
- ¼ teaspoon black pepper

Direction:
1. In a blender or in a large bowl, if using an immersion blender, combine the tomatoes, avocados, cucumber, bell pepper, yogurt, olive oil, cilantro, scallions, vinegar, and lime juice. Blend until smooth.
2. Season with salt and pepper and blend to combine the flavors.
3. Chill for 2 hours before serving. Serve cold.

Nutrition: 392 Calories 32g Fat 6g Protein

165. Tuscan Kale Salad with Anchovies

Preparation Time: 45 minutes
Cooking Time: 0 minute
Serving: 4
Ingredients:
- 1 large bunch Lacinato
- ¼ cup toasted pine nuts
- 1 cup Parmesan cheese
- ¼ cup extra-virgin olive oil
- 8 anchovy fillets
- 2 to 3 tablespoons lemon juice

- 2 teaspoons red pepper flakes (optional)

Direction:
1. Remove the rough center stems from the kale leaves and roughly tear each leaf into about 4-by-1-inch strips. Place torn kale in a large bowl and add the pine nuts and cheese.
2. Blend the olive oil, anchovies, lemon juice, and red pepper flakes (if using). Sprinkle over the salad and toss to coat well. Let sit at room temperature 30 minutes before serving, tossing again just prior to serving.

Nutrition: 337 Calories 25g Fat 16g Protein

166. Classic Hummus

Preparation Time: 8 minutes
Cooking Time: 30 minutes
Serving: 6
Ingredient:
- 1 cup dried chickpeas
- 4 cups water
- 1 tablespoon plus ¼ cup extra-virgin olive oil
- 1/3 cup tahini
- 1½ teaspoons ground cumin
- ¾ teaspoon salt
- ½ teaspoon ground black pepper
- ½ teaspoon ground coriander
- 1/3 cup lemon juice
- 1 teaspoon minced garlic

Direction:
1. Position chickpeas, water, and 1 tablespoon oil in the Instant Pot®. Close, select steam release to Sealing, click Manual, and time to 30 minutes.
2. When the timer rings, quick-release the pressure and open lid. Press the Cancel button and open lid. Drain, reserving the cooking liquid.
3. Blend chickpeas, remaining ¼ cup oil, tahini, cumin, salt, pepper, coriander, lemon juice, and garlic in a food processor. Serve.

Nutrition: 152 Calories 12g Fat 4g Protein

167. Roasted Garlic Hummus

Preparation Time: 9 minutes
Cooking Time: 33 minutes
Serving: 4
Ingredients:
- 1 cup dried chickpeas
- 4 cups water
- 1 tablespoon plus ¼ cup extra-virgin olive oil, divided
- 1/3 cup tahini
- 1 teaspoon ground cumin
- ½ teaspoon onion powder
- ¾ teaspoon salt
- ½ teaspoon ground black pepper
- 1/3 cup lemon juice

- 3 tablespoons mashed roasted garlic
- 2 tablespoons chopped fresh parsley

Direction:
1. Situate chickpeas, water, and 1 tablespoon oil in the Instant Pot®. Cover, press steam release to Sealing, set Manual button, and time to 30 minutes.
2. When the timer beeps, quick-release the pressure. Select Cancel button and open. Strain, reserving the cooking liquid.
3. Process chickpeas, remaining ¼ cup oil, tahini, cumin, onion powder, salt, pepper, lemon juice, and roasted garlic in a food processor. Top with parsley. Serve at room temperature.

Nutrition 104 Calories 6g Fat 4g Protein

168. Red Pepper Hummus

Preparation Time: 7 minutes
Cooking Time: 34 minutes
Serving: 4
Ingredients:
- 1 cup dried chickpeas
- 4 cups water
- 1 tablespoon plus ¼ cup extra-virgin olive oil, divided
- ½ cup chopped roasted red pepper, divided
- 1/3 cup tahini
- 1 teaspoon ground cumin
- ¾ teaspoon salt
- ½ teaspoon ground black pepper
- ¼ teaspoon smoked paprika
- 1/3 cup lemon juice
- ½ teaspoon minced garlic

Direction:
1. Put chickpeas, water, and 1 tablespoon oil in the Instant Pot®. Seal, put steam release to Sealing, select Manual and time to 30 minutes.
2. When the timer rings, quick-release the pressure. Click Cancel button and open it. Drain, set aside the cooking liquid.
3. Process chickpeas, 1/3 cup roasted red pepper, remaining ¼ cup oil, tahini, cumin, salt, black pepper, paprika, lemon juice, and garlic using food processor. Serve, garnished with reserved roasted red pepper on top.

Nutrition: 96 Calories 8g Fat 2g Protein

169. White Bean Hummus

Preparation Time: 11 minutes
Cooking Time: 40 minutes
Serving: 12
Ingredients:
- 2/3 cup dried white beans
- 3 cloves garlic, peeled and crushed
- ¼ cup olive oil
- 1 tablespoon lemon juice

- ½ teaspoon salt

Direction

1. Place beans and garlic in the Instant Pot® and stir well. Add enough cold water to cover ingredients. Cover, set steam release to Sealing, select Manual button, and time to 30 minutes.
2. Once the timer stops, release pressure for 20 minutes. Select Cancel and open lid. Use a fork to check that beans are tender. Drain off excess water and transfer beans to a food processor.
3. Add oil, lemon juice, and salt to the processor and pulse until mixture is smooth with some small chunks. Pour into container and refrigerate for at least 4 hours. Serve cold or at room temperature.

Nutrition: 57 Calories 5g Fat 1g Protein

170. Kidney Bean Dip with Cilantro, Cumin, and Lime

Preparation Time: 13 minutes
Cooking Time: 51 minutes
Serving: 16
Ingredients:
- 1 cup dried kidney beans
- 4 cups water
- 3 cloves garlic
- ¼ cup cilantro
- ¼ cup extra-virgin olive oil
- 1 tablespoon lime juice
- 2 teaspoons grated lime zest
- 1 teaspoon ground cumin
- ½ teaspoon salt

Direction

1. Place beans, water, garlic, and 2 tablespoons cilantro in the Instant Pot®. Close the lid, select steam release to Sealing, click Bean button, and cook for 30 minutes.
2. When the timer alarms, let pressure release naturally, about 20 minutes. Press the Cancel button, open lid, and check that beans are tender. Drain off extra water and transfer beans to a medium bowl. Gently mash beans with potato masher. Add oil, lime juice, lime zest, cumin, salt, and remaining 2 tablespoons cilantro and stir to combine. Serve warm or at room temperature.

Nutrition: 65 Calories 3g Fat 2g Protein

171. White Bean Dip with Garlic and Herbs

Preparation Time: 10 minutes
Cooking Time: 48 minutes
Serving: 16
Ingredients:
- 1 cup dried white beans
- 3 cloves garlic
- 8 cups water

- ¼ cup extra-virgin olive oil
- ¼ cup chopped fresh flat-leaf parsley
- 1 tablespoon fresh oregano
- 1 tablespoon d fresh tarragon
- 1 teaspoon fresh thyme leaves
- 1 teaspoon lemon zest
- ¼ teaspoon salt
- ¼ teaspoon black pepper

Direction

1. Place beans and garlic in the Instant Pot® and stir well. Add water, close lid, put steam release to Sealing, press the Manual, and adjust time to 30 minutes.
2. When the timer beeps, release naturally, about 20 minutes. Open and check if beans are soft. Press the Cancel button, drain off excess water, and transfer beans and garlic to a food processor with olive oil. Add parsley, oregano, tarragon, thyme, lemon zest, salt, and pepper, and pulse 3–5 times to mix. Chill for 4 hours or overnight. Serve cold or at room temperature.

Nutrition: 47 Calories 3g Fat 1g Protein

172. Black Bean Dip

Preparation Time: 14 minutes
Cooking Time: 53 minutes
Serving: 16
Ingredients:
- 1 tablespoon olive oil
- 2 slices bacon
- 1 small onion,
- 3 cloves garlic
- 1 cup low-sodium chicken broth
- 1 cup dried black beans
- 1 (14.5-ounce) can diced tomatoes
- 1 small jalapeño pepper
- 1 teaspoon ground cumin
- ½ teaspoon smoked paprika
- 1 tablespoon lime juice
- ½ teaspoon dried oregano
- ¼ cup minced fresh cilantro
- ¼ teaspoon sea salt

Direction:

1. Press the Sauté button on the Instant Pot® and heat oil. Add bacon and onion. Cook for 5 minutes. Cook garlic for 30 seconds. Fill in broth. Add beans, tomatoes, jalapeño, cumin, paprika, lime juice, oregano, cilantro, and salt. Press the Cancel button.
2. Close lid, let steam release to Sealing, set Bean button, and default time of 30 minutes. When the timer rings, let pressure release naturally for 10 minutes. Press the Cancel button and open lid.
3. Use an immersion blender blend the ingredients. Serve warm.

Nutrition: 60 Calories 2g Fat 3g Protein

173. Salsa Verde

Preparation Time: 9 minutes
Cooking Time: 21 minutes
Serving: 8
Ingredients:
- 1-pound tomatillos
- 2 small jalapeño peppers
- 1 small onion
- ½ cup chopped fresh cilantro
- 1 teaspoon ground coriander
- 1 teaspoon sea salt
- 1½ cups water

Direction:
1. Cut tomatillos in half and place in the Instant Pot®. Add enough water to cover.
2. Close lids, set steam release to Sealing, press the Manual button, and set time to 2 minutes. Once timer beeps, release pressure naturally, for 20 minutes. Press the Cancel and open lid.
3. Drain off excess water and transfer tomatillos to a food processor or blender, and add jalapeños, onion, cilantro, coriander, salt, and water. Pulse until well combined, about 20 pulses.
4. Wrap and cool for 2 hours before serving.

Nutrition: 27 Calories 1g Fat 1g Protein

174. Greek Eggplant Dip

Preparation Time: 16 minutes
Cooking Time: 3 minutes
Serving: 8
Ingredients:
- 1 cup water
- 1 large eggplant
- 1 clove garlic
- ½ teaspoon salt
- 1 tablespoon red wine vinegar
- ½ cup extra-virgin olive oil
- 2 tablespoons minced fresh parsley

Direction
1. Add water to the Instant Pot®, add the rack to the pot, and place the steamer basket on the rack.
2. Place eggplant in steamer basket. Close, set steam release to Sealing, turn on Manual button, and set time to 3 minutes. When the timer stops, quick-release the pressure. Click Cancel button and open.
3. Situate eggplant to a food processor and add garlic, salt, and vinegar. Pulse until smooth, about 20 pulses.
4. Slowly add oil to the eggplant mixture while the food processor runs continuously until oil is completely incorporated. Stir in parsley. Serve at room temperature.

Nutrition: 134 Calories 14g Fat 1g Protein

175. Baba Ghanoush

Preparation Time: 9 minutes
Cooking Time: 11 minutes
Serving: 8
Ingredients:
- 2 tablespoons extra-virgin olive oil
- 1 large eggplant
- 3 cloves garlic
- ½ cup water
- 3 tablespoons fresh flat-leaf parsley
- ½ teaspoon salt
- ¼ teaspoon smoked paprika
- 2 tablespoons lemon juice
- 2 tablespoons tahini

Direction
1. Press the Sauté button on the Instant Pot® and add 1 tablespoon oil. Add eggplant and cook until it begins to soften, about 5 minutes. Add garlic and cook 30 seconds.
2. Add water and close lid, click steam release to Sealing, select Manual, and time to 6 minutes. Once the timer rings, quick-release the pressure. Select Cancel and open lid.
3. Strain cooked eggplant and garlic and add to a food processor or blender along with parsley, salt, smoked paprika, lemon juice, and tahini. Add remaining 1 tablespoon oil and process. Serve warm or at room temperature.

Nutrition: 79 Calories 6g Fat 2g Protein

176. Chickpea, Parsley, and Dill Dip

Preparation Time: 11 minutes
Cooking Time: 22 minutes
Serving: 6
Ingredients:
- 8 cups water
- 1 cup dried chickpeas
- 3 tablespoons olive oil
- 2 garlic cloves
- 2 tablespoons fresh parsley
- 2 tablespoons fresh dill
- 1 tablespoon lemon juice
- ¼ teaspoon salt

Direction
1. Add 4 cups water and chickpeas to the Instant Pot®. Cover, place steam release to Sealing. Set Manual, and time to 1 minute. When the timer beeps, quick-release the pressure until the float valve drops, press the Cancel button, and open lid.
2. Drain water, rinse chickpeas, and return to pot with 4 cups fresh water. Set aside to soak for 1 hour.
3. Add 1 tablespoon oil to pot. Close, adjust steam release to Sealing, click Manual, and the time to 20 minutes. When alarm beeps, let pressure release for

20 minutes. Click the Cancel, open and drain chickpeas.

4. Place chickpeas to a food processor or blender, and add garlic, parsley, dill, lemon juice, and remaining 2 tablespoons water. Blend for about 30 seconds.

5. With the processor or blender lid still in place, slowly add remaining 2 tablespoons oil while still blending, then add salt. Serve warm or at room temperature.

Nutrition 76 Calories 4g Fat 2g Protein

177. Instant Pot® Salsa

Preparation Time: 9 minutes
Cooking Time: 22 minutes
Serving: 12
Ingredients:
- 12 cups seeded diced tomatoes
- 6 ounces tomato paste
- 2 medium yellow onions
- 6 small jalapeño peppers
- 4 cloves garlic
- ¼ cup white vinegar
- ¼ cup lime juice
- 2 tablespoons granulated sugar
- 2 teaspoons salt
- ¼ cup chopped fresh cilantro

Direction:
1. Place tomatoes, tomato paste, onions, jalapeños, garlic, vinegar, lime juice, sugar, and salt in the Instant Pot® and stir well. Close it, situate steam release to Sealing. Click Manual button, and time to 20 minutes.
2. Once timer beeps, quick-release the pressure. Open, stir in cilantro, and press the Cancel button.
3. Let salsa cool to room temperature, about 40 minutes, then transfer to a storage container and refrigerate overnight.

Nutrition: 68 Calories 0.1g Fat 2g Protein

178. Sfougato

Preparation Time: 9 minutes
Cooking Time: 13 minutes
Serving: 4
Ingredients:
- ½ cup crumbled feta cheese
- ¼ cup bread crumbs
- 1 medium onion
- 4 tablespoons all-purpose flour
- 2 tablespoons fresh mint
- ½ teaspoon salt
- ½ teaspoon ground black pepper
- 1 tablespoon dried thyme
- 6 large eggs, beaten
- 1 cup water

Direction:

1. In a medium bowl, mix cheese, bread crumbs, onion, flour, mint, salt, pepper, and thyme. Stir in eggs.
2. Grease an 8" round baking dish with nonstick cooking spray. Pour egg mixture into dish.
3. Place rack in the Instant Pot® and add water. Crease a long piece of foil in half lengthwise. Lay foil over rack to form a sling and top with dish. Cover loosely with foil. Seal lid, put steam release in Sealing, select Manual, and time to 8 minutes.
4. When the timer alarms, release the pressure. Uncover. Let stand 5 minutes, then remove dish from pot.

Nutrition: 274 Calories 14g Fat 17g Protein

179. Skordalia

Preparation Time: 7 minutes
Cooking Time: 11 minutes
Serving: 16
Ingredients:
- 1-pound russet potatoes
- 3 cups plus ¼ cup water
- 2 teaspoons salt
- 8 cloves garlic
- ¾ cup blanched almonds
- ½ cup extra-virgin olive oil
- 2 tablespoons lemon juice
- 2 tablespoons white wine vinegar
- ½ teaspoon ground black pepper

Direction
1. Place potatoes, 3 cups water, and 1 teaspoon salt in the Instant Pot® and stir well. Close, set steam release to Sealing, click Manual button, and set to 10 minutes.
2. While potatoes cook, place garlic and remaining 1 teaspoon salt on a cutting board. With the side of a knife, press garlic and salt until it forms a paste. Transfer garlic paste into a food processor along with almonds and olive oil. Purée into a paste. Set aside.
3. When the timer beeps, quick-release the pressure. Select Cancel button and open lid. Strain potatoes then situate to a medium bowl. Add garlic mixture and mash with a potato masher until smooth. Stir in lemon juice, vinegar, and pepper. Stir in ¼ cup water a little at a time until mixture is thin enough for dipping. Serve warm or at room temperature.

Nutrition: 115 Calories 10g Fat 2g Protein

180. Pinto Bean Dip with Avocado Pico

Preparation Time: 6 minutes
Cooking Time: 52 minutes
Serving: 16
Ingredients:
- 1 cup dried pinto beans

- 4 cups water
- 4 tablespoons cilantro, divided
- 3 tablespoons extra-virgin olive oil
- 1 teaspoon ground cumin
- 1 clove garlic, peeled and minced
- ½ teaspoon salt
- 1 medium avocado
- 1 large ripe tomato
- 1 small jalapeño pepper
- ½ medium white onion
- 2 teaspoons lime juice

Direction

1. Place beans, water, and 2 tablespoons cilantro in the Instant Pot®. Close lid, place steam release to Sealing, click Bean and set default time of 30 minutes.
2. When the timer rings, let pressure release naturally. Open then check the beans are tender. Drain off excess water. Crush beans with fork. Add oil, cumin, garlic, and salt and mix well.
3. Toss remaining 2 tablespoons cilantro with avocado, tomato, jalapeño, onion, and lime juice. Spoon topping over bean dip. Serve.

Nutrition: 59 Calories 4g Fat 1g Protein

181. Power Pods & Hearty Hazelnuts with Mustard-y Mix

Preparation Time: 15 minutes
Cooking Time: 15 minutes
Serving: 4
Ingredients:

- 1-lb. green beans, trimmed
- 3-tbsp extra-virgin olive oil (divided)
- 2-tsp whole grain mustard
- 1-tbsp red wine vinegar
- ¼-tsp salt
- ¼-tsp ground pepper
- ¼-cup toasted hazelnuts, chopped

Directions:

1. Preheat your grill to high heat.
2. In a big mixing bowl, toss the green beans with a tablespoon of olive oil. Place the beans in a grill basket. Grill for 8 minutes until charring a few spots, stirring occasionally.
3. Combine and whisk together the remaining oil, mustard, vinegar, salt, and pepper in the same mixing bowl. Add the grilled beans and toss to coat evenly.
4. To serve, top the side dish with hazelnuts.

Nutrition: 181 Calories 15g Fats 3g Protein

182. Peppery Potatoes

Preparation Time: 10 minutes
Cooking Time: 18 minutes
Serving: 4

Ingredients:

- 4-pcs large potatoes, cubed
- 4-tbsp extra-virgin olive oil (divided)
- 3-tbsp garlic, minced
- ½-cup coriander or cilantro, finely chopped
- 2-tbsp fresh lemon juice
- 1¾-tbsp paprika
- 2-tbsp parsley, minced

Directions:

1. Place the potatoes in a microwave-safe dish. Pour over a tablespoon of olive oil. Cover the dish tightly with plastic wrap. Heat the potatoes for seven minutes in your microwave to par-cook them.
2. Cook 2 tablespoons of olive oil in a pan placed over medium-low heat. Add the garlic and cover. Cook for 3 minutes. Add the coriander, and cook 2 minutes. Transfer the garlic-coriander sauce in a bowl, and set aside.
3. In the same pan placed over medium heat, heat 1 tablespoon of olive oil. Add the par-cooked potatoes. Do not stir! Cook for 3 minutes until browned, flipping once with a spatula. Continue cooking until browning all the sides.
4. Pull out the potatoes then situate them on a dish. Pour over the garlic-coriander sauce and lemon juice. Add the paprika, parsley, and salt. Toss gently to coat evenly.

Nutrition: 316.2 Calories 14.2g Fats 4.5g Protein

183. Turkey Spheroids with Tzatziki Sauce

Preparation Time: 10 minutes
Cooking Time: 20 minutes
Serving: 8
Ingredients:
For Meatballs:

- 2-lbs ground turkey
- 2-tsp salt
- 2-cups zucchini, grated
- 1-tbsp lemon juice
- 1-cup crumbled feta cheese
- 1½-tsp pepper
- 1½-tsp garlic powder
- 1½-tbsp oregano
- ¼-cup red onion, finely minced

For Tzatziki Sauce:

- 1-tsp garlic powder
- 1-tsp dill
- 1-tbsp white vinegar
- 1-tbsp lemon juice
- 1-cup sour cream
- ½-cup grated cucumber
- Salt and pepper

Directions:

1. Preheat your oven to 350 °F.
2. For the Meatballs:

3. Incorporate all the meatball ingredients in a large mixing bowl. Mix well until fully combined. Form the turkey mixture into spheroids, using ¼-cup of the mixture per spheroid.
4. Heat a non-stick skillet placed over high heat. Add the meatballs, and sear for 2 minutes.
5. Transfer the meatballs in a baking sheet. Situate the sheet in the oven, and bake for 15 minutes.
6. For the Tzatziki Sauce:
7. Combine and whisk together all the sauce ingredients in a medium-sized mixing bowl. Mix well until fully combined. Chill the sauce and serve.

Nutrition: 280 Calories 16g Fats 26.6g Protein

184. Cheesy Caprese Salad Skewers

Preparation Time: 15 minutes
Cooking Time: 0 minute
Serving: 10
Ingredients:
- 8-oz cherry tomatoes, sliced in half
- A handful of fresh basil leaves, rinsed and drained
- 1-lb fresh mozzarella, cut into bite-sized slices
- Balsamic vinegar
- Extra virgin olive oil
- Freshly ground black pepper

Directions:
1. Sandwich a folded basil leaf and mozzarella cheese between the halves of tomato onto a toothpick.
2. Drizzle with olive oil and balsamic vinegar each skewer. To serve, sprinkle with freshly ground black pepper.

Nutrition: 94 Calories 3.7g Fats 2.1g Protein

185. Leafy Lacinato Tuscan Treat

Preparation Time: 10 minutes
Cooking Time: 0 minute
Serving: 1
Ingredients:
- 1-tsp Dijon mustard
- 1-tbsp light mayonnaise
- 3-pcs medium-sized Lacinato kale leaves
- 3-oz. cooked chicken breast, thinly sliced
- 6-bulbs red onion, thinly sliced
- 1-pc apple, cut into 9-slices

Directions:
1. Mix the mustard and mayonnaise until fully combined.
2. Spread the mixture generously on each of the kale leaves. Top each leaf with 1-oz. chicken slices, 3-apple slices, and 2-red onion slices. Roll each kale leaf into a wrap.

Nutrition: 370 Calories 14g Fats 29g Protein

186. Greek Guacamole Hybrid Hummus

Preparation Time: 10 minutes
Cooking Time: 0 minute
Serving: 1
Ingredients:
- 1-15 oz. canned chickpeas
- 1-pc ripe avocado
- ¼-cup tahini paste
- 1-cup fresh cilantro leaves
- ¼-cup lemon juice
- 1-tsp ground cumin
- ¼-cup extra-virgin olive oil
- 1-clove garlic
- ½ tsp salt

Directions:
1. Drain the chickpeas and reserve 2-tablespoons of the liquid. Pour the reserved liquid in your food processor and add in the drained chickpeas.
2. Add the avocado, tahini, cilantro, lemon juice, cumin, oil, garlic, and salt. Puree the mixture into a smooth consistency.
3. Serve with pita chips, veggie chips, or crudités.

Nutrition: 156 Calories 12g Fats 3g Protein

187. Packed Picnic

Preparation Time: 5 minutes
Cooking Time: 0 minute
Serving: 1
Ingredients:
- 1-slice of whole-wheat bread, cut into bite-size pieces
- 10-pcs cherry tomatoes
- ¼-oz. aged cheese, sliced
- 6-pcs oil-cured olives

Directions:
1. Pack each of the ingredients in a portable container to serve you while snacking on the go.

Nutrition: 197 Calories 9g Fats 7g Protein

188. Pizza & Pastry

Preparation Time: 35 minutes
Cooking Time: 15 minutes
Serving: 10
Ingredients:
For Pizza Dough:
- 2-tsp honey
- ¼-oz. active dry yeast
- 1¼-cups warm water (about 120 °F)
- 2-tbsp olive oil
- 1-tsp sea salt
- 3-cups whole grain flour + ¼-cup, as needed for rolling

For Pizza Topping:
- 1-cup pesto sauce (refer to Perky Pesto recipe)
- 1-cup artichoke hearts
- 1-cup wilted spinach leaves
- 1-cup sun-dried tomato
- ½-cup Kalamata olives
- 4-oz. feta cheese
- 4-oz. mixed cheese of equal parts low-fat mozzarella, asiago, and provolone

Optional:
- Bell pepper
- Chicken breast, strips
- Fresh basil
- Pine nuts

Directions:
2. For the Pizza Dough:
3. Preheat your oven to 350 °F.
4. Combine the honey and yeast with the warm water in your food processor with a dough attachment. Blend the mixture until fully combined. Set aside the mixture for 5 minutes to ensure the activity of the yeast through the appearance of bubbles on the surface.
5. Pour in the olive oil. Add the salt, and blend for half a minute. Add gradually 3 cups of flour, about half a cup at a time, blending for a couple of minutes between each addition.
6. Let your processor knead the mixture for 10 minutes until smooth and elastic, sprinkling it with flour whenever necessary to prevent the dough from sticking to the processor bowl's surfaces.
7. Take the dough from the bowl. Let it stand for 15 minutes, covered with a moist, warm towel.
8. .Using a rolling pin, roll out the dough to a half-inch thickness, dusting it with flour as needed. Poke holes indiscriminately on the dough using a fork to prevent crust bubbling.
9. . Place the perforated, rolled dough on a pizza stone or baking sheet. Bake for 5 minutes.
10. For Pizza Topping:
11. . Lightly brush the baked pizza shell with olive oil.
12. . Pour over the pesto sauce and spread thoroughly over the pizza shell's surface, leaving out a half-inch space around its edge as the crust.
13. . Top the pizza with artichoke hearts, wilted spinach leaves, sun-dried tomatoes, and olives. Cover the top with the cheese.
14. . Situate pizza directly on the oven rack. Bake for 10 minutes. Set aside for 5 minutes before slicing.

Nutrition: 242.8 Calories 15g Fats 14g Protein

189. Mediterranean Margherita

Preparation Time: 15 minutes
Cooking Time: 15 minutes
Serving: 10
Ingredients:
- 1-batch pizza shell

- 2-tbsp olive oil
- ½-cup crushed tomatoes
- 3-Roma tomatoes, sliced ¼-inch thick
- ½-cup fresh basil leaves, thinly sliced
- 6-oz. block mozzarella
- ½-tsp sea salt

Directions:
1. Preheat your oven to 450 °F.
2. Lightly brush the pizza shell with olive oil. Thoroughly spread the crushed tomatoes over the pizza shell, leaving a half-inch space around its edge as the crust.
3. Top the pizza with the Roma tomato slices, basil leaves, and mozzarella slices. Sprinkle salt over the pizza.
4. Situate pizza directly on the oven rack. Bake for 15 minutes. Put aside for 5 minutes before slicing.

Nutrition: 251 Calories 8g Fats 9g Protein

190. Fowl & Feta Fettuccini

Preparation Time: 5 minutes
Cooking Time: 30 minutes
Serving: 6
Ingredients:
- 2-tbsp extra-virgin olive oil
- 1½-lb chicken breasts
- ¼-tsp freshly ground black pepper
- 1-tsp kosher salt
- 2-cups water
- 2-14.5-oz. cans tomatoes with garlic, oregano and basil
- 1-lb whole-wheat fettuccini pasta
- 4-oz. reduced-fat feta cheese
- Fresh basil leaves, finely chopped (optional)

Directions:
1. Heat up olive oil for 1 minute in your Dutch oven placed over high heat for 1 minute. Add the chicken, and sprinkle over with freshly ground black pepper and half a teaspoon of kosher salt. Cook the chicken for 8 minutes, flipping once. Sprinkle over with the remaining salt after flipping each chicken on its side. Cook further for 5 minutes until the chicken cooks through.
2. Pour in the water, and add the tomatoes. Stir in the fettuccini pasta, cook for 5 minutes, uncovered. Cover the dish, and cook further for 10 minutes.
3. Uncover the dish, and stir the pasta. Add 3-oz. of the feta cheese, and stir again. Cook further for 5 minutes, uncovered.
4. To serve, sprinkle over with the chopped basil and the remaining feta cheese.

Nutrition: 390 Calories 11g Fats 19g Protein

191. Very Vegan Patras Pasta

Preparation Time: 5 minutes
Cooking Time: 10 minutes

Serving: 6
Ingredients:

- 4-quarts salted water
- 10-oz. gluten-free and whole grain pasta
- 5-cloves garlic, minced
- 1-cup hummus
- Salt and pepper
- 1/3cup water
- ½-cup walnuts
- ½-cup olives
- 2-tbsp dried cranberries (optional)

Directions:

1. Bring the salted water to a boil for cooking the pasta.
2. In the meantime, prepare for the hummus sauce. Combine the garlic, hummus, salt, and pepper with water in a mixing bowl. Add the walnuts, olive, and dried cranberries, if desired. Set aside.
3. Put pasta in the boiling water. Cook the pasta according to the package's specifications. Drain the pasta.
4. Transfer the pasta to a large serving bowl and combine with the sauce.

Nutrition: 329 Calories 12.6g Fats12g Protein

192. Scrumptious Shrimp Pappardelle Pasta

Preparation Time: 10 minutes
Cooking Time: 20 minutes
Serving: 4
Ingredients:

- 3-quarts salted water
- 1-lb. jumbo shrimp
- ½-tsp kosher salt
- ¼-tsp black pepper
- 3-tbsp olive oil
- 2-cups zucchini
- 1-cup grape tomatoes
- 1/8 tsp red pepper flakes
- 2-cloves garlic
- 1 tsp zest of 1-pc lemon
- 2-tbsp lemon juice
- 1-tbsp Italian parsley, chopped
- 8-oz. fresh pappardelle pasta

Directions:

1. Bring the salted water to a boil for cooking the pasta.
2. In the meantime, prepare for the shrimp. Combine the shrimp with salt and pepper. Set aside.
3. Cook 1 tablespoon of oil in a big sauté pan placed over medium heat. Add the zucchini slices and sauté for 4 minutes.
4. Add the grape tomatoes and sauté for 2 minutes. Stir in the salt to combine with the vegetables. Transfer the cooked vegetables to a medium-sized bowl. Set aside.

5. In the same sauté pan, pour in the remaining oil. Switch the heat to medium-low. Add the red pepper flakes and garlic. Cook for 2 minutes.
6. Add the seasoned shrimp, and keep the heat on medium-low. Cook the shrimp for 3 minutes on each side until they turn pinkish.
7. Stir in the zest of lemon and the lemon juice. Mix cooked vegetables back to the pan. Stir to combine with the shrimp. Set aside.
8. Situate pasta in the boiling water. Cook following the manufacturer's specifications until al dente texture. Drain the pasta.
9. Transfer the cooked pasta in a large serving bowl and combine with the lemony-garlic shrimp and vegetables.

Nutrition: 474 Calories 15g Fats 37g Protein

193. Mixed Mushroom Palermitani Pasta

Preparation Time: 5 minutes
Cooking Time: 30 minutes
Serving: 8
Ingredients:

- 5-quarts salted water
- 3-tbsp olive oil
- 26-oz. assorted wild mushrooms
- 4-cloves garlic, minced
- 1-bulb red onion, diced
- 1-tsp sea salt
- 2-tbsp sherry cooking wine
- 2½-tsp fresh thyme, diced
- 1-lb. linguine pasta
- ¾-cup reserved liquid from cooked pasta
- 6-oz. goat cheese
- ¼-cup hazelnuts

Directions:

1. Bring the salted water to a boil for cooking the pasta.
2. Cook olive oil in a large skillet placed over medium-high heat. Add the mushrooms and sauté for 10 minutes until they brown.
3. Add the garlic, onions, and salt. Sauté for 4 minutes.
4. Stir in the wine, and cook down until the liquid evaporates. Sprinkle with thyme, and set aside.
5. Cook pasta in the boiling water in accordance with the manufacturer's specifications.
6. Before draining the pasta completely, reserve ¾-cup of the pasta liquid.
7. Transfer the cooked pasta in a large serving bowl and combine with the mushroom mixture, pasta liquid, and goat cheese. Toss gently to combine fully until the goat cheese melts completely.
8. To serve, top the pasta with chopped hazelnuts.

Nutrition: 331 Calories 12g Fats 13g Protein

194. Mediterranean Macaroni with Seasoned Spinach

Preparation Time: 5 minutes
Cooking Time: 20 minutes
Serving: 4
Ingredients:
- 2-tbsp olive oil
- 2-cloves garlic
- 1-pc yellow onion
- 10-oz. fresh baby spinach
- 2-pcs fresh tomatoes
- ¼-cup skim mozzarella cheese
- ½-cup crumbled feta cheese
- ½-cup white cheddar cheese, cubed
- 1-cup low-sodium vegetable broth
- 2-cups elbow whole-grain macaroni
- 1-cup unsweetened almond milk
- ½-tsp organic Italian Seasoning

Directions:
1. Cook olive oil in a large pan placed over medium-high heat. Add the garlic, onions, and a pinch of salt, and sauté for 3 minutes.
2. Add the spinach, tomatoes, cheese, vegetable broth, macaroni, milk, and seasonings. Mix well until fully combined. Boil the mixture, stirring frequently.
3. Lower heat to medium-low, and cover the pan. Cook further for 15 minutes, stirring every 3 minutes to prevent the pasta mixture from sticking on the pan's surfaces.
4. Take out the pasta from the heat and stir. To serve, garnish the pasta with parsley.

Nutrition: 544 Calories 23g Fats 22g Protein

195. Frittata Filled with Zucchini & Tomato Toppings

Preparation Time: 10 minutes
Cooking Time: 15 minutes
Serving: 4
Ingredients:
- 8-pcs eggs
- ¼-tsp red pepper, crushed
- ¼-tsp salt
- 1-tbsp olive oil
- 1-pc small zucchini
- ½-cup red or yellow cherry tomatoes
- 1/3-cup walnuts, coarsely chopped
- 2-oz. bite-sized fresh mozzarella balls (bocconcini)

Directions:
1. Preheat your broiler. Meanwhile, whisk together the eggs, crushed red pepper, and salt in a medium-sized bowl. Set aside.
2. In a 10-inch broiler-proof skillet placed over medium-high heat, heat the olive oil. Spread the slices of zucchini in an even layer on the bottom of the skillet. Cook for 3 minutes, turning them once, halfway through.
3. Top the zucchini layer with cherry tomatoes. Fill in the egg mixture over vegetables in skillet. Top with walnuts and mozzarella balls.
4. Switch to medium heat. Cook for 5 minutes. By using a spatula, lift the frittata for the uncooked portions of the egg mixture to flow underneath.
5. Place the skillet on the broiler. Broil the frittata 4-inches from the heat for 5 minutes until the top is set. To serve, cut the frittata into wedges.

Nutrition: 281 Calories 14g Fats 17g Protein

196. Peppers and Lentils Salad

Preparation Time: 10 minutes
Cooking Time: 0 minutes
Servings: 4
Ingredients:
- 14 ounces canned lentils
- 2 spring onions
- 1 red bell pepper
- 1 green bell pepper
- 1 tablespoon fresh lime juice
- 1/3 cup coriander
- 2 teaspoon balsamic vinegar

Directions:
1. In a salad bowl, combine the lentils with the onions, bell peppers, and the rest of the ingredients, toss and serve.

Nutrition: 200 Calories 2.45g Fat 5.6g Protein

197. Cashews and Red Cabbage Salad

Preparation Time: 10 minutes
Cooking Time: 0 minutes
Servings: 4
Ingredients:
- 1-pound red cabbage, shredded
- 2 tablespoons coriander, chopped
- ½ cup cashews halved
- 2 tablespoons olive oil
- 1 tomato, cubed
- A pinch of salt and black pepper
- 1 tablespoon white vinegar

Directions:
1. Mix the cabbage with the coriander and the rest of the ingredients in a salad bowl, toss and serve cold.

Nutrition: 210 Calories 6.3g Fat 8g Protein

198. Apples and Pomegranate Salad

Preparation Time: 10 minutes
Cooking Time: 0 minutes
Servings: 4

Ingredients:
- 3 big apples, cored and cubed
- 1 cup pomegranate seeds
- 3 cups baby arugula
- 1 cup walnuts, chopped
- 1 tablespoon olive oil
- 1 teaspoon white sesame seeds
- 2 tablespoons apple cider vinegar

Directions:
1. Mix the apples with the arugula and the rest of the ingredients in a bowl, toss and serve cold.

Nutrition: 160 Calories 4.3g Fat 10g Protein

199. Cranberry Bulgur Mix

Preparation Time: 10 minutes
Cooking Time: 0 minutes
Servings: 4

Ingredients:
- 1 and ½ cups hot water
- 1 cup bulgur
- Juice of ½ lemon
- 4 tablespoons cilantro, chopped
- ½ cup cranberries
- 1 and ½ teaspoons curry powder
- ¼ cup green onions
- ½ cup red bell peppers
- ½ cup carrots, grated
- 1 tablespoon olive oil

Directions:
1. Put bulgur into a bowl, add the water, stir, cover, leave aside for 10 minutes, fluff with a fork, and situate to a bowl. Add the rest of the ingredients, toss, and serve cold.

Nutrition: 300 Calories 6.4g Fat 13g Protein

200. Chickpeas, Corn and Black Beans Salad

Preparation Time: 10 minutes
Cooking Time: 0 minutes
Servings: 4

Ingredients:
- 1 and ½ cups canned black beans
- ½ teaspoon garlic powder
- 2 teaspoons chili powder
- 1 and ½ cups canned chickpeas
- 1 cup baby spinach
- 1 avocado, pitted, peeled, and chopped
- 1 cup corn kernels, chopped
- 2 tablespoons lemon juice
- 1 tablespoon olive oil
- 1 tablespoon apple cider vinegar
- 1 teaspoon chives, chopped

Directions:

1. Mix the black beans with the garlic powder, chili powder, and the rest of the ingredients in a bowl, toss and serve cold.

Nutrition: 300 Calories 13.4g Fat 13g Protein

201. Olives and Lentils Salad

Preparation Time: 10 minutes
Cooking Time: 0 minutes
Servings: 2

Ingredients:
- 1/3 cup canned green lentils
- 1 tablespoon olive oil
- 2 cups baby spinach
- 1 cup black olives
- 2 tablespoons sunflower seeds
- 1 tablespoon Dijon mustard
- 2 tablespoons balsamic vinegar
- 2 tablespoons olive oil

Directions:
1. Mix the lentils with the spinach, olives, and the rest of the ingredients in a salad bowl, toss and serve cold.

Nutrition: 279 Calories 6.5g Fat 12g Protein

202. Lime Spinach and Chickpeas Salad

Preparation Time: 10 minutes
Cooking Time: 0 minutes
Servings: 4

Ingredients:
- 16 ounces canned chickpeas
- 2 cups baby spinach leaves
- ½ tablespoon lime juice
- 2 tablespoons olive oil
- 1 teaspoon cumin, ground
- ½ teaspoon chili flakes

Directions:
1. Mix the chickpeas with the spinach and the rest of the ingredients in a large bowl, toss and serve cold.

Nutrition: 240 calories 8.2g fat 12g protein

203. Minty Olives and Tomatoes Salad

Preparation Time: 10 minutes
Cooking Time: 0 minutes
Servings: 4

Ingredients:
- 1 cup kalamata olives
- 1 cup black olives
- 1 cup cherry tomatoes
- 4 tomatoes
- 1 red onion, chopped
- 2 tablespoons oregano, chopped

- 1 tablespoon mint, chopped
- 2 tablespoons balsamic vinegar
- ¼ cup olive oil
- 2 teaspoons Italian herbs, dried

Directions:
1. In a salad bowl, mix the olives with the tomatoes and the rest of the ingredients, toss, and serve cold.

Nutrition: 190 Calories 8.1g Fat 4.6g Protein

204. Beans and Cucumber Salad

Preparation Time: 10 minutes
Cooking Time: 0 minutes
Servings: 4

Ingredients:
- 15 oz canned great northern beans
- 2 tablespoons olive oil
- ½ cup baby arugula
- 1 cup cucumber
- 1 tablespoon parsley
- 2 tomatoes, cubed
- 2 tablespoon balsamic vinegar

Directions:
1. Mix the beans with the cucumber and the rest of the ingredients in a large bowl, toss and serve cold.

Nutrition: 233 calories 9g fat 8g protein

205. Tomato and Avocado Salad

Preparation Time: 10 minutes
Cooking Time: 0 minutes
Servings: 4

Ingredients:
- 1-pound cherry tomatoes
- 2 avocados
- 1 sweet onion, chopped
- 2 tablespoons lemon juice
- 1 and ½ tablespoons olive oil
- Handful basil, chopped

Directions:
1. Mix the tomatoes with the avocados and the rest of the ingredients in a serving bowl, toss and serve right away.

Nutrition: 148 Calories 7.8g Fat 5.5g Protein

206. Arugula Salad

Preparation Time: 5 minutes
Cooking Time: 0 minutes
Servings: 4

Ingredients:
- Arugula leaves (4 cups)
- Cherry tomatoes (1 cup)
- Pine nuts (.25 cup)
- Rice vinegar (1 tbsp.)
- Olive/grapeseed oil (2 tbsp.)

- Grated parmesan cheese (.25 cup)
- Black pepper & salt (as desired)
- Large sliced avocado (1)

Directions:
1. Peel and slice the avocado. Rinse and dry the arugula leaves, grate the cheese, and slice the cherry tomatoes into halves.
2. Combine the arugula, pine nuts, tomatoes, oil, vinegar, salt, pepper, and cheese.
3. Toss the salad to mix and portion it onto plates with the avocado slices to serve.

Nutrition: 257 Calories 23g Fats 6.1g Protein

207. Chickpea Salad

Preparation Time: 15 minutes
Cooking Time: 0 minutes
Servings: 4

Ingredients:
- Cooked chickpeas (15 oz.)
- Diced Roma tomato (1)
- Diced green medium bell pepper (half of 1)
- Fresh parsley (1 tbsp.)
- Small white onion (1)
- Minced garlic (.5 tsp.)
- Lemon (1 juiced)

Directions:
1. Chop the tomato, green pepper, and onion. Mince the garlic. Combine each of the fixings into a salad bowl and toss well.
2. Cover the salad to chill for at least 15 minutes in the fridge. Serve when ready.

Nutrition: 163 Calories 7g Fats 4g Protein

208. Chopped Israeli Mediterranean Pasta Salad

Preparation Time: 15 minutes
Cooking Time: 2 minutes
Servings: 8

Ingredients:
- Small bow tie or other small pasta (.5 lb.)
- 1/3 cup Cucumber
- 1/3 cup Radish
- 1/3 cup Tomato
- 1/3 cup Yellow bell pepper
- 1/3 cup Orange bell pepper
- 1/3 cup Black olives
- 1/3 cup Green olives
- 1/3 cup Red onions
- 1/3 cup Pepperoncini
- 1/3 cup Feta cheese
- 1/3 cup Fresh thyme leaves
- Dried oregano (1 tsp.)

Dressing:
- 0.25 cup + more, olive oil

- juice of 1 lemon

Directions:
1. Slice the green olives into halves. Dice the feta and pepperoncini. Finely dice the remainder of the veggies.
2. Prepare a pot of water with the salt, and simmer the pasta until it's al dente (checking at two minutes under the listed time). Rinse and drain in cold water.
3. Combine a small amount of oil with the pasta. Add the salt, pepper, oregano, thyme, and veggies. Pour in the rest of the oil, lemon juice, mix and fold in the grated feta.
4. Pop it into the fridge within two hours, best if overnight. Taste test and adjust the seasonings to your liking; add fresh thyme.

Nutrition: 65 Calories 5.6g Fats 0.8g Protein

209. Feta Tomato Salad

Preparation Time: 5 minutes
Cooking Time: 0 minutes
Servings: 4

Ingredients:
- Balsamic vinegar (2 tbsp.)
- Freshly minced basil (1.5 tsp.) or Dried (.5 tsp.)
- Salt (.5 tsp.)
- Coarsely chopped sweet onion (.5 cup)
- Olive oil (2 tbsp.)
- Cherry or grape tomatoes (1 lb.)
- Crumbled feta cheese (.25 cup.)

Directions:
1. Whisk the salt, basil, and vinegar. Toss the onion into the vinegar mixture for 5 minutes
2. Slice the tomatoes into halves and stir in the tomatoes, feta cheese, and oil to serve.

Nutrition: 121 Calories 9g Fats 3g Protein

210. Greek Pasta Salad

Preparation Time: 5 minutes
Cooking Time: 11 minutes
Servings: 4

Ingredients:
- Penne pasta (1 cup)
- Lemon juice (1.5 tsp.)
- Red wine vinegar (2 tbsp.)
- Garlic (1 clove)
- Dried oregano (1 tsp.)
- Black pepper and sea salt (as desired)
- Olive oil (.33 cup)
- Halved cherry tomatoes (5)
- Red onion (half of 1 small)
- Green & red bell pepper (half of 1 - each)
- Cucumber (¼ of 1)
- Black olives (.25 cup)
- Crumbled feta cheese (.25 cup)

Directions:
1. Slice the cucumber and olives. Chop/dice the onion, peppers, and garlic. Slice the tomatoes into halves.
2. Arrange a large pot with water and salt using the high-temperature setting. Once it's boiling, add the pasta and cook for 11 minutes Rinse it using cold water and drain in a colander.
3. Whisk the oil, juice, salt, pepper, vinegar, oregano, and garlic. Combine the cucumber, cheese, olives, peppers, pasta, onions, and tomatoes in a large salad dish.
4. Add the vinaigrette over the pasta and toss. Chill in the fridge (covered) for about three hours and serve as desired.

Nutrition: 307 Calories 23.6g Fat 5.4g Protein

211. Pork and Greens Salad

Preparation Time: 10 minutes
Cooking Time: 15 minutes
Servings: 4

Ingredients:
- 1-pound pork chops
- 8 ounces white mushrooms, sliced
- ½ cup Italian dressing
- 6 cups mixed salad greens
- 6 ounces jarred artichoke hearts, drained
- Salt and black pepper to the taste
- ½ cup basil, chopped
- 1 tablespoon olive oil

Directions:
1. Heat a pan with the oil over medium-high heat, add the pork and brown for 5 minutes.
2. Add the mushrooms, stir and sauté for 5 minutes more.
3. Add the dressing, artichokes, salad greens, salt, pepper and the basil, cook for 4-5 minutes, divide everything into bowls and serve.

Nutrition: 235 Calories 6g Fat 11g Protein

212. Mediterranean Duck Breast Salad

Preparation Time: 10 minutes
Cooking Time: 20 minutes
Servings: 4

Ingredients:
- 3 tablespoons white wine vinegar
- 2 tablespoons sugar
- 2 oranges, peeled and cut into segments
- 1 teaspoon orange zest, grated
- 1 tablespoons lemon juice
- 1 teaspoon lemon zest, grated
- 3 tablespoons shallot, minced
- 2 duck breasts
- 1 head of frisée, torn

- 2 small lettuce heads
- 2 tablespoons chives

Directions:
1. Heat a small saucepan over medium high heat, add vinegar and sugar, stir and boil for 5 minutes and take off heat.
2. Add orange zest, lemon zest and lemon juice, stir and leave aside for a few minutes. Stir in shallot, salt and pepper to taste and the oil, whisk well and leave aside for now.
3. Pat dry duck pieces, score skin, trim and season with salt and pepper. Heat a pan over medium high heat for 1 minute, arrange duck breast pieces skin side down, brown for 8 minutes, reduce heat to medium and cook for 4 more minutes.
4. Flip pieces, cook for 3 minutes, transfer to a cutting board and cover them with foil. Put frisée and lettuce in a bowl, stir and divide between plates.
5. Slice duck, arrange on top, add orange segments, sprinkle chives and drizzle the vinaigrette.

Nutrition: 320 Calories 4g Fat 14g Protein

213. **Mediterranean Chicken Bites**

Preparation Time: 10 minutes
Cooking Time: 10 minutes
Servings: 4
Ingredients:
- 20 ounces canned pineapple slices
- A drizzle of olive oil
- 3 cups chicken thighs
- A tablespoon of smoked paprika

Directions:
1. Situate pan over medium high heat, add pineapple slices, cook them for a few minutes on each side, transfer to a cutting board, cool them down and cut into medium cubes.
2. Heat another pan with a drizzle of oil over medium high heat, rub chicken pieces with paprika, add them to the pan and cook for 5 minutes on each side.
3. Arrange chicken cubes on a platter, add a pineapple piece on top of each and stick a toothpick in each, and serve.

Nutrition: 120 Calories 3g Fat 2g Protein

214. **Mediterranean Chicken and Tomato Dish**

Preparation Time: 10 minutes
Cooking Time: 20 minutes
Servings: 4
Ingredients:
- Chicken thighs
- 1 Tablespoon thyme, chopped
- Garlic cloves, minced
- 1 Teaspoon red pepper flakes, crushed
- ½ cup heavy cream

- ¾ cup chicken stock
- ½ cup sun dried tomatoes in olive oil
- ¼ cup parmesan cheese, grated
- Basil leaves, chopped for serving

Directions:
1. Preheat pan with the oil over medium high heat, add chicken, salt and pepper to taste, cook for 6 minutes on both sides, transfer to a plate and leave aside for now.
2. Return pan to heat, add thyme, garlic and pepper flakes, stir and cook for 1 minute.
3. Add stock, tomatoes, salt and pepper, heavy cream and parmesan, stir and bring to a simmer.
4. Add chicken pieces, stir, place in the oven at 350 degrees F and bake for 15 minutes.
5. Take pan out of the oven, leave chicken aside for 2-3 minutes, divide between plates and serve with basil sprinkled on top.

Nutrition: 212 Calories 4g Fat 3g Protein

215. **Creamy Chicken Salad**

Preparation Time: 10 minutes
Cooking Time: 0 minute
Servings: 6
Ingredients:
- 20 ounces chicken meat
- ½ cup pecans, chopped
- 1 cup green grapes
- ½ cup celery, chopped
- 2 ounces canned mandarin oranges, drained
- For the creamy cucumber salad dressing:
- 1 cup Greek yogurt cucumber, chopped garlic clove
- 1 teaspoon lemon juice

Directions:
1. In a bowl, mix cucumber with salt, pepper to taste, lemon juice, garlic and yogurt and stir very well.
2. In a salad bowl, mix chicken meat with grapes, pecans, oranges and celery.
3. Add cucumber salad dressing, toss to coat and keep in the fridge until you serve it.

Nutrition: 200 Calories 3g Fat 8g Protein

216. **Chicken and Cabbage Mix**

Preparation Time: 10 minutes
Cooking Time: 6 minutes
Servings: 4
Ingredients:
- 3 medium chicken breasts
- 4 ounces green cabbage
- 5 tablespoon extra-virgin olive oil
- Salt and black pepper to taste
- 2 tablespoons sherry vinegar tablespoon chives
- ¼ cup feta cheese, crumbled
- ¼ cup barbeque sauce
- Bacon slices, cooked and crumbled

Directions:

1. In a bowl, mix 4 tablespoon oil with vinegar, salt and pepper to taste and stir well.
2. Add the shredded cabbage, toss to coat and leave aside for now.
3. Season chicken well, preheat a pan with remaining oil over medium high heat, add chicken, cook for 6 minutes, take off heat, transfer to a bowl and mix well with barbeque sauce.
4. Arrange salad on serving plates, add chicken strips, sprinkle cheese, chives and crumbled bacon and serve right away.

Nutrition: 200 Calories 15g Fat 33g Protein

217. Chicken and Quinoa Salad

Preparation Time: 10 minutes
Cooking Time: 20 minutes
Servings: 2
Ingredients:

- 2 tablespoons olive oil
- 2 ounces quinoa
- 2 ounces cherry tomatoes, cut in quarters
- 3 ounces sweet corn
- Lime juice from 1 lime
- Lime zest from 1 lime, grated
- 2 spring onions, chopped
- Small red chili pepper, chopped
- Avocado
- 2 ounces chicken meat

Directions:

1. Fill water in a pan, bring to a boil over medium high heat, add quinoa, stir and cook for 12 minutes.
2. Meanwhile, put corn in a pan, heat over medium high heat, cook for 5 minutes and leave aside for now.
3. Drain quinoa, transfer to a bowl, add tomatoes, corn, coriander, onions, chili, lime zest, olive oil, salt and black pepper to taste and toss.
4. In another bowl, mix avocado with lime juice and stir well.
5. Add this to quinoa salad, and chicken, toss to coat and serve.

Nutrition: 320 Calories 4g Fat 7g Protein

218. Simple Pork Stir Fry

Preparation Time: 10 minutes
Cooking Time: 15 minutes
Servings: 4
Ingredients:

- 4 ounces bacon, chopped
- 4 ounces snow peas
- 2 tablespoons butter
- 1-pound pork loin, cut into thin strips
- 2 cups mushrooms, sliced
- ¾ cup white wine

- ½ cup yellow onion, chopped
- 3 tablespoons sour cream

Directions:

1. Put snow peas in a saucepan, add water to cover, add a pinch of salt, boil over medium heat, cook until soft, drain and leave aside.
2. Preheat pan over medium high heat, add bacon, cook for a few minutes, drain grease, transfer to a bowl and also leave aside.
3. Heat a pan with 1 tablespoon butter over medium heat, add pork strips, salt and pepper to taste, brown for a few minutes and transfer to a plate as well.
4. Return pan to medium heat, add remaining butter and melt it. Add onions and mushrooms, stir and cook for 4 minutes.
5. Add wine, and simmer until it's reduced. Add cream, peas, pork, salt and pepper to taste, stir, heat up, divide between plates, top with bacon and serve.

Nutrition: 310 Calories 4g Fat 10g Protein

219. Beef Tartar

Preparation Time: 10 minutes
Cooking Time: 0 minutes
Servings: 1
Ingredients:

- 1 shallot, chopped
- 4 ounces beef fillet
- 5 small cucumbers
- 1 egg yolk
- 2 teaspoons mustard
- 1 tablespoon parsley
- 1 parsley spring

Direction:

1. Incorporate meat with shallot, egg yolk, salt, pepper, mustard, cucumbers and parsley.
2. Stir well and arrange on a platter.
3. Garnish with the chopped parsley spring and serve.

Nutrition: 210 Calories 3g Fat 8g Protein

220. Melon Salad

Preparation Time: 20 Minutes
Cooking Time: 0 minutes
Servings: 6
Ingredients:

- ¼ teaspoon sea salt
- ¼ teaspoon black pepper
- 1 tablespoon balsamic vinegar
- 1 cantaloupe
- 12 watermelons
- 2 cups mozzarella balls, fresh
- 1/3 cup basil, fresh & torn
- 2 tablespoons olive oil

Directions:

1. Spoon out balls of cantaloupe, then situate them in a colander over bowl.
2. Using melon baller to cut the watermelon as well
3. Drain fruits for ten minutes, then chill the juice.
4. Wipe the bowl dry, and then place your fruit in it.
5. Mix in basil, oil, vinegar, mozzarella and tomatoes before seasoning.
6. Gently mix and serve.

Nutrition: 218 Calories 10g Protein 13g Fat

221. Celery Citrus Salad

Preparation Time: 15 minutes
Cooking Time: 0 minutes
Servings: 6
Ingredients:
- 1 tablespoon lemon juice, fresh
- ¼ teaspoon sea salt, fine
- ¼ teaspoon black pepper
- 1 tablespoon olive brine
- 1 tablespoon olive oil
- ¼ cup red onion, sliced
- ½ cup green olives
- 2 oranges, peeled & sliced
- 3 celery stalks

Directions:
1. Put your oranges, olives, onion and celery in a shallow bowl.
2. Blend oil, olive brine and lemon juice, pour this over your salad.
3. Season with salt and pepper before serving.

Nutrition: 65 Calories 2g Protein 0.1g Fat

222. Broccoli Crunch Salad

Preparation Time: 10 minutes
Cooking Time: 20 minutes
Servings: 4
Ingredients:
- 1 lb. Broccoli
- 3 tablespoons olive oil, divided
- 1-pint cherry tomatoes
- 1 ½ teaspoons honey, raw & divided
- 3 cups cubed bread, whole grain
- 1 tablespoon balsamic vinegar
- ½ teaspoon black pepper
- ¼ teaspoon sea salt, fine

Directions:
1. Set oven to 450, and preheat rimmed baking sheet.
2. Drizzle your broccoli with a tablespoon of oil, and toss to coat.
3. Pull out baking sheet from the oven, and scoop the broccoli on it. Leave oil in it, add in your tomatoes, then toss tomatoes with a tablespoon of honey. Put on the same baking sheet.
4. Roast for fifteen minutes, and stir halfway through your cooking time.

5. Add in your bread, and then roast for three more minutes.
6. Whisk two tablespoons of oil, vinegar, and remaining honey. Season. Drizzle over broccoli mix to serve.

Nutrition: 226 Calories 7g Protein 12g Fat

223. Summer Tomato Salad

Preparation Time: 20 minutes
Cooking Time: 0 minutes
Servings: 4
Ingredients:
- 1 cucumber, sliced
- ¼ cup sun dried tomatoes
- 1 lb. Tomatoes, cubed
- ½ cup black olives
- 1 red onion, sliced
- 1 tablespoon balsamic vinegar
- ¼ cup parsley, fresh & chopped
- 2 tablespoons olive oil

Directions:
1. Mix all of your vegetables together. For dressing, mix all your seasoning, olive oil and vinegar. Toss with your salad and serve fresh.

Nutrition: 126 Calories 2.1g Protein 9.2g Fat

224. Cheese Beet Salad

Preparation Time: 15 minutes
Cooking Time: 0 minutes
Servings: 4
Ingredients:
- 6 red beets
- 3 ounces feta cheese
- 2 tablespoons olive oil
- 2 tablespoons balsamic vinegar

Directions:
1. Combine everything together, and then serve.

Nutrition: 230 Calories 7.3g Protein 12g Fat

225. Cauliflower and Cherry Tomato Salad

Preparation Time: 15 minutes
Cooking Time: 0 minutes
Servings: 4
Ingredients:
- 1 head cauliflower
- 2 tablespoons parsley
- 2 cups cherry tomatoes, halved
- 2 tablespoons lemon juice, fresh
- 2 tablespoons pine nuts

Direction:
1. Blend lemon juice, cherry tomatoes, cauliflower and parsley then season. Garnish with pine nuts, and mix well before serving.

Nutrition: 64 Calories 2.8g Protein 3.3g Fat

226. Watermelon Salad

Preparation Time: 18 minutes
Cooking Time: 0 minute
Serving: 6
Ingredients:
- ¼ teaspoon sea salt
- ¼ teaspoon black pepper
- 1 tablespoon balsamic vinegar
- 1 cantaloupe, quartered & seeded
- 12 watermelon, small & seedless
- 2 cups mozzarella balls, fresh
- 1/3 cup basil, fresh & torn
- 2 tablespoons olive oil

Directions:
1. Scoop out balls of cantaloupe, and the put them in a colander over bowl.
2. With a melon baller slice the watermelon.
3. Allow your fruit to drain for ten minutes, and then refrigerate the juice.
4. Wipe the bowl dry, and then place your fruit in it.
5. Stir in basil, oil, vinegar, mozzarella and tomatoes before seasoning.
6. Mix well and serve.

Nutrition: 218 Calories 10g Protein 13g Fat

227. Orange Celery Salad

Preparation Time: 16 minutes
Cooking Time: 0 minute
Serving: 6
Ingredients:
- 1 tablespoon lemon juice, fresh
- ¼ teaspoon sea salt, fine
- ¼ teaspoon black pepper
- 1 tablespoon olive brine
- 1 tablespoon olive oil
- ¼ cup red onion, sliced
- ½ cup green olives
- 2 oranges, peeled & sliced
- 3 celery stalks, sliced diagonally in ½ inch slices

Directions:
1. Put your oranges, olives, onion and celery in a shallow bowl.
2. Stir oil, olive brine and lemon juice, pour this over your salad.
3. Season with salt and pepper before serving.

Nutrition: 65 Calories 2g Protein 0.2g Fat

228. Roasted Broccoli Salad

Preparation Time: 9 minutes
Cooking Time: 17 minutes
Serving: 4
Ingredients:

- 1 lb. broccoli
- 3 tablespoons olive oil, divided
- 1-pint cherry tomatoes
- 1 ½ teaspoons honey
- 3 cups cubed bread, whole grain
- 1 tablespoon balsamic vinegar
- ½ teaspoon black pepper
- ¼ teaspoon sea salt, fine
- grated parmesan for serving

Directions:
1. Set oven to 450, and then place rimmed baking sheet.
2. Drizzle your broccoli with a tablespoon of oil, and toss to coat.
3. Take out from oven, and spoon the broccoli. Leave oil at bottom of the bowl and add in your tomatoes, toss to coat, then mix tomatoes with a tablespoon of honey. place on the same baking sheet.
4. Roast for fifteen minutes, and stir halfway through your cooking time.
5. Add in your bread, and then roast for three more minutes.
6. Whisk two tablespoons of oil, vinegar, and remaining honey. Season. Pour this over your broccoli mix to serve.

Nutrition: 226 Calories 7g Protein 12g Fat

229. Tomato Salad

Preparation Time: 22 minutes
Cooking Time: 0 minute
Serving: 4
Ingredients:
- 1 cucumber, sliced
- ¼ cup sun dried tomatoes, chopped
- 1 lb. tomatoes, cubed
- ½ cup black olives
- 1 red onion, sliced
- 1 tablespoon balsamic vinegar
- ¼ cup parsley, fresh & chopped
- 2 tablespoons olive oil

Directions:
1. Get out a bowl and combine all of your vegetables together. To make your dressing mix all your seasoning, olive oil and vinegar.
2. Toss with your salad and serve fresh.

Nutrition 126 Calories 2.1g Protein 9.2g Fat

230. Feta Beet Salad

Preparation Time: 16 minutes
Cooking Time: 0 minute
Serving: 4
Ingredients:
- 6 Red Beets, Cooked & Peeled
- 3 Ounces Feta Cheese, Cubed
- 2 Tablespoons Olive Oil

- 2 Tablespoons Balsamic Vinegar

Directions:
1. Combine everything together, and then serve.

Nutrition: 230 Calories 7.3g Protein 12g Fat

231. Cauliflower & Tomato Salad

Preparation Time: 17 minutes
Cooking Time: 0 minute
Serving: 4

Ingredients:
- 1 Head Cauliflower, Chopped
- 2 Tablespoons Parsley, Fresh & chopped
- 2 Cups Cherry Tomatoes, Halved
- 2 Tablespoons Lemon Juice, Fresh
- 2 Tablespoons Pine Nuts

Directions:
1. Incorporate lemon juice, cherry tomatoes, cauliflower and parsley and season well. Sprinkle the pine nuts, and mix.

Nutrition: 64 Calories 2.8g Protein 3.3g Fat

232. Tahini Spinach

Preparation Time: 11 minutes
Cooking Time: 6 minutes
Serving: 3

Ingredients:
- 10 spinach, chopped
- ½ cup water
- 1 tablespoon tahini
- 2 cloves garlic, minced
- ¼ teaspoon cumin
- ¼ teaspoon paprika
- ¼ teaspoon cayenne pepper
- 1/3 cup red wine vinegar

Direction:
1. Add your spinach and water to the saucepan, and then boil it on high heat. Once boiling reduce to low, and cover. Allow it to cook on simmer for five minutes.
2. Add in your garlic, cumin, cayenne, red wine vinegar, paprika and tahini. Whisk well, and season with salt and pepper.
3. Drain your spinach and top with tahini sauce to serve.

Nutrition: 69 Calories 5g Protein 3g Fat

233. Pilaf with Cream Cheese

Preparation Time: 11 minutes
Cooking Time: 34 minutes
Serving: 6

Ingredients:
- 2 cups yellow long grain rice, parboiled
- 1 cup onion
- 4 green onions

- 3 tablespoons butter
- 3 tablespoons vegetable broth
- 2 teaspoons cayenne pepper
- 1 teaspoon paprika
- ½ teaspoon cloves, minced
- 2 tablespoons mint leaves
- 1 bunch fresh mint leaves to garnish
- 1 tablespoons olive oil

Cheese Cream:
- 3 tablespoons olive oil
- sea salt & black pepper to taste
- 9 ounces cream cheese

Directions:
1. Start by heating your oven to 360, and then get out a pan. Heat your butter and olive oil together, and cook your onions and spring onions for two minutes.
2. Add in your salt, pepper, paprika, cloves, vegetable broth, rice and remaining seasoning. S
3. Sauté for three minutes.
4. Wrap with foil, and bake for another half hour. Allow it to cool.
5. Mix in the cream cheese, cheese, olive oil, salt and pepper. Serve your pilaf garnished with fresh mint leaves.

Nutrition: 364 Calories 5g Protein 30g Fat

234. Easy Spaghetti Squash

Preparation Time: 13 minutes
Cooking Time: 45 minutes
Serving: 6

Ingredients:
- 2 spring onions, chopped fine
- 3 cloves garlic, minced
- 1 zucchini, diced
- 1 red bell pepper, diced
- 1 tablespoon Italian seasoning
- 1 tomato, small & chopped fine
- 1 tablespoons parsley, fresh & chopped
- pinch lemon pepper
- dash sea salt, fine
- 4 ounces feta cheese, crumbled
- 3 Italian sausage links, casing removed
- 2 tablespoons olive oil
- 1 spaghetti sauce, halved lengthwise

Directions:
1. Prep oven to 350, and get out a large baking sheet. Coat it with cooking spray, and then put your squash on it with the cut side down.
2. Bake at 350 for forty-five minutes. It should be tender.
3. Turn the squash over, and bake for five more minutes. Scrape the strands into a larger bowl.
4. Cook tablespoon of olive oil in a skillet, and then add in your Italian sausage. Cook at eight minutes before removing it and placing it in a bowl.

5. Pour in additional tablespoon of olive oil to the skillet and cook your garlic and onions until softened. This will take five minutes. Throw in your Italian seasoning, red peppers and zucchini. Cook for another five minutes. Your vegetables should be softened.
6. Mix in your feta cheese and squash, cooking until the cheese has melted.
7. Stir in your sausage, and then season with lemon pepper and salt. Serve with parsley and tomato.

Nutrition: 423 Calories 18g Protein 30g Fat

235. <u>Roasted Eggplant Salad</u>

Preparation Time: 14 minutes
Cooking Time: 36 minutes
Serving: 6
Ingredients:

- 1 red onion, sliced
- 2 tablespoons parsley
- 1 teaspoon thyme
- 2 cups cherry tomatoes
- 1 teaspoon oregano
- 3 tablespoons olive oil
- 1 teaspoon basil
- 3 eggplants, peeled & cubed

Directions:

1. Start by heating your oven to 350.
2. Season your eggplant with basil, salt, pepper, oregano, thyme and olive oil.
3. Arrange it on a baking tray, and bake for a half hour.
4. Toss with your remaining ingredients before serving.

Nutrition: 148 Calories 3.5g Protein 7.7g Fat

236. <u>Penne with Tahini Sauce</u>

Preparation Time: 16 minutes
Cooking Time: 22 minutes
Serving: 8
Ingredients:

- 1/3 cup water
- 1 cup yogurt, plain
- 1/8 cup lemon juice
- 3 tablespoons tahini
- 3 cloves garlic
- 1 onion, chopped
- ¼ cup olive oil
- 2 portobello mushrooms, large & sliced
- ½ red bell pepper, diced
- 16 ounces penne pasta
- ½ cup parsley, fresh & chopped

Directions:

1. Start by getting out a pot and bring a pot of salted water to a boil. Cook your pasta al dente per package instructions.

2. Mix your lemon juice and tahini together, and then place it in a food processor. Process with garlic, water and yogurt.
3. Situate pan over medium heat. Heat up your oil, and cook your onions until soft.
4. Add in your mushroom and continue to cook until softened.
5. Add in your bell pepper, and cook until crispy.
6. Drain your pasta, and then toss with your tahini sauce, top with parsley and pepper and serve with vegetables.

Nutrition: 332 Calories 11g Proteins 12g Fat

237. <u>Roasted Veggies</u>

Preparation Time: 14 minutes
Cooking Time: 26 minutes
Serving: 12
Ingredients:

- 6 cloves garlic
- 6 tablespoons olive oil
- 1 fennel bulb, diced
- 1 zucchini, diced
- 2 red bell peppers, diced
- 6 potatoes, large & diced
- 2 teaspoons sea salt
- ½ cup balsamic vinegar
- ¼ cup rosemary, chopped & fresh
- 2 teaspoons vegetable bouillon powder

Directions:

1. Start by heating your oven to 400.
2. Get out a baking dish and place your potatoes, fennel, zucchini, garlic and fennel on a baking dish, drizzling with olive oil. Sprinkle with salt, bouillon powder, and rosemary. Mix well, and then bake at 450 for thirty to forty minutes. Mix your vinegar into the vegetables before serving.

Nutrition 675 Calories 13g Protein 21g Fat

238. <u>Zucchini Pasta</u>

Preparation Time: 9 minutes
Cooking Time: 32 minutes
Serving: 4
Ingredients:

- 3 tablespoons olive oil
- 2 cloves garlic, minced
- 3 zucchinis, large & diced
- sea salt & black pepper to taste
- ½ cup milk, 2%
- ¼ teaspoon nutmeg
- 1 tablespoon lemon juice, fresh
- ½ cup parmesan, grated
- 8 ounces uncooked farfalle pasta

Directions:

1. Get out a skillet and place it over medium heat, and then heat up the oil. Stir in your garlic and cook for

a minute. Stir often so that it doesn't burn. Add in your salt, pepper and zucchini. Stir well, and cook covered for fifteen minutes. During this time, you'll want to stir the mixture twice.

2. Get out a microwave safe bowl, and heat the milk for thirty seconds. Stir in your nutmeg, and then pour it into the skillet. Cook uncovered for five minutes. Stir occasionally to keep from burning.

3. Get out a stockpot and cook your pasta per package instructions. Drain the pasta, and then save two tablespoons of pasta water.

4. Stir everything together, and add in the cheese and lemon juice and pasta water.

Nutrition 410 Calories 15g Protein 17g Fat

239. Asparagus Pasta

Preparation Time: 8 minutes
Cooking Time: 33 minutes
Serving: 6
Ingredients:
- 8 ounces farfalle pasta, uncooked
- 1 ½ cups asparagus
- 1-pint grape tomatoes, halved
- 2 tablespoons olive oil
- 2 cups mozzarella, fresh & drained
- 1/3 cup basil leaves, fresh & torn
- 2 tablespoons balsamic vinegar

Directions:
1. Start by heating the oven to 400, and then get out a stockpot. Cook your pasta per package instructions, and reserve ¼ cup of pasta water.
2. Get out a bowl and toss the tomatoes, oil, asparagus, and season with salt and pepper. Spread this mixture on a baking sheet, and bake for fifteen minutes. Stir twice in this time.
3. Remove your vegetables from the oven, and then add the cooked pasta to your baking sheet. Mix with a few tablespoons of pasta water so that your sauce becomes smoother.
4. Mix in your basil and mozzarella, drizzling with balsamic vinegar. Serve warm.

Nutrition: 307 Calories 18g Protein 14g Fat

240. Feta & Spinach Pita Bake

Preparation Time: 11 minutes
Cooking Time: 36 minutes
Serving: 6
Ingredients:
- 2 roma tomatoes
- 6 whole wheat pita bread
- 1 jar sun dried tomato pesto
- 4 mushrooms, fresh & sliced
- 1 bunch spinach
- 2 tablespoons parmesan cheese
- 3 tablespoons olive oil
- ½ cup feta cheese

Directions:
1. Start by heating the oven to 350, and get to your pita bread. Spread the tomato pesto on the side of each one. Put them in a baking pan with the tomato side up.
2. Top with tomatoes, spinach, mushrooms, parmesan and feta. Pour in olive oil and season with pepper.
3. Bake for twelve minutes, and then serve cut into quarters.

Nutrition: 350 Calories 12g Protein 17g Fat

241. Spelled Salad

Preparation Time: 15 minutes
Cooking Time: 30 minutes
Servings: 4
Ingredients:
Salad
- 2 ½ cups of vegetable broth
- ¾ cup of crumbled feta cheese
- 1 can chickpeas, drained
- 1 cucumber, chopped
- 1 ½ cup pearl spelled
- 1 tablespoon of olive oil
- ½ sliced onion
- 2 cups of baby spinach, chopped
- 1 pint of cherry tomatoes
- 1 ¼ cups of water

Dressing:
- 2 tablespoons of lemon juice
- 1 tablespoon of honey
- ¼ cup olive oil
- ¼ tsp oregano
- 1 pinch of red pepper flakes
- ¼ teaspoon of salt
- 1 tablespoon of red wine vinegar

Directions:
1. Heat the oil in a skillet. Add the spelled and cook for a minute. Be sure to stir it regularly during cooking. Fill in water and broth, then bring to a boil. Reduce the heat and simmer until the spelled is tender, about 30 minutes. Drain the water and transfer the spelled to a bowl.
2. Add the spinach and mix. Let cool for about 20 minutes. Add the cucumber, onions, tomatoes, peppers, chickpeas and feta. Mix well to get a good mixture. Step back and prepare the dressing.
3. Mix all the dressing ingredients and mix well until smooth. Pour it into the bowl and mix it well. Season well to taste.

Nutrition 365 Calories 10g Fat 43g Carbohydrates 13g Protein

242. Chickpea and Zucchini Salad

Preparation Time: 10 minutes
Cooking Time: 0 minute

Servings: 3

Ingredients:

- ¼ cup balsamic vinegar
- 1/3 cup chopped basil leaves
- 1 tablespoon of capers, drained and chopped
- ½ cup crumbled feta cheese
- 1 can chickpeas, drained
- 1 garlic clove, chopped
- ½ cup Kalamata olives, chopped
- 1/3 cup of olive oil
- ½ cup sweet onion, chopped
- ½ tsp oregano
- 1 pinch of red pepper flakes, crushed
- ¾ cup red bell pepper, chopped
- 1 tablespoon chopped rosemary
- 2 cups of zucchini, diced
- salt and pepper, to taste

Directions:

1. Combine the vegetables in a bowl and cover well.
2. Serve at room temperature. But for best results, refrigerate the bowl for a few hours before serving, to allow the flavors to blend.

Nutrition 258 Calories 12g Fat 19g Carbohydrates 5.6g Protein

243. Provencal Artichoke Salad

Preparation Time: 15 minutes
Cooking Time: 5 minutes
Servings: 3

Ingredients:

- 9 oz artichoke hearts
- 1 teaspoon of chopped basil
- 2 garlic cloves, chopped
- 1 lemon zest
- 1 tablespoon olives, chopped
- 1 tablespoon of olive oil
- ½ chopped onion
- 1 pinch, ½ teaspoon of salt
- 2 tomatoes, chopped
- 3 tablespoons of water
- ½ glass of white wine
- salt and pepper, to taste

Directions:

1. Heat the oil in a skillet. Sauté the onion and garlic. Cook until the onions are translucent and season with a pinch of salt. Pour in the white wine and simmer until the wine is reduced by half.
2. Add the chopped tomatoes, artichoke hearts and water. Simmer then add the lemon zest and about ½ teaspoon of salt. Cover and cook for about 6 minutes.
3. Add the olives and basil. Season well and enjoy!

Nutrition 147 Calories 13g Fat 18g Carbohydrates 4g Protein

244. Bulgarian Salad

Preparation Time: 10 minutes
Cooking Time: 20 minutes
Servings: 2

Ingredients:

- 2 cups of bulgur
- 1 tablespoon of butter
- 1 cucumber, cut into pieces
- ¼ cup dill
- ¼ cup black olives, cut in half
- 1 tablespoon, 2 teaspoons of olive oil
- 4 cups of water
- 2 teaspoons of red wine vinegar
- salt, to taste

Directions:

1. In a saucepan, toast the bulgur on a mixture of butter and olive oil. Leave to cook until the bulgur is golden brown and begins to crack.
2. Add water and season with salt. Wrap everything and simmer for about 20 minutes or until the bulgur is tender.
3. In a bowl, mix the cucumber pieces with the olive oil, dill, red wine vinegar and black olives. Mix everything well.
4. It combines cucumber and bulgur.

Nutrition 386 Calories 14g Fat 55g Carbohydrates 9g Protein

245. Falafel Salad Bowl

Preparation Time: 15 minutes
Cooking Time: 5 minutes
Servings: 2

Ingredients

- 1 tablespoon of chili garlic sauce
- 1 tablespoon of garlic and dill sauce
- 1 pack of vegetarian falafels
- 1 box of humus
- 2 tablespoons of lemon juice
- 1 tablespoon of pitted kalamata olives
- 1 tablespoon of extra virgin olive oil
- ¼ cup onion, diced
- 2 cups of chopped parsley
- 2 cups of crisp pita
- 1 pinch of salt
- 1 tablespoon of tahini sauce
- ½ cup diced tomato

Directions:

1. Cook the prepared falafels. Put it aside. Prepare the salad. Mix the parsley, onion, tomato, lemon juice, olive oil and salt. Throw it all out and put everything aside.
2. Transfer everything to the serving bowls. Add the parsley and cover with humus and falafel. Sprinkle bowl with tahini sauce, chili garlic sauce and dill

sauce. Upon serving, add the lemon juice and mix the salad well. Serve with pita bread on the side.

Nutrition 561 Calories 11g Fat 60.1g Carbohydrates 18.5g Protein

246. Easy Greek Salad

Preparation Time: 15 minutes
Cooking Time: 0 minute
Servings: 2
Ingredients:

- 4 oz Greek feta cheese, cubed
- 5 cucumbers, cut lengthwise
- 1 teaspoon of honey
- 1 lemon, chewed and grated
- 1 cup kalamata olives, pitted and halved
- ¼ cup extra virgin olive oil
- 1 onion, sliced
- 1 teaspoon of oregano
- 1 pinch of fresh oregano (for garnish)
- 12 tomatoes, quartered
- ¼ cup red wine vinegar
- salt and pepper, to taste

Directions:
1. In a bowl, soak the onions in salted water for 15 minutes. In a large bowl, combine the honey, lemon juice, lemon peel, oregano, salt and pepper.
2. Mix everything. Gradually add the olive oil, beating as you do, until the oil emulsifies. Add the olives and tomatoes. Put it right. Add the cucumbers
3. Drain the onions soaked in salted water and add them to the salad mixture. Top the salad with fresh oregano and feta. Dash with olive oil and season with pepper, to taste.

Nutrition 292 Calories 17g Fat 12g Carbohydrates 6g Protein

247. Arugula Salad with Figs and Walnuts

Preparation Time: 15 minutes
Cooking Time: 10 minutes
Servings: 2
Ingredients:

- 5 oz arugula
- 1 carrot, scraped
- 1/8 teaspoon of cayenne pepper
- 3 oz of goat cheese, crumbled
- 1 can salt-free chickpeas, drained
- ½ cup dried figs, cut into wedges
- 1 teaspoon of honey
- 3 tablespoons of olive oil
- 2 teaspoons of balsamic vinegar
- ½ walnuts cut in half
- salt, to taste

Directions:

1. Preheat the oven to 175 degrees. In a baking dish, combine the nuts, 1 tablespoon of olive oil, cayenne pepper and 1/8 teaspoon of salt. Transfer the baking sheet in the oven and bake it until the nuts are golden. Set it aside when you are done.
2. In a bowl, incorporate the honey, balsamic vinegar, 2 tablespoons of oil and ¾ teaspoon of salt.
3. In a large bowl, combine the arugula, carrot and figs. Add nuts and goat cheese and drizzle with balsamic honey vinaigrette. Make sure you cover everything.

Nutrition 403 Calories 9g Fat 35g Carbohydrates 13g Protein

248. Cauliflower Salad with Tahini Vinaigrette

Preparation Time: 15 minutes
Cooking Time: 5 minutes
Servings: 2
Ingredients:

- 1 ½ lb. of cauliflower
- ¼ cup of dried cherries
- 3 tablespoons of lemon juice
- 1 tablespoon of fresh mint, chopped
- 1 teaspoon of olive oil
- ½ cup chopped parsley
- 3 tablespoons of roasted salted pistachios, chopped
- ½ teaspoon of salt
- ¼ Cup of shallot, chopped
- 2 tablespoons of tahini

Directions:
1. Grate the cauliflower in a microwave-safe container Add olive oil and ¼ salt. Be sure to cover and season the cauliflower evenly. Wrap the bowl with plastic wrap and heat it in the microwave for about 3 minutes.
2. Put the rice with the cauliflower on a baking sheet and let cool for about 10 minutes. Add the lemon juice and the shallots. Let it rest to allow the cauliflower to absorb the flavor.
3. Add the mixture of tahini, cherries, parsley, mint and salt. Mix everything well. Sprinkle with roasted pistachios before serving.

Nutrition 165 Calories 10g Fat 20g Carbohydrates 6g Protein

249. Mediterranean Potato Salad

Preparation Time: 15 minutes
Cooking Time: 10 minutes
Servings: 2
Ingredients:

- 1 bunch of basil leaves, torn
- 1 garlic clove, crushed
- 1 tablespoon of olive oil
- 1 onion, sliced

- 1 teaspoon of oregano
- 100 g of roasted red pepper. Slices
- 300g potatoes, cut in half
- 1 can of cherry tomatoes
- salt and pepper, to taste

Directions:
1. Sauté the onions in a saucepan. Add oregano and garlic. He cooks everything for a minute. Add the pepper and tomatoes. Season well, then simmer for about 10 minutes. Put that aside.
2. In a saucepan, boil the potatoes in salted water. Cook until tender, about 15 minutes. Drain well. Mix the potatoes with the sauce and add the basil and olives. Finally, throw everything away before serving.

Nutrition 111 Calories 9g Fat 16g Carbohydrates 3g Protein

250. Quinoa and Pistachio Salad

Preparation Time: 10 minutes
Cooking Time: 15 minutes
Servings: 2
Ingredients:
- ¼ teaspoon of cumin
- ½ cup of dried currants
- 1 teaspoon grated lemon zest
- 2 tablespoons of lemon juice
- ½ cup green onions, chopped
- 1 tablespoon of chopped mint
- 2 tablespoons of extra virgin olive oil
- ¼ cup chopped parsley
- ¼ teaspoon ground pepper
- 1/3 cup pistachios, chopped
- 1 ¼ cups uncooked quinoa
- 1 2/3 cup of water

Directions:
1. In a saucepan, combine 1 2/3 cups of water, raisins and quinoa. Cook everything until boiling then reduce the heat. Simmer everything for about 10 minutes and let the quinoa become frothy.
2. Set it aside for about 5 minutes. In a container, transfer the quinoa mixture. Add the nuts, mint, onions and parsley. Mix everything. In separate bowl, incorporate the lemon zest, lemon juice, currants, cumin and oil. Beat them together. Mix the dry and wet ingredients.

Nutrition 248 Calories 8g Fat 35g Carbohydrates 7g Protein

251. Cucumber Chicken Salad with Spicy Peanut Dressing

Preparation Time: 15 minutes
Cooking Time: 0 minute
Servings: 2
Ingredients
- 1/2 cup peanut butter
- 1 tablespoon sambal oelek (chili paste)

- 1 tablespoon low-sodium soy sauce
- 1 teaspoon grilled sesame oil
- 4 tablespoons of water, or more if necessary
- 1 cucumber with peeled and cut into thin strips
- 1 cooked chicken fillet, grated into thin strips
- 2 tablespoons chopped peanuts

Directions:
1. Combine peanut butter, soy sauce, sesame oil, sambal oelek, and water in a bowl. Place the cucumber slices on a dish. Garnish with grated chicken and sprinkle with sauce. Sprinkle the chopped peanuts.

Nutrition 720 calories 54 g fat 8.9g carbohydrates 45.9g protein

252. German Hot Potato Salad

Preparation Time: 10 minutes
Cooking Time: 30 minutes
Servings: 12
Ingredients
- 9 peeled potatoes
- 6 slices of bacon
- 1/8 teaspoon ground black pepper
- 1/2 teaspoon celery seed
- 2 tablespoons white sugar
- 2 teaspoons salt
- 3/4 cup water
- 1/3 cup distilled white vinegar
- 2 tablespoons all-purpose flour
- 3/4 cup chopped onions

Directions:
1. Boil salted water in a large pot. Put in the potatoes and cook until soft but still firm, about 30 minutes. Drain, let cool and cut finely. Over medium heat, cook bacon in a pan. Drain, crumble and set aside. Save the cooking juices. Cook onions in bacon grease until golden brown.
2. Combine flour, sugar, salt, celery seed, and pepper in a small bowl. Add sautéed onions and cook, stirring until bubbling, and remove from heat. Stir in the water and vinegar, then bring back to the fire and bring to a boil, stirring constantly. Boil and stir. Slowly add bacon and potato slices to the vinegar/water mixture, stirring gently until the potatoes are warmed up.

Nutrition 205 calories 6.5g fat 32.9g carbohydrates 4.3g protein

253. Chicken Fiesta Salad

Preparation Time: 20 minutes
Cooking Time: 20 minutes
Servings: 4
Ingredients
- 2 halves of chicken fillet without skin or bones
- 1 packet of herbs for fajitas, divided

- 1 tablespoon vegetable oil
- 1 can black beans, rinsed and drained
- 1 box of Mexican-style corn
- 1/2 cup of salsa
- 1 packet of green salad
- 1 onion, minced
- 1 tomato, quartered

Directions:
1. Rub the chicken evenly with 1/2 of the herbs for fajitas. Cook the oil in a frying pan over medium heat and cook the chicken for 8 minutes on the side by side or until the juice is clear; put aside.
2. Combine beans, corn, salsa, and other 1/2 fajita spices in a large pan. Heat over medium heat until lukewarm. Prepare the salad by mixing green vegetables, onion, and tomato. Cover the chicken salad and dress the beans and corn mixture.

Nutrition 311 calories 6.4g fat 42.2g carbohydrates 23g protein

254. Corn & Black Bean Salad

Preparation Time: 10 minutes
Cooking Time: 0 minute
Servings: 4
Ingredients
- 2 tablespoons vegetable oil
- 1/4 cup balsamic vinegar
- 1/2 teaspoon of salt
- 1/2 teaspoon of white sugar
- 1/2 teaspoon ground cumin
- 1/2 teaspoon ground black pepper
- 1/2 teaspoon chili powder
- 3 tablespoons chopped fresh coriander
- 1 can black beans (15 oz)
- 1 can of sweetened corn (8.75 oz) drained

Directions:
1. Combine balsamic vinegar, oil, salt, sugar, black pepper, cumin and chili powder in a small bowl. Combine black corn and beans in a medium bowl.
2. Mix with vinegar and oil vinaigrette and garnish with coriander. Cover and refrigerate overnight.

Nutrition 214 calories 8.4 g fat 28.6g carbohydrates 7.5g protein

255. Awesome Pasta Salad

Preparation Time: 30 minutes
Cooking Time: 10 minutes
Servings: 16
Ingredients
- 1 (16-oz) fusilli pasta package
- 3 cups of cherry tomatoes
- 1/2 pound of provolone, diced
- 1/2 pound of sausage, diced
- 1/4 pound of pepperoni, cut in half
- 1 large green pepper

- 1 can of black olives, drained
- 1 jar of chilis, drained
- 1 bottle (8 oz) Italian vinaigrette

Directions:
1. Boil a lightly salted water in a pot. Stir in the pasta and cook for about 8 to 10 minutes or until al dente. Drain and rinse with cold water.
2. Combine pasta with tomatoes, cheese, salami, pepperoni, green pepper, olives, and peppers in a large bowl. Pour the vinaigrette and mix well.

Nutrition 310 calories 17.7g fat 25.9g carbohydrates 12.9g protein

256. Tuna Salad

Preparation Time: 20 minutes
Cooking Time: 0 minute
Servings: 4
Ingredients
- 1 (19 ounce) can of garbanzo beans
- 2 tablespoons mayonnaise
- 2 teaspoons of spicy brown mustard
- 1 tablespoon sweet pickle
- Salt and pepper to taste
- 2 chopped green onions

Directions:
1. Combine green beans, mayonnaise, mustard, sauce, chopped green onions, salt and pepper in a medium bowl. Mix well.

Nutrition 220 calories 7.2g fat 32.7g carbohydrates 7g protein

257. Southern Potato Salad

Preparation Time: 15 minutes
Cooking Time: 15 minutes
Servings: 4
Ingredients
- 4 potatoes
- 4 eggs
- 1/2 stalk of celery, finely chopped
- 1/4 cup sweet taste
- 1 clove of garlic minced
- 2 tablespoons mustard
- 1/2 cup mayonnaise
- salt and pepper to taste

Directions:
1. Boil water in a pot then situate the potatoes and cook until soft but still firm, about 15 minutes; drain and chop. Transfer the eggs in a pan and cover with cold water.
2. Boil the water; cover, remove from heat, and let the eggs soak in hot water for 10 minutes. Remove then shell and chop.
3. Combine potatoes, eggs, celery, sweet sauce, garlic, mustard, mayonnaise, salt, and pepper in a large bowl. Mix and serve hot.

Nutrition 460 calories 27.4g fat 44.6g carbohydrates 11.3g protein

258. Seven-Layer Salad

Preparation Time: 15 minutes
Cooking Time: 5 minutes
Servings: 10
Ingredients
- 1-pound bacon
- 1 head iceberg lettuce
- 1 red onion, minced
- 1 pack of 10 frozen peas, thawed
- 10 oz grated cheddar cheese
- 1 cup chopped cauliflower
- 1 1/4 cup mayonnaise
- 2 tablespoons white sugar
- 2/3 cup grated Parmesan cheese

Directions:
1. Put the bacon in a huge, shallow frying pan. Bake over medium heat until smooth. Crumble and set aside. Situate the chopped lettuce in a large bowl and cover with a layer of an onion, peas, grated cheese, cauliflower, and bacon.
2. Prepare the vinaigrette by mixing the mayonnaise, sugar, and parmesan cheese. Pour over the salad and cool to cool.

Nutrition 387 calories 32.7g fat 9.9g carbohydrates 14.5g protein

259. Kale, Quinoa & Avocado Salad

Preparation Time: 5 minutes
Cooking Time: 25 minutes
Servings: 4
Ingredients
- 2/3 cup of quinoa
- 1 1/3 cup of water
- 1 bunch of kale, torn into bite-sized pieces
- 1/2 avocado - peeled, diced and pitted
- 1/2 cup chopped cucumber
- 1/3 cup chopped red pepper
- 2 tablespoons chopped red onion
- 1 tablespoon of feta crumbled

Directions:
1. Boil the quinoa and 1 1/3 cup of water in a pan. Adjust heat and simmer until quinoa is tender and water is absorbed for about 15 to 20 minutes. Set aside to cool.
2. Place the cabbage in a steam basket over more than an inch of boiling water in a pan. Seal the pan with a lid and steam until hot, about 45 seconds; transfer to a large plate. Garnish with cabbage, quinoa, avocado, cucumber, pepper, red onion, and feta cheese.

3. Combine olive oil, lemon juice, Dijon mustard, sea salt, and black pepper in a bowl until the oil is emulsified in the dressing; pour over the salad.

Nutrition 342 calories 20.3g fat 35.4g carbohydrates 8.9g protein

260. Chicken Salad

Preparation Time: 20 minutes
Cooking Time: 0 minute
Servings: 9
Ingredients
- 1/2 cup mayonnaise
- 1/2 teaspoon of salt
- 3/4 teaspoon of poultry herbs
- 1 tablespoon lemon juice
- 3 cups cooked chicken breast, diced
- 1/4 teaspoon ground black pepper
- 1/4 teaspoon garlic powder
- 1/4 teaspoon onion powder
- 1/2 cup finely chopped celery
- 1 (8 oz) box of water chestnuts, drained and chopped
- 1/2 cup chopped green onions
- 1 1/2 cups green grapes cut in half
- 1 1/2 cups diced Swiss cheese

Directions:
1. Combine mayonnaise, salt, chicken spices, onion powder, garlic powder, pepper, and lemon juice in a medium bowl.
2. Combine chicken, celery, green onions, water chestnuts, Swiss cheese, and raisins in a big bowl. Stir in the mayonnaise mixture and coat. Cool until ready to serve.

Nutrition 293 calories 19.5g fat 10.3g carbohydrates 19.4g protein

261. Cobb Salad

Preparation Time: 5 minutes
Cooking Time: 15 minutes
Servings: 6
Ingredients
- 6 slices of bacon
- 3 eggs
- 1 cup Iceberg lettuce, grated
- 3 cups cooked minced chicken meat
- 2 tomatoes, seeded and minced
- 3/4 cup of blue cheese, crumbled
- 1 avocado - peeled, pitted and diced
- 3 green onions, minced
- 1 bottle (8 oz.) Ranch Vinaigrette

Directions:
1. Situate the eggs in a pan and soak them completely with cold water. Boil the water. Cover and remove from heat and let the eggs rest in hot water for 10 to 12 minutes. Remove from hot water, let cool,

peel, and chop. Situate the bacon in a big, deep frying pan. Bake over medium heat until smooth. Set aside.

2. Divide the grated lettuce into separate plates. Spread chicken, eggs, tomatoes, blue cheese, bacon, avocado, and green onions in rows on lettuce. Sprinkle with your favorite vinaigrette and enjoy.

Nutrition 525 calories 39.9g fat 10.2g carbohydrates 31.7g protein

262. **Broccoli Salad**

Preparation Time: 10 minutes
Cooking Time: 15 minutes
Servings: 6
Ingredients
- 10 slices of bacon
- 1 cup fresh broccoli
- ¼ cup red onion, minced
- ½ cup raisins
- 3 tablespoons white wine vinegar
- 2 tablespoons white sugar
- 1 cup mayonnaise
- 1 cup of sunflower seeds

Directions:
1. Cook the bacon in a deep-frying pan over medium heat. Drain, crumble, and set aside. Combine broccoli, onion, and raisins in a medium bowl. Mix vinegar, sugar, and mayonnaise in a small bowl. Pour over the broccoli mixture and mix. Cool for at least two hours.
2. Before serving, mix the salad with crumbled bacon and sunflower seeds.

Nutrition 559 calories 48.1g fat 31g carbohydrates 18g protein

263. **Strawberry Spinach Salad**

Preparation Time: 10 minutes
Cooking Time: 0 minute
Servings: 4
Ingredients
- 2 tablespoons sesame seeds
- 1 tablespoon poppy seeds
- 1/2 cup white sugar
- 1/2 cup olive oil
- 1/4 cup distilled white vinegar
- 1/4 teaspoon paprika
- 1/4 teaspoon Worcestershire sauce
- 1 tablespoon minced onion
- 10 ounces fresh spinach
- 1-quart strawberries - cleaned, hulled and sliced
- 1/4 cup almonds, blanched and slivered

Directions:
1. In a medium bowl, whisk together the same seeds, poppy seeds, sugar, olive oil, vinegar, paprika,

Worcestershire sauce, and onion. Cover, and chill for one hour.

2. In a large bowl, incorporate the spinach, strawberries, and almonds. Drizzle dressing over salad and toss. Refrigerate 10 to 15 minutes before serving.

Nutrition 491 calories 35.2g fat 42.9g carbohydrates 6g protein

264. **Pear Salad with Roquefort Cheese**

Preparation Time: 20 minutes
Cooking Time: 10 minutes
Servings: 2
Ingredients
- 1 leaf lettuce, torn into bite-sized pieces
- 3 pears - peeled, cored and diced
- 5 ounces Roquefort, crumbled
- 1 avocado - peeled, seeded and diced
- 1/2 cup chopped green onions
- 1/4 cup white sugar
- 1/2 cup pecan nuts
- 1/3 cup olive oil
- 3 tablespoons red wine vinegar
- 1 1/2 teaspoon of white sugar
- 1 1/2 teaspoon of prepared mustard
- 1/2 teaspoon of salted black pepper
- 1 clove of garlic

Directions:
1. Stir in 1/4 cup of sugar with the pecans in a pan over medium heat. Continue to stir gently until the sugar caramelized with pecans. Cautiously transfer the nuts to wax paper. Let it chill and break into pieces.
2. Mix for vinaigrette oil, marinade, 1 1/2 teaspoon of sugar, mustard, chopped garlic, salt, and pepper.
3. In a deep bowl, combine lettuce, pears, blue cheese, avocado, and green onions. Put vinaigrette over salad, sprinkle with pecans and serve.

Nutrition 426 calories 31.6g fat 33.1g carbohydrates 8g protein

265. **Mexican Bean Salad**

Preparation Time: 15 minutes
Cooking Time: 0 minute
Servings: 6
Ingredients
- 1 can black beans (15 oz), drained
- 1 can red beans (15 oz), drained
- 1 can white beans (15 oz), drained
- 1 green pepper, minced
- 1 red pepper, minced
- 1 pack of frozen corn kernels
- 1 red onion, minced

- 2 tablespoons fresh lime juice
- 1/2 cup olive oil
- 1/2 cup red wine vinegar
- 1 tablespoon lemon juice
- 1 tablespoon salt
- 2 tablespoons white sugar
- 1 clove of crushed garlic
- 1/4 cup chopped coriander
- 1/2 tablespoon ground cumin
- 1/2 tablespoon ground black pepper
- 1 dash of hot pepper sauce
- 1/2 teaspoon chili powder

Directions:
1. Combine beans, peppers, frozen corn, and red onion in a large bowl. Combine olive oil, lime juice, red wine vinegar, lemon juice, sugar, salt, garlic, coriander, cumin, and black pepper in a small bowl — season with hot sauce and chili powder.
2. Pour the vinaigrette with olive oil over the vegetables; mix well. Cool well and serve cold.

Nutrition 334 calories 14.8g fat 41.7g carbohydrates 11.2g protein

266. Melon-Mozzarella Salad

Preparation Time:20 minutes
Cooking Time: 0 minute
Servings: 6
Ingredients:
- ¼ teaspoon sea salt
- ¼ teaspoon black pepper
- 1 tablespoon balsamic vinegar
- 1 cantaloupe, quartered & seeded
- 12 watermelon, small & seedless
- 2 cups mozzarella balls, fresh
- 1/3 cup basil, fresh & torn
- 2 tbsp. olive oil

Directions:
1. Scrape out balls of cantaloupe, and the place them in a colander over a serving bowl. Use your melon baller to cut the watermelon as well, and then put them in with your cantaloupe.
2. Allow your fruit to drain for ten minutes, and then refrigerate the juice for another recipe. It can even be added to smoothies. Wipe the bowl dry, and then place your fruit in it.
3. Add in your basil, oil, vinegar, mozzarella and tomatoes before seasoning with salt and pepper. Gently mix and serve immediately or chilled.

Nutrition 218 Calories 13g Fat 9g Carbohydrates 10g Protein

267. Citrus Celery Salad

Preparation Time: 15 minutes
Cooking Time: 0 minute
Servings: 6

Ingredients:
- 1 tablespoon lemon juice, fresh
- ¼ teaspoon sea salt, fine
- ¼ teaspoon black pepper
- 1 tablespoon olive brine
- 1 tablespoon olive oil
- ¼ cup red onion, sliced
- ½ cup green olives
- 2 oranges, peeled & sliced
- 3 celery stalks, sliced diagonally in ½ inch slices

Directions:
1. Put your oranges, olives, onion and celery in a shallow bowl. In a different bowl whisk your oil, olive brine and lemon juice, pour this over your salad. Season with salt and pepper before serving.

Nutrition 65 Calories 7g Fats 9g Carbohydrates 2g Protein

268. Oven-Roasted Broccoli Salad

Preparation Time: 20 minutes
Cooking Time: 10 minutes
Servings: 4
Ingredients:
- 1 lb. broccoli, cut into florets & stem sliced
- 3 tablespoons olive oil, divided
- 1-pint cherry tomatoes
- 1 ½ teaspoons honey, raw & divided
- 3 cups cubed bread, whole grain
- 1 tablespoon balsamic vinegar
- ½ teaspoon black pepper
- ¼ teaspoon sea salt, fine
- grated parmesan for serving

Directions:
1. Prepare oven at 450 degrees, and then get out a rimmed baking sheet. Place it in the oven to heat up. Drizzle your broccoli with a tablespoon of oil, and toss to coat.
2. Remove the baking sheet form the oven, and spoon the broccoli on it. Leave oil it eh bottom of the bowl and add in your tomatoes, toss to coat, and then toss your tomatoes with a tablespoon of honey. Pour them on the same baking sheet as your broccoli.
3. Roast for fifteen minutes, and stir halfway through your cooking time. Add in your bread, and then roast for three more minutes. Whisk two tablespoons of oil, vinegar, and remaining honey. Season with salt and pepper. Pour this over your broccoli mix to serve.

Nutrition 226 Calories 12g Fat 26g Carbohydrates 7g Protein

269. Sun-dried Tomato Salad

Preparation Time: 20 minutes
Cooking Time: 0 minute
Servings: 4

Ingredients:
- 1 cucumber, sliced
- ¼ cup sun dried tomatoes, chopped
- 1 lb. tomatoes, cubed
- ½ cup black olives
- 1 red onion, sliced
- 1 tablespoon balsamic vinegar
- ¼ cup parsley, fresh & chopped
- 2 tablespoons olive oil
- sea salt & black pepper to taste

Directions:
1. Get out a bowl and combine all of your vegetables together. To make your dressing mix all your seasoning, olive oil and vinegar. Toss with your salad and serve fresh.

Nutrition 126 Calories 9.2g Fat 11.5g Carbohydrates 2.1g Protein

270. Feta Cheese and Beet Salad

Preparation Time: 15 minutes
Cooking Time: 0 minute
Servings: 4

Ingredients:
- 6 red beets, cooked & peeled
- 3 ounces feta cheese, cubed
- 2 tablespoons olive oil
- 2 tablespoons balsamic vinegar

Directions:
1. Combine everything together, and then serve.

Nutrition 230 Calories 12g Fat 26.3g Carbohydrates 7.3g Protein

271. Cauliflower-Tomato Salad

Preparation Time: 15 minutes
Cooking Time: 0 minute
Servings: 4

Ingredients:
- 1 head cauliflower, chopped
- 2 tablespoons parsley, fresh & chopped
- 2 cups cherry tomatoes, halved
- 2 tablespoons lemon juice, fresh
- 2 tablespoons pine nuts
- sea salt & black pepper to taste

Directions:
1. Mix your lemon juice, cherry tomatoes, cauliflower and parsley together, and then season. Top with pine nuts, and mix well before serving.

Nutrition 64 Calories 3.3g Fat 7.9g Carbohydrates 2.8g Protein

272. Cheesy and Spiced Pilaf

Preparation Time: 20 minutes
Cooking Time: 10 minutes
Servings: 6

Ingredients:
- 2 cups yellow long grain rice, parboiled
- 1 cup onion
- 4 green onions
- 3 tablespoons butter
- 3 tablespoons vegetable broth
- 2 teaspoons cayenne pepper
- 1 teaspoon paprika
- ½ teaspoon cloves, minced
- 2 tablespoons mint leaves, fresh & chopped
- 1 bunch fresh mint leaves to garnish
- 1 tablespoons olive oil
- sea salt & black pepper to taste

Cheese Cream:
- 3 tablespoons olive oil
- sea salt & black pepper to taste
- 9 ounces cream cheese

Directions:
1. Ready the oven at 360 degrees, and then pull out a pan. Heat your butter and olive oil together, and cook your onions and spring onions for two minutes.
2. Add in your salt, pepper, paprika, cloves, vegetable broth, rice and remaining seasoning. Sauté for three minutes. Wrap with foil, and bake for another half hour. Allow it to cool.
3. Mix in the cream cheese, cheese, olive oil, salt and pepper. Serve your pilaf garnished with fresh mint leaves.

Nutrition 364 Calories 30g Fat 20g Carbohydrates 5g Protein

273. Oven-Roasted Vegetable Salad

Preparation Time: 10 minutes
Cooking Time: 20 minutes
Servings: 6

Ingredients:
- 1 red onion, sliced
- 2 tablespoons parsley, fresh & chopped
- 1 teaspoon thyme
- 2 cups cherry tomatoes, halved
- sea salt & black pepper to taste
- 1 teaspoon oregano
- 3 tablespoons olive oil
- 1 teaspoon basil
- 3 eggplants, peeled & cubed

Directions:
1. Start by heating your oven to 350. Season your eggplant with basil, salt, pepper, oregano, thyme and olive oil. Situate it on a baking tray, and bake for a half hour. Toss with your remaining ingredients before serving.

Nutrition 148 Calories 7.7g Fat 20.5g Carbohydrates 3.5g Protein

274. Herb-Roasted Vegetables

Preparation Time: 5 minutes
Cooking Time: 15 minutes
Servings: 12
Ingredients:
- 6 cloves garlic
- 6 tablespoons olive oil
- 1 fennel bulb, diced
- 1 zucchini, diced
- 2 red bell peppers, diced
- 6 potatoes, large & diced
- 2 teaspoons sea salt
- ½ cup balsamic vinegar
- ¼ cup rosemary, chopped & fresh
- 2 teaspoons vegetable bouillon powder

Directions:
1. Start by heating your oven to 400. Put your potatoes, fennel, zucchini, garlic and fennel on a baking dish, drizzling with olive oil. Sprinkle with salt, bouillon powder, and rosemary. Mix well, and then bake at 450 for thirty to forty minutes. Mix your vinegar into the vegetables before serving.

Nutrition 675 Calories 21g Fat 112g Carbohydrates 13g Protein

275. Cheesy Pistachio Salad

Preparation Time: 20 minutes
Cooking Time: 0 minute
Servings: 6
Ingredients:
- 6 cups kale, chopped
- ¼ cup olive oil
- 2 tablespoons lemon juice, fresh
- ½ teaspoon smoked paprika
- 2 cups arugula
- 1/3 cup pistachios, unsalted & shelled
- 6 tablespoons parmesan cheese, grated

Directions:
1. Get out a salad bowl and combine your oil, lemon, smoked paprika and kale. Gently massage the leaves for half a minute. Your kale should be coated well. Gently mix your arugula and pistachios when ready to serve.

Nutrition 150 Calories 12g Fat 8g Carbohydrates 5g Protein

276. Parmesan Barley Risotto

Preparation Time: 10 minutes
Cooking Time: 20 minutes
Servings: 6
Ingredients:
- 1 cup yellow onion, chopped
- 1 tablespoon olive oil
- 4 cups vegetable broth, low sodium
- 2 cups pearl barley, uncooked
- ½ cup dry white wine
- 1 cup parmesan cheese, grated fine & divided
- sea salt & black pepper to taste
- fresh chives, chopped for serving
- lemon wedges for serving

Directions:
1. Add your broth into a saucepan and bring it to a simmer over medium-high heat. Get out a stock pot and put it over medium-high heat as well. Heat up your oil before adding in your onion. Cook for eight minutes and stir occasionally. Add in your barley and cook for two minutes more. Stir in your barley, cooking until it's toasted.
2. Pour in the wine, cooking for a minute more. Most of the liquid should have evaporated before adding in a cup of warm broth. Cook and stir for two minutes. Your liquid should be absorbed. Add in the remaining broth by the cup, and cook until ach cup is absorbed fore adding more. It should take about two minutes each time.
3. Pull out from the heat, and add in half a cup of cheese, and top with remaining cheese, chives and lemon wedges.

Nutrition 345 Calories 7g Fat 56g Carbohydrates 14g Protein

277. Seafood & Avocado Salad

Preparation Time: 10 minutes
Cooking Time: 0 minute
Servings: 4
Ingredients:
- 2 lbs. salmon, cooked & chopped
- 2 lbs. shrimp, cooked & chopped
- 1 cup avocado, chopped
- 1 cup mayonnaise
- 4 tablespoons lime juice, fresh
- 2 cloves garlic
- 1 cup sour cream
- sea salt & black pepper to taste
- ½ red onion, minced
- 1 cup cucumber, chopped

Directions:
1. Start by getting out a bowl and combine your garlic, salt, pepper, onion, mayonnaise, sour cream and lime juice,
2. Get out a different bowl and mix together your salmon, shrimp, cucumber, and avocado.
3. Add the mayonnaise mixture to your shrimp, and then allow it to sit for twenty minutes in the fridge before serving.

Nutrition 394 Calories 30g Fat 3g Carbohydrates 27g Protein

278. Mediterranean Shrimp Salad

Preparation Time: 40 minutes
Cooking Time: 0 minute
Servings: 6
Ingredients:

- 1 ½ lbs. shrimp, cleaned & cooked
- 2 celery stalks, fresh
- 1 onion
- 2 green onions
- 4 eggs, boiled
- 3 potatoes, cooked
- 3 tablespoons mayonnaise
- sea salt & black pepper to taste

Directions:

1. Start by slicing your potatoes and chopping your celery. Slice your eggs, and season. Mix everything together. Put your shrimp over the eggs, and then serve with onion and green onions.

Nutrition 207 Calories 6g Fat 15g Carbohydrates 17g Protein

279. Chickpea Pasta Salad

Preparation Time: 10 minutes
Cooking Time: 15 minutes
Servings: 6
Ingredients:

- 2 tablespoons olive oil
- 16 ounces rotelle pasta
- ½ cup cured olives, chopped
- 2 tablespoons oregano, fresh & minced
- 2 tablespoons parsley, fresh & chopped
- 1 bunch green onions, chopped
- ¼ cup red wine vinegar
- 15 ounces canned garbanzo beans, drained & rinsed
- ½ cup parmesan cheese, grated
- sea salt & black pepper to taste

Directions:

1. Boil water and put the pasta al dente and follow per package instructions. Drain it and rinse it using cold water.
2. Get out a skillet and heat up your olive oil over medium heat. Add in your scallions, chickpeas, parsley, oregano and olives. Decrease the heat, and sauté for twenty minutes more. Allow this mixture to cool.
3. Toss your chickpea mixture with your pasta, and then add in your grated cheese, salt, pepper and vinegar. Let it chill for four hours or overnight before serving.

Nutrition 424 Calories 10g Fat 69g Carbohydrates 16g Protein

280. Mediterranean Stir Fry

Preparation Time: 10 minutes

Cooking Time: 30 minutes
Servings: 4
Ingredients:

- 2 zucchinis
- 1 onion
- ¼ teaspoon sea salt
- 2 cloves garlic
- 3 teaspoons olive oil, divided
- 1 lb. chicken breasts, boneless
- 1 cup quick cooking barley
- 2 cups water
- ¼ teaspoon black pepper
- 1 teaspoon oregano
- ¼ teaspoon red pepper flakes
- ½ teaspoon basil
- 2 plum tomatoes
- ½ cup Greek olives, pitted
- 1 tablespoons parsley, fresh

Directions:

1. Start by removing the skin from your chicken, and then chop it into smaller pieces. Chop the garlic and parsley, and then chop your olives, zucchini, tomatoes and onions. Get out a saucepan and bring your water to a boil. Mix in your barley, letting it simmer for eight to ten minutes.
2. Turn off heat. Let it rest for five minutes. Get out a skillet and add in two teaspoons of olive oil. Stir fry your chicken once it's hot, and then remove it from heat. Cook the onion in your remaining oil. Mix in your remaining ingredients, and cook for an additional three to five minutes. Serve warm.

Nutrition 337 Calories 8.6g Fat 32.3g Carbohydrates 31.7g Protein

281. Balsamic Cucumber Salad

Preparation Time: 15 minutes
Cooking Time: 0 minute
Servings: 4
Ingredients

- 2/3 large English cucumber, halved and sliced
- 2/3 medium red onion, halved and thinly sliced
- 5 1/2 tablespoons balsamic vinaigrette
- 1 1/3 cups grape tomatoes, halved
- 1/2 cup crumbled reduced-fat feta cheese

Directions

1. In a big bowl, mix cucumber, tomatoes and onion. Add vinaigrette; toss to coating. Refrigerate, covered, till serving. Just prior to serving, stir in cheese. Serve with a slotted teaspoon.

Nutrition 250 calories 12g fats 15g carbohydrates 34g protein

282. Beef Kefta Patties with Cucumber Salad

Preparation Time: 10 minutes

Cooking Time: 15 minutes
Servings: 2
Ingredients

- cooking spray
- 1/2-pound ground sirloin
- 2 tablespoons plus 2 tablespoons chopped fresh flat-leaf parsley, divided
- 1 1/2 teaspoons chopped peeled fresh ginger
- 1 teaspoon ground coriander
- 2 tablespoons chopped fresh cilantro
- 1/4 teaspoon salt
- 1/2 teaspoon ground cumin
- 1/4 teaspoon ground cinnamon
- 1 cup thinly sliced English cucumbers
- 1 tablespoon rice vinegar
- 1/4 cup plain fat-free Greek yogurt
- 1 1/2 teaspoons fresh lemon juice
- 1/4 teaspoon freshly ground black pepper
- 1 (6-inch) pitas, quartered

Directions

1. Warmth a grill skillet over medium-high warmth. Coat pan with cooking spray. Combine beef, 1/4 glass parsley, cilantro, and next 5 elements in a medium bowl.
2. Divide combination into 4 the same portions, shaping each into a 1/2-inch-thick patty. Add patties to pan; cook both sides until desired degree of doneness.
3. Mix cucumber and vinegar in a medium bowl; throw well. Combine fat-free yogurt, remaining 2 tablespoons parsley, juice, and pepper in a little bowl; stir with a whisk. Set up 1 patty and 1/2 cup cucumber mixture on each of 4 china.
4. Top each offering with about 2 tablespoons yogurt spices. Serve each with 2 pita wedges.

Nutrition 116 calories 5g fats 11g carbohydrates 28g protein

283. <u>Chicken and Cucumber Salad with Parsley Pesto</u>

Preparation Time: 15 minutes
Cooking Time: 5 minutes
Servings: 8
Ingredients

- 2 2/3 cups packed fresh flat-leaf parsley leaves
- 1 1/3 cups fresh baby spinach
- 1 1/2 tablespoons toasted pine nuts
- 1 1/2 tablespoons grated Parmesan cheese
- 2 1/2 tablespoons fresh lemon juice
- 1 1/3 teaspoons kosher salt
- 1/3 teaspoon black pepper
- 1 1/3 medium garlic cloves, smashed
- 2/3 cup extra-virgin olive oil
- 5 1/3 cups shredded rotisserie chicken (from 1 chicken)
- 2 2/3 cups cooked shelled edamame

- 1 1/2 cans 1 (15-oz.) unsalted chickpeas, drained and rinsed
- 1 1/3 cups chopped English cucumbers
- 5 1/3 cups loosely packed arugula

Directions

1. Combine parsley, spinach, lemon juice, pine nuts, cheese, garlic, salt, and pepper in food processor; process about 1 minute. With processor running, add oil; process until smooth, about 1 minute.
2. Stir together chicken, edamame, chickpeas, and cucumber in a large bowl. Add pesto; toss to combine.
3. Place 2/3 cup arugula in each of 6 bowls; top each with 1 cup chicken salad mixture. Serve immediately.

Nutrition 116 calories 12g fats 3g carbohydrates 9g protein

284. <u>Easy Arugula Salad</u>

Preparation Time: 15 minutes
Cooking Time: 0 minute
Servings: 6
Ingredients

- 6 cups young arugula leaves, rinsed and dried
- 1 1/2 cups cherry tomatoes, halved
- 6 tablespoons pine nuts
- 3 tablespoons grapeseed oil or olive oil
- 1 1/2 tablespoons rice vinegar
- 3/8 teaspoon freshly ground black pepper to taste
- 6 tablespoons grated Parmesan cheese
- 3/4 teaspoon salt to taste
- 1 1/2 large avocados - peeled, pitted and sliced

Directions

1. In a sizable plastic dish with a cover, incorporate arugula, cherry tomatoes, pine nut products, oil, vinegar, and Parmesan cheese. Period with salt and pepper to flavor. Cover, and wring to mix.
2. Separate salad onto china, and top with slices of avocado.

Nutrition 120 calories 12g fats 14g carbohydrates 25g protein

285. <u>Feta Garbanzo Bean Salad</u>

Preparation Time: 10 minutes
Cooking Time: 0 minute
Servings: 6
Ingredients

- 1 1/2 cans (15 ounces) garbanzo beans
- 1 1/2 cans (2-1/4 ounces) sliced ripe olives, drained
- 1 1/2 medium tomatoes
- 6 tablespoons thinly sliced red onions
- 2 1/4 cups 1-1/2 coarsely chopped English cucumbers
- 6 tablespoons chopped fresh parsley
- 4 1/2 tablespoons olive oil
- 3/8 teaspoon salt

- 1 1/2 tablespoons lemon juice
- 3/16 teaspoon pepper
- 7 1/2 cups mixed salad greens
- 3/4 cup crumbled feta cheese

Directions

1. Transfer all ingredients in a big bowl; toss to combine. Add parmesan cheese.

Nutrition 140 calories 16g fats 10g carbohydrates 24g protein

286. Greek Brown and Wild Rice Bowls

Preparation Time: 15 minutes
Cooking Time: 5 minutes
Servings: 4

Ingredients

- 2 packages (8-1/2 ounces) ready-to-serve whole grain brown and wild rice medley
- 1 medium ripe avocado, peeled and sliced
- 1 1/2 cups cherry tomatoes, halved
- 1/2 cup Greek vinaigrette, divided
- 1/2 cup crumbled feta cheese
- 1/2 cup pitted Greek olives, sliced
- minced fresh parsley, optional

Directions

1. Inside a microwave-safe dish, mix the grain mix and 2 tablespoons vinaigrette. Cover and cook on high until warmed through, about 2 minutes. Divide between 2 bowls. Best with avocado, tomato vegetables, cheese, olives, leftover dressing and, if desired, parsley.

Nutrition 116 calories 10g fats 9g carbohydrates 26g protein

287. Greek Dinner Salad

Preparation Time: 10 minutes
Cooking Time: 0 minute
Servings: 4

Ingredients

- 2 1/2 tablespoons coarsely chopped fresh parsley
- 2 tablespoons coarsely chopped fresh dill
- 2 teaspoons fresh lemon juice
- 2/3 teaspoon dried oregano
- 2 teaspoons extra virgin olive oil
- 4 cups shredded Romaine lettuce
- 2/3 cup thinly sliced red onions
- 1/2 cup crumbled feta cheese
- 2 cups diced tomatoes
- 2 teaspoons capers
- 2/3 cucumber, peeled, quartered lengthwise, and thinly sliced
- 2/3 (19-ounce) can chickpeas, drained and rinsed
- 4 (6-inch) whole wheat pitas, each cut into 8 wedges

Directions

1. Combine the first 5 substances in a sizable dish; stir with a whisk. Add a member of the lettuce family and the next 6 ingredients (lettuce through chickpeas); throw well. Serve with pita wedges.

Nutrition 103 calories 12g fats 8g carbohydrates 36g protein

288. Halibut Salad

Preparation Time: 15 minutes
Cooking Time: 5 minutes
Servings: 2

Ingredients

- 1/2 teaspoon ground coriander
- 1/4 teaspoon salt
- 1/8 teaspoon freshly ground black pepper
- 2 1/2 teaspoons extra-virgin olive oils, divided
- 1/4 teaspoon ground cumin
- 1 garlic clove, minced
- 2 (6-ounce) halibut fillets
- 1 cup fennel bulb
- 2 tablespoons thinly vertically sliced red onions
- 1 tablespoon fresh lemon juice
- 1 1/2 teaspoons chopped flat-leaf parsley
- 1/2 teaspoon fresh thyme leaves

Directions

1. Combine the first 4 substances in a little dish. Combine 1/2 tsp spice mixture, 2 teaspoons oil, and garlic in a little bowl; rub garlic clove mixture evenly over fish. Heat 1 teaspoon oil in a sizable nonstick frying pan over medium-high high temperature. Add fish to pan; cook 5 minutes on each side or until the desired level of doneness.
2. Combine remaining 3/4 teaspoon spice mix, remaining 2 tsp oil, fennel light bulb, and remaining substances in a medium bowl, tossing well to coat. Provide salad with seafood.

Nutrition 110 calories 9g fats 11g carbohydrates 29g protein

289. Herbed Greek Chicken Salad

Preparation Time: 10 minutes
Cooking Time: 10 minutes
Servings: 2

Ingredients

- 1/2 teaspoon dried oregano
- 1/4 teaspoon garlic powder
- 3/8 teaspoon black pepper, divided
- cooking spray
- 1/2-pound skinless, boneless chicken breasts, cut into 1-inch cubes
- 1/4 teaspoon salt, divided
- 1/2 cup plain fat-free yogurt
- 1 teaspoon tahini (sesame-seed paste)
- 2 1/2 tsps. fresh lemon juice
- 1/2 teaspoon bottled minced garlic
- 4 cups chopped Romaine lettuce

- 1/2 cup peeled chopped English cucumbers
- 1/2 cup grape tomatoes, halved
- 3 pitted kalamata olives, halved
- 2 tablespoons (1 ounce) crumbled feta cheese

Directions

1. Combine oregano, garlic natural powder, 1/2 teaspoon pepper, and 1/4 tsp salt in a bowl. Heat a nonstick skillet over medium-high heat. Coating pan with cooking food spray. Add poultry and spice combination; sauté until poultry is done. Drizzle with 1 teaspoon juice; stir. Remove from pan.
2. Combine remaining 2 teaspoons juice, leftover 1/4 teaspoon sodium, remaining 1/4 tsp pepper, yogurt, tahini, and garlic in a little bowl; mix well. Combine member of the lettuce family, cucumber, tomatoes, and olives. Put 2 1/2 cups of lettuce mixture on each of 4 plates. Top each serving with 1/2 cup chicken combination and 1 teaspoon cheese. Drizzle each serving with 3 tablespoons yogurt combination

Nutrition 116 calories 11g fats 15g carbohydrates 28g protein

290. Greek Couscous Salad

Preparation Time: 10 minutes
Cooking Time: 15 minutes
Servings: 10
Ingredients:

- 1 can (14-1/2 ounces) reduced-sodium chicken broth
- 1 1/2 cups 1-3/4 uncooked whole wheat couscous (about 11 ounces)

Dressing:

- 6 1/2 tablespoons olive oil
- 1 1/4 teaspoons 1-1/2 grated lemon zest
- 3 1/2 tablespoons lemon juice
- 13/16 teaspoon adobo seasonings
- 3/16 teaspoon salt

Salad:

- 1 2/3 cups grape tomatoes, halved
- 5/6 English cucumber, halved lengthwise and sliced
- 3/4 cup coarsely chopped fresh parsley
- 1 can (6-1/2 ounces) sliced ripe olives, drained
- 6 1/2 tablespoons crumbled feta cheese
- 3 1/3 green onions, chopped

Directions

1. In a sizable saucepan, bring broth to a boil. Stir in couscous. Remove from heat; let stand, covered, until broth is absorbed, about 5 minutes. Transfer to a sizable dish; cool completely.
2. Beat together dressing substances. Add cucumber, tomato vegetables, parsley, olives and green onions to couscous; stir in dressing. Gently mix in cheese. Provide immediately or refrigerate and serve frosty.

Nutrition 114 calories 13g fats 18g carbohydrates 27g protein

291. Cucumber Sandwich Bites

Preparation Time: 5 minutes
Cooking Time: 0 minute
Servings: 12
Ingredients:
- 1 cucumber, sliced
- 8 slices whole wheat bread
- 2 tablespoons cream cheese, soft
- 1 tablespoon chives, chopped
- ¼ cup avocado, peeled, pitted and mashed
- 1 teaspoon mustard
- Salt and black pepper to the taste

Directions:
1. Spread the mashed avocado on each bread slice, also spread the rest of the ingredients except the cucumber slices.
2. Divide the cucumber slices on the bread slices, cut each slice in thirds, arrange on a platter and serve as an appetizer.

Nutrition 187 Calories 12.4g Fat 4.5g Carbohydrates 8.2g Protein

292. Yogurt Dip

Preparation Time: 10 minutes
Cooking Time: 0 minute
Servings: 6
Ingredients:
- 2 cups Greek yogurt
- 2 tablespoons pistachios, toasted and chopped
- A pinch of salt and white pepper
- 2 tablespoons mint, chopped
- 1 tablespoon kalamata olives, pitted and chopped
- ¼ cup zaatar spice
- ¼ cup pomegranate seeds
- 1/3 cup olive oil

Directions:
1. Mix the yogurt with the pistachios and the rest of the ingredients, whisk well, divide into small cups and serve with pita chips on the side.

Nutrition 294 Calories 18g Fat 2g Carbohydrates 10g Protein

293. Tomato Bruschetta

Preparation Time: 10 minutes
Cooking Time: 10 minutes
Servings: 6
Ingredients:
- 1 baguette, sliced
- 1/3 cup basil, chopped
- 6 tomatoes, cubed
- 2 garlic cloves, minced
- A pinch of salt and black pepper
- 1 teaspoon olive oil
- 1 tablespoon balsamic vinegar
- ½ teaspoon garlic powder
- Cooking spray

Directions:
1. Situate the baguette slices on a baking sheet lined with parchment paper, grease with cooking spray. Bake for 10 minutes at 400 degrees.
2. Combine the tomatoes with the basil and the remaining ingredients, toss well and leave aside for 10 minutes. Divide the tomato mix on each baguette slice, arrange them all on a platter and serve.

Nutrition 162 Calories 4g Fat 29g Carbohydrates 4g Protein

294. Olives and Cheese Stuffed Tomatoes

Preparation Time: 10 minutes
Cooking Time: 0 minute
Servings: 24
Ingredients:
- 24 cherry tomatoes, top cut off and insides scooped out
- 2 tablespoons olive oil
- ¼ teaspoon red pepper flakes
- ½ cup feta cheese, crumbled
- 2 tablespoons black olive paste
- ¼ cup mint, torn

Directions:
1. In a bowl, mix the olives paste with the rest of the ingredients except the cherry tomatoes and whisk well. Stuff the cherry tomatoes with this mix, arrange them all on a platter and serve as an appetizer.

Nutrition 136 Calories 8.6g Fat 5.6g Carbohydrates 5.1g Protein

295. Pepper Tapenade

Preparation Time: 10 minutes
Cooking Time: 0 minute
Servings: 4
Ingredients:
- 7 ounces roasted red peppers, chopped
- ½ cup parmesan, grated
- 1/3 cup parsley, chopped
- 14 ounces canned artichokes, drained and chopped
- 3 tablespoons olive oil

- ¼ cup capers, drained
- 1 and ½ tablespoons lemon juice
- 2 garlic cloves, minced

Directions:
1. In your blender, combine the red peppers with the parmesan and the rest of the ingredients and pulse well. Divide into cups and serve as a snack.

Nutrition 200 Calories 5.6g Fat 12.4g Carbohydrates 4.6g Protein

296. Coriander Falafel

Preparation Time: 10 minutes
Cooking Time: 10 minutes
Servings: 8
Ingredients:
- 1 cup canned garbanzo beans
- 1 bunch parsley leaves
- 1 yellow onion, chopped
- 5 garlic cloves, minced
- 1 teaspoon coriander, ground
- A pinch of salt and black pepper
- ¼ teaspoon cayenne pepper
- ¼ teaspoon baking soda
- ¼ teaspoon cumin powder
- 1 teaspoon lemon juice
- 3 tablespoons tapioca flour
- Olive oil for frying

Directions:
1. In your food processor, combine the beans with the parsley, onion and the rest the ingredients except the oil and the flour and pulse well. Transfer the mix to a bowl, add the flour, stir well, shape 16 balls out of this mix and flatten them a bit.
2. Preheat pan over medium-high heat, add the falafels, cook them for 5 minutes on both sides, put in paper towels, drain excess grease, arrange them on a platter and serve as an appetizer.

Nutrition 122 Calories 6.2g Fat 12.3g Carbohydrates 3.1g Protein

297. Chickpeas and Red Pepper Hummus

Preparation Time: 10 minutes
Cooking Time: 0 minute
Servings: 6
Ingredients:
- 6 ounces roasted red peppers, peeled and chopped
- 16 ounces canned chickpeas, drained and rinsed
- ¼ cup Greek yogurt
- 3 tablespoons tahini paste
- Juice of 1 lemon
- 3 garlic cloves, minced
- 1 tablespoon olive oil
- A pinch of salt and black pepper

- 1 tablespoon parsley, chopped

Directions:
1. In your food processor, combine the red peppers with the rest of the ingredients except the oil and the parsley and pulse well. Add the oil, pulse again, divide into cups, sprinkle the parsley on top and serve as a party spread.

Nutrition 255 Calories 11.4g Fat 17.4g Carbohydrates 6.5g Protein

298. White Bean Dip

Preparation Time: 10 minutes
Cooking Time: 0 minute
Servings: 4
Ingredients:
- 15 ounces canned white beans, drained and rinsed
- 6 ounces canned artichoke hearts, drained and quartered
- 4 garlic cloves, minced
- 1 tablespoon basil, chopped
- 2 tablespoons olive oil
- Juice of ½ lemon
- Zest of ½ lemon, grated
- Salt and black pepper to the taste

Directions:
1. In your food processor, combine the beans with the artichokes and the rest of the ingredients except the oil and pulse well. Add the oil gradually, pulse the mix again, divide into cups and serve as a party dip.

Nutrition 27 Calories 11.7g Fat 18.5g Carbohydrates 16.5g Protein

299. Hummus with Ground Lamb

Preparation Time: 10 minutes
Cooking Time: 15 minutes
Servings: 8
Ingredients:
- 10 ounces hummus
- 12 ounces lamb meat, ground
- ½ cup pomegranate seeds
- ¼ cup parsley, chopped
- 1 tablespoon olive oil
- Pita chips for serving

Directions:
1. Preheat pan over medium-high heat, cook the meat, and brown for 15 minutes stirring often. Spread the hummus on a platter, spread the ground lamb all over, also spread the pomegranate seeds and the parsley and serve with pita chips as a snack.

Nutrition 133 Calories 9.7g Fat 6.4g Carbohydrates 5.4g Protein

300. Eggplant Dip

Preparation Time: 10 minutes

Cooking Time: 40 minutes
Servings: 4
Ingredients:
- 1 eggplant, poked with a fork
- 2 tablespoons tahini paste
- 2 tablespoons lemon juice
- 2 garlic cloves, minced
- 1 tablespoon olive oil
- Salt and black pepper to the taste
- 1 tablespoon parsley, chopped

Directions:
1. Put the eggplant in a roasting pan, bake at 400 degrees F for 40 minutes, cool down, peel and transfer to your food processor. Blend the rest of the ingredients except the parsley, pulse well, divide into small bowls and serve as an appetizer with the parsley sprinkled on top.

Nutrition 121 Calories 4.3g Fat 1.4g Carbohydrates 4.3g Protein

301. Veggie Fritters

Preparation Time: 10 minutes
Cooking Time: 10 minutes
Servings: 8
Ingredients:
- 2 garlic cloves, minced
- 2 yellow onions, chopped
- 4 scallions, chopped
- 2 carrots, grated
- 2 teaspoons cumin, ground
- ½ teaspoon turmeric powder
- Salt and black pepper to the taste
- ¼ teaspoon coriander, ground
- 2 tablespoons parsley, chopped
- ¼ teaspoon lemon juice
- ½ cup almond flour
- 2 beets, peeled and grated
- 2 eggs, whisked
- ¼ cup tapioca flour
- 3 tablespoons olive oil

Directions:
1. In a bowl, combine the garlic with the onions, scallions and the rest of the ingredients except the oil, stir well and shape medium fritters out of this mix.
2. Preheat pan over medium-high heat, place the fritters, cook for 5 minutes on each side, arrange on a platter and serve.

Nutrition 209 Calories 11.2g Fat 4.4g Carbohydrates 4.8g Protein

302. Bulgur Lamb Meatballs

Preparation Time: 10 minutes
Cooking Time: 15 minutes
Servings: 6

Ingredients:
- 1 and ½ cups Greek yogurt
- ½ teaspoon cumin, ground
- 1 cup cucumber, shredded
- ½ teaspoon garlic, minced
- A pinch of salt and black pepper
- 1 cup bulgur
- 2 cups water
- 1-pound lamb, ground
- ¼ cup parsley, chopped
- ¼ cup shallots, chopped
- ½ teaspoon allspice, ground
- ½ teaspoon cinnamon powder
- 1 tablespoon olive oil

Directions:
1. Mix the bulgur with the water, cover the bowl, leave aside for 10 minutes, drain and transfer to a bowl. Add the meat, the yogurt and the rest of the ingredients except the oil, stir well and shape medium meatballs out of this mix. Preheat pan over medium-high heat, place the meatballs, cook them for 7 minutes on each side, arrange them all on a platter and serve as an appetizer.

Nutrition 300 Calories 9.6g Fat 22.6g Carbohydrates 6.6g Protein

303. Cucumber Bites

Preparation Time: 10 minutes
Cooking Time: 0 minute
Servings: 12
Ingredients:
- 1 English cucumber, sliced into 32 rounds
- 10 ounces hummus
- 16 cherry tomatoes, halved
- 1 tablespoon parsley, chopped
- 1-ounce feta cheese, crumbled

Directions:
1. Spread the hummus on each cucumber round, divide the tomato halves on each, sprinkle the cheese and parsley on to and serve as an appetizer.

Nutrition 162 Calories 3.4g Fat 6.4g Carbohydrates 2.4g Protein

304. Stuffed Avocado

Preparation Time: 10 minutes
Cooking Time: 0 minute
Servings: 2
Ingredients:
- 1 avocado, halved and pitted
- 10 ounces canned tuna, drained
- 2 tablespoons sun-dried tomatoes, chopped
- 1 and ½ tablespoon basil pesto
- 2 tablespoons black olives, pitted and chopped
- Salt and black pepper to the taste

- 2 teaspoons pine nuts, toasted and chopped
- 1 tablespoon basil, chopped

Directions:
1. Mix the tuna with the sun-dried tomatoes and the rest of the ingredients except the avocado and stir. Stuff the avocado halves with the tuna mix and serve as an appetizer.

Nutrition 233 Calories 9g Fat 11.4g Carbohydrates 5.6g Protein

305. Wrapped Plums

Preparation Time: 5 minutes
Cooking Time: 0 minute
Servings: 8

Ingredients:
- 2 ounces prosciutto, cut into 16 pieces
- 4 plums, quartered
- 1 tablespoon chives, chopped
- A pinch of red pepper flakes, crushed

Directions:
1. Wrap each plum quarter in a prosciutto slice, arrange them all on a platter, sprinkle the chives and pepper flakes all over and serve.

Nutrition 30 Calories 1g Fat4g Carbohydrates 2g Protein

306. Herb-Marinated Feta and Artichokes

Preparation Time: 10 minutes, plus 4 hours inactive time
Cooking Time: 10 minutes
Servings: 2

Ingredients:
- 4 ounces traditional Greek feta, cut into ½-inch cubes
- 4 ounces drained artichoke hearts, quartered lengthwise
- 1/3 cup extra-virgin olive oil
- Zest and juice of 1 lemon
- 2 tablespoons roughly chopped fresh rosemary
- 2 tablespoons roughly chopped fresh parsley
- ½ teaspoon black peppercorns

Directions:
1. In a glass bowl combine the feta and artichoke hearts. Add the olive oil, lemon zest and juice, rosemary, parsley, and peppercorns and toss gently to coat, being sure not to crumble the feta.
2. Cool for 4 hours, or up to 4 days. Take out of the refrigerator 30 minutes before serving.

Nutrition 235 Calories 23g Fat 1g Carbohydrates 4g Protein

307. Yellowfin Croquettes

Preparation Time: 40 minutes, plus hours to overnight to chill
Cooking Time: 25 minutes
Servings: 36

Ingredients:
- 6 tablespoons extra-virgin olive oil, plus 1 to 2 cups
- 5 tablespoons almond flour, plus 1 cup, divided
- 1¼ cups heavy cream
- 1 (4-ounce) can olive oil-packed yellowfin tuna
- 1 tablespoon chopped red onion
- 2 teaspoons minced capers
- ½ teaspoon dried dill
- ¼ teaspoon freshly ground black pepper
- 2 large eggs
- 1 cup panko breadcrumbs (or a gluten-free version)

Directions:
1. In a large skillet, warm up6 tablespoons olive oil over medium-low heat. Add 5 tablespoons almond flour and cook, stirring constantly, until a smooth paste forms and the flour browns slightly, 2 to 3 minutes.
2. Select the heat to medium-high and gradually mix in the heavy cream, whisking constantly until completely smooth and thickened, another 4 to 5 minutes. Remove and add in the tuna, red onion, capers, dill, and pepper.
3. Transfer the mixture to an 8-inch square baking dish that is well coated with olive oil and set aside at room temperature. Wrap and cool for 4 hours or up to overnight. To form the croquettes, set out three bowls. In one, beat together the eggs. In another, add the remaining almond flour. In the third, add the panko. Line a baking sheet with parchment paper.
4. Scoop about a tablespoon of cold prepared dough into the flour mixture and roll to coat. Shake off excess and, using your hands, roll into an oval.
5. Dip the croquette into the beaten egg, then lightly coat in panko. Set on lined baking sheet and repeat with the remaining dough.
6. In a small saucepan, warm up the remaining 1 to 2 cups of olive oil, over medium-high heat.
7. Once the oil is heated, fry the croquettes 3 or 4 at a time, depending on the size of your pan, removing with a slotted spoon when golden brown. You will need to adjust the temperature of the oil occasionally to prevent burning. If the croquettes get dark brown very quickly, lower the temperature.

Nutrition 245 Calories 22g Fat 1g Carbohydrates 6g Protein

308. Spiced Salmon Crudités

Preparation Time: 10 minutes
Cooking Time: 15 minutes
Servings: 4

Ingredients:
- 6 ounces smoked wild salmon
- 2 tablespoons Roasted Garlic Aioli
- 1 tablespoon Dijon mustard
- 1 tablespoon chopped scallions, green parts only
- 2 teaspoons chopped capers
- ½ teaspoon dried dill

- 4 endive spears or hearts of romaine
- ½ English cucumber, cut into ¼-inch-thick rounds

Directions:

1. Roughly cut the smoked salmon and transfer in a small bowl. Add the aioli, Dijon, scallions, capers, and dill and mix well. Top endive spears and cucumber rounds with a spoonful of smoked salmon mixture and enjoy chilled.

Nutrition 92 Calories 5g Fat 1g Carbohydrates 9g Protein

309. All-Spiced Olives

Preparation Time: 4 hours and 10 minutes
Cooking Time: 0 minute
Servings: 2
Ingredients:

- 2 cups mixed green olives with pits
- ¼ cup red wine vinegar
- ¼ cup extra-virgin olive oil
- 4 garlic cloves, finely minced
- Zest and juice of 1 large orange
- 1 teaspoon red pepper flakes
- 2 bay leaves
- ½ teaspoon ground cumin
- ½ teaspoon ground allspice

Directions:

1. Incorporate the olives, vinegar, oil, garlic, orange zest and juice, red pepper flakes, bay leaves, cumin, and allspice and mix well. Seal and chill for 4 hours or up to a week to allow the olives to marinate, tossing again before serving.

Nutrition 133 Calories 14g Fat 2g Carbohydrates 1g Protein

310. Pitted Olives and Anchovies

Preparation Time: 1 hour and 10 minutes
Cooking Time: 0 minute
Servings: 2
Ingredients:

- 2 cups pitted Kalamata olives or other black olives
- 2 anchovy fillets, chopped
- 2 teaspoons chopped capers
- 1 garlic clove, finely minced
- 1 cooked egg yolk
- 1 teaspoon Dijon mustard
- ¼ cup extra-virgin olive oil
- Seedy Crackers, Versatile Sandwich Round, or vegetables, for serving (optional)

Directions:

1. Wash the olives in cold water and strain well. In a food processor, blender, or a large jar (if using an immersion blender) place the drained olives, anchovies, capers, garlic, egg yolk, and Dijon. Process until it forms a thick paste. While running, gradually stream in the olive oil.
2. Handover to a small bowl, cover, and refrigerate at least 1 hour to let the flavors develop. Serve with

Seedy Crackers, atop a Versatile Sandwich Round, or with your favorite crunchy vegetables.

Nutrition 179 Calories 19g Fat 2g Carbohydrates 2g Protein

311. Medi Deviled Eggs

Preparation Time: 45 minutes
Cooking Time: 15 minutes
Servings: 4
Ingredients:

- 4 large hardboiled eggs
- 2 tablespoons Roasted Garlic Aioli
- ½ cup finely crumbled feta cheese
- 8 pitted Kalamata olives, finely chopped
- 2 tablespoons chopped sun-dried tomatoes
- 1 tablespoon minced red onion
- ½ teaspoon dried dill
- ¼ teaspoon freshly ground black pepper

Directions:

1. Chop the hardboiled eggs in half lengthwise, remove the yolks, and place the yolks in a medium bowl. Reserve the egg white halves and set aside. Smash the yolks well with a fork. Add the aioli, feta, olives, sun-dried tomatoes, onion, dill, and pepper and stir to combine until smooth and creamy.
2. Spoon the filling into each egg white half and chill for 30 minutes, or up to 24 hours, covered.

Nutrition 147 Calories 11g Fat 6g Carbohydrates 9g Protein

312. Cheese Crackers

Preparation Time: 1 hour and 15 minutes
Cooking Time: 15 minutes
Servings: 20
Ingredients:

- 4 tablespoons butter, at room temperature
- 1 cup finely shredded Manchego cheese
- 1 cup almond flour
- 1 teaspoon salt, divided
- ¼ teaspoon freshly ground black pepper
- 1 large egg

Directions:

1. Using an electric mixer, scourge together the butter and shredded cheese until well combined and smooth. Incorporate the almond flour with ½ teaspoon salt and pepper. Gradually put the almond flour mixture to the cheese, mixing constantly until the dough just comes together to form a ball.
2. Situate a piece of parchment or plastic wrap and roll into a cylinder log about 1½ inches thick. Seal tightly then freeze for at least 1 hour. Preheat the oven to 350°F. Put parchment paper or silicone baking mats into 2 baking sheets.
3. To make the egg wash, scourge together the egg and remaining ½ teaspoon salt. Slice the refrigerated dough into small rounds, about ¼ inch thick, and place on the lined baking sheets.

4. Egg wash the tops of the crackers and bake until the crackers are golden and crispy. Situate on a wire rack to cool.
5. Serve warm or, once fully cooled, store in an airtight container in the refrigerator for up to 1 week.

Nutrition 243 Calories 23g Fat 1g Carbohydrates 8g Protein

313. Cheesy Caprese Stack

Preparation Time: 5 minutes
Cooking Time: 0 minute
Servings: 4
Ingredients:
- 1 large organic tomato, preferably heirloom
- ½ teaspoon salt
- ¼ teaspoon freshly ground black pepper
- 1 (4-ounce) ball burrata cheese
- 8 fresh basil leaves, thinly sliced
- 2 tablespoons extra-virgin olive oil
- 1 tablespoon red wine or balsamic vinegar

Directions:
1. Slice the tomato into 4 thick slices, removing any tough center core and sprinkle with salt and pepper. Place the tomatoes, seasoned-side up, on a plate. On a separate rimmed plate, slice the burrata into 4 thick slices and place one slice on top of each tomato slice. Top each with one-quarter of the basil and pour any reserved burrata cream from the rimmed plate over top.
2. Dash with olive oil and vinegar and serve with a fork and knife.

Nutrition 153 Calories 13g Fat 1g Carbohydrates 7g Protein

314. Zucchini-Cheese Fritters with Aioli

Preparation Time: 10 minutes, plus 20 minutes rest time
Cooking Time: 25 minutes
Servings: 4
Ingredients:
- 1 large or 2 small/medium zucchini
- 1 teaspoon salt, divided
- ½ cup whole-milk ricotta cheese
- 2 scallions
- 1 large egg
- 2 garlic cloves, finely minced
- 2 tablespoons chopped fresh mint (optional)
- 2 teaspoons grated lemon zest
- ¼ teaspoon freshly ground black pepper
- ½ cup almond flour
- 1 teaspoon baking powder
- 8 tablespoons extra-virgin olive oil
- 8 tablespoons Roasted Garlic Aioli or avocado oil mayonnaise

Directions:
1. Situate the shredded zucchini in a colander or on several layers of paper towels. Sprinkle with ½ teaspoon salt and let sit for 10 minutes.
2. Using another layer of paper towel press down on the zucchini to release any excess moisture and pat dry. Incorporate the drained zucchini, ricotta, scallions, egg, garlic, mint (if using), lemon zest, remaining ½ teaspoon salt, and pepper.
3. Scourge together the almond flour and baking powder. Fold in the flour mixture into the zucchini mixture and let rest for 10 minutes. In a large skillet, working in four batches, fry the fritters.
4. For each batch of four, heat 2 tablespoons olive oil over medium-high heat. Add 1 heaping tablespoon of zucchini batter per fritter, pressing down with the back of a spoon to form 2- to 3-inch fritters. Cover and let fry 2 minutes before flipping. Fry another 2 to 3 minutes, covered, or until crispy and golden and cooked through. You may need to reduce heat to medium to prevent burning. Remove from the pan and keep warm.
5. Repeat for the remaining three batches, using 2 tablespoons of the olive oil for each batch. Serve fritters warm with aioli.

Nutrition 448 Calories 42g Fat 2g Carbohydrates 8g Protein

315. Cucumbers Filled with Salmon

Preparation Time: 10 minutes
Cooking Time: 0 minute
Servings: 4
Ingredients:
- 2 large cucumbers, peeled
- 1 (4-ounce) can red salmon
- 1 medium very ripe avocado
- 1 tablespoon extra-virgin olive oil
- Zest and juice of 1 lime
- 3 tablespoons chopped fresh cilantro
- ½ teaspoon salt
- ¼ teaspoon freshly ground black pepper

Directions:
1. Slice the cucumber into 1-inch-thick segments and using a spoon, scrape seeds out of center of each segment and stand up on a plate. In a medium bowl, mix the salmon, avocado, olive oil, lime zest and juice, cilantro, salt, and pepper and mix until creamy.
2. Scoop the salmon mixture into the center of each cucumber segment and serve chilled.

Nutrition 159 Calories 11g Fat 3g Carbohydrates 9g Protein

316. Smoked Mackerel Pâté

Preparation Time: 10 minutes
Cooking Time: 0 minute
Servings: 4
Ingredients:

- 4 ounces olive oil-packed wild-caught mackerel
- 2 ounces goat cheese
- Zest and juice of 1 lemon
- 2 tablespoons chopped fresh parsley
- 2 tablespoons chopped fresh arugula
- 1 tablespoon extra-virgin olive oil
- 2 teaspoons chopped capers
- 1 to 2 teaspoons fresh horseradish (optional)
- Crackers, cucumber rounds, endive spears, or celery, for serving (optional)

Directions:
1. In a food processor, blender, or large bowl with immersion blender, combine the mackerel, goat cheese, lemon zest and juice, parsley, arugula, olive oil, capers, and horseradish (if using). Process or blend until smooth and creamy.
2. Serve with crackers, cucumber rounds, endive spears, or celery. Seal covered in the refrigerator for up to 1 week.

Nutrition 118 Calories 8g Fat 6g Carbohydrates 9g Protein

317. Medi Fat Bombs

Preparation Time: 4 hours and 15 minutes
Cooking Time: 0 minute
Servings: 6
Ingredients:
- 1 cup crumbled goat cheese
- 4 tablespoons jarred pesto
- 12 pitted Kalamata olives, finely chopped
- ½ cup finely chopped walnuts
- 1 tablespoon chopped fresh rosemary

Directions:
1. In a medium bowl, scourge the goat cheese, pesto, and olives and mix well using a fork. Freeze for 4 hours to toughen.
2. With your hands, create the mixture into 6 balls, about ¾-inch diameter. The mixture will be sticky.
3. In a small bowl, place the walnuts and rosemary and roll the goat cheese balls in the nut mixture to coat. Store the fat bombs in the refrigerator for up to 1 week or in the freezer for up to 1 month.

Nutrition 166 Calories 15g Fat 1g Carbohydrates 5g Protein

318. Avocado Cold Soup

Preparation Time: 15 minutes
Cooking Time: 10 minutes
Servings: 4
Ingredients:
- 2 cups chopped tomatoes
- 2 large ripe avocados, halved and pitted
- 1 large cucumber, peeled and seeded
- 1 medium bell pepper (red, orange or yellow), chopped
- 1 cup plain whole-milk Greek yogurt
- ¼ cup extra-virgin olive oil

- ¼ cup chopped fresh cilantro
- ¼ cup chopped scallions, green part only
- 2 tablespoons red wine vinegar
- Juice of 2 limes or 1 lemon
- ½ to 1 teaspoon salt
- ¼ teaspoon freshly ground black pepper

Directions:
1. Using an immersion blender, combine the tomatoes, avocados, cucumber, bell pepper, yogurt, olive oil, cilantro, scallions, vinegar, and lime juice. Blend until smooth.
2. Season and blend to combine the flavors. Serve cold.

Nutrition 392 Calories 32g Fat 9g Carbohydrates 6g Protein

319. Crab Cake Lettuce Cups

Preparation Time: 35 minutes
Cooking Time: 20 minutes
Servings: 4
Ingredients:
- 1-pound jumbo lump crab
- 1 large egg
- 6 tablespoons Roasted Garlic Aioli
- 2 tablespoons Dijon mustard
- ½ cup almond flour
- ¼ cup minced red onion
- 2 teaspoons smoked paprika
- 1 teaspoon celery salt
- 1 teaspoon garlic powder
- 1 teaspoon dried dill (optional)
- ½ teaspoon freshly ground black pepper
- ¼ cup extra-virgin olive oil
- 4 large Bibb lettuce leaves, thick spine removed

Directions:
1. Situate the crabmeat in a large bowl and pick out any visible shells, then break apart the meat with a fork. In a small bowl, scourge together the egg, 2 tablespoons aioli, and Dijon mustard. Add to the crabmeat and blend with a fork. Add the almond flour, red onion, paprika, celery salt, garlic powder, dill (if using), and pepper and combine well. Allow rest at room temperature for 10 to 15 minutes.
2. Form into 8 small cakes, about 2 inches in diameter. Cook the olive oil over medium-high heat. Fry the cakes until browned, 2 to 3 minutes per side. Wrap, decrease the heat to low, and cook for another 6 to 8 minutes, or until set in the center. Remove from the skillet.
3. To serve, wrap 2 small crab cakes in each lettuce leaf and top with 1 tablespoon aioli.

Nutrition 344 Calories 24g Fat 2g Carbohydrates 24g Protein

320. Orange-Tarragon Chicken Salad Wrap

Preparation Time: 15 minutes
Cooking Time: 0 minute
Servings: 4
Ingredients:

- ½ cup plain whole-milk Greek yogurt
- 2 tablespoons Dijon mustard
- 2 tablespoons extra-virgin olive oil
- 2 tablespoons fresh tarragon
- ½ teaspoon salt
- ¼ teaspoon freshly ground black pepper
- 2 cups cooked shredded chicken
- ½ cup slivered almonds
- 4 to 8 large Bibb lettuce leaves, tough stem removed
- 2 small ripe avocados, peeled and thinly sliced
- Zest of 1 clementine, or ½ small orange (about 1 tablespoon)

Directions:

1. In a medium bowl, mix the yogurt, mustard, olive oil, tarragon, orange zest, salt, and pepper and whisk until creamy. Add the shredded chicken and almonds and stir to coat.
2. To assemble the wraps, place about ½ cup chicken salad mixture in the center of each lettuce leaf and top with sliced avocados.

Nutrition 440 Calories 32g 1 Fat 8g Carbohydrates 26g Protein

321. Feta and Quinoa Stuffed Mushrooms

Preparation Time: 5 minutes
Cooking Time: 8 minutes
Servings: 6
Ingredients:

- 2 tablespoons finely diced red bell pepper
- 1 garlic clove, minced
- ¼ cup cooked quinoa
- 1/8 teaspoon salt
- ¼ teaspoon dried oregano
- 24 button mushrooms, stemmed
- 2 ounces crumbled feta
- 3 tablespoons whole wheat bread crumbs
- Olive oil cooking spray

Directions:

1. Preheat the air fryer to 360°F. In a small bowl, mix the bell pepper, garlic, quinoa, salt, and oregano. Spoon the quinoa stuffing into the mushroom caps until just filled. Add a small piece of feta to the top of each mushroom. Sprinkle a pinch bread crumbs over the feta on each mushroom.
2. Put the basket of the air fryer with olive oil cooking spray, then gently place the mushrooms into the basket, making sure that they don't touch each other.
3. Lay the basket into the air fryer and bake for 8 minutes. Remove from the air fryer and serve.

Nutrition 97 Calories 4g Fat 11g Carbohydrates 7g Protein

322. Five-Ingredient Falafel with Garlic-Yogurt Sauce

Preparation Time: 5 minutes
Cooking Time: 15 minutes
Servings: 4
Ingredients:
For the falafel

- 1 (15-ounce) can chickpeas, drained and rinsed
- ½ cup fresh parsley
- 2 garlic cloves, minced
- ½ tablespoon ground cumin
- 1 tablespoon whole wheat flour
- Salt

For the garlic-yogurt sauce

- 1 cup nonfat plain Greek yogurt
- 1 garlic clove, minced
- 1 tablespoon chopped fresh dill
- 2 tablespoons lemon juice

Directions:
To make the falafel

1. Preheat the air fryer to 360°F. Put the chickpeas into a food processor. Pulse until mostly chopped, then add the parsley, garlic, and cumin and pulse for another minutes, until the ingredients turn into a dough.
2. Add the flour. Pulse a few more times until combined. The dough will have texture, but the chickpeas should be pulsed into small bits. Using clean hands, roll the dough into 8 balls of equal size, then pat the balls down a bit so they are about ½-thick disks.
3. Put the basket of the air fryer with olive oil cooking spray, then place the falafel patties in the basket in a single layer, making sure they don't touch each other. Fry in the air fryer for 15 minutes.

To make the garlic-yogurt sauce

4. Mix the yogurt, garlic, dill, and lemon juice. Once the falafel is done cooking and nicely browned on all sides, remove them from the air fryer and season with salt. Serve hot side it dipping sauce.

Nutrition 151 Calories 2g Fat 10g Carbohydrates 12g Protein

323. Lemon Shrimp with Garlic Olive Oil

Preparation Time: 5 minutes
Cooking Time: 6 minutes
Servings: 4
Ingredients:

- 1-pound medium shrimp, cleaned and deveined
- ¼ cup plus 2 tablespoons olive oil, divided
- Juice of ½ lemon
- 3 garlic cloves, minced and divided
- ½ teaspoon salt
- ¼ teaspoon red pepper flakes
- Lemon wedges, for serving (optional)
- Marinara sauce, for dipping (optional)

Directions:
1. Preheat the air fryer to 380°F. Toss in the shrimp with 2 tablespoons of the olive oil, lemon juice, 1/3 of minced garlic, salt, and red pepper flakes and coat well.
2. In a small ramekin, combine the remaining ¼ cup of olive oil and the remaining minced garlic. Tear off a 12-by-12-inch sheet of aluminum foil. Place the shrimp into the center of the foil, then fold the sides up and crimp the edges so that it forms an aluminum foil bowl that is open on top. Place this packet into the air fryer basket.
3. Roast the shrimp for 4 minutes, then open the air fryer and place the ramekin with oil and garlic in the basket beside the shrimp packet. Cook for 2 more minutes. Transfer the shrimp on a serving plate or platter with the ramekin of garlic olive oil on the side for dipping. You may also serve with lemon wedges and marinara sauce, if desired.

Nutrition 264 Calories 21g Fat 10g Carbohydrates 16g Protein

324. Crispy Green Bean Fries with Lemon-Yogurt Sauce

Preparation Time: 5 minutes
Cooking Time: 5 minutes
Servings: 4
Ingredients:
For the green beans
- 1 egg
- 2 tablespoons water
- 1 tablespoon whole wheat flour
- ¼ teaspoon paprika
- ½ teaspoon garlic powder
- ½ teaspoon salt
- ¼ cup whole wheat bread crumbs
- ½ pound whole green beans

For the lemon-yogurt sauce
- ½ cup nonfat plain Greek yogurt
- 1 tablespoon lemon juice
- ¼ teaspoon salt
- 1/8 teaspoon cayenne pepper

Direction:
1. To make the green beans
2. Preheat the air fryer to 380°F.
3. In a medium shallow bowl, combine together the egg and water until frothy. In a separate medium shallow bowl, whisk together the flour, paprika,

garlic powder, and salt, then mix in the bread crumbs.
4. Spread the bottom of the air fryer with cooking spray. Dip each green bean into the egg mixture, then into the bread crumb mixture, coating the outside with the crumbs. Situate the green beans in a single layer in the bottom of the air fryer basket.
5. Fry in the air fryer for 5 minutes, or until the breading is golden brown.
6. To make the lemon-yogurt sauce
7. Incorporate the yogurt, lemon juice, salt, and cayenne. Serve the green bean fries alongside the lemon-yogurt sauce as a snack or appetizer.

Nutrition 88 Calories 2g Fat 10g Carbohydrates 7g Protein

325. Homemade Sea Salt Pita Chips

Preparation Time: 2 minutes
Cooking Time: 8 minutes
Servings: 2
Ingredients:
- 2 whole wheat pitas
- 1 tablespoon olive oil
- ½ teaspoon kosher salt

Directions
1. Preheat the air fryer to 360°F. Cut each pita into 8 wedges. In a medium bowl, mix the pita wedges, olive oil, and salt until the wedges are coated and the olive oil and salt are evenly distributed.
2. Place the pita wedges into the air fryer basket in an even layer and fry for 6 to 8 minutes.
3. Season with additional salt, if desired. Serve alone or with a favorite dip.

Nutrition 230 Calories 8g Fat 11g Carbohydrates 6g Protein

326. Baked Spanakopita Dip

Preparation Time: 10 minutes
Cooking Time: 15 minutes
Servings: 2
Ingredients:
- Olive oil cooking spray
- 3 tablespoons olive oil, divided
- 2 tablespoons minced white onion
- 2 garlic cloves, minced
- 4 cups fresh spinach
- 4 ounces cream cheese, softened
- 4 ounces feta cheese, divided
- Zest of 1 lemon
- ¼ teaspoon ground nutmeg
- 1 teaspoon dried dill
- ½ teaspoon salt
- Pita chips, carrot sticks, or sliced bread for serving (optional)

Directions:

1. Preheat the air fryer to 360°F. Coat the inside of a 6-inch ramekin or baking dish with olive oil cooking spray.
2. Using skillet over medium heat, cook 1 tablespoon of the olive oil. Add the onion, then cook for 1 minute. Add in the garlic and cook, stirring for 1 minute more.
3. Lower heat and combine the spinach and water. Cook until the spinach has wilted. Remove the skillet from the heat. In a medium bowl, scourge the cream cheese, 2 ounces of the feta, and the rest of olive oil, lemon zest, nutmeg, dill, and salt. Mix until just combined.
4. Add the vegetables to the cheese base and stir until combined. Pour the dip mixture into the prepared ramekin and top with the remaining 2 ounces of feta cheese.
5. Place the dip into the air fryer basket and cook for 10 minutes, or until heated through and bubbling. Serve with pita chips, carrot sticks, or sliced bread.

Nutrition 550 Calories 52g Fat 21g Carbohydrates

327. Roasted Pearl Onion Dip

Preparation Time: 5 minutes
Cooking Time: 12 minutes plus 1 hour to chill
Servings: 4
Ingredients:
- 2 cups peeled pearl onions
- 3 garlic cloves
- 3 tablespoons olive oil, divided
- ½ teaspoon salt
- 1 cup nonfat plain Greek yogurt
- 1 tablespoon lemon juice
- ¼ teaspoon black pepper
- 1/8 teaspoon red pepper flakes
- Pita chips, vegetables, or toasted bread for serving (optional)

Directions:
1. Preheat the air fryer to 360°F. In a large bowl, combine the pearl onions and garlic with 2 tablespoons of the olive oil until the onions are well coated.
2. Pour the garlic-and-onion mixture into the air fryer basket and roast for 12 minutes. Place the garlic and onions to a food processor. Pulse the vegetables several times, until the onions are minced but still have some chunks.
3. Toss in the garlic and onions and the remaining 1 tablespoon of olive oil, along with the salt, yogurt, lemon juice, black pepper, and red pepper flakes. Chill for 1 hour before serving with pita chips, vegetables, or toasted bread.

Nutrition 150 Calories 10g Fat 6g Carbohydrates 7g Protein

328. Red Pepper Tapenade

Preparation Time: 5 minutes

Cooking Time: 5 minutes
Servings: 4
Ingredients:
- 1 large red bell pepper
- 2 tablespoons plus 1 teaspoon olive oil
- ½ cup Kalamata olives, pitted and roughly chopped
- 1 garlic clove, minced
- ½ teaspoon dried oregano
- 1 tablespoon lemon juice

Directions:
1. Preheat the air fryer to 380°F. Brush the outside of a whole red pepper with 1 teaspoon olive oil and place it inside the air fryer basket. Roast for 5 minutes. For the meantime, in a medium bowl incorporate the remaining 2 tablespoons of olive oil with the olives, garlic, oregano, and lemon juice.
2. Remove the red pepper from the air fryer, then gently slice off the stem and remove the seeds. Roughly chop the roasted pepper into small pieces.
3. Add the red pepper to the olive mixture and stir all together until combined. Serve with pita chips, crackers, or crusty bread.

Nutrition 104 Calories 10g Fat 9g Carbohydrates 1g Protein

329. Greek Potato Skins with Olives and Feta

Preparation Time: 5 minutes
Cooking Time: 45 minutes
Servings: 4
Ingredients:
- 2 russet potatoes
- 3 tablespoons olive oil
- 1 teaspoon kosher salt, divided
- ¼ teaspoon black pepper
- 2 tablespoons fresh cilantro
- ¼ cup Kalamata olives, diced
- ¼ cup crumbled feta
- Chopped fresh parsley, for garnish (optional)

Directions:
1. Preheat the air fryer to 380°F. Using a fork, poke 2 to 3 holes in the potatoes, then coat each with about ½ tablespoon olive oil and ½ teaspoon salt.
2. Situate the potatoes into the air fryer basket and bake for 30 minutes. Remove the potatoes from the air fryer, and slice in half. Scrape out the flesh of the potatoes using a spoon, leaving a ½-inch layer of potato inside the skins, and set the skins aside.
3. In a medium bowl, combine the scooped potato middles with the remaining 2 tablespoons of olive oil, ½ teaspoon of salt, black pepper, and cilantro. Mix until well combined. Divide the potato filling into the now-empty potato skins, spreading it evenly over them. Top each potato with a tablespoon each of the olives and feta.
4. Place the loaded potato skins back into the air fryer and bake for 15 minutes. Serve with additional

chopped cilantro or parsley and a drizzle of olive oil, if desired.

Nutrition 270 Calories 13g Fat 34g Carbohydrates 5g Protein

330. Artichoke and Olive Pita Flatbread

Preparation Time: 5 minutes
Cooking Time: 10 minutes
Servings: 4
Ingredients:
- 2 whole wheat pitas
- 2 tablespoons olive oil, divided
- 2 garlic cloves, minced
- ¼ teaspoon salt
- ½ cup canned artichoke hearts, sliced
- ¼ cup Kalamata olives
- ¼ cup shredded Parmesan
- ¼ cup crumbled feta
- Chopped fresh parsley, for garnish (optional)

Directions:
1. Preheat the air fryer to 380°F. Brush each pita with 1 tablespoon olive oil, then sprinkle the minced garlic and salt over the top.
2. Distribute the artichoke hearts, olives, and cheeses evenly between the two pitas, and place both into the air fryer to bake for 10 minutes. Remove the pitas and cut them into 4 pieces each before serving. Sprinkle parsley over the top, if desired.

Nutrition 243 Calories 15g Fat 10g Carbohydrates 7g Protein

331. Mini Crab Cakes

Preparation Time: 10 minutes
Cooking Time: 10 minutes
Servings: 6
Ingredients:
- 8 ounces lump crab meat
- 2 tablespoons diced red bell pepper
- 1 scallion, white parts and green parts, diced
- 1 garlic clove, minced
- 1 tablespoon capers, minced
- 1 tablespoon nonfat plain Greek yogurt
- 1 egg, beaten
- ¼ cup whole wheat bread crumbs
- ¼ teaspoon salt
- 1 tablespoon olive oil
- 1 lemon, cut into wedges

Directions:
1. Preheat the air fryer to 360°F. In a medium bowl, mix the crab, bell pepper, scallion, garlic, and capers until combined. Add the yogurt and egg. Stir until incorporated. Mix in the bread crumbs and salt.
2. Portion this mixture into 6 equal parts and pat out into patties. Place the crab cakes inside the air fryer

basket on single layer, separately. Grease the tops of each patty with a bit of olive oil. Bake for 10 minutes.
3. Pull out the crab cakes from the air fryer and serve with lemon wedges on the side.

Nutrition 87 Calories 4g Fat 6g Carbohydrates 9g Protein

332. Zucchini Feta Roulades

Preparation Time: 10 minutes
Cooking Time: 10 minutes
Servings: 6
Ingredients:
- ½ cup feta
- 1 garlic clove, minced
- 2 tablespoons fresh basil, minced
- 1 tablespoon capers, minced
- 1/8 teaspoon salt
- 1/8 teaspoon red pepper flakes
- 1 tablespoon lemon juice
- 2 medium zucchinis
- 12 toothpicks

Directions:
1. Preheat the air fryer to 360°F. (If using a grill attachment, make sure it is inside the air fryer during preheating.) In a small bowl, mix the feta, garlic, basil, capers, salt, red pepper flakes, and lemon juice.
2. Slice the zucchini into 1/8-inch strips lengthwise. (Each zucchini should yield around 6 strips.) Spread 1 tablespoon of the cheese filling onto each slice of zucchini, then roll it up and locked it with a toothpick through the middle.
3. Place the zucchini roulades into the air fryer basket in a one layer, individually. Bake or grill in the air fryer for 10 minutes. Remove the zucchini roulades from the air fryer and gently remove the toothpicks before serving.

Nutrition 46 Calories 3g Fat 6g Carbohydrates 3g Protein

333. Garlic-Roasted Tomatoes and Olives

Preparation Time: 5 minutes
Cooking Time: 20 minutes
Servings: 6
Ingredients:
- 2 cups cherry tomatoes
- 4 garlic cloves, roughly chopped
- ½ red onion, roughly chopped
- 1 cup black olives
- 1 cup green olives
- 1 tablespoon fresh basil, minced
- 1 tablespoon fresh oregano, minced
- 2 tablespoons olive oil
- ¼ to ½ teaspoon salt

Directions:

1. Preheat the air fryer to 380°F. In a large bowl, incorporate all of the ingredients and toss together so that the tomatoes and olives are coated well with the olive oil and herbs.
2. Pour the mixture into the air fryer basket, and roast for 10 minutes. Stir the mixture well, then continue roasting for an additional 10 minutes. Remove from the air fryer, transfer to a serving bowl, and enjoy.

Nutrition 109 Calories 10g Fat 5g Carbohydrates 1g Protein

334. Goat Cheese and Garlic Crostini

Preparation Time: 3 minutes
Cooking Time: 5 minutes
Servings: 4
Ingredients:
- 1 whole wheat baguette
- ¼ cup olive oil
- 2 garlic cloves, minced
- 4 ounces goat cheese
- 2 tablespoons fresh basil, minced

Directions:
1. Preheat the air fryer to 380°F. Cut the baguette into ½-inch-thick slices. In a small bowl, incorporate together the olive oil and garlic, then brush it over one side of each slice of bread.
2. Place the olive-oil-coated bread in a single layer in the air fryer basket and bake for 5 minutes. In the meantime, combine together the goat cheese and basil. Remove the toast from the air fryer, then spread a thin layer of the goat cheese mixture over on each piece and serve.

Nutrition 365 Calories 21g Fat 10g Carbohydrates 12g Protein

335. Rosemary-Roasted Red Potatoes

Preparation Time: 5 minutes
Cooking Time: 20 minutes
Servings: 6
Ingredients:
- 1-pound red potatoes, quartered
- ¼ cup olive oil
- ½ teaspoon kosher salt
- ¼ teaspoon black pepper
- 1 garlic clove, minced
- 4 rosemary sprigs

Directions:
1. Preheat the air fryer to 360°F.
2. In a large bowl, toss in the potatoes with the olive oil, salt, pepper, and garlic until well coated. Fill the air fryer basket with potatoes and top with the sprigs of rosemary.

3. Roast for 10 minutes, then stir or toss the potatoes and roast for 10 minutes more. Remove the rosemary sprigs and serve the potatoes. Season well.

Nutrition 133 Calories 9g Fat 5g Carbohydrates 1g Protein

336. Guaca Egg Scramble

Preparation Time: 8 minutes
Cooking Time: 15 minutes
Servings: 4
Ingredients
- 4 eggs, beaten
- 1 white onion, diced
- 1 tablespoon avocado oil
- 1 avocado, finely chopped
- ½ teaspoon chili flakes
- 1 oz Cheddar cheese, shredded
- ½ teaspoon salt
- 1 tablespoon fresh parsley

Directions:
1. Pour avocado oil in the skillet and bring it to boil. Then add diced onion and roast it until it is light brown. Meanwhile, mix up together chili flakes, beaten eggs, and salt.
2. Fill the egg mixture over the cooked onion and cook the mixture for 1 minute over the medium heat. After this, scramble the eggs well with the help of the fork or spatula. Cook the eggs until they are solid but soft.
3. After this, add chopped avocado and shredded cheese. Stir the scramble well and transfer in the serving plates. Sprinkle the meal with fresh parsley.

Nutrition 236 Calories 20g Fat 4g Carbohydrates 8.6g Protein

337. Morning Tostadas

Preparation Time: 15 minutes
Cooking Time: 6 minutes
Servings: 6
Ingredients
- ½ white onion, diced
- 1 tomato, chopped
- 1 cucumber, chopped
- 1 tablespoon fresh cilantro, chopped
- ½ jalapeno pepper, chopped
- 1 tablespoon lime juice
- 6 corn tortillas
- 1 tablespoon canola oil
- 2 oz Cheddar cheese, shredded
- ½ cup white beans, canned, drained
- 6 eggs
- ½ teaspoon butter
- ½ teaspoon Sea salt

Directions
1. Make Pico de Galo: in the salad bowl combine together diced white onion, tomato, cucumber,

fresh cilantro, and jalapeno pepper. Then add lime juice and a ½ tablespoon of canola oil. Mix up the mixture well. Pico de Galo is cooked.

2. After this, preheat the oven to 390F. Line the tray with baking paper. Arrange the corn tortillas on the baking paper and brush with remaining canola oil from both sides. Bake the tortillas until they start to be crunchy. Chill the cooked crunchy tortillas well. Meanwhile, toss the butter in the skillet.

3. Crack the eggs in the melted butter and sprinkle them with sea salt. Fry the eggs until the egg whites become white (cooked). Approximately for 3-5 minutes over the medium heat. After this, mash the beans until you get puree texture. Spread the bean puree on the corn tortillas.

4. Add fried eggs. Then top the eggs with Pico de Galo and shredded Cheddar cheese.

Nutrition 246 Calories 11g Fat 4.7g Carbohydrates 13.7g Protein

338. Cheese Omelet

Preparation Time: 5 minutes
Cooking Time: 10 minutes
Servings: 2
Ingredients
- 1 tablespoon cream cheese
- 2 eggs, beaten
- ¼ teaspoon paprika
- ½ teaspoon dried oregano
- ¼ teaspoon dried dill
- 1 oz Parmesan, grated
- 1 teaspoon coconut oil

Directions
1. Mix up together cream cheese with eggs, dried oregano, and dill. Pour coconut oil in the skillet and heat it up until it will coat all the skillet.
2. Then fill the skillet with the egg mixture and flatten it. Add grated Parmesan and close the lid. Cook omelet for 10 minutes over the low heat. Then transfer the cooked omelet in the serving plate and sprinkle with paprika.

Nutrition 148 Calories 11.5g Fat 0.3g Carbohydrates 10.6g Protein

339. Fruity Pizza

Preparation Time: 10 minutes
Cooking Time: 0 minute
Servings: 2
Ingredients
- 9 oz watermelon slice
- 1 tablespoon Pomegranate sauce
- 2 oz Feta cheese, crumbled
- 1 tablespoon fresh cilantro, chopped

Directions
1. Place the watermelon slice in the plate and sprinkle with crumbled Feta cheese. Add fresh cilantro.

After this, sprinkle the pizza with Pomegranate juice generously. Cut the pizza into the servings.

Nutrition 143 Calories 6.2g Fat 0.6g Carbohydrates 5.1g Protein

340. Herb and Ham Muffins

Preparation Time: 10 minutes
Cooking Time: 15 minutes
Servings: 4
Ingredients
- 3 oz ham, chopped
- 4 eggs, beaten
- 2 tablespoons coconut flour
- ½ teaspoon dried oregano
- ¼ teaspoon dried cilantro
- Cooking spray

Directions
1. Spray the muffin's molds with cooking spray from inside. In the bowl mix up together beaten eggs, coconut flour, dried oregano, cilantro, and ham. When the liquid is homogenous, pour it in the prepared muffin molds.
2. Bake the muffins for 15 minutes at 360F. Chill the cooked meal well and only after this remove from the molds.

Nutrition 128 Calories 7.2g Fat 2.9g Carbohydrates 10.1g Protein

341. Morning Sprouts Pizza

Preparation Time: 15 minutes
Cooking Time: 20 minutes
Servings: 6
Ingredients
- ½ cup wheat flour, whole grain
- 2 tablespoons butter, softened
- ¼ teaspoon baking powder
- ¾ teaspoon salt
- 5 oz chicken fillet, boiled
- 2 oz Cheddar cheese, shredded
- 1 teaspoon tomato sauce
- 1 oz bean sprouts

Directions
1. Make the pizza crust: mix up together wheat flour, butter, baking powder, and salt. Knead the soft and non-sticky dough. Add more wheat flour if needed. Leave the dough for 10 minutes to chill. Then place the dough on the baking paper. Cover it with the second baking paper sheet.
2. Roll up the dough with the help of the rolling pin to get the round pizza crust. After this, remove the upper baking paper sheet. Transfer the pizza crust in the tray.
3. Spread the crust with tomato sauce. Then shred the chicken fillet and arrange it over the pizza crust. Add shredded Cheddar cheese. Bake pizza for 20

minutes at 355F. Then top the cooked pizza with bean sprouts and slice into the servings.

Nutrition 157 Calories 8.8g Fat 0.3g Carbohydrates 10.5g Protein

342. Quinoa with Banana and Cinnamon

Preparation Time: 10 minutes
Cooking Time: 12 minutes
Servings: 4
Ingredients
- 1 cup quinoa
- 2 cup milk
- 1 teaspoon vanilla extract
- 1 teaspoon honey
- 2 bananas, sliced
- ¼ teaspoon ground cinnamon

Directions
1. Pour milk in the saucepan and add quinoa. Close the lid and cook it over the medium heat for 12 minutes or until quinoa will absorb all liquid. Then chill the quinoa for 10-15 minutes and place in the serving mason jars.
2. Add honey, vanilla extract, and ground cinnamon. Stir well. Top quinoa with banana and stirs it before serving.

Nutrition 279 Calories 5.3g Fat 4.6g Carbohydrates 10.7g Protein

343. Egg Casserole

Preparation Time: 10 minutes
Cooking Time: 28 minutes
Servings: 4
Ingredients
- 2 eggs, beaten
- 1 red bell pepper, chopped
- 1 chili pepper, chopped
- ½ red onion, diced
- 1 teaspoon canola oil
- ½ teaspoon salt
- 1 teaspoon paprika
- 1 tablespoon fresh cilantro, chopped
- 1 garlic clove, diced
- 1 teaspoon butter, softened
- ¼ teaspoon chili flakes

Directions
1. Brush the casserole mold with canola oil and pour beaten eggs inside. After this, toss the butter in the skillet and melt it over the medium heat. Add chili pepper and red bell pepper.
2. After this, add red onion and cook the vegetables for 7-8 minutes over the medium heat. Stir them from time to time. Transfer the vegetables in the casserole mold.

3. Add salt, paprika, cilantro, diced garlic, and chili flakes. Stir mildly with the help of a spatula to get a homogenous mixture. Bake the casserole for 20 minutes at 355F in the oven. Then chill the meal well and cut into servings. Transfer the casserole in the serving plates with the help of the spatula.

Nutrition 68 Calories 4.5g Fat 1g Carbohydrates 3.4g Protein

344. Cheese-Cauliflower Fritters

Preparation Time: 10 minutes
Cooking Time: 10 minutes
Servings: 2
Ingredients
- 1 cup cauliflower, shredded
- 1 egg, beaten
- 1 tablespoon wheat flour, whole grain
- 1 oz Parmesan, grated
- ½ teaspoon ground black pepper
- 1 tablespoon canola oil

Directions
1. In the mixing bowl mix up together shredded cauliflower and egg. Add wheat flour, grated Parmesan, and ground black pepper. Stir the mixture with the help of the fork until it is homogenous and smooth.
2. Pour canola oil in the skillet and bring it to boil. Make the fritters from the cauliflower mixture with the help of the fingertips or use spoon and transfer in the hot oil. Roast the fritters for 4 minutes from each side over the medium-low heat.

Nutrition 167 Calories 12.3g Fat 1.5g Carbohydrates 8.8g Protein

345. Creamy Oatmeal Figs

Preparation Time: 10 minutes
Cooking Time: 20 minutes
Servings: 5
Ingredients
- 2 cups oatmeal
- 1 ½ cup milk
- 1 tablespoon butter
- 3 figs, chopped
- 1 tablespoon honey

Directions
1. Pour milk in the saucepan. Add oatmeal and close the lid. Cook the oatmeal for 15 minutes over the medium-low heat. Then add chopped figs and honey.
2. Add butter and mix up the oatmeal well. Cook it for 5 minutes more. Close the lid and let the cooked breakfast rest for 10 minutes before serving.

Nutrition 222 Calories 6g Fat 4.4g Carbohydrates 7.1g Protein

346. Baked Cinnamon Oatmeal

Preparation Time: 10 minutes
Cooking Time: 25 minutes
Servings: 4
Ingredients

- 1 cup oatmeal
- 1/3 cup milk
- 1 pear, chopped
- 1 teaspoon vanilla extract
- 1 tablespoon Splenda
- 1 teaspoon butter
- ½ teaspoon ground cinnamon
- 1 egg, beaten

Directions

1. In the big bowl mix up together oatmeal, milk, egg, vanilla extract, Splenda, and ground cinnamon. Melt butter and add it in the oatmeal mixture. Then add chopped pear and stir it well.
2. Transfer the oatmeal mixture in the casserole mold and flatten gently. Cover it with the foil and secure edges. Bake the oatmeal for 25 minutes at 350F.

Nutrition 151 Calories 3.9g Fat 3.3g Carbohydrates 4.9g Protein

347. Chia and Nut Porridge

Preparation Time: 10 minutes
Cooking Time: 30 minutes
Servings: 4
Ingredients

- 3 cups organic almond milk
- 1/3 cup chia seeds, dried
- 1 teaspoon vanilla extract
- 1 tablespoon honey
- ¼ teaspoon ground cardamom

Directions

1. Pour almond milk in the saucepan and bring it to boil. Then chill the almond milk to the room temperature (or appx. For 10-15 minutes). Add vanilla extract, honey, and ground cardamom. Stir well. After this, add chia seeds and stir again. Close the lid and let chia seeds soak the liquid for 20-25 minutes. Transfer the cooked porridge into the serving ramekins.

Nutrition 150 Calories 7.3g Fat 6.1g Carbohydrates 3.7g Protein

348. Chocolate Oatmeal

Preparation Time: 10 minutes
Cooking Time: 15 minutes
Servings: 2
Ingredients

- 1 ½ cup oatmeal
- 1 tablespoon cocoa powder
- ½ cup heavy cream

- ¼ cup of water
- 1 teaspoon vanilla extract
- 1 tablespoon butter
- 2 tablespoons Splenda

Directions

1. Mix up together oatmeal with cocoa powder and Splenda. Transfer the mixture in the saucepan. Add vanilla extract, water, and heavy cream. Stir it gently with the help of the spatula.
2. Close the lid and cook it for 10-15 minutes over the medium-low heat. Remove the cooked cocoa oatmeal from the heat and add butter. Stir it well.

Nutrition 230 Calories 10.6g Fat 3.5g Carbohydrates 4.6g Protein

349. Cinnamon Roll Oats

Preparation Time: 7 minutes
Cooking Time: 10 minutes
Servings: 4
Ingredients

- ½ cup rolled oats
- 1 cup milk
- 1 teaspoon vanilla extract
- 1 teaspoon ground cinnamon
- 2 teaspoon honey
- 2 tablespoons Plain yogurt
- 1 teaspoon butter

Directions

1. Transfer milk in the saucepan and bring it to boil. Add rolled oats and stir well. Close the lid and simmer the oats for 5 minutes over the medium heat. The cooked oats will absorb all milk.
2. Then add butter and stir the oats well. In the separated bowl, whisk together Plain yogurt with honey, cinnamon, and vanilla extract. Transfer the cooked oats in the serving bowls. Top the oats with the yogurt mixture in the shape of the wheel.

Nutrition 243 Calories 20.2g Fat 1g Carbohydrates 13.3g Protein

350. Pumpkin Oatmeal with Spices

Preparation Time: 10 minutes
Cooking Time: 13 minutes
Servings: 6
Ingredients

- 2 cups oatmeal
- 1 cup of coconut milk
- 1 cup milk
- 1 teaspoon Pumpkin pie spices
- 2 tablespoons pumpkin puree
- 1 tablespoon Honey
- ½ teaspoon butter

Directions

1. Pour coconut milk and milk in the saucepan. Add

butter and bring the liquid to boil. Add oatmeal, stir well with the help of a spoon and close the lid.

2. Simmer the oatmeal for 7 minutes over the medium heat. Meanwhile, mix up together honey, pumpkin pie spices, and pumpkin puree. When the oatmeal is cooked, add pumpkin puree mixture and stir well. Transfer the cooked breakfast in the serving plates.

Nutrition 232 Calories 12.5g Fat 3.8g Carbohydrates 5.9g Protein

351. **Passion Fruit and Spicy Couscous**

Preparation Time: 15 minutes
Cooking Time: 15 minutes
Serving: 4
Ingredients:
- 1 pinch of salt
- 1 pinch of allspice
- 1 teaspoon of mixed spice
- 1 cup of boiling water
- 2 teaspoons of extra-virgin olive oil
- ½ cup of full-fat Greek yogurt
- ½ cup of honey
- 1 cup of couscous
- 1 teaspoon of orange zest
- 2 oranges, peeled and sliced
- 2 tablespoons of passion fruit pulp
- ½ cup of blueberries
- ½ cup of walnuts, roasted and unsalted
- 2 tablespoons of fresh mint

Directions:
1. In a mixing bowl, combine the salt, allspice, mixed spice, honey, couscous, and boiling water. Cover the bowl and allow to rest for five to ten minutes, or until the water has been absorbed. Stir well then add the diced walnuts.
2. In a separate bowl, combine the passion fruit, yogurt, and orange zest.
3. To serve, portion couscous up into four bowls, add the yogurt mixture, and top with the sliced orange, blueberries, and mint leaves.

Nutrition: 100 calories 10.5g fat 2.1g protein

352. **Spring Sandwich**

Preparation Time: 10 minutes
Cooking Time: 25 minutes
Serving: 4
Ingredient
- 1 pinch salt
- 1 pinch black pepper
- 4 tsp. extra-virgin olive oil
- 4 eggs
- 4 multigrain sandwich thins
- 1 onion

- 1 tomato
- 2 cups baby spinach leaves
- 4 tbsp. crumbled feta
- 1 sprig rosemary

Direction:
1. Prep oven to 375 F.
2. Chop multigrain sandwich thins open and brush each side with one teaspoon of olive oil. Situate them into the oven and toast for 6 minutes. Remove and kept aside.
3. Situate non-stick skillet over medium heat, pour in remaining 2 teaspoons of olive oil and strip the leaves of rosemary off into the pan. Mix in the eggs, one by one.
4. Cook until yolks stay runny. Flip once then remove from the heat.
5. Portion multigrain thins onto serving plates, then situate spinach leaves on top, followed by sliced tomato, one egg, and a sprinkling of feta cheese. Sprinkle salt and pepper, then close your sandwich using the remaining multigrain thins.

Nutrition: 150 calories 15g fat 3g protein

353. **Springtime Quinoa Salad**

Preparation Time: 10 minutes
Cooking Time: 25 minutes
Serving: 4
Ingredients
for vinaigrette:
- 1 pinch of salt
- 1 pinch of black pepper
- ½ teaspoon of dried thyme
- ½ teaspoon of dried oregano
- ¼ cup of extra-virgin olive oil
- 1 tablespoon of honey
- juice of 1 lemon
- 1 clove of garlic, minced
- 2 tablespoons of fresh basil, diced

for salad:
- 1 ½ cups of cooked quinoa
- 4 cups of mixed leafy greens
- ½ cup of kalamata olives, halved and pitted
- ¼ cup of sun-dried tomatoes, diced
- ½ cup of almonds, raw, unsalted and diced

Directions:
1. Combine all the vinaigrette ingredients together, either by hand or using a blender or food processor. Set the vinaigrette aside in the refrigerator.
2. Incorporate salad ingredients.
3. Pour the vinaigrette over the salad, then serve.

Nutrition: 201 calories 13g fat 4g protein

354. **Seafood Souvlaki Bowl**

Preparation Time: 20 minutes
Cooking Time: 20 minutes

Serving: 4
Ingredient
for salmon

- 1 pinch salt
- 1 pinch black pepper
- 1 tbsp. fresh oregano
- 1 tbsp. paprika
- 1 tbsp. fresh dill
- 3 tbsp. extra-virgin olive oil
- 2 tbsp. balsamic vinegar
- 6 tbsp. squeezed lemon juice
- 2 cloves of garlic
- 1 lb. of fresh salmon

Ingredient:

- 1 pinch salt
- 1 pinch black pepper
- 2 tablespoons extra-virgin olive oil
- 1 lemon juice
- 2 red bell peppers
- 1 large cucumber
- 1 zucchini
- 1 cup of cherry tomatoes
- ½ cup of kalamata olives
- 1 cup of dry pearled couscous
- 8 oz. of feta

Direction:

1. Cook the couscous using the package instructions and keep aside.
2. Incorporate all the souvlaki ingredients apart from the fish. Incorporate well, then coat each fish fillet. Keep aside for 15 minutes.
3. Mix sliced bell peppers and zucchini. Stir in two tablespoons of olive oil, salt, and pepper. Put aside.
4. Using medium skillet over medium heat, cook the salmon until tender, then remove from the heat.
5. Mix in sliced peppers and zucchini to the skillet and cook for three minutes until you see charring, then remove from the heat.
6. To serve, ladle couscous up into four serving bowls and top with the lemon juice. Add the cooked salmon, charred vegetables, cucumber, tomatoes, olives, and feta.

Nutrition: 159 calories 11g fat 2g protein

355. Spaghetti Niçoise

Preparation Time: 15 minutes
Cooking Time: 20 minutes
Serving: 4
Ingredient
for pasta:

- 1 pinch salt
- 1 pinch black pepper
- ½ teaspoon chili flakes
- 8 oz. spaghetti
- 14 oz. canned tuna chunks in oil

- 1/3 cup kalamata olives
- 8 oz. cherry tomatoes
- 3 oz. arugula
- ½ cup of pine nuts

for dressing:

- 1 pinch salt
- 1 pinch black pepper
- 2 tablespoons extra-virgin olive oil
- 1 tablespoon Dijon mustard
- ¼ cup lemon juice
- 1 tablespoon lemon zest
- 1 clove of garlic
- 1 tablespoon capers

Directions:

1. Stir all the ingredients for the dressing.
2. Cook the pasta according the package instructions.
3. Boil the eggs, deshell and cut them in half. Set this aside.
4. Rinse and drain cooked pasta.
5. Add the remaining ingredients, give it a toss, top with the eggs, and then drizzle with the mustard dressing.

Nutrition: 287 calories 14g fat 4g protein

356. Tomato Poached Fish with Herbs and Chickpeas

Preparation Time: 20 minutes
Cooking Time: 20 minutes
Serving: 2
Ingredients:

- 1 pinch of salt
- 1 pinch of black pepper
- 4 sprigs of fresh oregano
- 4 sprigs of fresh dill
- 1 ½ cups of water
- 1 cup of white wine
- 2 tablespoons of extra-virgin olive oil
- 1 tablespoon of tomato paste
- 2 cloves of garlic
- 2 shallots
- 1 lemon
- zest of 1 lemon
- 14 oz. can of chickpeas
- 8 oz. of cherry tomatoes
- 1 Fresno pepper
- 1 lb. of cod

Directions:

1. Situate saucepan over high heat, cook olive oil, garlic, and shallots for two minutes.
2. Add the salt, pepper, tomato paste, cherry tomatoes, chickpeas, and Fresno pepper.
3. Stir in the water and wine. Place the fish into the center of the pan, ensuring it is submerged in the liquid. Sprinkle the lemon zest over the broth, then add the lemon slices and fresh herbs.

4. Secure lid onto the saucepan and allow the broth to simmer for five to ten minutes.
5. When cooked, remove from the heat and serve over basmati rice. Top with a few toasted pistachios for added texture.

Nutrition: 351 calories 21g fat 9g protein

357. Garlic Prawn and Pea Risotto

Preparation Time: 15 minutes
Cooking Time: 30 minutes
Serving: 4
Ingredients:
- 1 pinch of salt
- 1 pinch of black pepper
- 1 red chili
- 3 tablespoons of extra-virgin olive oil
- oz. of butter
- Juice of 1 lemon
- Zest of 1 lemon
- 50 Fl oz. of fish stock
- 1 cup of white wine
- 1 clove of garlic, finely diced
- 1 onion, diced
- 7 oz. of frozen peas
- 14 oz. of raw prawns
- oz. of Arborio rice

Directions:
1. Rinse the prawns under running water and then remove their heads and shells. Keep these aside and keep the prawn meat aside.
2. Situate saucepan over medium heat, add one tablespoon of olive oil, garlic, half of the finely diced chili, prawn heads, and shells. Cook until the shells change color. Boil stock, then turn the heat down to a simmer.
3. In a separate medium saucepan over medium heat, add half the butter and the onions. Cook until the onions have softened. Add the risotto into the pan and stir continuously until you notice that the rice has become transparent in appearance.
4. Stir wine to the rice and cook
5. Begin to ladle the stock over the rice, one spoonful at a time. Ensure that the ladle of stock has evaporated before continuing to add the next. Stir in the peas and prawns.
6. Continue pouring stock until al dente texture, soft with a starchy center, around 20 to 30 minutes. Continue to cook until the prawn meat has changed color.
7. Remove the risotto from the heat, then add the remaining chili, olive oil, and lemon juice.
8. Top with salt, pepper, lemon zest and serve.

Nutrition: 341 calories 16g fat 7g protein

358. Honey and Vanilla Custard Cups with Crunchy Filo Pastry

Preparation Time: 25 minutes
Cooking Time: 2 hours
Serving: 4
Ingredients:
- 1 vanilla bean, cut lengthways
- 2 cups of full-fat milk
- 1/3 cup of honey
- 1 tablespoon of brown sugar
- 2 tablespoons of custard powder
- 4 to 6 ripe figs, quartered
- 1 sheet of filo pastry
- 2 tablespoons of raw pistachios

Directions:
1. Situate saucepan over medium heat, simmer vanilla bean, milk, and honey
2. In a heatproof dish, combine the sugar and custard powder. Transfer the milk mixture into the bowl containing the custard powder. Using a whisk, combine well and then transfer back into the saucepan.
3. Bring to a boil, constantly whisking until the custard thickens. Remove the vanilla bean.
4. Pour the custard into cups and allow to chill in the refrigerator for 2 hours.
5. Prep oven to 350 F and prep baking tray with parchment.
6. Put the pastry sheet onto an even surface and spray lightly with olive oil cooking spray.
7. Sprinkle half the pistachios over the pastry and then fold the pastry in half. Heat up 2 tablespoons of honey in the microwave, then coat the pastry.
8. Place the pastry into the oven and allow to bake for 10 minutes. Pull away from heat and allow it to cool.
9. Gently break the filo pastry into pieces, then top the custard with the shards and fresh-cut figs.

Nutrition: 307 calories 17g fat 4g protein

359. Mediterranean Tostadas

Preparation Time: 15 minutes
Cooking Time: 10 minutes
Serving: 4
Ingredients:
- 1 pinch salt
- 1 pinch black pepper
- 1 pinch oregano
- 1 pinch garlic powder
- 4 tostadas
- 1 tablespoon of extra-virgin olive oil
- ½ cup of milk
- ½ cup of roasted red pepper hummus
- 8 eggs, beaten
- ½ cup of green onion, finely diced

- ½ cup of red bell peppers, finely diced
- ½ cup of diced cucumber
- ½ cup of diced tomato
- ¼ cup of crumbled feta
- 1 handful of fresh basil

Directions:
1. Position non-stick skillet over medium heat, cook olive oil and red peppers. Cook until these have softened, then add the salt, pepper, oregano, garlic powder, milk, eggs, and onion.
2. Gently stir the mixture until you reach a scrambled egg consistency.
3. Once cooked through, remove from the heat.
4. Place a tostada onto each place, and top with the hummus, egg, tomato, cucumber, feta, and fresh basil leaves.

Nutrition: 251 calories 19g fat 6g protein

360. Vegetable Ratatouille

Preparation Time: 15 minutes
Cooking Time: 40 minutes
Serving: 8
Ingredients:
- 1 pinch salt
- 1 pinch black pepper
- 1 pinch brown sugar
- ¼ cup extra-virgin olive oil
- ¼ cup of white wine
- 3 cloves of garlic
- 1 onion, diced
- 1 lb. of eggplant
- 1 cup of zucchini
- 1 ½ cups of canned tomato
- 1 red bell pepper, diced
- 1 green bell pepper, diced
- ½ cup of fresh basil

Directions:
1. Place saucepan over medium heat, cook olive oil and finely diced garlic and onion.
2. Add the cubed eggplant and continue to cook for a further 5 minutes.
3. Add the salt, pepper, and diced bell peppers. Allow to cook for another 3 minutes.
4. Add the sliced zucchini to the saucepan and cook for 3 minutes.
5. Mix white wine and canned tomatoes.
6. Allow to simmer for another five minutes. Taste the ratatouille.
7. Pull away from the heat, add the basil, and serve with a side portion of barley or brown rice.

Nutrition: 401 calories 19g fat 7g protein

361. Citrus Cups

Preparation Time: 15 minutes
Cooking Time: 15 minutes

Serving: 4
Ingredients:
- ½ cup of water
- 1 tablespoon of orange juice
- 3 cups of full-fat Greek yogurt
- 1 vanilla bean
- 1 ruby grapefruit
- 2 mandarins
- 1 orange
- 6 strips of mandarin rind
- 1/3 cup of powdered sugar
- 1 small handful of fresh mint leaves

Directions:
1. Slice open the vanilla bean lengthways and transfer the seeds into a medium saucepan. Add the pod to the saucepan as well, followed by the water, sugar, and mandarin rind.
2. Boil mixture, then turn down to a simmer and cook for five minutes or until the syrup has thickened.
3. Allow to cool, remove the pod, and stir in the orange juice.
4. Pour the syrup over the sliced citrus fruits and allow to rest.
5. Dish the yogurt up into four bowls, top with the citrus and syrup, sprinkle with a bit of mint, then serve.

Nutrition: 217 calories 16g fat 4g protein

362. Mixed Berry Pancakes and Ricotta

Preparation Time: 15 minutes
Cooking Time: 25 minutes
Serving: 4
Ingredients:
- 1 pinch of salt
- ½ cup of milk
- 1 tablespoon of canola oil
- 2 eggs
- 1 ½ tablespoon of coarse brown sugar
- 1 teaspoon of baking powder
- ¼ teaspoon of baking soda
- 1 1/3 cup of all-purpose flour
- ½ cup of ricotta cheese
- 1 cup of mixed berries

Directions:
1. In a mixing bowl, combine the salt, sugar, baking powder, baking soda, and flour.
2. In a separate mixing bowl, combine the ricotta, eggs, oil, and milk.
3. Incorporate wet mixture with the dry mixture. Mix well. Put aside for 10 minutes.
4. Situate big, non-stick frying pan over medium heat. When the pan is hot to the touch, spoon even amounts of the batter into the pan, making sure that the batter dollops do not touch.

5. When they begin to bubble through, flip them over and cook for a further minute or two.
6. Follow this process until all the batter has been made into pancakes.
7. Evenly divide the pancakes between four plates. Garnish with mixed berries and drizzle with maple syrup and a few extra dollops of ricotta.

Nutrition: 281 calories 19g fat 5g protein

363. Mediterranean Frittata

Preparation Time: 5 minutes
Cooking Time: 25 minutes
Serving: 4
Ingredients:
- 1 pinch of salt
- 1 pinch of black pepper
- 1 tablespoon of extra-virgin olive oil
- 2 egg whites
- 6 eggs
- 1 cup of goat cheese
- 1 cup of Parmesan, shredded
- 8 oz. of mixed mushrooms
- 1 leek, diced
- 1 lb. of asparagus, finely sliced
- ½ cup of fresh basil leaves

Directions:
1. Preheat your oven to 400 F.
2. Scourge egg whites and eggs, salt, pepper, Parmesan cheese, and basil leaves. Set this aside.
3. In a large skillet, preferably non-stick, add the olive oil and leeks over medium heat. Cook until the leeks have softened, then add in the mushrooms, asparagus, stir to combine and cook for a further 5 minutes.
4. Put egg mixture to the skillet, using a spatula to spread the eggs evenly over the mixture. Allow to cook for two minutes and then top with the goat cheese.
5. Place the skillet into the oven and allow to bake for five minutes
6. Remove from the oven and serve.

Nutrition: 317 calories 11g fat 3g protein

364. Caponata

Preparation Time: 30 minutes
Cooking Time: 70 minutes
Serving: 6
Ingredient
for Caponata:
- 1 pinch salt
- 1 pinch black pepper
- Fl oz. extra-virgin olive oil
- Fl oz. red wine vinegar
- 2 shallots
- 4 sticks of celery

- 4 plum tomatoes
- ½ cup fresh basil leaves
- 3 eggplants
- 2 teaspoons capers
- oz. of raisins
- ½ cup pine nuts

for bruschetta
- Extra-virgin olive oil
- 1 garlic clove
- 8 pcs. ciabatta

Direction:
1. Situate casserole over medium heat, cook olive oil and cubed eggplant
2. Take out the eggplant and set aside.
3. Stir in diced shallots to the casserole then cook until softened. Stir in the plum tomatoes.
4. Let the tomatoes to break down and return the eggplant cubes to this mixture.
5. Stir in salt, pepper, vinegar, celery, capers, and raisins.
6. Adjust heat to low, cover and simmer for 40 minutes. Once the vegetables have cooked through, remove from the heat and set aside.
7. Rub the sliced ciabatta with olive oil and place onto a griddle pan over medium heat. Remove once charred on both sides. Rub the ciabatta slices with garlic cloves to enhance their flavor.
8. Drizzle pine nuts and basil leaves, and serve with the sliced ciabatta on the side.

Nutrition: 311 calories 12g fat 2g protein

365. Fresh Deli Pasta

Preparation Time: 15 minutes
Cooking Time: 30 minutes
Serving: 4
Ingredients:
- 1 pinch of salt
- 1 pinch of black pepper
- 2 tablespoons of extra-virgin olive oil
- 2 teaspoons of white wine vinegar
- 1 clove of garlic
- 1 tomato, diced
- 10 sun-dried tomatoes
- 7 oz. of frozen peas
- oz. of pasta of your choice
- oz. of prosciutto
- ½ cup of fresh basil leaves

Directions:
1. In a large saucepan, cover the pasta with water and add a pinch of salt. Bring to a boil and allow to cook for 10 minutes, then add the frozen peas and cook for another 2 minutes.
2. Once the pasta is tender, drain it by placing it into a colander and running cold water over it. Give the colander a few shakes and set aside.

3. Pulse salt, pepper, olive oil, vinegar, garlic, 10 leaves of basil, tomato, and 5 of the sun-dried tomatoes into a blender.
4. Put cooked pasta and peas to the serving bowl, add the remaining basil leaves, and lightly tear the prosciutto over the pasta.
5. Toss then serve.

Nutrition: 341 calories 11g fat 3g protein

366. Balsamic Asparagus

Preparation Time: 10 minutes
Cooking Time: 15 minutes
Servings: 4
Ingredients:
- 3 tablespoons olive oil
- 3 garlic cloves
- 2 tablespoons shallot
- 2 teaspoons balsamic vinegar
- 1 and ½ pound asparagus

Direction:
1. Preheat pan with the oil over medium-high heat, add the garlic and the shallot and sauté for 3 minutes.
2. Add the rest of the ingredients, cook for 12 minutes more, divide between plates and serve.

Nutrition: 100 calories 10.5g fat 2.1g protein

367. Lime Cucumber Mix

Preparation Time: 10 minutes
Cooking Time: 0 minute
Servings: 8
Ingredients:
- 4 cucumbers
- ½ cup green bell pepper
- 1 yellow onion
- 1 chili pepper
- 1 garlic clove
- 1 teaspoon parsley
- 2 tablespoons lime juice
- 1 tablespoon dill
- 1 tablespoon olive oil

Directions:
1. Incorporate cucumber with the bell peppers and the rest of the ingredients, toss and serve as a side dish.

Nutrition: 123 calories 4.3g fat 2g protein

368. Walnuts Cucumber Mix

Preparation Time: 5 minutes
Cooking Time: 0 minute
Servings: 2
Ingredients:
- 2 cucumbers
- 1 tablespoon olive oil
- 1 red chili pepper

- 1 tablespoon lemon juice
- 3 tablespoons walnuts
- 1 tablespoon balsamic vinegar
- 1 teaspoon chives

Directions:
1. Mix cucumbers with the oil and the rest of the ingredients, toss and serve

Nutrition: 121 calories 2.3g fat 2.4g protein

369. Cheesy Beet Salad

Preparation Time: 10 minutes
Cooking Time: 1 hour
Servings: 4
Ingredients:
- 4 beets
- 3 tablespoons olive oil
- ¼ cup lime juice
- 8 slices goat cheese
- 1/3 cup walnuts
- 1 tablespoon chives

Directions:
1. In a roasting pan, combine the beets with the oil, salt and pepper, toss and bake at 400 degrees F for 1 hour.
2. Cool the beets down, transfer them to a bowl, add the rest of the ingredients, toss and serve as a side salad.

Nutrition: 156 calories 4.2g fat 4g protein

370. Rosemary Beets

Preparation Time: 10 minutes
Cooking Time: 20 minutes
Servings: 4
Ingredients:
- 4 medium beets
- 1/3 cup balsamic vinegar
- 1 teaspoon rosemary, chopped
- 1 garlic clove, minced
- ½ teaspoon Italian seasoning
- 1 tablespoon olive oil

Direction:
1. Place pan with the oil over medium heat, add the beets and the rest of the ingredients, toss, and cook for 20 minutes.
2. Divide the mix between plates and serve.

Nutrition: 165 calories 3.4g fat 2.3g protein

371. Squash and Tomatoes Mix

Preparation Time: 10 minutes
Cooking Time: 20 minutes
Servings: 6
Ingredients:
- 5 medium squash
- 3 tablespoons olive oil

- 1 cup pine nuts
- ¼ cup goat cheese
- 6 tomatoes
- ½ yellow onion
- 2 tablespoons cilantro
- 2 tablespoons lemon juice

Direction:
1. Put pan with the oil over medium heat, cook onion and pine nuts for 3 minutes.
2. Add the squash and the rest of the ingredients, cook everything for 15 minutes, divide between plates and serve.

Nutrition: 200 calories 4.5g fat 4g protein

372. Balsamic Eggplant Mix

Preparation Time: 10 minutes
Cooking Time: 20 minutes
Servings: 6
Ingredients:
- 1/3 cup chicken stock
- 2 tablespoons balsamic vinegar
- 1 tablespoon lime juice
- 2 big eggplants
- 1 tablespoon rosemary
- ¼ cup cilantro
- 2 tablespoons olive oil

Directions:
1. In a roasting pan, combine the eggplants with the stock, the vinegar and the rest of the ingredients, introduce the pan in the oven and bake at 390 degrees F for 20 minutes.
2. Divide the mix between plates and serve.

Nutrition: 201 calories 4.5g fat 3g protein

373. Sage Barley Mix

Preparation Time: 10 minutes
Cooking Time: 45 minutes
Servings: 4
Ingredients:
- 1 tablespoon olive oil
- 1 red onion, chopped
- 1 tablespoon leaves
- 1 garlic clove, minced
- 14 ounces barley
- ½ tablespoon parmesan
- 6 cups veggie stock

Directions:
1. Preheat pan with the oil over medium heat, sauté onion and garlic for 5 minutes.
2. Add the sage, barley and the rest of the ingredients except the parmesan, stir, bring to a simmer and cook for 40 minutes,
3. Add the parmesan, stir, divide between plates.

Nutrition: 210 calories 6.5g fat 3.4g protein

374. Chickpeas and Beets Mix

Preparation Time: 10 minutes
Cooking Time: 25 minutes
Servings: 4
Ingredients:
- 3 tablespoons capers
- Juice of 1 lemon
- Zest of 1 lemon, grated
- 1 red onion, chopped
- 3 tablespoons olive oil
- 14 ounces canned chickpeas
- 8 ounces beets
- 1 tablespoon parsley

Direction:
1. Situate pan with the oil over medium heat, add the onion, lemon zest, lemon juice and the capers and sauté for 5 minutes.
2. Incorporate rest of the ingredients, stir and cook over medium-low heat for 20 minutes more.
3. Divide the mix between plates and serve.

Nutrition: 199 calories 4.5g fat 3.3 protein

375. Creamy Sweet Potatoes Mix

Preparation Time: 10 minutes
Cooking Time: 1 hour
Servings: 4
Ingredients:
- 4 tablespoons olive oil
- 1 garlic clove, minced
- 4 medium sweet potatoes
- 1 red onion, sliced
- 3 ounces baby spinach
- Zest and juice of 1 lemon
- 1 and ½ tablespoons Greek yogurt
- 2 tablespoons tahini paste

Directions:
1. Situate potatoes on a baking sheet lined with parchment paper, bake at 350 degrees F for 1 hour.
2. Skin the potatoes, slice them into wedges and put them in a bowl.
3. Add the garlic, the oil and the rest of the ingredients, toss, divide the mix between plates and serve.

Nutrition: 214 calories 5.6g fat 3.1g protein

376. Cabbage and Mushrooms Mix

Preparation Time: 10 minutes
Cooking Time: 15 minutes
Servings: 2
Ingredients:
- 1 yellow onion, sliced
- 2 tablespoons olive oil
- 1 tablespoon balsamic vinegar
- ½ pound white mushrooms

- 1 green cabbage head
- 4 spring onions

Directions:
1. Position pan with the oil over medium heat, add the yellow onion and the spring onions and cook for 5 minutes.
2. Add the rest of the ingredients, cook everything for 10 minutes, divide between plates and serve.

Nutrition: 199 calories 4.5g fat 2.2g protein

377. Lemon Mushroom Rice

Preparation Time: 10 minutes
Cooking Time: 30 minutes
Servings: 4
Ingredients:
- 2 cups chicken stock
- 1 yellow onion, chopped
- ½ pound white mushrooms
- 2 garlic cloves, minced
- 8 ounces wild rice
- Juice and zest of 1 lemon
- 1 tablespoon chives, chopped
- 6 tablespoons goat cheese

Directions:
1. Heat up a pot with the stock over medium heat, add the rice, onion and the rest of the ingredients excluding the chives and the cheese, bring to a simmer and cook for 25 minutes.
2. Add the remaining ingredients, cook everything for 5 minutes, divide between plates and serve.

Nutrition: 222 calories 5.5g fat 5.6g protein

378. Paprika and Chives Potatoes

Preparation Time: 10 minutes
Cooking Time: 68 minutes
Servings: 4
Ingredients:
- 4 potatoes
- 1 tablespoon olive oil
- 1 celery stalk, chopped
- 2 tomatoes, chopped
- 1 teaspoon sweet paprika
- 2 tablespoons chives, chopped

Directions:
1. Situate potatoes on a baking sheet lined with parchment paper bake at 350 degrees F for 1 hour.
2. Cool the potatoes down, peel and cut them into larger cubes.
3. Preheat pan with the oil over medium heat, add the celery and the tomatoes and sauté for 2 minutes.
4. Add the potatoes and the rest of the ingredients, toss, cook everything for 6 minutes, divide the mix between plates and serve.

Nutrition: 233 calories 8.7g fat 6.4g protein

379. Bulgur, Kale and Cheese Mix

Preparation Time: 10 minutes
Cooking Time: 10 minutes
Servings: 6
Ingredients:
- 4 ounces bulgur
- 4 ounces kale
- 1 tablespoon mint
- 3 spring onions
- 1 cucumber
- A pinch of allspice
- 2 tablespoons olive oil
- Zest and juice of ½ lemon
- 4 ounces feta cheese

Directions:
1. Put bulgur in a bowl, cover with hot water, aside for 10 minutes and fluff with a fork.
2. Warmup pan with the oil over medium heat, add the onions and the allspice and cook for 3 minutes.
3. Stir in bulgur and the rest of the ingredients, cook everything for 5-6 minutes more, divide between plates and serve.

Nutrition: 200 calories 6.7g fat 4.5g protein

380. Spicy Green Beans Mix

Preparation Time: 5 minutes
Cooking Time: 15 minutes
Servings: 4
Ingredients:
- 4 teaspoons olive oil
- 1 garlic clove, minced
- ½ teaspoon hot paprika
- ¾ cup veggie stock
- 1 yellow onion, sliced
- 1-pound green beans
- ½ cup goat cheese, shredded
- 2 teaspoon balsamic vinegar

Directions:
1. Put pan with the oil over medium heat, add the garlic, stir and cook for 1 minute.
2. Add the green beans and the rest of the ingredients, toss, cook everything for 15 minutes more, divide between plates and serve.

Nutrition: 188 calories 4g fat 4.4g protein

381. Pistachio Arugula Salad

Preparation Time: 20 minutes
Cooking Time: 0 minute
Serving: 6
Ingredients:
- ¼ cup olive oil
- 6 cups kale, chopped rough
- 2 cups arugula

- ½ teaspoon smoked paprika
- 2 tablespoons lemon juice, fresh
- 1/3 cup pistachios, unsalted & shelled
- 6 tablespoons parmesan, grated

Directions:
1. Get out a large bowl and combine your oil, lemon juice, kale and smoked paprika. Massage it into the leaves for about fifteen seconds. You then need to allow it to sit for ten minutes.
2. Mix everything together before serving with grated cheese on top.

Nutrition: 150 Calories 5g Protein 12g Fat

382. Potato Salad

Preparation Time: 9 minutes
Cooking Time: 13 minutes
Serving: 6
Ingredients:
- 2 lbs. golden potatoes
- 3 tablespoons olive oil
- 3 tablespoons lemon juice, fresh
- 1 tablespoon olive brine
- ¼ teaspoon sea salt, fine
- ½ cup olives, sliced
- 1 cup celery, sliced
- 2 tablespoons oregano
- 2 tablespoons mint leaves

Directions:
1. Boil potatoes in saucepan before turning the heat down to medium-low. Cook for fifteen more minutes.
2. Get out a small bowl and whisk your oil, lemon juice, olive brine and salt together.
3. Drain your potatoes using a colander and transfer it to a serving bowl. Pour in three tablespoons of dressing over your potatoes, and mix well with oregano, and min along with the remaining dressing.

Nutrition: 175 Calories 3g Protein 7g Fat

383. Raisin Rice Pilaf

Preparation Time: 13 minutes
Cooking Time: 8 minutes
Serving: 5
Ingredients:
- 1 tablespoon olive oil
- 1 teaspoon cumin
- 1 cup onion, chopped
- ½ cup carrot, shredded
- ½ teaspoon cinnamon
- 2 cups instant brown rice
- 1 ¾ cup orange juice
- 1 cup golden raisins
- ¼ cup water
- ½ cup pistachios, shelled

- fresh chives, chopped for garnish

Directions:
1. Place a medium saucepan over medium-high heat before adding in your oil. Add n your onion, and stir often so it doesn't burn. Cook for 6 minutes then add in your cumin, cinnamon and carrot. Cook for about another minute.
2. Add in your orange juice, water and rice. Boil before covering your saucepan. Put the heat down to medium-low and then allow it to simmer for six to seven minutes.
3. Stir in your pistachios, chives and raisins. Serve warm.

Nutrition: 320 Calories 6g Protein 7g Fat

384. Lebanese Delight

Preparation Time: 7 minutes
Cooking Time: 25 minutes
Serving: 5
Ingredients:
- 1 tablespoon olive oil
- 1 cup vermicelli
- 3 cups cabbage, shredded
- 3 cups vegetable broth, low sodium
- ½ cup water
- 1 cup instant brown rice
- ¼ teaspoon sea salt, fine
- 2 cloves garlic
- ¼ teaspoon crushed red pepper
- ½ cup cilantro fresh & chopped
- lemon slices to garnish

Directions:
1. Get out a saucepan and then place it over medium-high heat. Add in your oil and once it's hot you will need to add in your pasta. Cook for three minutes or until your pasta is toasted. You will have to stir often in order to keep it from burning.
2. Ad in your cabbage, cooking for another four minutes. Continue to stir often.
3. Add in your water and rice. Season with salt, red pepper and garlic before bringing it all to a boil over high heat. Stir, and then cover. Once it's covered turn the heat down to medium-low. Allow it all to simmer for ten minutes.
4. Pull away the pan from the burner and then allow it to sit without lifting the lid for five minutes. Take the garlic cloves out and then mash them using a fork. Place them back in, and stir them into the rice. Stir in your cilantro as well and serve warm. Garnish with lemon wedges if desired.

Nutrition: 259 Calories 7g Protein 4g Fat

385. Mediterranean Sweet Potato

Preparation Time: 6 minutes
Cooking Time: 25 minutes
Serving: 4

Ingredients:
- 4 sweet potatoes
- 15 ounce can chickpeas, rinsed & drained
- ½ tablespoon olive oil
- ½ teaspoon cumin
- ½ teaspoon coriander
- ½ teaspoon cinnamon
- 1 pinch sea salt, fine
- ½ teaspoon paprika
- ¼ cup hummus
- 1 tablespoon lemon juice, fresh
- 2-3 teaspoon dill, fresh
- 3 cloves garlic, minced
- unsweetened almond milk as needed

Directions:
1. Set oven to 400, and then get out a baking sheet. Line it with foil.
2. Wash your sweet potatoes before halving them lengthwise.
3. Take your olive oil, cumin, chickpeas, coriander, sea salt and paprika on your baking sheet. Rub the sweet potatoes with olive oil, placing them face down over the mixture.
4. Roast for twenty to twenty-five minutes.
5. Mix your dill, lemon juice, hummus, garlic and a dash of almond milk.
6. Smash the insides of the sweet potato down, topping with chickpea mixture and sauce before serving.

Nutrition: 313 Calories 8.6g Protein 9g fats

386. Flavorful Braised Kale

Preparation Time: 7 minutes
Cooking Time: 32 minutes
Serving: 6
Ingredients:
- 1 lb. Kale
- 1 Cup Cherry Tomatoes, Halved
- 2 Teaspoons Olive Oil
- 4 Cloves Garlic, Sliced Thin
- ½ Cup Vegetable Stock
- ¼ Teaspoon Sea Salt, Fine
- 1 Tablespoon Lemon Juice, Fresh
- 1/8 Teaspoon Black Pepper

Directions:
1. Preheat olive oil in a frying pan using medium heat, and add in your garlic. Sauté for a minute or two until lightly golden.
2. Mix your kale and vegetable stock with your garlic, adding it to your pan.
3. Cover the pan and then turn the heat down to medium-low.
4. Allow it to cook until your kale wilts and part of your vegetable stock should be dissolved.
5. Stir in your tomatoes and cook without a lid until your kale is tender, and then remove it from heat.

6. Mix in your salt, pepper and lemon juice before serving warm.

Nutrition: 70 Calories 4g Protein 0.5g Fat

387. Bean Salad

Preparation Time: 16 minutes
Cooking Time: 0 minutes
Serving: 6
Ingredients:
- 1 can garbanzo beans, rinsed & drained
- 2 tablespoons balsamic vinegar
- ¼ cup olive oil
- 4 cloves garlic, chopped fine
- 1/3 cup parsley, fresh & chopped
- ¼ cup olive oil
- 1 red onion, diced
- 6 lettuce leaves
- ½ cup celery, chopped fine/black pepper to taste

Directions:
1. Make the vinaigrette dressing by whipping together your garlic, parsley, vinegar and pepper in a bowl.
2. Add the olive oil to this mixture and whisk before setting it aside.
3. Add in your onion and beans, and then pour your dressing on top. Toss then cover it. Chill before serving
4. Place a lettuce leaf on the plate when serving and spoon the mixture in. garnish with celery.

Nutrition: 218 Calories 7g Protein 0.1g Fat

388. Basil Tomato Skewers

Preparation Time: 14 minutes
Cooking Time: 0 minute
Serving: 2
Ingredients:
- 16 mozzarella balls, fresh & small
- 16 basil leaves, fresh
- 16 cherry tomatoes
- olive oil to drizzle
- sea salt & black pepper to taste

Directions:
1. Start by threading your basil, cheese and tomatoes together on small skewers.
2. Drizzle with oil before seasoning. Serve.

Nutrition: 46 Calories 7.6g Protein 0.9g Fat

389. Olives with Feta

Preparation Time: 5 minutes
Cooking Time: 0 minute
Serving: 4
Ingredients:
- ½ Cup Feta Cheese
- 1 Cup Kalamata Olives
- 2 Cloves Garlic, Sliced

- 2 Tablespoons Olive Oil
- 1 Lemon, Zested & Juiced
- 1 Teaspoon Rosemary, Fresh & Chopped
- Crushed Red Pepper
- Black Pepper to Taste

Directions:
1. Mix everything together and serve over crackers.

Nutrition: 71 Calories 4g Protein 2.6g Fat

390. Black Bean Medley

Preparation Time: 5 minutes
Cooking Time: 0 minute
Serving: 4
Ingredients:
- 4 plum tomatoes, chopped
- 14.5 ounces black beans, canned & drained
- ½ red onion, sliced
- ¼ cup dill, fresh & chopped
- 1 lemon, juiced
- 2 tablespoons olive oil
- ¼ cup feta cheese, crumbled
- sea salt to taste

Directions:
1. Mix everything in a bowl except for your feta and salt. Top the beans with salt and feta.

Nutrition: 121 Calories 6g Protein 5g Fat

391. Mediterranean Quiche

Preparation Time: 7 minutes
Cooking Time: 25 minutes
Serving: 6
Ingredients
- ½ cup sundried tomatoes
- 2 cloves garlic, minced
- 1 onion, diced
- 2 tablespoons butter
- 1 prepared pie crust
- boiling water
- 1 red pepper, diced
- 2 cups spinach, fresh
- ¼ cup kalamata olives
- 1 teaspoon oregano
- 1 teaspoon parsley
- 1/3 cup feta cheese, crumbled
- 4 eggs, large
- 1 ¼ cup milk
- sea salt & black pepper to taste
- 1 cup cheddar cheese, shredded & divided

Directions:
1. Add your tomatoes to boiling water and allow it to cook for five minutes before draining.
2. Chop the tomatoes before setting them to the side, and adjust the oven to 375.

3. Spread the pie crust into a nine-inch pie pan, and heat the butter and add in your garlic and onion.
4. Cook for three minutes before adding in your red pepper, and then cook for another three minutes.
5. Add in your parsley and oregano before adding in your spinach and olives. Cook for about another five minutes. Take it off heat, and then add in your feta cheese and tomatoes.
6. Spread your mixture into the prepared pie crust, and then beat the egg and milk. Season well then add in half a cup of cheese.
7. Pour this mixture over your spinach, and then bake for fifty-five minutes. It should be golden, and serve warm.

Nutrition: 417 Calories 14.5g Protein 13.3g Fat

392. Grilled Fish with Lemons

Preparation Time: 8 minutes
Cooking Time: 20 minutes
Serving: 4
Ingredients:
- 3-4 Lemons
- 1 Tablespoon Olive Oil
- Sea Salt & Black Pepper to Taste
- 4 Catfish Fillets, 4 Ounces Each
- Nonstick Cooking Spray

Directions:
1. Pat your fillets dry using a paper towel and let them come to room temperature. This may take ten minutes. Coat the cooking grate of your grill with nonstick cooking spray while it's cold. Once it's coated preheat it to 400 degrees.
2. Cut one lemon in half, setting it to the side. Slice your remaining half of the lemon into ¼ inch slices. Get out a bowl and squeeze a tablespoon of juice from your reserved half. Add your oil to the bowl, mixing well.
3. Brush your fish down with the oil and lemon mixture.
4. Place your lemon slices on the grill and then put our fillets on top. Grill with your lid closed. Turn the fish halfway through if they're more than a half an inch thick.

Nutrition: 147 Calories 22g Protein 1g Fat

393. Pesto Walnut Noodles

Preparation Time: 7 minutes
Cooking Time: 25 minutes
Serving: 4
Ingredients:
- 4 Zucchini, Made into Zoodles
- ¼ Cup Olive Oil, Divided
- ½ Teaspoon Crushed Red Pepper
- 2 Cloves Garlic, Minced & Divided
- ¼ Teaspoon Black Pepper
- ¼ Teaspoon sea Salt

- 2 Tablespoons Parmesan Cheese, Grated & Divided
- 1 Cup Basil, Fresh & Packed
- ¾ Cup Walnut Pieces, Divided

Directions:
1. Start by making your zucchini noodles by using a spiralizer to get ribbons. Combine your zoodles with a minced garlic clove and tablespoon of oil. Season with salt and pepper and crushed red pepper. Set it to the side.
2. Get out a large skillet and heat a ½ tablespoon of oil over medium-high heat. Add in half of your zoodles, cooking for five minutes. Repeat with another ½ a tablespoon of oil and your remaining zoodles.
3. Make your pesto while your zoodles cook. Put your garlic clove, a tablespoon or parmesan, basil leaves and ¼ cup of walnuts in your food processor. Season well, and drizzle the remaining two tablespoons of oil in until completely blended.
4. Add the pesto to your zoodles, topping with remaining walnuts and parmesan to serve.

Nutrition: 301 Calories 7g Protein 28g Fat

394. Tomato Tabbouleh

Preparation Time: 6 minutes
Cooking Time: 30 minutes
Serving: 4
Ingredients:
- 8 beefsteak tomatoes
- ½ cup water
- 3 tablespoons olive oil, divided
- ½ cup whole wheat couscous, uncooked
- 1 ½ cups parsley, fresh & minced
- 2 scallions chopped
- 1/3 cup mint, fresh & minced
- sea salt & black pepper to taste
- 1 lemon
- 4 teaspoons honey, raw
- 1/3 cup almonds, chopped

Directions:
1. Set oven to 400 degrees. Take your tomato and slice the top off each one before scooping the flesh out. Put the tops flesh and seeds in a mixing bowl.
2. Get out a baking dish before adding in a tablespoon of oil to grease it. Place your tomatoes in the dish, and then cover your dish with foil.
3. Now you will make your couscous while your tomatoes cook. Bring the water to a boil using a saucepan and then add the couscous in and cover. Pull it out from heat, and allow it to sit for five minutes. Fluff it with a fork.
4. Chop your tomato flesh and tops up, and then drain the excess water using a colander. Measure a cup of your chopped tomatoes and place them back in the mixing bowl. Mix with mint scallions, pepper, salt and parsley.

5. Zest lemon, and then half the lemon. Crush the lemon juice then mix well.
6. Add your tomato mix to the couscous.
7. Carefully remove your tomatoes from the oven and then divide your tabbouleh among your tomatoes. Cover the pan with foil and then put it in the oven. Cook for another eight to ten minutes.
8. Drizzle with honey and top with almonds before serving.

Nutrition: 314 Calories 8g Protein 15g Fat

395. Lemon Faro Bowl

Preparation Time: 9 minutes
Cooking Time: 25 minutes
Serving: 6
Ingredients:
- 1 ½ tablespoon olive oil
- 1 cup onion, chopped
- 2 cloves garlic, minced
- 1 carrot, shredded
- 2 cups vegetable broth, low sodium
- 1 cup pearled faro
- 2 avocados, peeled, pitted & sliced
- 1 lemon, small

Directions:
1. Situate saucepan over medium-high heat. Add in a tablespoon of oil and then throw in your onion once the oil is hot. Cook for about five minutes, stirring frequently to keep it from burning.
2. Add in your carrot and garlic. Allow it to cook for additional minutes while you continue to stir.
3. Add in your broth and faro. Boil and adjust your heat to high to help. Once it boils, lower it to medium-low and cover your saucepan. Let it simmer for twenty minutes.
4. Pour the faro into a bowl and add in your avocado and zest. Drizzle with your remaining oil and add in your lemon wedges.

Nutrition: 279 Calories 7g Protein 14g Fat

396. Vermicelli Rice

Preparation Time: 5 minutes
Cooking Time: 45 minutes
Servings: 6
Ingredients:
- 2 cups short-grain rice
- 3½ cups water, plus more for rinsing and soaking the rice
- ¼ cup olive oil
- 1 cup broken vermicelli pasta
- Salt

Directions:
1. Soak the rice under cold water until the water runs clean. Situate rice in a bowl, cover with water, and let soak for 10 minutes. Strain and putt aside. Cook the olive oil in a medium pot over medium heat.

2. Stir in the vermicelli and cook for 3 minutes.
3. Put the rice and cook for 1 minute, stirring, so the rice is well coated in the oil. Mix in the water and a pinch of salt and bring the liquid to a boil. Adjust heat and simmer for 20 minutes. Pull out from the heat and let rest for 10 minutes. Fluff with a fork and serve.

Nutrition 346 calories 9g total fat 60g carbohydrates 2g protein

397. Fava Beans with Basmati Rice

Preparation Time: 10 minutes
Cooking Time: 35 minutes
Servings: 4
Ingredients:
- ¼ cup olive oil
- 4 cups fresh fava beans, shelled
- 4½ cups water, plus more for drizzling
- 2 cups basmati rice
- 1/8 teaspoon salt
- 1/8 teaspoon freshly ground black pepper
- 2 tablespoons pine nuts, toasted
- ½ cup chopped fresh garlic chives, or fresh onion chives

Directions:
1. Fill the sauce pan with olive oil and cook over medium heat. Add the fava beans and drizzle them with a bit of water to avoid burning or sticking. Cook for 10 minutes.
2. Gently stir in the rice. Add the water, salt, and pepper. Set up the heat and boil the mixture. Adjust the heat and let it simmer for 15 minutes.
3. Pull out from the heat and let it rest for 10 minutes before serving. Spoon onto a serving platter and sprinkle with the toasted pine nuts and chives.

Nutrition 587 calories 17g total fat 2g protein

398. Buttered Fava Beans

Preparation Time: 30 minutes
Cooking Time: 15 minutes
Servings: 4
Ingredients:
- ½ cup vegetable broth
- 4 pounds fava beans, shelled
- ¼ cup fresh tarragon, divided
- 1 teaspoon chopped fresh thyme
- ¼ teaspoon freshly ground black pepper
- 1/8 teaspoon salt
- 2 tablespoons butter
- 1 garlic clove, minced
- 2 tablespoons chopped fresh parsley

Directions:
1. Boil vegetable broth in a shallow pan over medium heat. Add the fava beans, 2 tablespoons of tarragon,

the thyme, pepper, and salt. Cook until the broth is almost absorbed and the beans are tender.
2. Stir in the butter, garlic, and remaining 2 tablespoons of tarragon. Cook for 2 to 3 minutes. Sprinkle with the parsley and serve hot.

Nutrition 458 calories 9g fat 81g carbohydrates 37g protein

399. Freekeh

Preparation Time: 10 minutes
Cooking Time: 40 minutes
Servings: 4
Ingredients:
- 4 tablespoons Ghee
- 1 onion, chopped
- 3½ cups vegetable broth
- 1 teaspoon ground allspice
- 2 cups freekeh
- 2 tablespoons pine nuts, toasted

Directions:
1. Melt ghee in a heavy-bottomed saucepan over medium heat. Stir in the onion and cook for about 5 minutes, stirring constantly, until the onion is golden.
2. Pour in the vegetable broth, add the allspice, and bring to a boil. Stir in the freekeh and return the mixture to a boil. Adjust heat and simmer for 30 minutes, stir occasionally. Spoon the freekeh into a serving dish and top with the toasted pine nuts.

Nutrition 459 calories 18g fat 64g carbohydrates 10g protein

400. Fried Rice Balls with Tomato Sauce

Preparation Time: 15 minutes
Cooking Time: 20 minutes
Servings: 8
Ingredients:
- 1 cup bread crumbs
- 2 cups cooked risotto
- 2 large eggs, divided
- ¼ cup freshly grated Parmesan cheese
- 8 fresh baby mozzarella balls, or 1 (4-inch) log fresh mozzarella, cut into 8 pieces
- 2 tablespoons water
- 1 cup corn oil
- 1 cup Basic Tomato Basil Sauce, or store-bought

Directions:
1. Situate the bread crumbs into a small bowl and set aside. Incorporate the risotto, 1 egg, and the Parmesan cheese until well combined. Split the risotto mixture into 8 pieces. Situate them on a clean work surface and flatten each piece.
2. Situate 1 mozzarella ball on each flattened rice disk. Wrap the rice around the mozzarella to form a ball. Repeat until you finish all the balls. In the same medium, now-empty bowl, scourge remaining egg

and the water. Soak each prepared risotto ball into the egg wash and roll it in the bread crumbs. Set aside.

3. Cook corn oil in a skillet over high heat. Mildly lower the risotto balls into the hot oil and fry for 5 to 8 minutes. Stir them, as needed. With a slotted spoon, place the fried balls to paper towels to drain.

4. Warm up the tomato sauce in a medium saucepan over medium heat for 5 minutes, stir then serve the warm sauce alongside the rice balls.

Nutrition 255 calories 15g fat 16g carbohydrates 2g protein

401. **Spanish-Style Rice**

Preparation Time: 10 minutes
Cooking Time: 35 minutes
Servings: 4
Ingredients:
- ¼ cup olive oil
- 1 small onion, finely chopped
- 1 red bell pepper, seeded and diced
- 1½ cups white rice
- 1 teaspoon sweet paprika
- ½ teaspoon ground cumin
- ½ teaspoon ground coriander
- 1 garlic clove, minced
- 3 tablespoons tomato paste
- 3 cups vegetable broth
- 1/8 teaspoon salt

Directions:
1. Cook the olive oil in a large heavy-bottomed skillet over medium heat. Stir in the onion and red bell pepper. Cook for 5 minutes or until softened. Add the rice, paprika, cumin, and coriander and cook for 2 minutes, stirring often.
2. Add the garlic, tomato paste, vegetable broth, and salt. Stir it well and season, as needed. Allow the mixture to a boil. Lower heat and simmer for 20 minutes.
3. Set aside for 5 minutes before serving.

Nutrition 414 calories 14g fat 63g carbohydrates 2g protein

402. **Zucchini with Rice and Tzatziki**

Preparation Time: 20 minutes
Cooking Time: 35 minutes
Servings: 4
Ingredients:
- ¼ cup olive oil
- 1 onion, chopped
- 3 zucchinis, diced
- 1 cup vegetable broth
- ½ cup chopped fresh dill
- Salt
- Freshly ground black pepper
- 1 cup short-grain rice

- 2 tablespoons pine nuts
- 1 cup Tzatziki Sauce, Plain Yogurt, or store-bought

Directions:
1. Cook oil in a heavy-bottomed pot over medium heat. Stir in the onion, turn the heat to medium-low, and sauté for 5 minutes. Mix in the zucchini and cook for 2 minutes more.
2. Fill in the vegetable broth and dill and season with salt and pepper. Turn up heat to medium and bring the mixture to a boil.
3. Stir in the rice and place the mixture back to a boil. Set the heat to very low, cover the pot, and cook for 15 minutes. Pull out from the heat and set aside, for 10 minutes. Scoop the rice onto a serving platter, sprinkle with the pine nuts, and serve with tzatziki sauce.

Nutrition 414 calories 17g fat 57g carbohydrates 5g protein

403. **Cannellini Beans with Rosemary and Garlic Aioli**

Preparation Time: 10 minutes
Cooking Time: 10 minutes
Servings: 4
Ingredients:
- 4 cups cooked cannellini beans
- 4 cups water
- ½ teaspoon salt
- 3 tablespoons olive oil
- 2 tablespoons chopped fresh rosemary
- ½ cup Garlic Aioli
- ¼ teaspoon freshly ground black pepper

Directions:
1. Mix the cannellini beans, water, and salt in a medium saucepan over medium heat. Bring to a boil. Cook for 5 minutes. Drain. Cook the olive oil in a skillet over medium heat.
2. Add the beans. Stir in the rosemary and aioli. Adjust heat to medium-low and cook, stirring, just to heat through. Season with pepper and serve.

Nutrition 545 calories 36g fat 42g carbohydrates 14g protein

404. **Jeweled Rice**

Preparation Time: 15 minutes
Cooking Time: 30 minutes
Servings: 6
Ingredients:
- ½ cup olive oil, divided
- 1 onion, finely chopped
- 1 garlic clove, minced
- ½ teaspoon chopped peeled fresh ginger
- 4½ cups water
- 1 teaspoon salt, divided, plus more as needed
- 1 teaspoon ground turmeric
- 2 cups basmati rice
- 1 cup fresh sweet peas

- 2 carrots, peeled and cut into ½-inch dice
- ½ cup dried cranberries
- Grated zest of 1 orange
- 1/8 teaspoon cayenne pepper
- ¼ cup slivered almonds, toasted

Directions:
1. Warm up ¼ cup of olive oil in a large pan. Place the onion and cook for 4 minutes. Sauté in the garlic and ginger.
2. Pour in the water, ¾ teaspoon of salt, and the turmeric. Boil the mixture. Put in the rice and return the mixture to a boil. Taste the broth and season with more salt, as needed. Select the heat to low, and cook for 15 minutes. Put off the heat. Allow the rice rest on the burner, covered, for 10 minutes. Using medium sauté pan over medium-low heat, cook the remaining ¼ cup of olive oil. Mix in the peas and carrots. Cook for 5 minutes.
3. Stir in the cranberries and orange zest. Dust with the remaining salt and the cayenne. Cook for 1 to 2 minutes. Ladle the rice onto a serving platter. Garnish with the peas and carrots and drizzle with the toasted almonds.

Nutrition 470 calories 29g fat 63g carbohydrates 4g protein

405. Asparagus Risotto

Preparation Time: 15 minutes
Cooking Time: 30 minutes
Servings: 4
Ingredients:
- 5 cups vegetable broth, divided
- 3 tablespoons unsalted butter, divided
- 1 tablespoon olive oil
- 1 small onion, chopped
- 1½ cups Arborio rice
- 1-pound fresh asparagus, ends trimmed, cut into 1-inch pieces, tips separated
- ¼ cup freshly grated Parmesan cheese

Directions:
1. Boil the vegetable broth over medium heat. Set the heat to low and simmer. Mix 2 tablespoons of butter with the olive oil. Mix in the onion and cook for 2 to 3 minutes.
2. Put the rice and stir with a wooden spoon while cooking for 1 minute until the grains are well covered with butter and oil.
3. Stir in ½ cup of warm broth. Cook and continue stirring until the broth is completely absorbed. Add the asparagus stalks and another ½ cup of broth. Cook and stir occasionally Continue adding the broth, ½ cup at a time, and cooking until it is completely absorbed upon adding the next ½ cup. Stir frequently to prevent sticking. Rice should be cooked but still firm.
4. Add the asparagus tips, the remaining 1 tablespoon of butter, and the Parmesan cheese. Stir vigorously to combine. Remove from the heat, top with

additional Parmesan cheese, if desired, and serve immediately.
Nutrition 434 calories 14g fat 67g carbohydrates 6g protein

406. Vegetable Paella

Preparation Time: 25 minutes
Cooking Time: 45 minutes
Servings: 6
Ingredients:
- ¼ cup olive oil
- 1 large sweet onion
- 1 large red bell pepper
- 1 large green bell pepper
- 3 garlic cloves, finely minced
- 1 teaspoon smoked paprika
- 5 saffron threads
- 1 zucchini, cut into ½-inch cubes
- 4 large ripe tomatoes, peeled, seeded, and chopped
- 1½ cups short-grain Spanish rice
- 3 cups vegetable broth, warmed

Directions:
1. Preheat the oven to 350°F. Cook the olive oil over medium heat. Stir in the onion and red and green bell peppers and cook for 10 minutes.
2. Mix in the garlic, paprika, saffron threads, zucchini, and tomatoes. Adjust heat to medium-low and cook for 10 minutes.
3. Mix in the rice and vegetable broth. Increase the heat to boil paella. Put the heat to medium-low and cook for 15 minutes. Cover the pan with aluminum foil then situate it in the oven.
4. Bake for 10 minutes.

Nutrition 288 calories 10g fat 46g carbohydrates 3g protein

407. Eggplant and Rice Casserole

Preparation Time: 30 minutes
Cooking Time: 35 minutes
Servings: 4
Ingredients:
For the Sauce
- ½ cup olive oil
- 1 small onion, chopped
- 4 garlic cloves, mashed
- 6 ripe tomatoes, peeled and chopped
- 2 tablespoons tomato paste
- 1 teaspoon dried oregano
- ¼ teaspoon ground nutmeg
- ¼ teaspoon ground cumin

For the Casserole
- 4 (6-inch) Japanese eggplants, halved lengthwise
- 2 tablespoons olive oil
- 1 cup cooked rice
- 2 tablespoons pine nuts, toasted
- 1 cup water

Directions:

To Make the Sauce

1. Cook the olive oil in a heavy-bottomed saucepan over medium heat. Place the onion and cook for 5 minutes. Mixing the garlic, tomatoes, tomato paste, oregano, nutmeg, and cumin. Boil then down heat to low, and simmer for 10 minutes. Remove and set aside.

To Make the Casserole

2. Preheat the broiler. While the sauce simmers, rub eggplant with the olive oil and situate them on a baking sheet. Broil for about 5 minutes until golden. Remove and let cool. Turn the oven to 375°F. Spread cooled eggplant, cut-side up, in a 9-by-13-inch baking dish. Mildly spoon out some flesh to make room for the stuffing.
3. Mix half the tomato sauce, the cooked rice, and pine nuts. Stuff each eggplant half with the rice mixture. In the same bowl, mix remaining tomato sauce and water. Pour over the eggplant. Bake, covered, for 20 minutes until the eggplant is soft.

Nutrition 453 calories 39g fat 29g carbohydrates 7g protein

408. Many Vegetable Couscous

Preparation Time: 15 minutes
Cooking Time: 45 minutes
Servings: 8
Ingredients:

- ¼ cup olive oil
- 1 onion, chopped
- 4 garlic cloves, minced
- 2 jalapeño peppers, pierced with a fork in several places
- ½ teaspoon ground cumin
- ½ teaspoon ground coriander
- 1 (28-ounce) can crushed tomatoes
- 2 tablespoons tomato paste
- 1/8 teaspoon salt
- 2 bay leaves
- 11 cups water, divided
- 4 carrots
- 2 zucchinis, cut into 2-inch pieces
- 1 acorn squash, halved, seeded, and cut into 1-inch-thick slices
- 1 (15-ounce) can chickpeas, drained and rinsed
- ¼ cup chopped Preserved Lemons (optional)
- 3 cups couscous

Directions:

1. Cook the olive oil in heavy-bottom pot. Place the onion and cook for 4 minutes. Mixing the garlic, jalapeños, cumin, and coriander. Cook for 1 minute. Stir tomatoes, tomato paste, salt, bay leaves, and 8 cups of water. Bring the mixture to a boil.
2. Stir carrots, zucchini, and acorn squash and return to a boil. Decrease heat slightly, cover, and cook for about 20 minutes. Fill 2 cups of the cooking liquid and set aside. Season as needed.

3. Stir chickpeas and preserved lemons (if using). Cook for few minutes, and put off the heat.
4. In a medium pan, boil remaining 3 cups of water over high heat. Mix in the couscous, cover, and turn off the heat. Let the couscous rest for 10 minutes. Fill in with 1 cup of reserved cooking liquid. Using a fork, fluff the couscous.
5. Mound it on a large platter. Drizzle it with the remaining cooking liquid. Pull out the vegetables from the pot and spread on top. Serve.

Nutrition 455 calories 9g fat 75g carbohydrates 9g protein

409. Kushari

Preparation Time: 25 minutes
Cooking Time: 1 hour and 20 minutes
Servings: 8
Ingredients:

For the sauce

- 2 tablespoons olive oil
- 2 garlic cloves, minced
- 1 (16-ounce) can tomato sauce
- ¼ cup white vinegar
- ¼ cup Harissa, or store-bought
- 1/8 teaspoon salt

For the rice

- 1 cup olive oil
- 2 onions, thinly sliced
- 2 cups dried brown lentils
- 4 quarts plus ½ cup water, divided
- 2 cups short-grain rice
- 1 teaspoon salt
- 1-pound short elbow pasta
- 1 (15-ounce) can chickpeas, drained and rinsed

Directions:

1. To make the sauce
2. In a saucepan, cook the olive oil. Sauté the garlic. Stir in the tomato sauce, vinegar, harissa, and salt. Bring the sauce to boil. Turn down the heat to low and cook for 20 minutes or until the sauce has thickened. Remove and set aside.
3. To make the rice
4. Ready the plate with paper towels and set aside. In a large pan over medium heat, heat the olive oil. Sauté the onions, stir often, until crisp and golden. Transfer the onions to the prepared plate and set aside. Reserve 2 tablespoons of the cooking oil. Reserve the pan.
5. Over high heat, combine the lentils and 4 cups of water in a pot. Allow it boil and cook for 20 minutes. Strain and toss with the reserved 2 tablespoons of cooking oil. Set aside. Reserve the pot.
6. Place the pan you used to fry the onions over medium-high heat and add the rice, 4½ cups of water, and sprinkle salt to it. Bring to a boil. Set heat to low, and cook for 20 minutes. Turn off and set aside for 10 minutes. Bring the remaining 8 cups

of water, salted, to a boil over high heat in the same pot used to cook the lentils. Fill in the pasta and cook for 6 minutes. Drain and set aside.

7. To assemble
8. Spoon the rice onto a serving platter. Top it with the lentils, chickpeas, and pasta. Drizzle with the hot tomato sauce and sprinkle with the crispy fried onions.

Nutrition 668 calories 13g fat 113g carbohydrates 18g protein

410. Bulgur with Tomatoes and Chickpeas

Preparation Time: 10 minutes
Cooking Time: 35 minutes
Servings: 6
Ingredients:
- ½ cup olive oil
- 1 onion, chopped
- 6 tomatoes, diced, or 1 (16-ounce) can diced tomatoes
- 2 tablespoons tomato paste
- 2 cups water
- 1 tablespoon Harissa, or store-bought
- 1/8 teaspoon salt
- 2 cups coarse bulgur
- 1 (15-ounce) can chickpeas, drained and rinsed

Directions:
1. Using heavy-bottomed pot over medium heat, cook the olive oil. Sauté the onion then add the tomatoes with their juice and cook for 5 minutes.
2. Stir in the tomato paste, water, harissa, and salt. Bring to a boil.
3. Stir in the bulgur and chickpeas. Return the mixture to a boil. Put heat to low and cook for 15 minutes. Let rest for 15 minutes before serving.

Nutrition 413 calories 19g fat 55g carbohydrates 14g protein

411. Mackerel Maccheroni

Preparation Time: 10 minutes
Cooking Time: 15 minutes
Servings: 4
Ingredients
- 12oz Maccheroni
- 1 clove garlic
- 14oz Tomato sauce
- 1 sprig chopped parsley
- 2 Fresh chili peppers
- 1 teaspoon salt
- 7oz mackerel in oil
- 3 tablespoons extra virgin olive oil

Directions
1. Start by putting the water to boil in a saucepan. While the water is heating up, take a pan, pour in a

little oil and a little garlic and cook over low heat. Once the garlic is cooked, pull it out from the pan.
2. Cut open the chili pepper, remove the internal seeds and cut into thin strips.
3. Add the cooking water and the chili pepper to the same pan as before. Then, take the mackerel, and after draining the oil and separating it with a fork, put it to the pan with the other ingredients. Lightly sauté it by adding some cooking water.
4. Incorporate all the ingredients, pour in tomato puree in the pan. Mix well to even out all the ingredients and then, cook on low heat for about 3 minutes.
5. Let's move on to the pasta:
6. After the water starts boiling, add the salt and the pasta. Drain the maccheroni once they are slightly al dente, and add them to the sauce you prepared.
7. Sauté for a few moments in the sauce and after tasting, season with salt and pepper according to your liking.

Nutrition 510 Calories 15.4g Fat 70g Carbohydrates 22.9g Protein

412. Maccheroni With Cherry Tomatoes and Anchovies

Preparation Time: 10 minutes
Cooking Time: 15 minutes
Servings: 4
Ingredients
- 14oz Maccheroni Pasta
- 6 Salted anchovies
- 4oz Cherry tomatoes
- 1 clove garlic
- 3 tablespoons extra virgin olive oil
- Fresh chili peppers to taste
- 3 basil leaves
- Salt to taste

Directions
1. Start by heating water in a pot and add salt when it is boiling. Meanwhile, prepare the sauce: Take the tomatoes after having washed them and cut them into 4 pieces.
2. Now, take a non-stick pan, sprinkle in a little oil and throw in a clove of garlic. Once cooked, remove it from the pan. Add the clean anchovies to the pan, melting them in the oil.
3. When the anchovies are well dissolved, add the cut tomatoes pieces and turn the heat up to high, until they begin to soften (be careful not to let them become too soft).
4. Add the chili peppers without seeds, cut into small pieces, and season.
5. Transfer the pasta in the pot of boiling water, drain it al dente, and let it sauté in the saucepan for a few moments.

Nutrition 476 Calories 11g Fat 81.4g Carbohydrates 12.9g Protein

413. Lemon and Shrimp Risotto

Preparation Time: 10 minutes
Cooking Time: 30 minutes
Servings: 4

Ingredients

- 1 lemon
- 14oz Shelled shrimp
- 1 ¾ cups risotto Rice
- 1 white onion
- 33 fl. oz (1 liter) vegetable broth (even less is fine)
- 2 ½ tablespoons butter
- ½ glass white wine
- Salt to taste
- Black pepper to taste
- Chives to taste

Directions

1. Start by boiling the shrimps in salted water for 3-4 minutes, drain and set aside.
2. Peel and finely chop an onion, stir fry it with melted butter and once the butter has dried, toast the rice in the pan for a few minutes.
3. Deglaze the rice with half a glass of white wine, then add the juice of 1 lemon. Stir and finish cooking the rice by continuing to add a ladle of vegetable stock as needed.
4. Mix well and a few minutes before the end of cooking, add the previously cooked shrimps (keeping some of them aside for garnish) and some black pepper.
5. Once the heat is off, add a knob of butter and stir. The risotto is ready to be served. Decorate with the remaining shrimp and sprinkle with some chives.

Nutrition 510 Calories 10g Fat 82.4g Carbohydrates 20.6g Protein

414. Spaghetti with Clams

Preparation Time: 10 minutes
Cooking Time: 40 minutes
Servings: 4

Ingredients

- 11.5oz of spaghetti
- 2 pounds of clams
- 7oz of tomato sauce, or tomato pulp, for the red version of this dish
- 2 cloves of garlic
- 4 tablespoons extra virgin olive oil
- 1 glass of dry white wine
- 1 tablespoon of finely chopped parsley
- 1 chili pepper

Directions

1. Start by washing the clams: never "purge" the clams — they must only be opened through the use of heat, otherwise their precious internal liquid is lost along with any sand. Wash the clams quickly using a colander placed in a salad bowl: this will filter out the sand on the shells.
2. Then immediately put the drained clams in a saucepan with a lid on high heat. Turn them over occasionally, and when they are almost all open take them off the heat. The clams that remain closed are dead and must be eliminated. Remove the mollusks from the open ones, leaving some of them whole to decorate the dishes. Strain the liquid left at the bottom of the pan, and set aside.
3. Take a large pan and pour a little oil in it. Heat a whole pepper and one or two cloves of crushed garlic on very low heat until the cloves become yellowish. Add the clams and season with dry white wine.
4. Now, add the clam liquid strained previously and a some finely chopped parsley.
5. Strain and immediately toss the spaghetti al dente in the pan, after having cooked them in plenty of salted water. Stir well until the spaghetti absorb all the liquid from the clams. If you did not use a chili pepper, complete with a light sprinkle of white or black pepper.

Nutrition 167 Calories 8g Fat 18.63g Carbohydrates 5g Protein

415. Greek Fish Soup

Preparation Time: 10 minutes
Cooking Time: 60 minutes
Servings: 4

Ingredients

- Hake or other white fish
- 4 Potatoes
- 4 Spring onions
- 2 Carrots
- 2 stalks of Celery
- 2 Tomatoes
- 4 tablespoons Extra virgin olive oil
- 2 Eggs
- 1 Lemon
- 1 cup Rice
- Salt to taste

Directions

1. Choose a fish not exceeding 2.2pounds in weight, remove its scales, gills and intestines and wash it well. Salt it and set aside.
2. Wash the potatoes, carrots and onions and put them in the saucepan whole with enough water to soak them and then bring to a boil.
3. Add in the celery still tied in bunches so it does not disperse while cooking, cut the tomatoes into four parts and add these too, together with oil and salt.
4. When the vegetables are almost cooked, add more water and the fish. Boil for 20 minutes then get rid of it from the broth together with the vegetables.
5. Place the fish in a serving dish by adorning it with the vegetables and strain the broth. Put the broth

back on the heat, diluting it with a little water. Once it boils, put in the rice and season with salt. When the rice is cooked, pull out the saucepan from the heat.

6. Prepare the avgolemono sauce:
7. Whisk the eggs well and slowly drizzle the lemon juice. Put some broth in a ladle and slowly pour it into the eggs, mixing constantly.
8. Finally, add the obtained sauce to the soup and mix well.

Nutrition 263 Calories 17.1g Fat 18.6g Carbohydrates 9g Protein

416. Venere Rice with Shrimp

Preparation Time: 10 minutes
Cooking Time: 55 minutes
Servings: 3
Ingredients
- 1 ½ cups of black Venere rice (better if parboiled)
- 5 teaspoons extra virgin olive oil
- 10.5oz shrimp
- 10.5oz zucchini
- 1 Lemon (juice and rind)
- Table Salt to taste
- Black pepper to taste
- 1 clove garlic
- Tabasco to taste

Directions
1. Let's start with the rice:
2. After filling a pot with plenty of water and bringing it to a boil, pour in the rice, add salt and cook for the necessary time (check the cooking instructions on the package).
3. Meanwhile, grate the zucchini with grater with large holes. In a pan, cook olive oil with the peeled garlic clove, add the grated zucchini, salt and pepper, and cook for 5 minutes, then, remove the garlic clove and set the vegetables aside.
4. Now clean the shrimp:
5. Remove the shell, cut the tail and divide them in half lengthwise, remove the intestine (the dark thread in their back). Situate the cleaned shrimps in a bowl and season with olive oil; give it some extra flavor by adding lemon zest, salt and pepper and by adding a few drops of Tabasco if you so choose.
6. Heat up the shrimps in a hot pan for a couple of minutes. Once cooked, set aside.
7. Once the Venere rice is ready, strain it in a bowl, add the zucchini mix and stir.

Nutrition 293 Calories 5g Fat 52g Carbohydrates 10g Protein

417. Pennette with Salmon and Vodka

Preparation Time: 10 minutes
Cooking Time: 18 minutes

Servings: 4
Ingredients
- 14oz Pennette Rigate
- 7oz Smoked salmon
- 1.2oz Shallot
  - fl. oz(40ml) Vodka
- 5 oz cherry tomatoes
- 7 oz fresh liquid cream (I recommend the vegetable one for a lighter dish)
- Chives to taste
- 3 tablespoons extra virgin olive oil
- Salt to taste
- Black pepper to taste
- Basil to taste (for garnish)

Directions
1. Wash and cut the tomatoes and the chives. After having peeled the shallot, chop it with a knife, put it in a saucepan and let it marinate in extra virgin olive oil for a few moments.
2. Meanwhile, cut the salmon into strips and sauté it together with the oil and shallot.
3. Blend everything with the vodka, being careful as there could be a flare (if a flame should rise, don't worry, it will lower as soon as the alcohol has evaporated completely). Add the chopped tomatoes and add a pinch of salt and, if you like, some pepper. Finally, add the cream and chopped chives.
4. While the sauce continues cooking, prepare the pasta. Once the water boils, pour in the Pennette and let them cook until al dente.
5. Strain the pasta, and pour the Pennette into the sauce, letting them cook for a few moments so as allow them to absorb all the flavor. If you like, garnish with a basil leaf.

Nutrition 620 Calories 21.9g Fat 81.7g Carbohydrates 24g Protein

418. Seafood Carbonara

Preparation Time: 15 minutes
Cooking Time: 50 minutes
Servings: 3
Ingredients
- 11.5oz Spaghetti
- 3.5oz Tuna
- 3.5oz Swordfish
- 3.5oz Salmon
- 6 Yolks
- 4 tablespoons Parmesan cheese (Parmigiano Reggiano)
- 2 fl. oz (60ml) White wine
- 1 clove garlic
- Extra virgin olive oil to taste
- Table Salt to taste
- Black pepper to taste

Directions
1. Prepare a boiling water in a pot and add a little salt.

2. Meanwhile, pour 6 egg yolks in a bowl and add the grated parmesan, pepper and salt. Beat with a whisk, and dilute with a little cooking water from the pot.
3. Remove any bones from the salmon, the scales from the swordfish, and proceed by dicing the tuna, salmon and swordfish.
4. Once it boils, toss in the pasta and cook it slightly al dente.
5. Meanwhile, heat a little oil in a large pan, add the whole peeled garlic clove. When hot, throw in the fish cubes and sauté over high heat for about 1 minute. Remove the garlic and add the white wine.
6. Once the alcohol evaporates, take out the fish cubes and lower the heat. As soon as the spaghetti are ready, add them to the pan and sauté for about a minute, stirring constantly and adding the cooking water, as needed.
7. Pour in the egg yolk mixture and the fish cubes. Mix well. Serve.

Nutrition 375 Calories 17g Fat 41.40g Carbohydrates 14g Protein

419. Garganelli with Zucchini Pesto and Shrimp

Preparation Time: 10 minutes
Cook time: 30 minutes
Servings: 4
Ingredients
- 14 oz egg-based Garganelli
For the zucchini pesto:
- 7oz Zucchini
- 1 cup Pine nuts
- 8 tablespoons (0.35oz) Basil
- 1 teaspoon of table Salt
- 9 tablespoons extra virgin olive oil
- 2 tablespoons Parmesan cheese to be grated
- 1oz of Pecorino to be grated
For the sautéed shrimp:
- 8.8oz shrimp
- 1 clove garlic
- 7 teaspoons extra virgin olive oil
- Pinch of Salt
Directions
1. Start by preparing the pesto:
2. After washing the zucchini, grate them, place them in a colander (to allow them to lose some excess liquid), and lightly salt them. Put the pine nuts, zucchini and basil leaves in the blender. Add the grated Parmesan, the pecorino and the extra virgin olive oil.
3. Blend everything until the mixture is creamy, stir in a pinch of salt and set aside.
4. Switch to the shrimp:
5. First of all, pull out the intestine by cutting the shrimp's back with a knife along its entire length

and, with the tip of the knife, remove the black thread inside.
6. Cook the clove of garlic in a non-stick pan with extra virgin olive oil. When its browned, remove the garlic and add the shrimps. Sauté them for about 5 minutes over medium heat, until you see a crispy crust form on the outside.
7. Then, boil a pot of water with sprinkle of salt and cook the Garganelli. Set a couple of ladles of cooking water aside, and drain the pasta al dente.
8. Put the Garganelli in the pan where you cooked the shrimp. Cook together for a minute, add a ladle of cooking water and finally, add the zucchini pesto.
9. Mix everything well to combine the pasta with the sauce.

Nutrition 776 Calories 46g Fat 68g Carbohydrates 22.5g Protein

420. Salmon Risotto

Preparation Time: 10 minutes
Cooking Time: 30 minutes
Serving: 4
Ingredients
- 1 ¾ cup (12.3 oz) of Rice
- 8.8oz Salmon steaks
- 1 Leek
- Extra virgin olive oil to taste
- 1 clove of garlic
- ½ glass white wine
- 3 ½ tablespoons grated Grana Padano
- salt to taste
- Black pepper to taste
- 17 fl. oz (500ml) Fish broth
- 1 cup butter
Directions
1. Start by cleaning the salmon and cutting it into small pieces. Cook 1 tablespoon of oil in a pan with a whole garlic clove and brown the salmon for 2/3 minutes, add salt and set the salmon aside, removing the garlic.
2. Now, start preparing the risotto:
3. Cut the leek into very small pieces and let it simmer in a pan over a low heat with two tablespoons of oil. Mix in the rice and cook it for a few seconds over medium-high heat, stirring with a wooden spoon.
4. Fill in the white wine and continue cooking, stirring occasionally, trying not to let the rice stick to the pan, and add the stock (vegetable or fish) gradually.
5. Halfway through cooking, add the salmon, butter, and a pinch of salt if necessary. When the rice is well cooked, remove from heat. Combine with a couple of tablespoons of grated Grana Padano and serve.

Nutrition 521 Calories 13g Fat 82g Carbohydrates 19g Protein

421. Pasta with Cherry Tomatoes and Anchovies

Preparation Time: 15 minutes
Cooking Time: 35 minutes
Serving: 4

Ingredients

- 10.5oz Spaghetti
- 1.3-pound Cherry tomatoes
- 9oz Anchovies (pre-cleaned)
- 2 tablespoons Capers
- 1 clove of garlic
- 1 Small red onion
- Parsley to taste
- Extra virgin olive oil to taste
- Table salt to taste
- Black pepper to taste
- Black olives to taste

Directions

1. Cut the garlic clove, obtaining thin slices.
2. Cut the cherry tomatoes in 2. Peel the onion and slice it thinly.
3. Put a little oil with the sliced garlic and onions in a saucepan. Heat everything over medium heat for 5 minutes; stir occasionally.
4. Once everything has been well flavored, add the cherry tomatoes and a pinch of salt and pepper. Cook for 15 minutes. In the meantime, situate a pot with water on the stove and as soon as it boils, add the salt and the pasta.
5. Once the sauce is almost ready, mix in the anchovies and cook for a couple of minutes. Stir gently.
6. Turn off the heat, chop the parsley and place it in the pan.
7. When its cooked, strain the pasta and stir in directly to the sauce. Turn the heat back on again for a few seconds.

Nutrition 446 Calories 10g Fat 66.1g Carbohydrates 22.8g Protein

422. Broccoli and Sausage Orecchiette

Preparation Time: 10 minutes
Cooking Time: 32 minutes
Serving: 4

Ingredients

- 11.5oz Orecchiette
- 10.5 Broccoli
- 10.5oz Sausage
- fl. oz(40ml) White wine
- 1 clove of garlic
- 2 sprigs of thyme
- 7 teaspoons extra virgin olive oil
- Black pepper to taste
- Table salt to taste

Directions

1. Boil the pot with full of water and salt. Remove the broccoli florets from the stalk and cut them in half or in 4 parts if they are too big; then, situate them into the boiling water and covering the pot, cook for 6-7 minutes.
2. Meanwhile, finely chop thyme and set aside. Pull the gut from the sausage and with the help of a fork crush it gently.
3. Fry the garlic clove with a little olive oil and add the sausage. After a few seconds, add the thyme and a little white wine.
4. Without tossing out the cooking water, remove the cooked broccoli with the help of a slotted spoon and add them to the meat a little at a time. Cook everything for 3-4 minutes. Remove the garlic and add a pinch of black pepper.
5. Allow the water where you cooked the broccoli to reach a boil, then toss in the pasta and let it cook. Once the pasta is cooked, strain it with a slotted spoon, transferring it directly to the broccoli and sausage sauce. Then, mix well, adding black pepper and sautéing everything in the pan for a couple of minutes.

Nutrition 683 Calories 36g Fat 69.6g Carbohydrates 20g Protein

423. Radicchio and Smoked Bacon Risotto

Preparation Time: 10 minutes
Cooking Time: 30 minutes
Serving: 3

Ingredients

- 1 ½ cup of Rice
- 14oz Radicchio
- 5.3oz Smoked bacon
- 34 fl. oz (1l) Vegetable broth
- fl. oz(100ml) Red wine
- 7 teaspoons extra virgin olive oil
- 1.7oz Shallots
- Table salt to taste
- Black pepper to taste
- 3 sprigs of thyme

Directions

1. Let's begin with the preparation of the vegetable broth.
2. Start with the radicchio: cut it in half and remove the central part (the white part). Cut it into strips, rinse well and set it aside. Cut the smoked bacon into tiny strips as well.
3. Finely chop the shallot and situate it in a pan with a little oil. Let it simmer over medium heat, adding a ladle of broth, then, add the bacon and let it brown.
4. After about 2 minutes, add the rice and toast it, stirring often. At this point, pour the red wine over high heat.

5. Once all the alcohol has evaporated, continue cooking adding a ladle of broth at a time. Let the previous one dry before adding another, until fully cooked. Add salt and black pepper (it's up to how much you decide to add).
6. At the end of cooking, add the strips of radicchio. Mix them well until they are blended with the rice, but without cooking them. Add the chopped thyme.

Nutrition 482 Calories 17.5g Fat 68.1g Carbohydrates 13g Protein

424. **Pasta ala Genovese**

Preparation Time: 10 minutes
Cooking Time: 25 minutes
Serving: 3
Ingredients
- 11.5oz of Ziti
- 1 pound of Beef
- pounds golden onions
- 2oz Celery
- 2oz Carrots
- 1 tuft of parsley
- fl. oz(100ml) White wine
- Extra virgin olive oil to taste
- Table salt to taste
- Black pepper to taste
- Parmesan to taste

Directions
1. Peeling and finely chopping the onions and carrots. Then, wash and finely chop the celery (do not throw away the leaves, which must also be chopped and set aside). Next, switch to the meat, clean it of any excess fat and cut it into 5/6 large pieces. Finally, tie the celery leaves and parsley sprig with kitchen twine to create a fragrant bunch.
2. Fill plenty of oil in a large pan. Add the onions, celery, and carrots (which you had previously set aside) and let them cook for a couple of minutes.
3. Then, add the pieces of meat, a pinch of salt and the fragrant bunch. Stir and cook for a few minutes. Next, lower the heat and cover with a lid.
4. Cook for at least 3 hours (do not add water or broth because the onions will release all the liquid needed to prevent the bottom of the pan from drying). Occasionally, check on everything and stir.
5. After 3 hours of cooking, remove the bunch of herbs, increase the heat slightly, add a part of the wine and stir.
6. Cook the meat without a lid for about an hour, stirring often and adding the wine when the bottom of the pan dries.
7. At this point, take a piece of meat, cut it into slices on a cutting board and set aside. Chop the ziti and cook them in boiling salted water.
8. Once cooked, drain it and place it back in the pot. Dash a few tablespoons of cooking water and stir.

Place on a plate and add a little sauce and crumbled meat (the one set aside in step
9. Add pepper and grated Parmesan to taste.

Nutrition 450 Calories 8g Fat80g Carbohydrates 14.5g Protein

425. **Cauliflower Pasta from Naples**

Preparation Time: 15 minutes
Cooking Time: 35 minutes
Servings: 3
Ingredients
- 10.5 oz Pasta
- 1 cauliflower
- fl. oz (100 ml) of tomato puree
- 1 clove of garlic
- 1 chili pepper
- 3 tablespoons extra virgin olive oil (or teaspoons)
- Salt to taste
- Pepper to taste

Directions
1. Clean the cauliflower well: remove the outer leaves and the stalk. Cut it into small florets.
2. Peel the garlic clove, chop it and brown it in a saucepan with the oil and the chili pepper.
3. Add the tomato puree and cauliflower florets and let them brown for a few minutes over medium heat, then cover with a few ladles of water and cook for 15-20 minutes or at least until the cauliflower begins to become creamy.
4. If you see that the bottom of the pan is too dry, add as much water as needed so that the mixture remains liquid.
5. At this point, cover the cauliflower with hot water and, once it comes to a boil, add in the pasta.
6. Season with salt and pepper.

Nutrition 458 Calories 18g Fat 65g Carbohydrates 9g Protein

426. **Pasta e Fagioli with Orange and Fennel**

Preparation Time: 10 minutes
Cooking Time: 30 minutes
Servings: 5
Ingredients
- Extra-virgin olive oil – 1 tbsp. plus extra for serving
- Pancetta – 2 ounces, chopped fine
- Onion – 1, chopped fine
- Fennel – 1 bulb, stalks discarded, bulb halved, cored, and chopped fine
- Celery – 1 rib, minced
- Garlic – 2 cloves, minced
- Anchovy fillets – 3, rinsed and minced
- Minced fresh oregano – 1 tbsp.
- Grated orange zest – 2 tsp.

- Fennel seeds – ½ tsp.
- Red pepper flakes – ¼ tsp.
- Diced tomatoes – 1 (28-ounce) can
- Parmesan cheese – 1 rind, plus more for serving
- Cannellini beans – 1 (7-ounce) cans, rinsed
- Chicken broth – 2 ½ cups
- Water – 2 ½ cups
- Salt and pepper
- Orzo – 1 cup
- Minced fresh parsley – ¼ cup

Directions:
1. Cook oil in a Dutch oven over medium heat. Add pancetta. Stir-fry for 3 to 5 minutes or until beginning to brown. Stir in celery, fennel, and onion and stir-fry until softened (about 5 to 7 minutes).
2. Stir in pepper flakes, fennel seeds, orange zest, oregano, anchovies, and garlic. Cook for 1 minute. Stir in tomatoes and their juice. Stir in Parmesan rind and beans.
3. Simmer and cook for 10 minutes. Stir in water, broth, and 1 tsp. salt. Let it boil on high heat. Stir in pasta and cook until al dente.
4. Remove from heat and discard parmesan rind.
5. Sprinkle parsley and season with salt and pepper to taste. Pour some olive oil and topped with grated Parmesan. Serve.

Nutrition 502 Calories 8.8g Fat 72.2g Carbohydrates 34.9g Protein

427. Spaghetti al Limone

Preparation Time: 10 minutes
Cooking Time: 15 minutes
Servings: 6
Ingredients
- Extra-virgin olive oil – ½ cup
- Grated lemon zest – 2 tsp.
- Lemon juice – 1/3 cup
- Garlic – 1 clove, minced to pate
- Salt and pepper
- Parmesan cheese – 2 ounces, grated
- Spaghetti – 1 pound
- Shredded fresh basil – 6 tbsp.

Directions:
1. In a bowl, whisk garlic, oil, lemon zest, juice, ½ tsp. salt and ¼ tsp. pepper. Stir in the Parmesan and mix until creamy.
2. Meanwhile, cook the pasta according to package directions. Drain and reserve ½ cup cooking water. Add the oil mixture and basil to the pasta and toss to combine. Season well and stir in the cooking water as needed. Serve.

Nutrition 398 Calories 20.7g Fat 42.5g Carbohydrates 11.9g Protein

428. Spiced Vegetable Couscous

Preparation Time: 10 minutes
Cooking Time: 20 minutes
Servings: 6
Ingredients
- Cauliflower – 1 head, cut into 1 –inch florets
- Extra-virgin olive oil – 6 tbsp. plus extra for serving
- Salt and pepper
- Couscous – 1 ½ cups
- Zucchini – 1, cut into ½ inch pieces
- Red bell pepper – 1, stemmed, seeded, and cut into ½ inch pieces
- Garlic – 4 cloves, minced
- Ras el hanout – 2 tsp.
- Grated lemon zest -1 tsp. plus lemon wedges for serving
- Chicken broth – 1 ¾ cups
- Minced fresh marjoram – 1 tbsp.

Directions:
1. In a skillet, heat 2 tbsp. oil over medium heat. Add cauliflowers, ¾ tsp. salt, and ½ tsp. pepper. Mix. Cook until the florets turn brown and the edges are just translucent.
2. Remove the lid and cook, stirring for 10 minutes, or until the florets turn golden brown. Transfer to a bowl and clean the skillet. Heat 2 tbsp. oil in the skillet.
3. Add the couscous. Cook and continue stirring for 3 to 5 minutes, or until grains are just beginning to brown. Transfer to a bowl and clean the skillet. Heat the remaining 3 tbsp. oil in the skillet and add bell pepper, zucchini, and ½ tsp. salt. Cook for 8 minutes.
4. Stir in lemon zest, ras el hanout, and garlic. Cook until fragrant (about 30 seconds). Place in the broth and simmer. Stir in the couscous. Pull out from the heat, and set aside until tender.
5. Add marjoram and cauliflower; then gently fluff with a fork to incorporate. Drizzle with extra oil and season well. Serve with lemon wedges.

Nutrition 787 Calories 18.3g Fat 129.6g Carbohydrates 24.5g Protein

429. Spiced Baked Rice with Fennel

Preparation Time: 10 minutes
Cooking Time: 45 minutes
Servings: 8
Ingredients
- Sweet potatoes – 1 ½ pounds, peeled and cut into 1-inch pieces
- Extra-virgin olive oil – ¼ cup
- Salt and pepper
- Fennel – 1 bulb, chopped fine
- Small onion – 1, chopped fine

- Long-grain white rice – 1 ½ cups, rinsed
- Garlic – 4 cloves, minced
- Ras el hanout – 2 tsp.
- Chicken broth – 2 ¾ cups
- Large pitted brine-cured green olives – ¾ cup, halved
- Minced fresh cilantro – 2 tbsp.
- Lime wedges

Directions:
1. Situate the oven rack to the middle and preheat oven to 400F. Toss the potatoes with ½ tsp. salt and 2 tbsp. oil.
2. Situate potatoes in a single layer in a rimmed baking sheet and roast for 25 to 30 minutes, or until tender. Stir the potatoes halfway through roasting.
3. Pull out the potatoes and lower the oven temperature to 350F. In a Dutch oven, heat the remaining 2 tbsp. oil over medium heat.
4. Add onion and fennel; next, cook for 5 to 7 minutes, or until softened. Stir in ras el hanout, garlic, and rice. Stir-fry for 3 minutes.
5. Stir in the olives and broth and let sit for 10 minutes. Add the potatoes to the rice and fluff gently with a fork to combine. Season with salt and pepper to taste. Drizzle with cilantro and serve with lime wedges.

Nutrition 207 Calories 8.9g Fat 29.4g Carbohydrates 3.9g Protein

430. Moroccan-Style Couscous with Chickpeas

Preparation Time:5 minutes
Cooking Time: 18 minutes
Servings: 6
Ingredients
- Extra-virgin olive oil – ¼ cup, extra for serving
- Couscous – 1 ½ cups
- Peeled and chopped fine carrots – 2
- Chopped fine onion – 1
- Salt and pepper
- Garlic – 3 cloves, minced
- Ground coriander – 1 tsp.
- Ground ginger - tsp.
- Ground anise seed – ¼ tsp.
- Chicken broth – 1 ¾ cups
- Chickpeas - 1 (15-ounce) can, rinsed
- Frozen peas – 1 ½ cups
- Chopped fresh parsley or cilantro – ½ cup
- Lemon wedges

Directions:
1. Heat 2 tbsp. oil in a skillet over medium heat. Mix in the couscous and cook for 3 to 5 minutes, or until just beginning to brown. Transfer to a bowl and clean the skillet.
2. Heat remaining 2 tbsp. oil in the skillet and add the onion, carrots, and 1 tsp. salt. Cook for 5 to 7

minutes. Stir in anise, ginger, coriander, and garlic. Cook until fragrant (about 30 seconds).
3. Combine the chickpeas and broth and bring to simmer. Stir in the couscous and peas. Cover and remove from the heat. Set aside until the couscous is tender.
4. Add the parsley to the couscous and lint with a fork to combine. Dash with extra oil and season well. Serve with lemon wedges.

Nutrition 649 Calories 14.2g Fat 102.8g Carbohydrates 30.1g Protein

431. Vegetarian Paella with Green Beans and Chickpeas

Preparation Time: 10 minutes
Cooking Time: 35 minutes
Servings: 4
Ingredients
- Pinch of saffron
- Vegetable broth – 3 cups
- Olive oil – 1 tbsp.
- Yellow onion – 1 large, diced
- Garlic – 4 cloves, sliced
- Red bell pepper – 1, diced
- Crushed tomatoes – ¾ cup, fresh or canned
- Tomato paste – 2 tbsp.
- Hot paprika – 1 ½ tsp.
- Salt – 1 tsp.
- Freshly ground black pepper – ½ tsp.
- Green beans – 1 ½ cups, trimmed and halved
- Chickpeas – 1 (15-ounce) can, drained and rinsed
- Short-grain white rice – 1 cup
- Lemon – 1, cut into wedges

Directions:
1. Mix the saffron threads with 3 tbsp. warm water in a small bowl. In a saucepan, simmer the water over medium heat. Reduce the heat and allow to simmer.
2. Cook the oil in a skillet over medium heat. Mix in the onion and stir-fry for 5 minutes. Add the bell pepper and garlic and stir-fry for 7 minutes or until pepper is softened. Stir in the saffron-water mixture, salt, pepper, paprika, tomato paste, and tomatoes.
3. Add the rice, chickpeas, and green beans. Stir in the warm broth and bring to a boil. Lower the heat and simmer uncovered for 20 minutes.
4. Serve hot, garnished with lemon wedges.

Nutrition 709 Calories 12g Fat 121g Carbohydrates 33g Protein

432. Garlic Prawns with Tomatoes and Basil

Preparation Time: 10 minutes
Cooking Time: 10 minutes
Servings: 4

Ingredients

- Olive oil – 2 tbsp.
- Prawns – 1 ¼ pounds, peeled and deveined
- Garlic – 3 cloves, minced
- Crushed red pepper flakes – 1/8 tsp.
- Dry white wine – ¾ cup
- Grape tomatoes – 1 ½ cups
- Finely chopped fresh basil – ¼ cup, plus more for garnish
- Salt – ¾ tsp.
- Ground black pepper – ½ tsp.

Directions:

1. In a skillet, cook oil over medium-high heat. Stir in prawns and cook for 1 minute. Transfer to a plate.
2. Place the red pepper flakes, and garlic to the oil in the pan and cook, stirring, for 30 seconds. Stir in the wine and cook until it's reduced by about half.
3. Add the tomatoes and stir-fry until tomatoes begin to break down (about 3 to 4 minutes). Stir in the reserved shrimp, salt, pepper, and basil. Cook for 1 to 2 minutes more.
4. Serve garnished with the remaining basil.

Nutrition 282 Calories 10g Fat 7g Carbohydrates 33g Protein

433. Shrimp Paella

Preparation Time: 10 minutes
Cooking Time: 25 minutes
Servings: 4
Ingredients

- Olive oil – 2 tbsp.
- Medium onion – 1, diced
- Red bell pepper – 1, diced
- Garlic – 3 cloves, minced
- Pinch of saffron
- Hot paprika – ¼ tsp.
- Salt – 1 tsp.
- Freshly ground black pepper – ½ tsp.
- Chicken broth – 3 cups, divided
- Short-grain white rice - 1 cup
- Peeled and deveined large shrimp – 1 pound
- Frozen peas – 1 cup, thawed

Directions:

1. Heat olive oil in a skillet. Fill in the onion and bell pepper and stir-fry for 6 minutes, or until softened. Add the salt, pepper, paprika, saffron, and garlic and mix. Stir in 2 ½ cups of broth and rice.
2. Allow the mixture to boil, then simmer until the rice is cooked, about 12 minutes. Lay the shrimp and peas over the rice and add the remaining ½ cup broth.
3. Situate the lid back on the skillet and cook until all shrimp are just cooked through (about 5 minutes). Serve.

Nutrition 409 Calories 10g Fat 51g Carbohydrates 25g Protein

434. Lentil Salad with Olives, Mint, and Feta

Preparation Time: 1 hour
Cooking Time: 1 hour
Servings: 6
Ingredients

- Salt and pepper
- French lentils – 1 cup, picked over and rinsed
- Garlic – 5 cloves, lightly crushed and peeled
- Bay leaf – 1
- Extra-virgin olive oil – 5 tbsp.
- White wine vinegar – 3 tbsp.
- Pitted Kalamata olives – ½ cup, chopped
- Chopped fresh mint – ½ cup
- Shallot – 1 large, minced
- Feta cheese – 1 ounce, crumbled

Directions:

1. Add 4 cups warm water and 1 tsp. salt in a bowl. Add the lentils and soak at room temperature for 1 hour. Drain well.
2. Situate oven rack to the middle and heat the oven to 325F. Combine the lentils, 4 cups water, garlic, bay leaf, and ½ tsp. salt in a saucepan. Cover and situate the saucepan to the oven, and cook for 40 to 60 minutes, or until the lentils are tender.
3. Drain the lentils well, discarding garlic and bay leaf. In a large bowl, scourge oil and vinegar together. Add the shallot, mint, olives, and lentils and toss to combine.
4. Season with salt and pepper to taste. Place nicely in the serving dish and garnish with feta. Serve.

Nutrition 249 Calories 14.3g Fat 22.1g Carbohydrates 9.5g Protein

435. Chickpeas with Garlic and Parsley

Preparation Time: 5 minutes
Cooking Time: 20 minutes
Servings: 6
Ingredients

- Extra-virgin olive oil – ¼ cup
- Garlic – 4 cloves, sliced thin
- Red pepper flakes – 1/8 tsp.
- Onion – 1, chopped
- Salt and pepper
- Chickpeas – 2 (15-ounce) cans, rinsed
- Chicken broth – 1 cup
- Minced fresh parsley – 2 tbsp.
- Lemon juice – 2 tsp.

Directions:

1. In a skillet, add 3 tbsp. oil and cook garlic, and pepper flakes for 3 minutes. Stir in onion and ¼ tsp. salt and cook for 5 to 7 minutes.

2. Mix in the chickpeas and broth and bring to a simmer. Lower heat and simmer on low heat for 7 minutes, covered.
3. Uncover and set the heat to high and cook for 3 minutes, or until all liquid has evaporated. Set aside and mix in the lemon juice and parsley.
4. Season with salt and pepper to taste. Drizzle with 1 tbsp. oil and serve.

Nutrition 611 Calories 17.6g Fat 89.5g Carbohydrates 28.7g Protein

436. <u>Stewed Chickpeas with Eggplant and Tomatoes</u>

Preparation Time: 10 minutes
Cooking Time: 1 hour
Servings: 6
Ingredients
- Extra-virgin olive oil – ¼ cup
- Onions – 2, chopped
- Green bell pepper – 1, chopped fine
- Salt and pepper
- Garlic – 3 cloves, minced
- Minced fresh oregano – 1 tbsp.
- Bay leaves – 2
- Eggplant – 1 pound, cut into 1-inch pieces
- Whole peeled tomatoes – 1, can, drained with juice reserved, chopped
- Chickpeas – 2(15-ounce) cans, drained with 1 cup liquid reserved

Directions:
1. Situate the oven rack on the lower-middle part and heat the oven to 400F. Heat oil in the Dutch oven. Add bell pepper, onions, ½ tsp. salt, and ¼ tsp. pepper. Stir-fry for 5 minutes.
2. Stir in 1 tsp. oregano, garlic, and bay leaves and cook for 30 seconds. Stir in tomatoes, eggplant, reserved juice, chickpeas, and reserved liquid and bring to a boil. Transfer the pot to oven and cook, uncovered, for 45 to 60 minutes. Stirring twice.
3. Discard the bay leaves. Stir in the remaining 2 tsp. oregano and season with salt and pepper. Serve.

Nutrition 642 Calories 17.3g Fat 93.8g Carbohydrates 29.3g Protein

437. <u>Greek Lemon Rice</u>

Preparation Time: 20 minutes
Cooking Time: 45 minutes
Servings: 6
Ingredients
- Long grain rice – 2 cups, uncooked (soaked in cold water for 20 minutes, then drained)
- Extra virgin olive oil – 3 tbsp.
- Yellow onion – 1 medium, chopped
- Garlic - 1 clove, minced
- Orzo pasta – ½ cup

- Juice of 2 lemons, plus zest of 1 lemon
- Low sodium broth – 2 cups
- Pinch salt
- Chopped parsley – 1 large handful
- Dill weed – 1 tsp.

Directions:
1. In a saucepan, heat 3 tbsp. extra virgin olive oil. Add the onions and stir-fry for 3 to 4 minutes. Add the orzo pasta and garlic and toss to mix.
2. Then toss in the rice to coat. Add the broth and lemon juice. Boil and lower the heat. Close and cook for 20 minutes.
3. Remove from the heat. Cover and set aside for 10 minutes. Uncover and stir in the lemon zest, dill weed, and parsley. Serve.

Nutrition 145 Calories 6.9g Fat 18.3g Carbohydrates 3.3g Protein

438. <u>Garlic-Herb Rice</u>

Preparation Time: 10 minutes
Cooking Time: 30 minutes
Servings: 4
Ingredients
- Extra-virgin olive oil – ½ cup, divided
- Large garlic cloves – 5, minced
- Brown jasmine rice – 2 cups
- Water – 4 cups
- Sea salt – 1 tsp.
- Black pepper – 1 tsp.
- Chopped fresh chives – 3 tbsp.
- Chopped fresh parsley – 2 tbsp.
- Chopped fresh basil – 1 tbsp.

Directions:
1. In a saucepan, add ¼-cup olive oil, garlic, and rice. Stir and heat over medium heat. Stir in the water, sea salt, and black pepper. Next, mix again.
2. Boil and lower the heat. Simmer, uncovered, stirring occasionally.
3. When the water is almost absorbed, mix the remaining ¼-cup olive oil, along with the basil, parsley, and chives.
4. Stir until the herbs are incorporated and all the water is absorbed.

Nutrition 304 Calories 25.8g Fat 19.3g Carb 2g Protein

439. <u>Mediterranean Rice Salad</u>

Preparation Time: 10 minutes
Cooking Time: 25 minutes
Servings: 4
Ingredients
- Extra virgin olive oil – ½ cup, divided
- Long-grain brown rice – 1 cup
- Water – 2 cups
- Fresh lemon juice – ¼ cup
- Garlic clove – 1, minced

- Minced fresh rosemary – 1 tsp.
- Minced fresh mint – 1 tsp.
- Belgian endives – 3, chopped
- Red bell pepper – 1 medium, chopped
- Hothouse cucumber – 1, chopped
- Chopped whole green onion – ½ cup
- Chopped Kalamata olives – ½ cup
- Red pepper flakes – ¼ tsp.
- Crumbled feta cheese – ¾ cup
- Sea salt and black pepper

Directions:
1. Heat ¼-cup olive oil, rice, and a pinch of salt in a saucepan over low heat. Stir to coat the rice. Add the water and let simmer until the water is absorbed. Stirring occasionally. Fill in the rice into a big bowl and cool.
2. Scourge remaining ¼ cup olive oil, red pepper flakes, olives, green onion, cucumber, bell pepper, endives, mint, rosemary, garlic, and lemon juice.
3. Place the rice to the mixture and toss to combine. Gently mix in the feta cheese.
4. Taste and adjust the seasoning. Serve.

Nutrition 415 Calories 34g Fat 28.3g Carbohydrates 7g Protein

440. **Fresh Bean and Tuna Salad**

Preparation Time: 5 minutes
Cooking Time: 20 minutes
Servings: 6
Ingredients
- Shelled (shucked) fresh beans – 2 cups
- Bay leaves – 2
- Extra-virgin olive oil – 3 tbsp.
- Red wine vinegar – 1 tbsp.
- Salt and black pepper
- Best-quality tuna - 1 (6-ounce) can, packed in olive oil
- Salted capers – 1 tbsp. soaked and dried
- Finely minced flat-leaf parsley – 2 tbsp.
- Red onion – 1, sliced

Directions:
1. Boil lightly salted water in a pot. Add the beans and bay leaves; next, cook for 15 to 20 minutes, or until the beans are tender but still firm. Drain, discard aromatics, and transfer to a bowl.
2. Immediately dress the beans with vinegar and oil. Add the salt and black pepper. Mix well and adjust seasoning. Drain the tuna and flake the tuna flesh into the bean salad. Add the parsley and capers. Toss to mix and scatter the red onion slices over the top. Serve.

Nutrition 85 Calories 7.1g Fat 4.7g Carbohydrates 1.8g Protein

441. **Delicious Chicken Pasta**

Preparation Time: 10 minutes
Cooking Time: 17 minutes
Serving: 4
Ingredients:
- 3 chicken breasts, skinless, boneless, cut into pieces
- 9 oz whole-grain pasta
- 1/2 cup olives, sliced
- 1/2 cup sun-dried tomatoes
- 1 tbsp roasted red peppers, chopped
- 14 oz can tomato, diced
- 2 cups marinara sauce
- 1 cup chicken broth
- Pepper
- Salt

Directions:
1. Stir in all ingredients except whole-grain pasta into the instant pot.
2. Close the lid and cook on high for 12 minutes.
3. Once done, allow to release pressure naturally. Remove lid.
4. Add pasta and stir well. Seal pot again and select manual and set timer for 5 minutes.
5. When finished, release the pressure for 5 minutes then release remaining using quick release. Remove lid. Stir well and serve.

Nutrition 615 Calories 15.4g Fat 71g Carbohydrates 48g Protein

442. **Flavors Taco Rice Bowl**

Preparation Time: 10 minutes
Cooking Time: 14 minutes
Serving: 8
Ingredients:
- 1 lb. ground beef
- 8 oz cheddar cheese, shredded
- 14 oz can red beans
- 2 oz taco seasoning
- 16 oz salsa
- 2 cups of water
- 2 cups brown rice
- Pepper
- Salt

Directions:
1. Set instant pot on sauté mode.
2. Add meat to the pot and sauté until brown.
3. Add water, beans, rice, taco seasoning, pepper, and salt and stir well.
4. Top with salsa. Close then cook on high for 14 minutes.
5. Once done, release pressure using quick release. Remove lid.
6. Sprinkle cheddar cheese and stir until cheese is melted.
7. Serve and enjoy.

Nutrition 464 Calories 15.3g Fat 48.9g Carbohydrates 32.2g Protein

443. Flavorful Mac & Cheese

Preparation Time: 10 minutes
Cooking Time: 10 minutes
Serving: 6
Ingredients:
- 16 oz whole-grain elbow pasta
- 4 cups of water
- 1 cup can tomato, diced
- 1 tsp garlic, chopped
- 2 tbsp olive oil
- 1/4 cup green onions, chopped
- 1/2 cup parmesan cheese, grated
- 1/2 cup mozzarella cheese, grated
- 1 cup cheddar cheese, grated
- 1/4 cup passata
- 1 cup unsweetened almond milk
- 1 cup marinated artichoke, diced
- 1/2 cup sun-dried tomatoes, sliced
- 1/2 cup olives, sliced
- 1 tsp salt

Directions:
1. Add pasta, water, tomatoes, garlic, oil, and salt into the instant pot and stir well. Cover lid and cook on high.
2. Once done, release pressure for few minutes then release remaining using quick discharge. Remove lid.
3. Set pot on sauté mode. Add green onion, parmesan cheese, mozzarella cheese, cheddar cheese, passata, almond milk, artichoke, sun-dried tomatoes, and olive. Mix well.
4. Stir well and cook until cheese is melted.
5. Serve and enjoy.

Nutrition 519 Calories 17.1g Fat 66.5g Carbohydrates 25g Protein

444. Cucumber Olive Rice

Preparation Time: 10 minutes
Cooking Time: 10 minutes
Serving: 8
Ingredients:
- 2 cups rice, rinsed
- 1/2 cup olives, pitted
- 1 cup cucumber, chopped
- 1 tbsp red wine vinegar
- 1 tsp lemon zest, grated
- 1 tbsp fresh lemon juice
- 2 tbsp olive oil
- 2 cups vegetable broth
- 1/2 tsp dried oregano
- 1 red bell pepper, chopped

- 1/2 cup onion, chopped
- 1 tbsp olive oil
- Pepper
- Salt

Directions:
1. Add oil into the inner pot of instant pot and select the pot on sauté mode. Add onion and sauté for 3 minutes. Add bell pepper and oregano and sauté for 1 minute.
2. Add rice and broth and stir well. Secure the lid and cook at high for 6 minutes. Once done, allow pressure release for 10 minutes then release remaining using quick release. Remove lid.
3. Add remaining ingredients and stir everything well to mix. Serve immediately and enjoy it.

Nutrition 229 Calories 5.1g Fat 40.2g Carbohydrates 4.9g Protein

445. Flavors Herb Risotto

Preparation Time: 10 minutes
Cooking Time: 15 minutes
Serving: 4
Ingredients:
- 2 cups of rice
- 2 tbsp parmesan cheese, grated
- oz heavy cream
- 1 tbsp fresh oregano, chopped
- 1 tbsp fresh basil, chopped
- 1/2 tbsp sage, chopped
- 1 onion, chopped
- 2 tbsp olive oil
- 1 tsp garlic, minced
- 4 cups vegetable stock
- Pepper
- Salt

Directions:
1. Add oil into the inner vessel of instant pot and click the pot on sauté mode. Add garlic and onion the inner pan of instant pot and press the pot on sauté mode. Add garlic and onion and sauté for 2-3 minutes.
2. Add remaining ingredients except for parmesan cheese and heavy cream and stir well. Seal lid and cook on high for 12 minutes.
3. Once done, discharge the pressure for 10 minutes then release remaining using quick release. Remove lid. Stir in cream and cheese and serve.

Nutrition 514 Calories 17.6g Fat 79.4g Carbohydrates 8.8g Protein

446. Delicious Pasta Primavera

Preparation Time: 10 minutes
Cooking Time: 4 minutes
Serving: 4
Ingredients:

- 8 oz whole wheat penne pasta
- 1 tbsp fresh lemon juice
- 2 tbsp fresh parsley, chopped
- 1/4 cup almonds slivered
- 1/4 cup parmesan cheese, grated
- 14 oz can tomato, diced
- 1/2 cup prunes
- 1/2 cup zucchini, chopped
- 1/2 cup asparagus
- 1/2 cup carrots, chopped
- 1/2 cup broccoli, chopped
- 1 3/4 cups vegetable stock
- Pepper
- Salt

Directions:
1. Add stock, pars, tomatoes, prunes, zucchini, asparagus, carrots, and broccoli into the instant pot and stir well. Close and cook on high for 4 minutes. Once done, release pressure using quick release. Take out lid. Stir remaining ingredients well and serve.

Nutrition 303 Calories 2.6g Fat 63.5g Carbohydrates 12.8g Protein

447. **Roasted Pepper Pasta**

Preparation Time: 10 minutes
Cooking Time: 13 minutes
Serving: 6
Ingredients:
- 1 lb. whole wheat penne pasta
- 1 tbsp Italian seasoning
- 4 cups vegetable broth
- 1 tbsp garlic, minced
- 1/2 onion, chopped
- 14 oz jar roasted red peppers
- 1 cup feta cheese, crumbled
- 1 tbsp olive oil
- Pepper
- Salt

Directions:
1. Add roasted pepper into the blender and blend until smooth. Add oil into the inner pot of instant pot and set the jug on sauté mode. Add garlic and onion the inner cup of instant pot and set the pot on sauté. Add garlic and onion and sauté for 2-3 minutes.
2. Add blended roasted pepper and sauté for 2 minutes.
3. Add remaining ingredients except feta cheese and stir well. Seal it tight and cook on high for 8 minutes. When done, release pressure naturally for 5 minutes then releases the remaining using quick release. Remove lid. Top with feta cheese and serve.

Nutrition 459 Calories 10.6g Fat 68.1g Carbohydrates 21.3g Protein

448. **Cheese Basil Tomato Rice**

Preparation Time: 10 minutes
Cooking Time: 26 minutes
Serving: 8
Ingredients:
- 1 1/2 cups brown rice
- 1 cup parmesan cheese, grated
- 1/4 cup fresh basil, chopped
- 2 cups grape tomatoes, halved
- 8 oz can tomato sauce
- 1 3/4 cup vegetable broth
- 1 tbsp garlic, minced
- 1/2 cup onion, diced
- 1 tbsp olive oil
- Pepper
- Salt

Directions:
1. Add oil into the inner basin of instant pot and select the pot on sauté. Put garlic and onion the inner vessel of instant pot and set it on sauté manner. Mix in garlic and onion and sauté for 4 minutes. Add rice, tomato sauce, broth, pepper, and salt and stir well.
2. Seal it and cook on high for 22 minutes.
3. Once done, let it release pressure for 10 minutes then release remaining using quick release. Remove cap. Stir in remaining ingredients and mix. Serve and enjoy.

Nutrition 208 Calories 5.6g Fat 32.1g Carbohydrates 8.3g Protein

449. **Mac & Cheese**

Preparation Time: 10 minutes
Cooking Time: 4 minutes
Serving: 8
Ingredients:
- 1 lb. whole grain pasta
- 1/2 cup parmesan cheese, grated
- 4 cups cheddar cheese, shredded
- 1 cup milk
- 1/4 tsp garlic powder
- 1/2 tsp ground mustard
- 2 tbsp olive oil
- 4 cups of water
- Pepper
- Salt

Directions:
1. Add pasta, garlic powder, mustard, oil, water, pepper, and salt into the instant pot. Seal tight and cook on high for 4 minutes. When done, release pressure using quick release. Open lid. Put remaining ingredients and stir well and serve.

Nutrition 509 Calories 25.7g Fat 43.8g Carbohydrates 27.3g Protein

450. Tuna Pasta

Preparation Time: 10 minutes
Cooking Time: 8 minutes
Serving: 6

Ingredients:

- 10 oz can tuna, drained
- 15 oz whole wheat rotini pasta
- 4 oz mozzarella cheese, cubed
- 1/2 cup parmesan cheese, grated
- 1 tsp dried basil
- 14 oz can tomato
- 4 cups vegetable broth
- 1 tbsp garlic, minced
- 8 oz mushrooms, sliced
- 2 zucchinis, sliced
- 1 onion, chopped
- 2 tbsp olive oil
- Pepper
- Salt

Directions:

1. Pour oil into the inner pot of instant pot and press the pot on sauté. Add mushrooms, zucchini, and onion and sauté until onion is softened. Add garlic and sauté for a minute.
2. Add pasta, basil, tuna, tomatoes, and broth and stir well. Secure and cook on high for 4 minutes. When completed, release pressure for 5 minutes then releases the remaining using quick release. Remove lid. Add remaining ingredients and stir well and serve.

Nutrition 346 Calories 11.9g Fat 31.3g Carbohydrates 6.3g Protein

451. Avocado and Turkey Mix Panini

Preparation Time: 5 minutes
Cooking Time: 8 minutes
Servings: 2

Ingredients:

- 2 red peppers, roasted and sliced into strips
- ¼ lb. thinly sliced mesquite smoked turkey breast
- 1 cup whole fresh spinach leaves, divided
- 2 slices provolone cheese
- 1 tbsp olive oil, divided
- 2 ciabatta rolls
- ¼ cup mayonnaise
- ½ ripe avocado

Directions:

1. In a bowl, mash thoroughly together mayonnaise and avocado. Then preheat Panini press.
2. Chop the bread rolls in half and spread olive oil on the insides of the bread. Then fill it with filling, layering them as you go: provolone, turkey breast, roasted red pepper, spinach leaves and spread

avocado mixture and cover with the other bread slice.
3. Place sandwich in the Panini press and grill for 5 to 8 minutes until cheese has melted and bread is crisped and ridged.

Nutrition 546 Calories 34.8g Fat31.9g Carbohydrates27.8g Protein

452. Cucumber, Chicken and Mango Wrap

Preparation Time: 5 minutes
Cooking Time: 20 minutes
Serving: 1

Ingredients:

- ½ of a medium cucumber cut lengthwise
- ½ of ripe mango
- 1 tbsp salad dressing of choice
- 1 whole wheat tortilla wrap
- 1-inch thick slice of chicken breast around 6-inch in length
- 2 tbsp oil for frying
- 2 tbsp whole wheat flour
- 2 to 4 lettuce leaves
- Salt and pepper to taste

Directions:

1. Slice a chicken breast into 1-inch strips and just cook a total of 6-inch strips. That would be like two strips of chicken. Store remaining chicken for future use.
2. Season chicken with pepper and salt. Dredge in whole wheat flour.
3. On medium fire, place a small and nonstick fry pan and heat oil. Once oil is hot, add chicken strips and fry until golden brown around 5 minutes per side.
4. While chicken is cooking, place tortilla wraps in oven and cook for 3 to 5 minutes. Then set aside and transfer in a plate.
5. Slice cucumber lengthwise, use only ½ of it and store remaining cucumber. Peel cucumber cut into quarter and remove pith. Place the two slices of cucumber on the tortilla wrap, 1-inch away from the edge.
6. Slice mango and store the other half with seed. Peel the mango without seed, slice into strips and place on top of the cucumber on the tortilla wrap.
7. Once chicken is cooked, place chicken beside the cucumber in a line.
8. Add cucumber leaf, drizzle with salad dressing of choice.
9. Roll the tortilla wrap, serve and enjoy.

Nutrition 434 Calories 10g Fat65g Carbohydrates21g Protein

453. Fattoush –Middle East Bread

Preparation Time: 10 minutes
Cooking Time: 15 minutes

Servings: 6
Ingredients:
- 2 loaves pita bread
- 1 tbsp Extra Virgin Olive Oil
- 1/2 tsp sumac, more for later
- Salt and pepper
- 1 heart of Romaine lettuce
- 1 English cucumber
- 5 Roma tomatoes
- 5 green onions
- 5 radishes
- 2 cups chopped fresh parsley leaves
- 1 cup chopped fresh mint leaves

Dressing Ingredients:
- 1 1/2 lime, juice of
- 1/3 cup Extra Virgin Olive Oil
- Salt and pepper
- 1 tsp ground sumac
- 1/4 tsp ground cinnamon
- scant 1/4 tsp ground allspice

Directions:
1. For 5 minutes toast the pita bread in the toaster oven. And then break the pita bread into pieces.
2. In a large pan on medium fire, heat 3 tbsp of olive oil in for 3 minutes. Add pita bread and fry until browned, around 4 minutes while tossing around.
3. Add salt, pepper and 1/2 tsp of sumac. Set aside the pita chips from the heat and put in paper towels to drain.
4. Toss well the chopped lettuce, cucumber, tomatoes, green onions, sliced radish, mint leaves and parsley in a large salad bowl.
5. To make the lime vinaigrette, whisk together all ingredients in a small bowl.
6. Stir in the dressing onto the salad and toss well. Mix in the pita bread.
7. Serve and enjoy.

Nutrition 192 Calories 13.8g Fats16.1g Carbohydrates3.9g Protein

454. Garlic & Tomato Gluten Free Focaccia

Preparation Time: 5 minutes
Cooking Time: 20 minutes
Serving: 8
Ingredients:
- 1 egg
- ½ tsp lemon juice
- 1 tbsp honey
- 4 tbsp olive oil
- A pinch of sugar
- 1 ¼ cup warm water
- 1 tbsp active dry yeast
- 2 tsp rosemary, chopped
- 2 tsp thyme, chopped

- 2 tsp basil, chopped
- 2 cloves garlic, minced
- 1 ¼ tsp sea salt
- 2 tsp xanthan gum
- ½ cup millet flour
- 1 cup potato starch, not flour
- 1 cup sorghum flour
- Gluten free cornmeal for dusting

Directions:
1. For 5 minutes, turn on the oven and then turn it off, while keeping oven door closed.
2. Combine warm water and pinch of sugar. Add yeast and swirl gently. Leave for 7 minutes.
3. In a large mixing bowl, whisk well herbs, garlic, salt, xanthan gum, starch, and flours. Once yeast is done proofing, pour into bowl of flours. Whisk in egg, lemon juice, honey, and olive oil.
4. Mix thoroughly and place in a well-greased square pan, dusted with cornmeal. Top with fresh garlic, more herbs, and sliced tomatoes. Place in the warmed oven and let it rise for half an hour.
5. Turn on oven to 375oF and after preheating time it for 20 minutes. Focaccia is done once tops are lightly browned. Remove from oven and pan immediately and let it cool. Best served when warm.

Nutrition 251 Calories 9g Fat38.4g Carbohydrates5.4g Protein

455. Grilled Burgers with Mushrooms

Preparation Time: 15 minutes
Cooking Time: 10 minutes
Serving: 4
Ingredients:
- 2 Bibb lettuce, halved
- 4 slices red onion
- 4 slices tomato
- 4 whole wheat buns, toasted
- 2 tbsp olive oil
- ¼ tsp cayenne pepper, optional
- 1 garlic clove, minced
- 1 tbsp sugar
- ½ cup water
- 1/3 cup balsamic vinegar
- 4 large Portobello mushroom caps, around 5-inches in diameter

Directions:
1. Remove stems from mushrooms and clean with a damp cloth. Transfer into a baking dish with gill-side up.
2. In a bowl, mix thoroughly olive oil, cayenne pepper, garlic, sugar, water and vinegar. Pour over mushrooms and marinate mushrooms in the ref for at least an hour.
3. Once the one hour is nearly up, preheat grill to medium high fire and grease grill grate.

4. Grill mushrooms for five minutes per side or until tender. Baste mushrooms with marinade so it doesn't dry up.
5. To assemble, place ½ of bread bun on a plate, top with a slice of onion, mushroom, tomato and one lettuce leaf. Cover with the other top half of the bun. Repeat process with remaining ingredients, serve and enjoy.

Nutrition 244 Calories 9.3g Fat32g Carbohydrates8.1g Protein

456. Mediterranean Baba Ghanoush

Preparation Time: 10 minutes
Cooking Time: 25 minutes
Serving: 4
Ingredients:
- 1 bulb garlic
- 1 red bell pepper, halved and seeded
- 1 tbsp chopped fresh basil
- 1 tbsp olive oil
- 1 tsp black pepper
- 2 eggplants, sliced lengthwise
- 2 rounds of flatbread or pita
- Juice of 1 lemon

Directions:
1. Brush grill grate with cooking spray and preheat grill to medium high.
2. Slice tops of garlic bulb and wrap in foil. Place in the cooler portion of the grill and roast for at least 20 minutes. Place bell pepper and eggplant slices on the hottest part of grill. Grill for both sides.
3. Once bulbs are done, peel off skins of roasted garlic and place peeled garlic into food processor. Add olive oil, pepper, basil, lemon juice, grilled red bell pepper and grilled eggplant. Puree and pour into a bowl.
4. Grill bread at least 30 seconds per side to warm. Serve bread with the pureed dip and enjoy.

Nutrition 231.6 Calories 4.8g Fat36.3g Carbohydrates6.3g Protein

457. Multi Grain & Gluten Free Dinner Rolls

Preparation Time: 10 minutes
Cooking Time: 20 minutes
Serving: 8
Ingredients:
- ½ tsp apple cider vinegar
- 3 tbsp olive oil
- 2 eggs
- 1 tsp baking powder
- 1 tsp salt
- 2 tsp xanthan gum
- ½ cup tapioca starch

- ¼ cup brown teff flour
- ¼ cup flax meal
- ¼ cup amaranth flour
- ¼ cup sorghum flour
- ¾ cup brown rice flour

Directions:
1. Mix well water and honey in a small bowl and add yeast. Leave it for exactly 10 minutes.
2. Combine the following with a paddle mixer: baking powder, salt, xanthan gum, flax meal, sorghum flour, teff flour, tapioca starch, amaranth flour, and brown rice flour.
3. In a medium bowl, whisk well vinegar, olive oil, and eggs.
4. Into bowl of dry ingredients pour in vinegar and yeast mixture and mix well.
5. Grease a 12-muffin tin with cooking spray. Transfer dough evenly into 12 muffin tins and leave it for an hour to rise.
6. Then preheat oven to 375oF and bake dinner rolls until tops are golden brown, around 20 minutes.
7. Remove dinner rolls from oven and muffin tins immediately and let it cool.
8. Best served when warm.

Nutrition 207 Calories 8.3g Fat27.8g Carbohydrates4.6g Protein

458. Quinoa Pizza Muffins

Preparation Time: 15 minutes
Cooking Time: 30 minutes
Serving: 4
Ingredients:
- 1 cup uncooked quinoa
- 2 large eggs
- ½ medium onion, diced
- 1 cup diced bell pepper
- 1 cup shredded mozzarella cheese
- 1 tbsp dried basil
- 1 tbsp dried oregano
- 2 tsp garlic powder
- 1/8 tsp salt
- 1 tsp crushed red peppers
- ½ cup roasted red pepper, chopped*
- Pizza Sauce, about 1-2 cups

Directions:
1. Preheat oven to 350oF. Cook quinoa according to directions. Combine all ingredients (except sauce) into bowl. Mix all ingredients well.
2. Scoop quinoa pizza mixture into muffin tin evenly. Makes 12 muffins. Bake for 30 minutes until muffins turn golden in color and the edges are getting crispy.
3. Top with 1 or 2 tbsp pizza sauce and enjoy!

Nutrition 303 Calories 6.1g Fat41.3g Carbohydrates21g Protein

459. Rosemary-Walnut Loaf Bread

Preparation Time: 5 minutes
Cooking Time: 45 minutes
Serving: 8
Ingredients:

- ½ cup chopped walnuts
- 4 tbsp fresh, chopped rosemary
- 1 1/3 cups lukewarm carbonated water
- 1 tbsp honey
- ½ cup extra virgin olive oil
- 1 tsp apple cider vinegar
- 3 eggs
- 5 tsp instant dry yeast granules
- 1 tsp salt
- 1 tbsp xanthan gum
- ¼ cup buttermilk powder
- 1 cup white rice flour
- 1 cup tapioca starch
- 1 cup arrowroot starch
- 1 ¼ cups all-purpose Bob's Red Mill gluten-free flour mix

Directions:

1. In a large mixing bowl, whisk well eggs. Add 1 cup warm water, honey, olive oil, and vinegar.
2. While beating continuously, incorporate the rest of the ingredients except for rosemary and walnuts.
3. Continue beating. If dough is too firm, stir a bit of warm water. Dough should be shaggy and thick.
4. Then add rosemary and walnuts continue kneading until evenly distributed.
5. Cover bowl of dough with a clean towel, place in a warm spot, and let it rise for 30 minutes.
6. Fifteen minutes into rising time, preheat oven to 400oF.
7. Generously grease with olive oil a 2-quart Dutch oven and preheat inside oven without the lid.
8. Once dough is done rising, remove pot from oven, and place dough inside. With a wet spatula, spread top of dough evenly in pot.
9. Brush tops of bread with 2 tbsp of olive oil, cover Dutch oven and bake for 35 to 45 minutes. Once bread is done, remove from oven. And gently remove bread from pot. Allow bread to cool at least ten minutes before slicing. Serve and enjoy.

Nutrition 424 Calories 19g Fat56.8g Carbohydrates7g Protein

460. Tasty Crabby Panini

Preparation Time: 5 minutes
Cooking Time: 10 minutes
Servings: 4
Ingredients:

- 1 tbsp Olive oil
- French bread split and sliced diagonally
- 1 lb. shrimp crab
- ½ cup celery
- ¼ cup green onion chopped
- 1 tsp Worcestershire sauce
- 1 tsp lemon juice
- 1 tbsp Dijon mustard
- ½ cup light mayonnaise

Directions:

1. In a medium bowl mix the following thoroughly: celery, onion, Worcestershire, lemon juice, mustard and mayonnaise. Season with pepper and salt. Then gently add in the almonds and crabs.
2. Spread olive oil on sliced sides of bread and smear with crab mixture before covering with another bread slice.
3. Grill sandwich in a Panini press until bread is crisped and ridged.

Nutrition 248 Calories 10.9g Fat12g Carbohydrates24.5g Protein

461. Perfect Pizza

Preparation Time: 35 minutes
Cooking Time: 15 minutes
Servings: 10
Ingredients:
For the Pizza Dough:

- 2-tsp honey
- 1/4-oz. active dry yeast
- 11/4-cups warm water (about 120 °F)
- 2-tbsp olive oil
- 1-tsp sea salt
- 3-cups whole grain flour + 1/4-cup, as needed for rolling

For the Pizza Topping:

- 1-cup pesto sauce
- 1-cup artichoke hearts
- 1-cup wilted spinach leaves
- 1-cup sun-dried tomato
- 1/2-cup Kalamata olives
- 4-oz. feta cheese
- 4-oz. mixed cheese of equal parts low-fat mozzarella, asiago, and provolone Olive oil

Optional Topping Add-Ons:

- Bell pepper
- Chicken breast, strips Fresh basil
- Pine nuts

Directions:
For the Pizza Dough:

1. Preheat your oven to 350 °F.
2. Stir the honey and yeast with the warm water in your food processor with a dough attachment. Blend the mixture until fully combined. Let the mixture to rest for 5 minutes to ensure the activity of the yeast through the appearance of bubbles on the surface.
3. Pour in the olive oil. Add the salt, and blend for half a minute. Add gradually 3 cups of flour, about

half a cup at a time, blending for a couple of minutes between each addition.

4. Let your processor knead the mixture for 10 minutes until smooth and elastic, sprinkling it with flour whenever necessary to prevent the dough from sticking to the processor bowl's surfaces.
5. Take the dough from the bowl. Let it stand for 15 minutes, covered with a moist, warm towel.
6. Roll out the dough to a half-inch thickness, dusting it with flour as needed. Poke holes indiscriminately on the dough using a fork to prevent crust bubbling.
7. Place the perforated, rolled dough on a pizza stone or baking sheet. Bake for 5 minutes.

For the Pizza Topping:

8. Lightly brush the baked pizza shell with olive oil.
9. Pour over the pesto sauce and spread thoroughly over the pizza shell's surface, leaving out a half-inch space around its edge as the crust.
10. Top the pizza with artichoke hearts, wilted spinach leaves, sun-dried tomatoes, and olives. (Top with more add-ons, as desired.) Cover the top with the cheese.
11. Put the pizza directly to the oven rack. Bake for 10 minutes until the cheese is bubbling and melting from the center to the end. Let the pizza chill for 5 minutes before slicing.

Nutrition 242.8 Calories 15.1g Fats 15.7g Carbohydrates 14.1g Protein

462. Margherita Model

Preparation Time: 15 minutes
Cooking Time: 15 minutes
Serving: 10
Ingredients:
- 1-batch pizza shell
- 2-tbsp olive oil
- 1/2-cup crushed tomatoes
- 3-Roma tomatoes, sliced 1/4-inch thick
- 1/2-cup fresh basil leaves, thinly sliced
- 6-oz. block mozzarella, cut into 1/4-inch slices, blot-dry with a paper towel
- 1/2-tsp sea salt

Directions:
1. Preheat your oven to 450 °F.
2. Lightly brush the pizza shell with olive oil. Thoroughly spread the crushed tomatoes over the pizza shell, leaving a half-inch space around its edge as the crust.
3. Top the pizza with the Roma tomato slices, basil leaves, and mozzarella slices. Sprinkle salt over the pizza.
4. Transfer the pizza directly on the oven rack. Bake until the cheese melts from the center to the crust. Set aside before slicing.

Nutrition 251 Calories 8g Fats 34g Carbohydrates 9g Protein

463. Portable Picnic

Preparation Time: 5 minutes
Cooking Time: 0 minute
Serving: 1
Ingredients:
- 1-slice of whole-wheat bread, cut into bite-size pieces
- 10-pcs cherry tomatoes
- 1/4-oz. aged cheese, sliced
- 6-pcs oil-cured olives

Directions:
1. Pack each of the ingredients in a portable container to serve you while snacking on the go.

Nutrition 197 Calories 9g Fats 22g Carbohydrates 7g Protein

464. Stuffed-Frittata

Preparation Time: 10 minutes
Cooking Time: 15 minutes
Serving: 4
Ingredients:
- 8-pcs eggs
- 1/4-tsp red pepper, crushed
- 1/4-tsp salt
- 1-tbsp olive oil
- 1-pc small zucchini, sliced thinly lengthwise
- 1/2-cup red or yellow cherry tomatoes, halved
- 1/3 -cup walnuts, coarsely chopped
- 2-oz. bite-sized fresh mozzarella balls (bocconcini)

Directions:
1. Preheat your broiler. Meanwhile, whisk together the eggs, crushed red pepper, and salt in a medium-sized bowl. Set aside.
2. In a 10-inch broiler-proof skillet placed over medium-high heat, heat the olive oil. Spread the slices of zucchini in an even layer on the bottom of the skillet. Cook for 3 minutes, turning them once, halfway through.
3. Top the zucchini layer with cherry tomatoes. Fill the egg mixture over vegetables in skillet. Top with walnuts and mozzarella balls.
4. Switch to medium heat. Cook until the sides begin to set. By using a spatula, lift the frittata for the uncooked portions of the egg mixture to flow underneath.
5. Place the skillet on the broiler. Broil the frittata 4-inches from the heat for 5 minutes until the top is set. To serve, cut the frittata into wedges.

Nutritional 284 Calories 14g Fats 4g Carbohydrates 17g Protein

465. Greek Flatbread

Preparation Time: 5 minutes
Cooking Time: 10 minutes
Servings: 4

Ingredients:
- 2 whole wheat pitas
- 2 tablespoons olive oil, divided
- 2 garlic cloves, minced
- ¼ teaspoon salt
- ½ cup canned artichoke hearts, sliced
- ¼ cup Kalamata olives
- ¼ cup shredded Parmesan
- ¼ cup crumbled feta
- Chopped fresh parsley, for garnish (optional)

Directions:
1. Preheat the air fryer to 380°F. Brush each pita with 1 tablespoon olive oil, then sprinkle the minced garlic and salt over the top.
2. Distribute the artichoke hearts, olives, and cheeses evenly between the two pitas, and place both into the air fryer to bake for 10 minutes. Remove the pitas and cut them into 4 pieces each before serving. Sprinkle parsley over the top, if desired.

Nutrition 243 Calories 15g Fat 10g Carbohydrates 7g Protein

466. Banana Sour Cream Bread

Preparation Time: 10 minutes
Cooking Time: 1 hour 10 minutes
Servings: 32

Ingredients:
- White sugar (.25 cup)
- Cinnamon (1 tsp.+ 2 tsp.)
- Butter (.75)
- White sugar (3 cups)
- Eggs (3)
- Very ripe bananas, mashed (6)
- Sour cream (16 oz. container)
- Vanilla extract (2 tsp.)
- Salt (.5 tsp.)
- Baking soda (3 tsp.)
- All-purpose flour (4.5 cups)

Directions:
1. Set the oven to reach 300°Fahrenheit. Grease the loaf pans.
2. Sift the sugar and one teaspoon of the cinnamon. Dust the pan with the mixture.
3. Cream the butter with the rest of the sugar. Mash the bananas with the eggs, cinnamon, vanilla, sour cream, salt, baking soda, and the flour. Toss in the nuts last.
4. Dump the mixture into the pans. Bake it for one hour. Serve

Nutrition 263 Calories 10.4g Fat 9g Carbohydrates 3.7g Protein

467. Homemade Pita Bread

Preparation Time: 15 minutes
Cooking Time: 5 hours (includes rising times)

Servings: 7
Ingredients:
- Dried yeast (.25 oz.)
- Sugar (.5 tsp.)
- Bread flour /mixture of all-purpose & whole wheat (2.5 cups + more for dusting)
- Salt (.5 tsp.)
- Water (.25 cup or as needed)
- Oil as needed

Directions:
1. Dissolve the yeast and sugar in ¼ of a cup lukewarm water in a small mixing container. Wait for about 15 minutes (ready when it's frothy).
2. In another container, sift the flour and salt. Make a hole in the center and add the yeast mixture (+) one cup of water. Knead the dough.
3. Situate it onto a lightly floured surface and knead.
4. Put a drop of oil into the bottom of a large bowl and roll the dough in it to cover the surface.
5. Place a dampened tea towel over the container of dough. Seal the bowl with a damp cloth and situate it in a warm spot for at least two hours or overnight.
6. Punch the dough down and knead the bread and divide it into small balls. Flatten the balls into thick oval discs.
7. Dust a tea towel using the flour and place the oval discs on top, leaving enough room to expand between them. Powder with flour and lay another clean cloth on top. Allow it rise for extra one to two hours.
8. Set the oven at 425° Fahrenheit. Situate several baking sheets in the oven to heat briefly. Lightly grease the warmed baking sheets with oil and place the oval bread discs on them.
9. Sprinkle the ovals lightly with water, and bake until they are lightly browned or for six to eight minutes.
10. Serve them while they are warm. Arrange the flatbread on a wire rack and wrap them in a clean, dry cloth to keep soft for later.

Nutrition 210 Calories 4g Fat 6g Carbohydrates 6g Protein

468. Flatbread Sandwiches

Preparation Time: 10 minutes
Cooking Time: 20 minutes
Serving: 7

Ingredient:
- 1 tbsp. Olive oil
- 8.5 oz. 7-Grain pilaf
- 1 cup English seedless cucumber
- 1 cup Seeded tomato
- ¼ cup Crumbled feta cheese
- 2 tbsp. Fresh lemon juice
- ¼ tsp. Freshly cracked black pepper
- 7 oz. Plain hummus
- 3 (2.8 oz.) Whole grain white flatbread wraps

Direction:

1. Cook the pilaf following the package instructions and put aside.
2. Chop and incorporate tomato, cucumber, cheese, oil, pepper, and lemon juice. Fold in the pilaf.
3. Prep the wraps with the hummus on one side. Spoon in the pilaf and fold.
4. Cut into a sandwich and serve.

Nutrition 310 Calories 9g Fat 8g Carbohydrates 10g Protein

469. Mezze Platter with Toasted Zaatar Pita Bread

Preparation Time: 10 minutes
Cooking Time: 10 minutes
Serving: 4
Ingredients:
- Whole-wheat pita rounds (4)
- Olive oil (4 tbsp.)
- Zaatar (4 tsp.)
- Greek yogurt (1 cup)
- Black pepper & Kosher salt (to your liking)
- Hummus (1 cup)
- Marinated artichoke hearts (1 cup)
- Assorted olives (2 cups)
- Sliced roasted red peppers (1 cup)
- Cherry tomatoes (2 cups)
- Salami (4 oz.)

Directions:
1. Use the medium-high heat setting to heat a large skillet.
2. Lightly grease the pita bread with the oil on each side and add the zaatar for seasoning.
3. Prepare in batches by adding the pita into a skillet and toasting until browned. It should take about two minutes on each side. Slice each of the pitas into quarters.
4. Season the yogurt with pepper and salt.
5. To assemble, divide the potatoes and add the hummus, yogurt, artichoke hearts, olives, red peppers, tomatoes, and salami.

Nutrition 731 Calories 48g Fat 10g Carbohydrates 26g Protein

470. Mini Chicken Shawarma

Preparation Time: 10 minutes
Cooking Time: 1 hour 15 minutes
Serving: 8
Ingredients:
The Chicken:
- Chicken tenders (1 lb.)
- Olive oil (.25 cup)
- Lemon - zest & juice (1)
- Cumin (1 tsp.)
- Garlic powder (2 tsp.)
- Smoked paprika (.5 tsp.)
- Coriander (.75 tsp.)

- Freshly ground black pepper (1 tsp.)
The Sauce:
- Greek yogurt (1.25 cups)
- Lemon juice (1 tbsp.)
- Grated garlic clove (1)
- Freshly chopped dill (2 tbsp.)
- Black pepper (.125 tsp/to taste)
- Kosher salt (as desired)
- Chopped fresh parsley (.25 cup)
- Red onion (half of 1)
- Romaine lettuce (4 leaves)
- English cucumber (half of 1)
- Tomatoes (2)
- Mini pita bread (16)

Directions:
1. Toss the chicken into a zipper-type baggie. Whisk the chicken fixings and add it to the bag to marinate for up to an hour.
2. Prepare the sauce by combining the juice, garlic, and yogurt in a mixing container. Stir in the dill, parsley, pepper, and salt. Place in the fridge.
3. Heat a skillet using the medium temperature heat setting. Transfer the chicken from the marinade (let the excess drip off).
4. Cook until thoroughly cooked or about four minutes per side. Chop it into bite-sized strips.
5. Thinly slice the cucumber and onion. Shred the lettuce and chop the tomatoes. Assemble and add to the pitas - the chicken, lettuce, onion, tomato, and cucumber.

Nutrition 216 Calories 16g Fat 9g Carbohydrates 9g Protein

471. Eggplant Pizza

Preparation Time: 10 minutes
Cooking Time: 30 minutes
Serving: 6
Ingredients:
- Eggplants (1 large or 2 medium)
- Olive oil (.33 cup)
- Black pepper & salt (as desired)
- Marinara sauce - store-bought/homemade (1.25 cups)
- Shredded mozzarella cheese (1.5 cups)
- Cherry tomatoes (2 cups - halved)
- Torn basil leaves (.5 cup)

Directions:
1. Heat the oven to reach 400° Fahrenheit. Ready the baking sheet with a layer of parchment baking paper.
2. Slice the end/ends off of the eggplant and them it into ¾-inch slices. Arrange the slices on the prepared sheet and brush both sides with olive oil. Dust with pepper and salt to your liking.
3. Roast the eggplant until tender (10 to 12 min.).
4. Transfer the tray from the oven and add two tablespoons of sauce on top of each section. Top it

off with the mozzarella and three to five tomato pieces on top.

5. Bake it until the cheese is melted. The tomatoes should begin to blister in about five to seven more minutes.
6. Take the tray from the oven. Serve and garnish basil.

Nutrition 257 Calories 20g Fat 11g Carbohydrates 8g Protein

472. Mediterranean Whole Wheat Pizza

Preparation Time: 10 minutes
Cooking Time: 25 minutes
Serving: 4
Ingredients:
- Whole-wheat pizza crust (1)
- Basil pesto (4 oz. jar)
- Artichoke hearts (.5 cup)
- Kalamata olives (2 tbsp.)
- Pepperoncini (2 tbsp. drained)
- Feta cheese (.25 cup)

Directions:
1. Program the oven to 450° Fahrenheit.
2. Drain and pull the artichokes to pieces. Slice/chop the pepperoncini and olives.
3. Arrange the pizza crust onto a floured work surface and cover it using pesto. Arrange the artichoke, pepperoncini slices, and olives over the pizza. Lastly, crumble and add the feta.
4. Bake for 10-12 minutes. Serve.

Nutrition 277 Calories 18.6g Fat 8g Carbohydrates 9.7g Protein

473. Spinach & Feta Pita Bake

Preparation Time: 5 minutes
Cooking Time: 22 minutes
Serving: 6
Ingredients:
- Sun-dried tomato pesto (6 oz. tub)
- Roma - plum tomatoes (2 chopped)
- Whole-wheat pita bread (Six 6-inch)
- Spinach (1 bunch)
- Mushrooms (4 sliced)
- Grated Parmesan cheese (2 tbsp.)
- Crumbled feta cheese (.5 cup)
- Olive oil (3 tbsp.)
- Black pepper (as desired)

Directions:
1. Set the oven at 350° Fahrenheit.
2. Brush the pesto onto one side of each pita bread and arrange them onto a baking tray (pesto-side up).
3. Rinse and chop the spinach. Top the pitas with spinach, mushrooms, tomatoes, feta cheese, pepper, Parmesan cheese, pepper, and a drizzle of oil.

4. Bake in the hot oven until the pita bread is crispy (12 min.). Slice the pitas into quarters.

Nutrition 350 Calories 17.1g Fat 9g Carbohydrates 11.6g Protein

474. Watermelon Feta & Balsamic Pizza

Preparation Time: 10 minutes
Cooking Time: 15 minutes
Serving: 4
Ingredients:
- Watermelon (1-inch thick from the center)
- Crumbled feta cheese (1 oz.)
- Sliced Kalamata olives (5-6)
- Mint leaves (1 tsp.)
- Balsamic glaze (.5 tbsp.)

Directions:
1. Slice the widest section of the watermelon in half. Then, slice each half into four wedges.
2. Serve on a round pie dish like a pizza round and cover with the olives, cheese, mint leaves, and glaze.

Nutrition 90 Calories 3g Fat 4g Carbohydrates 2g Protein

475. Mixed Spice Burgers

Preparation Time: 10 minutes
Cooking Time: 30 minutes
Serving: 6
Ingredients:
- Medium onion (1)
- Fresh parsley (3 tbsp.)
- Clove of garlic (1)
- Ground allspice (.75 tsp.)
- Pepper (.75 tsp.)
- Ground nutmeg (.25 tsp.)
- Cinnamon (.5 tsp.)
- Salt (.5 tsp.)
- Fresh mint (2 tbsp.)
- 90% lean ground beef (1.5 lb.)
- Optional: Cold Tzatziki sauce

Directions:
1. Finely chop/mince the parsley, mint, garlic, and onions.
2. Whisk the nutmeg, salt, cinnamon, pepper, allspice, garlic, mint, parsley, and onion.
3. Add the beef and prepare six (6) 2x4-inch oblong patties.
4. Use the medium temperature setting to grill the patties or broil them four inches from the heat for 6 minutes per side.
5. When they're done, the meat thermometer will register 160° Fahrenheit. Serve with the sauce if desired.

Nutrition 231 Calories 9g Fat 10g Carbohydrates 32g Protein

476. Prosciutto - Lettuce - Tomato & Avocado Sandwiches

Preparation Time: 10 minutes
Cooking Time: 10 minutes
Serving: 4
Ingredients:

- Prosciutto (2 oz./8 thin slices)
- Ripe avocado (1 cut in half)
- Romaine lettuce (4 full leaves)
- Large ripe tomato (1)
- Whole grain or whole wheat bread slices (8)
- Black pepper and kosher salt (.25 tsp.)

Directions:
1. Tear the lettuce leaves into eight pieces (total). Slice the tomato into eight rounds. Toast the bread and place it on a plate.
2. Scrape out the avocado flesh from the skin and toss it to a mixing bowl. Lightly dust it using the pepper and salt. Whisk or gently mash the avocado until it's creamy. Spread over the bread.
3. Make one sandwich. Take a slice of avocado toast; top it with a lettuce leaf, a prosciutto slice, and a tomato slice. Top with another slice of lettuce tomato and continue.
4. Repeat the process until all ingredients are depleted.

Nutrition 240 Calories 9g Fat 8g Carbohydrates 12g Protein

477. Spinach Pie

Preparation Time: 10 minutes
Cooking Time: 60 minutes
Serving: 6
Ingredients:

- Melted butter (.5 cup)
- Frozen spinach (10 oz. pkg.)
- Fresh parsley (.5 cup)
- Green onions (.5 cup)
- Fresh dill (.5 cup)
- Crumbled feta cheese (.5 cup)
- Cream cheese (4 oz.)
- Cottage cheese (4 oz.)
- Parmesan (2 tbsp. - grated)
- Large eggs (2)
- Pepper and salt (as desired)
- Phyllo dough (40 sheets)

Directions:
1. Heat the oven setting at 350° Fahrenheit.
2. Mince/chop the onions, dill, and parsley. Thaw the spinach and sheets of dough. Dab the spinach dry by squeezing.
3. Combine the spinach, scallions, eggs, cheeses, parsley, dill, pepper, and salt in a blender until it's creamy.
4. Prepare the small phyllo triangles by filling them with one teaspoon of the spinach mixture.

5. Lightly brush the outside of the triangles with butter and arrange them with the seam-side facing downwards on an ungreased baking tray.
6. Place them in the heated oven to bake until golden brown and puffed (20-25 min.). Serve piping hot.

Nutrition 555 Calories 21.3g Fat 15g Carbohydrates 18.1g Protein

478. Feta Chicken Burgers

Preparation Time: 10 minutes
Cooking Time: 30 minutes
Serving: 6
Ingredients:

- ¼ cup Reduced-fat mayonnaise
- ¼ cup Finely chopped cucumber
- ¼ tsp Black pepper
- 1 tsp Garlic powder
- ½ cup Chopped roasted sweet red pepper
- ½ tsp Greek seasoning
- lb. Lean ground chicken
- 1 cup Crumbled feta cheese
- 6 Whole wheat burger buns

Directions:
1. Preheat the broiler to the oven ahead of time. Mix the mayo and cucumber. Set aside.
2. Combine each of the seasonings and red pepper for the burgers. Mix the chicken and the cheese well. Form the mixture into 6 ½-inch thick patties.
3. Cook the burgers in a broiler and place approximately four inches from the heat source. Cook until the thermometer reaches 165° Fahrenheit.
4. Serve with buns and cucumber sauce. Garnish with tomato and lettuce if desired and serve.

Nutrition 356 Calories 14g Fat 10g Carbohydrates 31g Protein

479. Roast Pork for Tacos

Preparation Time: 10 minutes
Cooking Time: 85 minutes
Serving: 6
Ingredients:

- Pork shoulder roast (4 lb.)
- Diced green chilies (2 - 4 oz. cans)
- Chili powder (.25 cup)
- Dried oregano (1 tsp.)
- Taco seasoning (1 tsp.)
- Garlic (2 tsp.)
- Salt (1.5 tsp. or as desired)

Directions:
1. Set the oven to reach 300° Fahrenheit.
2. Situate the roast on top of a large sheet of aluminum foil.
3. Drain the chilis. Mince the garlic.

4. Mix the green chilis, taco seasoning, chili powder, oregano, and garlic. Rub the mixture over the roast and cover using a layer of foil.
5. Place the wrapped pork on top of a roasting rack on a cookie sheet to catch any leaks.
6. Roast it for 3.5 to 4 hours in the hot oven until it's falling apart. Cook until the center reaches at least 145° Fahrenheit when tested with a meat thermometer (internal temperature).
7. Transfer the roast to a chopping block to shred into small pieces using two forks. Season it as desired.

Nutrition 290 Calories 17.6g Fat 12g Carbohydrates

480. Italian Apple - Olive Oil Cake

Preparation Time: 10 minutes
Cooking Time: 1 hour 10 minutes
Serving: 12
Ingredients:
- Gala apples (2 large)
- Orange juice - for soaking apples
- All-purpose flour (3 cups)
- Ground cinnamon (.5 tsp.)
- Nutmeg (.5 tsp.)
- Baking powder (1 tsp.)
- Baking soda (1 tsp.)
- Sugar (1 cup)
- Olive oil (1 cup)
- Large eggs (2)
- Gold raisins (.66 cup)
- Confectioner's sugar - for dusting

Directions:
1. Peel and finely chop the apples. Drizzle the apples with just enough orange juice to prevent browning.
2. Soak the raisins in warm water for 15 minutes and drain well.
3. Sift the baking soda, flour, baking powder, cinnamon, and nutmeg. Set it to the side for now.
4. Pour the olive oil and sugar into the bowl of a stand mixer. Mix on the low setting for 2 minutes or until well combined.
5. Blend it while running, break in the eggs one at a time and continue mixing for 2 minutes. The mixture should increase in volume; it should be thick - not runny.
6. Combine all of the ingredients well. Build hole in the center of the flour mixture and add in the olive and sugar mixture.
7. Remove the apples of any excess of juice and drain the raisins that have been soaking. Add them together with the batter, mixing well.
8. Prepare the baking pan with parchment paper. Place the batter onto the pan and level it with the back of a wooden spoon.
9. Bake it for 45 minutes at a 350° Fahrenheit.
10. When ready, remove the cake from the parchment paper and place it into a serving dish. Dust with the confectioner's sugar. Heat dark honey to garnish the top.

Nutrition 294 Calories 11g Fat 9g Carbohydrates 5.3g Protein

DINNER RECIPES

481. Chicken Shawarma

Preparation Time: 8 minutes
Cooking Time: 15 minutes
Servings: 8
Ingredients:
- 2 lb. chicken breast, sliced into strips
- 1 teaspoon paprika
- 1 teaspoon ground cumin
- 1/4 teaspoon granulated garlic
- 1/2 teaspoon turmeric
- 1/4 teaspoon ground allspice

Directions
1. Season the chicken with the spices, and a little salt and pepper.
2. Pour 1 cup chicken broth to the skillet.
3. Seal the skillet.
4. Choose poultry setting.
5. Cook for 15 minutes.
6. Release the pressure naturally. Serve with flatbread.

Nutrition: 481 calories 21g fats 9g protein

482. Honey Balsamic Chicken

Preparation Time: 7 minutes
Cooking Time: 30 minutes
Servings: 5
Ingredients:
- 1/4 cup honey
- 1/2 cup balsamic vinegar
- 1/4 cup soy sauce
- 2 cloves garlic minced
- 10 chicken drumsticks

Directions
1. Mix the honey, vinegar, soy sauce and garlic in a bowl.
2. Soak the chicken in the sauce for 30 minutes.
3. Cover the skillet.
4. Set it to manual.
5. Cook at high pressure for 10 minutes.
6. Release the pressure quickly.
7. Choose the sauté button to thicken the sauce.

Nutrition: 517 calories 26g fats 10g protein

483. Garlic and Lemon Chicken Dish

Preparation Time: 11 minutes
Cooking Time: 10 minutes
Servings: 4
Ingredients
- 2-3 pounds chicken breast
- 1 teaspoon salt
- 1 onion, diced
- 1 tablespoon ghee
- 5 garlic cloves, minced
- ½ cup organic chicken broth
- 1 teaspoon dried parsley
- 1 large lemon, juiced
- 3-4 teaspoon arrowroot flour

Directions
1. Set your skillet to Sauté mode. Add diced up onion and cooking fat
2. Allow the onions to cook for 5 -10 minutes
3. Add the rest of the ingredients except arrowroot flour
4. Lock up the lid and set the skillet to poultry mode. Cook until the timer runs out
5. Allow the pressure to release naturally
6. Once done, remove ¼ cup of the sauce from the skillet and add arrowroot to make a slurry
7. Add the slurry to the skillet to make the gravy thick. Keep stirring well. Serve!

Nutrition: 511 calories 29g fats 11g protein

484. High-Quality Belizean Chicken Stew

Preparation Time: 7 minutes
Cooking Time: 23 minutes
Servings: 4
Ingredients
- 4 whole chicken
- 1 tablespoon coconut oil
- 2 tablespoons achiote seasoning
- 2 tablespoons white vinegar
- 3 tablespoons Worcestershire sauce
- 1 cup yellow onion, sliced
- 3 garlic cloves, sliced
- 1 teaspoon ground cumin
- 1 teaspoon dried oregano
- ½ teaspoon black pepper
- 2 cups chicken stock

Directions
1. Take a large sized bowl and add achiote paste, vinegar, Worcestershire sauce, oregano, cumin and pepper. Mix well and add chicken pieces and rub the marinade all over them
2. Allow the chicken to sit overnight. Set your skillet to Sauté mode and add coconut oil
3. Once hot, cook chicken pieces to the skillet in batches. Remove the seared chicken and transfer them to a plate

4. Add onions, garlic to the skillet and Sauté for 2-3 minutes. Add chicken pieces back to the skillet
5. Pour chicken broth to the bowl with marinade and stir well. Add the mixture to the skillet
6. Seal up the lid and cook for about 20 minutes at high pressure
7. Once done, release the pressure naturally. Season with a bit of salt and serve!

Nutrition: 517 calories 21g fats 9g protein

485. Crispy Mediterranean Chicken Thighs

Preparation Time: 9 minutes
Cooking Time: 35 minutes
Servings: 6
Ingredients:
- 2 tablespoons extra-virgin olive oil
- 2 teaspoons dried rosemary
- 1½ teaspoons ground cumin
- 1½ teaspoons ground coriander
- ¾ teaspoon dried oregano
- 1/8 teaspoon salt
- 6 chicken thighs (about 3 pounds)

Directions
1. Preheat the oven to 450°F. Line a baking sheet with parchment paper.
2. Place the olive oil and spices into a large bowl and mix together, making a paste. Add the chicken and mix together until evenly coated. Place on the prepared baking sheet.
3. Bake for 30 to 35 minutes.

Nutrition: 491 calories 22g fats 10g protein

486. Greek Penne and Chicken

Preparation Time: 11 minutes
Cooking Time: 9 minutes
Servings: 4
Ingredients
- 16-ounce package of Penne Pasta
- 1-pound Chicken Breast Halves
- 1/2 cup of Chopped Red Onion
- 1 1/2 tablespoons of Butter
- 2 cloves of Minced Garlic
- 14-ounce can of Artichoke Hearts
- 1 Chopped Tomato
- 3 tablespoons of Chopped Fresh Parsley
- 1/2 cup of Crumbled Feta Cheese
- 2 tablespoons of Lemon Juice
- 1 teaspoon of Dried Oregano
- Ground Black Pepper
- Salt

Directions:
1. In a large sized skillet over a medium-high heat, melt your butter. Add your garlic and onion. Cook approximately 2 minutes. Add your chopped

chicken and continue to cook until golden brown. Should take approximately 5 to 6 minutes. Stir occasionally.
2. Reduce your heat to a medium-low. Drain and chop your artichoke hearts. Add them to your skillet along with your chopped tomato, fresh parsley, feta cheese, dried oregano, lemon juice, and drained pasta. Cook for 2 to 3.
3. Season. Serve!

Nutrition: 411 calories 20g fats 8g protein

487. Yogurt-Marinated Chicken Kebabs

Preparation Time: 31 minutes
Cooking Time: 20 minutes
Servings: 4
Ingredients:
- ½ cup plain Greek yogurt
- 1 tablespoon lemon juice
- ½ teaspoon ground cumin
- ½ teaspoon ground coriander
- ½ teaspoon kosher salt
- ¼ teaspoon cayenne pepper
- 1½ pound chicken breast

Direction
1. In a huge bowl, mix yogurt, lemon juice, cumin, coriander, salt, and cayenne pepper. Mix together thoroughly and then add the chicken. Marinate for at least 30 minutes, and up to overnight in the refrigerator.
2. Bake for 21 minutes, rotating the chicken over once halfway through the cooking time.

Nutrition: 391 calories 22g fats 9g protein

488. Braised Chicken with Roasted Bell Peppers

Preparation Time: 7 minutes
Cooking Time: 54 minutes
Servings: 8
Ingredients:
- 2 tablespoons extra-virgin olive oil
- 4 pounds bone-in chicken, breast and thighs, skin removed
- 1½ teaspoon kosher salt, divided
- ¼ teaspoon freshly ground black pepper
- 1 onion, julienned
- 6 garlic cloves, sliced
- 1 cup white wine
- 2 pounds tomatoes, chopped
- ¼ teaspoon red pepper flakes
- 3 bell peppers
- 1/3 cup fresh parsley, chopped
- 1 tablespoon lemon juice

Directions

1. Cook olive oil in a large Dutch oven or skillet over medium-high heat. Season the chicken with ¾ teaspoon of the salt and the pepper. Stir in half the chicken to the skillet and brown about 2 minutes on each side. Situate to a plate, and repeat with the remaining half of the chicken.
2. Decrease heat to medium and add the onion. Sauté for about 5 minutes. Sauté garlic for 30 seconds. Fill in wine, increase the heat to medium-high, and bring to a boil to deglaze the skillet. Reduce the liquid for 6 minutes. Add the tomatoes, red pepper flakes, and the remaining ¾ teaspoon salt and mix well. Put the chicken back to the skillet, cover, reduce the heat to low, and simmer for 40 minutes, rotating the chicken halfway through the cooking time.
3. While the chicken cooks, prepare the roasted bell peppers. If you are using raw peppers, please refer to the roasting method here. If using jarred roasted red peppers, move on to step 4.
4. Chop the bell peppers into 1-inch pieces and set aside.
5. Once the chicken is cooked through, transfer it to a plate.
6. Adjust the heat to high and bring the mixture to a boil. Reduce by half, about 10 minutes.
7. Once is cool enough to handle, remove the meat from the bone and return it to the skillet with the bell peppers. Simmer 5 minutes to heat through. Stir in the parsley and lemon juice.

Nutrition: 501 calories 25g fats 6g protein

489. Chicken Stew with Artichokes, Capers, and Olives

Preparation Time: 6 minutes
Cooking Time: 33 minutes
Servings: 4
Ingredients:
- 1½ pounds boneless, skinless chicken thighs
- 1 teaspoon kosher salt, divided
- ¼ teaspoon freshly ground black pepper
- 2 tablespoons olive oil
- 1 onion, julienned
- 4 garlic cloves, sliced
- 1 teaspoon ground turmeric
- 1 teaspoon ground cumin
- ½ teaspoon ground coriander
- ½ teaspoon ground cinnamon
- ¼ teaspoon red pepper flakes
- 1 dried bay leaf
- 1¼ cups no-salt-added chicken stock
- ¼ cup white wine vinegar
- 2 tablespoons lemon juice
- 1 tablespoon lemon zest
- 1 (14-ounce) can artichoke hearts, drained
- ¼ cup olives, pitted and chopped
- 1 teaspoon capers, rinsed and chopped
- 1 tablespoon fresh mint, chopped
- 1 tablespoon fresh parsley, chopped

Directions
1. Season the chicken with ½ teaspoon of salt and pepper.
2. Cook olive oil in a large skillet over medium heat. sauté chicken for 3 minutes per side. Transfer to a plate and set aside.
3. Stir in onion to the same pan and sauté until translucent, about 5 minutes. Add the garlic and sauté 30 seconds. Add the remaining ½ teaspoon salt, the turmeric, cumin, coriander, cinnamon, red pepper flakes, and bay leaf and sauté 30 seconds.
4. Add ¼ cup of the chicken stock and increase the heat to medium-high to deglaze the pan. Add the remaining 1 cup stock, the lemon juice, and lemon zest. Close, set the heat to low, and simmer for 10 minutes.
5. Add the artichokes, olives, and capers and mix well. Add the reserved chicken and nestle it into the mixture. Simmer for 15 minutes. Garnish with the mint and parsley.

Nutrition: 601 calories 30g fats 12g protein

490. Zaatar Chicken Tenders

Preparation Time: 8 minutes
Cooking Time: 15 minutes
Servings: 4
Ingredients:
- Olive oil cooking spray
- 1-pound chicken tenders
- 1½ tablespoons zaatar
- ½ teaspoon kosher salt
- ¼ teaspoon freshly ground black pepper

Directions
1. In a large bowl, combine the chicken, zaatar, salt, and black pepper.
2. Mix together well, covering the chicken tenders fully.
3. Lay out in a single layer on the baking sheet and bake for 15 minutes, turning the chicken over once midway through the cooking time.

Nutrition: 304 calories 19g fats 7g protein

491. Lemon Chicken with Artichokes and Crispy Kale

Preparation Time: 9 minutes
Cooking Time: 35 minutes
Servings: 4
Ingredients:
- 3 tablespoons extra-virgin olive oil, divided
- 2 tablespoons lemon juice
- Zest of 1 lemon
- 2 garlic cloves, minced

- 2 teaspoons dried rosemary
- ¼ teaspoon freshly ground black pepper
- 1½ pounds boneless, skinless chicken breast
- 2 (14-ounce) cans artichoke hearts, drained
- 1 bunch (about 6 ounces) Lacinato kale

Directions

1. In a bowl, combine 2 tablespoons of the olive oil, the lemon juice, lemon zest, garlic, rosemary, salt, and black pepper. Mix well and then add the chicken and artichokes. Marinate for at least 30 minutes, and up to 4 hours in the refrigerator.
2. Pull out chicken and artichokes from the marinade and spread them in a single layer on the baking sheet. Roast for 15 minutes, flip over, and roast another 15 minutes. Remove the baking sheet and put the chicken, artichokes, and juices on a platter or large plate. Tent with foil to keep warm.
3. Change the oven temperature to broil. Mix kale with the remaining 1 tablespoon of the olive oil. Arrange the kale on the baking sheet and broil until golden brown in skillets and as crispy as you like, about 3 to 5 minutes.
4. Place the kale on top of the chicken and artichokes.

Nutrition: 497 calories 24g fats 11g protein

492. Sumac Chicken with Cauliflower and Carrots

Preparation Time: 8 minutes
Cooking Time: 40 minutes
Servings: 4
Ingredients:

- 3 tablespoons extra-virgin olive oil
- 1 tablespoon ground sumac
- 1 teaspoon kosher salt
- ½ teaspoon ground cumin
- ¼ teaspoon freshly ground black pepper
- 1½ pounds bone-in chicken thighs and drumsticks
- 1 medium cauliflower, cut into 1-inch florets
- 2 carrots
- 1 lemon, cut into ¼-inch-thick slices
- 1 tablespoon lemon juice
- ¼ cup fresh parsley, chopped
- ¼ cup fresh mint, chopped

Directions

1. Set the oven to 425°F. Prep a baking sheet using foil.
2. In a large bowl, scourge the olive oil, sumac, salt, cumin, and black pepper. Add the chicken, cauliflower, and carrots and toss until thoroughly coated with the oil and spice mixture.
3. Arrange the cauliflower, carrots, and chicken in a single layer on the baking sheet. Top with the lemon slices. Roast for 40 minutes, tossing the vegetables once halfway through. Sprinkle the lemon juice over the chicken and vegetables and garnish with the parsley and mint.

Nutrition: 401 calories 24g fat 11g protein

493. Harissa Yogurt Chicken Thighs

Preparation Time: 9 minutes
Cooking Time: 23 minutes
Servings: 4
Ingredients:

- ½ cup plain Greek yogurt
- 2 tablespoons harissa
- 1 tablespoon lemon juice
- ¼ teaspoon freshly ground black pepper
- 1½ pounds boneless

Directions

1. Mix yogurt, harissa, lemon juice, salt, and black pepper. Add the chicken and mix together. Marinate for at least 15 minutes, and up to 4 hours in the refrigerator.
2. Pull out the chicken thighs from the marinade then arrange in a single layer on the baking sheet. Roast for 20 minutes, turning the chicken over halfway.
3. Change the oven temperature to broil. Broil the chicken until golden brown in skillets, 2 to 3 minutes.

Nutrition: 391 calories 20g fats 9g protein

494. Braised Chicken with Wild Mushrooms

Preparation Time: 11 minutes
Cooking Time: 28 minutes
Servings: 4
Ingredients

- 1/4 cup dried porcini or morel mushrooms
- 1/4 cup olive oil
- 2–3 slices low-salt turkey bacon, chopped
- 1 chicken, cut into pieces
- 1 small celery stalk, diced
- 1 small dried red chili, chopped
- 1/4 cup vermouth or white wine
- 1/4 cup tomato puree
- 1/4 cup low-salt chicken stock
- 1/2 teaspoon arrowroot
- 1/4 cup flat-leaf parsley, chopped
- 4 teaspoons fresh thyme, chopped
- 3 teaspoons fresh tarragon

Directions

1. Soak mushrooms onto boiling water over them for 20 minutes to soften.
2. Drain and chop, reserving the liquid.
3. Heat the olive oil on medium heat. Stir in bacon and cook until browned and lightly crisp. Drain the bacon on a paper towel.
4. Season the chicken, and add to the oil and bacon drippings.
5. Cook for 10–15 minutes.

6. Add the celery and the chopped chili, and cook for 3–5 minutes.
7. Deglaze the pan with the wine, with a wooden spoon to scrape up the brown bits stuck to the bottom.
8. Add the tomato puree, chicken stock, arrowroot, and mushroom liquid. Close and simmer on low for 45 minutes.
9. Add the fresh chopped herbs and cook an additional 10 minutes, until the sauce thickens.
10. Season well. Serve with wilted greens or crunchy green beans.

Nutrition: 501 calories 21g fats 12g protein

495. Braised Duck with Fennel Root

Preparation Time: 13 minutes
Cooking Time: 45 minutes
Servings: 6
Ingredients
- 1/4 cup olive oil
- 1 whole duck, cleaned
- 3 teaspoon fresh rosemary
- 2 garlic cloves, minced
- 3 fennel bulbs, cut into chunks
- 1/2 cup sherry

Directions
1. Preheat the oven to 375 degrees.
2. Cook olive oil in a Dutch oven.
3. Season the duck, including the cavity, with the rosemary, garlic, sea salt, and freshly ground pepper.
4. Place the duck in the oil, and cook it for 10–15 minutes, turning as necessary to brown all sides.
5. Add the fennel bulbs and cook an additional 5 minutes.
6. Pour the sherry over the duck and fennel, cover and cook in the oven for 30–45 minutes, or until internal temperature of the duck is 140–150 degrees at its thickest part.
7. Allow duck to sit for 15 minutes before serving.

Nutrition: 571 calories 24g fats 15g protein

496. Turkey Burgers

Preparation Time: 15 minutes
Cooking Time: 10 minutes
Serving: 6
Ingredients:
- 1½ pounds ground turkey breast
- 1 teaspoon sea salt, divided
- ¼ teaspoon freshly ground black pepper
- 2 tablespoons extra-virgin olive oil
- 2 mangos, peeled, pitted, and cubed
- ½ red onion, finely chopped
- Juice of 1 lime
- 1 garlic clove, minced

- ½ jalapeño pepper, seeded and finely minced
- 2 tablespoons chopped fresh cilantro leaves

Direction:
1. Form the turkey breast into 4 patties and season with ½ teaspoon of sea salt and the pepper.
2. Using nonstick skillet over medium-high heat, heat the olive oil until it shimmers.
3. Add the turkey patties and cook for about 5 minutes per side until browned.
4. While the patties cook, mix together the mango, red onion, lime juice, garlic, jalapeño, cilantro, and remaining ½ teaspoon of sea salt in a small bowl. Spoon the salsa over the turkey patties and serve.

Nutrition: 384 calories 3g protein 16g Fat

497. Herb-Roasted Turkey Breast

Preparation Time: 15 minutes
Cooking Time: 90 minutes
Serving: 6
Ingredients:
- 2 tablespoons extra-virgin olive oil
- 4 garlic cloves, minced
- Zest of 1 lemon
- 1 tablespoon fresh thyme leaves
- 1 tablespoon fresh rosemary leaves
- 2 tablespoons fresh Italian parsley leaves
- 1 teaspoon ground mustard
- 1 teaspoon sea salt
- ¼ teaspoon black pepper
- 1 (6-pound) bone-in, skin-on turkey breast
- 1 cup dry white wine

Direction
1. Preheat the oven to 325°F.
2. Scourge olive oil, garlic, lemon zest, thyme, rosemary, parsley, mustard, sea salt, and pepper. Lay out herb mixture evenly over the surface of the turkey breast, and loosen the skin and rub underneath as well. Situate turkey breast in a roasting pan on a rack, skin-side up.
3. Pour the wine in the pan. Roast for 1 to 1½ hour. Take out from the oven and rest for 20 minutes, tented with aluminum foil to keep it warm, before carving.

Nutrition: 392 calories 84 Protein 6g Fat

498. Chicken Sausage and Peppers

Preparation Time: 10 minutes
Cooking Time: 20 minutes
Serving: 6
Ingredients:
- 2 tablespoons extra-virgin olive oil
- 6 Italian chicken sausage links
- 1 onion
- 1 red bell pepper
- 1 green bell pepper

- 3 garlic cloves, minced
- ½ cup dry white wine
- ½ teaspoon sea salt
- ¼ teaspoon freshly ground black pepper
- Pinch red pepper flakes

Direction
1. In a skillet at medium-high heat, cook olive oil.
2. Add the sausages and cook for 5 to 7 minutes, turning occasionally, until browned, and they reach an internal temperature of 165°F. With tongs, remove the sausage from the pan and set aside on a platter, tented with aluminum foil to keep warm.
3. Put skillet back to the heat and add the onion, red bell pepper, and green bell pepper. Cook for 5 to 7 minutes.
4. Cook garlic 30 seconds, stirring constantly.
5. Stir in the wine, sea salt, pepper, and red pepper flakes. Scrape and fold in any browned bits from the bottom. Simmer for about 4 minutes more. Spoon the peppers over the sausages and serve.

Nutrition: 173 Calories 22g Protein 5g Fat

499. Chicken Piccata

Preparation Time: 10 minutes
Cooking Time: 15 minutes
Serving: 6
Ingredients:
- ½ cup whole-wheat flour
- ½ teaspoon sea salt
- 1/8 teaspoon freshly ground black pepper
- 1½ pounds boneless
- 3 tablespoons extra-virgin olive oil
- 1 cup unsalted chicken broth
- ½ cup dry white wine
- Juice of 1 lemon
- Zest of 1 lemon
- ¼ cup capers, drained and rinsed
- ¼ cup chopped fresh parsley leaves

Direction
1. In a shallow dish, whisk the flour, sea salt, and pepper. Dredge the chicken in the flour and tap off any excess.
2. In a pan over medium-high heat, cook olive oil.
3. Add the chicken and cook for about 4 minutes. Pull out chicken from the pan and set aside, tented with aluminum foil to keep warm.
4. Return back to the heat and mix broth, wine, lemon juice, and lemon zest, and capers. Simmer for 3 to 4 minutes, stirring. Put the skillet back from the heat and return the chicken to the pan. Turn to coat. Stir in the parsley and serve.

Nutrition: 153 Calories 8g Protein 9g Fat

500. One-Pan Tuscan Chicken

Preparation Time: 10 minutes

Cooking Time: 25 minutes
Serving: 6
Ingredients:
- ¼ cup extra-virgin olive oil, divided
- 1-pound boneless chicken
- 1 onion
- 1 red bell pepper
- 3 garlic cloves
- ½ cup dry white wine
- 2 (14-ounce) can tomatoes
- 1 (14-ounce) can white beans
- 1 tablespoon dried Italian seasoning
- ½ teaspoon sea salt
- 1/8 teaspoon freshly ground black pepper
- 1/8 teaspoon red pepper flakes
- ¼ cup chopped fresh basil leaves

Direction:
1. In a huge skillet over medium-high heat, preheat 2 tablespoons of olive oil.
2. Add the chicken and cook for about 6 minutes, stirring. Put out the chicken and set aside on a platter, tented with aluminum foil to keep warm.
3. Situate the skillet back to the heat and heat the remaining 2 tablespoons of olive oil.
4. Add the onion and red bell pepper. Cook for about 5 minutes.
5. Cook garlic for 30 seconds.
6. Stir in the wine. Cook for 1 minute, stirring.
7. Add the crushed and chopped tomatoes, white beans, Italian seasoning, sea salt, pepper, and red pepper flakes. Allow to a simmer and adjust the heat to medium. Cook for 5 minutes, stirring occasionally.
8. Take chicken and any juices that have collected back to the skillet. Cook for 1 to 2 minutes. Pull out from the heat and stir in the basil before serving.

Nutrition: 271 Calories 14g Protein 0.1g Fat

501. Chicken Kapama

Preparation Time: 10 minutes
Cooking Time: 2 hours
Serving: 4
Ingredients:
- 1 (32-ounce) can chopped tomatoes
- ¼ cup dry white wine
- 2 tablespoons tomato paste
- 3 tablespoons extra-virgin olive oil
- ¼ teaspoon red pepper flakes
- 1 teaspoon ground allspice
- ½ teaspoon dried oregano
- 2 whole cloves
- 1 cinnamon stick
- ½ teaspoon sea salt
- 1/8 teaspoon black pepper
- 4 boneless, skinless chicken breast halves

Direction:

1. In pot over medium-high heat, mix the tomatoes, wine, tomato paste, olive oil, red pepper flakes, allspice, oregano, cloves, cinnamon stick, sea salt, and pepper. Bring to a simmer, stirring occasionally. Adjust heat to medium-low then simmer for 30 minutes, stirring occasionally. Remove and discard the whole cloves and cinnamon stick from the sauce and let the sauce cool.
2. Preheat the oven to 350°F.
3. Situate chicken in a 9-by-13-inch baking dish. Drizzle sauce over the chicken and cover the pan with aluminum foil. Bake for 45 minutes.

Nutrition: 220 Calories 8g Protein 14g Fat

502. Spinach and Feta–Stuffed Chicken Breasts

Preparation Time: 10 minutes
Cooking Time: 45 minutes
Serving: 4
Ingredients:
- 2 tablespoons extra-virgin olive oil
- 1-pound fresh baby spinach
- 3 garlic cloves, minced
- Zest of 1 lemon
- ½ teaspoon sea salt
- 1/8 teaspoon freshly ground black pepper
- ½ cup crumbled feta cheese
- 4 chicken breast halves

Direction:
1. Preheat the oven to 350°F.
2. Preheat oil and skillet over medium-high heat
3. Cook spinach for 3 to 4 minutes.
4. Cook garlic, lemon zest, sea salt, and pepper. Cool slightly and mix in the cheese.
5. Spread the spinach and cheese mixture in an even layer over the chicken pieces and roll the breast around the filling. Hold closed with toothpicks or butcher's twine. Place the breasts in a 9-by-13-inch baking dish and bake for 30 to 40 minutes. Take away from the oven and let rest for 5 minutes before slicing and serving.

Nutrition: 263 Calories 17g Protein 20g Fat

503. Rosemary Baked Chicken Drumsticks

Preparation Time: 5 minutes
Cooking Time: 1 hour
Serving: 6
Ingredients:
- 2 tablespoons chopped fresh rosemary leaves
- 1 teaspoon garlic powder
- ½ teaspoon sea salt
- 1/8 teaspoon freshly ground black pepper
- Zest of 1 lemon
- 12 chicken drumsticks

Direction
1. Preheat the oven to 350°F.
2. Blend rosemary, garlic powder, sea salt, pepper, and lemon zest.
3. Situate drumsticks in a 9-by-13-inch baking dish and sprinkle with the rosemary mixture. Bake for about 1 hour.

Nutrition: 163 Calories 26g Protein 6g Fat

504. Chicken with Onions, Potatoes, Figs, and Carrots

Preparation Time: 5 minutes
Cooking Time: 45 minutes
Serving: 4
Ingredients:
- 2 cups fingerling potatoes, halved
- 4 fresh figs, quartered
- 2 carrots, julienned
- 2 tablespoons extra-virgin olive oil
- 1 teaspoon sea salt, divided
- ¼ teaspoon freshly ground black pepper
- 4 chicken leg-thigh quarters
- 2 tablespoons chopped fresh parsley leaves

Direction:
1. Preheat the oven to 425°F.
2. In a small bowl, toss the potatoes, figs, and carrots with the olive oil, ½ teaspoon of sea salt, and the pepper. Spread in a 9-by-13-inch baking dish.
3. Rub chicken with the remaining ½ teaspoon of sea salt. Place it on top of the vegetables. Bake for 35 to 45 minutes.
4. Sprinkle with the parsley and serve.

Nutrition: 429 Calories 52g Protein 12g Fat

505. Chicken Gyros with Tzatziki

Preparation Time: 10 minutes
Cooking Time: 80 minutes
Serving: 6
Ingredient:
- 1-pound ground chicken breast
- 1 onion
- 2 tablespoons dried rosemary
- 1 tablespoon dried marjoram
- 6 garlic cloves, minced
- ½ teaspoon sea salt
- ¼ teaspoon freshly ground black pepper
- Tzatziki Sauce

Direction:
1. Preheat the oven to 350°F.
2. In a stand mixer, blend chicken, onion, rosemary, marjoram, garlic, sea salt, and pepper.
3. Press the mixture into a loaf pan. Bake for about 1 hour. Pull out from the oven and set aside for 20 minutes before slicing.

4. Slice the gyro and spoon the tzatziki sauce over the top.

Nutrition: 289 Calories 50g Protein 1g Fat

506. Eggplant Casserole

Preparation Time: 10 minutes
Cooking Time: 45 minutes
Serving: 8
Ingredients:

- 5 tablespoons extra-virgin olive oil
- 1 eggplant
- 1 onion
- 1 green bell pepper
- 1-pound ground turkey
- 3 garlic cloves, minced
- 2 tablespoons tomato paste
- 1 (14-ounce) can chopped tomatoes
- 1 tablespoon Italian seasoning
- 2 teaspoons Worcestershire sauce
- 1 teaspoon dried oregano
- ½ teaspoon ground cinnamon
- 1 cup unsweetened nonfat plain Greek yogurt
- 1 egg, beaten
- ¼ teaspoon freshly ground black pepper
- ¼ teaspoon ground nutmeg
- ¼ cup grated Parmesan cheese
- 2 tablespoons chopped fresh parsley leaves

Direction:
1. Preheat the oven to 400°F.
2. Preheat skillet over medium-high heat, pour 3 tablespoons
3. Add the eggplant slices and brown for 3 to 4 minutes per side. Transfer to paper towels to drain.
4. Return to the heat and pour remaining 2 tablespoons of olive oil. Add the onion and green bell pepper. Cook for 5 minutes. Remove from the pan and set aside.
5. Put back to the heat and add the turkey. Cook for about 5 minutes
6. Cook garlic.
7. Stir in the tomato paste, tomatoes, Italian seasoning, Worcestershire sauce, oregano, and cinnamon. Return the onion and bell pepper to the pan. Cook for 5 minutes, stirring.
8. Scourge yogurt, egg, pepper, nutmeg, and cheese.
9. Using 9-by-13-inch baking dish, spread half the meat mixture. Layer with half the eggplant. Add the remaining meat mixture and the remaining eggplant. Spread with the yogurt mixture. Bake for about 20 minutes.
10. Garnish with the parsley and serve.

Nutrition: 338 Calories 28g Protein 20g Fat

507. Dijon and Herb Pork Tenderloin

Preparation Time: 10 minutes
Cooking Time: 30 minutes
Serving: 6
Ingredients:

- ½ cup fresh Italian parsley leaves
- 3 tablespoons fresh rosemary leaves
- 3 tablespoons fresh thyme leaves
- 3 tablespoons Dijon mustard
- 1 tablespoon extra-virgin olive oil
- 4 garlic cloves, minced
- ½ teaspoon sea salt
- ¼ teaspoon freshly ground black pepper
- 1 (1½-pound) pork tenderloin

Direction:
1. Preheat the oven to 400°F.
2. In a blender, pulse parsley, rosemary, thyme, mustard, olive oil, garlic, sea salt, and pepper. Spread the mixture evenly over the pork and place it on a rimmed baking sheet.
3. Bake for about 20 minutes. Pull out from the oven and put aside for 10 minutes before slicing and serving.

Nutrition: 393 Calories 74g Protein 12g Fat

508. Steak with Red Wine– Mushroom Sauce

Preparation Time: 10 minutes
Cooking Time: 20 minutes
Serving: 4
Ingredients:
For marinade and steak

- 1 cup dry red wine
- 3 garlic cloves, minced
- 2 tablespoons extra-virgin olive oil
- 1 tablespoon low-sodium soy sauce
- 1 tablespoon dried thyme
- 1 teaspoon Dijon mustard
- 2 tablespoons extra-virgin olive oil
- 1½ pounds skirt steak

For mushroom sauce

- 2 tablespoons extra-virgin olive oil
- 1-pound cremini mushrooms
- ½ teaspoon sea salt
- 1 teaspoon dried thyme
- 1/8 teaspoon black pepper
- 2 garlic cloves, minced
- 1 cup dry red wine

Direction:
For marinade and steak
1. In a small bowl, whisk the wine, garlic, olive oil, soy sauce, thyme, and mustard. Pour into a resealable bag and add the steak. Refrigerate the steak to

marinate for 4 to 8 hours. Remove the steak from the marinade and pat it dry with paper towels.

2. In a big skillet over medium-high heat, warm up olive oil.
3. Cook steak for 4 minutes per side. Pull out steak from the skillet and put it on a plate tented with aluminum foil to keep warm, while you prepare the mushroom sauce.
4. When the mushroom sauce is ready, slice the steak against the grain into ½-inch-thick slices.

For mushroom sauce
5. Preheat skillet over medium-high heat, heat the olive oil.
6. Add the mushrooms, sea salt, thyme, and pepper. Cook for about 6 minutes.
7. Cook garlic for 30 seconds.
8. Stir in the wine, and use the side of a wooden spoon to scrape and fold in any browned bits from the bottommost of the skillet. Cook for about 4 minutes. Serve the mushrooms spooned over the steak.

Nutrition: 405 Calories 33g Protein 22g Fat

509. Greek Meatballs

Preparation Time: 20 minutes
Cooking Time: 25 minutes
Serving: 4
Ingredients:
- 2 whole-wheat bread slices
- 1¼ pounds ground turkey
- 1 egg
- ¼ cup seasoned whole-wheat bread crumbs
- 3 garlic cloves, minced
- ¼ red onion, grated
- ¼ cup chopped fresh Italian parsley leaves
- 2 tablespoons chopped fresh mint leaves
- 2 tablespoons chopped fresh oregano leaves
- ½ teaspoon sea salt
- ¼ teaspoon freshly ground black pepper

Direction:
1. Preheat the oven to 350°F.
2. Prep baking sheet with foil.
3. Run the bread under water to wet it, and squeeze out any excess. Rip the wet bread into small pieces and put it in a medium bowl.
4. Add the turkey, egg, bread crumbs, garlic, red onion, parsley, mint, oregano, sea salt, and pepper. Mix well. Form the mixture into ¼-cup-size balls. Place the meatballs on the prepared sheet and bake for about 25 minutes

Nutrition: 350 Calories 42g Protein 18g Fat

510. Lamb with String Beans

Preparation Time: 10 minutes
Cooking Time: 1 hour
Serving: 6

Ingredients:
- ¼ cup extra-virgin olive oil
- 6 lamb chops
- 1 teaspoon sea salt
- ½ teaspoon black pepper
- 2 tablespoons tomato paste
- 1½ cups hot water
- 1-pound green beans
- 1 onion
- 2 tomatoes

Direction:
1. In a skillet at medium-high heat, pour 2 tablespoons of olive oil.
2. Season the lamb chops with ½ teaspoon of sea salt and 1/8 teaspoon of pepper. Cook the lamb in the hot oil for about 4 minutes. Transfer the meat to a platter and set aside.
3. Put back to the heat then put the 2 tablespoons of olive oil. Heat until it shimmers.
4. Blend tomato paste in the hot water. Mix to the hot skillet along with the green beans, onion, tomatoes, and the remaining ½ teaspoon of sea salt and ¼ teaspoon of pepper. Bring to a simmer.
5. Return the lamb chops to the pan. Boil and adjust the heat to medium-low. Simmer for 45 minutes, adding additional water as needed to adjust the thickness of the sauce.

Nutrition: 439 Calories 50g Protein 22g Fat

511. Greek Lamb Chop

Preparation Time: 10 minutes
Cooking Time: 8 minutes
Serving: 8
Ingredients:
- 8 trimmed lamb loin chops
- 2 tbsp lemon juice
- 1 tbsp dried oregano
- 1 tbsp minced garlic
- ½ tsp salt
- ¼ tsp black pepper

Direction:
1. Preheat the broiler
2. Combine oregano, garlic, lemon juice, salt and pepper and rub on both sides of the lamb. Situate lamb on a broiler pan coated with cooking spray and cook for 4 min on each side.

Nutrition: 457 Calories 49g Protein 20g Fat

512. Skillet Braised Cod with Asparagus and Potatoes

Preparation Time: 20 minutes
Cooking Time: 20 minutes
Serving: 4
Ingredients:
- 4 skinless cod fillets

- 1-pound asparagus
- 12 oz halved small purple potatoes
- Finely grated zest of ½ lemon
- Juice of ½ lemon
- ½ cup white wine
- ¼ cup torn fresh basil leaves
- 1 ½ tbsp olive oil
- 1 tbsp capers
- 3 cloves sliced garlic

Direction:
1. Take a large and tall pan on the sides and heat the oil over medium-high.
2. Season the cod abundantly with salt and pepper and put in the pan, with the hot oil, for 1 min. Carefully flip for 1 more min and after transferring the cod to a plate. Set aside.
3. Add the lemon zest, capers and garlic to the pan and mix to coat with the remaining oil in the pan and cook about 1 min. Add the wine and deglaze the pan. Add lemon juice, potatoes, ½ tsp salt, ¼ tsp pepper and 2 cups of water and boil, adjust heat and simmer until potatoes are tender, for 10 to 12 min.
4. Mix the asparagus and cook for 2 min. Bring back the cod filets and any juices accumulated in the pan. Cook until the asparagus are tender, for about 3 min.
5. Divide the cod fillets into shallow bowls and add the potatoes and asparagus. Mix the basil in the broth left in the pan and pour over the cod.

Nutrition: 461 Calories 40g Protein 16g Fat

513. Savory Vegetable Pancakes

Preparation Time: 10 minutes
Cooking Time: 40 minutes
Serving: 7
Ingredients:
- 8 peeled carrots
- 2 cloves garlic
- 1 zucchini
- 1 bunch green onions
- ½ bunch parsley
- 1 recipe pancake batter

Direction:
1. Grate chop the zucchini and carrots using grater. Finely chop the onions, mince the garlic and roughly chop the parsley.
2. Prepare pancakes with your favorite recipe or buy them in the store, but use ¼ cup of liquid less than required, zucchini will add a large amount of liquid to the mix. Fold the vegetables in the prepared pancake batter.
3. Heat a pan over medium-high heat and brush it mildly with olive oil. With a 1/3 measuring cup to scoop the batter on the heated pan. Cook 3 to 4 min, until the outer edge has set, then turn over. Cook for another 2 min and remove from the heat.

4. Season the pancakes with plenty of salt. Serve.
Nutrition: 291 Calories 24g Protein 10g Fat

514. Mediterranean Tuna Noodle Casserole

Preparation Time: 15 minutes
Cooking Time: 40 minutes
Serving: 5
Ingredients:
- 10 oz dried egg noodles
- 9 oz halved frozen artichoke hearts
- 6 oz drained olive oil packed tuna
- 4 sliced scallions
- 1-pound sliced ¼ inch thick small red potatoes
- 2 cup milk
- ¾ cup finely grated Parmesan cheese
- ¾ cup drained capers
- ½ cup finely chopped flat-leaf parsley
- ½ cup sliced black olives
- ¼ cup flour
- 4 tbsp unsalted butter
- 2 tsp Kosher salt, divided

Direction:
1. Place a grill in the middle of the oven and heat to 400° F. Lightly coat a 2-quart baking tray with oil. Set aside.
2. Using a big pan of salt water to a boil. Stir in noodles and cook for 2 min less than recommended in the package directions. Strain noodles. Season immediately with olive oil so that they don't pile up. Set aside.
3. Fill the pan with water again and boil. Stir in potato slices and cook for 4 min. Drain well, then bring them back to the pan.
4. Cook butter in a saucepan at medium heat, while the noodles and potatoes are cooking. When it melts and expands, add the flour and cook for about 5 min mixing constantly, until the sauce thickens slightly, about 5 min. Add 1 tsp salt and pepper to taste.
5. Add the egg noodles to the potato pan, then pour the sauce over it. Add and mix the remaining 1 tsp of salt, capers, olive oil, tuna, artichoke hearts, shallots, parsley and ½ cup of Parmesan. Season well.
6. Transfer to the baking tray and distribute it in a uniform layer. Season with the remaining ¼ cup of Parmesan and bake, uncovered, about 25 min.

Nutrition: 457 Calories 37g Protein 21g Fat

515. Acquapazza Snapper

Preparation Time: 10 minutes
Cooking Time: 35 minutes
Serving: 4
Ingredients:

- 1 ½ pounds cut into 4 pieces red snapper fillets
- 1 ½ coarsely chopped ripe tomatoes
- 3 cups water
- 2 tbsp olive oil
- 1 tbsp chopped thyme leaves
- 1 tbsp chopped oregano leaves
- ¼ tsp red pepper flakes
- 3 cloves minced garlic

Direction:

1. Cook oil in a casserole large enough to hold all 4 pieces of snapper fillets in a single layer over medium heat. Cook garlic and red pepper flakes
2. Add the water, tomatoes, thyme, oregano and simmer. Cover, reduce over medium-low heat and simmer for 15 min. Remove the lid and continue to simmer for another 10 min so that the liquid decreases slightly, pressing occasionally on the tomatoes. Taste and season with salt as needed.
3. Put the snapper fillets in the casserole with the skin facing down, if there is skin. Sprinkle with salt, and cook for 9 min.
4. Place the snapper fillets on 4 large, shallow bowls and put the broth around it. Serve immediately.

Nutrition: 501 Calories 52g Protein 26g Fat

516. Eggplant Brown Rice Bowl

Preparation Time: 20 minutes
Cooking Time: 40 minutes
Serving: 4
Ingredients:

- 2 pounds cut into ½ inch-thick rounds eggplants
- 15 oz drained and rinsed garbanzo beans
- 4 cup cooked brown rice
- ½ cup tahini
- ½ cup coarsely chopped cilantro
- ¼ cup coarsely chopped mint leaves
- ¼ cup pomegranate arils
- 4 tbsp olive oil
- 1 tbsp zaatar
- 1 ½ tsp maple syrup
- 1 tsp squeezed lemon juice
- ½ tsp ground turmeric
- 1 clove minced garlic

Direction:

1. Situate rack in the middle of the oven and preheat to 400° F.
2. Place the eggplant on a rimmed baking sheet. Season with 3 tbsp of olive oil, then sprinkle with zaatar and a large pinch of salt. Using your hands, mix until the eggplant is well coated. Place the eggplants in a single layer. Cook for 15 min. Flip the eggplants and cook for another 10 min. Remove from the oven and season with a pinch of salt and black pepper. Set aside.
3. Put the tahini and 1/3 cup of water in a small bowl and blend until smooth and thick. Pour in 1 tbsp of

olive oil, maple syrup, turmeric, squeezed lemon juice, garlic and season with salt.

4. Divide the rice into 4 bowls. Complete with the garbanzo beans and eggplants. Sprinkle with the mint, pomegranate arils and cilantro. Season generously the turmeric tahini on top.

Nutrition: 307 Calories 31g Protein 18g Fat

517. Extra-Crispy Veggie-Packed Pizza

Preparation Time: 15 minutes
Cooking Time: 18 minutes
Serving: 4
Ingredients:

- 1 (5 oz) thin whole-wheat pizza crust
- 2 ½ oz crumbled feta cheese
- 2 oz baby spring mix
- 2 thinly sliced tomatoes
- 1 cup shaved zucchini strips
- ½ cup thinly sliced red onion
- ¼ cup chopped basil
- ¼ cup basil pesto
- 1 tbsp canola oil
- 1 tbsp white wine vinegar
- ½ tsp kosher salt, divided
- ¼ tsp black pepper
- 1/8 tsp crushed red pepper

Direction:

1. Set oven to 400°F with the rack in the upper position. Combine the oil, vinegar, black pepper and ¼ tsp of salt in a bowl. Mix the zucchini in the mixture and let stand at room temperature for 10 min.
2. Meantime, place pizza crust on a baking tray, spread the basil pesto on the crust. Season the cheese over the pesto and garnish with the tomatoes and red pepper. Cook on the grill above 400°F for 6 min. Raise the grill and continue to cook for about 2 min. Pull out from the oven and leave to cool for 2 min.
3. Add the spring mixture, basil and onion to the zucchini mixture. Put the prepared mixture evenly on the pizza and season with the remaining ¼ tsp of salt.

Nutrition: 399 Calories 31g Protein 19g Fat

518. Greek Turkey Burgers

Preparation Time: 15 minutes
Cooking Time: 10 minutes
Serving: 4
Ingredients:

- 4 Whole-Wheat hamburger buns
- 1 pound 93% lean ground turkey
- 2 cups arugula
- ½ cup sliced cucumber

- ½ cup thinly sliced red onion
- 1/3 cup chopped kalamata olives
- 1/3 cup plain whole-milk Greek yogurt
- ¼ cup canola mayonnaise
- 1 tbsp lemon juice
- 2 tsp dried oregano
- 1 tsp ground cumin
- ¼ tsp kosher salt
- ¼ tsp black pepper, divided

Direction:
1. Combine turkey, oregano, cumin, mayonnaise, salt and 1/8 tsp of pepper. Form the mixture into 4 patties.
2. Heat a big cast-iron pan at high heat. Slightly coat the pan with cooking spray and add the turkey patties. Cook for about 4 to 5 min per side.
3. Combine the yogurt, lemon juice, olives and the remaining 1/8 tsp of pepper in a small bowl. Sprinkle the yogurt mixture on the cut sides of the top and bottom buns. Divide the arugula between the lower halves of the sandwiches, garnish with cooked patties, cucumber and red onion. Wrap with the top halves of the rolls and serve.

Nutrition: 459 Calories 48g Protein 19g Fat

519. Beef and Lamb Kofta Lettuce Wraps

Preparation Time: 20 minutes
Cooking Time: 40 minutes
Serving: 4
Ingredients:
- 12 Boston lettuce leaves
- 1 slice torn into pieces whole-grain bread
- 1 large egg
- 1 package (about 8.8 oz) precooked brown rice
- 8 oz ground sirloin
- 6 oz lean ground lamb
- ¾ cup 2% reduced-fat Greek yogurt
- 5 tbsp grated red onion divided
- 3 tbsp diced English cucumber
- 2 tbsp chopped parsley
- 1 tbsp olive oil, divided
- 1 tbsp chopped mint
- 1 tsp paprika
- ¾ tsp kosher salt, divided
- ½ tsp ground allspice
- ½ tsp ground cinnamon
- ½ tsp ground black pepper, divided

Direction:
1. Put the bread in a mini kitchen robot and blend until large crumbs are formed. Combine bread, sirloin, lamb, egg, allspice, mint, parsley, cinnamon, 2 tbsp of onion, ½ tsp of salt and ¼ tsp of black pepper. Form the mixture into 12 patties. Preheat nonstick pan over medium-high heat and add 1 tsp

of oil. Place the patties on the pan, cook 2 to 3 min on each side.
2. Combine the yogurt, the remaining ¼ tsp of pepper, ¼ tsp of salt, the cucumber and the 3 tbsp of onion in a medium bowl and mix.
3. Cook the rice according to package directions. Season with paprika and the remaining 2 tsp of oil.
4. Place the lettuce leaves on a large serving plate and put the rice, patties and yogurt mixture.

Nutrition: 471 Calories 47g Protein 16g Fat

520. Chicken Souvlaki

Preparation Time: 25 minutes
Cooking Time: 10 minutes
Serving: 4
Ingredients:
- 4 pocketless pitas
- 2 cut into thin wedges tomatoes
- 1 cut into thin wedges small onion
- 1 halved cucumber
- 1 1/3 pound chicken breasts
- 2 cups plain yogurt
- 1/3 cup black olives
- 6 tbsp butter
- 2 tbsp olive oil
- 1 tbsp dried oregano
- 1 ½ tsp lemon juice
- 1 ¼ tsp salt
- ¼ tsp dried dill
- 1 clove minced garlic

Direction:
1. Situate the yogurt in a colander lined with a paper towel and place it on a bowl, leave to dry in the refrigerator for 15 min. In a medium glass bowl combine the cucumber with 1 tsp of salt, let it rest for about 15 min. Squeeze the cucumber to remove the liquid. Place the cucumber back to the bowl and add the drained yogurt, garlic, dill and 1/8 tsp of pepper.
2. Preheat the grill or the broiler. Scourge oil oregano, lemon juice, the remaining ¼ tsp of salt and the remaining ¼ tsp of pepper. Dip the chicken cubes into the oil mixture and thread them onto the skewers. Grill the chicken over high heat, flipping once until cooked, about 5 min in total. Transfer the chicken to a plate.
3. Spread both sides of the pitas with butter and grill, flipping once for about 4 min in total. Cut into quarters.
4. Place the pitas on plates and garnish with the onion, tomatoes and chicken skewers with any sauce accumulated. Serve with the tzatziki and olives.

Nutrition: 460 Calories 40g Protein 18g Fat

521. Spicy Chicken Shawarma

Preparation Time: 15 minutes

Cooking Time: 6 minutes
Serving: 4
Ingredients:

- 1-pound chicken breast
- 4 (6-inch) halved pitas
- ½ cup chopped plum tomato
- ½ cup chopped cucumber
- ¼ cup chopped red onion
- 5 tbsp plain low-fat Greek-style yogurt, divided
- 2 tbsp lemon juice, divided
- 2 tbsp finely chopped parsley
- 2 tbsp extra-virgin olive oil
- 1 tbsp tahini
- ½ tsp salt
- ½ tsp crushed red pepper
- ¼ tsp ground cumin
- ¼ tsp ground ginger
- 1/8 tsp ground coriander

Direction:

1. Combine the parsley, salt, red pepper, ginger, cumin, coriander, 1 tbsp of yogurt, 1 tbsp of juice and 2 cloves of garlic. Add the chicken, stir to coat. Prep oil in nonstick pan over medium-high heat. Add the chicken mixture to the pan and cook for 6 min
2. Scourge remaining 1 tbsp of lemon juice, the remaining ¼ cup of yogurt, remaining 1 clove of garlic and the tahini, mixing well. Put 1 ½ tsp of the tahini mixture inside each half of the pita, divide the chicken between the halves of the pita. Fill each half of the pita with 1 tbsp of cucumber, 1 tbsp of tomato and 1 ½ tsp of onion.

Nutrition: 440 Calories 37g Protein 19g Fat

522. Lemon Chicken Pita Burgers with Spiced Yogurt Sauce

Preparation Time: 15 minutes
Cooking Time: 6 minutes
Serving: 4
Ingredients:

- 4 (6-inch) cut in half pitas
- 2 lightly beaten large egg whites
- 1-pound ground chicken
- 2 cups shredded lettuce
- ½ cup diced tomato
- ½ cup chopped green onions
- ½ cup plain low-fat yogurt
- 1/3 cup Italian-seasoned breadcrumbs
- 1 tbsp olive oil
- 1 tbsp Greek seasoning blend
- 2 tsp grated lemon zest, divided
- 1 ½ tsp chopped oregano
- ½ tsp coarsely ground black pepper

Direction:

1. Combine the chicken, eggs, onion, black pepper, breadcrumbs, Greek seasoning blend and 1 tsp of zest, mixing well. Split mixture into 8 equal portions and make patties ¼-inch thick.
2. Heat the oil in a large nonstick pan over medium-high heat. Put on the patties and cook for 2 min per side. Cover, lower the heat to medium and cook for 4 min.
3. Combine oregano, yogurt and the remaining zest. Fill each half of the pita with 1 patty, 1 tbsp of yogurt mix, 1 tbsp of tomato and ¼ cup of lettuce.

Nutrition: 391 Calories 40g Protein 20g Fat

523. Lamb Chop with Pistachio Gremolata

Preparation Time: 10 minutes
Cooking Time: 8 minutes
Serving: 4
Ingredients:

- 8 trimmed lamb loin chops
- 2 tbsp chopped flat-leaf parsley
- 2 tbsp finely chopped pistachios
- 1 tbsp chopped cilantro
- 2 tsp grated lemon zest
- ½ tsp salt
- ½ tsp ground cumin
- ¼ tsp ground coriander
- ¼ tsp black pepper
- 1/8 tsp salt
- 1/8 ground cinnamon
- 1 clove minced garlic

Direction:

1. Heat nonstick pan at medium-high heat. Combine the cumin, coriander, cinnamon, salt and black pepper and season evenly on both sides of the lamb. Grease the pan with cooking spray and add the lamb, cook for 4 min per side.
2. In the meantime, combine the pistachios, cilantro, parsley, lemon zest, salt and garlic, season over the lamb.

Nutrition: 409 Calories 41g Protein 22g Fat

524. Pita Salad with Cucumber, Fennel and Chicken

Preparation Time: 10 minutes
Cooking Time: 12 minutes
Serving: 4
Ingredients:

- 2 (6-inch) pitas
- ½ halved lengthwise and thinly sliced English cucumber
- 2 cups thinly sliced fennel bulb
- 1 cup shredded skinless, boneless rotisserie chicken breast
- ½ cup chopped flat-leaf parsley

- ¼ cup vertically sliced red onion
- ¼ cup lemon juice
- 3 tbsp extra-virgin olive oil
- 1 tbsp white wine vinegar
- ½ tsp chopped oregano
- ½ tsp salt, divided
- ¼ tsp black pepper, divided

Direction:
1. Preheat the oven to 350°F.
2. Situate pitas on a baking tray and bake for 12 min, cool down 1 min. Cut into small pieces and combine with fennel, chicken, parsley and red onion. Season with ¼ tsp of salt and 1/8 tsp of pepper.
3. Add the juice, oregano, vinegar, the remaining ¼ tsp of salt and 1/8 tsp of pepper. Gradually add the oil, mixing with a whisk. Season with dressing over the pita mixture to coat and serve.

Nutrition: 413 Calories 38g Protein 17g Fat

525. Halibut with Lemon-Fennel Salad

Preparation Time: 15 minutes
Cooking Time: 5 minutes
Serving: 4
Ingredients:
- 4 halibut fillets
- 2 cups thinly sliced fennel bulb
- ¼ cup thinly vertically sliced red onion
- 2 tbsp lemon juice
- 1 tbsp thyme leaves
- 1 tbsp chopped flat-leaf parsley
- 5 tsp extra-virgin olive oil, divided
- 1 tsp coriander
- ½ tsp salt
- ½ tsp cumin
- ¼ tsp ground black pepper
- 2 cloves minced garlic

Direction:
1. Combine the coriander, cumin, salt and black pepper in a small bowl. Combine 2 tsp of olive oil, garlic and 1 ½ tsp of spice mixture in another small bowl, evenly rub the garlic mixture on the halibut. Heat 1 tsp of oil in a large nonstick pan over medium-high heat. Cook the halibut to the pan for 5 min.
2. Combine the remaining 2 tsp of oil, ¾ tsp of spice mixture, the fennel bulb, onion, lemon juice, thyme leaves and parsley in a bowl, mix well to coat, and serve salad with halibut.

Nutrition: 427 Calories 39g Protein 20g Fat

526. Tuscan Beef Stew

Preparation Time 10 minutes
Cooking Time 4 hours

Serving: 8
Ingredients
- 2 pounds beef stew meat
- 4 carrots
- 2 (14½-ounce) cans tomatoes
- 1 medium onion
- 1 package McCormick Slow Cookers Hearty Beef Stew Seasoning
- ½ cup water
- ½ cup dry red wine
- 1 teaspoon rosemary leaves
- 8 slices Italian bread

Directions
1. Place the cubed beef in the slow cooker along with the carrots, diced tomatoes, and onion wedges.
2. Mix the seasoning package in the ½ cup of water and stir well, making sure there are no lumps remaining.
3. Add the red wine to the water and stir slightly. Add the rosemary leaves to the water-and-wine mixture and then pour over the meat, stirring to ensure the meat is completely covered.
4. Switch the slow cooker to low then cook for 8 hours, or cook for 4 hours on high.
5. Serve with toasted Italian bread.

Nutrition 329 Calories 15g fat 25.6g protein

527. Mediterranean Beef Stew

Preparation Time 25 minutes
Cooking Time 8 hours
Serving: 6
Ingredients
- 1 tablespoon olive oil
- 8 ounces sliced mushrooms
- 1 onion
- 2 pounds chuck roast
- 1 cup beef stock
- 1 (14½-ounce) can tomatoes with juice
- ½ cup tomato sauce
- ¼ cup balsamic vinegar
- 1 can black olives
- ½ cup garlic cloves
- 2 tablespoons fresh rosemary
- 2 tablespoons fresh parsley
- 1 tablespoon capers

Directions
1. Heat a skillet over high heat. Add 1 tablespoon of olive oil. Once heated, cook cubed roast.
2. Once cooked, stir rest of the olive oil (if needed), then toss in the onions and mushrooms. When they have softened, transfer to the slow cooker.
3. Add the beef stock to the skillet to deglaze the pan, then pour it over the meat in the slow cooker.
4. Mix rest of the ingredients to the slow cooker to coat.

5. Set the temperature on your slow cooker to low and cook for 8 hours.

Nutrition 471 Calories 23.4g fat 47.1g protein

528. Cabbage Roll Casserole with Veal

Preparation Time 5 minutes
Cooking Time 4–8 hours
Serving: 6
Ingredients
- 1-pound raw ground veal
- 1 head of cabbage
- 1 medium green pepper
- 1 medium onion, chopped
- 1 (15-ounce) can tomatoes
- 2 (15-ounce) cans tomato sauce
- 1 teaspoon minced garlic
- 1 tablespoon Worcestershire sauce
- 1 tablespoon beef bouillon
- ½ teaspoon salt
- ½ teaspoon pepper
- 1 cup uncooked brown rice

Directions
1. Situate all the ingredients to your slow cooker
2. Stir well to combine.
3. Adjust your slow cooker to high and cook for 4 hours, or cook for 8 hours on low.

Nutrition 335 Calories 18g fat 22.9g protein

529. Slow Cooked Daube Provencal

Preparation Time 15 minutes
Cooking Time: 4–8 hours
Serving: 8–10
Ingredients
- 1 tablespoon olive oil
- 10 garlic cloves, minced
- 2 pounds boneless chuck roast
- 1½ teaspoons salt
- ½ teaspoon black pepper
- 1 cup dry red wine
- 2 cups carrots, chopped
- 1½ cups onion, chopped
- ½ cup beef broth
- 1 (14-ounce) can diced tomatoes
- 1 tablespoon tomato paste
- 1 teaspoon fresh rosemary, chopped
- 1 teaspoon fresh thyme, chopped
- ½ teaspoon orange zest, grated
- ½ teaspoon ground cinnamon
- ¼ teaspoon ground cloves
- 1 bay leaf
1. **Directions**

2. Preheat skillet and then add the olive oil. Cook minced garlic and onions
3. Add the cubed meat, salt, and pepper and cook until the meat has browned.
4. Transfer the meat to the slow cooker.
5. Put beef broth to the skillet and let simmer for about 3 minutes to deglaze the pan, then pour into slow cooker over the meat.
6. Incorporate the rest of the ingredients to the slow cooker and stir well to combine.
7. Adjust your slow cooker to low and cook for 8 hours, or set to high and cook for 4 hours.
8. Serve with a side of egg noodles, rice or some crusty Italian bread.

Nutrition 547 Calories 30.5g fat 45.2g protein

530. Osso Bucco

Preparation Time 30 minutes
Cooking Time 8 hours
Serving: 2–4
Ingredients
- 4 beef shanks or veal shanks
- 1 teaspoon sea salt
- ½ teaspoon ground black pepper
- 3 tablespoons whole wheat flour
- 1–2 tablespoons olive oil
- 2 medium onions, diced
- 2 medium carrots, diced
- 2 celery stalks, diced
- 4 garlic cloves, minced
- 1 (14-ounce) can diced tomatoes
- 2 teaspoons dried thyme leaves
- ½ cup beef or vegetable stock

Directions
1. Season the shanks on both sides, then dip in the flour to coat.
2. Heat a large skillet over high heat. Add the olive oil. Once hot, situate the shanks and brown evenly on both sides. When browned, transfer to the slow cooker.
3. Pour the stock into the skillet and let simmer for 3–5 minutes while stirring to deglaze the pan.
4. Incorporate the rest of the ingredients to the slow cooker and pour the stock from the skillet over the top.
5. Click slow cooker to low and cook for 8 hours.
6. Serve the Osso Bucco over quinoa, brown rice, or even cauliflower rice.

Nutrition 589 Calories 21.3g fat 74.7g protein

531. Slow Cooker Beef Bourguignon

Preparation Time 5 minutes
Cooking Time 6–8 hours
Serving: 6–8
Ingredients

- 1 tablespoon extra-virgin olive oil
- 6 ounces bacon
- 3 pounds beef brisket
- 1 large carrot
- 1 large white onion
- 6 cloves garlic
- ½ teaspoon coarse salt
- ½ teaspoon pepper
- 2 tablespoons whole wheat
- 12 small pearl onions
- 3 cups red wine
- 2 cups beef stock
- 2 tablespoons tomato paste
- 1 beef bouillon cube
- 1 teaspoon fresh thyme
- 2 tablespoons fresh parsley
- 2 bay leaves
- 2 tablespoons butter
- 1-pound mushrooms

Directions

1. Preheat skillet over medium-high heat, pour olive oil. When the oil has heated, cook the bacon until it is crisp, then place it in your slow cooker. Save the bacon fat in the skillet.
2. Pat-dry the beef with a paper towel and cook it in the same skillet with the bacon fat until all sides have the same brown coloring.
3. Transfer to the slow cooker.
4. Add the onions and carrots to the slow cooker and season with the salt and pepper. Stir to combine the ingredients and make sure everything is seasoned.
5. Pour the red wine into the skillet and simmer for 4–5 minutes to deglaze the pan, then stir in the flour, stirring until smooth.
6. When the liquid has thickened, pour it into the slow cooker and stir to coat everything with the wine mixture. Add the tomato paste, bouillon cube, thyme, parsley, 4 cloves of garlic, and bay leaf.
7. Adjust your slow cooker to high and cook for 6 hours, or set to low and cook for 8 hours.
8. Before serving, heat up butter in a skillet over medium heat. When the oil is hot, add the remaining 2 cloves of garlic and cook for about 1 minute before adding the mushrooms.
9. Cook the mushrooms until soft, then add to the slow cooker and mix to combine.
10. Serve with mashed potatoes, rice or noodles.

Nutrition 672 Calories 32g fat 56g protein

532. **Balsamic Beef**

Preparation Time 5 minutes
Cooking Time 8 hours
Serving: 8–10
Ingredients
- 2 pounds boneless chuck roast
- 1 tablespoon olive oil

Rub
- 1 teaspoon garlic powder
- ½ teaspoon onion powder
- 1 teaspoon sea salt
- ½ teaspoon black pepper

Sauce
- ½ cup balsamic vinegar
- 2 tablespoons honey
- 1 tablespoon honey mustard
- 1 cup beef broth
- 1 tablespoon tapioca

Directions

1. Incorporate all of the ingredients for the rub.
2. In a separate bowl, mix the balsamic vinegar, honey, honey mustard, and beef broth.
3. Coat the roast in olive oil, then rub in the spices from the rub mix.
4. Situate the roast in the slow cooker and then pour the sauce over the top.
5. Select slow cooker to low and cook for 8 hours.
6. If you want to thicken, pour the liquid into a saucepan and heat to boiling on the stovetop. Stir in the flour until smooth and let simmer until the sauce thickens.

Nutrition 306 Calories 19g fat 25g protein

533. **Veal Pot Roast**

Preparation Time 20 minutes
Cooking Time 5 hours
Serving: 6–8
Ingredient
- 2 tbsp. olive oil
- Salt and pepper
- 3-lb. boneless veal roast
- 4 medium carrots
- 2 parsnips
- 2 white turnips
- 10 garlic cloves
- 2 sprigs fresh thyme
- 1 orange
- 1 cup veal stock

Directions

1. Preheat big skillet over medium-high heat.
2. Rub veal roast all over with olive oil, then season with salt and pepper.
3. Once hot, add the veal roast and sear on all sides.
4. Once roast is cooked on all sides, situate it to the slow cooker.
5. Throw the carrots, parsnips, turnips, and garlic into the skillet. Stir and cook for 5 minutes.
6. Situate the vegetables to the slow cooker, putting around the meat.
7. Top the roast with the thyme and the zest from the orange. Slice orange in half and squeeze the juice over the top of the meat.

8. Pour in chicken stock, then cook the roast on low for 5 hours.

Nutrition 426 Calories 12.8g fat 48.8g protein

534. Mediterranean Rice and Sausage

Preparation Time 15 minutes
Cooking Time 8 hours
Serving: 6
Ingredients

- 1½ pounds Italian sausage, crumbled
- 1 medium onion, chopped
- 2 tablespoons steak sauce
- 2 cups long grain rice, uncooked
- 1 (14-ounce) can diced tomatoes with juice
- ½ cup water
- 1 medium green pepper, diced

Directions

1. Spray your slow cooker with olive oil or nonstick cooking spray.
2. Add the sausage, onion, and steak sauce to the slow cooker.
3. Cook at low for 9 hours.
4. After 8 hours, add the rice, tomatoes, water and green pepper. Stir to combine thoroughly.
5. Cook for 20 to 25 minutes.

Nutrition 650 Calories 36g fat 22g protein

535. Spanish Meatballs

Preparation Time 20 minutes
Cooking Time 5 hours
Serving: 6
Ingredients

- 1-pound ground turkey
- 1-pound ground pork
- 2 eggs
- 1 (20-ounce) can diced tomatoes
- ¾ cup sweet onion, minced, divided
- ¼ cup plus 1 tablespoon breadcrumbs
- 3 tablespoons fresh parsley, chopped
- 1½ teaspoons cumin
- 1½ teaspoons paprika (sweet or hot)

Directions

1. Spray the slow cooker with olive oil.
2. In a mixing bowl, mix ground meat, eggs, about half of the onions, the breadcrumbs, and the spices.
3. Wash your hands and mix together until everything is well combined. Shape into meatballs.
4. Mix 2 tablespoons of olive oil over medium heat. Once hot, stir in meatballs and brown on all sides. When they are done, transfer them to the slow cooker.
5. Add the rest of the onions and the tomatoes to the skillet and allow them to cook for a few minutes,

scraping the brown bits from the meatballs up to add flavor.
6. Pour the tomatoes over the meatballs in the slow cooker and cook on low for 5 hours.

Nutrition 372 Calories 21.7g fat 28.5g protein

536. Lamb Shanks with Red Wine

Preparation Time 20 minutes
Cooking Time 5 hours
Serving: 4
Ingredients

- 2 tablespoons olive oil
- 2 tablespoons flour
- 4 lamb shanks, trimmed
- 1 onion, chopped
- 2 garlic cloves, crushed
- 2/3 cup red wine
- 3 cups tomato sauce

Directions

1. Heat a skillet over high heat. Add the olive oil.
2. Season the lamb shanks then roll in the flour. Shake off excess flour and place the shanks in the skillet to brown on all sides.
3. Spray the slow cooker with olive oil and place the browned shanks in the slow cooker.
4. Add the crushed garlic to the red wine. Mix with the tomato sauce and then pour the mixture over the lamb shanks and cook on low for 5–6 hours

Nutrition 354 Calories 12g fat 42g protein

537. Leg of Lamb with Rosemary and Garlic

Preparation Time 15 minutes
Cooking Time 8 hours
Serving: 4–6
Ingredients

- 3–4-pound leg of lamb
- 4 garlic cloves, sliced thin
- 5–8 sprigs fresh rosemary (more if desired)
- 2 tablespoons olive oil
- 1 lemon, halved
- ¼ cup flour

Directions

1. Put skillet over high heat and pour olive oil.
2. When the olive oil is hot, add the leg of lamb and sear on both sides until brown.
3. Spray the slow cooker with olive oil and then transfer the lamb to the slow cooker.
4. Squeeze the lemon over the meat and then place in the pot next to the lamb.
5. Create small incisions in the meat, then stuff the holes you created with rosemary and garlic.
6. Place any remaining rosemary and garlic on top of the roast.
7. Cook on low for 8 hours.

Nutrition 557 Calories 39g fat 46g protein

538. Lemon Honey Lamb Shoulder

Preparation Time 10 minutes
Cooking Time 8 hours
Serving: 4
Ingredients
- 3 cloves garlic, thinly sliced
- 1 tablespoon fresh rosemary, chopped
- 1 teaspoon lemon zest, grated
- ½ teaspoon each salt and pepper
- 4–5-pound boneless lamb shoulder roast
- 3 tablespoons lemon juice
- 1 tablespoon honey
- 6 shallots, quartered
- 2 teaspoons cornstarch

Directions
1. Stir garlic, rosemary, lemon zest, salt, and pepper.
2. Rub the spice mixture into the lamb shoulder. Make sure to coat the whole roast.
3. Spray the slow cooker with olive oil and add the lamb.
4. Mix together the honey and lemon juice and then pour over the meat.
5. Arrange the shallots beside the meat in the slow cooker.
6. Cook on low for 8 hours.
7. Serve. You can make a gravy by transferring the juice from the slow cooker to a medium saucepan. Thoroughly mix the cornstarch into a little water until smooth. Then mix into the juice and bring to a simmer. Simmer until mixture thickens.

Nutrition 240 Calories 11g fat 31g protein

539. Italian Shredded Pork Stew

Preparation Time 20 minutes
Cooking Time 8 hours
Serving: 8
Ingredients
- 2 medium sweet potatoes
- 2 cups fresh kale, chopped
- 1 large onion, chopped
- 4 cloves garlic, minced
- 1 2½–3½ pound boneless pork shoulder butt roast
- 1 (14-ounce) can cannellini beans
- 1½ teaspoons Italian seasoning
- ½ teaspoon salt
- ½ teaspoon pepper
- 3 (14½-ounce) cans chicken broth
- Sour cream (optional)

Directions
1. Coat slow cooker with nonstick cooking spray or olive oil.
2. Place the cubed sweet potatoes, kale, garlic and onion into the slow cooker.

3. Add the pork shoulder on top of the potatoes.
4. Add the beans, Italian seasoning salt, and pepper.
5. Pour the chicken broth over the meat.
6. Cook on low for 8 hours.
7. Serve with sour cream, if desired.

Nutrition 283 Calories 13g fat 24g protein

540. Parmesan Honey Pork Loin Roast

Preparation Time 10 minutes
Cooking Time 5 hours
Serving: 8
Ingredients
- 3-pound pork loin
- 2/3 cup grated parmesan cheese
- ½ cup honey
- 3 tablespoons soy sauce
- 1 tablespoon oregano
- 1 tablespoon basil
- 2 tablespoons garlic, chopped
- 2 tablespoons olive oil
- ½ teaspoon salt
- 2 tablespoons cornstarch
- ¼ cup chicken broth

Directions
1. Spray your slow cooker with olive oil or nonstick cooking spray.
2. Place the pork loin in the slow cooker.
3. Incorporate cheese, honey, soy sauce, oregano, basil, garlic, olive oil, and salt. Stir with a fork to combine well, then pour over the pork loin.
4. Cook in low for 5–6 hours.
5. Remove the pork loin and put on a serving platter.
6. Pour the juices from the slow cooker into a small saucepan.
7. Create a slurry by mixing the cornstarch into the chicken broth and whisking until smooth.
8. Allow to boil, then whisk in the slurry and let simmer until thickened. Pour over the pork loin and serve.

Nutrition 449 Calories 15g fat55g protein

541. Slow Cooker Mediterranean Beef Roast

Preparation Time: 10 minutes
Cooking Time: 10 hours and 10 minutes
Servings: 6
Ingredients:
- 3 pounds Chuck roast, boneless
- 2 teaspoons Rosemary
- ½ cup Tomatoes, sun-dried and chopped
- 10 cloves Grated garlic
- ½ cup Beef stock
- 2 tablespoons Balsamic vinegar
- ¼ cup Chopped Italian parsley, fresh

- ¼ cup Chopped olives
- 1 teaspoon Lemon zest
- ¼ cup Cheese grits

Directions:
1. In the slow cooker, put garlic, sun dried tomatoes, and the beef roast. Add beef stock and Rosemary. Close the cooker and slow cook for 10 hours.
2. After cooking is over, remove the beef, and shred the meet. Discard the fat. Add back the shredded meat to the slow cooker and simmer for 10 minutes. In a small bowl combine lemon zest, parsley, and olives. Cool the mixture until you are ready to serve. Garnish using the refrigerated mix.
3. Serve it over pasta or egg noodles. Top it with cheese grits.

Nutrition 314 Calories 19g Fat 1g Carbohydrate 32g Protein

542. Slow Cooker Mediterranean Beef with Artichokes

Preparation Time: 3 hours and 20 minutes
Cooking Time: 7 hours and 8 minutes
Servings: 6
Ingredients:
- 2 pounds Beef for stew
- 14 ounces Artichoke hearts
- 1 tablespoon Grape seed oil
- 1 Diced onion
- 32 ounces Beef broth
- 4 cloves Garlic, grated
- 14½ ounces Tinned tomatoes, diced
- 15 ounces Tomato sauce
- 1 teaspoon Dried oregano
- ½ cup Pitted, chopped olives
- 1 teaspoon Dried parsley
- 1 teaspoon Dried oregano
- ½ teaspoon Ground cumin
- 1 teaspoon Dried basil
- 1 Bay leaf
- ½ teaspoon Salt

Directions:
1. In a large non-stick skillet pour some oil and bring to medium-high heat. Roast the beef until it turns brown on both the sides. Transfer the beef into a slow cooker.
2. Add in beef broth, diced tomatoes, tomato sauce, salt and combine. Pour in beef broth, diced tomatoes, oregano, olives, basil, parsley, bay leaf, and cumin. Combine the mixture thoroughly.
3. Close and cook on low heat for 7 hours. Discard the bay leaf at the time serving. Serve hot.

Nutrition 416 Calories 5g Fat 14.1g Carbohydrates 29.9g Protein

543. Skinny Slow Cooker Mediterranean Style Pot Roast

Preparation Time: 30 minutes
Cooking Time: 8 hours
Servings: 10
Ingredients:
- 4 pounds Eye of round roast
- 4 cloves Garlic
- 2 teaspoons Olive oil
- 1 teaspoon Freshly ground black pepper
- 1 cup Chopped onions
- 4 Carrots, chopped
- 2 teaspoons Dried Rosemary
- 2 Chopped celery stalks
- 28 ounces Crushed tomatoes in the can
- 1 cup Low sodium beef broth
- 1 cup Red wine
- 2 teaspoons Salt

Directions:
1. Season the beef roast with salt, garlic, and pepper and set aside. Pour oil in a non-stick skillet and bring to medium-high heat. Put the beef into it and roast until it becomes brown on all sides. Now, transfer the roasted beef into a 6-quart slow cooker. Add carrots, onion, rosemary, and celery into the skillet. Continue cooking until the onion and vegetable become soft.
2. Stir in the tomatoes and wine into this vegetable mixture. Add beef broth and tomato mixture into the slow cooker along with the vegetable mixture. Close and cook on low for 8 hours.
3. Once the meat gets cooked, remove it from the slow cooker and place it on a cutting board and wrap with an aluminum foil. To thicken the sauce, then transfer it into a saucepan and boil it under low heat until it reaches to the required consistency. Discard fats before serving.

Nutrition 260 Calories 6g Fat 8.7g Carbohydrates 37.6g Protein

544. Slow Cooker Meatloaf

Preparation Time: 10 minutes
Cooking Time: 6 hours and 10 minutes
Servings: 8
Ingredients:
- 2 pounds Ground bison
- 1 Grated zucchini
- 2 large Eggs
- Olive oil cooking spray as required
- 1 Zucchini, shredded
- ½ cup Parsley, fresh, finely chopped
- ½ cup Parmesan cheese, shredded
- 3 tablespoons Balsamic vinegar
- 4 Garlic cloves, grated

- 2 tablespoons Onion minced
- 1 tablespoon Dried oregano
- ½ teaspoon Ground black pepper
- ½ teaspoon Kosher salt

For the topping:
- ¼ cup Shredded Mozzarella cheese
- ¼ cup Ketchup without sugar
- ¼ cup Freshly chopped parsley

Directions:
1. Stripe line the inside of a six-quart slow cooker with aluminum foil. Spray non-stick cooking oil over it.
2. In a large bowl combine ground bison or extra lean ground sirloin, zucchini, eggs, parsley, balsamic vinegar, garlic, dried oregano, sea or kosher salt, minced dry onion, and ground black pepper.
3. Situate this mixture into the slow cooker and form an oblong shaped loaf. Cover the cooker, set on a low heat and cook for 6 hours. After cooking, open the cooker and spread ketchup all over the meatloaf.
4. Now, place the cheese above the ketchup as a new layer and close the slow cooker. Let the meatloaf sit on these two layers for about 10 minutes or until the cheese starts to melt. Garnish with fresh parsley, and shredded Mozzarella cheese.

Nutrition 320 Calories 2g Fat 4g Carbohydrates 26g Protein

545. Slow Cooker Mediterranean Beef Hoagies

Preparation Time: 10 minutes
Cooking Time: 13 hours
Servings: 6
Ingredients:
- 3 pounds Beef top round roast fatless
- ½ teaspoon Onion powder
- ½ teaspoon Black pepper
- 3 cups Low sodium beef broth
- 4 teaspoons Salad dressing mix
- 1 Bay leaf
- 1 tablespoon Garlic, minced
- 2 Red bell peppers, thin strips cut
- 16 ounces Pepperoncino
- 8 slices Sargento Provolone, thin
- 2 ounces Gluten-free bread
- ½ teaspoon salt

For seasoning:
- 1½ tablespoon Onion powder
- 1½ tablespoon Garlic powder
- 2 tablespoon Dried parsley
- 1 tablespoon stevia
- ½ teaspoon Dried thyme
- 1 tablespoon Dried oregano
- 2 tablespoons Black pepper
- 1 tablespoon Salt
- 6 Cheese slices

Directions:
1. Dry the roast with a paper towel. Combine black pepper, onion powder and salt in a small bowl and rub the mixture over the roast. Place the seasoned roast into a slow cooker.
2. Add broth, salad dressing mix, bay leaf, and garlic to the slow cooker. Combine it gently. Close and set to low cooking for 12 hours. After cooking, remove the bay leaf.
3. Take out the cooked beef and shred the beef meet. Put back the shredded beef and add bell peppers and. Add bell peppers and pepperoncino into the slow cooker. Cover the cooker and low cook for 1 hour. Before serving, top each of the bread with 3 ounces of the meat mixture. Top it with a cheese slice. The liquid gravy can be used as a dip.

Nutrition 442 Calories 11.5g Fat 37g Carbohydrates 49g Protein

546. Mediterranean Pork Roast

Preparation Time: 10 minutes
Cooking Time: 8 hours and 10 minutes
Servings: 6
Ingredients:
- 2 tablespoons Olive oil
- 2 pounds Pork roast
- ½ teaspoon Paprika
- ¾ cup Chicken broth
- 2 teaspoons Dried sage
- ½ tablespoon Garlic minced
- ¼ teaspoon Dried marjoram
- ¼ teaspoon Dried Rosemary
- 1 teaspoon Oregano
- ¼ teaspoon Dried thyme
- 1 teaspoon Basil
- ¼ teaspoon Kosher salt

Directions:
1. In a small bowl mix broth, oil, salt, and spices. In a skillet pour olive oil and bring to medium-high heat. Put the pork into it and roast until all sides become brown.
2. Take out the pork after cooking and poke the roast all over with a knife. Place the poked pork roast into a 6-quart crock pot. Now, pour the small bowl mixture liquid all over the roast.
3. Seal crock pot and cook on low for 8 hours. After cooking, remove it from the crock pot on to a cutting board and shred into pieces. Afterward, add the shredded pork back into the crockpot. Simmer it another 10 minutes. Serve along with feta cheese, pita bread, and tomatoes.

Nutrition 361 Calories 10.4g Fat 0.7g Carbohydrates 43.8g Protein

547. Beef Pizza

Preparation Time: 20 minutes

Cooking Time: 50 minutes
Servings: 10
Ingredients:
For Crust:

- 3 cups all-purpose flour
- 1 tablespoon sugar
- 2¼ teaspoons active dry yeast
- 1 teaspoon salt
- 2 tablespoons olive oil
- 1 cup warm water

For Topping:

- 1-pound ground beef
- 1 medium onion, chopped
- 2 tablespoons tomato paste
- 1 tablespoon ground cumin
- Salt and ground black pepper, as required
- ¼ cup water
- 1 cup fresh spinach, chopped
- 8 ounces artichoke hearts, quartered
- 4 ounces fresh mushrooms, sliced
- 2 tomatoes, chopped
- 4 ounces feta cheese, crumbled

Directions:
For crust:

1. Mix the flour, sugar, yeast and salt with a stand mixer, using the dough hook. Add 2 tablespoons of the oil and warm water and knead until a smooth and elastic dough is formed.
2. Make a ball of the dough and set aside for about 15 minutes.
3. Situate the dough onto a lightly floured surface and roll into a circle. Situate the dough into a lightly, greased round pizza pan and gently, press to fit. Set aside for about 10-15 minutes. Coat the crust with some oil. Preheat the oven to 400 degrees F.

For topping:

4. Fry beef in a nonstick skillet over medium-high heat for about 4-5 minutes. Mix in the onion and cook for about 5 minutes, stirring frequently. Add the tomato paste, cumin, salt, black pepper and water and stir to combine.
5. Put heat to medium and cook for about 5-10 minutes. Remove from the heat and set aside. Place the beef mixture over the pizza crust and top with the spinach, followed by the artichokes, mushrooms, tomatoes, and Feta cheese.
6. Bake until the cheese is melted. Pullout from the oven and keep aside for about 3-5 minutes before slicing. Cut into desired sized slices and serve.

Nutrition 309 Calories 8.7g Fat 3.7g Carbohydrates 3.3g Protein

548. Beef & Bulgur Meatballs

Preparation Time: 20 minutes
Cooking Time: 28 minutes
Servings: 6
Ingredients:

- ¾ cup uncooked bulgur
- 1-pound ground beef
- ¼ cup shallots, minced
- ¼ cup fresh parsley, minced
- ½ teaspoon ground allspice
- ½ teaspoon ground cumin
- ½ teaspoon ground cinnamon
- ¼ teaspoon red pepper flakes, crushed
- Salt, as required
- 1 tablespoon olive oil

Directions:

1. In a large bowl of the cold water, soak the bulgur for about 30 minutes. Drain the bulgur well and then, squeeze with your hands to remove the excess water. In a food processor, add the bulgur, beef, shallot, parsley, spices and salt and pulse until a smooth mixture is formed.
2. Situate the mixture into a bowl and refrigerate, covered for about 30 minutes. Remove from the refrigerator and make equal sized balls from the beef mixture. Using big nonstick skillet, heat up the oil over medium-high heat and cook the meatballs in 2 batches for about 13-14 minutes, flipping frequently. Serve warm.

Nutrition 228 Calories 7.4g Fat 0.1g Carbohydrates 3.5g Protein

549. Tasty Beef and Broccoli

Preparation Time: 10 minutes
Cooking Time: 15 minutes
Servings: 4
Ingredients:

- 1 and ½ lbs. flanks steak
- 1 tbsp. olive oil
- 1 tbsp. tamari sauce
- 1 cup beef stock
- 1-pound broccoli, florets separated

Directions:

1. Combine steak strips with oil and tamari, toss and set aside for 10 minutes. Select your instant pot on sauté mode, place beef strips and brown them for 4 minutes on each side. Stir in stock, cover the pot again and cook on high for 8 minutes. Stir in broccoli, cover and cook on high for 4 minutes more. Portion everything between plates and serve. Enjoy!

Nutrition 312 Calories 5g Fat 20g Carbohydrates 4g Protein

550. Beef Corn Chili

Preparation Time: 8-10 minutes
Cooking Time: 30 minutes
Servings: 8
Ingredients:

- 2 small onions, chopped (finely)
- ¼ cup canned corn

- 1 tablespoon oil
- 10 ounces lean ground beef
- 2 small chili peppers, diced

Directions:
1. Turn on the instant pot. Click "SAUTE". Pour the oil then stir in the onions, chili pepper, and beef; cook until turn translucent and softened. Pour the 3 cups water in the Cooking pot; mix well.
2. Seal the lid. Select "MEAT/STEW". Adjust the timer to 20 minutes. Allow to cook until the timer turns to zero.
3. Click "CANCEL" then "NPR" for natural release pressure for about 8-10 minutes. Open then place the dish in serving plates. Serve.

Nutrition 94 Calories 5g Fat 2g Carbohydrates 7g Protein

551. Balsamic Beef Dish

Preparation Time: 5 minutes
Cooking Time: 55 minutes
Servings: 8
Ingredients:
- 3 pounds chuck roast
- 3 cloves garlic, thinly sliced
- 1 tablespoon oil
- 1 teaspoon flavored vinegar
- ½ teaspoon pepper
- ½ teaspoon rosemary
- 1 tablespoon butter
- ½ teaspoon thyme
- ¼ cup balsamic vinegar
- 1 cup beef broth

Directions:
1. Slice the slits in the roast and stuff in garlic slices all over. Combine flavored vinegar, rosemary, pepper, thyme and rub the mixture over the roast. Select the pot on sauté mode and mix in oil, allow the oil to heat up. Cook both side of the roast.
2. Take it out and set aside. Stir in butter, broth, balsamic vinegar and deglaze the pot. Return the roast and close the lid, then cook on HIGH pressure for 40 minutes.
3. Perform a quick release. Serve!

Nutrition 393 Calories 15g Fat 25g Carbohydrates 37g Protein

552. Soy Sauce Beef Roast

Preparation Time: 8 minutes
Cooking Time: 35 minutes
Servings: 2-3
Ingredients:
- ½ teaspoon beef bouillon
- 1 ½ teaspoon rosemary
- ½ teaspoon minced garlic
- 2 pounds roast beef
- 1/3 cup soy sauce

Directions:
1. Combine the soy sauce, bouillon, rosemary, and garlic together in a mixing bowl.
2. Turn on your instant pot. Place the roast, and pour enough water to cover the roast; gently stir to mix well. Seal it tight.
3. Click "MEAT/STEW" Cooking function; set pressure level to "HIGH" and set the Cooking time to 35 minutes. Let the pressure to build to cook the ingredients. Once done, click "CANCEL" setting then click "NPR" Cooking function to naturally release the pressure.
4. Gradually open the lid, and shred the meat. Mix in the shredded meat back in the potting mix and stir well. Transfer in serving containers. Serve warm.

Nutrition 423 Calories 14g Fat 12g Carbohydrates 21g Protein

553. Rosemary Beef Chuck Roast

Preparation Time: 5 minutes
Cooking Time: 45 minutes
Servings: 5-6
Ingredients:
- 3 pounds chuck beef roast
- 3 garlic cloves
- ¼ cup balsamic vinegar
- 1 sprig fresh rosemary
- 1 sprig fresh thyme
- 1 cup of water
- 1 tablespoon vegetable oil
- Salt and pepper to taste

Directions:
1. Chop slices in the beef roast and place the garlic cloves in them. Rub the roast with the herbs, black pepper, and salt. Preheat your instant pot using the sauté setting and pour the oil. When warmed, mix in the beef roast and stir-cook until browned on all sides. Add the remaining ingredients; stir gently.
2. Seal tight and cook on high for 40 minutes using manual setting. Allow the pressure release naturally, about 10 minutes. Uncover and put the beef roast the serving plates, slice and serve.

Nutrition 542 Calories 11.2g Fat 8.7g Carbohydrates 55.2g Protein

554. Pork Chops and Tomato Sauce

Preparation Time: 10 minutes
Cooking Time: 20 minutes
Servings: 4
Ingredients:
- 4 pork chops, boneless
- 1 tablespoon soy sauce
- ¼ teaspoon sesame oil
- 1 and ½ cups tomato paste

- 1 yellow onion
- 8 mushrooms, sliced

Directions:
1. In a bowl, mix pork chops with soy sauce and sesame oil, toss and leave aside for 10 minutes. Set your instant pot on sauté mode, add pork chops and brown them for 5 minutes on each side.
2. Stir in onion, and cook for 1-2 minutes more. Add tomato paste and mushrooms, toss, cover and cook on high for 8-9 minutes. Divide everything between plates and serve. Enjoy!

Nutrition 300 Calories 7g Fat 18g Carbohydrates 4g Protein

555. Chicken with Caper Sauce

Preparation Time: 20 minutes
Cooking Time: 18 minutes
Servings: 5
Ingredients:
For Chicken:
- 2 eggs
- Salt and ground black pepper, as required
- 1 cup dry breadcrumbs
- 2 tablespoons olive oil
- 1½ pounds skinless, boneless chicken breast halves, pounded into ¾inch thickness and cut into pieces

For Capers Sauce:
- 3 tablespoons capers
- ½ cup dry white wine
- 3 tablespoons fresh lemon juice
- Salt and ground black pepper, as required
- 2 tablespoons fresh parsley, chopped

Directions:
1. For chicken: in a shallow dish, add the eggs, salt and black pepper and beat until well combined. In another shallow dish, place breadcrumbs. Soak the chicken pieces in egg mixture then coat with the breadcrumbs evenly. Shake off the excess breadcrumbs.
2. Cook the oil over medium heat and cook the chicken pieces for about 5-7 minutes per side or until desired doneness. With a slotted spoon, situate the chicken pieces onto a paper towel lined plate. With a piece of the foil, cover the chicken pieces to keep them warm.
3. In the same skillet, incorporate all the sauce ingredients except parsley and cook for about 2-3 minutes, stirring continuously. Drizzle parsley and remove from heat. Serve the chicken pieces with the topping of capers sauce.

Nutrition 352 Calories 13.5g Fat 1.9g Carbohydrates 1.2g Protein

556. Mango Salsa Chicken Burgers

Preparation Time: 15 minutes
Cooking Time: 10 minutes
Servings: 6

Ingredients:
- 1½ pounds ground turkey breast
- 1 teaspoon sea salt, divided
- ¼ teaspoon freshly ground black pepper
- 2 tablespoons extra-virgin olive oil
- 2 mangos, peeled, pitted, and cubed
- ½ red onion, finely chopped
- Juice of 1 lime
- 1 garlic clove, minced
- ½ jalapeño pepper, seeded and finely minced
- 2 tablespoons chopped fresh cilantro leaves

Directions:
1. Form the turkey breast into 4 patties and season with ½ teaspoon of sea salt and the pepper. Cook the olive oil in a nonstick skillet until it shimmers.
2. Add the turkey patties and cook for about 5 minutes per side until browned. While the patties cook, mix together the mango, red onion, lime juice, garlic, jalapeño, cilantro, and remaining ½ teaspoon of sea salt in a small bowl. Spoon the salsa over the turkey patties and serve.

Nutrition 384 Calories 3g Fat 27g Carbohydrates 34g Protein

557. Roast Herb Turkey

Preparation Time: 15 minutes
Cooking Time: 1½ hours (plus 20 minutes to rest)
Servings: 6
Ingredients:
- 2 tablespoons extra-virgin olive oil
- 4 garlic cloves, minced
- Zest of 1 lemon
- 1 tablespoon chopped fresh thyme leaves
- 1 tablespoon chopped fresh rosemary leaves
- 2 tablespoons chopped fresh Italian parsley leaves
- 1 teaspoon ground mustard
- 1 teaspoon sea salt
- ¼ teaspoon freshly ground black pepper
- 1 (6-pound) bone-in, skin-on turkey breast
- 1 cup dry white wine

Directions:
1. Preheat the oven to 325°F. Combine the olive oil, garlic, lemon zest, thyme, rosemary, parsley, mustard, sea salt, and pepper. Brush the herb mixture evenly over the surface of the turkey breast, and loosen the skin and rub underneath as well. Situate the turkey breast in a roasting pan on a rack, skin-side up.
2. Pour the wine in the pan. Roast for 1 to 1½ hours until the turkey reaches an internal temperature of 165 degrees F. Pull out from the oven and set separately for 20 minutes, tented with aluminum foil to keep it warm, before carving.

Nutrition 392 Calories 1g Fat 2g Carbohydrates 84g Protein

558. Chicken Sausage with Bell Peppers

Preparation Time: 10 minutes
Cooking Time: 20 minutes
Servings: 6
Ingredients:

- 2 tablespoons extra-virgin olive oil
- 6 Italian chicken sausage links
- 1 onion
- 1 red bell pepper
- 1 green bell pepper
- 3 garlic cloves, minced
- ½ cup dry white wine
- ½ teaspoon sea salt
- ¼ teaspoon freshly ground black pepper
- Pinch red pepper flakes

Directions:

1. Cook the olive oil on large skillet until it shimmers. Add the sausages and cook for 5 to 7 minutes, turning occasionally, until browned, and they reach an internal temperature of 165°F. With tongs, remove the sausage from the pan and set aside on a platter, tented with aluminum foil to keep warm.
2. Return the skillet to the heat and mix in the onion, red bell pepper, and green bell pepper. Cook and stir occasionally, until the vegetables begin to brown. Put in the garlic and cook for 30 seconds, stirring constantly.
3. Stir in the wine, sea salt, pepper, and red pepper flakes. Pull out and fold in any browned bits from the bottom of the pan. Simmer for about 4 minutes more, stirring, until the liquid reduces by half. Spoon the peppers over the sausages and serve.

Nutrition 173 Calories 1g Fat 6g Carbohydrates 22g Protein

559. Lemon Chicken Piccata

Preparation Time: 10 minutes
Cooking Time: 15 minutes
Servings: 6
Ingredients:

- ½ cup whole-wheat flour
- ½ teaspoon sea salt
- 1/8 teaspoon freshly ground black pepper
- 1½ pounds chicken breasts, cut into 6 pieces
- 3 tablespoons extra-virgin olive oil
- 1 cup unsalted chicken broth
- ½ cup dry white wine
- Juice of 1 lemon
- Zest of 1 lemon
- ¼ cup capers, drained and rinsed
- ¼ cup chopped fresh parsley leaves

Directions:

1. In a shallow dish, whisk the flour, sea salt, and pepper. Scour the chicken in the flour and tap off any excess. Cook the olive oil until it shimmers.

2. Put the chicken and cook for about 4 minutes per side until browned. Pull out the chicken from the pan and set aside, tented with aluminum foil to keep warm.
3. Situate the skillet back to the heat and stir in the broth, wine, lemon juice, and lemon zest, and capers. Use the side of a spoon scoop and fold in any browned bits from the bottom of the pan. Simmer until the liquid thickens. Take out the skillet from the heat and take the chicken back to the pan. Turn to coat. Stir in the parsley and serve.

Nutrition 153 Calories 2g Fat 9g Carbohydrates 8g Protein

560. One Skillet Tuscan Chicken

Preparation Time: 10 minutes
Cooking Time: 25 minutes
Servings: 6
Ingredients:

- ¼ cup extra-virgin olive oil, divided
- 1-pound boneless, skinless chicken breasts, cut into ¾-inch pieces
- 1 onion, chopped
- 1 red bell pepper, chopped
- 3 garlic cloves, minced
- ½ cup dry white wine
- 1 (14-ounce) can crushed tomatoes, undrained
- 1 (14-ounce) can chopped tomatoes, drained
- 1 (14-ounce) can white beans, drained
- 1 tablespoon dried Italian seasoning
- ½ teaspoon sea salt
- 1/8 teaspoon freshly ground black pepper
- 1/8 teaspoon red pepper flakes
- ¼ cup chopped fresh basil leaves

Directions:

1. Cook 2 tablespoons of olive oil until it shimmers. Mix in the chicken and cook until browned. Pullout the chicken from the skillet and put aside on a platter, tented with aluminum foil to keep warm.
2. Situate the skillet back to the heat and heat up the remaining olive oil. Add the onion and red bell pepper. Cook and stir rarely, until the vegetables are soft. Put the garlic and cook for 30 seconds, stirring constantly.
3. Stir in the wine, and use the side of the spoon to scoop out any browned bits from the bottom of the pan. Cook for 1 minute, stirring.
4. Mix in the crushed and chopped tomatoes, white beans, Italian seasoning, sea salt, pepper, and red pepper flakes. Allow to simmer. Cook for 5 minutes, stirring occasionally.
5. Put the chicken back and any juices that have collected to the skillet. Cook until the chicken is cook through. Take out from the heat and stir in the basil before serving.

Nutrition 271 Calories 8g Fat 29g Carbohydrates 14g Protein

561. Tomato Chicken Kapama

Preparation Time: 10 minutes
Cooking Time: 2 hours
Servings: 4
Ingredients:

- 1 (32-ounce) can chopped tomatoes, drained
- ¼ cup dry white wine
- 2 tablespoons tomato paste
- 3 tablespoons extra-virgin olive oil
- ¼ teaspoon red pepper flakes
- 1 teaspoon ground allspice
- ½ teaspoon dried oregano
- 2 whole cloves
- 1 cinnamon stick
- ½ teaspoon sea salt
- 1/8 teaspoon freshly ground black pepper
- 4 boneless, skinless chicken breast halves

Directions:

1. Mix the tomatoes, wine, tomato paste, olive oil, red pepper flakes, allspice, oregano, cloves, cinnamon stick, sea salt, and pepper in large pot. Bring to a simmer, stirring occasionally. Allow to simmer for 30 minutes. Remove and discard the whole cloves and cinnamon stick from the sauce and let the sauce cool.
2. Preheat the oven to 350°F. Situate the chicken in a 9-by-13-inch baking dish. Pour the sauce over the chicken and cover the pan with aluminum foil. Continue baking until it reaches 165°F internal temperature.

Nutrition 220 Calories 3g Fat 11g Carbohydrates 8g Protein

562. Chicken Filled with Spinach and Cheese

Preparation Time: 10 minutes
Cooking Time: 45 minutes
Servings: 4
Ingredients:

- 2 tablespoons extra-virgin olive oil
- 1-pound fresh baby spinach
- 3 garlic cloves, minced
- Zest of 1 lemon
- ½ teaspoon sea salt
- 1/8 teaspoon freshly ground black pepper
- ½ cup crumbled feta cheese
- 4 boneless, skinless chicken breasts

Directions:

1. Preheat the oven to 350°F. Cook the olive oil over medium heat until it shimmers. Add the spinach. Continue cooking and stirring, until wilted.
2. Stir in the garlic, lemon zest, sea salt, and pepper. Cook for 30 seconds, stirring constantly. Cool slightly and mix in the cheese.
3. Spread the spinach and cheese mixture in an even layer over the chicken pieces and roll the breast

around the filling. Hold closed with toothpicks or butcher's twine. Place the breasts in a 9-by-13-inch baking dish and bake for 30 to 40 minutes, or until the chicken have an internal temperature of 165°F. Take out from the oven and set aside for 5 minutes before slicing and serving.

Nutrition 263 Calories 3g Fat 7g Carbohydrates 17g Protein

563. Baked Lemon Chicken

Preparation Time: 5 minutes
Cooking Time: 1 hour
Servings: 6
Ingredients:

- 2 tablespoons chopped fresh rosemary leaves
- 1 teaspoon garlic powder
- ½ teaspoon sea salt
- 1/8 teaspoon freshly ground black pepper
- Zest of 1 lemon
- 12 chicken drumsticks

Directions:

1. Preheat the oven to 350°F. Mix the rosemary, garlic powder, sea salt, pepper, and lemon zest.
2. Situate the drumsticks in a 9-by-13-inch baking dish and sprinkle with the rosemary mixture. Bake until the chicken reaches an internal temperature of 165°F.

Nutrition 163 Calories 1g Fat 2g Carbohydrates 26g Protein

564. Chicken with Veggies

Preparation Time: 5 minutes
Cooking Time: 45 minutes
Servings: 4
Ingredients:

- 2 cups fingerling potatoes, halved
- 4 fresh figs, quartered
- 2 carrots, julienned
- 2 tablespoons extra-virgin olive oil
- 1 teaspoon sea salt, divided
- ¼ teaspoon freshly ground black pepper
- 4 chicken leg-thigh quarters
- 2 tablespoons chopped fresh parsley leaves

Directions:

1. Preheat the oven to 425°F. In a small bowl, toss the potatoes, figs, and carrots with the olive oil, ½ teaspoon of sea salt, and the pepper. Spread in a 9-by-13-inch baking dish.
2. Season the chicken with the rest of t sea salt. Place it on top of the vegetables. Bake until the internal temperature of 165°F. Sprinkle with the parsley and serve.

Nutrition 429 Calories 4g Fat 27g Carbohydrates 52g Protein

565. Tzatziki Chicken Gyros

Preparation Time: 15 minutes
Cooking Time: 80 minutes
Servings: 6
Ingredients:
- 1-pound ground chicken breast
- 1 onion, grated with excess water wrung out
- 2 tablespoons dried rosemary
- 1 tablespoon dried marjoram
- 6 garlic cloves, minced
- ½ teaspoon sea salt
- ¼ teaspoon freshly ground black pepper
- Tzatziki Sauce

Directions:
1. Preheat the oven to 350°F. Mix the chicken, onion, rosemary, marjoram, garlic, sea salt, and pepper using food processor. Blend until the mixture forms a paste. Alternatively, mix these ingredients in a bowl until well combined (see preparation tip).
2. Press the mixture into a loaf pan. Bake until it reaches 165 degrees internal temperature. Take out from the oven and let rest for 20 minutes before slicing.
3. Slice the gyro and spoon the tzatziki sauce over the top.

Nutrition 289 Calories 1g Fat 20g Carbohydrates 50g Protein

566. Greek Lasagna

Preparation Time: 10 minutes
Cooking Time: 45 minutes
Servings: 8
Ingredients:
- 5 tablespoons extra-virgin olive oil, divided
- 1 eggplant, sliced (unpeeled)
- 1 onion, chopped
- 1 green bell pepper, seeded and chopped
- 1-pound ground turkey
- 3 garlic cloves, minced
- 2 tablespoons tomato paste
- 1 (14-ounce) can chopped tomatoes, drained
- 1 tablespoon Italian seasoning
- 2 teaspoons Worcestershire sauce
- 1 teaspoon dried oregano
- ½ teaspoon ground cinnamon
- 1 cup unsweetened nonfat plain Greek yogurt
- 1 egg, beaten
- ¼ teaspoon freshly ground black pepper
- ¼ teaspoon ground nutmeg
- ¼ cup grated Parmesan cheese
- 2 tablespoons chopped fresh parsley leaves

Directions:
1. Preheat the oven to 400°F. Cook 3 tablespoons of olive oil until it shimmers. Add the eggplant slices and brown for 3 to 4 minutes per side. Transfer to paper towels to drain.
2. Situate the skillet back to the heat and pour the remaining 2 tablespoons of olive oil. Add the onion and green bell pepper. Continue cooking until the vegetables are soft. Remove from the pan and set aside.
3. Pull out the skillet to the heat and stir in the turkey. Cook for about 5 minutes, crumbling with a spoon, until browned. Cook garlic for 30 seconds, stirring constantly.
4. Stir in the tomato paste, tomatoes, Italian seasoning, Worcestershire sauce, oregano, and cinnamon. Place the onion and bell pepper back to the pan. Cook for 5 minutes, stirring. Combine the yogurt, egg, pepper, nutmeg, and cheese.
5. Arrange half of the meat mixture in a 9-by-13-inch baking dish. Layer with half the eggplant. Add the remaining meat mixture and the remaining eggplant. Spread with the yogurt mixture. Bake until golden brown. Garnish with the parsley and serve.

Nutrition 338 Calories 5g Fat 16g Carbohydrates 28g Protein

567. Baked Pork Tenderloin

Preparation Time: 10 minutes
Cooking Time: 30 minutes
Servings: 6
Ingredients:
- ½ cup fresh Italian parsley leaves, chopped
- 3 tablespoons fresh rosemary leaves, chopped
- 3 tablespoons fresh thyme leaves, chopped
- 3 tablespoons Dijon mustard
- 1 tablespoon extra-virgin olive oil
- 4 garlic cloves, minced
- ½ teaspoon sea salt
- ¼ teaspoon freshly ground black pepper
- 1 (1½-pound) pork tenderloin

Directions:
1. Preheat the oven to 400°F. Blend the parsley, rosemary, thyme, mustard, olive oil, garlic, sea salt, and pepper. Process for about 30 seconds until smooth. Spread the mixture evenly over the pork and place it on a rimmed baking sheet.
2. Bake until the meat reaches an internal temperature of 140°F. Pull out from the oven and set aside for 10 minutes before slicing and serving.

Nutrition 393 Calories 3g Fat 5g Carbohydrates 74g Protein

568. Mushroom Sauce Steak

Preparation Time: 8 hours
Cooking Time: 20 minutes
Servings: 4
Ingredients:
For the Marinade and Steak
- 1 cup dry red wine

- 3 garlic cloves, minced
- 2 tablespoons extra-virgin olive oil
- 1 tablespoon low-sodium soy sauce
- 1 tablespoon dried thyme
- 1 teaspoon Dijon mustard
- 2 tablespoons extra-virgin olive oil
- 1 to 1½ pounds skirt steak, flat iron steak, or tri-tip steak

For the Mushroom Sauce
- 2 tablespoons extra-virgin olive oil
- 1-pound cremini mushrooms, quartered
- ½ teaspoon sea salt
- 1 teaspoon dried thyme
- 1/8 teaspoon freshly ground black pepper
- 2 garlic cloves, minced
- 1 cup dry red wine

Directions:

To Make the Marinade and Steak

1. In a small bowl, whisk the wine, garlic, olive oil, soy sauce, thyme, and mustard. Pour into a resealable bag and add the steak. Refrigerate the steak to marinate for 4 to 8 hours. Remove the steak from the marinade and pat it dry with paper towels.
2. Cook the olive oil in large pan until it shimmers.
3. Situate the steak and cook for about 4 minutes per side until deeply browned on each side and the steak reaches an internal temperature of 140°F. Remove the steak from the skillet and put it on a plate tented with aluminum foil to keep warm, while you prepare the mushroom sauce.
4. When the mushroom sauce is ready, slice the steak against the grain into ½-inch-thick slices.

To Make the Mushroom Sauce

5. Cook oil in the same skillet over medium-high heat. Add the mushrooms, sea salt, thyme, and pepper. Cook for about 6 minutes, stirring very infrequently, until the mushrooms are browned.
6. Sauté the garlic. Mix in the wine. Cook until the liquid reduces by half. Serve the mushrooms spooned over the steak.

Nutrition 405 Calories 5g Fat 7g Carbohydrates 33g Protein

569. Keftedes

Preparation Time: 20 minutes
Cooking Time: 25 minutes
Servings: 4
Ingredients:
- 2 whole-wheat bread slices
- 1¼ pounds ground turkey
- 1 egg
- ¼ cup seasoned whole-wheat bread crumbs
- 3 garlic cloves, minced
- ¼ red onion, grated
- ¼ cup chopped fresh Italian parsley leaves
- 2 tablespoons chopped fresh mint leaves
- 2 tablespoons chopped fresh oregano leaves

- ½ teaspoon sea salt
- ¼ teaspoon freshly ground black pepper

Directions:

1. Preheat the oven to 350°F. Situate parchment paper or aluminum foil onto the baking sheet. Run the bread under water to wet it, and squeeze out any excess. Shred wet bread into small pieces and place it in a medium bowl.
2. Add the turkey, egg, bread crumbs, garlic, red onion, parsley, mint, oregano, sea salt, and pepper. Mix well. Form the mixture into ¼-cup-size balls. Place the meatballs on the prepared sheet and bake for about 25 minutes, or until the internal temperature reaches 165°F.

Nutrition 350 Calories 6g Fat 10g Carbohydrates 42g Protein

570. String Beans and Tomatoes Lamb Chops

Preparation Time: 10 minutes
Cooking Time: 1 hour
Servings: 6
Ingredients:
- ¼ cup extra-virgin olive oil, divided
- 6 lamb chops, trimmed of extra fat
- 1 teaspoon sea salt, divided
- ½ teaspoon freshly ground black pepper
- 2 tablespoons tomato paste
- 1½ cups hot water
- 1-pound green beans, trimmed and halved crosswise
- 1 onion, chopped
- 2 tomatoes, chopped

Directions:

1. Cook 2 tablespoons of olive oil in large skillet until it shimmers. Season the lamb chops with ½ teaspoon of sea salt and 1/8 teaspoon of pepper. Cook the lamb in the hot oil for about 4 minutes per side until browned on both sides. Situate the meat to a platter and set aside.
2. Position the skillet back to the heat and put the remaining 2 tablespoons of olive oil. Heat until it shimmers.
3. In a bowl, melt the tomato paste in the hot water. Mix it to the hot skillet along with the green beans, onion, tomatoes, and the remaining ½ teaspoon of sea salt and ¼ teaspoon of pepper. Bring to a simmer, using the side of a spoon to scrape browned bits from the bottom of the pan.
4. Return the lamb chops to the pan. Allow to boil and adjust the heat to medium-low. Simmer for 45 minutes until the beans are soft, adding additional water as needed to adjust the thickness of the sauce.

Nutrition 439 Calories 4g Fat 10g Carbohydrates 50g Protein

571. Chicken in Tomato-Balsamic Pan Sauce

Preparation Time: 10 minutes
Cooking Time: 20 minutes
Servings: 4
Ingredients

- 2 (8 oz. or 226.7 g each) boneless chicken breasts, skinless
- ½ tsp. salt
- ½ tsp. ground pepper
- 3 tbsps. extra-virgin olive oil
- ½ c. halved cherry tomatoes
- 2 tbsps. sliced shallot
- ¼ c. balsamic vinegar
- 1 tbsp. minced garlic
- 1 tbsp. toasted fennel seeds, crushed
- 1 tbsp. butter

Directions;
1. Slice the chicken breasts into 4 pieces and beat them with a mallet till it reaches a thickness of a ¼ inch. Use ¼ teaspoons of pepper and salt to coat the chicken. Heat two tablespoons of oil in a skillet and keep the heat to a medium. Cook the chicken breasts on each side for three minutes. Place it to a serving plate and cover it with foil to keep it warm.
2. Add one tablespoon oil, shallot, and tomatoes in a pan and cook till it softens. Add vinegar and boil the mix till the vinegar gets reduced by half. Put fennel seeds, garlic, salt, and pepper and cook for about four minutes. Pull it out from the heat and stir it with butter. Pour this sauce over chicken and serve.

Nutrition 294 Calories 17g Fat 10g Carbohydrates 2g Protein

572. Brown Rice, Feta, Fresh Pea, and Mint Salad

Preparation Time: 10 minutes
Cooking Time: 25 minutes
Servings: 4
Ingredients

- 2 c. brown rice
- 3 c. water
- Salt
- 5 oz. or 141.7 g crumbled feta cheese
- 2 c. cooked peas
- ½ c. chopped mint, fresh
- 2 tbsps. olive oil
- Salt and pepper

Directions:
1. Place the brown rice, water, and salt into a saucepan over medium heat, cover, and bring to boiling point. Turn the lower heat and allow it to cook until the water has dissolved and the rice is soft but chewy. Leave to cool completely

2. Add the feta, peas, mint, olive oil, salt, and pepper to a salad bowl with the cooled rice and toss to combine Serve and enjoy!

Nutrition 613 Calories 18.2g Fat 45g Carbohydrates 12g Protein

573. Whole Grain Pita Bread Stuffed with Olives and Chickpeas

Preparation Time: 10 minutes
Cooking Time 20 minutes
Servings: 2
Ingredients

- 2 wholegrain pita pockets
- 2 tbsps. olive oil
- 2 garlic cloves, chopped
- 1 onion, chopped
- ½ tsp. cumin
- 10 black olives, chopped
- 2 c. cooked chickpeas
- Salt and pepper

Directions:
1. Slice open the pita pockets and set aside Adjust your heat to medium and set a pan in place. Add in the olive oil and heat. Mix in the garlic, onion, and cumin to the hot pan and stir as the onions soften and the cumin is fragrant Add the olives, chickpeas, salt, and pepper and toss everything together until the chickpeas become golden
2. Set the pan from heat and use your wooden spoon to roughly mash the chickpeas so that some are intact and some are crushed Heat your pita pockets in the microwave, in the oven, or on a clean pan on the stove
3. Fill them with your chickpea mixture and enjoy!

Nutrition 503 Calories 19g Fat 14g Carbohydrates 15.7g Protein

574. Roasted Carrots with Walnuts and Cannellini Beans

Preparation Time: 10 minutes
Cooking Time: 45 minutes
Servings: 4
Ingredients

- 4 peeled carrots, chopped
- 1 c. walnuts
- 1 tbsp. honey
- 2 tbsps. olive oil
- 2 c. canned cannellini beans, drained
- 1 fresh thyme sprig
- Salt and pepper

Directions:
1. Set oven to 400 F/204 C and line a baking tray or roasting pan with baking paper Lay the carrots and walnuts onto the lined tray or pan Sprinkle olive oil

and honey over the carrots and walnuts and give everything a rub to make sure each piece is coated Scatter the beans onto the tray and nestle into the carrots and walnuts

2. Add the thyme and sprinkle everything with salt and pepper   Set tray in your oven and roast for about 40 minutes.
3. Serve and enjoy

Nutrition 385 Calories 27g Fat 6g Carbohydrates 18g Protein

575. Seasoned Buttered Chicken

Preparation Time: 10 minutes
Cooking Time: 20 minutes
Servings: 4
Ingredients
- ½ c. Heavy Whipping Cream
- 1 tbsp. Salt
- ½ c. Bone Broth
- 1 tbsp. Pepper
- 4 tbsps. Butter
- 4 Chicken Breast Halves

Directions:
1. Place cooking pan on your oven over medium heat and add in one tablespoon of butter. Once the butter is warm and melted, place the chicken in and cook for five minutes on either side. At the end of this time, the chicken should be cooked through and golden; if it is, go ahead and place it on a plate.
2. Next, you are going to add the bone broth into the warm pan. Add heavy whipping cream, salt, and pepper. Then, leave the pan alone until your sauce begins to simmer. Allow this process to happen for five minutes to let the sauce thicken up.
3. Finally, you are going to add the rest of your butter and the chicken back into the pan. Be sure to use a spoon to place the sauce over your chicken and smother it completely. Serve

Nutrition 350 Calories 25g Fat 10g Carbohydrates 25g Protein

576. Double Cheesy Bacon Chicken

Preparation Time: 10 minutes
Cooking Time: 30 minutes
Servings: 4
Ingredients
- 4 oz. or 113 g. Cream Cheese
- 1 c. Cheddar Cheese
- 8 strips Bacon
- Sea salt
- Pepper
- 2 Garlic cloves, finely chopped
- Chicken Breast
- 1 tbsp. Bacon Grease or Butter

Directions:

1. Ready the oven to 400 F/204 C Slice the chicken breasts in half to make them thin
2. Season with salt, pepper, and garlic Grease a baking pan with butter and place chicken breasts into it. Add the cream cheese and cheddar cheese on top of the breasts
3. Add bacon slices as well Place the pan to the oven for 30 minutes Serve hot

Nutrition 610 Calories 32g Fat 3g Carbohydrates 38g Protein

577. Shrimps with Lemon and Pepper

Preparation Time: 10 minutes
Cooking Time: 10 minutes
Servings: 4
Ingredients
- 40 deveined shrimps, peeled
- 6 minced garlic cloves
- Salt and black pepper
- 3 tbsps. olive oil
- ¼ tsp. sweet paprika
- A pinch crushed red pepper flake
- ¼ tsp. grated lemon zest
- 3 tbsps. Sherry or another wine
- 1½ tbsps. sliced chives
- Juice of 1 lemon

Directions:
1. Adjust your heat to medium-high and set a pan in place.
2. Add oil and shrimp, sprinkle with pepper and salt and cook for 1 minute Add paprika, garlic and pepper flakes, stir and cook for 1 minute. Gently stir in sherry and allow to cook for an extra minute
3. Take shrimp off the heat, add chives and lemon zest, stir and transfer shrimp to plates.   Add lemon juice all over and serve

Nutrition 140 Calories 1g Fat 5g Carbohydrates 18g Protein

578. Breaded and Spiced Halibut

Preparation Time: 5 minutes
Cooking Time: 25 minutes
Servings: 4
Ingredients
- ¼ c. chopped fresh chives
- ¼ c. chopped fresh dill
- ¼ tsp. ground black pepper
- ¾ c. panko breadcrumbs
- 1 tbsp. extra-virgin olive oil
- 1 tsp. finely grated lemon zest
- 1 tsp. sea salt
- 1/3 c. chopped fresh parsley
- 4 (6 oz. or 170 g. each) halibut fillets

Directions:

1. In a medium bowl, mix olive oil and the rest ingredients except halibut fillets and breadcrumbs
2. Place halibut fillets into the mixture and marinate for 30 minutes Preheat your oven to 400 F/204 C Set a foil to a baking sheet, grease with cooking spray Dip the fillets to the breadcrumbs and put to the baking sheet Cook in the oven for 20 minutes Serve hot

Nutrition 667 Calories 24.5g Fat 2g Carbohydrates 54.8g Protein

579. Curry Salmon with Mustard

Preparation Time: 10 minutes
Cooking Time: 20 minutes
Servings: 4
Ingredients
- ¼ tsp. ground red pepper or chili powder
- ¼ tsp. turmeric, ground
- ¼ tsp. salt
- 1 tsp. honey
- ¼ tsp. garlic powder
- 2 tsps. whole grain mustard
- 4 (6 oz. or 170 g. each) salmon fillets

Directions:
1. In a bowl mix mustard and the rest ingredients except salmon Prep the oven to 350 F. Rub baking dish with cooking spray. Place salmon on baking dish with skin side down and spread evenly mustard mixture on top of fillets Place into the oven and cook for 10-15 minutes or until flaky

Nutrition 324 Calories 18.9g Fat 1.3g Carbohydrates 34g Protein

580. Walnut-Rosemary Crusted Salmon

Preparation Time: 10 minutes
Cooking Time: 25 minutes
Servings: 4
Ingredients
- 1 lb. or 450 g. frozen skinless salmon fillet
- 2 tsps. Dijon mustard
- 1 clove garlic, minced
- ¼ tsp. lemon zest
- ½ tsp. honey
- ½ tsp. kosher salt
- 1 tsp. freshly chopped rosemary
- 3 tbsps. panko breadcrumbs
- ¼ tsp. crushed red pepper
- 3 tbsps. chopped walnuts
- 2 tsp. extra-virgin olive oil

Directions:
1. Prepare the oven to 420 F/215 C and use parchment paper to line a rimmed baking sheet. In a bowl combine mustard, lemon zest, garlic, lemon juice, honey, rosemary, crushed red pepper, and salt.

In another bowl mix walnut, panko, and 1 tsp oil Place parchments paper on the baking sheet and lay the salmon on it
2. Spread mustard mixture on the fish, and top with the panko mixture. Spray the rest of olive oil lightly on the salmon. Bake for about 10 -12 minutes or until the salmon is being separated by a fork Serve hot

Nutrition 222 Calories 12g Fat 4g Carbohydrates 0.8g Protein

581. Quick Tomato Spaghetti

Preparation Time: 10 minutes
Cooking Time: 25 minutes
Servings: 4
Ingredients
- 8 oz. or 226.7g spaghetti
- 3 tbsps. olive oil
- 4 garlic cloves, sliced
- 1 jalapeno, sliced
- 2 c. cherry tomatoes
- Salt and pepper
- 1 tsp. balsamic vinegar
- ½ c. Parmesan, grated

Directions:
1. Boil a large pot of water on medium flame. Add a pinch of salt and bring to a boil then add the spaghetti. Allow cooking for 8 minutes. While the pasta cooks, heat the oil in a skillet and add the garlic and jalapeno. Cook for an extra 1 minute then stir in the tomatoes, pepper, and salt.
2. Cook for 5-7 minutes until the tomatoes' skins burst.
3. Add the vinegar and remove off heat. Drain spaghetti well and mix it with the tomato sauce. Sprinkle with cheese and serve right away.

Nutrition 298 Calories 13.5g Fat 10.5g Carbohydrates 8g Protein

582. Chili Oregano Baked Cheese

Preparation Time: 10 minutes
Cooking Time: 25 minutes
Servings: 4
Ingredients
- 8 oz. or 226.7g feta cheese
- 4 oz. or 113g mozzarella, crumbled
- 1 sliced chili pepper
- 1 tsp. dried oregano
- 2 tbsps. olive oil

Directions:
1. Place the feta cheese in a small deep-dish baking pan. Top with the mozzarella then season with pepper slices and oregano. cover your pan with lid. Bake in the prepared oven at 350 F/176 C for 20 minutes. Serve the cheese and enjoy it.

Nutrition 292 Calories 24.2g Fat 5.7g Carbohydrates 2g Protein

583. Crispy Italian Chicken

Preparation Time: 10 minutes
Cooking Time: 30 minutes
Servings: 4
Ingredients
- 4 chicken legs
- 1 tsp. dried basil
- 1 tsp. dried oregano
- Salt and pepper
- 3 tbsps. olive oil
- 1 tbsp. balsamic vinegar

Directions:
1. Season the chicken well with basil, and oregano. Using a skillet, add oil and heat. Add the chicken in the hot oil. Let each side cook for 5 minutes until golden then cover the skillet with a lid.
2. Adjust your heat to medium and cook for 10 minutes on one side then flip the chicken repeatedly, cooking for another 10 minutes until crispy. Serve the chicken and enjoy.

Nutrition 262 Calories 13.9g Fat 11g Carbohydrates 32.6g Protein

584. Sea Bass in a Pocket

Preparation Time: 10 minutes
Cooking Time: 25 minutes
Servings: 4
Ingredients
- 4 sea bass fillets
- 4 sliced garlic cloves
- 1 sliced celery stalk
- 1 sliced zucchini
- 1 c. halved cherry tomatoes halved
- 1 shallot, sliced
- 1 tsp. dried oregano
- Salt and pepper

Directions:
1. Mix the garlic, celery, zucchini, tomatoes, shallot, and oregano in a bowl. Add salt and pepper to taste. Take 4 sheets of baking paper and arrange them on your working surface. Spoon the vegetable mixture in the center of each sheet.
2. Top with a fish fillet then wrap the paper well so it resembles a pocket. Place the wrapped fish in a baking tray and cook in the preheated oven at 350 F/176 C for 15 minutes. Serve the fish warm and fresh.

Nutrition 149 Calories 2.8g Fat 5.2g Carbohydrates 25.2g Protein

585. Creamy Smoked Salmon Pasta

Preparation Time: 5 minutes
Cooking Time: 35 minutes
Servings: 4
Ingredients
- 2 tbsps. olive oil
- 2 chopped garlic cloves
- 1 shallot, chopped
- 4 oz. or 113 g chopped salmon, smoked
- 1 c. green peas
- 1 c. heavy cream
- Salt and pepper
- 1 pinch chili flakes
- 8 oz. or 230 g penne pasta
- 6 c. water

Directions:
1. Place skillet on medium-high heat and add oil. Add the garlic and shallot. Cook for 5 minutes or until softened. Add peas, salt, pepper, and chili flakes. Cook for 10 minutes
2. Add the salmon, and continue cooking for 5-7 minutes more. Add heavy cream, reduce heat and cook for an extra 5 minutes.
3. In the meantime, place a pan with water and salt to your taste on high heat as soon as it boils, add penne pasta and cook for 8-10 minutes or until softened   Drain the pasta, add to the salmon sauce and serve

Nutrition 393 Calories 20.8g Fat 38g Carbohydrates 3g Protein

586. Slow Cooker Greek Chicken

Preparation Time 20 minutes
Cooking Time: 3 hours
Servings: 4
Ingredients
- 1 tablespoon extra-virgin olive oil
- 2 pounds boneless, chicken breasts
- ½ tsp kosher salt
- ¼ tsp black pepper
- 1 (12-ounce) jar roasted red peppers
- 1 cup Kalamata olives
- 1 medium red onion, cut into chunks
- 3 tablespoons red wine vinegar
- 1 tablespoon minced garlic
- 1 teaspoon honey
- 1 teaspoon dried oregano
- 1 teaspoon dried thyme
- ½ cup feta cheese (optional, for serving)

Directions
1. Brush slow cooker with nonstick cooking spray or olive oil. Cook the olive oil in a large skillet. Season both side of the chicken breasts. Once hot, stir in

chicken breasts and sear on both sides (about 3 minutes).

2. Once cooked, transfer it to the slow cooker. Add the red peppers, olives, and red onion to the chicken breasts. Try to place the vegetables around the chicken and not directly on top.

3. In a small bowl, mix together the vinegar, garlic, honey, oregano, and thyme. Once combined, pour it over the chicken. Cook the chicken on low for 3 hours or until no longer pink in the middle. Serve with crumbled feta cheese and fresh herbs.

Nutrition 399 Calories 17g Fat 12g Carbohydrates 50g Protein

587. Chicken Gyros

Preparation Time 10 minutes
Cooking Time: 4 hours
Servings: 4
Ingredients
- 2 lbs. boneless chicken breasts or chicken tenders
- Juice of one lemon
- 3 cloves garlic
- 2 teaspoons red wine vinegar
- 2–3 tablespoons olive oil
- ½ cup Greek yogurt
- 2 teaspoons dried oregano
- 2–4 teaspoons Greek seasoning
- ½ small red onion, chopped
- 2 tablespoons dill weed
- Tzatziki Sauce
- 1 cup plain Greek yogurt
- 1 tablespoon dill weed
- 1 small English cucumber, chopped
- Pinch of salt and pepper
- 1 teaspoon onion powder

Directions
1. Slice the chicken breasts into cubes and place in the slow cooker. Add the lemon juice, garlic, vinegar, olive oil, Greek yogurt, oregano, Greek seasoning, red onion, and dill to the slow cooker and stir to make sure everything is well combined.

2. Cook on low for 5–6 hours or on high for 2–3 hours. In the meantime, incorporate all ingredients for the tzatziki sauce and stir. When well mixed, put in the refrigerator until the chicken is done.

3. When the chicken has finished cooking, serve with pita bread and any or all of the toppings listed above.

Nutrition 317 Calories 7.4g Fat 36.1g Carbohydrates 28.6g Protein

588. Slow Cooker Chicken Cassoulet

Preparation Time: 10 minutes
Cooking Time: 20 minutes

Servings: 16
Ingredients
- 1 cup dry navy beans, soaked
- 8 bone-in skinless chicken thighs
- 1 Polish sausage, cooked and chopped into bite-sized pieces (optional)
- 1¼ cup tomato juice
- 1 (28-ounce) can halved tomatoes
- 1 tbsp Worcestershire sauce
- 1 tsp instant chicken bouillon granules
- ½ tsp dried basil
- ½ teaspoon dried oregano
- ½ teaspoon paprika
- ½ cup chopped celery
- ½ cup chopped carrot
- ½ cup chopped onion

Directions
1. Brush the slow cooker with olive oil or nonstick cooking spray. In a mixing bowl, stir together the tomato juice, tomatoes, Worcestershire sauce, beef bouillon, basil, oregano, and paprika. Make sure the ingredients are well combined.

2. Place the chicken and sausage into the slow cooker and cover with the tomato juice mixture. Top with celery, carrot, and onion. Cook on low for 10–12 hours.

Nutrition 244 Calories 7g Fat 25g Carbohydrates 21g Protein

589. Slow Cooker Chicken Provencal

Preparation Time 5 minutes
Cooking Time: 8 hours
Servings: 4
Ingredients
- 4 (6-ounce) skinless bone-in chicken breast halves
- 2 teaspoons dried basil
- 1 teaspoon dried thyme
- 1/8 teaspoon salt
- 1/8 teaspoon freshly ground black pepper
- 1 yellow pepper, diced
- 1 red pepper, diced
- 1 (15.5-ounce) can cannellini beans
- 1 (14.5-ounce) can petite tomatoes with basil, garlic, and oregano, undrained

Directions
1. Brush the slow cooker with nonstick olive oil. Add all the ingredients to the slow cooker and stir to combine. Cook on low for 8 hours.

Nutrition 304 Calories 4.5g Fat 27.3g Carbohydrates 39.4g Protein

590. Greek Style Turkey Roast

Preparation Time: 20 minutes

Cooking Time: 7 hours and 30 minutes
Servings: 8
Ingredients

- 1 (4-pound) boneless turkey breast, trimmed
- ½ cup chicken broth, divided
- 2 tablespoons fresh lemon juice
- 2 cups chopped onion
- ½ cup pitted Kalamata olives
- ½ cup oil-packed sun-dried tomatoes, thinly sliced
- 1 teaspoon Greek seasoning
- ½ teaspoon salt
- ¼ teaspoon fresh ground black pepper
- 3 tablespoons all-purpose flour (or whole wheat)

Directions

1. Brush the slow cooker with nonstick cooking spray or olive oil. Add the turkey, ¼ cup of the chicken broth, lemon juice, onion, olives, sun-dried tomatoes, Greek seasoning, salt and pepper to the slow cooker.
2. Cook on low for 7 hours. Scourge the flour into the remaining ¼ cup of chicken broth, then stir gently into the slow cooker. Cook for an additional 30 minutes.

Nutrition 341 Calories 19g Fat 12g Carbohydrates 36.4g Protein

591. Garlic Chicken with Couscous

Preparation Time: 25 minutes
Cooking Time: 7 hours
Servings: 4
Ingredients

- 1 whole chicken, cut into pieces
- 1 tablespoon extra-virgin olive oil
- 6 cloves garlic, halved
- 1 cup dry white wine
- 1 cup couscous
- ½ teaspoon salt
- ½ teaspoon pepper
- 1 medium onion, thinly sliced
- 2 teaspoons dried thyme
- 1/3 cup whole wheat flour

Directions

1. Cook the olive oil in a heavy skillet. When skillet is hot, add the chicken to sear. Make sure the chicken pieces don't touch each other. Cook with the skin side down for about 3 minutes or until browned.
2. Brush your slow cooker with nonstick cooking spray or olive oil. Put the onion, garlic, and thyme into the slow cooker and sprinkle with salt and pepper. Stir in the chicken on top of the onions.
3. In a separate bowl, whisk the flour into the wine until there are no lumps, then pour over the chicken. Cook at low for 7 hours. You can cook on high for 3 hours as well. Serve the chicken over the cooked couscous and spoon sauce over the top.

Nutrition 440 Calories 17.5g Fat 14g Carbohydrates 35.8g Protein

592. Chicken Karahi

Preparation Time: 5 minutes
Cooking Time: 5 hours
Servings: 4
Ingredients

- 2 lbs. chicken breasts or thighs
- ¼ cup olive oil
- 1 small can tomato paste
- 1 tablespoon butter
- 1 large onion, diced
- ½ cup plain Greek yogurt
- ½ cup water
- 2 tablespoons ginger in garlic paste
- 3 tablespoons fenugreek leaves
- 1 teaspoon ground coriander
- 1 medium tomato
- 1 teaspoon red chili
- 2 green chilies
- 1 teaspoon turmeric
- 1 tablespoon garam masala
- 1 teaspoon cumin powder
- 1 teaspoon sea salt
- ¼ teaspoon nutmeg

Directions

1. Brush the slow cooker with nonstick cooking spray. In a small bowl, thoroughly mix together all of the spices. Mix in the chicken to the slow cooker followed by the rest of the ingredients, including the spice mixture. Stir until everything is well mixed with the spices.
2. Cook on low for 4–5 hours. Serve with naan or Italian bread.

Nutrition 345 Calories 9.9g Fat 10g Carbohydrates 53.7g Protein

593. Chicken Cacciatore with Orzo

Preparation Time: 20 minutes
Cooking Time: 4 hours
Servings: 6
Ingredients

- 2 pounds skin-on chicken thighs
- 1 tablespoon olive oil
- 1 cup mushrooms, quartered
- 3 carrots, chopped
- 1 small jar Kalamata olives
- 2 (14-ounce) cans diced tomatoes
- 1 small can tomato paste
- 1 cup red wine
- 5 garlic cloves
- 1 cup orzo

Directions

1. In a large skillet, cook the olive oil. When the oil is heated, add the chicken, skin side down, and sear it.
2. When the chicken is browned, add to the slow cooker along with all the ingredients except the orzo. Cook the chicken at low for 2 hours, then add the orzo and cook for an additional 2 hours. Serve with a crusty French bread.

Nutrition 424 Calories 16g Fat 10g Carbohydrates 11g Protein

594. Slow Cooker Beef Daube

Preparation Time: 15 minutes
Cooking Time: 8 hours
Servings: 8
Ingredients
- 1 tablespoon olive oil
- 10 garlic cloves, minced
- 2 pounds boneless chuck roast
- 1½ teaspoons salt, divided
- ½ teaspoon freshly ground black pepper
- 1 cup dry red wine
- 2 cups carrots, chopped
- 1½ cups onion, chopped
- ½ cup beef broth
- 1 (14-ounce) can diced tomatoes
- 1 tablespoon tomato paste
- 1 teaspoon fresh rosemary, chopped
- 1 teaspoon fresh thyme, chopped
- ½ teaspoon orange zest, grated
- ½ teaspoon ground cinnamon
- ¼ teaspoon ground cloves
- 1 bay leaf

Directions
1. Preheat a skillet and then add the olive oil. Add the minced garlic and onions and cook until the onions are soft and the garlic begins to brown.
2. Add the cubed meat, salt, and pepper and cook until the meat has browned. Transfer the meat to the slow cooker. Mix in the beef broth to the skillet and let simmer for about 3 minutes to deglaze the pan, then pour into slow cooker over the meat.
3. Incorporate the rest of the ingredients to the slow cooker and stir well to combine. Adjust slow cooker to low and cook for 8 hours, or set to high and cook for 4 hours. Serve with a side of egg noodles, rice or some crusty Italian bread.

Nutrition 547 Calories 30.5g Fat 22g Carbohydrates 45.2g Protein

595. Slow-Cooked Veal Shanks

Preparation Time: 30 minutes
Cooking Time: 8 hours
Servings: 3
Ingredients
- 4 beef shanks or veal shanks

- 1 teaspoon sea salt
- ½ teaspoon ground black pepper
- 3 tablespoons whole wheat flour
- 1–2 tablespoons olive oil
- 2 medium onions, diced
- 2 medium carrots, diced
- 2 celery stalks, diced
- 4 garlic cloves, minced
- 1 (14-ounce) can diced tomatoes
- 2 teaspoons dried thyme leaves
- ½ cup beef or vegetable stock

Directions
1. Season the shanks on both sides, then dip in the flour to coat. Heat a large skillet over high heat. Add the olive oil. Once hot, situate shanks and brown evenly on both sides. When browned, transfer to the slow cooker.
2. Pour the stock into the skillet and let simmer for 3–5 minutes while stirring to deglaze the pan. Transfer the rest of the ingredients to the slow cooker and pour the stock from the skillet over the top.
3. Adjust the slow cooker to low and cook for 8 hours. Serve the Osso Bucco over quinoa, brown rice, or even cauliflower rice.

Nutrition 589 Calories 21.3g Fat 15g Carbohydrates 74.7g Protein

596. Crockpot Beef Bourguignon

Preparation Time: 5 minutes
Cooking Time: 8 hours
Servings: 8
Ingredients
- 1 tablespoon extra-virgin olive oil
- 6 ounces bacon, roughly chopped
- 3 pounds beef brisket, trimmed of fat, cut into 2-inch cubes
- 1 large carrot, sliced
- 1 large white onion, diced
- 6 cloves garlic, minced and divided
- ½ teaspoon coarse salt
- ½ teaspoon freshly ground pepper
- 2 tablespoons whole wheat
- 12 small pearl onions
- 3 cups red wine (Merlot, Pinot Noir, or Chianti)
- 2 cups beef stock
- 2 tablespoons tomato paste
- 1 beef bouillon cube, crushed
- 1 teaspoon fresh thyme, finely chopped
- 2 tablespoons fresh parsley
- 2 bay leaves
- 2 tablespoons butter or 1 tablespoon olive oil
- 1 pound fresh small white or brown mushrooms, quartered

Directions

1. Preheat skillet over medium-high heat, then add the olive oil. When the oil has heated, cook the bacon until it is crisp, then place it in your slow cooker. Save the bacon fat in the skillet.
2. Pat dry the beef and cook it in the same skillet with the bacon fat until all sides have the same brown coloring. Transfer to the slow cooker.
3. Mix in the onions and carrots to the slow cooker and season with the salt and pepper. Stir to combine the ingredients and make sure everything is seasoned.
4. Stir in the red wine into the skillet and simmer for 4–5 minutes to deglaze the pan, then whisk in the flour, stirring until smooth. Continue cooking until the liquid reduces and thickens a bit.
5. When the liquid has thickened, pour it into the slow cooker and stir to coat everything with the wine mixture. Add the tomato paste, bouillon cube, thyme, parsley, 4 cloves of garlic, and bay leaf. Adjust your slow cooker to high and cook for 6 hours, or set to low and cook for 8 hours.
6. Soften the butter or heat the olive oil in a skillet over medium heat. When hot, stir in the remaining 2 cloves of garlic and cook for about 1 minute before adding the mushrooms. Cook the mushrooms until soft, then add to the slow cooker and mix to combine.
7. Serve with mashed potatoes, rice or noodles.

Nutrition 672 Calories 32g Fat 15g Carbohydrates 56g Protein

597. **Balsamic Chuck Roast**

Preparation Time: 5 minutes
Cooking Time: 8 hours
Servings: 10
Ingredients
- 2 pounds boneless chuck roast
- 1 tablespoon olive oil

Rub
- 1 teaspoon garlic powder
- ½ teaspoon onion powder
- 1 teaspoon sea salt
- ½ teaspoon freshly ground black pepper

Sauce
- ½ cup balsamic vinegar
- 2 tablespoons honey
- 1 tablespoon honey mustard
- 1 cup beef broth
- 1 tablespoon tapioca, whole wheat flour, or cornstarch (to thicken sauce when it is done cooking if desired)

Directions
1. Incorporate all of the ingredients for the rub.
2. In a separate bowl, mix the balsamic vinegar, honey, honey mustard, and beef broth. Coat the roast in olive oil, then rub in the spices from the rub mix. Situate roast in the slow cooker and then pour the

sauce over the top. Adjust the slow cooker to low and cook for 8 hours.
3. If you want to thicken the sauce when the roast is done cooking transfer it from the slow cooker to a serving plate. Then fill the liquid into a saucepan and heat to boiling on the stovetop. Mix the flour until smooth and let simmer until the sauce thickens.

Nutrition 306 Calories 19g Fat 13g Carbohydrates 25g Protein

598. **Pot-Roast Veal**

Preparation Time: 20 minutes
Cooking Time: 5 hours
Servings: 8
Ingredients
- 2 tablespoons olive oil
- Salt and pepper
- 3-pound boneless veal roast, tied
- 4 medium carrots, peeled
- 2 parsnips, peeled and halved
- 2 white turnips, peeled and quartered
- 10 garlic cloves, peeled
- 2 sprigs fresh thyme
- 1 orange, scrubbed and zested
- 1 cup chicken or veal stock

Directions
1. Heat a large skillet over medium-high heat. Scour veal roast all over with olive oil, then season with salt and pepper. Once hot, situate the veal roast and sear on all sides. This will take about 3 minutes on every side, but this process seals in the juices and makes the meat succulent.
2. When cooked, place it to the slow cooker. Throw in the carrots, parsnips, turnips, and garlic into the skillet. Cook for 5 minutes.
3. Situate vegetables to the slow cooker, placing them all around the meat. Top the roast with the thyme and the zest from the orange. Slice the orange into 2 and squeeze the juice over the top of the meat. Fill in chicken stock, then cook the roast on low for 5 hours.

Nutrition 421 Calories 12.8g Fat 10g Carbohydrates 48.8g Protein

599. **Medi Sausage with Rice**

Preparation Time: 15 minutes
Cooking Time 8 hours
Servings: 6
Ingredients
- 1½ pounds Italian sausage, crumbled
- 1 medium onion, chopped
- 2 tablespoons steak sauce
- 2 cups long grain rice, uncooked
- 1 (14-ounce) can diced tomatoes with juice

- ½ cup water
- 1 medium green pepper, diced

Directions

1. Spray your slow cooker with olive oil or nonstick cooking spray. Add the sausage, onion, and steak sauce to the slow cooker. Put on low for 9 hours.
2. After 8 hours, add the rice, tomatoes, water and green pepper. Stir to combine thoroughly. Cook an additional 20 to 25 minutes.

Nutrition 650 Calories 36g Fat 11g Carbohydrates 22g Protein

600. Albondigas

Preparation Time: 20 minutes
Cooking Time 5 hours
Servings: 6
Ingredients

- 1-pound ground turkey
- 1-pound ground pork
- 2 eggs
- 1 (20-ounce) can diced tomatoes
- ¾ cup sweet onion, minced, divided
- ¼ cup plus 1 tablespoon breadcrumbs
- 3 tablespoons fresh parsley, chopped
- 1½ teaspoons cumin
- 1½ teaspoons paprika (sweet or hot)

Directions

1. Spray the slow cooker with olive oil.
2. In a mixing bowl, incorporate the ground meat, eggs, about half of the onions, the breadcrumbs, and the spices.
3. Wash your hands and mix together until everything is well combined. Do not over-mix, though, as this makes for tough meatballs. Shape into meatballs. How big you make them will obviously determine how many total meatballs you get.
4. In a skillet, cook 2 tablespoons of olive oil over medium heat. Once hot, mix in the meatballs and brown on all sides. Make sure the balls aren't touching each other so they brown evenly. Once done, transfer them to the slow cooker.
5. Add the rest of the onions and the tomatoes to the skillet and allow them to cook for a few minutes, scraping the brown bits from the meatballs up to add flavor. Transfer the tomatoes over the meatballs in the slow cooker and cook on low for 5 hours.

Nutrition 372 Calories 21.7g Fat 15g Carbohydrates 28.6g Protein

601. Baked Bean Fish Meal

Preparation Time: 10 minutes
Cooking Time: 10 minutes
Servings: 4
Ingredients:

- 1 tablespoon balsamic vinegar

- 2 ½ cups green beans
- 1-pint cherry or grape tomatoes
- 4 (4-ounce each) fish fillets, such as cod or tilapia
- 2 tablespoons olive oil

Directions:

1. Preheat an oven to 400 degrees. Grease two baking sheets with some olive oil or olive oil spray. Arrange 2 fish fillets on each sheet. In a mixing bowl, pour olive oil and vinegar. Combine to mix well with each other.
2. Mix green beans and tomatoes. Combine to mix well with each other. Combine both mixtures well with each other. Add mixture equally over fish fillets. Bake for 6-8 minutes, until fish opaque and easy to flake. Serve warm.

Nutrition 229 Calories 13g Fat 2.5g Protein

602. Mushroom Cod Stew

Preparation Time: 10 minutes
Cooking Time: 20 minutes
Servings: 6
Ingredients:

- 2 tablespoons extra-virgin olive oil
- 2 garlic cloves, minced
- 1 can tomato
- 2 cups chopped onion
- ¾ teaspoon smoked paprika
- a (12-ounce) jar roasted red peppers
- 1/3 cup dry red wine
- ¼ teaspoon kosher or sea salt
- ¼ teaspoon black pepper
- 1 cup black olives
- 1 ½ pounds cod fillets, cut into 1-inch pieces
- 3 cups sliced mushrooms

Directions:

1. Get medium-large cooking pot, warm up oil over medium heat. Add onions and stir-cook for 4 minutes.
2. Add garlic and smoked paprika; cook for 1 minute, stirring often. Add tomatoes with juice, roasted peppers, olives, wine, pepper, and salt; stir gently.
3. Boil mixture. Add the cod and mushrooms; turn down heat to medium. Close and cook until the cod is easy to flake, stir in between. Serve warm.

Nutrition 238 Calories 7g Fat 3.5g Protein

603. Spiced Swordfish

Preparation Time: 10 minutes
Cooking Time: 15 minutes
Servings: 4
Ingredients:

- 4 (7 ounces each) swordfish steaks
- 1/2 teaspoon ground black pepper
- 12 cloves of garlic, peeled
- 3/4 teaspoon salt

- 1 1/2 teaspoon ground cumin
- 1 teaspoon paprika
- 1 teaspoon coriander
- 3 tablespoons lemon juice
- 1/3 cup olive oil

Directions:
1. Using food processor, incorporate all the ingredients excluding for swordfish. Secure the lid and blend until smooth mixture. Pat dry fish steaks; coat equally with the prepared spice mixture.
2. Situate them over an aluminum foil, cover and refrigerator for 1 hour. Prep a griddle pan over high heat, pour oil and heat it. Stir in fish steaks; stir-cook for 5-6 minutes per side. Serve warm.

Nutrition 255 Calories 12g Fat 0.5g Protein

604. Anchovy Pasta Mania

Preparation Time: 10 minutes
Cooking Time: 20 minutes
Servings: 4
Ingredients:
- 4 anchovy fillets, packed in olive oil
- ½ pound broccoli, cut into 1-inch florets
- 2 cloves garlic, sliced
- 1-pound whole-wheat penne
- 2 tablespoons olive oil
- ¼ cup Parmesan cheese, grated
- Salt and black pepper, to taste
- Red pepper flakes, to taste

Directions:
1. Cook pasta as directed over pack; drain and set aside. Take a medium saucepan or skillet, add oil. Heat over medium heat.
2. Add anchovies, broccoli, and garlic, and stir-cook until veggies turn tender for 4-5 minutes. Take off heat; mix in the pasta. Serve warm with Parmesan cheese, red pepper flakes, salt, and black pepper sprinkled on top.

Nutrition 328 Calories 8g Fat 7g Protein

605. Shrimp Garlic Pasta

Preparation Time: 10 minutes
Cooking Time: 15 minutes
Servings: 4
Ingredients:
- 1-pound shrimp
- 3 garlic cloves, minced
- 1 onion, finely chopped
- 1 package whole wheat or bean pasta
- 4 tablespoons olive oil
- Salt and black pepper, to taste
- ¼ cup basil, cut into strips
- ¾ cup chicken broth, low-sodium

Directions:

1. Cook pasta as directed over pack; rinse and set aside. Get medium saucepan, add oil then warm up over medium heat. Add onion, garlic and stir-cook until become translucent and fragrant for 3 minutes.
2. Add shrimp, black pepper (ground) and salt; stir-cook for 3 minutes until shrimps are opaque. Add broth and simmer for 2-3 more minutes. Add pasta in serving plates; add shrimp mixture over; serve warm with basil on top.

Nutrition 605 Calories 17g Fat 19g Protein

606. Vinegar Honeyed Salmon

Preparation Time: 10 minutes
Cooking Time: 5 minutes
Servings: 4
Ingredients:
- 4 (8-ounce) salmon filets
- 1/2 cup balsamic vinegar
- 1 tablespoon honey
- Black pepper and salt, to taste
- 1 tablespoon olive oil

Directions:
1. Combine honey and vinegar. Combine to mix well with each other.
2. Season fish fillets with the black pepper (ground) and sea salt; brush with honey glaze. Take a medium saucepan or skillet, add oil.
3. Heat over medium heat. Add salmon fillets and stir-cook until medium rare in center and lightly browned for 3-4 minutes per side. Serve warm.

Nutrition 481 Calories 16g Fat 1.5g Protein

607. Orange Fish Meal

Preparation Time: 10 minutes
Cooking Time: 5 minutes
Servings: 4
Ingredients:
- ¼ teaspoon kosher or sea salt
- 1 tablespoon extra-virgin olive oil
- 1 tablespoon orange juice
- 4 (4-ounce) tilapia fillets, with or without skin
- ¼ cup chopped red onion
- 1 avocado, pitted, skinned, and sliced

Directions:
1. Take a baking dish of 9-inch; add olive oil, orange juice, and salt. Combine well. Add fish fillets and coat well.
2. Add onions over fish fillets. Cover with a plastic wrap. Microwave for 3 minutes until fish is cooked well and easy to flake. Serve warm with sliced avocado on top.

Nutrition 231 Calories 9g Fat 2.5g Protein

608. Shrimp Zoodles

Preparation Time: 10 minutes

Cooking Time: 5 minutes
Servings: 2

Ingredients:
- 2 tablespoons chopped parsley
- 2 teaspoons minced garlic
- 1 teaspoon salt
- ½ teaspoon black pepper
- 2 medium zucchinis, spiralized
- 3/4 pounds medium shrimp, peeled & deveined
- 1 tablespoon olive oil
- 1 lemon, juiced and zested

Directions:
1. Take a medium saucepan or skillet, add oil, lemon juice, lemon zest. Heat over medium heat. Add shrimps and stir-cook 1 minute per side.
2. Sauté garlic and red pepper flakes for 1 more minute. Add Zoodles and stir gently; cook for 3 minutes until cooked to satisfaction. Season well, serve warm with parsley on top.

Nutrition 329 Calories 12g Fat 3g Protein

609. Asparagus Trout Meal

Preparation Time: 10 minutes
Cooking Time: 20 minutes
Servings: 4

Ingredients:
- 2 pounds trout fillets
- 1-pound asparagus
- 1 tablespoon olive oil
- 1 garlic clove, finely minced
- 1 scallion, thinly sliced
- 4 medium golden potatoes
- 2 Roma tomatoes, chopped
- 8 pitted kalamata olives, chopped
- 1 large carrot, thinly sliced
- 2 tablespoons dried parsley
- ¼ cup ground cumin
- 2 tablespoons paprika
- 1 tablespoon vegetable bouillon seasoning
- ½ cup dry white wine

Directions:
1. In a mixing bowl, add fish fillets, white pepper and salt. Combine to mix well with each other. Take a medium saucepan or skillet, add oil.
2. Heat over medium heat. Add asparagus, potatoes, garlic, white part scallion, and stir-cook until become softened for 4-5 minutes. Add tomatoes, carrot and olives; stir-cook for 6-7 minutes until turn tender. Add cumin, paprika, parsley, bouillon seasoning, and salt. Stir mixture well.
3. Mix in white wine and fish fillets. Over low heat, cover and simmer mixture for about 6 minutes until fish is easy to flake, stir in between. Serve warm with green scallions on top.

Nutrition 303 Calories 17g Fat 6g Protein

610. Kale Olive Tuna

Preparation Time: 10 minutes
Cooking Time: 15 minutes
Servings: 6

Ingredients:
- 1 cup chopped onion
- 3 garlic cloves, minced
- 1 (2.25-ounce) can sliced olives
- 1-pound kale, chopped
- 3 tablespoons extra-virgin olive oil
- ¼ cup capers
- ¼ teaspoon crushed red pepper
- 2 teaspoons sugar
- 1 (15-ounce) can cannellini beans
- 2 (6-ounce) cans tuna in olive oil, un-drained
- ¼ teaspoon black pepper
- ¼ teaspoon kosher or sea salt

Directions:
1. Soak kale in boiling water for 2 minutes; drain and set aside. Take a medium-large cooking pot or stock pot, heat oil over medium heat.
2. Add onion and stir-cook until become translucent and softened. Add garlic and stir-cook until become fragrant for 1 minute.
3. Add olives, capers, and red pepper, and stir-cook for 1 minute. Mix in cooked kale and sugar. Over low heat, cover and simmer mixture for about 8-10 minutes, stir in between.
4. Add tuna, beans, pepper, and salt. Stir well and serve warm.

Nutrition 242 Calories 11g Fat 7g Protein

611. Tangy Rosemary Shrimps

Preparation Time: 10 minutes
Cooking Time: 10 minutes
Servings: 6

Ingredients:
- 1 large orange, zested and peeled
- 3 garlic cloves, minced
- 1 ½ pounds raw shrimp, shells and tails removed
- 3 tablespoons olive oil
- 1 tablespoon chopped thyme
- 1 tablespoon chopped rosemary
- ¼ teaspoon black pepper
- ¼ teaspoon kosher or sea salt

Directions:
1. Take a zip-top plastic bag, add orange zest, shrimps, 2 tablespoons olive oil, garlic, thyme, rosemary, salt, and black pepper. Shake well and set aside to marinate for 5 minutes.
2. Take a medium saucepan or skillet, add 1 tablespoon olive oil. Heat over medium heat. Add shrimps and stir-cook for 2-3 minutes per side until totally pink and opaque.

3. Slice orange into bite-sized wedges and add in a serving plate. Add shrimps and combine well. Serve fresh.

Nutrition 187 Calories 7g Fat 0.5g Protein

612. Asparagus Salmon

Preparation Time: 10 minutes
Cooking Time: 15 minutes
Servings: 2
Ingredients:
- 8.8-ounce bunch asparagus
- 2 small salmon fillets
- 1 ½ teaspoon salt
- 1 teaspoon black pepper
- 1 tablespoon olive oil
- 1 cup hollandaise sauce, low-carb

Directions:
1. Season well the salmon fillets. Take a medium saucepan or skillet, add oil. Heat over medium heat.
2. Add salmon fillets and stir-cook until evenly seared and cooked well for 4-5 minutes per side. Add asparagus and stir cook for 4-5 more minutes. Serve warm with hollandaise sauce on top.

Nutrition 565 Calories 7g Fat 2.5g Protein

613. Tuna Nutty Salad

Preparation Time: 10 minutes
Cooking Time: 0 minutes
Servings: 4
Ingredient:
- 1 tablespoon tarragon
- 1 stalk celery
- 1 medium shallot
- 3 tablespoons chives
- 1 (5-oz.) can tuna
- 1 tsp. Dijon mustard
- 2-3 tbsp. mayonnaise
- 1/4 tsp. salt
- 1/8 tsp. pepper
- 1/4 cup pine nuts

Direction:
1. Incorporate tuna, shallot, chives, tarragon, and celery. In a mixing bowl, blend mayonnaise, mustard, salt, and black pepper.
2. Pour in mayonnaise mixture to salad bowl; toss well to combine. Add pine nuts and toss again. Serve fresh.

Nutrition 238 Calories 16g Fat 2g Protein

614. Creamy Shrimp Soup

Preparation Time: 10 minutes
Cooking Time: 35 minutes
Servings: 6
Ingredients:

- 1-pound medium shrimp
- 1 leek, both whites and light green parts, sliced
- 1 medium fennel bulb, chopped
- 2 tablespoons olive oil
- 3 stalks celery, chopped
- 1 clove garlic, minced
- Sea salt and ground pepper to taste
- 4 cups vegetable or chicken broth
- 1 tablespoon fennel seeds
- 2 tablespoons light cream
- Juice of 1 lemon

Directions:
1. Take a medium-large cooking pot or Dutch oven, heat oil over medium heat. Add celery, leek, and fennel and stir-cook for about 15 minutes, until vegetables are softened and browned. Add garlic; season with black pepper and sea salt to taste. Add fennel seed and stir.
2. Pour broth and bring to a boil. Over low heat, simmer mixture for about 20 minutes, stir in between. Add shrimp and cook until just pink for 3 minutes. Mix in cream and lemon juice; serve warm.

Nutrition 174 Calories 5g Fat 2g Protein

615. Spiced Salmon with Vegetable Quinoa

Preparation Time: 30 minutes
Cooking Time: 10 minutes
Servings: 4
Ingredients:
- 1 cup uncooked quinoa
- 1 teaspoon of salt, divided in half
- ¾ cup cucumbers, seeds removed, diced
- 1 cup of cherry tomatoes, halved
- ¼ cup red onion, minced
- 4 fresh basil leaves, cut in thin slices
- Zest from one lemon
- ¼ teaspoon black pepper
- 1 teaspoon cumin
- ½ teaspoon paprika
- 4 (5-oz.) salmon fillets
- 8 lemon wedges
- ¼ cup fresh parsley, chopped

Directions:
1. To a medium-sized saucepan, add the quinoa, 2 cups of water, and ½ teaspoons of the salt. Heat these until the water is boiling, then lower the temperature until it is simmering. Cover the pan and let it cook 20 minutes or as long as the quinoa package instructs. Turn off the burner under the quinoa and allow it to sit, covered, for at least another 5 minutes before serving.
2. Right before serving, scourge onion, tomatoes, cucumbers, basil leaves, and lemon zest to the quinoa. In the meantime (while the quinoa cooks),

prepare the salmon. Turn on the oven broiler to high and make sure a rack is in the lower part of the oven. To a small bowl, add the following components: black pepper, ½ teaspoon of the salt, cumin, and paprika. Stir them together.

3. Place foil over the top of a glass or aluminum baking sheet, then spray it with nonstick cooking spray. Place salmon fillets on the foil. Rub the spice mixture over each fillet (about ½ teaspoons of the spice mixture per fillet). Add the lemon wedges to the pan edges near the salmon.

4. Cook the salmon under the broiler for 8-10 minutes. Your goal is for the salmon to flake apart easily with a fork. Sprinkle the salmon with the parsley, then serve it with the lemon wedges and vegetable parsley. Enjoy!

Nutrition 385 Calories 12.5g Fat 35.5g Protein

616. **Baked Cod with Vegetables**

Preparation Time: 15 minutes
Cooking Time: 25 minutes
Serving: 2
Ingredient

- 1 pound (454 g) thick cod fillet
- ¼ teaspoon onion powder
- ¼ teaspoon paprika
- 3 tablespoons extra-virgin olive oil
- 4 medium scallions
- ½ cup fresh chopped basil, divided
- 3 tablespoons minced garlic
- 2 teaspoons salt
- 2 teaspoons ground black pepper
- ¼ teaspoon dry marjoram
- 6 pcs. sun-dried tomato slices
- ½ cup dry white wine
- ½ cup crumbled feta cheese
- 1 (15-ounce) can oil-packed artichoke hearts
- 1 lemon
- 1 cup pitted kalamata olives
- 1 teaspoon capers (optional)
- 4 small red potatoes, quartered

Direction:
1. Set oven to 375ºF (190ºC).
2. Rub the fish with paprika and onion powder (if desired).
3. Preheat ovenproof skillet over medium heat and sear the top side of the cod for about 1 minute until golden. Set aside.
4. Cook olive oil in the same skillet over medium heat. Stir in scallions, ¼ cup of basil, garlic (if desired), salt, pepper, marjoram (if desired), tomato slices, and white wine and stir to combine. Boil then pull away from heat.
5. Evenly lay the sauce on the bottom of skillet. Situate cod on top of the tomato basil sauce and scatter with feta cheese. Situate artichokes in the skillet and top with the lemon slices.

6. Spread the olives, capers (if desired), and the remaining ¼ cup of basil. Pull-out from the heat and situate to the preheated oven. Bake for 15 to 20 minutes
7. Situate quartered potatoes on a baking sheet or wrapped in aluminum foil. Bake in the oven for 15 minutes.
8. Cool for 5 minutes before serving.

Nutrition: 1168 calories60g fat64g protein

617. **Slow Cooker Salmon in Foil**

Preparation Time: 5 minutes
Cooking Time: 2 hours
Serving: 2
Ingredients:

- 2 (6-ounce / 170-g) salmon fillets
- 1 tablespoon olive oil
- 2 cloves garlic, minced
- ½ tablespoon lime juice
- 1 teaspoon finely chopped fresh parsley
- ¼ teaspoon black pepper

Direction
1. Spread a length of foil onto a work surface and place the salmon fillets in the middle.
2. Blend olive oil, garlic, lime juice, parsley, and black pepper. Brush the mixture over the fillets. Crease the foil over and crimp the sides to make a packet.
3. Place the packet into the slow cooker, cover, and cook on High for 2 hours
4. Serve hot.

Nutrition: 446 calories 21g fat 65g protein

618. **Dill Chutney Salmon**

Preparation Time: 5 minutes
Cooking Time: 3 minutes
Serving: 2
Ingredients:
Chutney:

- ¼ cup fresh dill
- ¼ cup extra virgin olive oil
- Juice from ½ lemon
- Sea salt, to taste

Fish:

- 2 cups water
- 2 salmon fillets
- Juice from ½ lemon
- ¼ teaspoon paprika
- Salt and freshly ground pepper to taste

Direction:
1. Pulse all the chutney ingredients in a food processor until creamy. Set aside.
2. Add the water and steamer basket to the Instant Pot. Place salmon fillets, skin-side down, on the steamer basket. Drizzle the lemon juice over salmon and sprinkle with the paprika.

3. Secure the lid. Click the Manual mode and set the cooking time for 3 minutes at High Pressure.
4. Once done, do a swift pressure release. Carefully open the lid.
5. Season the fillets with pepper and salt to taste. Serve topped with the dill chutney.

Nutrition 636 calories 41g fat 65g protein

619. Garlic-Butter Parmesan Salmon and Asparagus

Preparation Time: 10 minutes
Cooking Time: 15 minutes
Serving: 2
Ingredients:

- 2 (6-ounce / 170-g) salmon fillets, skin on and patted dry
- Pink Himalayan salt
- Freshly ground black pepper, to taste
- 1 pound (454 g) fresh asparagus, ends snapped off
- 3 tablespoons almond butter
- 2 garlic cloves, minced
- ¼ cup grated Parmesan cheese

Direction:
1. Prep oven to 400°F (205°C). Line a baking sheet with aluminum foil.
2. Season both sides of the salmon fillets.
3. Situate salmon in the middle of the baking sheet and arrange the asparagus around the salmon.
4. Heat the almond butter in a small saucepan over medium heat.
5. Cook minced garlic
6. Drizzle the garlic-butter sauce over the salmon and asparagus and scatter the Parmesan cheese on top.
7. Bake in the prepared oven for about 12 minutes. You can switch the oven to broil at the end of cooking time for about 3 minutes.
8. Let cool for 5 minutes before serving.

Nutrition: 435 calories 26g fat 42g protein

620. Lemon Rosemary Roasted Branzino

Preparation Time: 15 minutes
Cooking Time: 30 minutes
Serving: 2
Ingredients:

- 4 tablespoons extra-virgin olive oil, divided
- 2 (8-ounce) Branzino fillets
- 1 garlic clove, minced
- 1 bunch scallions
- 10 to 12 small cherry tomatoes, halved
- 1 large carrot, cut into ¼-inch rounds
- ½ cup dry white wine
- 2 tablespoons paprika
- 2 teaspoons kosher salt
- ½ tablespoon ground chili pepper

- 2 rosemary sprigs
- 1 small lemon, thinly sliced
- ½ cup sliced pitted kalamata olives

Direction:
1. Preheat big ovenproof skillet over high heat until hot, about 2 minutes. Add 1 tablespoon of olive oil and heat
2. Add the Branzino fillets, skin-side up, and sear for 2 minutes. Flip the fillets and cook. Set aside.
3. Twist 2 tablespoons of olive oil around the skillet to coat evenly.
4. Add the garlic, scallions, tomatoes, and carrot, and sauté for 5 minutes
5. Add the wine, stirring until all ingredients are well combined. Carefully place the fish over the sauce.
6. Prep the oven to 450°F (235°C).
7. Brush the fillets with the remaining 1 tablespoon of olive oil and season with paprika, salt, and chili pepper. Top each fillet with a rosemary sprig and lemon slices. Scatter the olives over fish and around the skillet.
8. Roast for about 10 minutes until the lemon slices are browned. Serve hot.

Nutrition: 724 calories 43g fat 57g protein

621. Grilled Lemon Pesto Salmon

Preparation Time: 5 minutes
Cooking Time: 10 minutes
Serving: 2
Ingredients:

- 10 ounces (283 g) salmon fillet
- 2 tablespoons prepared pesto sauce
- 1 large fresh lemon, sliced
- Cooking spray

Direction:
1. Preheat the grill to medium-high heat. Spray the grill grates with cooking spray.
2. Season the salmon well. Spread the pesto sauce on top.
3. Make a bed of fresh lemon slices about the same size as the salmon fillet on the hot grill, and place the salmon on top of the lemon slices. Put any additional lemon slices on top of the salmon.
4. Grill the salmon for 10 minutes.
5. Serve hot.

Nutrition: 316 calories 21g fat 29g protein

622. Steamed Trout with Lemon Herb Crust

Preparation Time: 10 minutes
Cooking Time: 15 minutes
Serving: 2
Ingredient:

- 3 tbsp. olive oil
- 3 garlic cloves
- 2 tbsp. fresh lemon juice

- 1 tbsp. fresh mint
- 1 tbsp. fresh parsley
- ¼ tsp. dried ground thyme
- 1 teaspoon sea salt
- 1-pound fresh trout (2 pieces)
- 2 cups fish stock

Direction:
1. Scourge olive oil, garlic, lemon juice, mint, parsley, thyme, and salt. Brush the marinade onto the fish.
2. Situate a trivet in the Instant Pot. Pour in the fish stock and situate the fish on the trivet.
3. Secure the lid. Click the Steam mode and set the cooking time for 15 minutes at High Pressure.
4. Once done, do a swift pressure release. Carefully open the lid. Serve warm.

Nutrition: 487 calories 38g fat 52g protein

623. Roasted Trout Stuffed with Veggies

Preparation Time: 10 minutes
Cooking Time: 25 minutes
Serving: 2
Ingredient:
- 2 (8-ounce) whole trout fillets
- 1 tablespoon extra-virgin olive oil
- ¼ teaspoon salt
- 1/8 teaspoon black pepper
- 1 small onion, thinly sliced
- ½ red bell pepper
- 1 poblano pepper
- 2 or 3 shiitake mushrooms, sliced
- 1 lemon, sliced

Direction:
1. Set oven to 425°F (220°C). Coat baking sheet with nonstick cooking spray.
2. Scour both trout fillets, inside and out, with the olive oil. Season with salt and pepper.
3. Incorporate onion, bell pepper, poblano pepper, and mushrooms in a large bowl. Fill half of this mix into the cavity of each fillet. Top the mixture with 2 or 3 lemon slices inside each fillet.
4. Situate fish on the prepared baking sheet side by side. Roast in the prepared oven for 25 minutes
5. Pull-out from the oven and serve on a plate.

Nutrition: 459 calories 26g fat 49g protein

624. Lemony Trout with Caramelized Shallots

Preparation Time: 10 minutes
Cooking Time: 20 minutes
Serving: 2
Ingredients:
Shallots:
- 1 teaspoon almond butter
- 2 shallots, thinly sliced

- Dash salt

Trout:
- 1 tablespoon almond butter
- 2 (4-ounce / 113-g) trout fillets
- 3 tablespoons capers
- ¼ cup freshly squeezed lemon juice
- ¼ teaspoon salt
- Dash freshly ground black pepper
- 1 lemon, thinly sliced

Direction:
For Shallots
1. Situate skillet over medium heat, cook the butter, shallots, and salt for 20 minutes, stirring every 5 minutes.

For Trout
2. Using huge skillet over medium heat, heat 1 teaspoon of almond butter.
3. Add the trout fillets and cook each side for 3 minutes, or until flaky. Transfer to a plate and set aside.
4. In the skillet used for the trout, stir in the capers, lemon juice, salt, and pepper, then bring to a simmer. Whisk in the remaining 1 tablespoon of almond butter. Spoon the sauce over the fish.
5. Garnish the fish with the lemon slices and caramelized shallots before serving.

Nutrition: 344 calories 18g fat 21g protein

625. Easy Tomato Tuna Melts

Preparation Time: 5 minutes
Cooking Time: 4 minutes
Serving: 2
Ingredients:
- 1 (5-oz) can chunk light tuna packed in water
- 2 tablespoons plain Greek yogurt
- 2 tablespoons finely chopped celery
- 1 tablespoon finely chopped red onion
- 2 teaspoons freshly squeezed lemon juice
- 1 large tomato, cut into ¾-inch-thick rounds
- ½ cup shredded Cheddar cheese

Direction:
1. Preheat the broiler to High.
2. Stir together the tuna, yogurt, celery, red onion, lemon juice, and cayenne pepper in a medium bowl.
3. Place the tomato rounds on a baking sheet. Top each with some tuna salad and Cheddar cheese.
4. Broil for 3 to 4 minutes. Cool for 5 minutes before serving.

Nutrition: 244 calories 10g fat 30g protein

626. Mackerel and Green Bean Salad

Preparation Time: 10 minutes
Cooking Time: 10 minutes
Serving: 2

Ingredients:

- 2 cups green beans
- 1 tablespoon avocado oil
- 2 mackerel fillets
- 4 cups mixed salad greens
- 2 hard-boiled eggs, sliced
- 1 avocado, sliced
- 2 tablespoons lemon juice
- 2 tablespoons olive oil
- 1 teaspoon Dijon mustard
- Salt and black pepper, to taste

Direction:

1. Cook the green beans in pot of boiling water for about 3 minutes. Drain and set aside.
2. Melt the avocado oil in a pan over medium heat. Add the mackerel fillets and cook each side for 4 minutes.
3. Divide the greens between two salad bowls. Top with the mackerel, sliced egg, and avocado slices.
4. Scourge lemon juice, olive oil, mustard, salt, and pepper, and drizzle over the salad. Toss in cooked green beans to combine, then serve.

Nutrition: 737 calories 57g fat 34g protein

627. Hazelnut Crusted Sea Bass

Preparation Time: 10 minutes
Cooking Time: 15 minutes
Serving: 2
Ingredients:

- 2 tablespoons almond butter
- 2 sea bass fillets
- 1/3 cup roasted hazelnuts
- A pinch of cayenne pepper

Direction

1. Ready oven to 425°F (220°C). Line a baking dish with waxed paper.
2. Brush the almond butter over the fillets.
3. Pulse the hazelnuts and cayenne in a food processor. Coat the sea bass with the hazelnut mixture, then transfer to the baking dish.
4. Bake in the prepared oven for about 15 minutes. Cool for 5 minutes before serving.

Nutrition: 468 calories 31g fat 40g protein

628. Shrimp and Pea Paella

Preparation Time: 20 minutes
Cooking Time: 60 minutes
Serving: 2
Ingredients:

- 2 tablespoons olive oil
- 1 garlic clove, minced
- ½ large onion, minced
- 1 cup diced tomato
- ½ cup short-grain rice
- ½ teaspoon sweet paprika
- ½ cup dry white wine
- 1¼ cups low-sodium chicken stock
- 8 ounces (227 g) large raw shrimp
- 1 cup frozen peas
- ¼ cup jarred roasted red peppers

Direction

1. Cook olive oil in a large skillet over medium-high heat.
2. Add the garlic and onion and sauté for 3 minutes, or until the onion is softened.
3. Add the tomato, rice, and paprika and stir for 3 minutes to toast the rice.
4. Fill in wine and chicken stock and stir to combine. Bring the mixture to a boil.
5. Close and set heat to medium-low, and simmer for 45 minutes
6. Add the shrimp, peas, and roasted red peppers. Close and cook for an additional 6 minutes. Season with salt to taste and serve.

Nutrition: 646 calories 27g fat 42g protein

629. Garlic Shrimp with Arugula Pesto

Preparation Time: 20 minutes
Cooking Time: 5 minutes
Serving: 2
Ingredients:

- 3 cups lightly packed arugula
- ½ cup lightly packed basil leaves
- ¼ cup walnuts
- 3 tablespoons olive oil
- 3 medium garlic cloves
- 2 tablespoons grated Parmesan cheese
- 1 tablespoon freshly squeezed lemon juice
- 1 (10-ounce) package zucchini noodles
- 8 ounces (227 g) cooked, shelled shrimp
- 2 Roma tomatoes, diced

Direction

1. Process the arugula, basil, walnuts, olive oil, garlic, Parmesan cheese, and lemon juice in a food processor until smooth. Season
2. Heat a skillet over medium heat. Add the pesto, zucchini noodles, and cooked shrimp. Toss to combine the sauce over the noodles and shrimp, and cook until heated through.
3. Season well. Serve topped with the diced tomatoes.

Nutrition: 435 calories 30.2g fat 33g protein

630. Baked Oysters with Vegetables

Preparation Time: 30 minutes
Cooking Time: 17 minutes
Serving: 2
Ingredients:

- 2 cups coarse salt, for holding the oysters

- 1 dozen fresh oysters, scrubbed
- 1 tablespoon almond butter
- ¼ cup finely chopped scallions
- ½ cup finely chopped artichoke hearts
- ¼ cup finely chopped red bell pepper
- 1 garlic clove, minced
- 1 tablespoon finely chopped fresh parsley
- Zest and juice of ½ lemon

Direction:

1. Pour the salt into a baking dish and spread to evenly fill the bottom of the dish.
2. Using a shucking knife, insert the blade at the joint of the shell, where it hinges open and shut. Firmly apply pressure to pop the blade in, and work the knife around the shell to open. Discard the empty half of the shell. Using the knife, gently loosen the oyster, and remove any shell particles. Sprinkle salt in the oysters
3. Set oven to 425°F (220°C).
4. Heat the almond butter in a large skillet over medium heat. Add the scallions, artichoke hearts, and bell pepper, and cook for 5 to 7 minutes. Cook garlic
5. Takeout from the heat and stir in the parsley, lemon zest and juice, and season to taste with salt and pepper.
6. Divide the vegetable mixture evenly among the oysters. Bake in the preheated oven for 10 to 12 minutes.

Nutrition: 135 calories 7g fat 6g protein

631. Grilled Whole Sea Bass

Preparation Time: 5 minutes
Cooking Time: 15 minutes
Serving: 2
Ingredients:

- 1 (1-pound) whole lavraki
- ¼ cup extra-virgin olive oil
- 1 bunch fresh thyme
- ¼ cup chopped fresh parsley
- 2 teaspoons minced garlic
- 1 small lemon, cut into ¼-inch rounds

Direction:

1. Preheat a grill to high heat.
2. Rub the olive oil all over the fish's surface and in its middle cavity.
3. Season liberally with salt and pepper.
4. Stuff the inner cavity with the thyme, parsley, garlic, and lemon slices.
5. Set the lavraki on the grill (see Cooking tip). Cook for 6 minutes per side.
6. Remove the head, backbone, and tail. Carve 2 fillets from each side for serving.

Nutrition: 480 Calories 34g Fat 43g Protein

632. Pan-Cooked Fish with Tomatoes

Preparation Time: 20 minutes
Cooking Time: 45 minutes
Serving: 8
Ingredients:

- 1½ cups extra-virgin olive oil
- 1½ cups tomato juice
- 2 (12-ounce) cans organic tomato paste
- 2 teaspoons sea salt
- 2 teaspoons cane sugar
- 1 teaspoon black pepper
- 1 teaspoon dried Greek oregano
- 3 pounds fresh white fish fillets
- 2 large sweet onions
- 1 cup white wine
- 1½ cups bread crumbs
- 4 garlic cloves
- ½ cup fresh parsley
- 4 large, firm tomatoes

Direction

1. Preheat the oven to 325°F.
2. Blend olive oil, tomato juice, tomato paste, salt, sugar, pepper, and oregano. Rub small amount of the mixture onto the bottom of 9-by-13-inch roasting pan.
3. Lay the fresh fish fillets side by side on top of the tomato mixture.
4. Cover with the onion slices, overlapping them.
5. Sprinkle the wine evenly over each piece of fish.
6. Pour half of the tomato and olive oil mixture over the fish.
7. Blend bread crumbs, garlic, and parsley. Spread over the fish.
8. Lay the tomato slices, overlapping them, over the fish. Drizzle remaining tomato mixture over the top.
9. Bake for 40 to 45 minutes.

Nutrition: 908 Calories 55g Fat 51g Protein

633. Fish Steamed in Parchment with Veggies

Preparation Time: 25 minutes
Cooking Time: 20 minutes
Serving: 4
Ingredients:

- Juice of 2 lemons
- 4 tablespoons extra-virgin olive oil
- 2 teaspoons sea salt
- 1 teaspoon freshly ground black pepper
- 4 (6- to 8-ounce) fish fillets
- ½ pound tomatoes, chopped
- ½ cup chopped scallion
- ¼ cup chopped Kalamata olives

- 1 tablespoon capers, drained
- ¼ cup white wine vinegar
- 2 garlic cloves, minced
- 1 fennel bulb

Direction

1. Preheat the oven to 375°F.
2. Scourge lemon juice, 2 tablespoons of olive oil, salt, and pepper.
3. Add the fish and marinate in the refrigerator for 10 minutes.
4. In a medium bowl, combine the tomatoes, scallion, olives, capers, vinegar, remaining 2 tablespoons of olive oil, and garlic.
5. Fold 4 (12-by-16-inch) pieces of parchment paper in half and cut out a half heart shape, keeping as much of the parchment as possible. Unfold the hearts and place ¼ of the fennel close to the center crease to make a bed for the fish. Top with 1 fish fillet and ¼ of the tomato mixture.
6. Fold the parchment back over the fish and, starting at the bottom end, start folding the edges, overlapping to seal the packet. Bake for 20 minutes.

Nutrition: 277 Calories 16g Fat 27g Protein

634. Swordfish Souvlaki

Preparation Time: 25 minutes
Cooking Time: 10 minutes
Serving: 4

Ingredients:

- ½ cup freshly squeezed lemon juice
- ½ cup extra-virgin olive oil
- 1 teaspoon kosher salt
- 1 teaspoon freshly ground black pepper
- 1 teaspoon dried Greek oregano
- 2 pounds swordfish steaks
- 8 ounces cherry tomatoes
- 1 red onion, quartered

Direction:

1. Scourge lemon juice, olive oil, salt, pepper, and oregano.
2. Add the fish and marinate in the refrigerator for 10 to 15 minutes.
3. Heat a grill to medium-high heat.
4. Skewer the swordfish, tomatoes, and red onion, alternating 1 to 2 pieces of fish for each tomato and onion quarter. Grill the kebabs for 10 minutes.
5. Alternatively, broil the skewers carefully for 3 to 5 minutes per side, checking frequently.
6. Serve with a squeeze of lemon and Avocado Skordalia / Avocado Garlic Spread.

Nutrition: 493 Calories 34g Fat 42g Protein

635. Stuffed Monkfish

Preparation Time: 20 minutes
Cooking Time: 8 minutes
Serving: 4

Ingredients:

- 4 (6-ounce) fresh white fish fillets
- 6 tablespoons extra-virgin olive oil, divided
- ½ teaspoon sea salt
- ½ teaspoon freshly ground black pepper
- ¼ cup feta cheese
- ¼ cup minced green olives
- ¼ cup minced orange pulp
- 1 tablespoon orange zest
- ½ teaspoon dried dill
- ¼ cup chopped fresh Greek basil

Direction:

1. Blend fish with 2 tablespoons of olive oil, salt, and pepper.
2. In another bowl, mix together the feta, olives, and orange pulp. Spoon the mixture onto the fish fillets and spread it to coat them. Roll the fillets, inserting 2 toothpicks through to the other side to hold them together.
3. In heavy-bottomed skillet over medium-high heat, heat the remaining olive oil for about 15 seconds.
4. Add the rolled fillets and cook for 6 to 8 minutes, depending on their thickness, rolling onto each side as they cook.
5. Top each piece with the orange zest, dill, and basil, equally divided.

Nutrition: 365 Calories 25g Fat 29g Protein

636. Shrimp Santorini

Preparation Time: 20 minutes
Cooking Time: 30 minutes
Serving: 4

Ingredients:

- 1-pound shrimp
- 5 tablespoons extra-virgin olive oil
- 2 teaspoons kosher salt
- 2 teaspoons freshly ground black pepper
- 1 onion, chopped
- 4 garlic cloves, minced
- 2 pounds tomatoes, chopped or grated
- ½ teaspoon red pepper flakes
- ½ teaspoon dried Greek oregano
- 6 ounces feta cheese
- 3 tablespoons chopped fresh parsley

Direction:

1. Preheat the oven to 400°F.
2. Throw shrimp with 1 tablespoon of olive oil and the salt, and season with black pepper.
3. Using medium oven-safe skillet over medium heat, cook 4 tablespoons of olive oil.
4. Add the onion and season with salt. Cook for 3 to 5 minutes.
5. Add the garlic and black pepper. Cook for 4 minutes.
6. Cook tomatoes, red pepper flakes, and oregano for 10 minutes.

7. Arrange the shrimp and olives (if using) over the tomato mixture in one layer.
8. Crumble the feta over the surface.
9. Bake for 10 to 12 minutes.
10. Pull away from the oven and garnish with parsley.

Nutrition: 458 Calories 29g Fat 35g Protein

637. Greek-Style Shrimp Cocktail

Preparation Time: 15 minutes
Cooking Time: 5 minutes
Serving: 4
Ingredients:
- 1 pound (20- to 30-count) wild shrimp
- 1 egg
- 1 tablespoon Greek oregano or dill
- 2 teaspoons minced Kalamata olives
- 1 garlic clove, minced
- 1 teaspoon mustard
- ½ cup walnut oil
- ¼ teaspoon sea salt
- ¼ teaspoon freshly ground black pepper

Direction:
Boil 8 cups of water in pot over high heat.
Add the shrimp and boil for 2 to 3 minutes, until pink. Drain and cool.
In a food processor, combine the egg, oregano, olives, garlic, and mustard. Blend to combine.
With the processor running on low speed, very gradually add the walnut oil through the feed tube on your food processor.
When it has thickened to a mayonnaise-like texture, blend in the salt and pepper. Serve.

Nutrition: 257 Calories 13g Fat 31g Protein

638. Fried Calamari

Preparation Time: 20 minutes
Cooking Time: 2 minutes
Serving: 6
Ingredient:
- 2 eggs
- 1 cup organic cornmeal
- 1 teaspoon sea salt
- ½ teaspoon dried dill
- 1-pound calamari rings and tentacles
- ½ cup Kalamata olives, pitted
- 1 lemon, cut into wedges and seeded
- 2 cups extra-virgin olive oil

Direction:
1. Beat the eggs in a flat shallow dish with a fork.
2. In another flat shallow dish, mix the cornmeal, salt, and dill with a fork.
3. . Prepare the calamari, olives, and lemon slices for frying by lightly coating each piece with egg and dredging through the seasoned cornmeal.

4. With a skillet over medium heat, heat the olive oil
5. . Add the calamari, lemon, and olives to the pan. Fry for about 2 minutes
6. . Pull out the items with a slotted spoon then place on paper towel to drain any excess oil.

Nutrition: 374 Calories 19g Fat 23g Protein

639. Stuffed Squid

Preparation Time: 20 minutes
Cooking Time: 45 minutes
Serving: 4
Ingredients:
For squid
- 1 tablespoon extra-virgin olive oil
- 1 onion, chopped
- 1 teaspoon sea salt
- 1 teaspoon freshly ground black pepper
- 3 garlic cloves, minced
- 1-pound small squid
- ½ pound cherry tomatoes, halved
- ¼ cup basmati or long-grain rice, rinsed
- ¼ cup pine nuts, toasted
- ¼ cup fresh basil

For sauce
- ¼ cup extra-virgin olive oil
- 1 onion, chopped
- 1 teaspoon sea salt
- 1 teaspoon black pepper
- 2 garlic cloves, chopped
- ¼ cup dry white wine
- 1 (28-ounce) can diced tomatoes
- ¼ cup fresh basil, cut into chiffonade
- Juice of 1 lemon
- Lemon slices, for serving

Direction:
1. For squid
2. Situate pot over medium-high heat, heat the olive oil.
3. Sauté onion, salt, and pepper for 5 minutes.
4. Add the garlic. Cook for 1 minute
5. If the squid came with tentacles, chop them up and put them in the pot now.. Add the cherry tomatoes, rice, and pine nuts. Cook for 3 minutes
6. Fold the fresh basil into the mixture.
7. . Prick the squid bodies all over with a toothpick and snip off the very end of the cavity.
8. Stuff each squid with filling so it is ¼-to-½ full. The rice will expand when the squid cooks in the sauce, so make sure there's room.
9. For sauce and cook the squid
10. In the same pot, cook olive oil over medium-high heat.
11. Add the onion, salt, and pepper. Cook for 3 to 5 minutes
12. Add the garlic. Cook for about 1 minute.
13. . Stir white wine to deglaze the pan

14. . Stir in the tomatoes. Cook for 10 minutes.
15. Add the basil.
16. . Add the stuffed squid in even layers to the pot. Seal the pot and simmer for 30 minutes. Check the squid by piercing it with a knife—if there is too much resistance, cook for 15 minutes more.
17. . When the squid is cooked through, squeeze the lemon into the pot and serve with additional lemon slices.

Nutrition: 429 Calories 25g Fat 22g Protein

640. Octopus with Figs and Peaches

Preparation Time: 15 minutes,
Cooking Time: 10 minutes
Serving: 4
Ingredient:
- 1-pound octopus tentacles
- ¼ cup extra-virgin olive oil
- 1 teaspoon sea salt
- 1 teaspoon black pepper
- 1 teaspoon granulated garlic
- ½ teaspoon dried Greek oregano
- 1 cup fig balsamic vinegar
- 6 fresh figs, halved
- 2 large peaches, quartered
- ¼ cup chopped fresh parsley

Direction:
1. In a large bowl, thoroughly mix the octopus, olive oil, salt, pepper, garlic, and oregano to coat well. Marinate in the refrigerator for 2 hours. Bring to room temperature before cooking.
2. In an 8- to 10-inch heavy-bottomed deep skillet over medium-high heat, bring the fig balsamic vinegar to a boil. Reduce the heat to a rolling simmer. Stir with the flat side of a metal spatula so any thickened vinegar is mixed into the liquid instead of sticking to the pan. After about 4 minutes, when the vinegar is foamy on top, add the octopus and stir quickly, cooking for only 2 to 3 minutes
3. Add the figs and peaches to the vinegar remaining in the skillet. Cook for about 1 minute, stirring them into the caramelized vinegar just until coated and soft. Transfer to the serving bowl and gently stir to combine.
4. Top with the parsley.

Nutrition: 304 Calories 14g Fat 21g Protein

641. Octopus with Potatoes

Preparation Time: 10 minutes
Cooking Time: 35 minutes
Serving: 4
Ingredients:
- 2 pounds octopus, cleaned
- 1-pound baby potatoes

- 1 fennel bulb, quartered
- 1 bay leaf
- 10 peppercorns
- Juice of 2 lemons
- ¼ cup extra-virgin olive oil
- 1 teaspoon kosher salt
- 1 teaspoon freshly ground black pepper
- 3 garlic cloves
- 1 cup chopped scallions
- ¼ cup chopped fresh parsley

Direction
1. Place 8-quart pot over medium-high heat, mix octopus, potatoes, fennel, bay leaf, and peppercorns. Cover with water. Close the pot, bring to a boil, reduce the heat to low, and simmer. Don't overcook the octopus or it will be rubbery.
2. Preheat a grill to high heat.
3. Remove the octopus and cut it into 2- to 3-inch pieces and place them on the grill for 4 minutes on both sides.
4. Scourge lemon juice, olive oil, salt, pepper, and garlic.
5. Remove the potatoes from the pot and add to the dressing, along with the scallions and parsley, and toss to combine.
6. Add the grilled octopus to the bowl and toss with the rest of the ingredients. Turn out onto a platter and serve.

Nutrition: 392 Calories 15g Fat 43g Protein

642. Feta Crab Cakes

Preparation Time: 30 minutes
Cooking Time: 15 minutes
Serving: 4
Ingredients:
- 1-pound crabmeat
- ½ cup minced scallion
- 1/3 cup bread crumbs
- ¼ cup feta cheese
- 2 eggs
- 2 garlic cloves
- 1 small Anaheim or pasilla chili
- 1 medium firm tomato
- 2 tablespoons minced fresh fennel
- 2 tablespoons minced fresh parsley
- ½ teaspoon dried dill
- ½ teaspoon dried Greek oregano
- ½ teaspoon sea salt
- ½ teaspoon freshly ground black pepper
- ¼ teaspoon ground nutmeg
- 3 tablespoons extra-virgin olive oil

Direction:
1. Blend crabmeat, scallion, bread crumbs, feta, eggs, garlic, chili, tomato, fennel, parsley, dill, oregano, salt, pepper, and nutmeg. Mix thoroughly. Split mixture into 8 equal portions and form each into a

2½-inch patty about ½ inch thick, creating a definitive edge for easier flipping when cooking.
2. Situate skillet over medium-high heat, heat the olive oil. Place the crab cakes in the heated pan and brown for 7 to 8 minutes per side.

Nutrition: 315 Calories 16g Fat 15g Protein

643. Steamed Mussels with White Wine and Fennel

Preparation Time: 20 minutes
Cooking Time: 30 minutes
Serving: 4

Ingredients:
- ¼ cup extra-virgin olive oil
- 1 onion, chopped
- 1 teaspoon sea salt
- 4 garlic cloves, minced
- 1 teaspoon red pepper flakes
- 1 fennel bulb
- 1 cup dry white wine
- 4 pounds mussels
- Juice of 2 lemons

Direction:
1. Position 8-quart pot over medium-high heat, heat the olive oil.
2. Add the onion and salt. Cook for 5 minutes, until translucent.
3. Add garlic and red pepper flakes. Cook for 1 minute.
4. Stir in the chopped fennel. Cook for 3 minutes.
5. Stir in the wine and simmer for about 7 minutes.
6. Carefully pour the mussels into the pot. Reduce the heat to medium, give everything a good stir, cover the pot, and cook for 5 to 7 minutes.
7. Remove the opened mussels and divide them among 4 bowls. Re-cover the pot and cook any unopened mussels for 3 minutes more. Divide any additional opened mussels among the bowls. Discard any unopened mussels. Evenly distribute the broth into the bowls. Garnish with the fennel leaves.

Nutrition: 578 Calories 23g Fat 55g Protein

644. Seafood Rice

Preparation Time: 10 minutes
Cooking Time: 40 minutes
Serving: 6

Ingredients:
- 1 tablespoon extra-virgin olive oil
- 1½ pounds seafood
- 1 onion, chopped
- 1 teaspoon sea salt
- 4 garlic cloves, minced
- 1 cup chopped celery
- 2 medium tomatoes

- ½ cup dry white wine
- 2 cups arborio rice
- ¼ cup chopped fresh parsley
- ¼ cup chopped fresh dill
- 4¼ cups chicken broth

Direction:
1. Put skillet over medium-high heat, heat 1 tablespoon of olive oil.
2. Add the squid and cook for about 2 minutes. Remove the squid and set aside.
3. Pour in remaining 1 teaspoon of olive oil to the skillet to heat.
4. Add the onion and salt. Cook for 5 minutes.
5. Cook garlic.
6. Add the celery and tomatoes. Cook for 3 minutes.
7. Pour in the wine and cook for about 3 minutes, stirring frequently.
8. Stir in the rice, parsley, dill, and 4 cups of broth. Close then simmer for 15 minutes.
9. Top the rice mixture with the shrimp and mussels, cover the skillet, and simmer for 6 minutes more.
10. Return the squid to the skillet. Discard any unopened mussels. Side with the lemon wedges

Nutrition: 246 Calories 5g Fat 28g Protein

645. Mixed Seafood with Wine and Capers

Preparation Time: 25 minutes
Cooking Time: 10 minutes
Serving: 4

Ingredients:
- 1 (1-pound) bag frozen mixed seafood
- ½ cup white wine
- ¼ cup extra-virgin olive oil
- ½ teaspoon sea salt
- ½ teaspoon freshly ground black pepper
- ½ cup capers, drained
- ¼ cup chopped fresh parsley

Direction:
1. Thaw the frozen seafood by rinsing in a colander under cold running water for several minutes, turning so that it will thaw evenly. Put aside for 5 minutes, and squeeze out excess water completely.
2. In a small bowl, whisk the white wine, olive oil, salt, and pepper.
3. In a 10-inch skillet over medium-high heat, bring the white wine mixture to a simmer.
4. Add the seafood and stir in the capers. Cook for 5 minutes.
5. Sprinkle with the parsley and serve.

Nutrition: 235 Calories 14g Fat 17g Protein

646. Speedy Tilapia with Red Onion and Avocado

Preparation Time: 10 minutes

Cooking Time: 5 minutes
Servings: 4
Ingredients:
- 1 tablespoon extra-virgin olive oil
- 1 tablespoon freshly squeezed orange juice
- ¼ teaspoon kosher or sea salt
- 4 (4-ounce) tilapia fillets, more oblong than square, skin-on or skinned
- ¼ cup chopped red onion
- 1 avocado

Directions:
1. In a 9-inch glass pie dish, combine together the oil, orange juice, and salt. Work on the fillet simultaneously, situate each in the pie dish and coat on all sides. Form the fillets in a wagon-wheel formation. Place each fillet with 1 tablespoon of onion, then fold the end of the fillet that's hanging over the edge in half over the onion. Once done, you should have 4 folded-over fillets with the fold against the outer edge of the dish and the ends all in the center.
2. Wrap the dish with plastic, leave small part open at the edge to vent the steam. Cook at high for 4 minutes in microwave. When done it should separate into flakes (chunks) when pressed gently with a fork. Garnish the fillets with the avocado and serve.

Nutrition 200 Calories 3g Fat 4g Carbohydrates 22g Protein

647. Grilled Fish on Lemons

Preparation Time: 10 minutes
Cooking Time: 10 minutes
Servings: 4
Ingredients:
- 4 (4-ounce) fish fillets
- Nonstick cooking spray
- 3 to 4 medium lemons
- 1 tablespoon extra-virgin olive oil
- ¼ teaspoon freshly ground black pepper
- ¼ teaspoon kosher or sea salt

Directions:
1. Using paper towels, pat the fillets dry and let stand at room temperature for 10 minutes. Meanwhile, coat the cold cooking grate of the grill with nonstick cooking spray, and preheat the grill to 400°F, or medium-high heat.
2. Slice one lemon in half and set half aside. Slice the remaining half of that lemon and the remaining lemons into ¼-inch-thick slices. (You should have about 12 to 16 lemon slices.) Into a small bowl, squeeze 1 tablespoon of juice out of the reserved lemon half.
3. Add the oil to the bowl with the lemon juice, and mix well. Put both sides of the fish with the oil mixture, and sprinkle evenly with pepper and salt.
4. Carefully place the lemon slices on the grill (or the grill pan), arranging 3 to 4 slices together in the

shape of a fish fillet, and repeat with the remaining slices. Place the fish fillets directly on top of the lemon slices, and grill with the lid closed. (If you're grilling on the stove top, cover with a large pot lid or aluminum foil.) Flip the fish midway through the cooking time only if the fillets are more than half an inch thick.

Nutrition 147 Calories 5g Fat 1g Carbohydrates 22g Protein

648. Weeknight Sheet Pan Fish Dinner

Preparation Time: 10 minutes
Cooking Time: 10 minutes
Servings: 4
Ingredients:
- Nonstick cooking spray
- 2 tablespoons extra-virgin olive oil
- 1 tablespoon balsamic vinegar
- 4 (4-ounce) fish fillets (½ inch thick)
- 2½ cups green beans
- 1-pint cherry or grape tomatoes

Directions:
1. Preheat the oven to 400°F. Brush two large, rimmed baking sheets with nonstick cooking spray. In a small bowl, combine together the oil and vinegar. Set aside. Place two pieces of fish on each baking sheet.
2. In a large bowl, combine the beans and tomatoes. Fill in the oil and vinegar, and toss gently to coat. Pour half of the green bean mixture over the fish on one baking sheet, and the remaining half over the fish on the other. Turn the fish over, and rub it in the oil mixture to coat. Lay the vegetables equally on the baking sheets so hot air can circulate around them.
3. Bake until the fish is just opaque. It is cooked when it just begins to separate into chunks when pricked gently with a fork.

Nutrition 193 Calories 8g Fat 3g Carbohydrates 23g Protein

649. Crispy Polenta Fish Sticks

Preparation Time: 15 minutes
Cooking Time: 10 minutes
Servings: 4
Ingredients:
- 2 large eggs, lightly beaten
- 1 tablespoon 2% milk
- 1-pound skinned fish fillets sliced into 20 (1-inch-wide) strips
- ½ cup yellow cornmeal
- ½ cup whole-wheat panko bread crumbs
- ¼ teaspoon smoked paprika
- ¼ teaspoon kosher or sea salt
- ¼ teaspoon freshly ground black pepper
- Nonstick cooking spray

Directions:
1. Situate a large, rimmed baking sheet in the oven. Preheat the oven to 400°F with the pan inside. Scourge eggs and milk. Using a fork, add the fish strips to the egg mixture and stir gently to coat.
2. Put the cornmeal, bread crumbs, smoked paprika, salt, and pepper in a quart-size zip-top plastic bag. Using a fork or tongs, transfer the fish to the bag, letting the excess egg wash drip off into the bowl before transferring. Seal tight and shake gently to completely coat each fish stick.
3. With oven mitts, carefully pull away the hot baking sheet from the oven and spray it with nonstick cooking spray. Using a fork or tongs, remove the fish sticks from the bag and arrange them on the hot baking sheet, with space between them so the hot air can circulate and crisp them up. Bake for 5 to 8 minutes, until gentle pressure with a fork causes the fish to flake, and serve.

Nutrition 256 Calories 6g Fat 2g Carbohydrates 29g Protein

650. Salmon Skillet Supper

Preparation Time: 15 minutes
Cooking Time: 15 minutes
Servings: 4
Ingredients:
- 1 tablespoon extra-virgin olive oil
- 2 garlic cloves minced
- 1 teaspoon smoked paprika
- 1-pint grape or cherry tomatoes, quartered
- 1 (12-ounce) jar roasted red peppers
- 1 tablespoon water
- ¼ teaspoon freshly ground black pepper
- ¼ teaspoon kosher or sea salt
- 1-pound salmon fillets, skin removed, cut into 8 pieces
- 1 tablespoon freshly squeezed lemon juice (from ½ medium lemon)

Directions:
1. Over medium heat, cook the oil in a skillet. Mix in the garlic and smoked paprika and cook for 1 minute, stirring often. Stir in the tomatoes, roasted peppers, water, black pepper, and salt. Adjust the heat to medium-high, simmer, and cook for 3 minutes and smash the tomatoes until the end of the cooking time.
2. Place the salmon to the skillet, and drizzle some of the sauce over the top. Cover and cook for 10 to 12 minutes (145°F using a meat thermometer) and just starts to flake.
3. Pull out the skillet from the heat, and sprinkle lemon juice over the top of the fish. Stir the sauce, then slice the salmon into chunks. Serve.

Nutrition 289 Calories 13g Fat 2g Carbohydrates 31g Protein

651. Tuscan Tuna and Zucchini Burgers

Preparation Time: 10 minutes
Cooking Time: 10 minutes
Servings: 4
Ingredients
- 3 slices whole-wheat sandwich bread, toasted
- 2 (5-ounce) cans tuna in olive oil
- 1 cup shredded zucchini
- 1 large egg, lightly beaten
- ¼ cup diced red bell pepper
- 1 tablespoon dried oregano
- 1 teaspoon lemon zest
- ¼ teaspoon freshly ground black pepper
- ¼ teaspoon kosher or sea salt
- 1 tablespoon extra-virgin olive oil
- Salad greens or 4 whole-wheat rolls, for serving (optional)

Directions
1. Crumble the toast into bread crumbs using your fingers (or use a knife to cut into ¼-inch cubes) until you have 1 cup of loosely packed crumbs. Pour the crumbs into a large bowl.
2. Add the tuna, zucchini, egg, bell pepper, oregano, lemon zest, black pepper, and salt. Mix well with a fork. Divide the mixture into four (½-cup-size) patties. Place on a plate, and press each patty flat to about ¾-inch thick.
3. Over medium-high heat, cook the oil in a skillet. Add the patties to the hot oil, then turn the heat down to medium. Cook the patties for 5 minutes, flip with a spatula, and cook for an additional 5 minutes. Enjoy as is or serve on salad greens or whole-wheat rolls.

Nutrition 191 Calories 10g Fat 2g Carbohydrates 15g Protein

652. Sicilian Kale and Tuna Bowl

Preparation Time: 15 minutes
Cooking Time: 15 minutes
Servings: 6
Ingredients:
- 1-pound kale
- 3 tablespoons extra-virgin olive oil
- 1 cup chopped onion
- 3 garlic cloves, minced
- 1 (2.25-ounce) can sliced olives, drained
- ¼ cup capers
- ¼ teaspoon red pepper
- 2 teaspoons sugar
- 2 (6-ounce) cans tuna in olive oil
- 1 (15-ounce) can cannellini beans
- ¼ teaspoon ground black pepper
- ¼ teaspoon kosher or sea salt

Directions:

1. Boil three-quarters full of water in a stock pot. Mix in the kale and cook for 2 minutes. Strain the kale with colander and set aside.
2. Return the empty pot back on the stove over medium heat, and put in the oil. Mix in the onion and cook for 4 minutes, continuous stirring. Place in the garlic and cook for 1 minute. Place the olives, capers, and crushed red pepper, and cook for 1 minute. Lastly, add the partially cooked kale and sugar, stir until the kale is completely coated with oil. Close pot and cook for 8 minutes.
3. Pull out the kale from the heat, add in the tuna, beans, pepper, and salt, and serve.

Nutrition 265 Calories 12g Fat 7g Carbohydrates 16g Protein

653. Mediterranean Cod Stew

Preparation Time: 10 minutes
Cooking Time: 20 minutes
Servings: 6
Ingredients:

- 2 tablespoons extra-virgin olive oil
- 2 cups chopped onion
- 2 garlic cloves, minced
- ¾ teaspoon smoked paprika
- 1 (14.5-ounce) can diced tomatoes, undrained
- 1 (12-ounce) jar roasted red peppers
- 1 cup sliced olives, green or black
- 1/3 cup dry red wine
- ¼ teaspoon freshly ground black pepper
- ¼ teaspoon kosher or sea salt
- 1½ pounds cod fillets, cut into 1-inch pieces
- 3 cups sliced mushrooms

Directions:

1. Cook the oil in a stockpot. Mix in the onion and cook for 4 minutes, stirring occasionally. Stir in the garlic and smoked paprika and cook for 1 minute, stirring often.
2. Mix in the tomatoes with their juices, roasted peppers, olives, wine, pepper, and salt, and turn the heat up to medium-high. Bring to a boil. Add the cod and mushrooms, and reduce the heat to medium.
3. Cook for about 10 minutes, stir occasionally, until the cod is cooked through and flakes easily, and serve.

Nutrition 220 Calories 8g Fat 3g Carbohydrates 28g Protein

654. Steamed Mussels in White Wine Sauce

Preparation Time: 5 minutes
Cooking Time: 10 minutes
Servings: 4
Ingredients:

- 2 pounds small mussels
- 1 tablespoon extra-virgin olive oil
- 1 cup thinly sliced red onion
- 3 garlic cloves, sliced
- 1 cup dry white wine
- 2 (¼-inch-thick) lemon slices
- ¼ teaspoon freshly ground black pepper
- ¼ teaspoon kosher or sea salt
- Fresh lemon wedges, for serving (optional)

Directions:

1. In a large colander in the sink, run cold water over the mussels (but don't let the mussels sit in standing water). All the shells should be closed tight; discard any shells that are a little bit open or any shells that are cracked. Leave the mussels in the colander until you're ready to use them.
2. In a large skillet, cook the oil. Mix in the onion and cook for 4 minutes, stirring occasionally. Place the garlic and cook for 1 minute, stirring constantly. Add the wine, lemon slices, pepper, and salt, and bring to a simmer. Cook for 2 minutes.
3. Add the mussels and cover. Cook until the mussels open their shells. Gently shake the pan two or three times while they are cooking.
4. All the shells should now be wide open. Using a slotted spoon, discard any mussels that are still closed. Spoon the opened mussels into a shallow serving bowl, and pour the broth over the top. Serve with additional fresh lemon slices, if desired.

Nutrition 222 Calories 7g Fat 1g Carbohydrates 18g Protein

655. Orange and Garlic Shrimp

Preparation Time: 20 minutes
Cooking Time: 10 minutes
Servings: 6
Ingredients:

- 1 large orange
- 3 tablespoons extra-virgin olive oil, divided
- 1 tablespoon chopped fresh rosemary
- 1 tablespoon chopped fresh thyme
- 3 garlic cloves, minced (about 1½ teaspoons)
- ¼ teaspoon freshly ground black pepper
- ¼ teaspoon kosher or sea salt
- 1½ pounds fresh raw shrimp, shells and tails removed

Directions:

1. Zest the entire orange using a citrus grater. Mix the orange zest and 2 tablespoons of oil with the rosemary, thyme, garlic, pepper, and salt. Stir in the shrimp, seal the bag, and gently massage the shrimp until all the ingredients are combined and the shrimp is completely covered with the seasonings. Set aside.
2. Heat a grill, grill pan, or a large skillet over medium heat. Brush on or swirl in the remaining 1 tablespoon of oil. Add half the shrimp, and cook for 4 to 6 minutes, or until the shrimp turn pink

and white, flipping halfway through if on the grill or stirring every minute if in a pan. Handover the shrimp to a large serving bowl. Repeat, and place them to the bowl.

3. While the shrimp cook, peel the orange and cut the flesh into bite-size pieces. Place to the serving bowl, and toss with the cooked shrimp. Serve immediately or refrigerate and serve cold.

Nutrition 190 Calories 8g Fat 1g Carbohydrates 24g Protein

656. Roasted Shrimp-Gnocchi Bake

Preparation Time: 10 minutes
Cooking Time: 20 minutes
Servings: 4
Ingredients:
- 1 cup chopped fresh tomato
- 2 tablespoons extra-virgin olive oil
- 2 garlic cloves, minced
- ½ teaspoon freshly ground black pepper
- ¼ teaspoon crushed red pepper
- 1 (12-ounce) jar roasted red peppers
- 1-pound fresh raw shrimp, shells and tails removed
- 1-pound frozen gnocchi (not thawed)
- ½ cup cubed feta cheese
- 1/3 cup fresh torn basil leaves

Directions:
1. Preheat the oven to 425°F. In a baking dish, mix the tomatoes, oil, garlic, black pepper, and crushed red pepper. Roast in the oven for 10 minutes.
2. Stir in the roasted peppers and shrimp. Roast for 10 more minutes, until the shrimp turn pink and white.
3. While the shrimp cooks, cook the gnocchi on the stove top according to the package directions. Drain in a colander and keep warm. Remove the dish from the oven. Mix in the cooked gnocchi, feta, and basil, and serve.

Nutrition 277 Calories 7g Fat 1g Carbohydrates 20g Protein

657. Spicy Shrimp Puttanesca

Preparation Time: 5 minutes
Cooking Time: 15 minutes
Servings: 4
Ingredients:
- 2 tablespoons extra-virgin olive oil
- 3 anchovy fillets, drained and chopped
- 3 garlic cloves, minced
- ½ teaspoon crushed red pepper
- 1 (14.5-ounce) can low-sodium or no-salt-added diced tomatoes, undrained
- 1 (2.25-ounce) can black olives
- 2 tablespoons capers
- 1 tablespoon chopped fresh oregano
- 1-pound fresh raw shrimp, shells and tails removed

Directions:

1. Over medium heat, cook the oil. Mix in the anchovies, garlic, and crushed red pepper. Cook for 3 minutes, stirring frequently and mashing up the anchovies with a wooden spoon, until they have melted into the oil.
2. Stir in the tomatoes with their juices, olives, capers, and oregano. Turn up the heat to medium-high, and bring to a simmer.
3. When the sauce is lightly bubbling, stir in the shrimp. Select heat to medium, and cook the shrimp until they turn pink and white then serve.

Nutrition 214 Calories 10g Fat 2g Carbohydrates 26g Protein

658. Italian Tuna Sandwiches

Preparation Time: 10 minutes
Cooking Time: 0 minute
Servings: 4
Ingredients:
- 3 tablespoons freshly squeezed lemon juice
- 2 tablespoons extra-virgin olive oil
- 1 garlic clove, minced
- ½ teaspoon freshly ground black pepper
- 2 (5-ounce) cans tuna, drained
- 1 (2.25-ounce) can sliced olives
- ½ cup chopped fresh fennel, including fronds
- 8 slices whole-grain crusty bread

Directions:
1. Combine the lemon juice, oil, garlic, and pepper. Add the tuna, olives, and fennel. Using a fork, separate the tuna into chunks and stir to combine all the ingredients.
2. Divide the tuna salad equally among 4 slices of bread. Top each with the remaining bread slices. Let the sandwiches sit for at least 5 minutes so the zesty filling can soak into the bread before serving.

Nutrition 347 Calories 17g Fat 5g Carbohydrates 25g Protein

659. Dill Salmon Salad Wraps

Preparation Time: 10 minutes
Cooking Time: 10 minutes
Servings: 6
Ingredients:
- 1-pound salmon filet, cooked and flaked
- ½ cup diced carrots
- ½ cup diced celery
- 3 tablespoons chopped fresh dill
- 3 tablespoons diced red onion
- 2 tablespoons capers
- 1½ tablespoons extra-virgin olive oil
- 1 tablespoon aged balsamic vinegar
- ½ teaspoon freshly ground black pepper
- ¼ teaspoon kosher or sea salt

- 4 whole-wheat flatbread wraps or soft whole-wheat tortillas

Directions:
1. Combine together the salmon, carrots, celery, dill, red onion, capers, oil, vinegar, pepper, and salt. Divide the salmon salad among the flatbreads. Crease the bottom of the flatbread, then roll up the wrap and serve.

Nutrition 336 Calories 16g Fat 5g Carbohydrates 32g Protein

660. White Clam Pizza Pie

Preparation Time: 10 minutes
Cooking Time: 20 minutes
Servings: 4

Ingredients:
- 1 pound refrigerated fresh pizza dough
- Nonstick cooking spray
- 2 tablespoons extra-virgin olive oil, divided
- 2 garlic cloves, minced (about 1 teaspoon)
- ½ teaspoon crushed red pepper
- 1 (10-ounce) can whole baby clams, drained
- ¼ cup dry white wine
- All-purpose flour, for dusting
- 1 cup diced mozzarella cheese
- 1 tablespoon Parmesan cheese
- 1 tablespoon chopped fresh flat-leaf (Italian) parsley

Directions:
1. Preheat the oven to 500°F. Brush large, rimmed baking sheet with nonstick cooking spray.
2. In a large skillet, cook 1½ tablespoons of the oil. Put the garlic and crushed red pepper and cook for 1 minute, stirring frequently to prevent the garlic from burning. Add the reserved clam juice and wine. Bring to a boil over high heat. Reduce to medium heat so the sauce is just simmering and cook for 10 minutes, stirring occasionally. The sauce will cook down and thicken.
3. Place the clams and cook for 3 minutes, stirring occasionally. While the sauce is cooking, on a lightly floured surface, form the pizza dough into a 12-inch circle or into a 10-by-12-inch rectangle with a rolling pin or by stretching with your hands. Situate the dough on the prepared baking sheet. Grease the dough with the remaining ½ tablespoon of oil. Set aside until the clam sauce is ready.
4. Spread the clam sauce over the prepared dough within ½ inch of the edge. Top with the mozzarella cheese, then sprinkle with the Pecorino Romano.
5. Bake for 10 minutes. Pull out the pizza from the oven and place onto a wooden cutting board. Top with the parsley, cut into eight pieces with a pizza cutter or a sharp knife, and serve.

Nutrition 541 Calories 21g Fat 1g Carbohydrates 32g Protein

661. Baked Balsamic Fish

Preparation Time: 10 minutes
Cooking Time: 10 minutes
Servings: 4

Ingredients:
- 1 tablespoon balsamic vinegar
- 2 ½ cups green beans
- 1-pint cherry or grape tomatoes
- 4 (4-ounce each) fish fillets, such as cod or tilapia
- 2 tablespoons olive oil

Directions:
1. Preheat an oven to 400 degrees. Grease two baking sheets with some olive oil or olive oil spray. Arrange 2 fish fillets on each sheet. In a mixing bowl, pour olive oil and vinegar. Combine to mix well with each other.
2. Mix green beans and tomatoes. Combine to mix well with each other. Combine both mixtures well with each other. Add mixture equally over fish fillets. Bake for 6-8 minutes, until fish opaque and easy to flake. Serve warm.

Nutrition 229 Calories 13g Fat 8g Carbohydrates 2.5g Protein

662. Cod-Mushroom Soup

Preparation Time: 10 minutes
Cooking Time: 20 minutes
Servings: 6

Ingredients:
- 2 tablespoons extra-virgin olive oil
- 2 garlic cloves, minced
- 1 can tomato
- 2 cups chopped onion
- ¾ teaspoon smoked paprika
- a (12-ounce) jar roasted red peppers
- 1/3 cup dry red wine
- ¼ teaspoon kosher or sea salt
- ¼ teaspoon black pepper
- 1 cup black olives
- 1 ½ pounds cod fillets, cut into 1-inch pieces
- 3 cups sliced mushrooms

Directions:
1. Get medium-large cooking pot, warm up oil over medium heat. Add onions and stir-cook for 4 minutes. Add garlic and smoked paprika; cook for 1 minute, stirring often. Add tomatoes with juice, roasted peppers, olives, wine, pepper, and salt; stir gently. Boil mixture. Add the cod and mushrooms; turn down heat to medium. Close and cook until the cod is easy to flake, stir in between. Serve warm.

Nutrition 238 Calories 7g Fat 15g Carbohydrates 3.5g Protein

663. Mediterranean-Spiced Swordfish

Preparation Time: 10 minutes
Cooking Time: 15 minutes
Servings: 4
Ingredients:

- 4 (7 ounces each) swordfish steaks
- 1/2 teaspoon ground black pepper
- 12 cloves of garlic, peeled
- 3/4 teaspoon salt
- 1 1/2 teaspoon ground cumin
- 1 teaspoon paprika
- 1 teaspoon coriander
- 3 tablespoons lemon juice
- 1/3 cup olive oil

Directions:

1. Using food processor, incorporate all the ingredients except for swordfish. Seal the lid and blend to make a smooth mixture. Pat dry fish steaks; coat equally with the prepared spice mixture.
2. Situate them over an aluminum foil, cover and refrigerator for 1 hour. Prep a griddle pan over high heat, cook oil. Put fish steaks; stir-cook for 5-6 minutes per side until cooked through and evenly browned. Serve warm.

Nutrition 275 Calories 17g Fat 5g Carbohydrates 0.5g Protein

664. Anchovy-Parmesan Pasta

Preparation Time: 10 minutes
Cooking Time: 20 minutes
Servings: 4
Ingredients:

- 4 anchovy fillets, packed in olive oil
- ½ pound broccoli, cut into 1-inch florets
- 2 cloves garlic, sliced
- 1-pound whole-wheat penne
- 2 tablespoons olive oil
- ¼ cup Parmesan cheese, grated
- Salt and black pepper, to taste
- Red pepper flakes, to taste

Directions:

1. Cook pasta as directed over pack; drain and set aside. Take a medium saucepan or skillet, add oil. Heat over medium heat.
2. Add anchovies, broccoli, and garlic, and stir-cook until veggies turn tender for 4-5 minutes. Take off heat; mix in the pasta. Serve warm with Parmesan cheese, red pepper flakes, salt, and black pepper sprinkled on top.

Nutrition 328 Calories 8g Fat 35g Carbohydrates 7g Protein

665. Garlic-Shrimp Pasta

Preparation Time: 10 minutes

Cooking Time: 15 minutes
Servings: 4
Ingredients:

- 1-pound shrimp, peeled and deveined
- 3 garlic cloves, minced
- 1 onion, finely chopped
- 1 package whole wheat or bean pasta of your choice
- 4 tablespoons olive oil
- Salt and black pepper, to taste
- ¼ cup basil, cut into strips
- ¾ cup chicken broth, low-sodium

Directions:

1. Cook pasta as directed over pack; rinse and set aside. Get medium saucepan, add oil then warm up over medium heat. Add onion, garlic and stir-cook until become translucent and fragrant for 3 minutes.
2. Add shrimp, black pepper (ground) and salt; stir-cook for 3 minutes until shrimps are opaque. Add broth and simmer for 2-3 more minutes. Add pasta in serving plates; add shrimp mixture over; serve warm with basil on top.

Nutrition 605 Calories 17g Fat 53g Carbohydrates 19g Protein

666. Sweet and Sour Salmon

Preparation Time: 10 minutes
Cooking Time: 5 minutes
Servings: 4
Ingredients:

- 4 (8-ounce) salmon filets
- 1/2 cup balsamic vinegar
- 1 tablespoon honey
- Black pepper and salt, to taste
- 1 tablespoon olive oil

Directions:

1. Combine honey and vinegar. Combine to mix well with each other.
2. Season fish fillets with the black pepper (ground) and sea salt; brush with honey glaze. Take a medium saucepan or skillet, add oil. Heat over medium heat. Add salmon fillets and stir-cook until medium rare in center and lightly browned for 3-4 minutes per side. Serve warm.

Nutrition 481 Calories 16g Fat 24g Carbohydrates 1.5g Protein

667. Citrus-Baked Fish

Preparation Time: 10 minutes
Cooking Time: 5 minutes
Servings: 4
Ingredients:

- ¼ teaspoon kosher or sea salt
- 1 tablespoon extra-virgin olive oil
- 1 tablespoon orange juice
- 4 (4-ounce) tilapia fillets, with or without skin

- ¼ cup chopped red onion
- 1 avocado, pitted, skinned, and sliced

Directions:
1. Take a baking dish of 9-inch; add olive oil, orange juice, and salt. Combine well. Add fish fillets and coat well. Add onions over fish fillets.
2. Cover with a plastic wrap. Microwave for 3 minutes until fish is cooked well and easy to flake. Serve warm with sliced avocado on top.

Nutrition 231 Calories 9g Fat 8g Carbohydrates 2.5g Protein

668. Lemon-Garlic Shrimp Zoodles

Preparation Time: 10 minutes
Cooking Time: 5 minutes
Servings: 2
Ingredients:
- 2 tablespoons chopped parsley
- 2 teaspoons minced garlic
- 1 teaspoon salt
- ½ teaspoon black pepper
- 2 medium zucchinis, spiralized
- 3/4 pounds medium shrimp, peeled & deveined
- 1 tablespoon olive oil
- 1 lemon, juiced and zested

Directions:
1. Take a medium saucepan or skillet, add oil, lemon juice, lemon zest. Heat over medium heat. Add shrimps and stir-cook 1 minute per side.
2. Sauté garlic and red pepper flakes for 1 more minute. Add Zoodles and stir gently; cook for 3 minutes until cooked to satisfaction. Season well, serve warm with parsley on top.

Nutrition 329 Calories 12g Fat 11g Carbohydrates 3g Protein

669. One-Pan Asparagus Trout

Preparation Time: 10 minutes
Cooking Time: 20 minutes
Servings: 4
Ingredients:
- 2 pounds trout fillets
- 1-pound asparagus
- Salt and ground white pepper, to taste
- 1 tablespoon olive oil
- 1 garlic clove, finely minced
- 1 scallion, thinly sliced (green and white part)
- 4 medium golden potatoes, thinly sliced
- 2 Roma tomatoes, chopped
- 8 pitted kalamata olives, chopped
- 1 large carrot, thinly sliced
- 2 tablespoons dried parsley
- ¼ cup ground cumin
- 2 tablespoons paprika
- 1 tablespoon vegetable bouillon seasoning

- ½ cup dry white wine

Directions:
1. In a mixing bowl, add fish fillets, white pepper and salt. Combine to mix well with each other. Take a medium saucepan or skillet, add oil. Heat over medium heat. Add asparagus, potatoes, garlic, white part scallion, and stir-cook until become softened for 4-5 minutes. Add tomatoes, carrot and olives; stir-cook for 6-7 minutes until turn tender. Add cumin, paprika, parsley, bouillon seasoning, and salt. Stir mixture well.
2. Mix in white wine and fish fillets. Over low heat, cover and simmer mixture for about 6 minutes until fish is easy to flake, stir in between. Serve warm with green scallions on top.

Nutrition 303 Calories 17g Fat 37g Carbohydrates 6g Protein

670. Olive Tuna

Preparation Time: 10 minutes
Cooking Time: 15 minutes
Servings: 6
Ingredients:
- 1 cup chopped onion
- 3 garlic cloves, minced
- 1 (2.25-ounce) can sliced olives, drained
- 1-pound kale, chopped
- 3 tablespoons extra-virgin olive oil
- ¼ cup capers
- ¼ teaspoon crushed red pepper
- 2 teaspoons sugar
- 1 (15-ounce) can cannellini beans
- 2 (6-ounce) cans tuna in olive oil, un-drained
- ¼ teaspoon black pepper
- ¼ teaspoon kosher or sea salt

Directions:
1. Soak kale in boiling water for 2 minutes; drain and set aside. Take a medium-large cooking pot or stock pot, heat oil over medium heat. Add onion and stir-cook until become translucent and softened. Add garlic and stir-cook until become fragrant for 1 minute.
2. Add olives, capers, and red pepper, and stir-cook for 1 minute. Mix in cooked kale and sugar. Over low heat, cover and simmer mixture for about 8-10 minutes, stir in between. Add tuna, beans, pepper, and salt. Stir well and serve warm.

Nutrition 242 Calories 11g Fat| 24g Carbohydrates 7g Protein

671. Rosemary-Citrus Shrimps

Preparation Time: 10 minutes
Cooking Time: 10 minutes
Servings: 6
Ingredients:
- 1 large orange, zested and peeled

- 3 garlic cloves, minced
- 1 ½ pounds raw shrimp, shells and tails removed
- 3 tablespoons olive oil
- 1 tablespoon chopped thyme
- 1 tablespoon chopped rosemary
- ¼ teaspoon black pepper
- ¼ teaspoon kosher or sea salt

Directions:
1. Take a zip-top plastic bag, add orange zest, shrimps, 2 tablespoons olive oil, garlic, thyme, rosemary, salt, and black pepper. Shake well and set aside to marinate for 5 minutes.
2. Take a medium saucepan or skillet, add 1 tablespoon olive oil. Heat over medium heat. Add shrimps and stir-cook for 2-3 minutes per side until totally pink and opaque. Slice orange into bite-sized wedges and add in a serving plate. Add shrimps and combine well. Serve fresh.

Nutrition 187 Calories 7g Fat 6g Carbohydrates 0.5g Protein

672. Pan-Seared Asparagus Salmon

Preparation Time: 10 minutes
Cooking Time: 15 minutes
Servings: 2
Ingredients:
- 8.8-ounce bunch asparagus
- 2 small salmon fillets
- 1 ½ teaspoon salt
- 1 teaspoon black pepper
- 1 tablespoon olive oil
- 1 cup hollandaise sauce, low-carb

Directions:
1. Season well the salmon fillets. Take a medium saucepan or skillet, add oil. Heat over medium heat.
2. Add salmon fillets and stir-cook until evenly seared and cooked well for 4-5 minutes per side. Add asparagus and stir cook for 4-5 more minutes. Serve warm with hollandaise sauce on top.

Nutrition 565 Calories 7g Fat 8g Carbohydrates 2.5g Protein

673. Pine Nut Tuna Salad

Preparation Time: 10 minutes
Cooking Time: 0 minute
Servings: 4
Ingredient:
- 1 tablespoon tarragon
- 1 stalk celery
- 1 medium shallot
- 3 tablespoons chives
- 1 (5-oz) can tuna
- 1 teaspoon Dijon mustard
- 2-3 tablespoons mayonnaise
- 1/4 teaspoon salt

- 1/8 teaspoon pepper
- 1/4 cup pine nuts, toasted

Directions:
1. Incorporate tuna, shallot, chives, tarragon, and celery. Blend mayonnaise, mustard, salt, and black pepper.
2. Stir in mayonnaise mixture to salad bowl; toss well to combine. Add pine nuts and toss again. Serve fresh.

Nutrition 276 Calories 16g Fat 4g Carbohydrates 1g Protein

674. Creamy Leek Shrimp Stew

Preparation Time: 10 minutes
Cooking Time: 35 minutes
Servings: 6
Ingredients:
- 1-pound medium shrimp, peeled and deveined
- 1 leek, both whites and light green parts, sliced
- 1 medium fennel bulb, chopped
- 2 tablespoons olive oil
- 3 stalks celery, chopped
- 1 clove garlic, minced
- Sea salt and ground pepper to taste
- 4 cups vegetable or chicken broth
- 1 tablespoon fennel seeds
- 2 tablespoons light cream
- Juice of 1 lemon

Directions:
1. Take a medium-large cooking pot or Dutch oven, heat oil over medium heat. Add celery, leek, and fennel and stir-cook for about 15 minutes, until vegetables are softened and browned. Add garlic; season with black pepper and sea salt to taste. Add fennel seed and stir.
2. Pour broth and bring to a boil. Over low heat, simmer mixture for about 20 minutes, stir in between. Add shrimp and cook until just pink for 3 minutes. Mix in cream and lemon juice; serve warm.

Nutrition 174 Calories 5g Fat 9.5g Carbohydrates 2g Protein

675. Salmon and Vegetable Quinoa

Preparation Time: 30 minutes
Cooking Time: 10 minutes
Servings: 4
Ingredients:
- 1 cup uncooked quinoa
- 1 teaspoon of salt, divided in half
- ¾ cup cucumbers, seeds removed, diced
- 1 cup of cherry tomatoes, halved
- ¼ cup red onion, minced
- 4 fresh basil leaves, cut in thin slices
- Zest from one lemon

- ¼ teaspoon black pepper
- 1 teaspoon cumin
- ½ teaspoon paprika
- 4 (5-oz.) salmon fillets
- 8 lemon wedges
- ¼ cup fresh parsley, chopped

Directions:
1. To a medium-sized saucepan, add the quinoa, 2 cups of water, and ½ teaspoons of the salt. Heat these until the water is boiling, then lower the temperature until it is simmering. Cover the pan and let it cook 20 minutes or as long as the quinoa package instructs. Turn off the burner under the quinoa and allow it to sit, covered, for at least another 5 minutes before serving.
2. Right before serving, mix onion, tomatoes, cucumbers, basil leaves, and lemon zest to the quinoa. In the meantime (while the quinoa cooks), prepare the salmon. Turn on the oven broiler to high and make sure a rack is in the lower part of the oven. To a small bowl, add the following components: black pepper, ½ teaspoon of the salt, cumin, and paprika. Stir them together.
3. Place foil over the top of a glass or aluminum baking sheet, then spray it with nonstick cooking spray. Place salmon fillets on the foil. Scour the spice mixture over the surface of each fillet (about ½ teaspoons of the spice mixture per fillet). Add the lemon wedges to the pan edges near the salmon.
4. Cook the salmon under the broiler for 8-10 minutes. Your goal is for the salmon to flake apart easily with a fork. Sprinkle the salmon with the parsley, then serve it with the lemon wedges and vegetable parsley. Enjoy!

Nutrition 385 Calories 12.5g Fat 32.5g Carbohydrates 35.5g Protein

676. Mustard Trout with Apples

Preparation Time: 15 minutes
Cooking Time: 55 minutes
Servings: 2
Ingredients:
- 1 Tablespoon Olive Oil
- 1 Small Shallot, Minced
- 2 Lady Apples, Halved
- 4 Trout Fillets, 3 Ounces Each
- 1 1/2 Tablespoons Bread Crumbs, Plain & Fine
- 1/2 Teaspoon Thyme, Fresh & Chopped
- 1/2 Tablespoon Butter, Melted & Unsalted
- 1/2 Cup Apple Cider
- 1 Teaspoon Light Brown Sugar
- 1/2 Tablespoon Dijon Mustard
- 1/2 Tablespoon Capers, Rinsed
- Sea Salt & Black Pepper to Taste

Directions:

1. Prepare oven to 375 degrees, and then get out a small bowl. Combine your bread crumbs, shallot and thyme before seasoning with salt and pepper.
2. Add in the butter, and mix well.
3. Put the apples cut side up in a baking dish, and then sprinkle with sugar. Top with bread crumbs, and then pour half of your cider around the apples, covering the dish. Bake for a half an hour.
4. Uncover, and then bake for twenty more minutes. The apples should be tender but your crumbs should be crisp. Remove the apples from the oven.
5. Turn the broiler on, and then put the rack four inches away. Pat your trout down, and then season with salt and pepper. Brush your oil on a baking sheet, and then put your trout with the skin side up. Brush your remaining oil over the skin, and broil for six minutes. Repeat the apples on the shelf right below the trout. This will keep the crumbs from burning, and it should only take two minutes to heat up.
6. Get out a saucepan, and whisk your remaining cider, capers, and mustard together. Add more cider if necessary, to thin, and cook for five minutes on medium-high. It should have a sauce like consistency. Scoop the juices over the fish, and serve with an apple on each plate.

Nutrition 366 calories 13g fats 10g carbohydrates 31g protein

677. Gnocchi with Shrimp

Preparation Time: 5 minutes
Cooking Time: 15 minutes
Servings: 4
Ingredients:
- 1/2 lb. Shrimp, Peeled & Deveined
- 1/4 Cup Shallots, Sliced
- 1/2 Tablespoon + 1 Teaspoon Olive Oil
- 8 Ounces Shelf Stable Gnocchi
- 1/2 Bunch Asparagus, Cut into Thirds
- 3 Tablespoons Parmesan Cheese
- 1 Tablespoon Lemon Juice, Fresh
- 1/3 Cup Chicken Broth
- Sea Salt & Black Pepper to Taste

Directions:
1. Start by heating a half a tablespoon of oil over medium heat, and then add in your gnocchi. Cook while stirring often until they turn plump and golden. This will take from seven to ten minutes. Place them in a bowl.
2. Heat your remaining teaspoon of oil with your shallots, cooking until they begin to brown. Make sure to stir, but this will take two minutes. Stir in the broth before adding your asparagus. Cover, and cook for three to four minutes.
3. Stir in shrimp, seasoning with salt and pepper. Cook until they are pink and cooked through, which will take roughly four minutes.

4. Return the gnocchi to the skillet with lemon juice, cooking for another two minutes. Stir well, and then remove it from heat.
5. Sprinkle with parmesan, and let it stand for two minutes. Your cheese should melt. Serve warm.

Nutrition 342 calories 11g fats 9g carbohydrates 38g protein

678. <u>Shrimp Saganaki</u>

Preparation Time: 15 minutes
Cooking Time: 30 minutes
Servings: 2
Ingredients:
- 1/2 lb. Shrimp with Shells
- 1 Small Onion, Chopped
- 1/2 Cup White Wine
- 1 Tablespoon Parsley, Fresh & Chopped
- 8 Ounces Tomatoes, Canned & Diced
- 3 Tablespoons Olive Oil
- 4 Ounces Feta Cheese
- Cubed Salt
- Dash Black Pepper
- 14 Teaspoon Garlic Powder

Directions:
1. Get out a saucepan and then pour in about two inches of water, bringing it to a boil. Boil for five minutes, and then drain but reserve the liquid. Set both the shrimp and the liquid to the side.
2. Heat two tablespoons of oil up next, and when heated add in your onions. Cook until the onions are translucent. Mix in your parsley, garlic, wine, olive oil and tomatoes. Simmer for a half hour, and stir until it's thickened.
3. Remove the legs of the shrimp, pulling off the shells, head and tail. Add the shrimp and shrimp stock into the sauce once it's thickened. Simmer for 5 minutes then add the feta cheese. Let it stand until the cheese starts to melt, and then serve warm.

Nutrition 329 calories 14g fat 10g carbohydrates 31g protein

679. <u>Mediterranean Salmon</u>

Preparation Time: 10 minutes
Cooking Time: 20 minutes
Servings: 2
Ingredients:
- 2 Salmon Fillets, Skinless & 6 Ounces Each
- 1 Cup Cherry Tomatoes
- 1 Tablespoon Capers
- 1/4 Cup Zucchini, Chopped Fine
- 1/8 Teaspoon Black Pepper
- 1/8 Teaspoon Sea Salt, Fine
- 1/2 Tablespoon Olive Oil
- Ounces Ripe Olives, Sliced

Directions:
1. Ready the oven to 425 degrees, and then sprinkle your salt and pepper over your fish on both sides.

Situate fish in a single layer on your baking dish after coating your baking dish using cooking spray.
2. Combine the tomatoes and remaining ingredients, spooning the mixture over your fillets, and then bake for twenty-two minutes. Serve warm.

Nutrition 322 calories 10g fats 15g carbohydrates 31g protein

680. <u>Seafood Linguine</u>

Preparation Time: 10 minutes
Cooking Time: 35 minutes
Servings: 2
Ingredients:
- 2 Cloves Garlic, Chopped
- 4 Ounces Linguine, Whole Wheat
- 1 Tablespoon Olive Oil
- 14 Ounces Tomatoes, Canned & Diced
- 1/2 Tablespoon Shallot, Chopped
- 1/4 Cup White Wine
- Sea Salt & Black Pepper to Taste
- 6 Cherrystone Clams, Cleaned
- 4 Ounces Tilapia, Sliced into 1 Inch Strips
- 4 Ounces Dry Sea Scallops
- 1/8 Cup Parmesan Cheese, Grated
- 1/2 Teaspoon Marjoram, Chopped & Fresh

Directions:
1. Boil the water in pot, then cook pasta until tender which should take roughly eight minutes. Drain and then rinse your pasta.
2. Heat your oil using a large skillet over medium heat, and then once your oil is hot stir in your garlic and shallot. Cook for a minute, and stir often.
3. Increase the heat to medium-high before adding your salt, wine, pepper and tomatoes, bringing it to a simmer. Cook for one minute more.
4. Add your clams next, covering and cooking for another two minutes.
5. Stir in your marjoram, scallops and fish next. Continue cooking until the fish is cook all the way through and your clams have opened up this will take up to five minutes, and get rid of any clams that do not open.
6. Spoon the sauce and your clams over the pasta, sprinkling with parmesan and marjoram before serving. Serve warm.

Nutrition 329 calories 12g fats 10g carbohydrates 33g protein

681. <u>Ginger Shrimp & Tomato Relish</u>

Preparation Time: 10 minutes
Cooking Time: 15 minutes
Servings: 2
Ingredients:
- 1 1/2 Tablespoons Vegetable Oil

- 1 Clove Garlic, Minced
- 10 Shrimp, Extra Large, Peeled & Tails Left On
- 3/4 Tablespoons Finger, Grated & Peeled
- 1 Green Tomatoes, Halved
- 2 Plum Tomatoes, Halved
- 1 Tablespoon Lime Juice, Fresh
- 1/2 Teaspoon Sugar
- 1/2 Tablespoon Jalapeno with Seeds, Fresh & Minced
- 1/2 Tablespoon Basil, Fresh & Chopped
- 1/2 Tablespoons Cilantro, Chopped & Fresh
- 10 Skewers

Directions:

1. Immerse your skewers in a pan of water for at least a half hour.
2. Stir your garlic and ginger together in a bowl, transferring half to a larger bowl and stirring it with two tablespoons of your oil. Add in the shrimp, and make sure they are well coated.
3. Cover and transfer it in the fridge for at least a half hour, and then allow it to refrigerate.
4. Preheat grill to high, and rub the grates lightly using oil. Get out a bowl and toss your plum and green tomatoes with the remaining tablespoon of oil, seasoning with salt and pepper.
5. Grill your tomatoes with the cut side up and the skins should be charred. The flesh of your tomato should be tender, which will take about four to six minutes for the plum tomato and about ten minutes for the green tomato.
6. Remove the skins once the tomatoes are cool enough to handle, and then discard the seeds. Chop the tomatoes flesh fine, adding it to the reserved ginger and garlic. Add in your sugar, jalapeno, lime juice and basil.
7. Season your shrimp using salt and pepper threading them onto the skewers, and then grill until they turn opaque, which is about two minutes on each side. Place the shrimp on a platter with your relish and enjoy.

Nutrition 391 calories 13g fats 11g carbohydrates 34g protein

682. Shrimp & Pasta

Preparation Time: 10 minutes
Cooking Time: 10 minutes
Servings: 2

Ingredients:

- 2 Cups Angel Hair Pasta, Cooked
- 1/2 lb. Medium Shrimp, Peeled
- 1 Clove Garlic, Minced
- 1 Cup Tomato, Chopped
- 1 Teaspoon Olive Oil
- 1/6 Cup Kalamata Olives, Pitted & Chopped
- 1/8 Cup Basil, Fresh & Sliced Thin
- 1 Tablespoon Capers, Drained

- 1/8 Cup Feta Cheese, Crumbled
- Dash Black Pepper

Directions:

1. Cook your pasta per package instructions, and then heat up your olive oil in a skillet using medium-high heat. Cook your garlic for half a minute, and then add your shrimp. Sauté for a minute more.
2. Add your basil and tomato, and then reduce the heat to allow it to simmer for three minutes. Your tomato should be tender.
3. Stir in your olives and capers. Add a dash of black pepper, and combine your shrimp mix and pasta together to serve. Top with cheese before serving warm.

Nutrition 357 calories 11g fats 9g carbohydrates 30g protein

683. Poached Cod

Preparation Time: 10 minutes
Cooking Time: 25 minutes
Servings: 2

Ingredients:

- 2 Cod Filets, 6 Ounces
- Sea Salt & Black Pepper to Taste
- 1/4 Cup Dry White Wine
- 1/4 Cup Seafood Stock
- 2 Cloves Garlic, Minced
- 1 Bay Leaf
- 1/2 Teaspoon Sage, Fresh & Chopped
- 2 Rosemary Sprigs to Garnish

Directions:

1. Start by turning your oven to 375, and then season the fillets with salt and pepper. Place them in a baking pan, and add in your stock, garlic, wine, sage and bay leaf. Cover well, and then bake for twenty minutes. Your fish should be flaky when tested with a fork.
2. Use a spatula to remove each fillet, placing the liquid over high heat and cooking to reduce in half. This should take ten minutes, and you need to stir frequently. Serve dripped in poaching liquid and garnished with a rosemary sprig.

Nutrition 361 calories 10g fats 9g carbohydrates 34g protein

684. Mussels in White Wine

Preparation Time: 5 minutes
Cooking Time: 10 minutes
Servings: 2

Ingredients:

- 2 lbs. Live Mussels, Fresh
- 1 Cup Dry White Wine
- 1/4 Teaspoon Sea Salt, Fine
- 3 Cloves Garlic, Minced
- 2 Teaspoons Shallots, Diced
- 1/4 Cup Parsley, Fresh & Chopped, Divided
- 2 Tablespoons olive Oil

- 1/4 Lemon, Juiced

Directions:
1. Get out a colander and scrub your mussels, rinsing them using cold water. Discard mussels that will not close if they're tapped, and then use a paring knife to remove the beard from each one.
2. Get out stockpot, placing it over medium-high heat, and add in your garlic, shallots, wine and parsley. Bring it to a simmer. Once it's at a steady simmer, add in your mussels and cover. Allow them to simmer for five to seven minutes. Make sure they do not overcook.
3. Use a slotted spoon to remove them, and add your lemon juice and olive oil into the pot. Stir well, and pour the broth over your mussels before serving with parsley.

Nutrition 345 calories 9g fats 18g carbohydrates 37g protein

685. Dilly Salmon

Preparation Time: 10 minutes
Cooking Time: 15 minutes
Servings: 2

Ingredients:
- 2 Salmon Fillets, 6 Ounces Each
- 1 Tablespoon Olive Oil
- 1/2 Tangerine, Juiced
- 2 Teaspoons Orange Zest
- 2 Tablespoons Dill, Fresh & Chopped
- Sea Salt & Black Pepper to Taste

Directions:
1. Prepare oven to 375 degrees, and then get out two ten-inch pieces of foil. Rub your filets down with olive oil on both side before seasoning with salt and pepper, placing each fillet into a piece of foil.
2. Drizzle your orange juice over each one, and then top with orange zest and dill. Fold your packet closed, making sure it has two inches of air space within the foil so your fish can steam, and then place them on a baking dish.
3. Bake for fifteen minutes before opening the packets, and transfer to two serving plates. Pour the sauce over the top of each before serving.

Nutrition 366 calories 14g fats 9g carbohydrates 36g protein

686. Smooth Salmon

Preparation Time: 8 minutes
Cooking Time: 8 minutes
Servings: 2

Ingredients:
- Salmon, 6-ounce fillet
- Lemon, 2 slices
- Capers, 1 tablespoon
- Sea salt and pepper, 1/8 teaspoon
- Extra virgin olive oil, 1 tablespoon

Directions:

1. Situate clean skillet over a medium heat to prepare for 3 minutes. Place olive oil on a plate, and coat the salmon completely. Cook the salmon over a high heat in the skillet.
2. Top the salmon with the rest of the ingredients, and turn to cook each side. Notice when both sides are brown. It may take 3-5 minutes each side. Make sure the salmon is cooked by testing with a fork.
3. Serve with lemon slices.

Nutrition 371 Calories 25.1g Fat 0.9g Carbohydrates 33.7g Protein

687. Tuna Melody

Preparation Time: 20 minutes
Cooking Time: 20 minutes
Servings: 2

Ingredients:
- Tuna, 12 ounces
- Green onions, 1 for garnish
- Bell pepper, ¼, chopped
- Vinegar, 1 dash
- Salt and pepper to taste
- Avocados, 1, halved and pitted
- Greek yogurt, 2 tablespoons

Directions:
1. Mix the tuna with the vinegar, onion, yogurt, avocado and pepper in a bowl.
2. Add the seasonings, mix, and serve with the green onion garnish.

Nutrition 294 Calories 19g Fat 10g Carbohydrates 12g Protein

688. Sea Cheese

Preparation Time: 12 minutes
Cooking Time: 25 minutes
Servings: 2

Ingredients:
- Salmon, 6-ounce fillet
- Dried basil, 1 tablespoon
- Cheese, 2 tablespoons, grated
- Tomato, 1, sliced
- Extra virgin olive oil, 1 tablespoon

Directions:
1. Prepare a baking oven at 375 F. Layer aluminum foil in a baking dish, and spray with cooking oil. Carefully transfer the salmon to the baking tray and top with the rest of the ingredients.
2. Let the salmon brown for 20 minutes. Allow to cool for five minutes, and transfer to a serving plate. You will see the topping in the middle of the salmon.

Nutrition 411 Calories 26.6g Fat 1.6g Carbohydrates 8g Protein

689. Healthy Steaks

Preparation Time: 10 minutes
Cooking Time: 20 minutes
Servings: 2
Ingredients:
- Olive oil, 1 teaspoon
- Halibut steak, 8 ounces
- Garlic, ½ teaspoon, minced
- Butter, 1 tablespoon
- Salt and pepper to taste

Directions:
1. Heat a skillet and add the oil. Over a medium flame, brown the steaks in a pan, melt the butter with the garlic, salt and pepper. Add the steaks, toss to coat, and serve.

Nutrition 284 Calories 17g Fat 0.2g Carbohydrates 8g Protein

690. Herbal Salmon

Preparation Time: 8 minutes
Cooking Time: 18 minutes
Servings: 2
Ingredients:
- Salmon, 2 fillets without skin
- Coarse salt to taste
- Extra virgin olive oil, 1 tablespoon
- Lemon, 1, sliced
- Fresh rosemary, 4 sprigs

Directions:
1. Preheat the oven to 400F. Situate aluminum foil in a baking dish, and place salmon on top. Top the salmon with the rest of the ingredients and bake for 20 minutes. Serve immediately with lemon slices.

Nutrition 257 Calories 18g Fat 2.7g Carbohydrates 7g Protein

691. Smokey Glazed Tuna

Preparation Time: 35 minutes
Cooking Time: 10 minutes
Servings: 2
Ingredients:
- Tuna, 4-ounce steaks
- Orange juice, 1 tablespoon
- Minced garlic, ½ clove
- Lemon juice, ½ teaspoon
- Fresh parsley, 1 tablespoon, chopped
- Soy sauce, 1 tablespoon
- Extra virgin olive oil, 1 tablespoon
- Ground black pepper, ¼ teaspoon
- Oregano, ¼ teaspoon

Directions:
1. Pick a mixing dish, and add all the ingredients, except the tuna. Mix well, and then add the tuna to marinade.

2. Refrigerate this mixture for half an hour. Heat a grill pan and cook the tuna on each side for 5 minutes. Serve when cooked.

Nutrition 200 Calories 7.9g Fat 0.3g Carbohydrates 10g Protein

692. Crusty Halibut

Preparation Time: 20 minutes
Cooking Time: 15 minutes
Servings: 2
Ingredients:
- Parsley to top
- Fresh dill, 2 tablespoons, chopped
- Fresh chives, 2 tablespoons, chopped
- Olive oil, 1 tablespoon
- Salt and pepper to taste
- Halibut, fillets, 6 ounces
- Lemon zest, ½ teaspoon, finely grated
- Greek yogurt, 2 tablespoons

Directions:
1. Preheat the oven to 400F. Line a baking sheet with foil. Add all the ingredients to a wide dish, and marinate the fillets. Rinse and dry the fillets; then add to the oven and bake for 15 minutes.

Nutrition 273 Calories 7.2g Fat 0.4g Carbohydrates 9g Protein

693. Fit Tuna

Preparation Time: 15 minutes
Cooking Time: 10 minutes
Servings: 2
Ingredients:
- Egg, ½
- Onion, 1 tablespoon, finely chopped
- Celery to top
- Salt and pepper to taste
- Garlic, 1 clove, minced
- Canned tuna, 7 ounces
- Greek yogurt, 2 tablespoons

Directions:
1. Drain the tuna, and add the egg and yogurt with the garlic, salt and pepper.
2. In a bowl, combine this mixture with onions and shape into patties. Take a large skillet and brown the patties for 3 minutes per side. Drain and serve.

Nutrition 230 Calories 13g Fat 0.8g Carbohydrates 10g Protein

694. Hot and Fresh Fishy Steaks

Preparation Time: 14 minutes
Cooking Time: 14 minutes
Servings: 2
Ingredients:
- Garlic, 1 clove, minced

- Lemon juice, 1 tablespoon
- Brown sugar, 1 tablespoon
- Halibut steak, 1 pound
- Salt and pepper to taste
- Soy sauce, ¼ teaspoon
- Butter, 1 teaspoon
- Greek yogurt, 2 tablespoons

Directions:

1. Over a medium flame, preheat the grill. Mix the butter, sugar, yogurt, lemon juice, soy sauce and seasonings in a bowl. Warm the mixture in a pan. Use this mixture to brush onto the steak while cooking on the griller. Serve hot.

Nutrition 412 Calories 19.4g Fat 7.6g Carbohydrates11g Protein

695. Mussels O' Marine

Preparation Time: 20 minutes
Cooking Time: 10 minutes
Servings: 2
Ingredients:

- Mussels, scrubbed and debearded, 1 pound
- Coconut milk, ½ cup
- Cayenne pepper, 1 teaspoon
- Fresh lemon juice, 1 tablespoon
- Garlic, 1 teaspoon, minced
- Cilantro, freshly chopped for topping
- Brown sugar, 1 teaspoon

Directions:

1. Mix all the ingredients, except the mussels in a pot. Heat the mixture and bring it to the boil. Add the mussels, and cook for 10 minutes. Serve in a dish with the boiled liquid.

Nutrition 483 Calories 24.4g Fat 21.6g Carbohydrates 1.2g Protein

696. Savory Salmon Fat Bombs

Preparation Time: 2 hours
Cooking Time: 0 minute
Serving: 6
Ingredients

- 1/2 cup full-fat cream cheese
- 1/3 cup butter
- 1/2 package smoked salmon
- 1 tbsp fresh lemon juice
- 1-2 tbsp freshly chopped dill

Direction

1. Put the cream cheese, butter and smoked salmon into a nourishment processor.
2. Add lemon juice and dill and beat until smooth.
3. Line a plate with parchment paper and make little fat bombs utilizing around 2 1/2 tablespoons of the blend per piece.
4. Trimming with more dill and put in the cooler for 1-2 hours or until firm

Nutrition: 300 Calories 30g Fat 3g Protein

697. Greek Stuffed Collard Greens

Preparation Time: 10 minutes
Cooking Time: 20 minutes
Serving: 4
Ingredients:

- 1 (28-ounce) can low-sodium crushed tomatoes
- 8 collard green leaves
- 2 (10-ounce) bags frozen grain medley
- 2 tablespoons grated Parmesan cheese

Direction:

1. Preheat the oven to 400°F. Pour the tomatoes into a baking pan and set aside.
2. Fill a large stockpot about three-quarters of the way with water and bring to a boil. Add the collard greens and cook for 2 minutes. Drain in a colander. Put the greens on a clean towel or paper towels and blot dry.
3. To assemble the stuffed collards, lay one leaf flat on the counter vertically. Add about ½ cup of the lentils and rice mixture to the middle of the leaf, and spread it evenly along the middle of the leaf. Fold one long side of the leaf over the rice filling, then fold over the other long side so it is slightly overlapping. Take the bottom end, where the stem was, and gently but firmly roll up until you have a slightly square package. Carefully transfer the stuffed leaf to the baking pan, and place it seam-side down in the crushed tomatoes. Repeat with the remaining leaves.
4. Sprinkle the leaves with the grated cheese, and cover the pan with aluminum foil. Bake for 20 minutes, or until the collards are tender-firm, and serve.

Nutrition: 205 Calories 8g Fat 6g Protein

698. Walnut Pesto Zoodles

Preparation Time: 15 minutes
Cooking Time: 10 minutes
Serving: 4
Ingredients:

- 4 medium zucchinis
- ¼ cup extra-virgin olive oil, divided
- 2 garlic cloves
- ½ teaspoon crushed red pepper
- ¼ teaspoon black pepper, divided
- ¼ teaspoon kosher or sea salt
- 2 tablespoons grated Parmesan cheese
- 1 cup packed fresh basil leaves
- ¾ cup walnut pieces, divided

Direction:

1. Make the zucchini noodles (zoodles) using a spiralizer or your vegetable peeler to make ribbons. Mix zoodles with 1 tablespoon of oil, 1 minced garlic clove, all the crushed red pepper, 1/8

teaspoon of black pepper, and 1/8 teaspoon of salt. Set aside.

2. Using huge skillet over medium-high heat, heat ½ tablespoon of oil. Add half of the zoodles to the pan and cook for 5 minutes, stirring every minute or so. Pour the cooked zoodles into a large serving bowl, and repeat with another ½ tablespoon of oil and the remaining zoodles. Add those zoodles to the serving bowl when they are done cooking.
3. While the zoodles are cooking, make the pesto. Using a high-powered blender, add the 2 tablespoons of oil first and then the rest of the pesto ingredients. Pulse until the pesto is completely blended.
4. Add the pesto to the zoodles along with the remaining 1 tablespoon of Parmesan and the remaining ½ cup of walnuts. Mix together well and serve.

Nutrition 301 Calories 28g Fat 7g Protein

699. Cauliflower Steaks with Eggplant Relish

Preparation Time: 5 minutes
Cooking Time: 25 minutes
Serving: 4
Ingredients
- 2 small heads cauliflower
- ¼ teaspoon kosher or sea salt
- ¼ teaspoon smoked paprika
- extra-virgin olive oil, divided
- 1 recipe Eggplant Relish Spread

Direction:
1. Situate large, rimmed baking sheet in the oven. Set oven to 400°F with the pan inside.
2. Stand one head of cauliflower on a cutting board, stem-end down. With a long chef's knife, slice down through the very center of the head, including the stem. Starting at the cut edge, measure about 1 inch and cut one thick slice from each cauliflower half, including as much of the stem as possible, to make two cauliflower "steaks." Reserve the remaining cauliflower for another use. Repeat with the second cauliflower head.
3. Dry each steak well with a clean towel. Sprinkle the salt and smoked paprika evenly over both sides of each cauliflower steak.
4. Put skillet over medium-high heat, cook 2 tablespoons of oil. When the oil is very hot, add two cauliflower steaks to the pan and cook for about 3 minutes. Flip and cook for 2 more minutes. Transfer the steaks to a plate. Wipe out the pan to remove most of the hot oil. Repeat the cooking process with the remaining 2 tablespoons of oil and the remaining two steaks.
5. Using oven mitts, carefully pull away the baking sheet from the oven and place the cauliflower on the baking sheet. Roast in the oven for 13 minutes. Serve with the Eggplant Relish Spread.

Nutrition: 282 calories 22g Fat 8g Protein

700. Mediterranean Lentil Sloppy Joes

Preparation Time: 5 minutes
Cooking Time: 15 minutes
Serving: 4
Ingredients:
- 1 tablespoon extra-virgin olive oil
- 1 cup chopped onion
- 1 cup chopped bell pepper
- 2 garlic cloves
- 1 (15-ounce) can lentils, drained and rinsed
- 1 (14.5-ounce) can low-sodium tomatoes
- 1 teaspoon ground cumin
- 1 teaspoon dried thyme
- ¼ teaspoon kosher or sea salt
- 4 whole-wheat pita breads, split open
- 1½ cups chopped seedless cucumber
- 1 cup chopped romaine lettuce

Direction
1. In a saucepan at medium-high heat, sauté onion and bell pepper for 4 minutes. Cook garlic and stir in lentils, tomatoes (with their liquid), cumin, thyme, and salt.
2. Put the heat to medium and cook, stirring occasionally, for 10 minutes.
3. Stuff the lentil mixture inside each pita. Lay the cucumbers and lettuce on top of mixture and serve.

Nutrition: 334 Calories 5g Fat 16g Protein

701. Gorgonzola Sweet Potato Burgers

Preparation Time: 10 minutes
Cooking Time: 15 minutes
Serving: 4
Ingredients:
- 1 large sweet potato (about 8 ounces)
- 2 tablespoons extra-virgin olive oil, divided
- 1 cup chopped onion (about ½ medium onion)
- 1 cup old-fashioned rolled oats
- 1 large egg
- 1 tablespoon balsamic vinegar
- 1 tablespoon dried oregano
- 1 garlic clove
- ¼ teaspoon kosher or sea salt
- ½ cup crumbled Gorgonzola

Direction
1. Prick sweet potato all over and microwave on high for 4 to 5 minutes. Cool slightly, then slice in half.
2. While the sweet potato is cooking, in a large skillet over medium-high heat, heat 1 tablespoon of oil. Cook onion

3. Using a spoon, carefully scoop the sweet potato flesh out of the skin and put the flesh in a food processor. Blend onion, oats, egg, vinegar, oregano, garlic, and salt. Add the cheese and pulse four times to barely combine. With your hands, form the mixture into four (½-cup-size) burgers. Place the burgers on a plate, and press to flatten each to about ¾-inch thick.

4. Clean out the skillet with a paper towel, then heat the remaining 1 tablespoon of oil over medium-high heat for 2 minutes. Stir in burgers to the hot oil, then turn the heat down to medium. Cook the burgers for 5 minutes, flip with a spatula, then cook an additional 5 minutes. Enjoy as is or serve on salad greens or whole-wheat rolls.

Nutrition: 223 Calories 13g Fat 7g Protein

702. Zucchini-Eggplant Gratin

Preparation Time: 10 minutes
Cooking Time: 20 minutes
Serving: 6
Ingredients:
- 1 large eggplant
- 2 large zucchinis
- ¼ teaspoon black pepper
- ¼ teaspoon kosher or sea salt
- 3 tablespoons extra-virgin olive oil
- 1 tablespoon all-purpose flour
- ¾ cup 2% milk
- 1/3 cup Parmesan cheese
- 1 cup chopped tomato
- 1 cup diced or shredded fresh mozzarella
- ¼ cup fresh basil leaves

Direction:
1. Preheat the oven to 425°F.
2. Mix eggplant, zucchini, pepper, and salt.
3. Situate skillet over medium-high heat, heat 1 tablespoon of oil. Add half the veggie mixture to the skillet. Stir a few times, then cover and cook for 5 minutes, stirring occasionally. Pour the cooked veggies into a baking dish. Situate skillet back on the heat, add 1 tablespoon of oil, and repeat with the remaining veggies. Add the veggies to the baking dish.
4. While the vegetables are cooking, heat the milk in the microwave for 1 minute. Set aside.
5. Place a medium saucepan over medium heat. Add the remaining tablespoon of oil and flour, and whisk together for about 1 minute
6. Slowly pour the warm milk into the oil mixture, whisking the entire time. Drizzle 1/3 cup of Parmesan cheese, and whisk until melted. Pour the cheese sauce over the vegetables in the baking dish and mix well.
7. Gently mix in the tomatoes and mozzarella cheese. Roast in the oven for 10 minutes, or until the gratin is almost set and not runny. Garnish with the fresh

basil leaves and the remaining 2 tablespoons of Parmesan cheese before serving.
Nutrition: 207 Calories 14g Fat 11g Protein

703. Grilled Stuffed Portobello Mushrooms

Preparation Time: 5 minutes
Cooking Time: 25 minutes
Serving: 6
Ingredients:
- 3 tablespoons extra-virgin olive oil
- 1 cup diced onion
- 2 garlic cloves
- 3 cups chopped mushrooms
- 2 small zucchinis
- 1 cup chopped tomato
- 1 teaspoon dried oregano
- ¼ teaspoon crushed red pepper
- ¼ teaspoon kosher or sea salt
- 6 large portobello mushrooms
- 4 ounces fresh mozzarella cheese
- Additional dried oregano, for serving (optional)

Direction:
1. Position skillet over medium heat, heat 2 tablespoons of oil. Cook onion for 4 minutes, stirring occasionally. Cook garlic for 1 minute, stirring often.
2. Stir in the mushrooms, zucchini, tomato, oregano, crushed red pepper, and salt. Cook for 10 minutes, stirring occasionally. Remove from the heat.
3. While the veggies are cooking, heat the grill or grill pan to medium-high heat.
4. Brush the remaining tablespoon of oil over the portobello mushroom caps. Place the mushrooms bottom-side (where the stem was removed) down on the grill or pan. Cover and cook for 5 minutes.
5. Flip the mushroom caps over, and spoon about ½ cup of the cooked vegetable mixture into each cap. Top each with about 2½ tablespoons of mozzarella and additional oregano, if desired.
6. Cover and grill for 4 to 5 minutes.
7. Remove each portobello with a spatula, and let them sit for about 5 minutes to cool slightly before serving.

Nutrition: 171 Calories 12g Fat 9g Protein

704. Stuffed Tomatoes with Tabbouleh

Preparation Time: 10 minutes
Cooking Time: 20 minutes
Serving: 4
Ingredients:
- 8 medium beefsteak tomatoes
- 3 tablespoons extra-virgin olive oil
- ½ cup water

- ½ cup whole-wheat couscous
- 1½ cups minced fresh curly parsley
- 1/3 cup minced fresh mint
- 2 scallions
- ¼ teaspoon black pepper
- ¼ teaspoon kosher or sea salt
- 1 medium lemon
- 4 teaspoons honey
- 1/3 cup chopped almonds

Direction:

1. Preheat the oven to 400°F.
2. Cut top off each tomato and set aside. Spoon out all the flesh inside, and put the tops, flesh, and seeds in a large mixing bowl.
3. Rub baking dish with 1 tablespoon of oil. Place the carved-out tomatoes in the baking dish, and cover with aluminum foil. Roast for 10 minutes.
4. While the tomatoes are cooking, make the couscous by bringing the water to boil in a medium saucepan. Pour in the couscous, remove from the heat, and cover. Keep aside for 5 minutes.
5. While the couscous is cooking, chop up the tomato flesh and tops. Drain off the excess tomato water using a colander. Measure out 1 cup of the chopped tomatoes (reserve any remaining chopped tomatoes for another use). Add the cup of tomatoes back into the mixing bowl. Mix in the parsley, mint, scallions, pepper, and salt.
6. Using a Micro plane or citrus grater, zest the lemon into the mixing bowl. Halve the lemon, and squeeze the juice through a strainer (to catch the seeds) from both halves into the bowl with the tomato mixture. Mix well.
7. When the couscous is ready, add it to the tomato mixture and mix well.
8. With oven mitts, carefully remove the tomatoes from the oven. Divide the tabbouleh evenly among the tomatoes and stuff them, using a spoon to press the filling down so it all fits. Wrap with the foil and return it to the oven. Cook for another 8 to 10 minutes. Before serving, top each tomato with a drizzle of ½ teaspoon of honey and about 2 teaspoons of almonds.

Nutrition: 314 Calories 15g Fat 8g Protein

705. Polenta with Mushroom Bolognese

Preparation Time: 5 minutes
Cooking Time: 25 minutes
Serving: 4
Ingredients:

- 2 (8-ounce) packages white button mushrooms
- 3 tablespoons extra-virgin olive oil, divided
- 1½ cups onion
- ½ cup carrot
- 4 garlic cloves
- 1 (18-ounce) tube plain polenta

- ¼ cup tomato paste
- 1 tablespoon dried oregano
- ¼ teaspoon ground nutmeg
- ¼ teaspoon kosher or sea salt
- ¼ teaspoon freshly ground black pepper
- ½ cup dry red wine
- ½ cup whole milk
- ½ teaspoon sugar

Direction:

1. Situate half the mushrooms in a food processor bowl and pulse about 15 times. Do with the remaining mushrooms and set aside.
2. Situate stockpot over medium-high heat, heat 2 tablespoons of oil. Cook onion and carrot then mushrooms and garlic for 10 minutes.
3. While cooking, add the remaining 1 tablespoon of oil to skillet at medium-high heat. Put 4 slices of polenta to the skillet and cook for 3 to 4 minutes. Remove the polenta from the skillet, place it on a shallow serving dish, and cover with aluminum foil to keep warm. Repeat with the remaining 4 slices of polenta.
4. To the mushroom mixture in the stockpot, add the tomato paste, oregano, nutmeg, salt, and pepper and stir. Continue cooking for additional 4 minutes. Pour wine and cook for 1 to 2 minutes. Lower the heat to medium.
5. Using microwave-safe bowl, scourge milk and sugar together and microwave on high for 30 to 45 seconds. Simmer the milk into the mushroom mixture. Drizzle the mushroom veggie sauce over the warm polenta slices.

Nutrition: 300 Calories 12g Fat 9g Protein

706. North African Peanut Stew over Cauliflower Rice

Preparation Time: 5 minutes
Cooking Time: 25 minutes
Serving: 4
Ingredients:

- 1 cup frozen corn
- 2 tablespoons extra-virgin olive oil
- 1 cup chopped onion
- 2 medium Yukon Gold potatoes
- 1 large sweet potato
- 3 garlic cloves
- 1½ teaspoons ground cumin
- 1 teaspoon ground allspice
- 1 teaspoon freshly grated ginger root
- ½ teaspoon crushed red pepper
- ¼ teaspoon kosher or sea salt
- ½ cup water
- 1 (28-ounce) can diced tomatoes, undrained
- 1 (12-ounce) package frozen plain cauliflower rice
- 1 (15-ounce) can lentils, undrained
- 1/3 cup creamy peanut butter

Direction:
1. Put the corn on the counter to partially thaw while making the stew.
2. In a large stockpot over medium-high heat, heat the oil. Add the onion, potatoes, and sweet potatoes. Cook for 7 minutes. Put the potatoes to the edges of the pot, and add the garlic, cumin, allspice, ginger, crushed red pepper, and salt. Cook for 1 minute, stirring constantly. Stir in the water and cook for 1 more minute, scraping up the crispy bits from the bottom of the pan.
3. Stir in tomatoes with their juices to the stockpot. Cook for 15 minutes uncovered, stirring occasionally.
4. While the tomatoes are cooking, cook the cauliflower rice according to the package directions.
5. Into the tomato mixture, stir in the lentils, partially thawed corn, and peanut butter. Adjust to medium heat and cook for 1 to 2 minutes. Serve over the cauliflower rice with hot peppers, peanuts, and fresh cilantro, if desired.

Nutrition: 467 Calories 20g Fat 21g Protein

707. Italian Baked Beans

Preparation Time: 5 minutes
Cooking Time: 15 minutes
Serving: 6
Ingredients:
- 2 teaspoons extra-virgin olive oil
- ½ cup minced onion
- 1 (12-ounce) can low-sodium tomato paste
- ¼ cup red wine vinegar
- 2 tablespoons honey
- ¼ teaspoon ground cinnamon
- ½ cup water
- 2 (15-ounce) cans cannellini

Direction:
1. Position saucepan over medium heat, heat the oil. Cook onion. Add the tomato paste, vinegar, honey, cinnamon, and water, and mix well. Turn the heat to low.
2. Strain and wash one can of the beans in a colander and add to the saucepan. Pour the entire second can of beans (including the liquid) into the saucepan. Let it cook for 10 minutes, stirring occasionally, and serve.

Nutrition: 236 Calories 3g Fat 10g Protein

708. Cannellini Bean Lettuce Wraps

Preparation Time: 10 minutes
Cooking Time: 10 minutes
Serving: 4
Ingredients:
- 1 tablespoon extra-virgin olive oil
- ½ cup diced red onion
- ¾ cup chopped fresh tomatoes
- ¼ teaspoon freshly ground black pepper
- 1 (15-ounce) can cannellini beans
- ¼ cup curly parsley
- ½ cup Lemony Garlic Hummus
- 8 romaine lettuce leaves

Direction:
1. Position skillet over medium heat, heat the oil. Add the onion and cook for 3 minutes, stirring occasionally. Add the tomatoes and pepper and cook for 3 more minutes, stirring occasionally. Add the beans and cook for 3 more minutes, stirring occasionally. Pullout from the heat, and mix in the parsley.
2. Spread 1 tablespoon of hummus over each lettuce leaf. Evenly spread the warm bean mixture down the center of each leaf. Fold one side of the lettuce leaf over the filling lengthwise, then fold over the other side to make a wrap and serve.

Nutrition: 211 Calories 8g Fat 10g Protein

709. Israeli Eggplant, Chickpea, and Mint Sauté

Preparation Time: 5 minutes
Cooking Time: 20 minutes
Serving: 6
Ingredients:
- 1 medium globe eggplant
- 1 tablespoon extra-virgin olive oil
- 2 tablespoons lemon juice
- 2 tablespoons balsamic vinegar
- 1 teaspoon ground cumin
- ¼ teaspoon salt
- 1 (15-ounce) can chickpeas
- 1 cup sliced sweet onion
- ¼ cup mint leaves
- 1 tablespoon sesame seeds
- 1 garlic clove

Direction:
1. Place one oven rack about 4 inches below the broiler element. Turn the broiler to the highest setting to preheat. Grease rimmed baking sheet using nonstick cooking spray.
2. Slice eggplant lengthwise into four slabs (½- to 5/8-inch thick). Place the eggplant slabs on the prepared baking sheet. Put aside.
3. Scourge oil, lemon juice, vinegar, cumin, and salt. Brush 2 tablespoons of the lemon dressing over both sides of the eggplant slabs.
4. Broil the eggplant under the heating element for 4 minutes, flip them, then broil for 4 minutes.
5. While the eggplant is broiling, combine the chickpeas, onion, mint, sesame seeds, and garlic. Add the reserved dressing, and gently mix.
6. When done, situate slabs from the baking sheet to a

cooling rack and cool for 3 minutes. When slightly cooled, cut each slab crosswise into ½-inch strips.

7. Toss eggplant to the mixture and serve warm.

Nutrition: 159 Calories 4g Fat 6g Protein

710. Mediterranean Lentils and Rice

Preparation Time: 5 minutes
Cooking Time: 25 minutes
Serving: 4
Ingredients:
- 2¼ cups low-sodium vegetable broth
- ½ cup lentils
- ½ cup uncooked instant brown rice
- ½ cup diced carrots
- ½ cup diced celery
- 1 (2.25-ounce) can sliced olives
- ¼ cup diced red onion
- ¼ cup chopped fresh curly-leaf parsley
- 1½ tablespoons extra-virgin olive oil
- 1 tablespoon freshly squeezed lemon juice
- 1 garlic clove
- ¼ teaspoon kosher or sea salt
- ¼ teaspoon black pepper

Direction:
1. Position saucepan over high heat, bring the broth and lentils to a boil, cover, and lower the heat to medium-low. Cook for 8 minutes.
2. Switch the heat to medium, then mix in the rice. Cover the pot and cook the mixture for 15 minutes. Take away pot from the heat and let it sit, covered, for 1 minute, then stir.
3. While cooking, incorporate carrots, celery, olives, onion, and parsley in a large serving bowl.
4. Blend oil, lemon juice, garlic, salt, and pepper. Set aside.
5. When cooked, put them to the serving bowl. Pour the dressing on top, and mix everything together. Serve.

Nutrition: 230 Calories 8g Fat 8g Protein

711. Brown Rice Pilaf with Golden Raisins

Preparation Time: 5 minutes
Cooking Time: 15 minutes
Serving: 6
Ingredients:
- 1 tablespoon extra-virgin olive oil
- 1 cup chopped onion
- ½ cup shredded carrot
- 1 teaspoon ground cumin
- ½ teaspoon ground cinnamon
- 2 cups instant brown rice
- 1¾ cups 100% orange juice

- ¼ cup water
- 1 cup golden raisins
- ½ cup shelled pistachios

Direction:
1. Put saucepan on medium-high heat, cook onion for 5 minutes. Sauté carrot, cumin, and cinnamon.
2. Stir in the rice, orange juice, and water. Bring to a boil, cover, then lower the heat to medium-low. Simmer for 7 minutes.
3. Stir in the raisins, pistachios, and chives (if using) and serve.

Nutrition: 320 Calories 7g Fat 6g Protein

712. Vegetarian Quinoa Pilaf

Preparation Time: 9 minutes
Cooking Time: 35 minutes
Servings: 1
Ingredients:
- 3 TB. extra-virgin olive oil
- 2 portobello mushrooms, sliced
- 1 medium red onion, finely chopped
- 1 TB. minced garlic
- 1 (16-oz.) can diced tomatoes, with juice
- 2 cups water
- 2 tsp. salt
- 1 TB. dried oregano
- 1 TB. turmeric
- 1 tsp. paprika
- 1 tsp. ground black pepper
- 2 cups red or yellow quinoa
- 1/2 cup fresh parsley, chopped

Directions:
1. In a huge, 3-quart pot over medium heat, cook extra-virgin olive oil. Cook portobello mushrooms
2. Cook red onion and garlic, stir for 5 minutes.
3. Stir in tomatoes with juice, water, salt, oregano, turmeric, paprika, and black pepper. Simmer for 6 minutes.
4. Mix in red quinoa to the pot, and stir. Cover, reduce heat to low, and cook for 20 minutes.
5. Pull away from heat, fluff with a fork, cover, and let sit for 10 minutes.
6. Ladle quinoa onto a plate, sprinkle with parsley, and serve warm.

Nutrition: 305 Calories 8g Fat 4g Protein

713. Roasted and Curried Cauliflower

Preparation Time: 8 minutes
Cooking Time: 50 Minutes
Serving: 6
Ingredients:
- 1 lime (juiced)
- 1 medium head of cauliflower
- 1 tsp cayenne pepper

- 1 tsp sea salt
- 1 tsp smoked paprika
- 1 ½ cups full fat Greek yogurt
- ½ tsp black pepper
- 2 tbsp yellow curry powder
- 2 tsp lime zest
- 1 clove garlic
- 1 tbsp cilantro
- 1/2 cup pine nuts
- 1/4 cup olive oil
- 1/4 cup sun-dried tomatoes
- 2 tbsp feta cheese (crumbled)

Directions:
1. Prep baking sheet using parchment paper and preheat the oven to 375oF.
2. Scourge lime zest, curry, black pepper, yogurt, paprika, sea salt, and lime in a bowl. Rub all over the cauliflower.
3. Situate cauliflower on the prepared pan and po in the oven. Bake for about 45 minutes.
4. Meanwhile, make the topping ingredients by pulsing sun-dried tomatoes, half of pine nits, and garlic in a food processor.
5. Situate mixture in a bowl and fold in remaining topping ingredients.
6. One cauliflower is done, remove from the oven and let it cool enough to handle. Break into bite sized pieces and pour topping ingredients over it.
7. Serve.

Nutrition: 384 Calories 15g Protein 30g Fat

714. **Easy and Healthy Baked Vegetables**

Preparation Time: 9 minutes
Cooking Time: 75 minutes
Serving: 6
Ingredients:
- 2 lbs. Brussels sprouts, trimmed
- 3 lbs. Butternut Squash
- 1 lb. Pork breakfast sausage
- 1 tbsp fat from fried sausage

Directions:
1. Grease a 9x inch baking pan and preheat oven to 350oF.
2. With medium high fire, situate nonstick saucepan and cook sausage. Break up sausages and cook until browned.
3. In a greased pan mix browned sausage, squash, sprouts, sea salt and fat. Toss to mix well. Pop into the oven and cook for an hour.
4. Remove from oven and serve warm.

Nutrition: 364 Calories 19g Protein 17g Fat

715. **Green Beans and Tomatoes**

Preparation Time: 7 minutes

Cooking Time: 30 minutes
Serving: 2
Ingredients:
- 1/4 cup extra-virgin olive oil
- 2 medium white onions, chopped
- 11/2 tsp. salt
- 3 medium tomatoes, chopped
- 1/4 cup minced garlic
- 1/2 tsp. ground black pepper
- 1/2 tsp. cayenne

Directions:
1. Situate 4 cups green beans, trimmed and cut into in. pieces
2. In a big, 3-quart pot over medium heat, cook extra-virgin olive oil. Sauté white onions for 5 minutes.
3. Stir in salt, tomatoes, and garlic, and cook for 10 minutes.
4. Add black pepper, cayenne, and green beans, and toss together. Cover and cook for 10 minutes.
5. Serve with pita bread.

Nutrition: 341 Calories 10g Fat 4g Protein

716. **Crunchy Kale Chips**

Preparation Time: 11 minutes
Cooking Time: 2 hours
Serving: 8
Ingredients:
- 2 tbsp filtered water
- ½ tsp sea salt
- 1 tbsp raw honey
- 2 tbsp nutritional yeast
- 1 lemon, juiced
- 1 cup sweet potato
- 1 cup fresh cashews
- 2 bunches green curly kale

Directions:
1. Prepare a baking sheet by covering with an unbleached parchment paper. Preheat oven to 0oF.
2. In a large mixing bowl, place kale.
3. Using food processor, process remaining ingredients until smooth. Pour over kale.
4. With your hands, coat kale with marinade.
5. Evenly spread kale onto parchment paper and pop in the oven. Dehydrate for 2 hours and turn leaves after the first hour of baking.
6. Remove from oven; let it cool completely before serving.

Nutrition: 209 Calories 7g Protein 15.9g Fat

717. **Zucchini Lasagna**

Preparation Time: 13 minutes
Cooking Time: 45 minutes
Serving: 4
Ingredients:
- 2 zucchinis, trimmed

- 1 cup Mozzarella, shredded
- ½ cup tomato sauce
- 1 onion, chopped
- 1 tablespoon olive oil
- ½ cup potato, boiled, mashed
- 1 teaspoon Italian seasonings
- ¼ cup tomato sauce
- 1 teaspoon butter, softened

Directions:
1. Heat up olive oil in the skillet.
2. Add onion and roast it until light brown.
3. Meanwhile, slice the zucchini lengthwise.
4. Grease the casserole mold with butter from inside.
5. Put ½ part of sliced zucchini in the casserole mold to get the layer.
6. Then add the layer of cooked onion and a ½ cup of Mozzarella cheese.
7. After this, make the layer from the remaining zucchini.
8. Top the vegetables with a layer of mashed potatoes and Mozzarella.
9. Pour the tomato sauce over the cheese and cover the surface of the mold with foil. Secure the edges.
10. Bake the lasagna for 30 minutes at 365F.
11. Then discard the foil and cook lasagna for 10 minutes more.

Nutrition: 103 calories 6.3g fat 4.1g protein

718. Garlic Parmesan Artichokes

Preparation Time: 9 minutes
Cooking Time: 10 minutes
Serving: 4
Ingredients:
- 4 artichokes, wash, trim, and cut top
- 1/2 cup vegetable broth
- 1/4 cup parmesan cheese, grated
- 1 tbsp olive oil
- 2 tsp garlic, minced
- Salt

Directions:
1. Pour broth into the instant pot then place steamer rack in the pot.
2. Place artichoke steam side down on steamer rack into the pot.
3. Sprinkle garlic and grated cheese on top of artichokes and season with salt. Drizzle oil over artichokes.
4. Seal pot with lid and cook on high for 10 minutes.
5. Once done, release pressure using quick release. Remove lid.
6. Serve and enjoy.

Nutrition: 132 Calories 5.2g Fat 7.9g Protein

719. Roasted Brussels Sprouts And Pecans

Preparation Time: 9 minutes
Cooking Time: 3 hours
Serving; 7
Ingredients:
- 1 ½ pounds fresh Brussels sprouts
- 4 tablespoons olive oil
- 4 cloves of garlic, minced
- 3 tablespoons water
- Salt and pepper to taste
- ½ cup chopped pecans

Directions:
1. Place all ingredients in the Instant Pot.
2. Combine all ingredients until well combined.
3. Close the lid and make sure that the steam release vent is set to "Venting."
4. Press the "Slow Cook" button and adjust the cooking time to 3 hours.
5. Sprinkle with a dash of lemon juice if desired.

Nutrition: 161 Calories 4.1g Protein 13g Fat

720. Parmesan Veggies Mix

Preparation Time: 8 minutes
Cooking Time: 40 minutes
Serving: 4
Ingredients:
- 1 zucchini, sliced
- 1 carrot, sliced
- 1 eggplant, sliced
- 1 red onion, sliced
- 1 sweet pepper, sliced
- ½ cup cream
- 1 teaspoon dried oregano
- 1 teaspoon ground black pepper
- 1 teaspoon dried basil
- 2 oz Parmesan, grated
- 1 teaspoon butter, softened

Directions:
1. Mix up together cream, dried oregano, ground black pepper, and dried basil.
2. Grease the springform pan with butter and arrange all vegetable one-by-one in it.
3. Then pour cream mixture over the vegetables.
4. Top the ratatouille with Parmesan and cover with foil. Secure the edges.
5. Bake the meal for 40 minutes at 36.
6. The remove the foil from the meal and chill it for 10 minutes before serving.

Nutrition: 139 calories 6.1g fat 7.4g protein

721. Almond Kale

Preparation Time: 7 minutes
Cooking Time: 10 minutes

Serving: 2

Ingredients:
- 2 cups kale, chopped
- 1 tablespoon butter
- 1 cup of water
- 1 tablespoon almond, chopped
- 1 teaspoon cumin seeds
- ½ teaspoon salt

Directions:
1. Bring the water to boil.
2. Add kale in the hot water and boil the greens for 3 minutes.
3. After this, drain the water.
4. Melt the butter in the skillet.
5. Add cumin seeds and roast them for 1 minute over the medium heat or until they start to give a smell.
6. Add boiled kale and mix up.
7. After this, sprinkle the kale with salt and almonds. Mix up well.
8. Roast the kale for 2 minutes.

Nutrition: 105 calories 7.5g fat 2.9g protein

722. Tomato Basil Cauliflower Rice

Preparation Time: 13 minutes
Cooking Time: 10 minutes
Serving: 4

Ingredients:
- Dried parsley for garnish
- ¼ cup tomato paste
- ½ teaspoon garlic, minced
- ½ teaspoon onion powder
- ½ teaspoon marjoram
- 1 ½ teaspoon dried basil
- 1 teaspoon dried oregano
- 1 large head of cauliflower
- 1 teaspoon oil

Direction:
1. Slice cauliflower into florets and put in the food processor.
2. Pulse until it has a coarse consistency similar with rice. Set aside.
3. In a skillet, heat the oil and sauté the garlic and onion for three minutes. Add the rest of the ingredients. Cook for 8 minutes.

Nutrition: 106 Calories 3.3g Protein 5g Fat

723. Allspice Okra

Preparation Time: 7 minutes
Cooking Time: 20 minutes
Serving: 2

Ingredients:
- 1 teaspoon allspices
- ¼ teaspoon ground cumin
- 1/3 teaspoon garlic, diced
- 1/3 cup crushed tomatoes

- 2 cups okra, chopped
- 1 teaspoon tomato paste
- ½ teaspoon salt
- 1 cup of water
- ½ teaspoon sunflower oil

Directions:
1. Heat up sunflower oil in the saucepan and add okra.
2. Sprinkle the vegetables with allspices and roast for 3 minutes.
3. After this, add ground cumin, garlic, and crushed tomatoes.
4. Bring the mixture to boil and add water.
5. Close the lid and simmer Baima for 10 minutes over the medium heat.
6. Then remove the cooked meal from the heat and let it rest for 10-15 minutes before serving.

Nutrition: 62 calories 1.6g fat 2.5g protein

724. Garlicky Rosemary Potatoes

Preparation Time: 9 minutes
Cooking Time: 2 minutes
Serving: 4

Ingredients:
- 1-pound potatoes
- 2 garlic cloves
- ½ teaspoon salt
- 1 tablespoon olive oil
- 2 sprigs of rosemary

Directions:
1. Situate trivet or steamer basket in the Instant Pot and pour in a cup of water.
2. In a baking dish that can fit inside the Instant Pot, combine all ingredients and toss to coat everything.
3. Wrap the baking dish using aluminum foil and place on the steamer basket.
4. Cover and press the Steam button.
5. Adjust the cooking time to 30 minutes
6. Do quick pressure release.
7. Once cooled, evenly divide into serving size, keep in your preferred container, and refrigerate until ready to eat.

Nutrition: 119 Calories 2.39g Protein3.48g Fat

725. Creamy Carrot Chowder

Preparation Time: 11 minutes
Cooking Time: 40 minutes
Serving: 8

Ingredients:
- 8 fresh mint sprigs
- ½ cup 2% Greek Style Plain yogurt
- 1 tsp fresh ginger
- 2 cups chicken broth
- 1 lb. baby carrots
- 1/3 cup sliced shallots
- 2 tsp sesame oil

Directions:

1. On medium fire, place a medium heavy bottom pot and heat oil.
2. Sauté shallots until tender around minutes.
3. Add carrots and sauté for another 4 minutes.
4. Pour broth, cover and bring to a boil. Once soup is boiling, slow fire to a simmer and cook carrots until tender around 22 minutes.
5. Add ginger and continue cooking while covered for another eight minutes.
6. Turn off fire and let it cool for 10 minutes.
7. Pour mixture into blender and puree. If needed, puree carrots in batches then return to pot.
8. Heat pureed carrots until heated through around 2 minutes.
9. Turn off fire and evenly pour into 8 serving bowls.
10. Serve and enjoy.

Nutrition: 47 Calories 2.2g Protein1.6g Fat

726. Cauliflower Hash Brown

Preparation Time: 11 minutes
Cooking Time: 6 minutes
Serving: 6

Ingredients:

- 12 eggs, beaten
- ½ cup coconut milk
- ½ teaspoon dry mustard
- Salt and pepper to taste
- 1 head cauliflower, shredded
- 2 cups shredded cheese

Directions:

1. Place all ingredients in a mixing bowl until well combined.
2. Put enough oil for frying in a skillet and heat over medium flame.
3. Add a large dollop of cauliflower mixture in the skillet and flatten with the back of a fork.
4. Fry until golden brown.
5. Place in a plate lined with a kitchen towel to absorb excess oil.
6. Place in individual containers.
7. Put a label and store in the fridge.
8. Allow to thaw at room temperature before heating in the microwave oven.

Nutrition: 340 Calories 22.8g Protein 25g Fat

727. Mediterranean Veggie Bowl

Preparation Time: 10 minutes
Cooking Time: 20 minutes
Serving: 4

Ingredients:

- 2 cups water
- 1 cup quinoa
- 1½ teaspoons salt, divided
- 1-pint (2 cups) cherry tomatoes
- 1 large bell pepper

- 1 large cucumber
- 1 cup Kalamata olives
- ½ cup freshly squeezed lemon juice
- 1 cup extra-virgin olive oil
- ½ teaspoon black pepper

Direction:

1. Situate medium pot over medium heat, boil the water. Add the bulgur (or quinoa) and 1 teaspoon of salt. Seal and cook for 17 minutes.
2. To arrange the veggies in your 4 bowls, visually divide each bowl into 5 sections. Place the cooked bulgur in one section. Follow with the tomatoes, bell pepper, cucumbers, and olives.
3. Scourge lemon juice, olive oil, remaining ½ teaspoon salt, and black pepper.
4. Evenly spoon the dressing over the 4 bowls.
5. Serve immediately or cover and refrigerate for later.

Nutrition: 772 Calories 6g Protein68g Fat

728. Grilled Veggie and Hummus Wrap

Preparation Time: 15 minutes
Cooking Time: 10 minutes
Serving: 6

Ingredients:

- 1 large eggplant
- 1 large onion
- ½ cup extra-virgin olive oil
- 1 teaspoon salt
- 6 lavash wraps or large pita bread
- 1 cup Creamy Traditional Hummus

Direction

1. Preheat a grill, large grill pan, or lightly oiled large skillet on medium heat.
2. Slice the eggplant and onion into circles. Rub vegetables with olive oil and sprinkle with salt.
3. Cook the vegetables on both sides, about 3 to 4 minutes each side.
4. To make the wrap, lay the lavash or pita flat. Spread 2 tbsp. of hummus on the wrap.
5. Evenly divide the vegetables among the wraps, layering them along one side of the wrap. Gently fold over the side of the wrap with the vegetables, tucking them in and making a tight wrap.
6. Lay the wrap seam side-down and cut in half or thirds.

Nutrition: 362 Calories 15g Protein 26g Fat

729. Spanish Green Beans

Preparation Time: 10 minutes
Cooking Time: 20 minutes
Serving: 4

Ingredients

- ¼ cup extra-virgin olive oil
- 1 large onion, chopped

- 4 cloves garlic, finely chopped
- 1-pound green beans
- 1½ teaspoons salt, divided
- 1 (15-ounce) can diced tomatoes
- ½ teaspoon freshly ground black pepper

Direction:
1. Position large pot over medium heat, cook olive oil, onion, and garlic.
2. Cut the green beans into 2-inch pieces.
3. Add the green beans and 1 teaspoon of salt to the pot and toss everything together; cook for 3 minutes.
4. Add the diced tomatoes, remaining ½ teaspoon of salt, and black pepper to the pot; continue to cook for another 12 minutes, stirring occasionally.
5. Serve warm.

Nutrition: 200 Calories 4g Protein 14g Fat

730. Rustic Cauliflower and Carrot Hash

Preparation Time: 10 minutes
Cooking Time: 10 minutes
Serving: 4

Ingredients:
- 3 tablespoons extra-virgin olive oil
- 1 large onion
- 1 tablespoon garlic
- 2 cups carrots
- 4 cups cauliflower pieces
- 1 teaspoon salt
- ½ teaspoon ground cumin

Direction:
1. Preheat a pan over medium heat, cook the olive oil, onion, garlic, and carrots for 3 minutes.
2. Cut the cauliflower into 1-inch or bite-size pieces. Add the cauliflower, salt, and cumin to the skillet and toss to combine with the carrots and onions.
3. Cover and cook for 3 minutes.
4. Toss the vegetables and continue to cook for 4 minutes.
5. Serve warm.

Nutrition: 159 Calories 3g Protein 11g Fat

731. Roasted Cauliflower and Tomatoes

Preparation Time: 5 minutes
Cooking Time: 25 minutes
Serving: 4

Ingredients:
- 4 cups cauliflower
- 6 tablespoons extra-virgin olive oil
- 1 teaspoon salt
- 4 cups cherry tomatoes
- ½ teaspoon black pepper
- ½ cup grated Parmesan cheese

Direction:
1. Preheat the oven to 425°F.
2. Add the cauliflower, 3 tablespoons of olive oil, and ½ teaspoon of salt to a large bowl and toss to evenly coat. Pour onto a baking sheet and spread the cauliflower out in an even layer.
3. In another large bowl, add the tomatoes, remaining 3 tablespoons of olive oil, and ½ teaspoon of salt, and toss to coat evenly. Pour onto a different baking sheet.
4. Put the sheet of cauliflower and the sheet of tomatoes in the oven to roast for 17 to 20 minutes until the cauliflower is lightly browned and tomatoes are plump.
5. Using a spatula, spoon the cauliflower into a serving dish, and top with tomatoes, black pepper, and Parmesan cheese. Serve warm.

Nutrition: 294 Calories 9g Protein 26g Fat

732. Roasted Acorn Squash

Preparation Time: 10 minutes
Cooking Time: 35 minutes
Serving: 6

Ingredients
- 2 acorn squash, medium to large
- 2 tablespoons extra-virgin olive oil
- 1 teaspoon salt, plus more for seasoning
- 5 tablespoons unsalted butter
- ¼ cup chopped sage leaves
- 2 tablespoons fresh thyme leaves
- ½ teaspoon freshly ground black pepper

Direction:
1. Preheat the oven to 400°F.
2. Cut the acorn squash in half lengthwise. Spoon out the seeds and cut it horizontally into ¾-inch-thick slices.
3. In a large bowl, drizzle the squash with the olive oil, sprinkle with salt, and toss together to coat.
4. Lay the acorn squash flat on a baking sheet.
5. Situate baking sheet in the oven and bake the squash for 20 minutes. Flip squash over with a spatula and bake for another 15 minutes.
6. Cook butter in a medium saucepan at medium heat.
7. Heat sage and thyme to the melted butter for 30 seconds.
8. Transfer the cooked squash slices to a plate. Spoon the butter/herb mixture over the squash. Season with salt and black pepper. Serve warm.

Nutrition: 188 Calories 1g Protein 15g Fat

733. Sautéed Garlic Spinach

Preparation Time: 5 minutes
Cooking Time: 10 minutes
Serving: 4

Ingredients:
- ¼ cup extra-virgin olive oil

- 1 large onion, thinly sliced
- 3 cloves garlic, minced
- 6 (1-pound) bags of baby spinach, washed
- ½ teaspoon salt
- 1 lemon, cut into wedges

Direction:
1. Cook the olive oil, onion, and garlic in a large skillet for 2 minutes over medium heat.
2. Add one bag of spinach and ½ teaspoon of salt. Cover the skillet and let the spinach wilt for 30 seconds. Repeat (omitting the salt), adding 1 bag of spinach at a time.
3. When all the spinach has been added, open and cook for 3 minutes, letting some of the moisture evaporate.
4. Serve with squeeze of lemon over the top.

Nutrition: 301 Calories 17g Protein 14g Fat

734. Garlicky Sautéed Zucchini with Mint

Preparation Time: 5 minutes
Cooking Time: 10 minutes
Serving: 4

Ingredients:
- 3 large green zucchinis
- 3 tablespoons extra-virgin olive oil
- 1 large onion, chopped
- 3 cloves garlic, minced
- 1 teaspoon salt
- 1 teaspoon dried mint

Direction
1. Cut the zucchini into ½-inch cubes.
2. Position skillet over medium heat, cook the olive oil, onions, and garlic for 3 minutes, stirring constantly.
3. Add the zucchini and salt to the skillet and toss to combine with the onions and garlic, cooking for 5 minutes.
4. Add the mint to the skillet, tossing to combine. Cook for another 2 minutes. Serve warm.

Nutrition: 147 Calories 4g Protein 11g Fat

735. Stewed Okra

Preparation Time: 5 minutes
Cooking Time: 25 minutes
Serving: 4

Ingredients:
- ¼ cup extra-virgin olive oil
- 1 large onion, chopped
- 4 cloves garlic, finely chopped
- 1 teaspoon salt
- 1 pound fresh or frozen okra, cleaned
- 1 (15-ounce) can plain tomato sauce
- 2 cups water
- ½ cup fresh cilantro, finely chopped

- ½ teaspoon freshly ground black pepper

Direction
1. Situate pot over medium heat, stir and cook the olive oil, onion, garlic, and salt for 1 minute.
2. Stir in the okra and cook for 3 minutes.
3. Add the tomato sauce, water, cilantro, and black pepper; stir, cover, and let cook for 15 minutes, stirring occasionally.
4. Serve warm.

Nutrition: 201 Calories 4g Protein 14g Fat

736. Sweet Veggie-Stuffed Peppers

Preparation Time: 20 minutes
Cooking Time: 30 minutes
Serving: 6

Ingredients:
- 6 large bell peppers, different colors
- 3 tablespoons extra-virgin olive oil
- 1 large onion, chopped
- 3 cloves garlic, minced
- 1 carrot, chopped
- 1 (16-ounce) can garbanzo beans
- 3 cups cooked rice
- 1½ teaspoons salt
- ½ teaspoon freshly ground black pepper

Direction:
1. Preheat the oven to 350°F.
2. Make sure to choose peppers that can stand upright. Cut off the pepper cap and remove the seeds, reserving the cap for later. Stand the peppers in a baking dish.
3. In a skillet over medium heat, sauté olive oil, onion, garlic, and carrots for 3 minutes.
4. Stir in the garbanzo beans. Cook for another 3 minutes.
5. Pull away the pan from the heat and spoon the cooked ingredients to a large bowl.
6. Add the rice, salt, and pepper; toss to combine.
7. Stuff each pepper to the top and then put the pepper caps back on.
8. Wrap baking dish with aluminum foil and bake for 25 minutes.
9. Peel out the foil and bake for another 5 minutes.
10. Serve warm.

Nutrition: 301 Calories 8g Protein 9g Fat

737. Moussaka

Preparation Time: 55 minutes
Cooking Time: 40 minutes
Serving: 6

Ingredients:
- 2 large eggplants
- 2 teaspoons salt, divided
- ¼ cup extra-virgin olive oil

- 2 large onions, sliced
- 10 cloves garlic, sliced
- 2 (15-ounce) cans diced tomatoes
- 1 (16-oz) can garbanzo beans
- 1 teaspoon dried oregano
- ½ teaspoon freshly ground black pepper

Direction:

1. Slice the eggplant horizontally into ¼-inch-thick round disks. Sprinkle the eggplant slices with 1 teaspoon of salt and place in a colander for 30 minutes.
2. Preheat the oven to 450°F. Pat the slices of eggplant dry with a paper towel and spray each side with an olive oil spray or lightly brush each side with olive oil.
3. Situate eggplant in a single layer on a baking sheet. Put in the oven and bake for 10 minutes. Then, using a spatula, flip the slices over and bake for another 10 minutes.
4. In a large skillet add the olive oil, onions, garlic, and remaining 1 teaspoon of salt. Cook for 4 minutes. Add the tomatoes, garbanzo beans, oregano, and black pepper. Simmer for 11 minutes, stirring occasionally.
5. Using a deep casserole dish, begin to layer, starting with eggplant, then the sauce. Repeat until all ingredients have been used. Bake in the oven for 20 minutes.
6. Remove from the oven and serve warm.

Nutrition: 262 Calories 8g Protein 11g Fat

738. **Vegetable-Stuffed Grape Leaves**

Preparation Time: 50 minutes
Cooking Time: 45 minutes
Serving: 8

Ingredients:

- 2 cups white rice
- 2 large tomatoes
- 1 large onion
- 1 green onion
- 1 cup fresh Italian parsley
- 3 cloves garlic, minced
- 2½ teaspoons salt
- ½ teaspoon black pepper
- 1 (16-ounce) jar grape leaves
- 1 cup lemon juice
- ½ cup extra-virgin olive oil
- 4 to 6 cups water

Direction:

1. Mix rice, tomatoes, onion, green onion, parsley, garlic, salt, and black pepper.
2. Drain and rinse the grape leaves.
3. Prepare a large pot by placing a layer of grape leaves on the bottom. Lay each leaf flat and trim off any stems.

4. Place 2 tablespoons of the rice mixture at the base of each leaf. Fold over the sides, then roll as tight as possible. Situate rolled grape leaves in the pot, lining up each rolled grape leaf. Continue to layer in the rolled grape leaves.
5. Gently pour the lemon juice and olive oil over the grape leaves, and add enough water to just cover the grape leaves by 1 inch.
6. Lay a heavy plate that is smaller than the opening of the pot upside down over the grape leaves. Cover the pot and cook the leaves over medium-low heat for 45 minutes. Let stand for 20 minutes before serving.
7. Serve warm or cold.

Nutrition: 532 Calories 12g Protein 21g Fat

739. **Grilled Eggplant Rolls**

Preparation Time: 30 minutes
Cooking Time: 10 minutes
Serving: 6

Ingredients:

- 2 large eggplants
- 1 teaspoon salt
- 4 ounces goat cheese
- 1 cup ricotta
- ¼ cup fresh basil, finely chopped
- ½ teaspoon black pepper

Direction

1. Cutoff the tops of the eggplants and cut the eggplants lengthwise into ¼-inch-thick slices. Sprinkle the slices with the salt and place the eggplant in a colander for 15 to 20 minutes.
2. In a large bowl, combine the goat cheese, ricotta, basil, and pepper.
3. Preheat a grill, grill pan, or lightly oiled skillet on medium heat. Dry eggplant slices using paper towel and lightly spray with olive oil spray. Place the eggplant on the grill, grill pan, or skillet and cook for 3 minutes on each side.
4. Pull out the eggplant from the heat and let cool for 5 minutes.
5. To roll, lay one eggplant slice flat, place a tablespoon of the cheese mixture at the base of the slice, and roll up. Serve immediately or chill until serving.

Nutrition: 255 Calories 15g Protein 15g Fat

740. **Crispy Zucchini Fritters**

Preparation Time: 15 minutes
Cooking Time: 20 minutes
Serving: 6

Ingredients:

- 2 large green zucchinis
- 2 tablespoons Italian parsley
- 3 cloves garlic, minced
- 1 teaspoon salt

- 1 cup flour
- 1 large egg, beaten
- ½ cup water
- 1 teaspoon baking powder
- 3 cups vegetable or avocado oil

Direction
1. Grate the zucchini into a large bowl.
2. Add the parsley, garlic, salt, flour, egg, water, and baking powder to the bowl and stir to combine.
3. In a large pot or fryer over medium heat, heat oil to 365°F.
4. Drop the fritter batter into the hot oil by spoonful. Turn the fritters over using a slotted spoon and fry until they are golden brown, about 2 to 3 minutes.
5. Take out the fritters from the oil and drain on a plate lined with paper towels.
6. Serve warm with Creamy Tzatziki dip.

Nutrition: 446 Calories 5g Protein 38g Fat

741. Cheesy Spinach Pies

Preparation Time: 20 minutes
Cooking Time: 40 minutes
Serving: 6 to 8
Ingredients:
- 2 tablespoons extra-virgin olive oil
- 1 large onion, chopped
- 2 cloves garlic, minced
- 3 (1-pound) bags of baby spinach, washed
- 1 cup feta cheese
- 1 large egg, beaten
- Puff pastry sheets

Direction:
1. Preheat the oven to 375°F.
2. Using big skillet over medium heat, cook the olive oil, onion, and garlic for 3 minutes.
3. Add the spinach to the skillet one bag at a time, letting it wilt in between each bag. Toss using tongs. Cook for 4 minutes. Once cooked, strain any excess liquid from the pan.
4. In a large bowl, combine the feta cheese, egg, and cooked spinach.
5. Lay the puff pastry flat on a counter. Cut the pastry into 3-inch squares.
6. Place a tablespoon of the spinach mixture in the center of a puff-pastry square. Fold over one corner of the square to the diagonal corner, forming a triangle. Crimp the edges of the pie by pressing down with the tines of a fork to seal them together. Repeat until all squares are filled.
7. Place the pies on a parchment-lined baking sheet and bake for 25 to 30 minutes or until golden brown. Serve warm or at room temperature.

Nutrition: 503 Calories 16g Protein 32g Fat

742. Fried Eggplant Rolls

Preparation Time: 20 minutes

Cooking Time: 10 minutes
Servings: 6
Ingredients:
- 2 large eggplants
- 1 teaspoon salt
- 1 cup shredded ricotta cheese
- 4 ounces (113 g) goat cheese, shredded
- ¼ cup finely chopped fresh basil
- ½ teaspoon freshly ground black pepper
- Olive oil spray

Directions:
1. Add the eggplant slices to a colander and season with salt. Set aside for 15 to 20 minutes.
2. Mix together the ricotta and goat cheese, basil, and black pepper in a large bowl and stir to combine. Set aside. Pat dry the eggplant slices with paper towels and lightly mist them with olive oil spray.
3. Warm up large skillet over medium heat and lightly spray it with olive oil spray. Arrange the eggplant slices in the skillet and fry each side for 3 minutes until golden brown.
4. Remove from the heat to a paper towel-lined plate and rest for 5 minutes. Make the eggplant rolls: Lay the eggplant slices on a flat work surface and top each slice with a tablespoon of the prepared cheese mixture. Roll them up and serve immediately.

Nutrition 254 Calories 14.9g Fat 7.1g Carbohydrates 15.3g Protein

743. Roasted Veggies and Brown Rice Bowl

Preparation Time: 15 minutes
Cooking Time: 20 minutes
Servings: 4
Ingredients:
- 2 cups cauliflower florets
- 2 cups broccoli florets
- 1 (15-ounce / 425-g) can chickpeas
- 1 cup carrot slices (about 1 inch thick)
- 2 to 3 tablespoons extra-virgin olive oil, divided
- Salt and black pepper, to taste
- Nonstick cooking spray
- 2 cups cooked brown rice
- 3 tablespoons sesame seeds

Dressing:
- 3 to 4 tablespoons tahini
- 2 tablespoons honey
- 1 lemon, juiced
- 1 garlic clove, minced
- Salt and black pepper, to taste

Directions
1. Ready the oven to 400°F (205°C). Spritz two baking sheets with nonstick cooking spray.
2. Spread the cauliflower and broccoli on the first baking sheet and the second with the chickpeas and carrot slices.

3. Drizzle each sheet with half of the olive oil and sprinkle with salt and pepper. Toss to coat well.
4. Roast the chickpeas and carrot slices in the preheated oven for 10 minutes, leaving the carrots tender but crisp, and the cauliflower and broccoli for 20 minutes until fork-tender. Stir them once halfway through the cooking time.
5. Meanwhile, make the dressing: Whisk together the tahini, honey, lemon juice, garlic, salt, and pepper in a small bowl.
6. Divide the cooked brown rice among four bowls. Top each bowl evenly with roasted vegetables and dressing. Sprinkle the sesame seeds on top for garnish before serving.

Nutrition 453 Calories 17.8g Fat 11.2g Carbohydrate 12.1g Protein

744. Cauliflower Hash with Carrots

Preparation Time: 10 minutes
Cooking Time: 10 minutes
Servings: 4
Ingredients:
- 3 tablespoons extra-virgin olive oil
- 1 large onion, chopped
- 1 tablespoon minced garlic
- 2 cups diced carrots
- 4 cups cauliflower florets
- ½ teaspoon ground cumin
- 1 teaspoon salt

Directions:
1. Cook the olive oil over medium heat. Mix in the onion and garlic and sauté for 1 minute. Stir in the carrots and stir-fry for 3 minutes. Add the cauliflower florets, cumin, and salt and toss to combine.
2. Cover and cook for 3 minutes until lightly browned. Stir well and cook, uncovered, for 3 to 4 minutes, until softened. Remove from the heat and serve warm.

Nutrition 158 Calories 10.8g Fat 5.1g Carbohydrates 3.1g Protein

745. Garlicky Zucchini Cubes with Mint

Preparation Time: 5 minutes
Cooking Time: 10 minutes
Servings: 4
Ingredients:
- 3 large green zucchinis
- 3 tablespoons extra-virgin olive oil
- 1 large onion, chopped
- 3 cloves garlic, minced
- 1 teaspoon salt
- 1 teaspoon dried mint

Directions:

1. Cook the olive oil in a large skillet over medium heat.
2. Mix in the onion and garlic and sauté for 3 minutes, stirring constantly, or until softened.
3. Stir in the zucchini cubes and salt and cook for 5 minutes, or until the zucchini is browned and tender.
4. Add the mint to the skillet and toss to combine, then continue cooking for 2 minutes. Serve warm.

Nutrition 146 Calories 10.6g Fat 3g Carbohydrates 4.2g Protein

746. Zucchini and Artichokes Bowl with Faro

Preparation Time: 15 minutes
Cooking Time: 10 minutes
Servings: 6
Ingredients:
- 1/3 cup extra-virgin olive oil
- 1/3 cup chopped red onions
- ½ cup chopped red bell pepper
- 2 garlic cloves, minced
- 1 cup zucchini, cut into ½-inch-thick slices
- ½ cup coarsely chopped artichokes
- ½ cup canned chickpeas, drained and rinsed
- 3 cups cooked faro
- Salt and black pepper, to taste
- ½ cup crumbled feta cheese, for serving (optional)
- ¼ cup sliced olives, for serving (optional)
- 2 tablespoons fresh basil, chiffonade, for serving (optional)
- 3 tablespoons balsamic vinegar, for serving (optional)

Directions:
1. Cook the olive oil in a large skillet over medium heat until it shimmers. Mix the onions, bell pepper, and garlic and sauté for 5 minutes, stirring occasionally, until softened.
2. Stir in the zucchini slices, artichokes, and chickpeas and sauté for about 5 minutes until slightly tender. Add the cooked faro and toss to combine until heated through. Sprinkle the salt and pepper to season.
3. Divide the mixture into bowls. Top each bowl evenly with feta cheese, olive slices, and basil and sprinkle with the balsamic vinegar, if desired.

Nutrition 366 Calories 19.9g Fat 9g Carbohydrates 9.3g Protein

747. 5-Ingredient Zucchini Fritters

Preparation Time: 15 minutes
Cooking Time: 5 minutes
Servings: 14
Ingredients:
- 4 cups grated zucchini

- Salt, to taste
- 2 large eggs, slightly beaten
- 1/3 cup sliced scallions
- 2/3 all-purpose flour
- 1/8 teaspoon black pepper
- 2 tablespoons olive oil

Directions:
1. Situate the grated zucchini in a colander and lightly season with salt. Set aside to rest for 10 minutes. Grip as much liquid from the grated zucchini as possible.
2. Pour the grated zucchini into a bowl. Fold in the beaten eggs, scallions, flour, salt, and pepper and stir until everything is well combined.
3. Cook the olive oil in a big skillet over medium heat until hot.
4. Drop 3 tablespoons mounds of the zucchini mixture onto the hot skillet to make each fritter, pin them lightly into rounds and spacing them about 2 inches apart.
5. Cook for 2 to 3 minutes. Flip the zucchini fritters and cook for 2 minutes more, or until they are golden brown and cooked through.
6. Remove from the heat to a plate lined with paper towels. Repeat with the remaining zucchini mixture. Serve hot.

Nutrition 113 Calories 6.1g Fat 9g Carbohydrates 4g Protein

748. Moroccan Tagine with Vegetables

Preparation Time: 20 minutes
Cooking Time: 40 minutes
Servings: 2
Ingredients:
- 2 tablespoons olive oil
- ½ onion, diced
- 1 garlic clove, minced
- 2 cups cauliflower florets
- 1 medium carrot, cut into 1-inch pieces
- 1 cup diced eggplant
- 1 can whole tomatoes with juices
- 1 (15-ounce / 425-g) can chickpeas
- 2 small red potatoes
- 1 cup water
- 1 teaspoon pure maple syrup
- ½ teaspoon cinnamon
- ½ teaspoon turmeric
- 1 teaspoon cumin
- ½ teaspoon salt
- 1 to 2 teaspoons harissa paste

Directions:
1. In a Dutch oven, heat up the olive oil over medium-high heat. Sauté the onion for 5 minutes, stirring occasionally, or until the onion is translucent.
2. Stir in the garlic, cauliflower florets, carrot, eggplant, tomatoes, and potatoes. Mash tomatoes by using a wooden spoon into smaller pieces.
3. Add the chickpeas, water, maple syrup, cinnamon, turmeric, cumin, and salt and stir to incorporate. Let it boil
4. Once done, reduce the heat to medium-low. Stir in the harissa paste, cover, allow to simmer for about 40 minutes, or until the vegetables are softened. Taste and adjust seasoning as needed. Let it rest before serving.

Nutrition 293 Calories 9.9g Fat 12.1g Carbohydrates 11.2g Protein

749. Chickpea Lettuce Wraps with Celery

Preparation Time: 10 minutes
Cooking Time: 0 minute
Servings: 4
Ingredients:
- 1 (15-ounce / 425-g) can low-sodium chickpeas
- 1 celery stalk, thinly sliced
- 2 tablespoons finely chopped red onion
- 2 tablespoons unsalted tahini
- 3 tablespoons honey mustard
- 1 tablespoon capers, undrained
- 12 butter lettuce leaves

Directions:
1. In a bowl, puree the chickpeas with a potato masher or the back of a fork until mostly smooth. Add the celery, red onion, tahini, honey mustard, and capers to the bowl and stir until well incorporated.
2. For each serving, place three overlapping lettuce leaves on a plate and top with ¼ of the mashed chickpea filling, then roll up. Repeat with the remaining lettuce leaves and chickpea mixture.

Nutrition 182 Calories 7.1g Fat 3g Carbohydrates 10.3g Protein

750. Grilled Vegetable Skewers

Preparation Time: 15 minutes
Cooking Time: 10 minutes
Servings: 4
Ingredient:
- 4 medium red onions sliced into 6 wedges
- 4 medium zucchinis, cut into 1-inch-thick slices
- 2 beefsteak tomatoes, cut into quarters
- 4 red bell peppers
- 2 orange bell peppers
- 2 yellow bell peppers
- 2 tablespoons plus 1 teaspoon olive oil

Directions:
1. Preheat the grill to medium-high heat. Skewer the vegetables by alternating between red onion, zucchini, tomatoes, and the different colored bell

peppers. Grease them with 2 tablespoons of olive oil.

2. Oil the grill grates with 1 teaspoon of olive oil and grill the vegetable skewers for 5 minutes. Flip the skewers and grill for 5 minutes more, or until they are cooked to your liking. Let the skewers cool for 5 minutes before serving.

Nutrition 115 Calories 3g Fat 4.7g Carbohydrates 3.5g Protein

751. Stuffed Portobello Mushroom with Tomatoes

Preparation Time: 10 minutes
Cooking Time: 15 minutes
Servings: 4
Ingredients:
- 4 large portobello mushroom caps
- 3 tablespoons extra-virgin olive oil
- Salt and black pepper, to taste
- 4 sun-dried tomatoes
- 1 cup shredded mozzarella cheese, divided
- ½ to ¾ cup low-sodium tomato sauce

Directions:
1. Preheat the broiler on high. Lay the mushroom caps on a baking sheet and drizzle with olive oil. Sprinkle with salt and pepper. Broil for 1o minutes, flipping the mushroom caps halfway through, until browned on the top.
2. Remove from the broil. Spoon 1 tomato, 2 tablespoons of cheese, and 2 to 3 tablespoons of sauce onto each mushroom cap. Return the mushroom caps to the broiler and continue broiling for 2 to 3 minutes. Cool for 5 minutes before serving.

Nutrition 217 Calories 15.8g Fat 9g Carbohydrates 11.2g Protein

752. Wilted Dandelion Greens with Sweet Onion

Preparation Time: 15 minutes
Cooking Time: 15 minutes
Servings: 4
Ingredients:
- 1 tablespoon extra-virgin olive oil
- 2 garlic cloves, minced
- 1 Vidalia onion, thinly sliced
- ½ cup low-sodium vegetable broth
- 2 bunches dandelion greens, roughly chopped
- Freshly ground black pepper, to taste

Directions:
1. Cook olive oil in a big skillet over low heat. Add the garlic and onion and cook for 2 to 3 minutes, stirring occasionally, or until the onion is translucent.

2. Fold in the vegetable broth and dandelion greens and cook for 5 to 7 minutes until wilted, stirring frequently. Sprinkle with the black pepper and serve on a plate while warm.

Nutrition 81 Calories 3.9g Fat 4g Carbohydrates 3.2g Protein

753. Celery and Mustard Greens

Preparation Time: 10 minutes
Cooking Time: 15 minutes
Serving: 4
Ingredients:
- ½ cup low-sodium vegetable broth
- 1 celery stalk, roughly chopped
- ½ sweet onion, chopped
- ½ large red bell pepper, thinly sliced
- 2 garlic cloves, minced
- 1 bunch mustard greens, roughly chopped

Directions:
1. Pour the vegetable broth into a large cast iron pan and bring it to a simmer over medium heat. Stir in the celery, onion, bell pepper, and garlic. Cook uncovered for 6 minutes.
2. Add the mustard greens to the pan and stir well. Decrease heat and cook until the liquid is evaporated and the greens are wilted. Remove from the heat and serve warm.

Nutrition 39 Calories 3.1g Protein 6.8g Carbohydrates 3g Protein

754. Vegetable and Tofu Scramble

Preparation Time: 5 minutes
Cooking Time: 10 minutes
Servings: 2
Ingredients:
- 2 tablespoons extra-virgin olive oil
- ½ red onion, finely chopped
- 1 cup chopped kale
- 8 ounces (227 g) mushrooms, sliced
- 8 ounces (227 g) tofu, cut into pieces
- 2 garlic cloves, minced
- Pinch red pepper flakes
- ½ teaspoon sea salt
- 1/8 teaspoon freshly ground black pepper

Directions:
1. Cook the olive oil in a medium nonstick skillet over medium-high heat until shimmering. Add the onion, kale, and mushrooms to the skillet. Cook and stirring irregularly, or until the vegetables start to brown.
2. Add the tofu and stir-fry for 3 to 4 minutes until softened. Stir in the garlic, red pepper flakes, salt, and black pepper and cook for 30 seconds. Let it rest before serving.

Nutrition 233 Calories 15.9g Fat 2g Carbohydrates 13.4g Protein

755. Simple Zoodles

Preparation Time: 10 minutes
Cooking Time: 5 minutes
Servings: 2
Ingredients:
- 2 tablespoons avocado oil
- 2 medium zucchinis, spiralized
- ¼ teaspoon salt
- Freshly ground black pepper, to taste

Directions:
1. Cook avocado oil in a big skillet over medium heat until it shimmers. Add the zucchini noodles, salt, and black pepper to the skillet and toss to coat. Cook and stir continuously, until tender. Serve warm.

Nutrition 128 Calories 14g Fat 0.3g Carbohydrates 0.3g Protein

756. Lentil and Tomato Collard Wraps

Preparation Time: 15 minutes
Cooking Time: 0 minute
Servings: 4
Ingredients:
- 2 cups cooked lentils
- 5 Roma tomatoes, diced
- ½ cup crumbled feta cheese
- 10 large fresh basil leaves, thinly sliced
- ¼ cup extra-virgin olive oil
- 1 tablespoon balsamic vinegar
- 2 garlic cloves, minced
- ½ teaspoon raw honey
- ½ teaspoon salt
- ¼ teaspoon freshly ground black pepper
- 4 large collard leaves, stems removed

Directions:
1. Combine the lentils, tomatoes, cheese, basil leaves, olive oil, vinegar, garlic, honey, salt, and black pepper and stir well.
2. Lay the collard leaves on a flat work surface. Spoon the equal-sized amounts of the lentil mixture onto the edges of the leaves. Roll them up and slice in half to serve.

Nutrition 318 Calories 17.6g Fat 27.5g Carbohydrates 13.2g Protein

757. Ultimate Mediterranean Bowl

Preparation Time: 10 minutes
Cooking Time: 20 minutes
Servings: 4
Ingredients:
- 2 cups water
- 1 cup of either bulgur wheat #3 or quinoa, rinsed
- 1½ teaspoons salt, divided
- 1-pint (2 cups) cherry tomatoes, cut in half
- 1 large bell pepper, chopped
- 1 large cucumber, chopped
- 1 cup Kalamata olives
- ½ cup freshly squeezed lemon juice
- 1 cup extra-virgin olive oil
- ½ teaspoon freshly ground black pepper

Directions:
1. Boil the water in a medium pot over medium heat. Add the bulgur (or quinoa) and 1 teaspoon of salt. Cover and cook for 18 minutes.
2. To arrange the veggies in your 4 bowls, visually divide each bowl into 5 sections. Place the cooked bulgur in one section. Follow with the tomatoes, bell pepper, cucumbers, and olives.
3. Scourge together the lemon juice, olive oil, remaining ½ teaspoon salt, and black pepper.
4. Evenly spoon the dressing over the 4 bowls. Serve immediately or cover and refrigerate for later.

Nutrition 772 Calories 9g Fat 6g Protein 41g Carbohydrates

758. Pan-Grilled Vegetable and Hummus Wrap

Preparation Time: 15 minutes
Cooking Time: 10 minutes
Servings: 6
Ingredients:
- 1 large eggplant
- 1 large onion
- ½ cup extra-virgin olive oil
- 1 teaspoon salt
- 6 lavash wraps or large pita bread
- 1 cup Creamy Traditional Hummus

Directions:
1. Preheat a grill, large grill pan, or lightly oiled large skillet on medium heat. Slice the eggplant and onion into circles. Grease the vegetables with olive oil and sprinkle with salt.
2. Cook the vegetables on both sides, about 3 to 4 minutes each side. To make the wrap, lay the lavash or pita flat. Lay about 2 tablespoons of hummus on the wrap.
3. Evenly divide the vegetables among the wraps, layering them along one side of the wrap. Gently fold over the side of the wrap with the vegetables, tucking them in and making a tight wrap.
4. Lay the wrap seam side-down and cut in half or thirds.
5. You can also wrap each sandwich with plastic wrap to help it hold its shape and eat it later.

Nutrition 362 Calories 10g Fat 28g Carbohydrates 15g Protein

759. Spanish-Style Green Beans and Tomatoes

Preparation Time: 10 minutes
Cooking Time: 20 minutes
Servings: 4
Ingredients:
- ¼ cup extra-virgin olive oil
- 1 large onion, chopped
- 4 cloves garlic, finely chopped
- 1-pound green beans, fresh or frozen, trimmed
- 1½ teaspoons salt, divided
- 1 (15-ounce) can diced tomatoes
- ½ teaspoon freshly ground black pepper

Directions:
1. Warm up the olive oil, onion, and garlic; cook for 1 minute. Cut the green beans into 2-inch pieces. Add the green beans and 1 teaspoon of salt to the pot and toss everything together; cook for 3 minutes.
2. Add the diced tomatoes, remaining ½ teaspoon of salt, and black pepper to the pot; continue to cook for another 12 minutes, stirring occasionally. Serve warm.

Nutrition 200 Calories 12g Fat 18g Carbohydrates 4g Protein

760. Roasted Cauliflower Hash brown

Preparation Time: 10 minutes
Cooking Time: 10 minutes
Servings: 4
Ingredients:
- 3 tablespoons extra-virgin olive oil
- 1 large onion, chopped
- 1 tablespoon garlic, minced
- 2 cups carrots, diced
- 4 cups cauliflower pieces, washed
- 1 teaspoon salt
- ½ teaspoon ground cumin

Directions:
1. Cook the olive oil, onion, garlic, and carrots for 3 minutes. Cut the cauliflower into 1-inch or bite-size pieces. Add the cauliflower, salt, and cumin to the skillet and toss to combine with the carrots and onions.
2. Cover and cook for 3 minutes. Toss in the vegetables and continue cooking for an additional 3 to 4 minutes. Serve warm.

Nutrition 159 Calories 17g Fat 15g Carbohydrates 3g Protein

761. Oven-Roasted Cauliflower and Cherry Tomatoes

Preparation Time: 5 minutes

Cooking Time: 25 minutes
Servings: 4
Ingredients:
- 4 cups cauliflower, cut into 1-inch pieces
- 6 tablespoons extra-virgin olive oil, divided
- 1 teaspoon salt, divided
- 4 cups cherry tomatoes
- ½ teaspoon freshly ground black pepper
- ½ cup grated Parmesan cheese

Directions:
1. Preheat the oven to 425°F. Add the cauliflower, 3 tablespoons of olive oil, and ½ teaspoon of salt to a large bowl and toss to evenly coat. Spread onto a baking sheet evenly.
2. In another large bowl, add the tomatoes, remaining 3 tablespoons of olive oil, and ½ teaspoon of salt, and toss to coat evenly. Pour onto a different baking sheet. Put the sheet of cauliflower and the sheet of tomatoes in the oven to roast for 17 to 20 minutes until the cauliflower is lightly browned and tomatoes are plump.
3. Using a spatula, spoon the cauliflower into a serving dish, and top with tomatoes, black pepper, and Parmesan cheese. Serve warm.

Nutrition 294 Calories 14g Fat 13g Carbohydrates 9g Protein

762. Oven-Roasted Acorn Squash

Preparation Time: 10 minutes
Cooking Time: 35 minutes
Servings: 6
Ingredients:
- 2 acorn squash, medium to large
- 2 tablespoons extra-virgin olive oil
- 1 teaspoon salt, plus more for seasoning
- 5 tablespoons unsalted butter
- ¼ cup chopped sage leaves
- 2 tablespoons fresh thyme leaves
- ½ teaspoon freshly ground black pepper

Directions:
1. Preheat the oven to 400°F. Cut the acorn squash in half lengthwise. Scrape out the seeds and cut it horizontally into ¾-inch-thick slices. In a large bowl, drizzle the squash with the olive oil, sprinkle with salt, and toss together to coat.
2. Lay the acorn squash flat on a baking sheet. Situate in the baking sheet in the oven and bake the squash for 20 minutes. Flip squash over with a spatula and bake for another 15 minutes.
3. Soften the butter in a medium saucepan over medium heat. Add the sage and thyme to the melted butter and let them cook for 30 seconds. Transfer the cooked squash slices to a plate. Spoon the butter/herb mixture over the squash. Season with salt and black pepper. Serve warm.

Nutrition 188 Calories 13g Fat 16g Carbohydrates 1g Protein

763. Stir-fried Garlic Spinach

Preparation Time: 5 minutes
Cooking Time: 10 minutes
Servings: 4
Ingredients:
- ¼ cup extra-virgin olive oil
- 1 large onion, thinly sliced
- 3 cloves garlic, minced
- 6 (1-pound) bags of baby spinach, washed
- ½ teaspoon salt
- 1 lemon, cut into wedges

Directions:
1. Cook the olive oil, onion, and garlic in a large skillet for 2 minutes over medium heat. Add one bag of spinach and ½ teaspoon of salt. Cover the skillet and let the spinach wilt for 30 seconds. Repeat (omitting the salt), adding 1 bag of spinach at a time.
2. When all the spinach has been added in, remove the cover and cook for 3 minutes, letting some of the moisture evaporate. Serve warm with lemon zest over the top.

Nutrition 301 Calories 12g Fat 29g Carbohydrates 17g Protein

764. Stir-fried Zucchini

Preparation Time: 5 minutes
Cooking Time: 10 minutes
Servings: 4
Ingredients:
- 3 large green zucchinis
- 3 tablespoons extra-virgin olive oil
- 1 large onion, chopped
- 3 cloves garlic, minced
- 1 teaspoon salt
- 1 teaspoon dried mint

Directions:
1. Cut the zucchini into ½-inch cubes. Cook the olive oil, onions, and garlic for 3 minutes, stirring constantly.
2. Add the zucchini and salt to the skillet and toss to combine with the onions and garlic, cooking for 5 minutes. Add the mint to the skillet, tossing to combine. Cook for another 2 minutes. Serve warm.

Nutrition 147 Calories 16g Fat 12g Carbohydrates 4g Protein

765. Tomatoes and Okra Stew

Preparation Time: 5 minutes
Cooking Time: 25 minutes
Servings: 4
Ingredients:
- ¼ cup extra-virgin olive oil
- 1 large onion, chopped
- 4 cloves garlic, finely chopped
- 1 teaspoon salt
- 1 pound fresh or frozen okra, cleaned
- 1 (15-ounce) can plain tomato sauce
- 2 cups water
- ½ cup fresh cilantro, finely chopped
- ½ teaspoon freshly ground black pepper

Directions:
1. Mix and cook the olive oil, onion, garlic, and salt for 1 minute. Stir in the okra and cook for 3 minutes.
2. Add the tomato sauce, water, cilantro, and black pepper; stir, cover, and let cook for 15 minutes, stirring occasionally. Serve warm.

Nutrition 201 Calories 6g Fat 18g Carbohydrates 4g Protein

766. Bean-Stuffed Bell Peppers

Preparation Time: 20 minutes
Cooking Time: 30 minutes
Servings: 6
Ingredients:
- 6 large bell peppers, different colors
- 3 tablespoons extra-virgin olive oil
- 1 large onion, chopped
- 3 cloves garlic, minced
- 1 carrot, chopped
- 1 (16-oz) can garbanzo beans
- 3 cups cooked rice
- 1½ teaspoons salt
- ½ teaspoon freshly ground black pepper

Directions:
1. Preheat the oven to 350°F. Make sure to choose peppers that can stand upright. Cut off the pepper cap and remove the seeds, reserving the cap for later. Stand the peppers in a baking dish.
2. Warm up the olive oil, onion, garlic, and carrots for 3 minutes. Stir in the garbanzo beans. Cook for another 3 minutes. Pull out from the pan from the heat and spoon the cooked ingredients to a large bowl. Add the rice, salt, and pepper; toss to combine.
3. Stuff each pepper to the top and then put the pepper caps back on. Tuck the baking dish with aluminum foil and bake for 25 minutes. Pull out the foil and bake for another 5 minutes. Serve warm.

Nutrition 301 Calories 15g Fat 50g Carbohydrates 8g Protein

767. Moussaka Eggplant

Preparation Time: 55 minutes
Cooking Time: 40 minutes
Servings: 6
Ingredients:
- 2 large eggplants
- 2 teaspoons salt, divided

- Olive oil spray
- ¼ cup extra-virgin olive oil
- 2 large onions, sliced
- 10 cloves garlic, sliced
- 2 (15-ounce) cans diced tomatoes
- 1 (16-oz) can garbanzo beans
- 1 teaspoon dried oregano
- ½ teaspoon freshly ground black pepper

Directions:
1. Slice the eggplant horizontally into ¼-inch-thick round disks. Sprinkle the eggplant slices with 1 teaspoon of salt and place in a colander for 30 minutes.
2. Preheat the oven to 450°F. Pat the slices of eggplant dry with a paper towel and spray each side with an olive oil spray or lightly brush each side with olive oil.
3. Assemble the eggplant in a single layer on a baking sheet. Situate in the oven and bake for 10 minutes. Then, using a spatula, flip the slices over and bake for another 10 minutes.
4. Sauté the olive oil, onions, garlic, and remaining 1 teaspoon of salt. Cook 5 minutes stirring seldom. Add the tomatoes, garbanzo beans, oregano, and black pepper. Simmer for 12 minutes, stirring irregularly.
5. Using a deep casserole dish, begin to layer, starting with eggplant, then the sauce. Repeat until all ingredients have been used. Bake in the oven for 20 minutes. Remove from the oven and serve warm.

Nutrition 262 Calories 11g Fat 35g Carbohydrates 8g Protein

768. Grape Leaves Filled with Veggies

Preparation Time: 50 minutes
Cooking Time: 45 minutes
Servings: 8
Ingredients:
- 2 cups white rice, rinsed
- 2 large tomatoes, finely diced
- 1 large onion, finely chopped
- 1 green onion, finely chopped
- 1 cup fresh Italian parsley, finely chopped
- 3 cloves garlic, minced
- 2½ teaspoons salt
- ½ teaspoon freshly ground black pepper
- 1 (16-ounce) jar grape leaves
- 1 cup lemon juice
- ½ cup extra-virgin olive oil
- 4 to 6 cups water

Directions:
1. Combine the rice, tomatoes, onion, green onion, parsley, garlic, salt, and black pepper. Drain and rinse the grape leaves. Prepare a large pot by placing a layer of grape leaves on the bottom. Lay each leaf flat and trim off any stems.
2. Place 2 tablespoons of the rice mixture at the base of each leaf. Fold over the sides, then roll as tight as possible. Put the rolled grape leaves in the pot, lining up each rolled grape leaf. Continue to layer in the rolled grape leaves.
3. Gently pour the lemon juice and olive oil over the grape leaves, and add enough water to just cover the grape leaves by 1 inch. Lay a heavy plate that is smaller than the opening of the pot upside down over the grape leaves. Cover the pot and cook the leaves over medium-low heat for 45 minutes. Let stand for 20 minutes before serving. Serve warm or cold.

Nutrition 532 Calories 15g Fat 80g Carbohydrates 12g Protein

769. Grilled-Pan Eggplant Rolls

Preparation Time: 30 minutes
Cooking Time: 10 minutes
Servings: 6
Ingredients:
- 2 large eggplants
- 1 teaspoon salt
- 4 ounces goat cheese
- 1 cup ricotta
- ¼ cup fresh basil, finely chopped
- ½ teaspoon freshly ground black pepper
- Olive oil spray

Directions:
1. Cut up the tops of the eggplants and cut the eggplants lengthwise into ¼-inch-thick slices. Sprinkle the slices with the salt and place the eggplant in a colander for 15 to 20 minutes.
2. Scourge the goat cheese, ricotta, basil, and pepper. Preheat a grill, grill pan, or lightly oiled skillet on medium heat. Pat dry the eggplant slices and lightly spray with olive oil spray. Place the eggplant on the grill, grill pan, or skillet and cook for 3 minutes on each side.
3. Take out the eggplant from the heat and let cool for 5 minutes. To roll, lay one eggplant slice flat, place a tablespoon of the cheese mixture at the base of the slice, and roll up. Serve immediately or chill until serving.

Nutrition 255 Calories 7g Fat 19g Carbohydrates 15g Protein

770. Crunchy Zucchini Fritters

Preparation Time: 15 minutes
Cooking Time: 20 minutes
Servings: 6
Ingredients:
- 2 large green zucchinis
- 2 tablespoons Italian parsley, finely chopped

- 3 cloves garlic, minced
- 1 teaspoon salt
- 1 cup flour
- 1 large egg, beaten
- ½ cup water
- 1 teaspoon baking powder
- 3 cups vegetable or avocado oil

Directions:
1. Grate the zucchini into a large bowl. Add the parsley, garlic, salt, flour, egg, water, and baking powder to the bowl and stir to combine. In a large pot or fryer over medium heat, heat oil to 365°F.
2. Drop the fritter batter into the hot oil by spoonful. Turn the fritters over using a slotted spoon and fry until they are golden brown, about 2 to 3 minutes. Strain the fritters from the oil and place on a plate lined with paper towels.
3. Serve warm with Creamy Tzatziki or Creamy Traditional Hummus as a dip.

Nutrition 446 Calories 2g Fat 19g Carbohydrates 5g Protein

771. Feta Cheese and Spinach Pies

Preparation Time: 20 minutes
Cooking Time: 40 minutes
Servings: 8
Ingredients:
- 2 tablespoons extra-virgin olive oil
- 1 large onion, chopped
- 2 cloves garlic, minced
- 3 (1-pound) bags of baby spinach, washed
- 1 cup feta cheese
- 1 large egg, beaten
- Puff pastry sheets

Directions:
1. Preheat the oven to 375°F. Warm up the olive oil, onion, and garlic for 3 minutes. Add the spinach to the skillet one bag at a time, letting it wilt in between each bag. Toss using tongs. Cook for 4 minutes. Once the spinach is cooked, scoop out any excess liquid from the pan.
2. In a large bowl, mix the feta cheese, egg, and cooked spinach. Lay the puff pastry flat on a counter. Cut the pastry into 3-inch squares. Place a tablespoon of the spinach mixture in the center of a puff-pastry square. Crease over one corner of the square to the diagonal corner, forming a triangle. Crimp the edges of the pie by pressing down with the tines of a fork to seal them together. Repeat until all squares are filled.
3. Situate the pies on a parchment-lined baking sheet and bake for 25 to 30 minutes or until golden brown. Serve warm or at room temperature.

Nutrition 503 Calories 6g Fat 38g Carbohydrates 16g Protein

772. Minestrone Soup

Preparation Time: 10 minutes
Cooking Time: 1 hour
Servings: 4
Ingredients:
- 1 small white onion
- 4 cloves garlic
- 1/2 cup carrots
- 1 medium zucchini
- 1 medium yellow squash
- 2 tablespoons minced fresh parsley
- 1/4 cup celery sliced
- 3 tablespoons olive oil
- 2 x 15 oz. cans cannellini beans
- 2 x 15 oz. can red kidney beans
- 1 x 14.5 oz. can fire-roasted diced tomatoes, drained
- 4 cups vegetable stock
- 2 cups of water
- 1 1/2 teaspoons oregano
- 1/2 teaspoon basil
- 1/4 teaspoon thyme
- 1 teaspoon salt
- 1/2 teaspoon pepper
- 3/4 cup small pasta shells
- 4 cups fresh baby spinach
- 1/4 cup Parmesan or Romano cheese

Direction:
1. Grab a stockpot and place over medium heat. Add the oil then the onions, garlic, carrots, zucchini, squash, parsley, and celery. Cook for five minutes until the veggies are getting soft.
2. Pour in the stock, water, beans, tomatoes, herbs, and salt and pepper. Stir well. Decrease heat, cover, and simmer for 30 minutes.
3. Add the pasta and spinach, stir well then cover and cook for a further 20 minutes until the pasta is cooked through. Stir through the cheese then serve and enjoy.

Nutrition: 34 calories 26.3 g protein 30.3 g fat

773. Chicken Wild Rice Soup

Preparation Time: 10 minutes
Cooking Time: 15 minutes
Servings: 6
Ingredients:
- 2/3 cup wild rice, uncooked
- 1 tablespoon onion, chopped finely
- 1 tablespoon fresh parsley, chopped
- 1 cup carrots, chopped
- 8-ounces chicken breast, cooked
- 2 tablespoon butter
- 1/4 cup all-purpose white flour
- 5 cups low-sodium chicken broth
- 1 tablespoon slivered almonds

Directions:
1. Start by adding rice and 2 cups broth along with ½ cup water to a cooking pot. Cook the chicken until the rice is al dente and set it aside. Add butter to a saucepan and melt it.
2. Stir in onion and sauté until soft then add the flour and the remaining broth.
3. Stir it and then cook for it 1 minute then add the chicken, cooked rice, and carrots. Cook for 5 minutes on simmer. Garnish with almonds. Serve fresh.

Nutrition: 287 calories 21g protein 35g fat

774. Classic Chicken Soup

Preparation Time: 10 minutes
Cooking Time: 25 minutes
Servings: 2
Ingredients:
- 1 1/2 cups low-sodium vegetable broth
- 1 cup of water
- 1/4 teaspoon poultry seasoning
- 1/4 teaspoon black pepper
- 1 cup chicken strips
- 1/4 cup carrot
- 2-ounces egg noodles, uncooked

Directions:
1. Gather all the ingredients into a slow cooker and toss it Cook soup on high heat for 25 minutes.
2. Serve warm.

Nutrition: 103 calories 8g protein 11g fat

775. Cucumber Soup

Preparation Time: 10 minutes
Cooking Time: 0 minute
Servings: 4
Ingredients:
- 2 medium cucumbers
- 1/3 cup sweet white onion
- 1 green onion
- 1/4 cup fresh mint
- 2 tablespoons fresh dill
- 2 tablespoons lemon juice
- 2/3 cup water
- 1/2 cup half and half cream
- 1/3 cup sour cream
- 1/2 teaspoon pepper
- Fresh dill sprigs for garnish

Directions:
1. Situate all of the ingredients into a food processor and toss. Puree the mixture and refrigerate for 2 hours. Garnish with dill sprigs. Enjoy fresh.

Nutrition: 77 calories 2g protein 6g fats

776. Squash and Turmeric Soup

Preparation Time: 10 minutes
Cooking Time: 30 minutes
Servings: 4
Ingredients:
- 4 cups low-sodium vegetable broth
- 2 medium zucchini squash
- 2 medium yellow crookneck squash
- 1 small onion
- 1/2 cup frozen green peas
- 2 tablespoons olive oil
- 1/2 cup plain nonfat Greek yogurt
- 2 teaspoon turmeric

Directions:
1. Warm the broth in a saucepan on medium heat. Toss in onion, squash, and zucchini. Let it simmer for approximately 25 minutes then add oil and green peas.
2. Cook for another 5 minutes then allow it to cool. Puree the soup using a handheld blender then add Greek yogurt and turmeric. Refrigerate it overnight and serve fresh.

Nutrition: 100 calories 4g protein 10g fat

777. Leek, Potato, and Carrot Soup

Preparation Time: 15 minutes
Cooking Time: 25 minutes
Servings: 4
Ingredients:
- 1 - leek
- ¾ - cup diced and boiled potatoes
- ¾ - cup diced and boiled carrots
- 1 - garlic clove
- 1 - tablespoon oil
- Crushed pepper to taste
- 3 - cups low sodium chicken stock
- Chopped parsley for garnish
- 1 - bay leaf
- ¼ - teaspoon ground cumin

Directions:
1. Trim off and take away a portion of the coarse inexperienced portions of the leek, at that factor reduce daintily and flush altogether in virus water. Channel properly. Warmth the oil in an extensively based pot. Include the leek and garlic, and sear over low warmth for two-3 minutes, till sensitive.
2. Include the inventory, inlet leaf, cumin, and pepper. Heat the mixture, mix constantly. Include the bubbled potatoes and carrots and stew for 10-15minutes Modify the flavoring, eliminate the inlet leaf, and serve sprinkled generously with slashed parsley.
3. To make a pureed soup, manner the soup in a blender or nourishment processor till smooth Come

again to the pan. Include ½ field milk. Bring to bubble and stew for 2-3minutes

Nutrition: 315 calories 8g fat 15g protein

778. Bell Pepper Soup

Preparation Time: 30 minutes
Cooking Time: 35 minutes
Servings: 4
Ingredients:

- 4 - cups low-sodium chicken broth
- 3 - red peppers
- 2 - medium onions
- 3 - tablespoon lemon juice
- 1 - tablespoon finely minced lemon zest
- A pinch cayenne peppers
- ¼ - teaspoon cinnamon
- ½ - cup finely minced fresh cilantro

Directions:

1. In a medium stockpot, consolidate each one of the fixings except for the cilantro and warmth to the point of boiling over excessive warm temperature.
2. Diminish the warmth and stew, ordinarily secured, for around 30 minutes, till thickened. Cool marginally. Utilizing a hand blender or nourishment processor, puree the soup. Include the cilantro and tenderly heat.

Nutrition: 265 calories 8g fat 5g protein

779. Yucatan Soup

Preparation Time: 10 minutes
Cooking Time: 20 minutes
Servings: 4
Ingredients:

- ½ cup onion, chopped
- 8 cloves garlic, chopped
- 2 Serrano chili peppers, chopped
- 1 medium tomato, chopped
- 1 ½ cups chicken breast, cooked, shredded
- 2 six-inch corn tortillas, sliced
- 1 tablespoon olive oil
- 4 cups chicken broth
- 1 bay leaf
- ¼ cup lime juice
- ¼ cup cilantro, chopped
- 1 teaspoon black pepper

Directions:

1. Spread the corn tortillas in a baking sheet and bake them for 3 minutes at 400°F. Place a suitably-sized saucepan over medium heat and add oil to heat.
2. Toss in chili peppers, garlic, and onion, then sauté until soft. Stir in broth, tomatoes, bay leaf, and chicken.
3. Let this chicken soup cook for 10 minutes on a simmer. Stir in cilantro, lime juice, and black pepper. Garnish with baked corn tortillas. Serve.

Nutrition: 215 calories 21g protein 32g fat

780. Zesty Taco Soup

Preparation Time: 10 minutes
Cooking Time: 7 hours
Servings: 2
Ingredients:

- 1 ½ pounds chicken breast
- 15 ½ ounces canned dark red kidney beans
- 15 ½ ounces canned white corn
- 1 cup canned tomatoes
- ½ cup onion
- 15 ½ ounces canned yellow hominy
- ½ cup green bell peppers
- 1 garlic clove
- 1 medium jalapeno
- 1 tablespoon package McCormick
- 2 cups chicken broth

Directions:

1. Add drained beans, hominy, corn, onion, garlic, jalapeno pepper, chicken, and green peppers to a Crockpot.
2. Cover the beans-corn mixture and cook for 1 hour on "high" temperature. Set heat to "low" and continue cooking for 6 hours. Shred the slow-cooked chicken and return to the taco soup. Serve warm.

Nutrition: 191 calories 21g protein 20g fat

781. Southwestern Posole

Preparation Time: 10 minutes
Cooking Time: 53 minutes
Servings: 4
Ingredients:

- 1 tablespoon olive oil
- 1-pound pork loin, diced
- ½ cup onion, chopped
- 1 garlic clove, chopped
- 28 ounces canned white hominy
- 4 ounces canned diced green chilis
- 4 cups chicken broth
- ¼ teaspoon black pepper

Directions:

1. Place a suitably-sized cooking pot over medium heat and add oil to heat. Toss in pork pieces and sauté for 4 minutes.
2. Stir in garlic and onion, then stir for 4 minutes, or until onion is soft. Add the remaining ingredients, then cover the pork soup. Cook this for 45 minutes, or until the pork is tender. Serve warm.

Nutrition: 286 calories 25g protein 15g fat

782. Spring Vegetable Soup

Preparation Time: 10 minutes

Cooking Time: 45 minutes
Servings: 4
Ingredients:
- 1 cup fresh green beans
- ¾ cup celery
- ½ cup onion
- ½ cup carrots
- ½ cup mushrooms
- ½ cup of frozen corn
- 1 medium Roma tomato
- 2 tablespoons olive oil
- ½ cup of frozen corn
- 4 cups vegetable broth
- 1 teaspoon dried oregano leaves
- 1 teaspoon garlic powder

Directions:
1. Place a suitably-sized cooking pot over medium heat and add olive oil to heat. Toss in onion and celery, then sauté until soft. Stir in the corn and rest of the ingredients and cook the soup to boil.
2. Now reduce its heat to a simmer and cook for 45 minutes. Serve warm.

Nutrition: 115 calories 3g protein 13g fat

783. Seafood Corn Chowder

Preparation Time: 10 minutes
Cooking Time: 12 minutes
Servings: 4
Ingredients:
- 1 tablespoon butter
- 1 cup onion
- 1/3 cup celery
- ½ cup green bell pepper
- ½ cup red bell pepper
- 1 tablespoon white flour
- 14 ounces chicken broth
- 2 cups cream
- 6 ounces evaporated milk
- 10 ounces surimi imitation crab chunks
- 2 cups frozen corn kernels
- ½ teaspoon black pepper
- ½ teaspoon paprika

Directions:
1. Place a suitably-sized saucepan over medium heat and add butter to melt. Toss in onion, green and red peppers, and celery, then sauté for 5 minutes. Stir in flour and whisk well for 2 minutes.
2. Pour in chicken broth and stir until it boils. Add evaporated milk, corn, surimi crab, paprika, black pepper, and creamer. Cook for 5 minutes then serves warm.

Nutrition: 175 calories 8g protein 7g fat

784. Beef Sage Soup

Preparation Time: 10 minutes
Cooking Time: 20 minutes
Servings: 4
Ingredients:
- ½ pound ground beef
- ½ teaspoon ground sage
- ½ teaspoon black pepper
- ½ teaspoon dried basil
- ½ teaspoon garlic powder
- 4 slices bread, cubed
- 2 tablespoons olive oil
- 1 tablespoon herb seasoning blend
- 2 garlic cloves, minced
- 3 cups chicken broth
- 1 ½ cups water
- 4 tablespoons fresh parsley
- 2 tablespoons parmesan cheese

Directions:
1. Preheat your oven to 375°F. Mix beef with sage, basil, black pepper, and garlic powder in a bowl, then set it aside. Throw in the bread cubes with olive oil in a baking sheet and bake them for 8 minutes.
2. Meanwhile, sauté the beef mixture in a greased cooking pot until it is browned. Stir in garlic and sauté for 2 minutes, then add parsley, water, and broth. Cover the beef soup and cook for 10 minutes on a simmer. Garnish the soup with parmesan cheese and baked bread. Serve warm.

Nutrition: 336 calories 26g protein 16g fat

785. Cabbage Borscht

Preparation Time: 10 minutes
Cooking Time: 90 minutes
Servings: 6
Ingredients:
- 2 pounds beef steaks
- 6 cups cold water
- 2 tablespoons olive oil
- ½ cup tomato sauce
- 1 medium cabbage, chopped
- 1 cup onion, diced
- 1 cup carrots, diced
- 1 cup turnips, peeled and diced
- 1 teaspoon pepper
- 6 tablespoons lemon juice
- 4 tablespoons sugar

Directions:
1. Start by placing steak in a large cooking pot and pour enough water to cover it. Cover the beef pot and cook it on a simmer until it is tender, then shred it using a fork. Add olive oil, onion, tomato

sauce, carrots, turnips, and shredded steak to the cooking liquid in the pot.
2. Stir in black pepper, sugar, and lemon juice to season the soup. Cover the cabbage soup and cook on low heat for 1 ½ hour. Serve warm.

Nutrition: 212 calories 19g protein 10g fat

786. Ground Beef Soup

Preparation Time: 10 minutes
Cooking Time: 30 minutes
Servings: 4
Ingredients:
- 1-pound lean ground beef
- ½ cup onion, chopped
- 2 teaspoons lemon-pepper seasoning blend
- 1 cup beef broth
- 2 cups of water
- 1/3 cup white rice, uncooked
- 3 cups of frozen mixed vegetables
- 1 tablespoon sour cream

Directions:
1. Spray a saucepan with cooking oil and place it over medium heat. Toss in onion and ground beef, then sauté until brown. Stir in broth and rest of the ingredients, then boil it.
2. Reduce heat to a simmer, then cover the soup to cook for 30 minutes. Garnish with sour cream. Enjoy.

Nutrition: 223 calories 20g protein 20g fat

787. Mexican Tortilla Soup

Preparation Time: 7 minutes
Cooking Time: 40 minutes
Serving: 4
Ingredients:
- 1-pound chicken breasts
- 1 can (15 ounces) whole peeled tomatoes
- 1 can (10 ounces) red enchilada sauce
- 1 and 1/2 teaspoons minced garlic
- 1 yellow onion, diced
- 1 can (4 ounces) fire-roasted diced green chili
- 1 can (15 ounces) black beans
- 1 can (15 ounces) fire-roasted corn
- 1 container (32 ounces) chicken stock
- 1 teaspoon ground cumin
- 2 teaspoons chili powder
- 3/4 teaspoons paprika
- 1 bay leaf
- 1 tablespoon chopped cilantro

Directions:
1. Set your Instant Pot on Sauté mode.
2. Toss olive oil, onion and garlic into the insert of the Instant Pot.
3. Sauté for 4 minutes then add chicken and remaining ingredients.

4. Mix well gently then seal and lock the lid.
5. Select Manual mode for 7 minutes at high pressure.
6. Once done, release the pressure completely then remove the lid.
7. Adjust seasoning as needed.
8. Garnish with desired toppings.

Nutrition: 390 Calories 29.5g Protein 26.5g Fat

788. Chicken Noodle Soup

Preparation Time: 9 minutes
Cooking Time: 35 minutes
Serving: 6
Ingredients:
- 1 tablespoon olive oil
- 1 1/2 cups carrots
- 1 1/2 cup diced celery
- 1 cup chopped yellow onion
- 3 tablespoons minced garlic
- 8 cups low-sodium chicken broth
- 2 teaspoons minced fresh thyme
- 2 teaspoons minced fresh rosemary
- 1 bay leaf
- 2 1/2 lbs. chicken thighs
- 3 cups wide egg noodles
- 1 tablespoon fresh lemon juice
- 1/4 cup chopped fresh parsley

Directions:
1. Preheat olive oil in the insert of the Instant Pot on Sauté mode.
2. Add onion, celery, and carrots and sauté them for minutes.
3. Stir in garlic and sauté for 1 minute.
4. Add bay leaf, thyme, broth, rosemary, salt, and pepper.
5. Seal and secure the Instant Pot lid and select Manual mode for 10 minutes at high pressure.
6. Once done, release the pressure completely then remove the lid.
7. Add noodles to the insert and switch the Instant Pot to sauté mode.
8. Cook the soup for 6 minutes until noodles are all done.
9. Pullout chicken and shred it using a fork.
10. Return the chicken to the soup then add lemon juice and parsley.

Nutrition: 333 Calories 44.7g Protein 13.7g Fat

789. Cheesy Broccoli Soup

Preparation Time: 11 minutes
Cooking Time: 30 minutes
Serving: 4
Ingredients:
- ½ cup heavy whipping cream
- 1 cup broccoli
- 1 cup cheddar cheese

- Salt, to taste
- 1½ cups chicken broth

Directions:
1. Cook chicken broth in a large pot and add broccoli.
2. Boil and stir in the rest of the ingredients.
3. Simmer on low heat for 21 minutes.
4. Ladle out into a bowl and serve hot.

Nutrition: 188 Calories 15g Fats 9.8g Protein

790. Rich Potato Soup

Preparation Time: 6 minutes
Cooking Time: 30 minutes
Serving: 4

Ingredients:
- 1 tablespoon butter
- 1 medium onion, diced
- 3 cloves garlic, minced
- 3 cups chicken broth
- 1 can/box cream of chicken soup
- 7-8 medium-sized russet potatoes
- 1 1/2 teaspoons salt
- 1 cup milk
- 1 tablespoon flour
- 2 cups shredded cheddar cheese

Garnish:
- 5-6 slices bacon, chopped
- Sliced green onions
- Shredded cheddar cheese

Directions:
1. Heat butter in the insert of the Instant Pot on sauté mode.
2. Add onions and sauté for 4 minutes until soft.
3. Stir in garlic and sauté it for 1 minute.
4. Add potatoes, cream of chicken, broth, salt, and pepper to the insert.
5. Mix well then seal and lock the lid.
6. Cook this mixture for 10 minutes at Manual Mode with high pressure.
7. Meanwhile, mix flour with milk in a bowl and set it aside.
8. Once the instant pot beeps, release the pressure completely.
9. Remove the Instant Pot lid and switch the instant pot to Sauté mode.
10. Pour in flour slurry and stir cook the mixture for 5 minutes until it thickens.
11. Add 2 cups of cheddar cheese and let it melt.
12. Garnish it as desired.

Nutrition: 784 Calories 34g Protein; 46.5g Fat

791. Mediterranean Lentil Soup

Preparation Time: 9 minutes
Cooking Time: 20 minutes
Serving: 4

Ingredients:

- 1 tablespoon olive oil
- 1/2 cup red lentils
- 1 medium yellow or red onion
- 2 garlic cloves
- 1/2 teaspoon ground cumin
- 1/2 teaspoon ground coriander
- 1/2 teaspoon ground sumac
- 1/2 teaspoon red chili flakes
- 1/2 teaspoon dried parsley
- 3/4 teaspoons dried mint flakes
- 2.5 cups water
- juice of 1/2 lime

Directions:
1. Preheat oil in the insert of your Instant Pot on Sauté mode.
2. Add onion and sauté until it turns golden brown.
3. Toss in the garlic, parsley sugar, mint flakes, red chili flakes, sumac, coriander, and cumin.
4. Stir cook this mixture for 2 minutes.
5. Add water, lentils, salt, and pepper. Stir gently.
6. Seal and lock the Instant Pot lid and select Manual mode for 8 minutes at high pressure.
7. Once done, release the pressure completely then remove the lid.
8. Stir well then add lime juice.

Nutrition: 525 Calories 30g Protein 19.3g Fat

792. Sausage Kale Soup with Mushrooms

Preparation Time: 8 minutes
Cooking Time: 70 minutes
Serving: 6

Ingredients:
- 2 cups fresh kale
- 6.5 ounces mushrooms, sliced
- 6 cups chicken bone broth
- 1-pound sausage, cooked and sliced

Directions:
1. Heat chicken broth with two cans of water in a large pot and bring to a boil.
2. Stir in the remaining ingredients and allow the soup to simmer on low heat for about 1 hour.
3. Dish out and serve hot.

Nutrition: 259 Calories 20g Fats 14g Proteins

793. Classic Minestrone

Preparation Time: 12 minutes
Cooking Time: 25 minutes
Serving: 6

Ingredients:
- 2 tablespoons olive oil
- 3 cloves garlic
- 1 onion, diced
- 2 carrots

- 2 stalks celery
- 1 1/2 teaspoons dried basil
- 1 teaspoon dried oregano
- 1/2 teaspoon fennel seed
- 6 cups low sodium chicken broth
- 1 (28-ounce) can tomatoes
- 1 (16-ounce) can kidney beans
- 1 zucchini
- 1 Parmesan rind
- 1 bay leaf
- 1 bunch kale leaves, chopped
- 2 teaspoons red wine vinegar
- 1/3 cup freshly grated Parmesan
- 2 tablespoons chopped fresh parsley leaves

Directions:
1. Preheat olive oil in the insert of the Instant Pot on Sauté mode.
2. Add carrots, celery, and onion, sauté for 3 minutes.
3. Stir in fennel seeds, oregano, and basil. Stir cook for 1 minute.
4. Add stock, beans, tomatoes, parmesan, bay leaf, and zucchini.
5. Secure and seal the Instant Pot lid then select Manual mode to cook for minutes at high pressure.
6. Once done, release the pressure completely then remove the lid.
7. Add kale and let it sit for 2 minutes in the hot soup.
8. Stir in red wine, vinegar, pepper, and salt.
9. Garnish with parsley and parmesan.

Nutrition: 805 Calories 124 Protein 34g Fat

794. Turkey Meatball and Ditalini Soup

Preparation Time: 15 minutes
Cooking Time: 40 minutes
Serving: 4
Ingredients:
meatballs:
- 1 pound 93% lean ground turkey
- 1/3 cup seasoned breadcrumbs
- 3 tablespoons grated Pecorino Romano cheese
- 1 large egg, beaten
- 1 clove crushed garlic
- 1 tablespoon fresh minced parsley
- 1/2 teaspoon kosher salt

Soup:
- 1 teaspoon olive oil
- 1/2 cup onion
- 1/2 cup celery
- 1/2 cup carrot
- 3 cloves garlic
- 1 can San Marzano tomatoes
- 4 cups reduced sodium chicken broth
- 4 torn basil leaves
- 2 bay leaves

- 1 cup ditalini pasta
- 1 cup zucchini, diced small
- Parmesan rind, optional
- Grated parmesan cheese, optional for serving

Directions:
1. Thoroughly combine turkey with egg, garlic, parsley, salt, pecorino and breadcrumbs in a bowl.
2. Make 30 equal sized meatballs out of this mixture.
3. Preheat olive oil in the insert of the Instant Pot on Sauté mode.
4. Sear the meatballs in the heated oil in batches, until brown.
5. Set the meatballs aside in a plate.
6. Add more oil to the insert of the Instant Pot.
7. Stir in carrots, garlic, celery, and onion. Sauté for 4 minutes.
8. Add basil, bay leaves, tomatoes, and Parmesan rind.
9. Return the seared meatballs to the pot along with the broth.
10. Secure and sear the Instant Pot lid and select Manual mode for 15 minutes at high pressure.
11. Once done, release the pressure completely then remove the lid.
12. Add zucchini and pasta, cook it for 4 minutes on Sauté mode.
13. Garnish with cheese and basil.

Nutrition: 261 Calories 37g Protein 7g Fat

795. Mint Avocado Chilled Soup

Preparation Time: 6 minutes
Cooking Time: 0 minutes
Serving: 2
Ingredients:
- 1 cup coconut milk, chilled
- 1 medium ripe avocado
- 1 tablespoon lime juice
- Salt, to taste
- 20 fresh mint leaves

Directions:
1. Put all the ingredients into an immersion blender and blend until a thick mixture is formed.
2. Allow to cool for 10 minutes and serve chilled.

Nutrition: 286 Calories 27g Fats 4.2g Proteins

796. Split Pea Soup

Preparation Time: 11 minutes
Cooking Time: 30 minutes
Serving: 6
Ingredients:
- 3 tablespoons butter
- 1 onion diced
- 2 ribs celery diced
- 2 carrots diced
- 6 oz. diced ham
- 1 lb. dry split peas sorted and rinsed

- 6 cups chicken stock
- 2 bay leaves

Directions:
1. Set your Instant Pot on Sauté mode and melt butter in it.
2. Stir in celery, onion, carrots, salt, and pepper.
3. Sauté them for 5 minutes then stir in split peas, ham bone, chicken stock, and bay leaves.
4. Seal and lock the Instant Pot lid then select Manual mode for 15 minutes at high pressure.
5. Once done, release the pressure completely then remove the lid.
6. Remove the ham bone and separate meat from the bone.
7. Shred meat and return it to the soup.
8. Adjust seasoning as needed then serve warm.

Nutrition: 190 Calories 8g Protein 3.5g Fat

797. <u>Butternut Squash Soup</u>

Preparation Time: 8 minutes
Cooking Time: 40 minutes
Serving: 4

Ingredients:
- 1 tablespoon olive oil
- 1 medium yellow onion chopped
- 1 large carrot chopped
- 1 celery rib chopped
- 3 cloves of garlic minced
- 2 lbs. butternut squash, peeled chopped
- 2 cups vegetable broth
- 1 green apple peeled, cored, and chopped
- 1/4 teaspoon ground cinnamon
- 1 sprig fresh thyme
- 1 sprig fresh rosemary
- 1 teaspoon kosher salt
- 1/2 teaspoon black pepper
- Pinch of nutmeg optional

Directions:
1. Preheat olive oil in the insert of the Instant Pot on Sauté mode.
2. Add celery, carrots, and garlic, sauté for 5 minutes.
3. Stir in squash, broth, cinnamon, apple nutmeg, rosemary, thyme, salt, and pepper.
4. Mix well gently then seal and secure the lid.
5. Select Manual mode to cook for 10 minutes at high pressure.
6. Once done, release the pressure completely then remove the lid.
7. Puree the soup using an immersion blender.
8. Serve warm.

Nutrition: 282 Calories 13g Protein 4.7g Fat

798. <u>Beef Stroganoff Soup</u>

Preparation Time: 9 minutes
Cooking Time: 35 minutes

Serving: 6

Ingredients:
- 1.5 pounds stew meat
- 6 cups beef broth
- 4 tablespoons Worcestershire sauce
- 1/2 teaspoon Italian seasoning blend
- 1 1/2 teaspoons onion powder
- 2 teaspoons garlic powder
- salt and pepper to taste
- 1/2 cup sour cream
- 8 ounces mushrooms, sliced
- 8 ounces short noodles, cooked
- 1/3 cup cold water
- 1/4 cup corn starch

Directions:
1. Add meat, 5 cups broth, Italian seasoning, Worcestershire sauce, garlic powder, salt, pepper, and onion powder to the insert of the Instant Pot.
2. Secure and seal the Instant Pot lid then select Manual mode for 1 hour at high pressure.
3. Once done, release the pressure completely then remove the lid.
4. Click Instant pot on Soup mode and add sour cream along with 1 cup broth.
5. Mix well then add mushrooms and mix well.
6. Whisk corn-starch with water and pour this mixture into the pot.
7. Cook this mixture until it thickens then add noodles, salt, and pepper.
8. Garnish with cheese parsley, black pepper.

Nutrition: 320 Calories 26.9g Protein 13.7g Fat

799. <u>Creamy Low Carb Butternut Squash Soup</u>

Preparation Time: 12 minutes
Cooking Time: 70 minutes
Serving: 8

Ingredients:
- 2 tablespoons avocado oil, divided
- 2 pounds butternut squash
- 1 (13.5-oz) can coconut milk
- 4 cups chicken bone broth

Direction:
1. Adjust oven at 400 degrees F and grease a baking sheet.
2. Spread the butternut squash halves with open side up on the baking sheet.
3. Pour half of the avocado oil and season with sea salt and black pepper.
4. Flip over and transfer into the oven.
5. Roast the butternut squash.
6. Cook remaining avocado oil over medium heat in a large pot and add the broth and coconut milk.
7. Let it simmer for 22 minutes and scoop the squash out of the shells to transfer into the soup.
8. Puree this mixture in an immersion blender until smooth and serve immediately.

Nutrition: 185 Calories 12.6g Fats 4.7g Proteins

800. Baked Shrimp Stew

Preparation Time:13 minutes
Cooking Time: 25 minutes
Serving: 6
Ingredients:

- Greek extra virgin olive oil
- 2 1/2 lb. prawns, peeled
- 1 large red onion
- 5 garlic cloves
- 1 red bell pepper
- 2 15-oz cans diced tomatoes
- 1/2 cup water
- 1 1/2 tsp ground coriander
- 1 tsp sumac
- 1 tsp cumin
- 1 tsp red pepper flakes
- 1/2 tsp ground green cardamom
- Salt and pepper, to taste
- 1 cup parsley leaves, stems removed
- 1/3 cup toasted pine nuts
- 1/4 cup toasted sesame seeds
- Lemon or lime wedges to serve

Directions:

1. Preheat the oven to 375 degrees F
2. Using frying pan, add 1 tbsp olive oil
3. Sauté the prawns for 2 minutes, until they are barely pink, then remove and set aside
4. In the same pan over medium-high heat, drizzle a little more olive oil and sauté the chopped onions, garlic and red bell peppers for 5 minutes, stirring regularly
5. Add in the canned diced tomatoes and water, allow to simmer for 10 minutes, until the liquid reduces, stir occasionally
6. Set heat to medium, put shrimp back to the pan, stir in the spices the ground coriander, sumac, cumin, red pepper flakes, green cardamom, salt and pepper, then the toasted pine nuts, sesame seeds and parsley leaves, stir to combined
7. Transfer the shrimp and sauce to an oven-safe earthenware or stoneware dish, cover tightly with foil Situate in the oven to bake for minutes, uncover and broil briefly.
8. allow the dish to cool completely
9. Distribute among the containers, store for 2-3 days
10. To Serve: Reheat on the stove for 1-2 minutes or until heated through. Serve with your favorite bread or whole grain. Garnish with a side of lime or lemon wedges.

Nutrition: 977 Calories 20g Fat 41g Protein

801. Cinnamon Squash Soup

Preparation Time: 11 minutes

Cooking Time: 1 hour
Serving: 6
Ingredients:

- 1 small butternut squash
- 4 tablespoons extra-virgin olive oil
- 1 small yellow onion
- 2 large garlic cloves
- 1 teaspoon salt, divided
- 1 pinch black pepper
- 1 teaspoon dried oregano
- 2 tablespoons fresh oregano
- 2 cups low sodium chicken stock
- 1 cinnamon stick
- ½ cup canned white kidney beans
- 1 small pear
- 2 tablespoons walnut pieces
- ¼ cup Greek yogurt
- 2 tablespoons parsley

Directions:

1. Preheat oven to 425 degrees F.
2. Place squash in bowl and season with a ½ teaspoon of salt and tablespoons of olive oil.
3. Arrange squash onto a roasting pan and roast for about 25 minutes until tender.
4. Keep aside squash to let cool.
5. Cook remaining 2 tablespoons of olive oil in a medium-sized pot at medium-high heat.
6. Sauté onions
7. Add dried oregano and garlic and sauté for 1 minute.
8. Mix squash, broth, pear, cinnamon stick, pepper, and remaining salt.
9. Bring mixture to a boil.
10. Once the boiling point is reached, add walnuts and beans.
11. Lower heat and cook for 20 minutes.
12. Remove the cinnamon stick.
13. Use an immersion blender and blend the entire mixture until smooth.
14. Add yogurt gradually while whisking
15. Season to your taste.
16. Garnish with parsley and fresh oregano.

Nutrition: 197 Calories 11.6g Fat 6.1g Protein

802. Bulgarian Lentil Soup

Preparation Time: 8 minutes
Cooking Time: 15 minutes
Serving: 10
Ingredients:

- 2 cups brown lentils
- 2 onions, chopped
- 5-6 cloves garlic, peeled
- 2-3 medium carrots, chopped
- 1-2 small tomatoes, ripe
- 4 tbsp olive oil
- 1 ½ tsp paprika

- 1 tsp summer savory

Directions:
1. Cook oil in a cooking pot, add the onions and carrots. Add the paprika and washed lentils with 4 cups of warm water; continue to simmer.
2. Chop the tomatoes and stir in them to the soup about 15 minutes after the lentils have started to simmer. Add savory and peeled garlic cloves. Simmer soup. Salt to taste.

Nutrition: 201 Calories 12g Fat 5g Protein

803. White Bean Soup

Preparation Time: 13 minutes
Cooking Time: 17 minutes
Serving: 6
Ingredients:
- 1 cup white beans
- 2-3 carrots
- 2 onions, finely chopped
- 1-2 tomatoes, grated
- 1 red bell pepper, chopped
- 4-5 springs of fresh mint and parsley
- 1 tsp paprika
- 3 tbsp sunflower oil

Directions:
1. Submerge beans in cold water for 3-4 hours, drain and discard the water.
2. Cover the beans with cold water. Add the oil, finely chopped carrots, onions and bell pepper. Boil and simmer until tender.
3. Add the grated tomatoes, mint, paprika and salt. Simmer for another 15 minutes. Serve sprinkled with finely chopped parsley.

Nutrition: 210 Calories 11g Fat 5g Protein

804. Cauliflower Soup

Preparation Time: 9 minutes
Cooking Time: 40 minutes
Serving: 8
Ingredients:
- 1 large onion finely cut
- 1 medium head cauliflower
- 2-3 garlic cloves, crushed
- 3 cups water
- ½ cup whole cream
- 4 tbsp olive oil

Direction:
1. Cook olive oil in a large pot over medium heat and sauté the onion, cauliflower and garlic. Stir in the water and bring the soup to a boil.
2. Reduce heat, cover, and simmer for 40 minutes. Remove the soup from heat add the cream and blend in a blender. Season with salt and pepper.

Nutrition: 221 Calories 19g Fat 8g Protein

805. Moroccan Pumpkin Soup

Preparation Time: 7 minutes
Cooking Time: 54 minutes
Serving: 6
Ingredients:
- 1 leek, white part only
- 3 cloves garlic
- ½ tsp ground ginger
- ½ tsp ground cinnamon
- ½ tsp ground cumin
- 2 carrots
- 2 lb. pumpkin
- 1/3 cup chickpeas
- 5 tbsp olive oil
- juice of ½ lemon

Directions:
1. Cook oil in a huge saucepan and sauté leek, garlic and 2 teaspoons of salt, stirring occasionally, until soft. Add cinnamon, ginger and cumin and stir. Add in carrots, pumpkin and chickpeas. Stir to combine.
2. Add 5 cups of water and bring the soup to the boil, then reduce heat and simmer for 50 minutes.
3. Pullout from heat, add lemon juice and blend the soup. Heat again over low heat for 4-5 minutes. Serve topped with parsley sprigs.

Nutrition: 241Calories 21g Fat 4g Protein

806. Potato Soup

Preparation Time: 16 minutes
Cooking Time: 7 minutes
Serving: 5
Ingredients:
- 4-5 medium potatoes
- 2 carrots
- 1 zucchini
- 1 celery rib
- 3 cups water
- 3 tbsp olive oil
- 1 cup whole milk
- ½ tsp dried rosemary

Directions:
1. Cook olive oil over medium heat and sauté the vegetables for 2-3 minutes. Pour 3 cups of water, add the rosemary and bring the soup to a boil, then lower heat and simmer until tender.
2. Blend the soup in a blender until smooth. Add a cup of warm milk and blend some more. Serve warm, seasoned with black pepper and parsley sprinkled over each serving.

Nutrition: 211 Calories 18g Fat 6g Protein

807. Leek, Rice and Potato Soup

Preparation Time: 9 minutes
Cooking Time: 17 minutes

Serving: 6

Ingredients:

- 1/3 cup rice
- 4 cups of water
- 2-3 potatoes, diced
- 1 small onion, cut
- 1 leek, halved lengthwise and sliced
- 3 tbsp olive oil
- lemon juice, to serve

Directions:

1. Heat a soup pot over medium heat. Add olive oil and onion and sauté for 2 minutes. Add leeks and potatoes and stir for a few minutes more. Fill in three cups of water, boil, reduce heat and simmer for 5 minutes.
2. Add the very well washed rice and simmer for 10 minutes. Serve with lemon juice to taste.

Nutrition: 180 Calories 11g Fat 5g Protein

808. Carrot and Chickpea Soup

Preparation Time: 9 minutes
Cooking Time: 18 minutes
Serving: 5

Ingredients:

- 3-4 big carrots
- 1 leek, chopped
- 4 cups vegetable broth
- 1 cup canned chickpeas
- ½ cup orange juice
- 2 tbsp olive oil
- ½ tsp cumin
- ½ tsp ginger
- 4-5 tbsp yogurt, to serve

Directions:

1. Cook oil in a huge saucepan over medium heat. Add leek and carrots and sauté until soft. Add orange juice, broth, chickpeas and spices. Bring to the boil.
2. Switch heat to medium-low and simmer for 15 minutes.
3. Blend the soup until smooth; return to pan. Season with salt and pepper. Stir over low heat until heated through. Pour in 4-5 bowls, top with yogurt, and serve.

Nutrition: 207 Calories 13g Fat 4g Protein

809. Broccoli, Zucchini and Blue Cheese Soup

Preparation Time: 11 minutes
Cooking Time: 22 minutes
Serving: 6

Ingredients:

- 2 leeks, white part only
- 1 head broccoli
- 2 zucchinis, chopped

- 1 potato, chopped
- 2 cups vegetable broth
- 2 cups water
- 3 tbsp olive oil
- oz blue cheese, crumbled
- 1/3 cup light cream

Directions:

1. Cook oil in a saucepan over medium heat. Sauté the leeks, stirring, for 5 minutes. Stir in bite sized pieces of broccoli, zucchinis, potato, water and broth and bring to a boil.
2. Reduce heat to low and simmer, stirring occasionally, for 10 minutes, or until vegetables are just tender. Remove from heat and set aside for 5 minutes to cool slightly.
3. Transfer the soup to a blender. Drizzle cheese and blend in batches until smooth. Return to saucepan and place over low heat. Add cream and stir to combine. Season with salt and pepper to taste.

Nutrition: 301 Calories 16g Fat 4g Protein

810. Beetroot and Carrot Soup

Preparation Time: 12 minutes
Cooking Time: 32 minutes
Serving: 6

Ingredients:

- 4 beets
- 2 carrots
- 2 potatoes
- 1 medium onion
- 4 cups vegetable broth
- 2 cups water
- 2 tbsp yogurt
- 2 tbsp olive oil

Direction

1. Peel and chop the beets. Cook olive oil in a saucepan over medium high heat and sauté the onion and carrot until onion is tender. Add beets, potatoes, broth and water. Bring to the boil. Switch heat to medium and simmer, partially covered, for 30-40 minutes. Cool slightly.
2. Blend the soup in batches until smooth. Return it to pan over low heat and cook, stirring, for 4 to 5 minutes or until heated through. Season with salt and pepper. Serve soup topped with yogurt and sprinkled with spring onions.

Nutrition: 301 Calories 21g Fat 11g Protein

811. Roasted Red Pepper Soup

Preparation Time: 16 minutes
Cooking Time: 23 minutes
Serving: 7

Ingredients:

- 5-6 red peppers
- 1 large brown onion

- 2 garlic cloves
- 4 medium tomatoes
- 3 cups chicken broth
- 3 tbsp olive oil
- 2 bay leaves

Directions:

1. Roast peppers in the oven at 450 F until the skins are a little burnt. Place the roasted peppers in a brown paper bag or a lidded container and leave covered for about 10 minutes. This makes it easier to peel them. Peel the skins and remove the seeds. Cut the peppers in small pieces.
2. Cook oil in a big saucepan over medium-high heat. Add onion and garlic and sauté, stirring, for 3 minutes or until onion has softened. Add the red peppers, bay leaves, tomato and simmer for 5 minutes.
3. Add in the broth. Season with pepper. Boil then reduce heat and simmer for 23 minutes. Set aside to cool slightly. Blend, in batches, until smooth and serve.

Nutrition: 311 Calories 13g Fat 5g Protein

812. Lentil, Barley and Mushroom Soup

Preparation Time: 4 minutes
Cooking Time: 38 minutes
Serving: 6
Ingredients:

- 2 medium leeks
- 10 white mushrooms
- 3 garlic cloves
- 2 bay leaves
- 2 cans tomatoes
- 3/4 cup red lentils
- 1/3 cup barley
- 3 tbsp olive oil
- 1 tsp paprika
- 1 tsp summer savory
- ½ tsp cumin

Direction:

1. Cook oil in a large saucepan over medium-high heat. Sauté leeks and mushrooms for 3 to 4 minutes or until softened. Add cumin, paprika, savory and tomatoes, lentils, barley, and 5 cups cold water. Season with salt and pepper.
2. Cover and bring to the boil. Reduce heat to low. Simmer for 37 minutes.

Nutrition: 314 Calories 19g Fat 5g Protein

813. Spinach Soup

Preparation Time: 10 minutes
Cooking Time: 21 minutes
Serving: 6
Ingredients:

- 14 oz frozen spinach
- 1 large onion
- 1 carrot
- 4 cups water
- 3-4 tbsp olive oil
- 1/4 cup white rice
- 1-2 cloves garlic, crushed

Directions:

1. Cook oil in a cooking pot, stir in onion and carrot and sauté together for a few minutes, until just softened. Add chopped garlic and rice and stir for a minute. Remove from heat.
2. Add in the chopped spinach along with about 2 cups of hot water and season with salt and pepper. Bring back to a boil, then reduce the heat and simmer for around 30 minutes.

Nutrition: 291 Calories 16g Fat 7g Protein

814. Spinach and Feta Cheese Soup

Preparation Time: 8 minutes
Cooking Time: 24 minutes
Serving: 4
Ingredients:

- 14 oz frozen spinach
- oz feta cheese
- 1 large onion or 4-5 scallions
- 2 -3 tbsp light cream
- 3-4 tbsp olive oil
- 1-2 cloves garlic
- 4 cups water

Directions:

1. Cook oil in a cooking pot, add the onion and spinach and sauté together for a few minutes, until just softened. Add garlic and stir for a minute. Remove from heat. Fill 2 cups of hot water and season with salt and pepper.
2. Bring back to the boil, then reduce the heat and simmer for around 30 minutes. Blend soup in a blender. Crumble the cheese with a fork. Stir in the crumbled feta cheese and the cream. Serve hot.

Nutrition: 251 Calories 13g Fat 5g Protein

815. Nettle Soup

Preparation Time: 4 minutes
Cooking Time: 26 minutes
Serving: 6
Ingredients:

- lb. young top shoots of nettles
- 3-4 tbsp sunflower oil
- 2 potatoes, diced small
- 1 bunch spring onions
- 1 ½ cup freshly boiled water
- 1 tsp salt

Directions:

1. Clean the young nettles, wash and cook them in slightly salted water. Drain, rinse, drain again and then chop or pass through a sieve. Sauté the chopped spring onions and potatoes.
2. Turn off the heat, add the nettles, then gradually stir in the water. Simmer until the potatoes are cooked through.

Nutrition: 251 Calories 13g Fat 4g Protein

816. Thick Herb Soup

Preparation Time: 11 minutes
Cooking Time: 23 minutes
Serving: 4
Ingredients:
- 2 oz mint leaves
- 2 oz celery leaves
- 4 tbsp butter or olive oil
- 2 tbsp flour
- 3 cups water
- ½ cup thick yogurt
- juice of a lemon
- 2 egg yolks
- 1 tsp salt

Directions:
1. Rinse the herbs, remove stalks and snip or chop finely. Cook butter or oil in a cooking pot, add prepared herbs, cover and simmer gently.
2. When the herbs are tender, add in the flour and stir to combine. Cook for a few moments before slowly adding the water, stirring all the time. Simmer for about 10-15 min.
3. Mix separately egg yolks, thick yogurt (or sour cream) and lemon juice. Add to the soup slowly, then stir well.

Nutrition: 247 Calories 13g Fat 7g Protein

817. Rice with Vermicelli

Preparation Time: 5 minutes
Cooking Time: 45 minutes
Serving: 6
Ingredients
- 2 cups short-grain rice
- 3½ cups water
- ¼ cup olive oil
- 1 cup broken vermicelli pasta
- Salt

Direction
1. Drench the rice under cold water until the water runs clean. Situate the rice in a bowl, cover with water, and let soak for 10 minutes. Drain and set aside.
2. Using medium pot over medium heat, heat the olive oil.
3. Stir in the vermicelli and cook for 2 to 3 minutes, stirring continuously, until golden.

4. Stir in rice and cook for 1 minute, stirring, so the rice is well coated in the oil.
5. Pour in water and a pinch of salt and bring the liquid to a boil. Adjust the heat to low, cover the pot, and simmer for 20 minutes.
6. Pull away from the heat and let rest, covered, for 10 minutes. Fluff with a fork and serve.

Nutrition: 349 calories 19g fat 17g protein

818. Fava Beans and Rice

Preparation Time: 10 minutes
Cooking Time: 35 minutes
Serving: 4
Ingredients:
- ¼ cup olive oil
- 4 cups fresh fava beans
- 4½ cups water
- 2 cups basmati rice
- 1/8 teaspoon salt
- 1/8 teaspoon black pepper
- 2 tablespoons pine nuts, toasted
- ½ cup chopped fresh garlic chives

Direction:
1. In a large saucepan over medium heat, heat the olive oil.
2. Add the fava beans and drizzle them with a bit of water. Cook for 10 minutes.
3. Gently stir in the rice. Add the water, salt, and pepper. Increase the heat and bring the mixture to a boil. Close, set the heat to low, then simmer for 15 minutes.
4. Turn off the heat and let the mixture rest for 10 minutes before serving. Sprinkle with toasted pine nuts and chives.

Nutrition: 587 calories 17g fat 17g protein.

819. Fresh Buttery Fava Beans

Preparation Time: 30 minutes
Cooking Time: 15 minutes
Serving: 4
Ingredients
- ½ cup vegetable broth
- 4 pounds fava beans
- ¼ cup fresh tarragon
- 1 teaspoon chopped fresh thyme
- ¼ teaspoon black pepper
- 1/8 teaspoon salt
- 2 tablespoons butter
- 1 garlic clove, minced
- 2 tablespoons chopped fresh parsley

Direction:
1. In a shallow pan over medium heat, bring the vegetable broth to a boil.
2. Add the fava beans, 2 tablespoons of tarragon, the thyme, pepper, and salt. Cook for 10 minutes.

3. Stir in the butter, garlic, and remaining 2 tablespoons of tarragon. Cook for 2 to 3 minutes.
4. Sprinkle with the parsley.

Nutrition: 458 calories 9g fat 37g protein

820. Farik

Preparation Time: 10 minutes
Cooking Time: 40 minutes
Serving: 4

Ingredients:
- 4 tablespoons Ghee
- 1 onion, chopped
- 3½ cups vegetable broth
- 1 teaspoon ground allspice
- 2 cups freekeh
- 2 tablespoons pine nuts

Direction
1. In a heavy-bottomed saucepan over medium heat, melt the ghee.
2. Stir in the onion and cook for about 5 minutes, stirring constantly, until the onion is golden.
3. Pour in the vegetable broth, add the allspice, and bring to a boil.
4. Stir in the freekeh and return the mixture to a boil. Switch heat to low, close, and simmer for 30 minutes, stirring occasionally.
5. Spoon the freekeh into a serving dish and top with the toasted pine nuts.

Nutrition: 459 calories 18g fat 19g protein

821. Pan-Fried Rice Balls

Preparation Time: 15 minutes
Cooking Time: 20 minutes
Serving: 4

Ingredients:
- 1 cup bread crumbs
- 2 cups cooked risotto
- 2 large eggs, divided
- ¼ cup freshly grated Parmesan cheese
- 8 fresh baby mozzarella balls
- 2 tablespoons water
- 1 cup corn oil
- 1 cup Basic Tomato Basil Sauce

Direction
1. Situate bread crumbs into a small bowl and set aside.
2. Incorporate risotto, 1 egg, and the Parmesan cheese until well combined.
3. Moisten your hands with a little water to prevent sticking and portion the risotto mixture into 8 pieces. Put them on a clean work surface and flatten each piece.
4. Situate 1 mozzarella ball on each flattened rice disk. Close the rice around the mozzarella to form a ball. Repeat until you finish all the balls.

5. In the same medium, now-empty bowl, scourge remaining egg and the water.
6. Soak each prepared risotto ball into the egg wash and roll it in the bread crumbs. Set aside.
7. Using big sauté pan or skillet over high heat, heat the corn oil for about 3 minutes.
8. Mildly lower the risotto balls into the hot oil and fry for 5 to 8 minutes. Stir them, as needed, to ensure the entire surface is fried. Using a slotted spoon, transfer the fried balls to paper towels to drain.
9. Using medium saucepan over medium heat, heat the tomato sauce for 5 minutes, stirring occasionally, and serve the warm sauce alongside the rice balls.

Nutrition: 255 calories 15g fat 11g protein

822. Tomato-Garlic Spanish Rice

Preparation Time: 10 minutes
Cooking Time: 35 minutes
Serving: 4

Ingredients:
- ¼ cup olive oil
- 1 small onion
- 1 red bell pepper
- 1½ cups white rice
- 1 teaspoon sweet paprika
- ½ teaspoon ground cumin
- ½ teaspoon ground coriander
- 1 garlic clove, minced
- 3 tablespoons tomato paste
- 3 cups vegetable broth
- 1/8 teaspoon salt

Direction:
1. Using big heavy-bottomed skillet over medium heat, heat the olive oil.
2. Stir in the onion and red bell pepper. Cook for 5 minutes or until softened.
3. Add the rice, paprika, cumin, and coriander and cook for 2 minutes, stirring often.
4. Add the garlic, tomato paste, vegetable broth, and salt. Stir and season with more salt, as needed.
5. Increase the heat to bring the mixture to a boil. Reduce the heat to low, cover the skillet, and simmer for 20 minutes.
6. Let the rice rest, covered, for 5 minutes before serving.

Nutrition: 414 calories 14g fat 6g protein

823. Zucchini and Rice with Tzatziki Sauce

Preparation Time: 20 minutes
Cooking Time: 35 minutes
Serving: 4

Ingredients:
- ¼ cup olive oil

- 1 onion
- 3 zucchinis
- 1 cup vegetable broth
- ½ cup chopped fresh dill
- 1 cup short-grain rice
- 2 tablespoons pine nuts
- 1 cup Tzatziki Sauce, Plain Yogurt

Direction:
1. Using heavy-bottomed pot over medium heat, heat the olive oil.
2. Mix in onion, turn the heat to medium-low, and sauté for 5 minutes.
3. Stir in zucchini and cook for 2 minutes more.
4. Fill in the vegetable broth and dill and season with salt and pepper. Increase the heat to medium and bring the mixture to a boil.
5. Mix in the rice and let it boil. Set to very low heat, cover the pot, and cook for 15 minutes. Remove from the heat and let the rice rest, covered, for 10 minutes.
6. Ladle the rice onto a serving platter, sprinkle with the pine nuts, and serve with tzatziki sauce.

Nutrition: 414 calories 17g fat 11g protein

824. Rosemary, Garlic Aioli and Cannellini Beans

Preparation Time: 10 minutes
Cooking Time: 10 minutes
Serving: 4
Ingredients:
- 4 cups cooked cannellini beans
- 4 cups water
- ½ teaspoon salt
- 3 tablespoons olive oil
- 2 tablespoons chopped fresh rosemary
- ½ cup Garlic Aioli
- ¼ teaspoon freshly ground black pepper

Direction:
1. Using medium saucepan over medium heat, mix cannellini beans, water, and salt. Bring to a boil. Cook for 5 minutes. Drain.
2. In a skillet over medium heat, cook olive oil.
3. Add the beans. Stir in the rosemary and aioli. Switch heat to medium-low and cook, stirring, just to heat through. Season with pepper and serve.

Nutrition: 545 calories 36g fat 15g protein

825. Jeweled Basmati Rice

Preparation Time: 15 minutes
Cooking Time: 30 minutes
Serving: 6
Ingredients:
- ½ cup olive oil, divided
- 1 onion, finely chopped
- 1 garlic clove, minced

- ½ teaspoon fresh ginger
- 4½ cups water
- 1 teaspoon salt
- 1 teaspoon ground turmeric
- 2 cups basmati rice
- 1 cup fresh sweet peas
- 2 carrots
- ½ cup dried cranberries
- Grated zest of 1 orange
- 1/8 teaspoon cayenne pepper
- ¼ cup slivered almonds

Direction:
1. Using huge heavy-bottomed pot over medium heat, heat ¼ cup of olive oil.
2. Stir in onion and cook for 4 minutes. Add the garlic and ginger and cook for 1 minute more.
3. Pour in the water, ¾ teaspoon of salt, and the turmeric. Bring the mixture to a boil. Mix in the rice and boil. Select heat to low, cover the pot, and cook for 15 minutes. Turn off the heat. Let the rice rest on the burner, covered, for 10 minutes.
4. Meanwhile, using medium sauté pan or skillet over medium-low heat, cook remaining ¼ cup of olive oil. Stir in the peas and carrots. Cook for 5 minutes.
5. Drizzle cranberries and orange zest. Season with the remaining ¼ teaspoon of salt and the cayenne. Cook for 1 to 2 minutes.
6. Ladle the rice onto a serving platter. Top with the peas and carrots and sprinkle with the toasted almonds.

Nutrition: 460 calories 19g fat 7g protein

826. Cheese Asparagus Risotto

Preparation Time: 15 minutes
Cooking Time: 30 minutes
Serving: 4
Ingredients:
- 5 cups vegetable broth
- 3 tablespoons unsalted butter
- 1 tablespoon olive oil
- 1 small onion, chopped
- 1½ cups Arborio rice
- 1-pound fresh asparagus
- ¼ cup grated Parmesan cheese

Direction:
1. In a saucepan over medium heat, bring the vegetable broth to a boil. Switch heat to low and keep the broth at a steady simmer.
2. In a 4-quart heavy-bottomed saucepan over medium heat, melt 2 tablespoons of butter with the olive oil. Add the onion and cook for 2 to 3 minutes.
3. Add the rice and stir with a wooden spoon while cooking for 1 minute.
4. Stir in ½ cup of warm broth. Cook, stirring often, for about 5 minutes until the broth is completely absorbed.

5. Add the asparagus stalks and another ½ cup of broth. Cook, stirring often, until the liquid is absorbed. Continue adding the broth, ½ cup at a time, and cooking until it is completely absorbed before adding the next ½ cup. Stir frequently to prevent sticking. After about 20 minutes, the rice should be cooked but still firm.
6. Add the asparagus tips, the remaining 1 tablespoon of butter, and the Parmesan cheese. Stir vigorously to combine.
7. Remove from the heat, top with additional Parmesan cheese, if desired, and serve immediately.

Nutrition: 434 calories 14g fat 10g protein

827. Spanish Vegan Paella

Preparation Time: 25 minutes
Cooking Time: 45 minutes
Serving: 6
Ingredients:
- ¼ cup olive oil
- 1 large sweet onion
- 1 large red bell pepper
- 1 large green bell pepper
- 3 garlic cloves
- 1 teaspoon smoked paprika
- 5 saffron threads
- 1 zucchini, cut into ½-inch cubes
- 4 large ripe tomatoes
- 1½ cups short-grain Spanish rice
- 3 cups vegetable broth, warmed

Direction:
1. Preheat the oven to 350°F.
2. Using oven-safe skillet over medium heat, heat the olive oil.
3. Stir in onion and red and green bell peppers and cook for 10 minutes.
4. Mix in the garlic, paprika, saffron threads, zucchini, and tomatoes. Turn the heat to medium-low and cook for 10 minutes.
5. Pour in the rice and vegetable broth. Increase the heat to bring the paella to a boil. Reduce the heat to medium-low and cook for 15 minutes. Cover the pan with aluminum foil and put it in the oven.
6. Bake for 10 minutes.

Nutrition: 288 calories 10g fat 5g protein

828. Japanese Eggplant Casserole

Preparation Time: 30 minutes
Cooking Time: 35 minutes
Serving: 4
Ingredients:
For sauce
- ½ cup olive oil
- 1 small onion
- 4 garlic cloves
- 6 ripe tomatoes

- 2 tablespoons tomato paste
- 1 teaspoon dried oregano
- ¼ teaspoon ground nutmeg
- ¼ teaspoon ground cumin

For casserole
- 4 (6-inch) Japanese eggplants
- 2 tablespoons olive oil
- 1 cup cooked rice
- 2 tablespoons pine nuts
- 1 cup water

Direction:
For sauce
1. Using heavy-bottomed saucepan over medium heat, heat the olive oil. Stir in onion and cook for 5 minutes.
2. Mix in the garlic, tomatoes, tomato paste, oregano, nutmeg, and cumin. Bring to a boil. Close, switch heat to low, and simmer for 10 minutes. Remove and set aside.

For casserole
3. Prep the broiler.
4. While the sauce simmers, rub eggplant with the olive oil and situate them on a baking sheet. Broil for about 5 minutes until golden. Remove and let cool.
5. Switch the oven to 375°F. Arrange the cooled eggplant, cut-side up, in a 9-by-13-inch baking dish. Gently spoon out some flesh to make room for the stuffing.
6. Incorporate half the tomato sauce, the cooked rice, and pine nuts. Fill each eggplant half with the rice mixture.
7. Mix remaining tomato sauce and water. Pour over the eggplant.
8. Bake for 20 minutes.

Nutrition: 453 calories 39g fat 6g protein

829. Veggie Couscous

Preparation Time: 15 minutes
Cooking Time: 45 minutes
Serving: 8
Ingredient
- ¼ cup olive oil
- 1 onion
- 4 garlic cloves
- 2 jalapeño peppers
- ½ tsp. ground cumin
- ½ tsp. ground coriander
- 1 (28-oz) can crushed tomatoes
- 2 tbsp. tomato paste
- 1/8 tsp. salt
- 2 bay leaves
- 11 cups water
- 4 carrots, cut into 2-inch pieces
- 2 zucchinis
- 1 acorn squash

- 1 (15-oz) can chickpeas
- ¼ cup Preserved Lemons
- 3 cups couscous

Direction:
1. Using big heavy-bottomed pot over medium heat, heat the olive oil. Stir in the onion and cook for 4 minutes. Stir in the garlic, jalapeños, cumin, and coriander. Cook for 1 minute.
2. Mix in tomatoes, tomato paste, salt, bay leaves, and 8 cups of water. Bring the mixture to a boil.
3. Stir in carrots, zucchini, and acorn squash and return to a boil. Reduce the heat slightly, cover, and cook for about 20 minutes until the vegetables are tender but not mushy. Remove 2 cups of the cooking liquid and set aside. Season as needed.
4. Mix in chickpeas and preserved lemons (if using). Cook for 2 to 3 minutes, and turn off the heat.
5. Using medium pan, bring the remaining 3 cups of water to a boil over high heat. Stir in the couscous, cover, and turn off the heat. Let the couscous rest for 10 minutes. Drizzle with 1 cup of reserved cooking liquid. Using a fork, fluff the couscous.
6. Drizzle with the remaining cooking liquid. Remove the vegetables from the pot and arrange on top. Serve the remaining stew in a separate bowl.

Nutrition: 415 calories 7g fat 14g protein

830. Egyptian Koshari

Preparation Time: 25 minutes
Cooking Time: 80 minutes
Serving: 8
Ingredients:
For sauce
- 2 tablespoons olive oil
- 2 garlic cloves, minced
- 1 (16-ounce) can tomato sauce
- ¼ cup white vinegar
- ¼ cup Harissa, or store-bought
- 1/8 teaspoon salt

For rice
- 1 cup olive oil
- 2 onions, thinly sliced
- 2 cups dried brown lentils
- 4 quarts plus ½ cup water
- 2 cups short-grain rice
- 1 teaspoon salt
- 1-pound short elbow pasta
- 1 (15-ounce) can chickpeas

Direction:
For sauce
1. In a saucepan over medium heat, heat the olive oil.
2. Stir in garlic and cook for 1 minute.
3. Stir in the tomato sauce, vinegar, harissa, and salt. Increase the heat to bring the sauce to a boil. Adjust the heat to low and cook for 20 minutes or until the sauce has thickened. Remove and set aside.

For rice

4. Prep the plate with paper towels and put aside.
5. In a large pan over medium heat, heat the olive oil.
6. Add the onions and cook for 7 to 10 minutes, stirring often, until crisp and golden. Transfer the onions to the prepared plate and set aside. Reserve 2 tablespoons of the cooking oil. Reserve the pan.
7. Using big pot over high heat, mix the lentils and 4 cups of water. Bring to a boil and cook for 20 minutes. Drain, situate to a bowl, and pour in the reserved 2 tablespoons of cooking oil. Set aside. Reserve the pot.
8. Place the pan you used to fry the onions over medium-high heat and add the rice, 4½ cups of water, and sprinkle salt to it. Bring to a boil then switch heat to low, then cook for 20 minutes. Turn off the heat and let the rice rest for 10 minutes.6.
9. In the pot used to cook the lentils, bring the remaining 8 cups of water, salted, to a boil over high heat. Stir in the pasta and cook for 7 minutes or according to the package instructions. Drain and set aside.
10. To assemble: Spoon the rice onto a serving platter. Top it with the lentils, chickpeas, and pasta. Drizzle with the hot tomato sauce and sprinkle with the crispy fried onions.

Nutrition: 668 calories 13g fat 25g protein

831. Tomatoes and Chickpeas Bulgur

Preparation Time: 10 minutes
Cooking Time: 35 minutes
Serving: 6
Ingredients:
- ½ cup olive oil
- 1 onion, chopped
- 6 tomatoes
- 2 tablespoons tomato paste
- 2 cups water
- 1 tablespoon Harissa
- 1/8 teaspoon salt
- 2 cups coarse bulgur #3
- 1 (15-ounce) can chickpeas

Direction:
1. Using heavy-bottomed pot over medium heat, heat the olive oil.
2. Cook onion for 5 minutes.
3. Add the tomatoes with their juice and cook for 5 minutes.
4. Stir in the tomato paste, water, harissa, and salt. Bring to a boil.
5. Stir in the bulgur and chickpeas. Return the mixture to a boil. Switch heat to low, cover then cook for 15 minutes. Let rest for 15 minutes before serving.

Nutrition: 413 calories 19g fat 11g protein

832. Cauliflower Steaks with Olive Citrus Sauce

Preparation Time: 15 minutes
Cooking Time: 30 minutes
Serving: 4
Ingredients:

- 2 large heads cauliflowers
- 1/3 cup extra-virgin olive oil
- ¼ teaspoon kosher salt
- 1/8 teaspoon black pepper
- Juice of 1 orange
- Zest of 1 orange
- ¼ cup black olives
- 1 tablespoon Dijon mustard
- 1 tablespoon red wine vinegar
- ½ teaspoon ground coriander

Direction

1. Preheat the oven to 400°F. Prep baking sheet with parchment paper or foil.
2. Cut off the stem of the cauliflower so it will sit upright. Slice it vertically into four thick slabs. Situate cauliflower on the prepared baking sheet. Drizzle with the olive oil, salt, and black pepper. Bake for 31 minutes, turning over once.
3. In a medium bowl, combine the orange juice, orange zest, olives, mustard, vinegar, and coriander; mix well.
4. Serve at room temperature with the sauce.

Nutrition: 265 Calories 21g fat 5g Protein

833. Pistachio Mint Pesto Pasta

Preparation Time: 10 minutes
Cooking Time: 10 minutes
Serving: 4
Ingredients:

- 8 ounces whole-wheat pasta
- 1 cup fresh mint
- ½ cup fresh basil
- 1/3 cup unsalted pistachios, shelled
- 1 garlic clove, peeled
- ½ teaspoon kosher salt
- Juice of ½ lime
- 1/3 cup extra-virgin olive oil

Direction:

1. Cook the pasta following the package directions. Strain, reserving ½ cup of the pasta water, and set aside.
2. In a food processor, add the mint, basil, pistachios, garlic, salt, and lime juice. Process until the pistachios are coarsely ground. Add the olive oil in a slow, steady stream and process until incorporated.
3. In a large bowl, mix the pasta with the pistachio pesto; toss well to incorporate. If a thinner, more saucy consistency is desired, add some of the reserved pasta water and toss well.

Nutrition: 420 Calories 3g fat 11g Protein

834. Burst Cherry Tomato Sauce with Angel Hair Pasta

Preparation Time: 10 minutes
Cooking Time: 20 minutes
Serving: 4
Ingredients:

- 8 ounces angel hair pasta
- 2 tablespoons extra-virgin olive oil
- 3 garlic cloves, minced
- 3 pints cherry tomatoes
- ½ teaspoon kosher salt
- ¼ teaspoon red pepper flakes
- ¾ cup fresh basil, chopped
- 1 tablespoon white balsamic vinegar (optional)
- ¼ cup grated Parmesan cheese (optional)

Direction:

1. Cook the pasta following the package directions. Drain and set aside.
2. Heat the olive oil in a skillet or large sauté pan over medium-high heat. Stir in garlic and sauté for 30 seconds. Mix in the tomatoes, salt, and red pepper flakes and cook, stirring occasionally, until the tomatoes burst, about 15 minutes.
3. Pull away from the heat then mix in the pasta and basil. Toss together well. (For out-of-season tomatoes, add the vinegar, if desired, and mix well.)
4. Serve with the grated Parmesan cheese, if desired.

Nutrition: 305 Calories 8g fat 11g Protein

835. Baked Tofu with Sun-Dried Tomatoes and Artichokes

Preparation Time: 30 minutes
Cooking Time: 30 minutes
Serving: 4
Ingredients:

- 1 (16-ounce) package extra-firm tofu
- 2 tablespoons extra-virgin olive oil, divided
- 2 tablespoons lemon juice, divided
- 1 tablespoon low-sodium soy sauce
- 1 onion, diced
- ½ teaspoon kosher salt
- 2 garlic cloves, minced
- 1 (14-ounce) can artichoke hearts, drained
- 8 sun-dried tomato halves packed in oil
- ¼ teaspoon freshly ground black pepper
- 1 tablespoon white wine vinegar
- Zest of 1 lemon
- ¼ cup fresh parsley, chopped

Direction:

1. Preheat the oven to 400°F. Prep baking sheet with foil or parchment paper.

2. Mix tofu, 1 tablespoon of the olive oil, 1 tablespoon of the lemon juice, and the soy sauce. Allow to sit and marinate for 15 to 30 minutes. Arrange the tofu in a single layer on the prepared baking sheet and bake for 20 minutes, turning once, until light golden brown.

3. Cook remaining 1 tablespoon olive oil in a sauté pan over medium heat. Cook onion and salt for6 minutes. Stir garlic and sauté for 30 seconds. Add the artichoke hearts, sun-dried tomatoes, and black pepper and sauté for 5 minutes. Add the white wine vinegar and the remaining 1 tablespoon lemon juice and deglaze the pan, scraping up any brown bits. Pull away the pan from the heat and stir in the lemon zest and parsley. Gently mix in the baked tofu.

Nutrition: 230 Calories 14g fat 14g Protein

836. Baked Mediterranean Tempeh with Tomatoes and Garlic

Preparation Time: 25 minutes
Cooking Time: 35 minutes
Serving: 4
Ingredient:
For tempeh
- 12 ounces tempeh
- ¼ cup white wine
- 2 tablespoons extra-virgin olive oil
- 2 tablespoons lemon juice
- Zest of 1 lemon
- ¼ teaspoon kosher salt
- ¼ teaspoon freshly ground black pepper

For tomatoes and garlic sauce
- 1 tablespoon extra-virgin olive oil
- 1 onion, diced
- 3 garlic cloves, minced
- 1 (14.5-ounce) can no-salt-added crushed tomatoes
- 1 beefsteak tomato, diced
- 1 dried bay leaf
- 1 teaspoon white wine vinegar
- 1 teaspoon lemon juice
- 1 teaspoon dried oregano
- 1 teaspoon dried thyme
- ¾ teaspoon kosher salt
- ¼ cup basil, cut into ribbons

Direction:
For tempeh
1. Place the tempeh in a medium saucepan. Add enough water to cover it by 1 to 2 inches. Bring to a boil over medium-high heat, cover, and lower heat to a simmer. Cook for 10 to 15 minutes. Remove the tempeh, pat dry, cool, and cut into 1-inch cubes.

2. Incorporate white wine, olive oil, lemon juice, lemon zest, salt, and black pepper. Add the tempeh, cover the bowl, and put in the refrigerator for 4 hours, or up to overnight.

3. Preheat the oven to 375°F. Place the marinated tempeh and the marinade in a baking dish and cook for 15 minutes.

For tomatoes and garlic sauce
4. Cook olive oil in a large skillet over medium heat. Stir in onion and sauté until transparent, 3 to 5 minutes. Mix in garlic and sauté for 30 seconds. Add the crushed tomatoes, beefsteak tomato, bay leaf, vinegar, lemon juice, oregano, thyme, and salt. Mix well. Simmer for 15 minutes.

5. Add the baked tempeh to the tomato mixture and gently mix together. Garnish with the basil.

Nutrition: 330 Calorie 20g fat 18g Protein

837. Roasted Portobello Mushrooms with Kale and Red Onion

Preparation Time: 30 minutes
Cooking Time: 30 minutes
Serving: 4
Ingredients
- ¼ cup white wine vinegar
- 3 tablespoons extra-virgin olive oil, divided
- ½ teaspoon honey
- ¾ teaspoon kosher salt, divided
- ¼ teaspoon freshly ground black pepper
- 4 (4 to 5 ounces) portobello mushrooms, stems removed
- 1 red onion, julienned
- 2 garlic cloves, minced
- 1 (8-ounce) bunch kale, stemmed and chopped small
- ¼ teaspoon red pepper flakes
- ¼ cup grated Parmesan or Romano cheese

Direction:
1. Prep baking sheet with foil. In a medium bowl, whisk together the vinegar, 1½ tablespoons of the olive oil, honey, ¼ teaspoon of the salt, and the black pepper. Spread the mushrooms on the baking sheet and pour the marinade over them. Marinate for 15 to 30 minutes.

2. Meanwhile, preheat the oven to 400°F.

3. Bake the mushrooms for 20 minutes, turning over halfway through.

4. Heat the remaining 1½ tablespoons olive oil in a large skillet or ovenproof sauté pan over medium-high heat. Add the onion and the remaining ½ teaspoon salt and sauté until golden brown, 5 to 6 minutes. Stir in garlic and sauté for 30 seconds. Mix kale and red pepper flakes and sauté until the kale cooks down, about 5 minutes.

5. Remove the mushrooms from the oven and increase the temperature to broil.

6. Carefully pour the liquid from the baking sheet into the pan with the kale mixture; mix well.

7. Turn the mushrooms over so that the stem side is facing up. Spoon some of the kale mixture on top

of each mushroom. Sprinkle 1 tablespoon Parmesan cheese on top of each.

8. Broil until golden brown, 3 to 4 minutes.

Nutrition 200 Calories 13g fat 8g Protein

838. Balsamic Marinated Tofu with Basil and Oregano

Preparation Time: 40 minutes
Cooking Time: 30 minutes
Serving: 4
Ingredients:
- ¼ cup extra-virgin olive oil
- ¼ cup balsamic vinegar
- 2 tablespoons gluten-free tamari
- 3 garlic cloves, grated
- 2 teaspoons pure maple syrup
- Zest of 1 lemon
- 1 teaspoon dried basil
- 1 teaspoon dried oregano
- ½ teaspoon dried thyme
- ½ teaspoon dried sage
- ¼ teaspoon kosher salt
- ¼ teaspoon freshly ground black pepper
- ¼ teaspoon red pepper flakes (optional)
- 1 (16-ounce) block extra firm tofu

Direction:
1. In a bowl or gallon zip-top bag, mix together the olive oil, vinegar, soy sauce, garlic, maple syrup, lemon zest, basil, oregano, thyme, sage, salt, black pepper, and red pepper flakes, if desired. Add the tofu and mix gently. Put in the refrigerator and marinate for 30 minutes, or up to overnight if you desire.
2. Prep the oven to 425°F. Line a baking sheet with parchment paper or foil. Arrange the marinated tofu in a single layer on the prepared baking sheet. Bake for 28 minutes, turning over halfway through, until slightly crispy on the outside and tender on the inside.

Nutrition: 225 Calories 16g fat 13g Protein

839. Ricotta, Basil, and Pistachio–Stuffed Zucchini

Preparation Time: 15 minutes
Cooking Time: 25 minutes
Serving: 4
Ingredients:
- 2 medium zucchinis
- 1 tablespoon extra-virgin olive oil
- 1 onion, diced
- 1 teaspoon kosher salt
- 2 garlic cloves, minced
- ¾ cup ricotta cheese
- ¼ cup unsalted pistachios

- ¼ cup fresh basil
- 1 large egg, beaten
- ¼ teaspoon freshly ground black pepper

Direction:
1. Prep the oven to 425°F. Prep baking sheet with parchment paper or foil.
2. Scoop out the seeds/pulp from the zucchini, leaving ¼-inch flesh around the edges. Transfer the pulp to a cutting board and chop the pulp.
3. Heat the olive oil in a huge skillet over medium heat, sauté onion, pulp, and salt for 5 minutes. Add the garlic and sauté 30 seconds.
4. Mix ricotta cheese, pistachios, basil, egg, and black pepper. Add the onion mixture and mix together well.
5. Place the 4 zucchini halves on the prepared baking sheet. Stuff the zucchini halves with the ricotta mixture. Bake for 20 minutes.

Nutrition: 200 Calories 12g fat 11g Protein

840. Farro with Roasted Tomatoes and Mushrooms

Preparation Time: 20 minutes
Cooking Time: 1 hour
Serving: 4
Ingredients:
For tomatoes
- 2 pints cherry tomatoes
- 1 teaspoon extra-virgin olive oil
- ¼ teaspoon kosher salt
For farro
- 3 to 4 cups water
- ½ cup farro
- ¼ teaspoon kosher salt
For mushrooms
- 2 tablespoons extra-virgin olive oil
- 1 onion, julienned
- ½ teaspoon kosher salt
- ¼ teaspoon freshly ground black pepper
- 10 ounces baby Bella mushrooms
- ½ cup no-salt-added vegetable stock
- 1 (15-ounce) can low-sodium cannellini beans
- 1 cup baby spinach
- 2 tablespoons fresh basil
- ¼ cup pine nuts, toasted
- Aged balsamic vinegar (optional)

Direction:
For tomatoes
1. Preheat the oven to 400°F. Prep baking sheet using parchment paper or foil. Toss the tomatoes, olive oil, and salt together on the baking sheet and roast for 30 minutes.
For farro
2. Bring the water, farro, and salt to a boil in a medium saucepan or pot over high heat. Cover, switch heat to low, and simmer, and cook for 30

minutes, or until the farro is al dente. Drain and set aside.

For mushrooms

3. Cook olive oil in a large skillet or sauté pan over medium-low heat. Add the onions, salt, and black pepper and sauté until golden brown and starting to caramelize, about 15 minutes. Add the mushrooms, increase the heat to medium, and sauté until the liquid has evaporated and the mushrooms brown, about 10 minutes. Pour in vegetable stock then deglaze the pan, scraping up any brown bits, and reduce the liquid for about 5 minutes. Add the beans and warm through, about 3 minutes.

4. Remove from the heat and mix in the spinach, basil, pine nuts, roasted tomatoes, and farro. Garnish with a drizzle of balsamic vinegar, if desired.

Nutrition: 375 Calories 15g fat 14g Protein

841. **Baked Orzo**

Preparation Time: 20 minutes
Cooking Time: 1 hour
Serving: 4
Ingredient:

- 2 tablespoons extra-virgin olive oil
- 1 large (1-pound) eggplant, diced small
- 2 carrots, peeled and diced small
- 2 celery stalks, diced small
- 1 onion, diced small
- ½ teaspoon kosher salt
- 3 garlic cloves, minced
- ¼ teaspoon freshly ground black pepper
- 1 cup whole-wheat orzo
- 1 teaspoon no-salt-added tomato paste
- 1½ cups no-salt-added vegetable stock
- 1 cup Swiss chard, stemmed and chopped small
- 2 tablespoons fresh oregano, chopped
- Zest of 1 lemon
- 4 ounces mozzarella cheese, diced small
- ¼ cup grated Parmesan cheese
- 2 tomatoes, sliced ½-inch-thick

Direction:

1. Preheat the oven to 400°F.
2. Heat the olive oil in a large oven-safe sauté pan over medium heat. Add the eggplant, carrots, celery, onion, and salt and sauté about 10 minutes. Add the garlic and black pepper and sauté about 30 seconds. Add the orzo and tomato paste and sauté 1 minute. Fill in vegetable stock and deglaze the pan, scraping up the brown bits. Add the Swiss chard, oregano, and lemon zest and stir until the chard wilts.
3. Remove from the heat and mix in the mozzarella cheese. Smooth the top of the orzo mixture flat. Sprinkle the Parmesan cheese over the top. Spread tomatoes in one layer on top of the Parmesan cheese. Bake for 45 minutes.

Nutrition: 470 Calories 17g fat 19g Protein

842. **Barley Risotto with Tomatoes**

Preparation Time: 20 minutes
Cooking Time: 45 minutes
Serving: 4
Ingredients:

- 2 tablespoons extra-virgin olive oil
- 2 celery stalks, diced
- ½ cup shallots, diced
- 4 garlic cloves, minced
- 3 cups no-salt-added vegetable stock
- 2 (14.5-ounce) can no-salt-added diced tomatoes
- 1 cup pearl barley
- Zest of 1 lemon
- 1 teaspoon kosher salt
- ½ teaspoon smoked paprika
- ¼ teaspoon red pepper flakes
- ¼ teaspoon freshly ground black pepper
- 4 thyme sprigs
- 1 dried bay leaf
- 2 cups baby spinach
- ½ cup crumbled feta cheese
- 1 tablespoon fresh oregano, chopped
- 1 tablespoon fennel seeds, toasted (optional)

Direction:

1. Cook olive oil in a large saucepan over medium heat. Stir in celery and shallots and sauté, about 4 to 5 minutes. Add the garlic and sauté 30 seconds. Add the vegetable stock, diced tomatoes, crushed tomatoes, barley, lemon zest, salt, paprika, red pepper flakes, black pepper, thyme, and the bay leaf, and mix well. Bring to a boil, then lower to low, and simmer. Cook, stirring occasionally, for 40 minutes.
2. Remove the bay leaf and thyme sprigs. Stir in the spinach.
3. In a small bowl, combine the feta, oregano, and fennel seeds. Serve the barley risotto in bowls topped with the feta mixture.

Nutrition: 375 Calories 12g fat 11g Protein

843. **Chickpeas and Kale with Spicy Pomodoro Sauce**

Preparation Time: 10 minutes
Cooking Time: 35 minutes
Serving: 4
Ingredient:

- 2 tablespoons extra-virgin olive oil
- 4 garlic cloves, sliced
- 1 teaspoon red pepper flakes
- 1 (28-ounce) can no-salt-added crushed tomatoes
- 1 teaspoon kosher salt
- ½ teaspoon honey
- 1 bunch kale, stemmed and chopped

- 2 (15-ounce) cans no-salt-added or low-sodium chickpeas
- ¼ cup fresh basil, chopped
- ¼ cup grated pecorino Romano cheese

Direction:
1. Heat the olive oil in sauté pan over medium heat. Cook garlic and red pepper flakes for 2 minutes. Add the tomatoes, salt, and honey and mix well. Switch heat to low and simmer for 20 minutes.
2. Add the kale and mix in well. Cook about 5 minutes. Add the chickpeas and simmer about 5 minutes.
3. Remove from heat and stir in the basil. Serve topped with pecorino cheese.

Nutrition: 420 Calories 13g fat 20g Protein

844. Roasted Feta with Kale and Lemon Yogurt

Preparation Time: 15 minutes
Cooking Time: 20 minutes
Serving: 4
Ingredients:
- 1 tablespoon extra-virgin olive oil
- 1 onion, julienned
- ¼ teaspoon kosher salt
- 1 teaspoon ground turmeric
- ½ teaspoon ground cumin
- ½ teaspoon ground coriander
- ¼ teaspoon freshly ground black pepper
- 1 bunch kale, stemmed and chopped
- 7-ounce block feta cheese
- ½ cup plain Greek yogurt
- 1 tablespoon lemon juice

Direction:
1. Preheat the oven to 400°F.
2. Cook olive oil in a huge ovenproof skillet or sauté pan over medium heat. Add the onion and salt; sauté until lightly golden brown, about 5 minutes. Add the turmeric, cumin, coriander, and black pepper; sauté for 30 seconds. Add the kale and sauté about 2 minutes. Add ½ cup water and continue to cook down the kale, about 3 minutes.
3. Remove from the heat and place the feta cheese slices on top of the kale mixture. Place in the oven and bake until the feta softens, 10 to 12 minutes.
4. In a small bowl, combine the yogurt and lemon juice.
5. Serve the kale and feta cheese topped with the lemon yogurt.

Nutrition: 210 Calories 14g fat 11g Protein

845. Roasted Eggplant and Chickpeas with Tomato Sauce

Preparation Time: 15 minutes
Cooking Time: 1 hour

Serving: 4
Ingredients:
- Olive oil cooking spray
- 1 large (about 1 pound) eggplant
- 1 teaspoon kosher salt, divided
- 1 tablespoon extra-virgin olive oil
- 3 garlic cloves, minced
- 1 (28-ounce) can no-salt-added crushed tomatoes
- ½ teaspoon honey
- ¼ teaspoon freshly ground black pepper
- 2 tablespoons fresh basil, chopped
- 1 (15-ounce) can no-salt-added or low-sodium chickpeas, drained and rinsed
- ¾ cup crumbled feta cheese
- 1 tablespoon fresh oregano, chopped

Direction:
1. Preheat the oven to 425°F. Prep two baking sheets with foil and lightly spray with olive oil cooking spray. Arrange the eggplant in a single layer and sprinkle with ½ teaspoon of the salt. Bake for 22 minutes.
2. Cook olive oil in a big saucepan over medium heat. Cook garlic and sauté for 30 seconds. Add the crushed tomatoes, honey, the remaining ½ teaspoon salt, and black pepper. Simmer about 20 minutes, until the sauce reduces a bit and thickens. Stir in the basil.
3. After removing the eggplant from the oven, reduce the oven temperature to 375°F. In a large rectangular or oval baking dish, ladle in the chickpeas and 1 cup sauce. Layer the eggplant slices on top, overlapping as necessary to cover the chickpeas. Drizzle remaining sauce on top of the eggplant. Sprinkle the feta cheese and oregano on top.
4. Cover the baking dish with foil and bake for 15 minutes. Take out foil and bake an additional 15 minutes.

Nutrition: 320 Calories 11g fat 14g Protein

846. Baked Falafel Sliders

Preparation Time: 10 minutes
Cooking Time: 30 minutes
Serving: 6
Ingredients
- Olive oil cooking spray
- 1 (15-ounce) can low-sodium chickpeas
- 1 onion, roughly chopped
- 2 garlic cloves, peeled
- 2 tablespoons fresh parsley, chopped
- 2 tablespoons whole-wheat flour
- ½ teaspoon ground coriander
- ½ teaspoon ground cumin
- ½ teaspoon baking powder
- ½ teaspoon kosher salt
- ¼ teaspoon freshly ground black pepper

Direction:

1. Preheat the oven to 350°F. Prep baking sheet with parchment paper or foil and lightly spray with olive oil cooking spray.
2. Using food processor, mix in chickpeas, onion, garlic, parsley, flour, coriander, cumin, baking powder, salt, and black pepper.
3. Make 6 slider patties, each with a heaping ¼ cup of mixture, and arrange on the prepared baking sheet. Bake it for 30 minutes

Nutrition: 90 Calories 1g fat 4g Protein

847. Portobello Caprese

Preparation Time: 15 minutes
Cooking Time: 30 minutes
Serving: 2
Ingredient:

- 1 tablespoon olive oil
- 1 cup cherry tomatoes
- 4 large fresh basil leaves, thinly sliced, divided
- 3 medium garlic cloves, minced
- 2 large portobello mushrooms, stems removed
- 4 pieces mini Mozzarella balls
- 1 tablespoon Parmesan cheese, grated

Direction:

1. Prep oven to 350°F (180°C). Grease a baking pan with olive oil.
2. Drizzle 1 tablespoon olive oil in a nonstick skillet, and heat over medium-high heat.
3. Add the tomatoes to the skillet, and sprinkle salt and black pepper to season. Prick some holes on the tomatoes for juice during the cooking. Put the lid on and cook the tomatoes for 10 minutes or until tender.
4. Reserve 2 teaspoons of basil and add the remaining basil and garlic to the skillet. Crush the tomatoes with a spatula, then cook for half a minute. Stir constantly during the cooking. Set aside.
5. Arrange the mushrooms in the baking pan, cap side down, and sprinkle with salt and black pepper to taste.
6. Spoon the tomato mixture and Mozzarella balls on the gill of the mushrooms, then scatter with Parmesan cheese to coat well.
7. Bake for 20 minutes
8. Remove the stuffed mushrooms from the oven and serve with basil on top.

Nutrition 285 calories 21.8g fat 14.3g protein

848. Mushroom and Cheese Stuffed Tomatoes

Preparation Time: 15 minutes
Cooking Time: 20 minutes
Serving: 4
Ingredients:

- 4 large ripe tomatoes
- 1 tablespoon olive oil
- ½ pound (454 g) white or cremini mushrooms
- 1 tablespoon fresh basil, chopped
- ½ cup yellow onion, diced
- 1 tablespoon fresh oregano, chopped
- 2 garlic cloves, minced
- ½ teaspoon salt
- ¼ teaspoon freshly ground black pepper
- 1 cup part-skim Mozzarella cheese, shredded
- 1 tablespoon Parmesan cheese, grated

Direction:

1. Set oven to 375°F (190°C).
2. Chop a ½-inch slice off the top of each tomato. Scoop the pulp into a bowl and leave ½-inch tomato shells. Spread the tomatoes on a baking sheet lined with aluminum foil.
3. Heat the olive oil in a nonstick skillet over medium heat.
4. Add the mushrooms, basil, onion, oregano, garlic, salt, and black pepper to the skillet and sauté for 5 minutes
5. Pour the mixture to the bowl of tomato pulp, then add the Mozzarella cheese and stir to combine well.
6. Spoon the mixture into each tomato shell, then top with a layer of Parmesan.
7. Bake for 15 minutes
8. Remove the stuffed tomatoes from the oven and serve warm.

Nutrition: 254 calories 14.7g fat 17.5g protein

849. Tabbouleh

Preparation Time: 15 minutes
Cooking Time: 5 minutes
Serving: 6
Ingredients:

- 4 tablespoons olive oil
- 4 cups riced cauliflower
- 3 garlic cloves
- ½ large cucumber
- ½ cup Italian parsley
- Juice of 1 lemon
- 2 tablespoons red onion
- ½ cup mint leaves, chopped
- ½ cup pitted Kalamata olives
- 1 cup cherry tomatoes
- 2 cups baby arugula
- 2 medium avocados

Direction:

1. Warm 2 tablespoons olive oil in a nonstick skillet over medium-high heat.
2. Add the rice cauliflower, garlic, salt, and black pepper to the skillet and sauté for 3 minutes or until fragrant. Transfer them to a large bowl.
3. Add the cucumber, parsley, lemon juice, red onion, mint, olives, and remaining olive oil to the bowl.

Toss to combine well. Reserve the bowl in the refrigerator for at least 30 minutes.

4. Remove the bowl from the refrigerator. Add the cherry tomatoes, arugula, avocado to the bowl. Sprinkle with salt and black pepper, and toss to combine well. Serve chilled.

Nutrition: 198 calories 17.5g fat 4.2g protein

850. Spicy Broccoli Rabe and Artichoke Hearts

Preparation Time: 5 minutes
Cooking Time: 15 minutes
Serving: 4
Ingredient:

- 3 tablespoons olive oil, divided
- 2 pounds fresh broccoli rabe
- 3 garlic cloves, finely minced
- 1 teaspoon red pepper flakes
- 1 teaspoon salt, plus more to taste
- 13.5 ounces artichoke hearts
- 1 tablespoon water
- 2 tablespoons red wine vinegar

Direction:

1. Warm 2 tablespoons olive oil in a nonstick skillet over medium-high skillet.
2. Add the broccoli, garlic, red pepper flakes, and salt to the skillet and sauté for 5 minutes or until the broccoli is soft.
3. Add the artichoke hearts to the skillet and sauté for 2 more minutes or until tender.
4. Add water to the skillet and turn down the heat to low. Put the lid on and simmer for 5 minutes.
5. Meanwhile, combine the vinegar and 1 tablespoon of olive oil in a bowl.
6. Drizzle the simmered broccoli and artichokes with oiled vinegar, and sprinkle with salt and black pepper. Toss to combine well before serving.

Nutrition: 272 calories 21.5g fat 11.2g protein

851. Shakshuka

Preparation Time: 10 minutes
Cooking Time: 25 minutes
Serving: 4
Ingredient:

- 5 tablespoons olive oil, divided
- 1 red bell pepper, finely diced
- ½ small yellow onion, finely diced
- 14 ounces crushed tomatoes, with juices
- 6 ounces frozen spinach
- 1 teaspoon smoked paprika
- 2 garlic cloves
- 2 teaspoons red pepper flakes
- 1 tablespoon capers
- 1 tablespoon water
- 6 large eggs

- ¼ teaspoon freshly ground black pepper
- ¾ cup feta or goat cheese
- ¼ cup fresh flat-leaf parsley

Direction:

1. Prep oven to 300°F (150°C).
2. Cook 2 tablespoons olive oil in an oven-safe skillet over medium-high heat.
3. Cook bell pepper and onion to the skillet for 6 minutes.
4. Add the tomatoes and juices, spinach, paprika, garlic, red pepper flakes, capers, water, and 2 tablespoons olive oil to the skillet. Stir and boil.
5. Put down the heat to low, then close to simmer for 5 minutes.
6. Crack the eggs over the sauce, and keep a little space between each egg, leave the egg intact and sprinkle with freshly ground black pepper.
7. Cook for another 8 minutes
8. Scatter the cheese over the eggs and sauce, and bake in the preheated oven for 5 minutes
9. Drizzle 1 tablespoon olive oil and spread the parsley on top before serving warm.

Nutrition: 335 calories 26.5g fat 16.8g protein

852. Spanakopita

Preparation Time: 15 minutes
Cooking Time: 50 minutes
Serving: 6
Ingredients:

- 6 tablespoons olive oil
- 1 small yellow onion
- 4 cups frozen chopped spinach
- 4 garlic cloves, minced
- ½ teaspoon salt
- ½ teaspoon freshly ground black pepper
- 4 large eggs, beaten
- 1 cup ricotta cheese
- ¾ cup feta cheese, crumbled
- ¼ cup pine nuts

Direction

1. Set oven to 375°F (190°C). Coat a baking dish with 2 tablespoons olive oil.
2. Heat 2 tablespoons olive oil in a nonstick skillet over medium-high heat.
3. Stir in onion to the skillet and sauté for 6 minutes or until translucent and tender.
4. Add the spinach, garlic, salt, and black pepper to the skillet and sauté for 5 minutes more. Keep aside
5. Combine the beaten eggs and ricotta cheese in a separate bowl, then pour them in to the bowl of spinach mixture. Stir to mix well.
6. Fill in mixture into the baking dish, and tilt the dish so the mixture coats the bottom evenly.
7. Bake for 20 minutes. Pull away baking dish from the oven, and spread the feta cheese and pine nuts on top, then drizzle with remaining 2 tablespoons olive oil.

8. Situate baking dish to the oven and bake for additional 15 minutes
9. Remove the dish from the oven. Allow the spanakopita to cool for a few minutes and slice to serve.

Nutrition: 340 calories 27.3g fat 18.2g protein

853. Tagine

Preparation Time: 20 minutes
Cooking Time: 1 hour
Serving: 6
Ingredients:
- ½ cup olive oil
- 6 celery stalks
- 2 medium yellow onions
- 1 teaspoon ground cumin
- ½ teaspoon ground cinnamon
- 1 teaspoon ginger powder
- 6 garlic cloves, minced
- ½ teaspoon paprika
- 1 teaspoon salt
- ¼ teaspoon freshly ground black pepper
- 2 cups low-sodium vegetable stock
- 2 medium zucchinis
- 2 cups cauliflower, cut into florets
- 1 medium eggplant
- 1 cup green olives
- 13.5 ounces artichoke hearts
- ½ cup chopped fresh cilantro leaves, for garnish
- ½ cup plain Greek yogurt, for garnish
- ½ cup chopped fresh flat-leaf parsley, for garnish

Direction:
1. Cook olive oil in a stockpot over medium-high heat.
2. Add the celery and onion to the pot and sauté for 6 minutes or until the celery is tender and the onion is translucent.
3. Add the cumin, cinnamon, ginger, garlic, paprika, salt, and black pepper to the pot and sauté for 2 minutes more until aromatic.
4. Pour the vegetable stock to the pot and bring to a boil.
5. Turn down the heat to low, and add the zucchini, cauliflower, and eggplant to the pot. Close to simmer for 30 minutes or until the vegetables are soft.
6. Then add the olives and artichoke hearts to the pot and simmer for 15 minutes more.
7. Pour them into a large serving bowl or a Tagine, then serve with cilantro, Greek yogurt, and parsley on top.

Nutrition 312 calories 21.2g fat 6.1g protein

854. Citrus Pistachios and Asparagus

Preparation Time: 10 minutes
Cooking Time: 10 minutes
Serving: 4
Ingredients:
- Zest and juice of 2 clementine
- Zest and juice of 1 lemon
- 1 tablespoon red wine vinegar
- 3 tablespoons extra-virgin olive oil
- 1 teaspoon salt
- ¼ teaspoon black pepper
- ½ cup pistachios, shelled
- 1-pound fresh asparagus
- 1 tablespoon water

Direction:
1. Combine the zest and juice of clementine and lemon, vinegar, 2 tablespoons of olive oil, ½ teaspoon of salt, and black pepper in a bowl. Stir to mix well. Set aside.
2. Toast the pistachios in a nonstick skillet over medium-high heat for 2 minutes or until golden brown. Transfer the roasted pistachios to a clean work surface, then chop roughly. Mix the pistachios with the citrus mixture. Set aside.
3. Heat the remaining olive oil in the nonstick skillet over medium-high heat.
4. Add the asparagus to the skillet and sauté for 2 minutes, then season with remaining salt.
5. Add the water to the skillet. Turn down the heat to low, and put the lid on. Simmer for 4 minutes until the asparagus is tender.
6. Remove the asparagus from the skillet to a large dish. Pour the citrus and pistachios mixture over the asparagus. Toss to coat well before serving.

Nutrition: 211 calories 17.5g fat 5.9g protein

855. Tomato and Parsley Stuffed Eggplant

Preparation Time: 25 minutes
Cooking Time: 2 hours
Serving: 6
Ingredients:
- ¼ cup extra-virgin olive oil
- 3 small eggplants, cut in half lengthwise
- 1 teaspoon sea salt
- ½ teaspoon freshly ground black pepper
- 1 large yellow onion, finely chopped
- 4 garlic cloves, minced
- 15 ounces diced tomatoes
- ¼ cup fresh flat-leaf parsley

Direction:
1. Brush insert of the slow cooker with 2 tablespoons of olive oil.
2. Cut some slits on the cut side of each eggplant half, keep a ¼-inch space between each slit.
3. Place the eggplant halves in the slow cooker, skin side down. Sprinkle with salt and black pepper.

4. Cook remaining olive oil in a nonstick skillet over medium-high heat.
5. Add the onion and garlic to the skillet and sauté for 3 minutes or until the onion is translucent.
6. Add the parsley and tomatoes with the juice to the skillet, and sprinkle with salt and black pepper. Sauté for 5 more minutes or until they are tender.
7. Divide and spoon the mixture in the skillet on the eggplant halves.
8. Close and cook on HIGH for 2 hours.
9. Transfer the eggplant to a plate, and allow to cool for a few minutes before serving.

Nutrition: 455 calories 13g fat 14g protein

856. Ratatouille

Preparation Time: 15 minutes
Cooking Time: 7 hours
Serving: 6
Ingredient:
- 3 tablespoons extra-virgin olive oil
- 1 large eggplant
- 2 large onions
- 4 small zucchinis
- 2 green bell peppers
- 6 large tomatoes
- 2 tablespoons fresh flat-leaf parsley
- 1 teaspoon dried basil
- 2 garlic cloves, minced
- 2 teaspoons sea salt
- ¼ teaspoon black pepper

Direction
1. Grease insert of the slow cooker with 2 tablespoons olive oil.
2. Arrange the vegetables slices, strips, and wedges alternately in the insert of the slow cooker.
3. Spread the parsley on top of the vegetables, and season with basil, garlic, salt, and black pepper. Drizzle with the remaining olive oil.
4. Cover on and cook on LOW for 7 hours until the vegetables are tender.
5. Transfer the vegetables on a plate and serve warm.

Nutrition: 265 calories 1.7g fat 8.3g protein

857. Gemista

Preparation time: 15 minutes
Cooking time: 4 hours
Serving: 4
Ingredients:
- 2 tablespoons extra-virgin olive oil
- 4 large bell peppers, any color
- ½ cup uncooked couscous
- 1 teaspoon oregano
- 1 garlic clove, minced
- 1 cup crumbled feta cheese
- 1 (15-ounce) can cannellini beans

- 4 green onions

Direction:
1. Brush insert of the slow cooker with 2 tablespoons olive oil.
2. Cut a ½-inch slice below the stem from the top of the bell pepper. Discard the stem only and chop the sliced top portion under the stem, and reserve in a bowl. Hollow the bell pepper with a spoon.
3. Mix remaining ingredients, except for the green parts of the green onion and lemon wedges, to the bowl of chopped bell pepper top. Stir to mix well.
4. Spoon the mixture in the hollowed bell pepper, and arrange the stuffed bell peppers in the slow cooker, then drizzle with more olive oil.
5. Close and cook at HIGH for 4 hours or until the bell peppers are soft.
6. Remove the bell peppers from the slow cooker and serve on a plate. Sprinkle with green parts of the green onions, and squeeze the lemon wedges on top before serving.

Nutrition: 246 calories 9g fat 11.1g protein

858. Stuffed Cabbage Rolls

Preparation Time: 15 minutes
Cooking Time: 2 hours
Serving: 4
Ingredients:
- 4 tablespoons olive oil
- 1 large head green cabbage
- 1 large yellow onion
- 3 ounces (85 g) feta cheese
- ½ cup dried currants
- 3 cups cooked pearl barley
- 2 tablespoons fresh flat-leaf parsley
- 2 tablespoons pine nuts, toasted
- ½ teaspoon sea salt
- ½ teaspoon black pepper
- 15 ounces (425 g) crushed tomatoes, with the juice
- ½ cup apple juice
- 1 tablespoon apple cider vinegar

Direction:
1. Rub insert of the slow cooker with 2 tablespoons olive oil.
2. Blanch the cabbage in a pot of water for 8 minutes. Remove it from the water, and allow to cool, then separate 16 leaves from the cabbage. Set aside.
3. Drizzle the remaining olive oil in a nonstick skillet, and heat over medium heat.
4. sauté onion for 6 minutes. Transfer the onion to a bowl.
5. Add the feta cheese, currants, barley, parsley, and pine nuts to the bowl of cooked onion, then sprinkle with ¼ teaspoon of salt and ¼ teaspoon of black pepper.
6. Arrange the cabbage leaves on a clean work surface. Spoon 1/3 cup of the mixture on the center of each leaf, then fold the edge of the leaf on the mixture

and roll it up. Place the cabbage rolls in the slow cooker, seam side down.

7. Combine the remaining ingredients in a separate bowl, then pour the mixture over the cabbage rolls.
8. Close and cook in HIGH for 2 hours.
9. Remove the cabbage rolls from the slow cooker and serve warm.

Nutrition: 383 calories 17g fat 11g protein

859. Brussels Sprouts with Balsamic Glaze

Preparation Time: 15 minutes
Cooking Time: 2 hours
Serving: 6
Ingredients
Balsamic glaze:
- 1 cup balsamic vinegar
- ¼ cup honey

Other:
- 2 tablespoons extra-virgin olive oil
- 2 pounds (907 g) Brussels sprouts
- 2 cups low-sodium vegetable soup
- 1 teaspoon sea salt
- Freshly ground black pepper, to taste
- ¼ cup Parmesan cheese, grated
- ¼ cup pine nuts, toasted

Direction:
1. Brush insert of the slow cooker with olive oil.
2. Make the balsamic glaze: Combine the balsamic vinegar and honey in a saucepan. Stir to mix well. Over medium-high heat, bring to a boil. Turn down the heat to low, then simmer for 20 minutes or until the glaze reduces in half and has a thick consistency.
3. Put the Brussels sprouts, vegetable soup, and ½ teaspoon of salt in the slow cooker, stir to combine.
4. Cover and cook at HIGH for 2 hours.
5. Transfer the Brussels sprouts to a plate, and sprinkle the remaining salt and black pepper to season. Pour in balsamic glaze over the Brussels sprouts, then serve with Parmesan and pine nuts.

Nutrition: 270 calories 11g fat 8.7g protein

860. Spinach Salad with Citrus Vinaigrette

Preparation Time: 10 minutes
Cooking Time: 0 minutes
Servings: 4
Ingredients:
Citrus Vinaigrette:
- ¼ cup extra-virgin olive oil
- 3 tablespoons balsamic vinegar
- ½ teaspoon fresh lemon zest
- ½ teaspoon salt

Salad:
- 1-pound (454 g) baby spinach

- 1 large ripe tomato
- 1 medium red onion

Direction:
1. Make the citrus vinaigrette: Stir together the olive oil, balsamic vinegar, lemon zest, and salt in a bowl until mixed well.
2. Make the salad: Place the baby spinach, tomato and onions in a separate salad bowl. Drizzle the citrus vinaigrette over the salad and gently toss until the vegetables are coated thoroughly.

Nutrition: 173 Calories 14g fat 4.1g protein

861. Kale Salad with Pistachio and Parmesan

Preparation Time: 20 minutes
Cooking Time: 0 minutes
Serving: 6
Ingredients:
- 6 cups raw kale
- ¼ cup extra-virgin olive oil
- 2 tablespoons lemon juice
- ½ teaspoon smoked paprika
- 2 cups chopped arugula
- 1/3 cup unsalted pistachios
- 6 tablespoons Parmesan cheese

Direction:
1. Put the kale, olive oil, lemon juice, and paprika in a large bowl. Using your hands to massage the sauce into the kale until coated completely. Allow the kale to marinate for about 10 minutes.
2. When ready to serve, add the arugula and pistachios into the bowl of kale. Toss well and divide the salad into six salad bowls. Serve sprinkled with 1 tablespoon shredded Parmesan cheese.

Nutrition: 106 Calories 9.2g fat 4.2g protein

862. Olive Citrus Sauce Cauliflower Steaks

Preparation Time: 15 minutes
Cooking Time: 30 minutes
Servings: 4
Ingredients:
- 1 or 2 large heads cauliflower
- 1/3 cup extra-virgin olive oil
- ¼ teaspoon kosher salt
- 1/8 teaspoon ground black pepper
- Juice of 1 orange
- Zest of 1 orange
- ¼ cup black olives, pitted and chopped
- 1 tablespoon Dijon or grainy mustard
- 1 tablespoon red wine vinegar
- ½ teaspoon ground coriander

Directions:

1. Preheat the oven to 400°F. Put parchment paper or foil into the baking sheet. Cut off the stem of the cauliflower so it will sit upright. Slice it vertically into four thick slabs. Situate cauliflower on the prepared baking sheet. Dash with the olive oil, salt, and black pepper. Bake for about 30 minutes.
2. In a medium bowl, stir the orange juice, orange zest, olives, mustard, vinegar, and coriander; mix well. Serve with the sauce.

Nutrition 265 Calories 21g Fat 4g Carbohydrates 5g Protein

863. <u>Pistachio Pesto</u>

Preparation Time: 10 minutes
Cooking Time: 10 minutes
Servings: 4
Ingredients:
- 8 ounces whole-wheat pasta
- 1 cup fresh mint
- ½ cup fresh basil
- 1/3 cup unsalted pistachios, shelled
- 1 garlic clove, peeled
- ½ teaspoon kosher salt
- Juice of ½ lime
- 1/3 cup extra-virgin olive oil

Directions:
1. Cook the pasta following the package directions. Drain, reserving ½ cup of the pasta water, and set aside. In a food processor, add the mint, basil, pistachios, garlic, salt, and lime juice. Process until the pistachios are coarsely ground. Pour in the olive oil in a slow, steady stream and process until incorporated.
2. In a large bowl, incorporate the pasta with the pistachio pesto. If a thinner, more saucy consistency is desired, add some of the reserved pasta water and toss well.

Nutrition 420 Calories 3g Fat 2g Carbohydrates 11g Protein

864. <u>Tomato Sauce Angel Hair Pasta</u>

Preparation Time: 10 minutes
Cooking Time: 20 minutes
Servings: 4
Ingredients:
- 8 ounces angel hair pasta
- 2 tablespoons extra-virgin olive oil
- 3 garlic cloves, minced
- 3 pints cherry tomatoes
- ½ teaspoon kosher salt
- ¼ teaspoon red pepper flakes
- ¾ cup fresh basil, chopped
- 1 tablespoon white balsamic vinegar (optional)
- ¼ cup grated Parmesan cheese (optional)

Directions:

1. Cook the pasta following the package directions. Drain and set aside.
2. Cook the olive oil in a skillet or large sauté pan over medium-high heat. Stir in the garlic and sauté for 30 seconds. Mix in the tomatoes, salt, and red pepper flakes and cook, stirring occasionally, until the tomatoes burst, about 15 minutes.
3. Take out from the heat and stir in the pasta and basil. Toss together well. (For out-of-season tomatoes, add the vinegar, if desired, and mix well.) Serve.

Nutrition 305 Calories 8g Fat 3g Carbohydrates 11g Protein

865. <u>Baked Tofu</u>

Preparation Time: 30 minutes
Cooking Time: 30 minutes
Servings: 4
Ingredients:
- 1 (16-ounce) package extra-firm tofu, cut into 1-inch cubes
- 2 tablespoons extra-virgin olive oil, divided
- 2 tablespoons lemon juice, divided
- 1 tablespoon low-sodium soy sauce
- 1 onion, diced
- ½ teaspoon kosher salt
- 2 garlic cloves, minced
- 1 (14-ounce) can artichoke hearts, drained
- 8 sun-dried tomato
- ¼ teaspoon freshly ground black pepper
- 1 tablespoon white wine vinegar
- Zest of 1 lemon
- ¼ cup fresh parsley, chopped

Directions:
1. Prepare the oven to 400°F. Position the foil or parchment paper into the baking sheet. In a bowl, combine the tofu, 1 tablespoon of the olive oil, 1 tablespoon of the lemon juice, and the soy sauce.
2. Set aside and marinate for 15 to 30 minutes. Arrange the tofu in a single layer on the prepared baking sheet and bake for 20 minutes, turning once, until light golden brown.
3. Cook the remaining 1 tablespoon olive oil in a large skillet or sauté pan over medium heat. Add the onion and salt; sauté until translucent, 5 to 6 minutes.
4. Mix in the garlic and sauté for 30 seconds. Then put the artichoke hearts, sun-dried tomatoes, and black pepper and sauté for 5 minutes. Add the white wine vinegar and the remaining 1 tablespoon lemon juice and deglaze the pan, scraping up any brown bits. Take the pan from the heat and put in the lemon zest and parsley. Gently mix in the baked tofu.

Nutrition 230 Calories 14g Fat 5g Carbohydrates 14g Protein

866. Oven-Baked Mediterranean Tempeh

Preparation Time: 25 minutes, plus 4 hours to marinate
Cooking Time: 35 minutes
Servings: 4
Ingredients:
For the Tempeh
- 12 ounces tempeh
- ¼ cup white wine
- 2 tablespoons extra-virgin olive oil
- 2 tablespoons lemon juice
- Zest of 1 lemon
- ¼ teaspoon kosher salt
- ¼ teaspoon freshly ground black pepper

For the Tomatoes and Garlic Sauce
- 1 tablespoon extra-virgin olive oil
- 1 onion, diced
- 3 garlic cloves, minced
- 1 (14.5-ounce) can no-salt-added crushed tomatoes
- 1 beefsteak tomato, diced
- 1 dried bay leaf
- 1 teaspoon white wine vinegar
- 1 teaspoon lemon juice
- 1 teaspoon dried oregano
- 1 teaspoon dried thyme
- ¾ teaspoon kosher salt
- ¼ cup basil, cut into ribbons

Directions:
To Make the Tempeh
1. Place the tempeh in a medium saucepan. Fill enough water to cover it by 1 to 2 inches. Bring to a boil over medium-high heat, cover, and lower heat to a simmer. Cook for 10 to 15 minutes. Remove the tempeh, pat dry, cool, and cut into 1-inch cubes.
2. Mix the white wine, olive oil, lemon juice, lemon zest, salt, and black pepper. Add the tempeh, cover the bowl, and put in the refrigerator for 4 hours, or up to overnight. Preheat the oven to 375°F. Place the marinated tempeh and the marinade in a baking dish and cook for 15 minutes.

To Make the Tomatoes and Garlic Sauce
3. Cook the olive oil in a large skillet over medium heat. Add the onion and sauté until transparent, 3 to 5 minutes. Mix in the garlic and sauté for 30 seconds. Add the crushed tomatoes, beefsteak tomato, bay leaf, vinegar, lemon juice, oregano, thyme, and salt. Mix well. Simmer for 15 minutes.
4. Add the baked tempeh to the tomato mixture and gently mix together. Garnish with the basil.

Nutrition 330 Calories 20g Fat 4g Carbohydrates 18g Protein

867. Oven-Roasted Portobello Mushrooms

Preparation Time: 30 minutes
Cooking Time: 30 minutes
Servings: 4
Ingredients:
- ¼ cup white wine vinegar
- 3 tablespoons extra-virgin olive oil, divided
- ½ teaspoon honey
- ¾ teaspoon kosher salt, divided
- ¼ teaspoon freshly ground black pepper
- 4 large portobello mushrooms, stems removed
- 1 red onion, julienned
- 2 garlic cloves, minced
- 1 (8-ounce) bunch kale, stemmed and chopped small
- ¼ teaspoon red pepper flakes
- ¼ cup grated Parmesan or Romano cheese

Directions:
1. Situate parchment paper or foil into the baking sheet. In a medium bowl, whisk together the vinegar, 1½ tablespoons of the olive oil, honey, ¼ teaspoon of the salt, and the black pepper. Lay the mushrooms on the baking sheet and pour the marinade over them. Marinate for 15 to 30 minutes.
2. Meanwhile, preheat the oven to 400°F. Bake the mushrooms for 20 minutes, turning over halfway through. Heat the remaining 1½ tablespoons olive oil in a large skillet or ovenproof sauté pan over medium-high heat. Add the onion and the remaining ½ teaspoon salt and sauté until golden brown, 5 to 6 minutes. Mix in the garlic and sauté for 30 seconds. Mix in the kale and red pepper flakes and sauté until the kale cooks down, about 5 minutes.
3. Remove the mushrooms from the oven and increase the temperature to broil. Carefully pour the liquid from the baking sheet into the pan with the kale mixture; mix well. Turn the mushrooms over so that the stem side is facing up. Spoon some of the kale mixture on top of each mushroom. Sprinkle 1 tablespoon Parmesan cheese on top of each. Broil until golden brown.

Nutrition 200 Calories 13g Fat 4g Carbohydrates 8g Protein

868. Tofu with Balsamic, Basil and Oregano

Preparation Time: 40 minutes
Cooking Time: 30 minutes
Servings: 4
Ingredients:
- ¼ cup extra-virgin olive oil
- ¼ cup balsamic vinegar
- 2 tablespoons low-sodium soy sauce
- 3 garlic cloves, grated

- 2 teaspoons pure maple syrup
- Zest of 1 lemon
- 1 teaspoon dried basil
- 1 teaspoon dried oregano
- ½ teaspoon dried thyme
- ½ teaspoon dried sage
- ¼ teaspoon kosher salt
- ¼ teaspoon freshly ground black pepper
- ¼ teaspoon red pepper flakes (optional)
- 1 (16-ounce) block extra firm tofu

Directions:
1. In a bowl or gallon zip-top bag, mix together the olive oil, vinegar, soy sauce, garlic, maple syrup, lemon zest, basil, oregano, thyme, sage, salt, black pepper, and red pepper flakes, if desired. Add the tofu and mix gently. Put in the refrigerator and marinate for 30 minutes, or up to overnight if you desire.
2. Prepare the oven to 425°F. Place parchment paper or foil into the baking sheet. Arrange the marinated tofu in a single layer on the prepared baking sheet. Bake for 20 to 30 minutes, flip over halfway through, until slightly crispy.

Nutrition 225 Calories 16g Fat 2g Carbohydrates 13g Protein

869. Zucchini Filled with Ricotta, Basil, and Pistachio

Preparation Time: 15 minutes
Cooking Time: 25 minutes
Servings: 4

Ingredients:
- 2 medium zucchinis, halved lengthwise
- 1 tablespoon extra-virgin olive oil
- 1 onion, diced
- 1 teaspoon kosher salt
- 2 garlic cloves, minced
- ¾ cup ricotta cheese
- ¼ cup unsalted pistachios, shelled and chopped
- ¼ cup fresh basil, chopped
- 1 large egg, beaten
- ¼ teaspoon freshly ground black pepper

Directions:
1. Ready the oven to 425°F. Situate parchment paper or foil into the baking sheet. Scoop out the seeds/pulp from the zucchini, leaving ¼-inch flesh around the edges. Situate the pulp to a cutting board and chop off the pulp.
2. Cook the olive oil in a sauté pan over medium heat. Add the onion, pulp, and salt and sauté about 5 minutes. Add the garlic and sauté 30 seconds. Mix the ricotta cheese, pistachios, basil, egg, and black pepper. Add the onion mixture and mix together well.

3. Place the 4 zucchini halves on the prepared baking sheet. Spread the zucchini halves with the ricotta mixture. Bake until golden brown.

Nutrition 200 Calories 12g Fat 3g Carbohydrates 11g Protein

870. Roasted Tomatoes and Mushrooms Farro

Preparation Time: 20 minutes
Cooking Time: 1 hour
Servings: 4

Ingredients:
For the Tomatoes
- 2 pints cherry tomatoes
- 1 teaspoon extra-virgin olive oil
- ¼ teaspoon kosher salt
- For the Farro
- 3 to 4 cups water
- ½ cup farro
- ¼ teaspoon kosher salt

For the Mushrooms
- 2 tablespoons extra-virgin olive oil
- 1 onion, julienned
- ½ teaspoon kosher salt
- ¼ teaspoon freshly ground black pepper
- 10 ounces baby bell mushrooms, stemmed and sliced thin
- ½ cup no-salt-added vegetable stock
- 1 (15-ounce) can low-sodium cannellini beans, drained and rinsed
- 1 cup baby spinach
- 2 tablespoons fresh basil, cut into ribbons
- ¼ cup pine nuts, toasted
- Aged balsamic vinegar (optional)

Directions:
To Make the Tomatoes
1. Preheat the oven to 400°F. Put parchment paper or foil into the baking sheet. Mix the tomatoes, olive oil, and salt together on the baking sheet and roast for 30 minutes.

To Make the Farro
2. Bring the water, farro, and salt to a boil in a medium saucepan or pot over high heat. Allow to simmer, and cook for 30 minutes, or until the farro is al dente. Drain and set aside.

To Make the Mushrooms
3. Cook the olive oil in a large skillet or sauté pan over medium-low heat. Add the onions, salt, and black pepper and sauté until golden brown and starting to caramelize, about 15 minutes. Stir in the mushrooms, increase the heat to medium, and sauté until the liquid has evaporated and the mushrooms brown, about 10 minutes. Stir in the vegetable stock and deglaze the pan, scraping up any brown bits, and reduce the liquid for about 5 minutes. Add the beans and warm through, about 3 minutes.

4. Remove and stir in the spinach, basil, pine nuts, roasted tomatoes, and farro. Dash with balsamic vinegar, if desired.

Nutrition 375 Calories 15g Fat 10g Carbohydrates 14g Protein

871. Baked Orzo with Cheese and Eggplant

Preparation Time: 20 minutes
Cooking Time: 1 hour
Servings: 4
Ingredients:

- 2 tablespoons extra-virgin olive oil
- 1 large (1-pound) eggplant, diced small
- 2 carrots, peeled and diced small
- 2 celery stalks, diced small
- 1 onion, diced small
- ½ teaspoon kosher salt
- 3 garlic cloves, minced
- ¼ teaspoon freshly ground black pepper
- 1 cup whole-wheat orzo
- 1 teaspoon no-salt-added tomato paste
- 1½ cups no-salt-added vegetable stock
- 1 cup Swiss chard, stemmed and chopped small
- 2 tablespoons fresh oregano, chopped
- Zest of 1 lemon
- 4 ounces mozzarella cheese, diced small
- ¼ cup grated Parmesan cheese
- 2 tomatoes, sliced ½-inch-thick

Directions:
1. Preheat the oven to 400°F. Cook the olive oil in a large oven-safe sauté pan over medium heat. Add the eggplant, carrots, celery, onion, and salt and sauté about 10 minutes. Add the garlic and black pepper and sauté about 30 seconds. Add the orzo and tomato paste and sauté 1 minute. Mix in the vegetable stock and deglaze the pan, scraping up the brown bits. Add the Swiss chard, oregano, and lemon zest and stir until the chard wilts.
2. Pull out and put in the mozzarella cheese. Smooth the top of the orzo mixture flat. Sprinkle the Parmesan cheese over the top. Spread the tomatoes in a single layer on top of the Parmesan cheese. Bake for 45 minutes.

Nutrition 470 Calories 17g Fat 7g Carbohydrates 18g Protein

872. Tomato Barley Risotto

Preparation Time: 20 minutes
Cooking Time: 45 minutes
Servings: 4
Ingredients:

- 2 tablespoons extra-virgin olive oil
- 2 celery stalks, diced
- ½ cup shallots, diced

- 4 garlic cloves, minced
- 3 cups no-salt-added vegetable stock
- 1 (14.5-ounce) can no-salt-added diced tomatoes
- 1 (14.5-ounce) can no-salt-added crushed tomatoes
- 1 cup pearl barley
- Zest of 1 lemon
- 1 teaspoon kosher salt
- ½ teaspoon smoked paprika
- ¼ teaspoon red pepper flakes
- ¼ teaspoon freshly ground black pepper
- 4 thyme sprigs
- 1 dried bay leaf
- 2 cups baby spinach
- ½ cup crumbled feta cheese
- 1 tablespoon fresh oregano, chopped
- 1 tablespoon fennel seeds, toasted (optional)

Directions:
1. Cook the olive oil in a large saucepan over medium heat. Add the celery and shallots and sauté, about 4 to 5 minutes. Add the garlic and sauté 30 seconds. Add the vegetable stock, diced tomatoes, crushed tomatoes, barley, lemon zest, salt, paprika, red pepper flakes, black pepper, thyme, and the bay leaf, and mix well. Let it boil, then lower to low, and simmer. Cook, stirring occasionally, for 40 minutes.
2. Remove the bay leaf and thyme sprigs. Stir in the spinach. In a small bowl, combine the feta, oregano, and fennel seeds. Serve the barley risotto in bowls topped with the feta mixture.

Nutrition 375 Calories 12g Fat 13g Carbohydrates 11g Protein

873. Spicy Pomodoro Chickpeas and Kale

Preparation Time: 10 minutes
Cooking Time: 35 minutes
Servings: 4
Ingredients:

- 2 tablespoons extra-virgin olive oil
- 4 garlic cloves, sliced
- 1 teaspoon red pepper flakes
- 1 (28-ounce) can no-salt-added crushed tomatoes
- 1 teaspoon kosher salt
- ½ teaspoon honey
- 1 bunch kale, stemmed and chopped
- 2 (15-ounce) cans low-sodium chickpeas, drained and rinsed
- ¼ cup fresh basil, chopped
- ¼ cup grated pecorino Romano cheese

Directions:
1. Cook the olive oil in a sauté pan over medium heat. Stir in the garlic and red pepper flakes and sauté until the garlic is a light golden brown, about 2 minutes. Add the tomatoes, salt, and honey and mix well. Switch heat to low and simmer for 23 minutes.

2. Add the kale and mix in well. Cook about 5 minutes. Add the chickpeas and simmer about 5 minutes. Remove from heat and stir in the basil. Serve topped with pecorino cheese.

Nutrition 420 Calories 13g Fat 12g Carbohydrates 20g Protein

874. Cheesy and Citrusy Roasted Kale

Preparation Time: 15 minutes
Cooking Time: 20 minutes
Servings: 4
Ingredients:
- 1 tablespoon extra-virgin olive oil
- 1 onion, julienned
- ¼ teaspoon kosher salt
- 1 teaspoon ground turmeric
- ½ teaspoon ground cumin
- ½ teaspoon ground coriander
- ¼ teaspoon freshly ground black pepper
- 1 bunch kale, stemmed and chopped
- 7-ounce block feta cheese, cut into ¼-inch-thick slices
- ½ cup plain Greek yogurt
- 1 tablespoon lemon juice

Directions:
1. Preheat the oven to 400°F. Fry the olive oil in a large ovenproof skillet or sauté pan over medium heat. Add the onion and salt; sauté until lightly golden brown, about 5 minutes.
2. Add the turmeric, cumin, coriander, and black pepper; sauté for 30 seconds. Add the kale and sauté about 2 minutes. Add ½ cup water and continue to cook down the kale, about 3 minutes.
3. Remove from the heat and place the feta cheese slices on top of the kale mixture. Introduce in the oven and bake until the feta softens, 10 to 12 minutes. In a small bowl, combine the yogurt and lemon juice. Serve the kale and feta cheese topped with the lemon yogurt.

Nutrition 210 Calories 14g Fat 2g Carbohydrates 11g Protein

875. Roasted Eggplant and Chickpeas in Tomato Sauce

Preparation Time: 15 minutes
Cooking Time: 1 hour
Servings: 4
Ingredients:
- Olive oil cooking spray
- 1 large (about 1 pound) eggplant, sliced into ¼-inch-thick rounds
- 1 teaspoon kosher salt, divided
- 1 tablespoon extra-virgin olive oil
- 3 garlic cloves, minced
- 1 (28-ounce) can no-salt-added crushed tomatoes
- ½ teaspoon honey
- ¼ teaspoon freshly ground black pepper
- 2 tablespoons fresh basil, chopped
- 1 (15-ounce) can no-salt-added or low-sodium chickpeas, drained and rinsed
- ¾ cup crumbled feta cheese
- 1 tablespoon fresh oregano, chopped

Directions:
1. Preheat the oven to 425°F. Grease and line two baking sheets with foil and lightly spray with olive oil cooking spray. Spread the eggplant in a single layer and sprinkle with ½ teaspoon of the salt. Bake for 23 minutes.
2. Meanwhile, heat up the olive oil in a large saucepan over medium heat. Mix in the garlic and sauté for 30 seconds. Add the crushed tomatoes, honey, the remaining ½ teaspoon salt, and black pepper. Simmer about 20 minutes, until the sauce reduces a bit and thickens. Stir in the basil.
3. After removing the eggplant from the oven, reduce the oven temperature to 375°F. In a large rectangular or oval baking dish, ladle in the chickpeas and 1 cup sauce. Layer the eggplant slices on top, overlapping as necessary to cover the chickpeas. Lay the remaining sauce on top of the eggplant. Sprinkle the feta cheese and oregano on top.
4. Wrap the baking dish with foil and bake for 15 minutes. Pull out the foil and bake an additional 15 minutes.

Nutrition 320 Calories 11g Fat 12g Carbohydrates 14g Protein

876. Oven-Baked Falafel Sliders

Preparation Time: 10 minutes
Cooking Time: 30 minutes
Servings: 6
Ingredients:
- Olive oil cooking spray
- 1 (15-ounce) can low-sodium chickpeas, drained and rinsed
- 1 onion, roughly chopped
- 2 garlic cloves, peeled
- 2 tablespoons fresh parsley, chopped
- 2 tablespoons whole-wheat flour
- ½ teaspoon ground coriander
- ½ teaspoon ground cumin
- ½ teaspoon baking powder
- ½ teaspoon kosher salt
- ¼ teaspoon freshly ground black pepper

Directions:
1. Preheat the oven to 350°F. Put parchment paper or foil and lightly spray with olive oil cooking spray in the baking sheet.
2. In a food processor, mix in the chickpeas, onion,

garlic, parsley, flour, coriander, cumin, baking powder, salt, and black pepper. Blend until smooth.

3. Make 6 slider patties, each with a heaping ¼ cup of mixture, and arrange on the prepared baking sheet. Bake for 30 minutes. Serve.

Nutrition 90 Calories 1g Fat 3g Carbohydrates 4g Protein

877. Mushroom Caprese

Preparation Time: 15 minutes
Cooking Time: 30 minutes
Servings: 2
Ingredients:
- 1 tablespoon olive oil
- 1 cup cherry tomatoes
- Salt and black pepper, to taste
- 4 large fresh basil leaves, thinly sliced, divided
- 3 medium garlic cloves, minced
- 2 large portobello mushrooms, stems removed
- 4 pieces mini Mozzarella balls
- 1 tablespoon Parmesan cheese, grated

Directions:
1. Prepare the oven to 350°F (180°C). Grease a baking pan with olive oil. Drizzle 1 tablespoon olive oil in a nonstick skillet, and heat over medium-high heat. Add the tomatoes to the skillet, and sprinkle salt and black pepper to season. Prick some holes on the tomatoes for juice during the cooking. Put the lid on and cook the tomatoes for 10 minutes or until tender.
2. Reserve 2 teaspoons of basil and add the remaining basil and garlic to the skillet. Crush the tomatoes with a spatula, then cook for half a minute. Stir constantly during the cooking. Set aside. Arrange the mushrooms in the baking pan, cap side down, and sprinkle with salt and black pepper to taste.
3. Spoon the tomato mixture and Mozzarella balls on the gill of the mushrooms, then scatter with Parmesan cheese to coat well. Bake until the mushrooms are fork-tender and the cheeses are browned. Pull out the stuffed mushrooms from the oven and serve with basil on top.

Nutrition 285 Calories 21.8g Fat 2.1g Carbohydrates 14.3g Protein

878. Tomatoes Filled with Cremini and Cheese

Preparation Time: 15 minutes
Cooking Time: 20 minutes
Servings: 4
Ingredients:
- 4 large ripe tomatoes
- 1 tablespoon olive oil
- ½ pound (454 g) white or cremini mushrooms, sliced
- 1 tablespoon fresh basil, chopped
- ½ cup yellow onion, diced
- 1 tablespoon fresh oregano, chopped
- 2 garlic cloves, minced
- ½ teaspoon salt
- ¼ teaspoon freshly ground black pepper
- 1 cup part-skim Mozzarella cheese, shredded
- 1 tablespoon Parmesan cheese, grated

Directions:
1. Ready the oven to 375°F (190°C). Cut a ½-inch slice off the top of each tomato. Scoop the pulp into a bowl and leave ½-inch tomato shells. Spread tomatoes on a baking sheet lined with aluminum foil. Heat up the olive oil in a nonstick skillet over medium heat.
2. Add the mushrooms, basil, onion, oregano, garlic, salt, and black pepper to the skillet and sauté for 5 minutes.
3. Pour the mixture to the bowl of tomato pulp, then add the Mozzarella cheese and stir to combine well. Spoon the mixture into each tomato shell, then top with a layer of Parmesan.
4. Bake in the prepared oven for 15 minutes. Pull out the stuffed tomatoes from the oven and serve warm.

Nutrition 254 Calories 14.7g Fat 5.2g Carbohydrates 17.5g Protein

879. Tabouli Salad

Preparation Time: 15 minutes
Cooking Time: 5 minutes
Servings: 6
Ingredients:
- 4 tablespoons olive oil, divided
- 4 cups riced cauliflower
- 3 garlic cloves, finely minced
- Salt and black pepper, to taste
- ½ large cucumber, peeled, seeded, and chopped
- ½ cup Italian parsley, chopped
- Juice of 1 lemon
- 2 tablespoons minced red onion
- ½ cup mint leaves, chopped
- ½ cup pitted Kalamata olives, chopped
- 1 cup cherry tomatoes, quartered
- 2 cups baby arugula or spinach leaves
- 2 medium avocados, peeled, pitted, and diced

Directions:
1. Warm 2 tablespoons olive oil in a nonstick skillet over medium-high heat. Add the rice cauliflower, garlic, salt, and black pepper to the skillet and sauté for 3 minutes or until fragrant. Transfer them to a large bowl.
2. Add the cucumber, parsley, lemon juice, red onion, mint, olives, and remaining olive oil to the bowl. Toss to combine well. Reserve the bowl in the refrigerator for at least 30 minutes.

3. Remove the bowl from the refrigerator. Add the cherry tomatoes, arugula, avocado to the bowl. Season well, and toss to combine well. Serve chilled.

Nutrition 198 Calories 17.5g Fat 6.2g Carbohydrates 4.2g Protein

880. Spicy Broccoli Rabe And Artichoke Hearts

Preparation Time: 5 minutes
Cooking Time: 15 minutes
Servings: 4
Ingredients:
- 3 tablespoons olive oil, divided
- 2 pounds (907 g) fresh broccoli rabe
- 3 garlic cloves, finely minced
- 1 teaspoon red pepper flakes
- 1 teaspoon salt, plus more to taste
- 13.5 ounces (383 g) artichoke hearts
- 1 tablespoon water
- 2 tablespoons red wine vinegar
- Freshly ground black pepper, to taste

Directions:
1. Warm 2 tablespoons olive oil in a nonstick skillet over medium-high skillet. Add the broccoli, garlic, red pepper flakes, and salt to the skillet, sauté for 5 minutes or until the broccoli is soft.
2. Put the artichoke hearts to the skillet and sauté for 2 more minutes or until tender. Add water to the skillet and turn down the heat to low. Put the lid on and simmer for 5 minutes. Meanwhile, combine the vinegar and 1 tablespoon of olive oil in a bowl.
3. Drizzle the simmered broccoli and artichokes with oiled vinegar, and sprinkle with salt and black pepper. Toss to combine well before serving.

Nutrition 272 Calories 21.5g Fat 9.8g Carbohydrates 11.2g Protein

881. Poached Egg in Tomato Sauce

Preparation Time: 10 minutes
Cooking Time: 25 minutes
Servings: 4
Ingredients:
- 5 tablespoons olive oil, divided
- 1 red bell pepper, finely diced
- ½ small yellow onion, finely diced
- 14 ounces (397 g) crushed tomatoes, with juices
- 6 ounces (170 g) frozen spinach, thawed and drained of excess liquid
- 1 teaspoon smoked paprika
- 2 garlic cloves, finely minced
- 2 teaspoons red pepper flakes
- 1 tablespoon capers, roughly chopped
- 1 tablespoon water
- 6 large eggs
- ¼ teaspoon freshly ground black pepper
- ¾ cup feta or goat cheese, crumbled
- ¼ cup fresh flat-leaf parsley or cilantro, chopped

Directions:
1. Ready the oven to 300ºF (150ºC). Heat 2 tablespoons olive oil in an oven-safe skillet over medium-high heat. Sauté the bell pepper and onion to the skillet until the onion is translucent and the bell pepper is soft.
2. Add the tomatoes and juices, spinach, paprika, garlic, red pepper flakes, capers, water, and 2 tablespoons olive oil to the skillet. Stir well and bring to a boil. Set down the heat to low, then put the lid on and simmer for 5 minutes.
3. Crack the eggs over the sauce, and keep a little space between each egg, leave the egg intact and sprinkle with freshly ground black pepper. Cook until the eggs reach the right doneness.
4. Scatter the cheese over the eggs and sauce, and bake in the preheated oven for 5 minutes or until the cheese is frothy and golden brown. Drizzle with the remaining 1 tablespoon olive oil and spread the parsley on top before serving warm.

Nutrition 335 Calories 26.5g Fat 5g Carbohydrates 16.8g Protein

882. Greek Spinach Pie

Preparation Time: 15 minutes
Cooking Time: 50 minutes
Serving: 6
Ingredients:
- 6 tablespoons olive oil, divided
- 1 small yellow onion, diced
- 4 cups frozen chopped spinach
- 4 garlic cloves, minced
- ½ teaspoon salt
- ½ teaspoon freshly ground black pepper
- 4 large eggs, beaten
- 1 cup ricotta cheese
- ¾ cup feta cheese, crumbled
- ¼ cup pine nuts

Directions:
1. Rub baking dish with 2 tablespoons olive oil. Organize the oven at 375 degrees F. Heat 2 tablespoons olive oil in a nonstick skillet over medium-high heat. Mix in the onion to the skillet and sauté for 6 minutes or until translucent and tender.
2. Add the spinach, garlic, salt, and black pepper to the skillet and sauté for 5 minutes more. Place them to a bowl and set aside. Combine the beaten eggs and ricotta cheese in a separate bowl, then pour them in to the bowl of spinach mixture. Stir to mix well.
3. Fill the mixture into the baking dish, and tilt the dish so the mixture coats the bottom evenly. Bake until it begins to set. Take out the baking dish from

the oven then spread the feta cheese and pine nuts on top, then dash with remaining 2 tablespoons olive oil.

4. Situate baking dish to the oven and bake for another 15 minutes or until the top is golden brown. Remove the dish from the oven. Allow the spanakopita to cool for a few minutes and slice to serve.

Nutrition 340 Calories 27.3g Fat 10.1g Carbohydrates 18.2g Protein

883. Vegetable Tagine

Preparation Time: 20 minutes
Cooking Time: 1 hour
Servings: 6
Ingredients:
- ½ cup olive oil
- 6 celery stalks, sliced into ¼-inch crescents
- 2 medium yellow onions, sliced
- 1 teaspoon ground cumin
- ½ teaspoon ground cinnamon
- 1 teaspoon ginger powder
- 6 garlic cloves, minced
- ½ teaspoon paprika
- 1 teaspoon salt
- ¼ teaspoon freshly ground black pepper
- 2 cups low-sodium vegetable stock
- 2 medium zucchinis, cut into ½-inch-thick semicircles
- 2 cups cauliflower, cut into florets
- 1 medium eggplant, cut into 1-inch cubes
- 1 cup green olives, halved and pitted
- 13.5 ounces (383 g) artichoke hearts, drained and quartered
- ½ cup chopped fresh cilantro leaves, for garnish
- ½ cup plain Greek yogurt, for garnish
- ½ cup chopped fresh flat-leaf parsley, for garnish

Directions:
1. Cook the olive oil in a stockpot over medium-high heat. Add the celery and onion to the pot and sauté for 6 minutes. Put the cumin, cinnamon, ginger, garlic, paprika, salt, and black pepper to the pot and sauté for 2 minutes more until aromatic.
2. Pour the vegetable stock to the pot and bring to a boil. Turn down the heat to low, and add the zucchini, cauliflower, and eggplant to the pot. Cover and simmer for 30 minutes or until the vegetables are soft. Then add the olives and artichoke hearts to the pot and simmer for 15 minutes more. Fill them into a large serving bowl or a Tagine, then serve with cilantro, Greek yogurt, and parsley on top.

Nutrition 312 Calories 21.2g Fat 9.2g Carbohydrates 6.1g Protein

884. Tangy Pistachios Asparagus

Preparation Time: 10 minutes
Cooking Time: 10 minutes
Servings: 4
Ingredients:
- Zest and juice of 2 clementine or 1 orange
- Zest and juice of 1 lemon
- 1 tablespoon red wine vinegar
- 3 tablespoons extra-virgin olive oil, divided
- 1 teaspoon salt, divided
- ¼ teaspoon freshly ground black pepper
- ½ cup pistachios, shelled
- 1 pound (454 g) fresh asparagus, trimmed
- 1 tablespoon water

Directions:
1. Combine the zest and juice of clementine and lemon, vinegar, 2 tablespoons of olive oil, ½ teaspoon of salt, and black pepper. Stir to mix well. Set aside.
2. Toast the pistachios in a nonstick skillet over medium-high heat for 2 minutes or until golden brown. Transfer the roasted pistachios to a clean work surface, then chop roughly. Mix the pistachios with the citrus mixture. Set aside.
3. Heat the remaining olive oil in the nonstick skillet over medium-high heat. Add the asparagus to the skillet and sauté for 2 minutes, then season with remaining salt. Add the water to the skillet. Put down the heat to low, and put the lid on. Simmer for 4 minutes until the asparagus is tender.
4. Remove the asparagus from the skillet to a large dish. Pour the citrus and pistachios mixture over the asparagus. Toss to coat well before serving.

Nutrition 211 Calories 17.5g Fat 3.8g Carbohydrates 5.9g Protein

885. Eggplant Filled with Tomato and Parsley

Preparation Time: 15 minutes
Cooking Time: 2 hours and 10 minutes
Servings: 6
Ingredients:
- ¼ cup extra-virgin olive oil
- 3 small eggplants, cut in half lengthwise
- 1 teaspoon sea salt
- ½ teaspoon freshly ground black pepper
- 1 large yellow onion, finely chopped
- 4 garlic cloves, minced
- 15 ounces (425 g) diced tomatoes, with the juice
- ¼ cup fresh flat-leaf parsley, finely chopped

Directions:
1. Put the insert of the slow cooker with 2 tablespoons of olive oil. Cut some slits on the cut side of each eggplant half, keep a ¼-inch space between each

slit. Place the eggplant halves in the slow cooker, skin side down. Sprinkle with salt and black pepper.

2. Warm up the remaining olive oil in a nonstick skillet over medium-high heat. Add the onion and garlic to the skillet and sauté for 3 minutes or until the onion is translucent.

3. Add the parsley and tomatoes with the juice to the skillet, and sprinkle with salt and black pepper. Sauté for 5 more minutes or until they are tender. Divide and spoon the mixture in the skillet on the eggplant halves.

4. Situate the slow cooker lid on and cook on HIGH for 2 hours until the eggplant is soft. Transfer the eggplant to a plate, and allow to cool for a few minutes before serving.

Nutrition 455 Calories 13g Fat 14g Carbohydrates 14g Protein

886. Stewed Vegetable

Preparation Time: 15 minutes
Cooking Time: 7 hours
Servings: 6
Ingredients:
- 3 tablespoons extra-virgin olive oil
- 1 large eggplant, unpeeled, sliced
- 2 large onions, sliced
- 4 small zucchinis, sliced
- 2 green bell peppers
- 6 large tomatoes, cut in ½-inch wedges
- 2 tablespoons fresh flat-leaf parsley, chopped
- 1 teaspoon dried basil
- 2 garlic cloves, minced
- 2 teaspoons sea salt
- ¼ teaspoon freshly ground black pepper

Direction:
1. Fill the insert of the slow cooker with 2 tablespoons olive oil. Arrange the vegetables slices, strips, and wedges alternately in the insert of the slow cooker.

2. Spread the parsley on top of the vegetables, and season with basil, garlic, salt, and black pepper. Drizzle with the remaining olive oil. Close and cook on LOW for 7 hours until the vegetables are tender. Transfer the vegetables on a plate and serve warm.

Nutrition 265 Calories 1.7g Fat 13.7g Carbohydrates 8.3g Protein

887. Stuffed Peppers

Preparation Time: 15 minutes
Cooking Time: 4 hours
Servings: 4
Ingredients:
- 2 tablespoons extra-virgin olive oil
- 4 large bell peppers, any color
- ½ cup uncooked couscous
- 1 teaspoon oregano

- 1 garlic clove, minced
- 1 cup crumbled feta cheese
- 1 (15-ounce / 425-g) can cannellini beans, rinsed and drained
- Salt and pepper, to taste
- 1 lemon wedges
- 4 green onions

Direction:
1. Cut a ½-inch slice below the stem from the top of the bell pepper. Discard the stem only and chop the sliced top portion under the stem, and reserve in a bowl. Hollow the bell pepper with a spoon. Grease the slow cooker with oil.

2. Incorporate the remaining ingredients, except for the green parts of the green onion and lemon wedges, to the bowl of chopped bell pepper top. Stir to mix well. Spoon the mixture in the hollowed bell pepper, and arrange the stuffed bell peppers in the slow cooker, then drizzle with more olive oil.

3. Seal the slow cooker lid on and cook on HIGH for 4 hours or until the bell peppers are soft.

4. Remove the bell peppers from the slow cooker and serve on a plate. Sprinkle with green parts of the green onions, and squeeze the lemon wedges on top before serving.

Nutrition 246 Calories 9g Fat 6.5g Carbohydrates 11.1g Protein

888. Cabbage-Filled Rolls

Preparation Time: 15 minutes
Cooking Time: 2 hours
Servings: 4
Ingredients:
- 4 tablespoons olive oil, divided
- 1 large head green cabbage, cored
- 1 large yellow onion, chopped
- 3 ounces (85 g) feta cheese, crumbled
- ½ cup dried currants
- 3 cups cooked pearl barley
- 2 tablespoons fresh flat-leaf parsley, chopped
- 2 tablespoons pine nuts, toasted
- ½ teaspoon sea salt
- ½ teaspoon black pepper
- 15 ounces (425 g) crushed tomatoes, with the juice
- 1 tablespoon apple cider vinegar
- ½ cup apple juice

Directions:
1. Brush off the insert of the slow cooker with 2 tablespoons olive oil. Blanch the cabbage in a pot of water for 8 minutes. Take it from the water, and set aside, then separate 16 leaves from the cabbage. Set aside.

2. Drizzle the remaining olive oil in a nonstick skillet, and heat over medium heat. Stir in the onion to the skillet and cook until the onion and bell pepper is tender. Transfer the onion to a bowl.

3. Add the feta cheese, currants, barley, parsley, and pine nuts to the bowl of cooked onion, then sprinkle with ¼ teaspoon of salt and ¼ teaspoon of black pepper.
4. Arrange the cabbage leaves on a clean work surface. Scoop 1/3 cup of the mixture on the center of each leaf, then fold the edge onto the mixture and roll it up. Place the cabbage rolls in the slow cooker, seam side down.
5. Incorporate the remaining ingredients in a separate bowl, then pour the mixture over the cabbage rolls. Seal slow cooker lid on and cook on HIGH for 2 hours. Remove the cabbage rolls from the slow cooker and serve warm.

Nutrition 383 Calories 14.7g Fat 12.9g Carbohydrates 10.7g Protein

889. Balsamic Glaze Brussels Sprouts

Preparation Time: 15 minutes
Cooking Time: 2 hours
Servings: 6
Ingredients:
- 1 cup balsamic vinegar
- ¼ cup honey
- 2 tablespoons extra-virgin olive oil
- 2 pounds (907 g) Brussels sprouts, trimmed and halved
- 2 cups low-sodium vegetable soup
- 1 teaspoon sea salt
- Freshly ground black pepper, to taste
- ¼ cup Parmesan cheese, grated
- ¼ cup pine nuts

Directions:
1. Make the balsamic glaze: Combine the balsamic vinegar and honey in a saucepan. Stir to mix well. Over medium-high heat, bring to a boil. Set down the heat to low, then simmer for 20 minutes or until the glaze reduces in half and has a thick consistency. Impose some olive oil inside the insert of the slow cooker.
2. Put the Brussels sprouts, vegetable soup, and ½ teaspoon of salt in the slow cooker, stir to combine. Seal the slow cooker lid on and cook on HIGH for 2 hours until the Brussels sprouts are soft.
3. Put the Brussels sprouts to a plate, and sprinkle the remaining salt and black pepper to season. Dash the balsamic glaze over the Brussels sprouts, then serve with Parmesan and pine nuts.

Nutrition 270 Calories 10.6g Fat 6.9g Carbohydrates 8.7g Protein

890. Citrus Vinaigrette Spinach Salad

Preparation Time: 10 minutes

Cooking Time: 0 minute
Servings: 4
Ingredients:
Citrus Vinaigrette:
- ¼ cup extra-virgin olive oil
- 3 tablespoons balsamic vinegar
- ½ teaspoon fresh lemon zest
- ½ teaspoon salt
Salad:
- 1-pound (454 g) baby spinach, washed, stems removed
- 1 large ripe tomato, cut into ¼-inch pieces
- 1 medium red onion, thinly sliced

Directions:
1. Make the citrus vinaigrette: Stir together the olive oil, balsamic vinegar, lemon zest, and salt in a bowl until mixed well.
2. Make the salad: Place the baby spinach, tomato and onions in a separate salad bowl. Fill the citrus vinaigrette over the salad and gently toss until the vegetables are coated thoroughly.

Nutrition 173 Calories 14.2g Fat 4.2g Carbohydrates 4.1g Protein

891. Simple Celery and Orange Salad

Preparation Time: 15 minutes
Cooking Time: 0 minute
Servings: 6
Ingredients:
Salad:
- 3 celery stalks, including leaves, sliced diagonally into ½-inch slices
- ½ cup green olives
- ¼ cup sliced red onion
- 2 large peeled oranges, cut into rounds
Dressing:
- 1 tablespoon extra-virgin olive oil
- 1 tablespoon lemon or orange juice
- 1 tablespoon olive brine
- ¼ teaspoon kosher or sea salt
- ¼ teaspoon freshly ground black pepper

Directions:
1. Make the salad: Put the celery stalks, green olives, onion, and oranges in a shallow bowl. Mix well and set aside.
2. Make the dressing: Stir the olive oil, lemon juice, olive brine, salt, and pepper well.
3. Fill the dressing into the bowl of salad and lightly toss until coated thoroughly.
4. Serve chilled or at room temperature.

Nutrition 24 Calories 1.2g Fat 1.2g Carbohydrates 1.1g Protein

892. Vanilla Cream

Preparation Time: 2 hours
Cooking Time: 10 minutes
Servings: 4
Ingredients:
- 1 cup almond milk
- 1 cup coconut cream
- 2 cups coconut sugar
- 2 tablespoons cinnamon powder
- 1 teaspoon vanilla extract

Directions:
1. Heat up a pan with the almond milk over medium heat, add the rest of the ingredients, whisk, and cook for 10 minutes more.
2. Divide the mix into bowls, cool down and keep in the fridge for 2 hours before serving.

Nutrition: 254 calories 7.5g fat 9.5g protein

893. Blueberries Bowls

Preparation Time: 10 minutes
Cooking Time: 0 minutes
Servings: 4
Ingredients:
- 1 teaspoon vanilla extract
- 2 cups blueberries
- 1 teaspoon coconut sugar
- 8 ounces Greek yogurt

Directions:
1. Mix strawberries with the vanilla and the other ingredients, toss and serve cold.

Nutrition: 343 calories 13.4g fat 5.5g protein

894. Brownies

Preparation Time: 10 minutes
Cooking Time: 25 minutes
Servings: 8
Ingredients:
- 1 cup pecans, chopped
- 3 tablespoons coconut sugar
- 2 tablespoons cocoa powder
- 3 eggs, whisked
- ¼ cup avocado oil
- ½ teaspoon baking powder
- 2 teaspoons vanilla extract
- Cooking spray

Directions:
1. In your food processor, combine the pecans with the coconut sugar and the other ingredients except the cooking spray and pulse well.
2. Grease a square pan with cooking spray, add the brownies mix, spread, introduce in the oven, bake at 350 degrees F for 25 minutes, leave aside to cool down, slice and serve.

Nutrition: 370 calories 14.3g fat 5.6g protein

895. Strawberries Coconut Cake

Preparation Time: 10 minutes
Cooking Time: 25 minutes
Servings: 6
Ingredients:
- 2 cups almond flour
- 1 cup strawberries, chopped
- ½ teaspoon baking soda
- ½ cup coconut sugar
- ¾ cup coconut milk
- ¼ cup avocado oil
- 2 eggs, whisked
- 1 teaspoon vanilla extract
- Cooking spray

Directions:
1. In a bowl, combine the flour with the strawberries and the other ingredients except the cooking spray and whisk well.
2. Grease a cake pan with cooking spray, pour the cake mix, spread, bake in the oven at 350 degrees F for 25 minutes, cool down, slice and serve.

Nutrition: 465 calories 22g fat 13.4g protein

896. Cocoa Almond Pudding

Preparation Time: 10 minutes
Cooking Time: 10 minutes
Servings: 4
Ingredients:
- 2 tablespoons coconut sugar
- 3 tablespoons coconut flour
- 2 tablespoons cocoa powder
- 2 cups almond milk
- 2 eggs, whisked
- ½ teaspoon vanilla extract

Directions:
1. Fill milk in a pan, add the cocoa and the other ingredients, whisk, simmer over medium heat for 10 minutes, pour into small cups and serve cold.

Nutrition: 385 calories 31.7g fat 7.3g protein

897. Nutmeg Cream

Preparation Time: 10 minutes
Cooking Time: 0 minutes

Servings: 6

Ingredients:
- 3 cups almond milk
- 1 teaspoon nutmeg, ground
- 2 teaspoons vanilla extract
- 4 teaspoons coconut sugar
- 1 cup walnuts, chopped

Directions:
1. In a bowl, combine milk with the nutmeg and the other ingredients, whisk well, divide into small cups and serve cold.

Nutrition: 243 calories 12.4g fat 9.7g protein

898. Vanilla Avocado Cream

Preparation Time: 70 minutes
Cooking Time: 0 minutes
Servings: 4

Ingredients:
- 2 cups coconut cream
- 2 avocados, peeled, pitted and mashed
- 2 tablespoons coconut sugar
- 1 teaspoon vanilla extract

Directions:
1. Blend cream with the avocados and the other ingredients, pulse well, divide into cups and keep in the fridge for 1 hour before serving.

Nutrition: 532 calories 48.2g fat 5.2g protein

899. Raspberries Cream Cheese Bowls

Preparation Time: 10 minutes
Cooking Time: 25 minutes
Servings: 4

Ingredients:
- 2 tablespoons almond flour
- 1 cup coconut cream
- 3 cups raspberries
- 1 cup coconut sugar
- 8 ounces cream cheese

Directions:
1. In a bowl, the flour with the cream and the other ingredients, whisk, transfer to a round pan, cook at 360 degrees F for 25 minutes, divide into bowls and serve.

Nutrition: 429 calories 36.3g fat 7.8g protein

900. Mediterranean Watermelon Salad

Preparation time: 4 minutes
Cooking time: 0 minutes
Servings: 4

Ingredients:
- 1 cup watermelon, peeled and cubed

- 2 apples, cored and cubed
- 1 tablespoon coconut cream
- 2 bananas, cut into chunks

Directions:
1. Incorporate watermelon with the apples and the other ingredients, toss and serve.

Nutrition: 131 calories 1.3g fat 1.3g protein

901. Coconut Apples

Preparation Time: 10 minutes
Cooking Time: 10 minutes
Servings: 4

Ingredients:
- 2 teaspoons lime juice
- ½ cup coconut cream
- ½ cup coconut, shredded
- 4 apples, cored and cubed
- 4 tablespoons coconut sugar

Directions:
1. Incorporate apples with the lime juice and the other ingredients, stir, bring to a simmer over medium heat and cook for 10 minutes.
2. Divide into bowls and serve cold.

Nutrition: 320 calories 7.8g fat 4.7g protein

902. Orange Compote

Preparation Time: 10 minutes
Cooking Time: 15 minutes
Servings: 4

Ingredients:
- 5 tablespoons coconut sugar
- 2 cups orange juice
- 4 oranges, peeled and cut into segments

Directions:
1. In a pot, combine oranges with the sugar and the orange juice, toss, boil over medium heat, cook for 16 minutes, divide into bowls and serve cold.

Nutrition: 220 calories 5.2g fat 5.6g protein

903. Pears Stew

Preparation Time: 10 minutes
Cooking Time: 15 minutes
Servings: 4

Ingredients:
- 2 cups pears, cored and cut into wedges
- 2 cups water
- 2 tablespoons coconut sugar
- 2 tablespoons lemon juice

Directions:
1. In a pot, combine the pears with the water and the other ingredients, toss, cook over medium heat for 15 minutes, divide into bowls and serve.

Nutrition: 260 calories 6.2g fat 6g protein

904. Lemon Watermelon Mix

Preparation Time: 10 minutes
Cooking Time: 10 minutes
Servings: 4
Ingredients:
- 2 cups watermelon
- 4 tablespoons coconut sugar
- 2 teaspoons vanilla extract
- 2 teaspoons lemon juice

Directions:
1. In a small pan, combine the watermelon with the sugar and the other ingredients, toss, heat up over medium heat, cook for about 10 minutes, divide into bowls and serve cold.

Nutrition: 140 calories 4g fat 5g protein

905. Rhubarb Cream

Preparation Time: 10 minutes
Cooking Time: 14 minutes
Servings: 4
Ingredients:
- 1/3 cup cream cheese
- ½ cup coconut cream
- 2-pound rhubarb, roughly chopped
- 3 tablespoons coconut sugar

Directions:
1. Blend cream cheese with the cream and the other ingredients well.
2. Divide into small cups, introduce in the oven and bake at 350 degrees F for 14 minutes.
3. Serve cold.

Nutrition: 360 calories 14.3g fat 5.2g protein

906. Mango Bowls

Preparation Time: 10 minutes
Cooking Time: 0 minutes
Servings: 4
Ingredients:
- 3 cups mango, peeled and cubed
- 1 teaspoon chia seeds
- 1 cup coconut cream
- 1 teaspoon vanilla extract
- 1 tablespoon mint, chopped

Directions:
1. Mix mango with the cream and the other ingredients, toss, divide into smaller bowls and keep in the fridge for 10 minutes before serving.

Nutrition: 238 calories 16.6g fat 3.3g protein

907. Chocolate Ganache

Preparation time: 10 minutes
Cooking Time: 16 minutes
Servings: 16

Ingredients
- 9 ounces bittersweet chocolate, chopped
- 1 cup heavy cream
- 1 tablespoon dark rum (optional)

Direction
1. Situate chocolate in a medium bowl. Cook cream in a small saucepan over medium heat.
2. Bring to a boil. When the cream has reached a boiling point, pour the chopped chocolate over it and beat until smooth. Stir the rum if desired.
3. Allow the ganache to cool slightly before you pour it on a cake. Begin in the middle of the cake and work outside. For a fluffy icing or chocolate filling, let it cool until thick and beat with a whisk until light and fluffy.

Nutrition: 142 calories 10.8g fat 1.4g protein

908. Chocolate Covered Strawberries

Preparation Time: 15 minutes
Cooking Time: 0 minute
Servings: 24
Ingredients
- 16 ounces milk chocolate chips
- 2 tablespoons shortening
- 1-pound fresh strawberries with leaves

Direction
1. In a bain-marie, melt chocolate and shortening, occasionally stirring until smooth. Pierce the tops of the strawberries with toothpicks and immerse them in the chocolate mixture.
2. Turn the strawberries and put the toothpick in Styrofoam so that the chocolate cools.

Nutrition: 115 calories 7.3g fat 1.4g protein

909. Strawberry Angel Food Dessert

Preparation Time: 15 minutes
Cooking Time: 0 minutes
Servings: 18
Ingredients
- 1 angel cake (10 inches)
- 2 packages of softened cream cheese
- 1 cup of white sugar
- 1 container (8 oz) of frozen fluff, thawed
- 1 liter of fresh strawberries, sliced
- 1 jar of strawberry icing

Direction
1. Crumble the cake in a 9 x 13-inch dish.
2. Beat the cream cheese and sugar in a medium bowl until the mixture is light and fluffy. Stir in the whipped topping. Crush the cake with your hands, and spread the cream cheese mixture over the cake.
3. Combine the strawberries and the frosting in a bowl

until the strawberries are well covered. Spread over the layer of cream cheese. Cool until ready to serve.

Nutrition: 261 calories 11g fat 3.2g protein

910. Fruit Pizza

Preparation Time: 30 minutes
Cooking Time: 0 minute
Servings: 8
Ingredients
- 1 (18-oz) package sugar cookie dough
- 1 (8-oz) package cream cheese, softened
- 1 (8-oz) frozen filling, defrosted
- 2 cups of freshly cut strawberries
- 1/2 cup of white sugar
- 1 pinch of salt
- 1 tablespoon corn flour
- 2 tablespoons lemon juice
- 1/2 cup orange juice
- 1/4 cup water
- 1/2 teaspoon orange zest

Direction
1. Ready oven to 175 ° C Slice the cookie dough then place it on a greased pizza pan. Press the dough flat into the mold. Bake for 10 to 12 minutes. Let cool.
2. Soften the cream cheese in a large bowl and then stir in the whipped topping. Spread over the cooled crust.
3. Start with strawberries cut in half. Situate in a circle around the outer edge. Continue with the fruit of your choice by going to the center. If you use bananas, immerse them in lemon juice. Then make a sauce with a spoon on the fruit.
4. Combine sugar, salt, corn flour, orange juice, lemon juice, and water in a pan. Boil and stir over medium heat. Boil for 1 or 2 minutes until thick. Remove from heat and add the grated orange zest. Place on the fruit.
5. Allow to cool for two hours, cut into quarters, and serve.

Nutrition 535 calories 30g fat 5.5g protein

911. Bananas Foster

Preparation Time: 5 minutes
Cooking Time: 6 minutes
Servings: 4
Ingredients
- 2/3 cup dark brown sugar
- 1/4 cup butter
- 3 1/2 tablespoons rum
- 1 1/2 teaspoons vanilla extract
- 1/2 teaspoon of ground cinnamon
- 3 bananas, peeled and cut lengthwise and broad
- 1/4 cup coarsely chopped nuts
- vanilla ice cream

Direction
1. Melt the butter in a deep-frying pan over medium heat. Stir in sugar, rum, vanilla, and cinnamon.
2. When the mixture starts to bubble, place the bananas and nuts in the pan. Bake until the bananas are hot, 1 to 2 minutes. Serve immediately with vanilla ice cream.

Nutrition: 534 calories 23.8g fat 4.6g protein

912. Cranberry Orange Cookies

Preparation Time: 20 minutes
Cooking Time: 16 minutes
Servings: 24
Ingredients
- 1 cup of soft butter
- 1 cup of white sugar
- 1/2 cup brown sugar
- 1 egg
- 1 teaspoon grated orange peel
- 2 tablespoons orange juice
- 2 1/2 cups flour
- 1/2 teaspoon baking powder
- 1/2 teaspoon salt
- 2 cups chopped cranberries
- 1/2 cup chopped walnuts (optional)

Icing:
- 1/2 teaspoon grated orange peel
- 3 tablespoons orange juice
- 1 ½ cup confectioner's sugar

Direction
1. Preheat the oven to 190 ° C.
2. Blend butter, white sugar, and brown sugar. Beat the egg until everything is well mixed. Mix 1 teaspoon of orange zest and 2 tablespoons of orange juice. Mix the
3. flour, baking powder, and salt; stir in the orange mixture.
4. Mix the cranberries and, if used, the nuts until well distributed. Place the dough with a spoon on ungreased baking trays.
5. Bake in the preheated oven for 12 to 14 minutes. Cool on racks.
6. In a small bowl, mix icing ingredients. Spread over cooled cookies.

Nutrition: 110 calories 4.8g fat 1.1 g protein

913. Key Lime Pie

Preparation time: 15 minutes
Cooking Time: 8 minutes
Servings: 8
Ingredients
- 1 (9-inch) prepared graham cracker crust
- 3 cups of sweetened condensed milk
- 1/2 cup sour cream
- 3/4 cup lime juice
- 1 tablespoon grated lime zest

Direction

1. Prepare oven to 175 ° C
2. Combine the condensed milk, sour cream, lime juice, and lime zest in a medium bowl. Mix well and transfer into the graham cracker crust.
3. Bake in the preheated oven for 5 to 8 minutes
4. Cool the cake well before serving. Decorate with lime slices and whipped cream if desired.

Nutrition: 553 calories 20.5g fat 10.9g protein

914. Rhubarb Strawberry Crunch

Preparation time: 15 minutes
Cooking Time: 45 minutes
Servings: 18
Ingredients

- 1 cup of white sugar
- 3 tablespoons all-purpose flour
- 3 cups of fresh strawberries, sliced
- 3 cups of rhubarb, cut into cubes
- 1 1/2 cup flour
- 1 cup packed brown sugar
- 1 cup butter
- 1 cup oatmeal

Direction

1. Preheat the oven to 190 ° C.
2. Incorporate white sugar, 3 tablespoons flour, strawberries and rhubarb in a large bowl. Place the mixture in a 9 x 13-inch baking dish.
3. Mix 1 1/2 cups of flour, brown sugar, butter, and oats until a crumbly texture is obtained. You may want to use a blender for this. Crumble the mixture of rhubarb and strawberry.
4. Bake for 45 minutes.

Nutrition: 253 calories 10.8g fat 2.3g protein

915. Chocolate Chip Banana Dessert

Preparation Time: 20 minutes
Cooking Time: 20 minutes
Servings: 24
Ingredients

- 2/3 cup white sugar
- 3/4 cup butter
- 2/3 cup brown sugar
- 1 egg, beaten slightly
- 1 teaspoon vanilla extract
- 1 cup of banana puree
- 1 3/4 cup flour
- 2 teaspoons baking powder
- 1/2 teaspoon of salt
- 1 cup of semi-sweet chocolate chips

Direction:

1. Ready the oven to 175 ° C Grease and bake a 10 x 15-inch baking pan.

2. Beat the butter, white sugar, and brown sugar in a large bowl until light. Beat the egg and vanilla. Fold in the banana puree: mix baking powder, flour, and salt in another bowl. Mix flour mixture into the butter mixture. Stir in the chocolate chips. Spread in pan.
3. Bake for 20 minutes. Cool before cutting into squares.

Nutrition: 174 calories 8.2g fat 1.7g protein

916. Apple Pie Filling

Preparation time: 20 minutes
Cooking Time: 12 minutes
Servings: 40
Ingredients

- 18 cups chopped apples
- 3 tablespoons lemon juice
- 10 cups of water
- 4 1/2 cups of white sugar
- 1 cup corn flour
- 2 teaspoons of ground cinnamon
- 1 teaspoon of salt
- 1/4 teaspoon ground nutmeg

Direction

1. Mix apples with lemon juice in a large bowl and set aside. Pour the water in a Dutch oven over medium heat. Combine sugar, corn flour, cinnamon, salt, and nutmeg in a bowl. Add to water, mix well, and bring to a boil. Cook for 2 minutes with continuous stirring.
2. Boil apples again. Reduce the heat, cover, and simmer for 8 minutes. Allow cooling for 30 minutes.
3. Pour into five freezer containers and leave 1/2 inch of free space. Cool to room temperature.
4. Seal and freeze

Nutrition: 129 calories 0.1g fat0.2g protein

917. Ice Cream Sandwich Dessert

Preparation Time: 20 minutes
Cooking Time: 0 minute
Servings: 12
Ingredients

- 22 ice cream sandwiches
- Frozen whipped topping in 16 oz container, thawed
- 1 jar (12 oz) Caramel ice cream
- 1 1/2 cups of salted peanuts

Direction

1. Cut a sandwich with ice in two. Place a whole sandwich and a half sandwich on a short side of a 9 x 13-inch baking dish. Repeat this until the bottom is covered, alternate the full sandwich, and the half sandwich.
2. Spread half of the whipped topping. Pour the caramel over it. Sprinkle with half the peanuts. Do

layers with the rest of the ice cream sandwiches, whipped cream, and peanuts.

3. Cover and freeze for 2 months. Remove from the freezer 20 minutes before serving. Cut into squares.

Nutrition: 559 calories 28.8g fat 10g protein

918. Cranberry and Pistachio Biscotti

Preparation time: 15 minutes
Cooking Time: 35 minutes
Servings: 36
Ingredients
- 1/4 cup light olive oil
- 3/4 cup white sugar
- 2 teaspoons vanilla extract
- 1/2 teaspoon almond extract
- 2 eggs
- 1 3/4 cup all-purpose flour
- 1/4 teaspoon salt
- 1 teaspoon baking powder
- 1/2 cup dried cranberries
- 1 1/2 cup pistachio nuts

Direction
1. Prep oven to 150 ° C
2. Scourge oil and sugar in a large bowl until a homogeneous mixture is obtained. Stir in the vanilla and almond extract and add the eggs. Mix flour, salt, and baking powder; gradually add to the egg mixture — mix cranberries and nuts by hand.
3. Divide the dough in half — form two 12 x 2-inch logs on a parchment baking sheet. The dough can be sticky, wet hands with cold water to make it easier to handle the dough.
4. Bake in the preheated oven for 35 minutes or until the blocks are golden brown. Pullout from the oven and let cool for 10 minutes. Lower oven heat to 275 degrees F (135 degrees C).
5. Cut diagonally into 3/4-inch-thick slices. Place on the sides on the baking sheet covered with parchment — Bake for about 8 to 10 minutes

Nutrition: 92 calories 4.3g fat 2.1g protein

919. Cream Puff Dessert

Preparation time: 20 minutes
Cooking Time: 36 minutes
Servings: 12
Ingredients
Puff
- 1 cup water
- 1/2 cup butter
- 1 cup all-purpose flour
- 4 eggs
Filling
- 1 (8-oz) package cream cheese, softened
- 3 1/2 cups cold milk

- 2 (4-oz) packages instant chocolate pudding mix
Topping
- 1 (8-oz) package frozen whipped cream topping, thawed
- 1/4 cup topping with milk chocolate flavor
- 1/4 cup caramel filling
- 1/3 cup almond flakes

Direction:
1. Set oven to 200 degrees C (400 degrees F). Grease a 9 x 13-inch baking dish.
2. Melt the butter in the water in a medium-sized pan over medium heat. Pour the flour in one go and mix vigorously until the mixture forms a ball. Pull away from heat and let stand for 5 minutes. Beat the eggs one by one until they are smooth and shiny. Spread in the prepared pan.
3. Bake in the preheated oven for 30 to 35 minutes, until puffed and browned. Cool completely on a rack.
4. While the puff pastry cools, mix the cream cheese mixture, the milk, and the pudding. Spread over the cooled puff pastry. Cool for 20 minutes.
5. Spread whipped cream on cooled topping and sprinkle with chocolate and caramel sauce. Sprinkle with almonds. Freeze 1 hour before serving.

Nutrition: 355 calories 22.3g fat 8.7g protein

920. Fresh Peach Dessert

Preparation time: 30 minutes
Cooking Time: 27 minutes
Servings: 15
Ingredients
- 16 whole graham crackers, crushed
- 3/4 cup melted butter
- 1/2 cup white sugar
- 4 1/2 cups of miniature marshmallows
- 1/4 cup of milk
- 1 pint of heavy cream
- 1/3 cup of white sugar
- 6 large fresh peaches - peeled, seeded and sliced

Direction:
1. In a bowl, mix the crumbs from the graham cracker, melted butter, and 1/2 cup of sugar. Mix until a homogeneous mixture is obtained, save 1/4 cup of the mixture for filling. Squeeze the rest of the mixture into the bottom of a 9 x 13-inch baking dish.
2. Heat marshmallows and milk in a large pan over low heat and stir until marshmallows are completely melted. Remove from heat and let cool.
3. Beat the cream in a large bowl until soft peaks occur. Beat 1/3 cup of sugar until the cream forms firm spikes. Add the whipped cream to the cooled marshmallow mixture.
4. Divide half of the cream mixture over the crust, place the peaches over the cream and divide the rest of the cream mixture over the peaches. Sprinkle the

crumb mixture on the cream. Cool until ready to serve.

Nutrition: 366 calories 22.5g fat 1.9g protein

921. Blueberry Dessert

Preparation time: 30 minutes
Cooking Time: 20 minutes
Servings: 28
Ingredients
- 1/2 cup butter
- 2 cups white sugar
- 36 graham crackers, crushed
- 4 eggs
- 2 packets of cream cheese, softened
- 1 teaspoon vanilla extract
- 2 cans of blueberry pie filling
- 1 package (16-oz) frozen whipped cream, thawed

Direction:
1. Cook butter and sprinkle 1 cup of sugar and graham crackers. Squeeze this mixture into a 9x13 dish.
2. Beat the eggs. Gradually beat the cream cheese, sugar, and vanilla in the eggs.
3. Pour the mixture of eggs and cream cheese over the graham cracker crust. Bake for 15 to 20 minutes at 165 ° C (325 ° F). Cool.
4. Pour the blueberry pie filling on top of the baked dessert. Spread non-dairy whipped topping on fruit. Cool until ready to serve.

Nutrition: 354 calories 15.4g fat 3.8g protein

922. Good Sweet

Preparation Time: 10 minutes
Cooking Time: 10 minutes
Servings: 2
Ingredients:
- Tomatoes, ¼ teaspoon, chopped
- Cucumber, ¼ teaspoon, chopped
- Honey, 2 tablespoons
- Other veggies/beans optional

Directions:
1. Whisk the ingredients well.
2. In a bowl, toss to coat with honey as smoothly as possible.

Nutrition: 187 Calories 15.6g Fat 2g Protein

923. A Taste of Dessert

Preparation Time: 15 minutes
Cooking Time: 0 minutes
Servings: 2
Ingredients:
- Cilantro, 1 tablespoon
- Green onion, 1 tablespoon
- Mango, 1 peeled, seeded and chopped

- Bell pepper, ¼ cup, chopped
- Honey, 2 tablespoons

Directions:
1. Incorporate all the ingredients.
2. Serve when combined well.

Nutrition: 21 Calories 0.1g Fat 0.3g Protein

924. Honey Carrots

Preparation Time: 5 minutes
Cooking Time: 15 minutes
Servings: 2
Ingredients:
- Baby carrots, 16 ounces
- Brown sugar, ¼ cup

Directions:
1. Boil carrots with water in a huge pot
2. Drain after 15 minutes, and steam for 2 minutes.
3. Stir in the sugar, and serve when mixed well.

Nutrition: 402 Calories 23.3g Fat 1.4g Protein

925. Fresh Cherry Treat

Preparation Time: 10 minutes
Cooking Time: 10 minutes
Servings: 2
Ingredients:
- Honey, 1 tablespoon
- Almonds, 1 tablespoon, crushed
- Cherries, 12 ounces

Directions:
1. Preheat the oven to 350F, and for 5 minutes, bake the cherries.
2. Coat them with honey, and serve with almonds on top.

Nutrition: 448 Calories 36.4g Fat 3.5g Protein

926. Milky Peachy Dessert

Preparation Time: 15 minutes
Cooking Time: 10 minutes
Servings: 2
Ingredients:
- Peach, 1 fresh, peeled and sliced
- Brown sugar, 1 teaspoon
- Milk, 1 tablespoon

Directions:
1. Prepare a baking dish with a layer of peaches and toss in the milk.
2. Top the peaches with sugar, and bake at 350F for 5 minutes.

Nutrition: 366 Calories 22.5g Fat 1.9g Protein

927. Citrus Sections

Preparation Time: 20 minutes
Cooking Time: 5 minutes

Servings: 2

Ingredients:

- Grapefruit, 1, peeled and sectioned
- Pineapple, ½ cup, chunks
- Oranges, 1 small, sectioned into chunks
- Brown sugar, ½ tablespoon
- Butter, low fat and unsalted, ½ teaspoon, melted

Directions:

1. Preheat an oven tray at 350F.
2. Set the fruits on the tray, and top with the brown sugar, mixed with the butter, and bake for 5 minutes.
3. Transfer to a platter.

Nutrition: 279 Calories 5.9g Fat 2.2g Protein

928. After Meal Apples

Preparation Time: 15 minutes
Cooking Time: 25 minutes
Servings: 2

Ingredients:

- Apple, 1 whole, cut into chunks
- Pineapple chunks, ½ cups
- Grapes, seedless, ½ cup
- Orange juice, ¼ cup
- Cinnamon, ¼ teaspoon

Directions:

1. Preheat the oven to 350F.
2. Add all the fruits to a baking dish.
3. Drizzle with the orange juice and sprinkle with cinnamon.
4. Bake for 25 minutes, and serve hot.

Nutrition: 124 Calories 3.2g Fat 0.8g Protein

929. Warm Nut Bites

Preparation Time: 10 minutes
Cooking Time: 20 minutes
Servings: 2

Ingredients:

- Honey, 4 tablespoons
- Almonds, 2 cups
- Almond oil, 1 tablespoon

Directions:

1. Layer the almonds, whole, on a baking sheet.
2. Bake for 15 minutes at 350F.
3. Turn half way, and roll the almonds in honey.
4. Serve.

Nutrition: 268 Calories 19.7g Fat 7.6g Protein

930. Dipped Sprouts

Preparation time: 12 minutes
Cooking time: 10 minutes
Servings: 2

Ingredients:

- Brussels sprouts, 16 ounces
- Honey, 4 tablespoons

- Raisins and nuts, crushed, 6 tablespoons

Directions:

1. Boil water in a pot.
2. Add sprouts, and cook for 10 minutes until soft.
3. Glaze the sprouts in honey, and coat well. Add nuts and raisins.

Nutrition: 221 Calories 15.1g Fat 5.3g Protein

931. Pecans and Cheese

Preparation Time: 20 minutes
Cooking Time: 0 minutes
Servings: 2

Ingredients:

- Cinnamon, ground, 1 teaspoon
- Feta cheese, 4 ounces
- Pecans, finely chopped, 2 ounces
- Honey, 2 tablespoons
- Rosemary, fresh, 2 sprigs, minced

Directions:

1. Make small balls of the cheese.
2. Crush the pecans and situate them in a shallow bowl with the cinnamon.
3. Roll the cheese in the pecans and cinnamon.
4. Drizzle honey over the balls.
5. Serve with rosemary on top.

Nutrition: 234 Calories 18.6g Fat 7.5g Protein

932. Hazelnut Cookies

Preparation Time: 8 minutes
Cooking Time: 21 minutes
Servings: 5

Ingredients:

- 1 1/4 cups hazelnut meal
- 6 tbsp. flour
- 1 tbsp. brown sugar
- 2 tbsp. powdered sugar
- 1/2 tsp. kosher salt
- 1/2 lemon zest
- 1/2 lemon juice
- 1/2 tsp. vanilla
- 1/4 cup extra virgin olive oil

Directions:

1. Heat the oven at 375 degrees F.
2. Take a bowl, add the hazelnut meal, brown sugar, flour, half of the powdered sugar, lemon zest, and salt. Next, whisk it well.
3. Whisk olive oil and vanilla.
4. Once the dough is crumbly, shape them into cookies and line them on the baking sheet.
5. Bake it until the edges are lightly brown, around 20 minutes.
6. Take out on a cooling rack Let it sit to cool.
7. Meanwhile, take a small bowl and add lemon juice, and the remaining powdered sugar.
8. Drizzle the syrup over the cookies before serving.

Nutrition: 276 Calories 3.6g Protein 21.2g Fat

933. Fruit Dessert Nachos

Preparation Time: 9 minutes
Cooking Time: 13 minutes
Servings: 3
Ingredients:
- 1 tbsp. sugar
- a pinch of ground cinnamon
- 1 1/2 whole wheat tortillas
- 1/4 cup softened light cream cheese
- 1 cup chopped assorted melon
- 2 1/2 tbsp. light dairy sour cream
- 1/2 tsp. finely shredded orange peel
- 1 tbsp. orange juice

Directions:
1. Preheat oven at 425 degrees F.
2. Grease huge baking sheet with cooking spray.
3. Take a small bowl, combine the cinnamon and half of the sugar.
4. Take the tortillas and lightly coat with cooking spray. Sprinkle each side with the sugar mix.
5. Cut the tortillas to make 8 wedges and place them on the baking sheet.
6. Bake the tortillas until they turn light browned, for about 7 to 8 minutes. Turn once halfway.
7. Meanwhile, take a small sized bowl and mix together the sour cream, cream cheese, 30 grams of orange juice, orange peel and the remaining sugar. Once smooth, set it aside.
8. Take a medium bowl and combine together melon and remaining orange juice.
9. Serve by adding a spoon of melon mix on each tortilla wedge, and a spoon of cream cheese mixture.

Nutrition: 121 Calories 5.3g Protein 5.2g Fat

934. Honey Yogurt with Berries

Preparation Time: 12 minutes
Cooking Time: 0 minute
Servings: 2
Ingredients:
- 4 oz. hulled, halved strawberries
- 1/6 cup Greek yogurt
- 1/2 cup blueberries
- 1/2 cup raspberries
- 1 tsp. honey
- 1/2 tbsp. balsamic vinegar

Directions:
1. Take a large bowl and toss the berries with the balsamic vinegar.
2. Set it aside for 8 to 10 minutes.
3. Meanwhile, mix together the honey and yogurt in a bowl.
4. Serve it by topping the berries with honey yogurt.

Nutrition: 111 Calories 4.6g Protein 3g Fat

935. Caramelized Apples with Yogurt

Preparation Time: 14 minutes
Cooking Time: 9 minutes
Servings: 4
Ingredients:
- 1/2 cup Greek yogurt
- 2 tbsp. toasted, chopped walnuts
- 1/4 cup heavy cream
- 1 tbsp. sugar
- 1/2 tbsp. honey
- 1 tbsp. unsalted butter
- 1 apple
- a pinch of ground cinnamon

Directions:
1. Take a bowl and add the yogurt, honey, and cream. Next, beat it with a hand blender or a whisk. Beat it until the mixture forms peaks and has thickened.
2. Place a large skillet on medium heat and warm the butter.
3. Add 21 grams of sugar and the apples in to the pan and mix it well.
4. Cook the apples for five to seven minutes while occasionally stirring, so it doesn't stick.
5. Once the apples soften, sprinkle the cinnamon and the remaining sugar on them.
6. Cook for 3 more minutes before removing from the heat.
7. Wait for the apples to appear warm.
8. Serve the whipped yogurt topped with apples and almonds.

Nutrition: 315 Calories 6.4g Protein 22g Fat

936. Ricotta Brulee

Preparation Time: 7 minutes
Cooking Time: 14 minutes
Servings: 4
Ingredients:
- fresh raspberries
- 1 cup whole milk ricotta cheese
- 1 tbsp. granulated sugar
- 1/2 tsp. finely grated lemon zest
- 1 tbsp. honey

Directions:
1. Take a large bowl, stir in the lemon zest, ricotta, and honey.
2. Combine the ingredients well.
3. Place four ramekins and divide the batter among them.
4. Add sugar on top if you don't have a kitchen torch.
5. Add all of the ramekins on a baking sheet and place it on the oven rack.
6. Keep the rack on the highest level and turn the broiler on.

7. Once the ricotta is golden-brown and starts to bubble, turn the oven off.
8. Top with raspberries once it has cooled down. Serve it cold.

Nutrition: 254 Calories 12.8g Protein 14.7g Fat

937. Chocolate Quinoa Bars

Preparation time: 19 minutes
Cooking Time: 6 minutes
Servings: 10
Ingredients:
- 1/4 tsp. vanilla
- 2 oz. semi-sweet chocolate
- 1/2 cup dry quinoa
- 1/2 tbsp. powdered peanut butter

Peanut Butter Drizzle:
- 1 tbsp. water
- 9 tsp. powdered peanut butter

Directions:
1. Place a large pot on medium heat.
2. Once the pot is hot, add the quinoa, 45 grams at a time.
3. Stir the quinoa occasionally, until you start hearing it pop.
4. Once the popping starts, stir continuously for a minute.
5. Once you see that the quinoa has popped, place it in a small bowl.
6. Set up a double boiler and melt your chocolate.
7. Take a large bowl and add the chocolate, peanut butter powder, vanilla, and quinoa.
8. Mix it well to combine.
9. Place a parchment paper on the baking sheet.
10. Spread the chocolate batter across, making it around half an inch thick.
11. Mix together water and peanut butter to make the drizzle, and then drizzle it over the chocolate.
12. Swirl it around with a fork.
13. Refrigerate for it to set, and then slice them into small bars.

Nutrition: 170 Calories 4g Protein 8g Fat

938. Almond Honey Ricotta Spread

Preparation Time: 7 minutes
Cooking Time: 15 minutes
Servings: 3
Ingredients:
- 1/2 cup whole milk ricotta
- orange zest
- 1/4 cup sliced almonds
- 1/8 tsp. almond extract
- 1/2 tsp. honey
- sliced peaches
- honey to drizzle

Directions:
1. Take a medium bowl, and combine almonds, almond extract and ricotta.
2. Once you have stirred it well, place it in a bowl to serve.
3. Sprinkle with sliced almonds and drizzle some honey on the ricotta.
4. Spread a tablespoon of the spread to your choice of bread, top it with some honey and sliced peaches.

Nutrition: 199 Calories 8.5g Protein 12g Fat

939. Apricot Energy Bites

Preparation Time: 16 minutes
Cooking Time: 0 minute
Servings: 10
Ingredients:
- 1 cup unsalted raw cashew nuts
- 1/4 tsp. ground ginger
- 1/2 cup dried apricots
- 2 3/4 tbsp. shredded, unsweetened coconut
- 2 tbsp. chopped dates
- 1 tsp. orange zest
- 1 tsp. lemon zest
- 1/4 tsp. cinnamon
- salt to taste

Directions:
1. Grind apricots, coconut, dates and cashew nuts in a processor.
2. Pulse until all a crumbly mixture has formed.
3. Add the spices, salt and citrus zest in the mixture.
4. Pulse it again to mix well.
5. Process the batter on high till it sticks together.
6. Take a dish or a tray and line it with parchment paper.
7. Shape the balls in your palm, make around 20 balls.
8. Keep in the refrigerator. Serve as needed.

Nutrition: 102 Calories 2g Protein 6g Fat

940. Pistachio Snack Bars

Preparation time: 17 minutes
Cooking Time: 0 minute
Servings: 4
Ingredients:
- 10 pitted dates
- 1/2 tsp. vanilla extract
- 1 tbsp. pistachio butter
- 10 tbsp. roasted, salted pistachios
- 1/2 cup rolled oats, old fashioned
- 2 tbsp. unsweetened, applesauce

Directions:
1. Grind dates until pureed, in a processor.
2. Add the oats and 123 grams of pistachios and pulse a few times for 15 seconds each time.

3. Once there's a coarse and crumbly consistency, add the pistachio butter, vanilla extract, and applesauce until the dough becomes sticky.
4. Line a standard pan with parchment paper.
5. Place the dough on the pan, place another parchment paper on top, and press it down to evenly flatten the dough.
6. Sprinkle the remaining pistachios after removing the parchment paper.
7. Place the paper on top of the dough again and freeze for a while before cutting it into 8 equal bars.

Nutrition: 220 Calories 6g Protein 12g Fat

941. Oat Berry Smoothie

Preparation Time: 4 minutes
Cooking Time: 0 minute
Servings: 2
Ingredients:
- 1/2 cup frozen berries
- 1/2 cup Greek yogurt
- milk
- 4 1/2 tbsp. oats
- 1 tsp. honey

Directions:
1. Blend the berries, milk, and yogurt together until it's smooth.
2. Mix in the porridge oats, pour in a glass once it's mixed well, and drizzle some honey on top.

Nutrition: 295 Calories 18g Protein 5g Fat

942. Stewed Cinnamon Apples with Dates

Preparation Time: 15 minutes
Cooking Time: 10 minutes
Servings: 6
Ingredients:
- 4 large Pink Lady apples
- ½ cup water
- ¼ cup chopped pitted dates
- 1 teaspoon ground cinnamon
- ¼ teaspoon vanilla extract
- 1 teaspoon unsalted butter

Directions:
1. Place apples, water, dates, and cinnamon in the Instant Pot®. Close, let steam release, press the Manual button, and set the timer to 3 minutes.
2. When the alarm beeps, quick-release the pressure until the float valve sets. Click the Cancel button and open lid. Stir in vanilla and butter. Serve hot or chilled.

Nutrition 111 Calories 2g Fat 6g Carbohydrates 1g Protein

943. Spiced Poached Pears

Preparation Time: 10 minutes

Cooking Time: 15 minutes
Servings: 4
Ingredients:
- 2 cups water
- 2 cups red wine
- ¼ cup honey
- 4 whole cloves
- 2 cinnamon sticks
- 1-star anise
- 1 teaspoon vanilla bean paste
- 4 Bartlett pears, peeled

Directions:
1. Place all elements in the Instant Pot® and mix. Cover, set steam release to Sealing, press the Manual Instant Pot®. Stir to couple. Close lid, let steam release to Seal click the Manual button, and alarm to 3 minutes.
2. When the timer beeps, swiftly-release the pressure until the float valve drops. Select the Cancel and open. Take out pears to a plate and allow to cool for 5 minutes. Serve warm.

Nutrition 194 Calories 1g Protein 4g Carbohydrates 5g Fiber

944. Cranberry Applesauce

Preparation Time: 10 minutes
Cooking Time: 20 minutes
Servings: 8
Ingredients:
- 1 cup whole cranberries
- 4 medium tart apples, peeled, cored, and grated
- 4 medium sweet apples, peeled, cored, and grated
- 1½ tablespoons grated orange zest
- ¼ cup orange juice
- ¼ cup dark brown sugar
- ¼ cup granulated sugar
- 1 tablespoon unsalted butter
- 2 teaspoons ground cinnamon
- ½ teaspoon ground cloves
- ¼ teaspoon ground black pepper
- 1/8 teaspoon salt
- 1 tablespoon lemon juice

Directions:
1. Incorporate all ingredients in the Instant Pot®. Seal then, set the Manual button, and time to 5 minutes. When the timer beeps, let pressure release naturally, about 25 minutes. Open the lid. Lightly mash fruit with a fork. Stir well. Serve warm or cold.

Nutrition 136 Calories 4g Fat 3g Carbohydrates 9g Protein

945. Blueberry Compote

Preparation Time: 10 minutes
Cooking Time: 0 minute
Servings: 8

Ingredients:
- 1 (16-ounce) bag frozen blueberries, thawed
- ¼ cup sugar
- 1 tablespoon lemon juice
- 2 tablespoons cornstarch
- 2 tablespoons water
- ¼ teaspoon vanilla extract
- ¼ teaspoon grated lemon zest

Directions:
1. Add blueberries, sugar, and lemon juice to the Instant Pot®. Cover and press the Manual button, and adjust time to 1 minute.
2. When the timer beeps, sharply-release the pressure until the float valve falls. Press the Cancel button and open it.
3. Press the Sauté button. Combine cornstarch and water. Stir into blueberry mixture and cook until mixture comes to a boil and thickens, about 3–4 minutes. Press the Cancel button and stir in vanilla and lemon zest. Serve immediately or refrigerate until ready to serve.

Nutrition 57 Calories 2g Fat14g Carbohydrates 7g Protein

946. Dried Fruit Compote

Preparation Time: 5 minutes
Cooking Time: 20 minutes
Servings: 6
Ingredients:
- 8 ounces dried apricots, quartered
- 8 ounces dried peaches, quartered
- 1 cup golden raisins
- 1½ cups orange juice
- 1 cinnamon stick
- 4 whole cloves

Directions:
1. Stir to merge. Close, select the Manual button, and adjust the time to 3 minutes. When the timer beeps, let pressure release naturally, about 20 minutes. Press the Cancel button and open lid.
2. Remove and discard cinnamon stick and cloves. Press the Sauté button and simmer for 5–6 minutes. Serve warm then cover and refrigerate for up to a week.

Nutrition 258 Calories 5g Fat 8g Carbohydrates 4g Protein

947. Chocolate Rice Pudding

Preparation Time: 10 minutes
Cooking Time: 20 minutes
Servings: 6
Ingredients:
- 2 cups almond milk
- 1 cup long-grain brown rice
- 2 tablespoons Dutch-processed cocoa powder
- ¼ cup maple syrup
- 1 teaspoon vanilla extract

- ½ cup chopped dark chocolate

Directions:
1. Place almond milk, rice, cocoa, maple syrup, and vanilla in the Instant Pot®. Close then select the Manual button, and set time to 20 minutes.
2. When the timer beeps, let pressure release naturally for 15 minutes, then quick-release the remaining pressure. Press the Cancel button and open lid. Serve warm, sprinkled with chocolate.

Nutrition 271 Calories 8g Fat 4g Carbohydrates 3g Protein

948. Fruit Compote

Preparation Time: 10 minutes
Cooking Time: 15 minutes
Servings: 6
Ingredients:
- 1 cup apple juice
- 1 cup dry white wine
- 2 tablespoons honey
- 1 cinnamon stick
- ¼ teaspoon ground nutmeg
- 1 tablespoon grated lemon zest
- 1½ tablespoons grated orange zest
- 3 large apples, peeled, cored, and chopped
- 3 large pears, peeled, cored, and chopped
- ½ cup dried cherries

Directions:
1. Situate all ingredients in the Instant Pot® and stir well. Close and select the Manual button, and allow to sit for 1 minute. When the timer beeps, rapidly-release the pressure until the float valve hit the bottom. Click the Cancel then open lid.
2. Use a slotted spoon to transfer fruit to a serving bowl. Remove and discard cinnamon stick. Press the Sauté button and bring juice in the pot to a boil. Cook, stirring constantly, until reduced to a syrup that will coat the back of a spoon, about 10 minutes.
3. Stir syrup into fruit mixture. Once cool slightly, then wrap with plastic and chill overnight.

Nutrition 211 Calories 1g Fat 4g Carbohydrates 2g Protein

949. Stuffed Apples

Preparation Time: 10 minutes
Cooking Time: 15 minutes
Servings: 6
Ingredients:
- ½ cup apple juice
- ¼ cup golden raisins
- ¼ cup chopped toasted walnuts
- 2 tablespoons sugar
- ½ teaspoon grated orange zest
- ½ teaspoon ground cinnamon
- 4 large cooking apples
- 4 teaspoons unsalted butter

- 1 cup water

Directions:
1. Put apple juice in a microwave-safe container; heat for 1 minute on high or until steaming and hot. Pour over raisins. Soak raisins for 30 minutes. Drain, reserving apple juice. Add nuts, sugar, orange zest, and cinnamon to raisins and stir to mix.
2. Cut off the top fourth of each apple. Peel the cut portion and chop it, then stir diced apple pieces into raisin mixture. Hollow out and core apples by cutting to, but not through, the bottoms.
3. Situate each apple on a piece of aluminum foil that is large enough to wrap apple completely. Fill apple centers with raisin mixture.
4. Top each with 1 teaspoon butter. Cover the foil around each apple, folding the foil over at the top and then pinching it firmly together.
5. Stir in water to the Instant Pot® and place rack inside. Place apples on the rack. Close lid, set steam release to Sealing, press the Manual, and alarm to 10 minutes.
6. When the timer beeps, quick-release the pressure until the float valve drops and open the lid. Carefully lift apples out of the Instant Pot®. Unwrap and transfer to plates. Serve hot, at room temperature, or cold.

Nutrition 432 Calories 16g Fat 6g Carbohydrates 3g Protein

950. Cinnamon-Stewed Dried Plums with Greek Yogurt

Preparation Time: 10 minutes
Cooking Time: 15 minutes
Servings: 6
Ingredients:
- 3 cups dried plums
- 2 cups water
- 2 tablespoons sugar
- 2 cinnamon sticks
- 3 cups low-fat plain Greek yogurt

Directions:
1. Add dried plums, water, sugar, and cinnamon to the Instant Pot®. Close allow steam release to Sealing, press the Manual button, and start the time to 3 minutes.
2. Once the timer beeps, quick-release the pressure. Click the Cancel button and open. Remove and discard cinnamon sticks. Serve warm over Greek yogurt.

Nutrition 301 Calories 2g Fat 3g Carbohydrates 14g Protein

951. Vanilla-Poached Apricots

Preparation Time: 10 minutes
Cooking Time: 20 minutes
Servings: 6
Ingredients:
- 1¼ cups water

- ¼ cup marsala wine
- ¼ cup sugar
- 1 teaspoon vanilla bean paste
- 8 medium apricots, sliced in half and pitted

Directions:
1. Place all pieces in the Instant Pot® and combine well. Seal tight, click the Manual Instant Pot®. Stir to combine. Close lid, set steam release to Sealing, press the Manual button, and set second to 1 minute.
2. When the alarm beeps, quick-release the pressure until the float valve drops. Set the Cancel and open lid. Let stand for 10 minutes. Carefully remove apricots from poaching liquid with a slotted spoon. Serve warm or at room temperature.

Nutrition 62 Calories 1g Fat 5g Carbohydrates 2g Protein

952. Creamy Spiced Almond Milk

Preparation Time: 10 minutes
Cooking Time: 15 minutes
Servings:6
Ingredients:
- 1 cup raw almonds
- 5 cups filtered water, divided
- 1 teaspoon vanilla bean paste
- ½ teaspoon pumpkin pie spice

Directions:
1. Stir in almonds and 1 cup water to the Instant Pot®. Close and select the Manual, and set time to 1 minute.
2. When the timer alarms, quick-release the pressure until the float valve drops. Click the Cancel button and open cap. Strain almonds and rinse under cool water. Transfer to a high-powered blender with remaining 4 cups water. Purée for 2 minutes on high speed.
3. Incorporate mixture into a nut milk bag set over a large bowl. Squeeze bag to extract all liquid. Stir in vanilla and pumpkin pie spice. Transfer to a Mason jar or sealed jug and refrigerate for 8 hours. Stir or shake gently before serving.

Nutrition 86 Calories 8g Fat 5g Carbohydrates 3g Protein

953. Poached Pears with Greek Yogurt and Pistachio

Preparation Time: 10 minutes
Cooking Time: 15 minutes
Servings: 8
Ingredients:
- 2 cups water
- 1¾ cups apple cider
- ¼ cup lemon juice
- 1 cinnamon stick
- 1 teaspoon vanilla bean paste
- 4 large Bartlett pears, peeled

- 1 cup low-fat plain Greek yogurt
- ½ cup unsalted roasted pistachio meats

Directions:

1. Add water, apple cider, lemon juice, cinnamon, vanilla, and pears to the Instant Pot®. Close lid, set steam release, switch the Manual, and set time to 3 minutes.
2. When the timer stops, swift-release the pressure until the float valve drops. Select the Cancel button and open cap. Take out pears to a plate and allow to cool to room temperature.
3. To serve, carefully slice pears in half with a sharp paring knife and scoop out core with a melon baller. Lay pear halves on dessert plates or in shallow bowls. Top with yogurt and garnish with pistachios. Serve immediately.

Nutrition 181 Calories 7g Fat 5g Carbohydrates 7g Protein

954. Peaches Poached in Rose Water

Preparation Time: 10 minutes
Cooking Time: 20 minutes
Servings: 6

Ingredients:

- 1 cup water
- 1 cup rose water
- ¼ cup wildflower honey
- 8 green cardamom pods, lightly crushed
- 1 teaspoon vanilla bean paste
- 6 large yellow peaches, pitted and quartered
- ½ cup chopped unsalted roasted pistachio meats

Directions:

1. Add water, rose water, honey, cardamom, and vanilla to the Instant Pot®. Whisk well, then add peaches. Close lid, allow to steam release to Seal, press the Manual button, and alarm time to 1 minute.
2. When done, release the pressure until the float valve hits the bottom. Press the Remove and open it. Allow peaches to stand for 10 minutes. Carefully remove peaches from poaching liquid with a slotted spoon.
3. Slip skins from peach slices. Arrange slices on a plate and garnish with pistachios. Serve warm or at room temperature.

Nutrition 145 Calories 3g Fat 6g Carbohydrates 2g Protein

955. Brown Betty Apple Dessert

Preparation Time: 10 minutes
Cooking Time: 10 minutes
Servings: 8

Ingredients:

- 2 cups dried bread crumbs
- ½ cup sugar
- 1 teaspoon ground cinnamon
- 3 tablespoons lemon juice
- 1 tablespoon grated lemon zest
- 1 cup olive oil, divided
- 8 medium apples, peeled, cored, and diced
- 2 cups water

Directions:

1. Combine crumbs, sugar, cinnamon, lemon juice, lemon zest, and ½ cup oil in a medium mixing bowl. Set aside.
2. In a greased oven-safe dish that will fit in your cooker loosely, add a thin layer of crumbs, then one diced apple. Continue filling the container with alternating layers of crumbs and apples until all ingredients are finished. Pour remaining ½ cup oil on top.
3. Pour water to the Instant Pot® and place rack inside. Make a foil sling by folding a long piece of foil in half lengthwise and lower the uncovered container into the pot using the sling.
4. Seal and press the Manual button, and set time to 10 minutes. When the timer stops, let pressure release naturally, about 20 minutes. Press the Cancel button and open lid. Using the sling, remove the baking dish from the pot and let stand for 5 minutes before serving.

Nutrition 422 Calories 27g Fat 4g Carbohydrates 7g Protein

956. Blueberry Oat Crumble

Preparation Time: 10 minutes
Cooking Time: 10 minutes
Servings: 8

Ingredients:

- 1 cup water
- 4 cups blueberries
- 2 tablespoons packed light brown sugar
- 2 tablespoons cornstarch
- 1/8 teaspoon ground nutmeg
- 1/3 cup rolled oats
- ¼ cup granulated sugar
- ¼ cup all-purpose flour
- ¼ teaspoon ground cinnamon
- ¼ cup unsalted butter, melted and cooled

Directions:

1. Brush baking dish that fits inside the Instant Pot® with nonstick cooking spray. Add water to the pot and add rack. Crease a long piece of aluminum foil in half lengthwise. Lay foil over rack to form a sling.
2. In a medium bowl, combine blueberries, brown sugar, cornstarch, and nutmeg. Transfer mixture to prepared dish.
3. In a separate medium bowl, add oats, sugar, flour, and cinnamon. Mix well. Add butter and combine until mixture is crumbly. Sprinkle crumbles over blueberries, cover dish with aluminum foil, and crimp edges tightly.
4. Add baking dish to rack in pot so it rests on the sling and seal tight. Switch the Manual button, and

set time to 10 minutes. When the timer beeps, let pressure release naturally for 10 minutes, then quick-release the remaining pressure until the float valve drops. Press the Cancel button and open lid. Carefully remove dish with sling and remove foil cover.

5. Heat broiler on high. Broil crumble until topping is golden brown, about 5 minutes. Serve warm or at room temperature.

Nutrition 159 Calories 6g Fat 3g Carbohydrates 2g Protein

957. Date and Walnut Cookies

Preparation Time: 10 minutes
Cooking Time: 2 minutes
Servings: 30
Ingredients:
- 2 cups flour
- 1/4 cup sour cream
- 1/2 cup butter, softened
- 1 1/2 cups brown sugar
- 1/2 cup white sugar
- 1 egg
- 1 cup dates, pitted and chopped
- 1/3 cup water
- 1/4 cup walnuts, finely chopped
- 1/2 tsp salt
- 1/2 tsp baking soda
- a pinch of cinnamon

Directions:
1. Cook the dates together with the white sugar and water over medium-high heat, stirring constantly, until mixture is thick like jam. Add in the nuts, stir and remove from heat. Leave to cool.
2. In a medium bowl, scourge the butter and brown sugar. Stir in the egg and the sour cream. Mix the flour together with salt, baking soda and cinnamon and stir it into the butter mixture.
3. Drop a teaspoon of dough onto a cookie sheet, place 1/4 teaspoon of the filling on top of it and top with an additional 1/2 teaspoon of dough. Repeat with the rest of the dough. Bake cookies for about 10 minutes in a preheated to 340 F oven, or until golden.

Nutrition 134 Calories 7.9g Fats 2g Carbohydrates 1.4g Protein

958. Moroccan Stuffed Dates

Preparation Time: 15 minutes
Cooking Time: 0 minute
Servings: 30
Ingredients:
- 1 lb. dates
- 1 cup blanched almonds
- 1/4 cup sugar
- 1 1/2 tbsp orange flower water

- 1 tbsp butter, melted
- 1/4 teaspoon cinnamon

Directions:
1. Incorporate the almonds, sugar and cinnamon in a food processor. Stir in the butter and orange flower water and process until a smooth paste is formed. Roll small pieces of almond paste the same length as a date.
2. Take one date, make a vertical cut and discard the pit. Insert a piece of the almond paste and press the sides of the date firmly around. Repeat with all the remaining dates and almond paste.

Nutrition 102 Calories 7g Fats 5g Carbohydrates 2g Protein

959. Fig Cookies

Preparation Time: 10 minutes
Cooking Time: 15 minutes
Servings: 24
Ingredients:
- 1 cup flour
- 1 egg
- 1/2 cup sugar
- 1/2 cup figs, chopped
- 1/2 cup butter
- 1/4 cup water
- 1/2 tsp vanilla extract
- 1 tsp baking powder
- a pinch of salt

Directions:
1. Cook figs with water, stirring, for 4-5 minutes, or until thickened. Set aside to cool. Scourge butter with sugar until light and fluffy. Put in the egg and vanilla and beat to blend well. In separate bowl, incorporate together flour, baking powder and salt. Blend this into the egg mixture. Stir in the cooled figs.
2. Drop teaspoonfuls of dough on a greased baking tray. Bake in a preheated to 375 degrees F oven until lightly browned. Remove cookies and cool on wire racks.

Nutrition 111 Calories 9g Fats 5g Carbohydrates 3g Protein

960. Almond Cookies

Preparation Time: 10 minutes
Cooking Time: 15 minutes
Servings: 30
Ingredient:
- 1 cup almonds, blanched, toasted and finely chopped
- 1 cup powdered sugar
- 4 egg whites
- 2 tbsp flour
- 1/2 tsp vanilla extract
- 1 pinch ground cinnamon
- powdered sugar, to dust

Directions:

1. Preheat oven to 320 F. Blend the almonds in a food processor until finely chopped. Beat egg whites and sugar until thick. Add in vanilla extract and cinnamon. Gently stir in almonds and flour. Place tablespoonfuls of mixture on two lined baking trays. Bake for 10 minutes, or until firm. Turn it off, and leave cookies to cool. Dust with powdered sugar.

Nutrition 106 Calories 6g Fats 7g Carbohydrates 1g Protein

961. Turkish Delight Cookies

Preparation Time: 5 minutes
Cooking Time: 20 minutes
Servings: 48
Ingredients:

- 4 cups flour
- 3/4 cup sugar
- 1 cup lard (or butter)
- 3 eggs
- 1 tsp baking powder
- 1 tsp vanilla extract
- 8 oz Turkish delight, chopped
- powdered sugar, for dusting

Directions:

1. Ready oven to 375 F. Put parchment paper onto the baking sheet. Beat the eggs well, adding sugar a bit at a time. Beat for at least 3 minutes. Melt the lard, then let it cool enough and slowly combine it with the egg mixture.
2. Mix the flour and the baking powder. Lightly add the flour mixture to the egg and lard mixture to create a smooth dough. Divide dough into two or three smaller balls and roll it out until ¼ inch thick. Cut squares 3x2 inch. Situate a piece of Turkish delight in each square, roll each cookie into a stick and nip the end. Bake in a preheated to 350 degrees F oven until light pink. Dust in powdered sugar and store in an airtight container when completely cool.

Nutrition 109 Calories 7g Fats 5g Carbohydrates 3g Protein

962. Anise Cookies

Preparation Time: 10 minutes
Cooking Time: 20 minutes
Servings: 24
Ingredients:

- 1 ½ cups flour
- 1/3 cup sugar
- 1/3 cup olive oil
- 1 egg, whisked
- 3 tsp fennel seeds
- 1 tsp cinnamon
- zest of one orange
- 3 tbsp anise liqueur
- sugar, for sprinkling

Directions:

1. Cook olive oil in a small pan and sauté fennel seeds for 20-30 seconds. In a large bowl, combine together flour, sugar, and cinnamon. Add in olive oil, stirring, until well combined. Add orange zest and anise liqueur. Mix well then knead with hands until a smooth dough is formed. Add a little water if necessary.
2. On a well-floured surface, form two 1-inch long logs. Cut 1/8-inch cookies, arrange them on greased baking sheets. Egg wash each cookie and sprinkle with sugar. Bake cookies in a preheated to 350 F oven, for about 10 minutes, or until golden and crisp. Once cool, put in an airtight container.

Nutrition 113 Calories 8g Fats 5g Carbohydrates 2g Protein

963. Spanish Nougat

Preparation Time: 5 minutes
Cooking Time: 20 minutes
Servings: 24
Ingredients:

- 11/2 cup honey
- 3 egg whites
- 1 ¾ cup almonds, roasted and chopped

Directions:

1. Put the honey into a saucepan and boil over medium-high heat, then set aside to cool. Beat the egg whites to a thick glossy meringue and fold them into the honey. Bring the mixture back to medium-high heat and let it simmer, constantly stirring, for 15 minutes. When the color and consistency change to dark caramel, remove from heat, add the almonds and mix trough.
2. Put foil in a 9x13 inch pan and pour the hot mixture on it. Cover with another piece of foil and even out. Let cool completely. Place a wooden board weighted down with some heavy cans on it. Leave like this for 3-4 days, so it hardens and dries out. Slice into 1-inch squares.

Nutrition 110 Calories 5g Fats 7g Carbohydrates 1g Protein

964. Spanish Crumble Cakes

Preparation Time: 10 minutes
Cooking Time: 25 minutes
Servings: 30
Ingredients:

- 2 cups flour
- 1 cup butter, softened
- 1 cup sugar
- 1 egg
- 1 tsp lemon zest
- 1 tsp orange zest
- 1 tbsp orange juice
- 1/2 cup almonds, blanched and finely ground

Directions:

1. Beat butter with sugar, lemon and orange zest until light. Combine in the flour, using a wooden spoon.

Add ground almonds, stir, then knead with your hands until dough clings together. Divide it in three parts. Seal and chill for at least half an hour.

2. On a well-floured surface, roll out each piece of dough until it is 1/4 inch thick. Cut into different shapes. Arrange cookies on an ungreased baking sheet.

3. Beat together egg and orange juice and brush this over the cookies. Bake in a preheated to 350 degrees F oven for 7-8 minutes, or until edges are lightly golden. Set aside and keep in an airtight container.

Nutrition 113 Calories 8g Fats 5g Carbohydrates 4g Protein

965. Greek Honey Cookies

Preparation Time: 10 minutes
Cooking Time: 15 minutes
Servings: 40
Ingredients:
- 1 ¾ cups olive oil
- 2 cups walnuts, coarsely ground
- 1 cup sugar
- 1 cup fresh orange juice
- 3 tbsp orange peel
- 1/3 cup cognac
- 1 ½ tsp baking soda
- 1 tsp baking powder
- sifted flour, enough to make soft oily dough

for the syrup
- 2 cups honey
- 1 cup water

for sprinkling
- 1 cup very finely ground walnuts
- 1 tsp ground cinnamon
- 1 tsp ground cloves

Directions:
1. Line 2 baking trays with baking paper. In a very large bowl, scourge together oil, sugar, orange zest, orange juice, cognac, baking soda, baking powder, and salt until well combined. Fold in flour with a wooden spoon until a soft dough is formed.

2. Roll tablespoonfuls of the mixture into balls. Place them, about 1.5 inch apart, on the prepared trays. With a fork to prick the top of each cookie by cross-pressing. Bake in a preheated to 350 degrees F oven, for 30-35 minutes, or until golden.

3. Situate the water and honey in a medium saucepan over medium-high heat. Simmer for 5 minutes, removing foam. Set heat to low and with the help of a perforated spoon, dip 5-6 cookies at a time into the syrup. Once the cookies have absorbed a little of the syrup, remove them with the same spoon and situate them on a tray to cool and get rid of any excess syrup. After dipping the cookies, sprinkle with a mixture of cinnamon, cloves and finely ground walnuts.

Nutrition 116 Calories 7g Fats 6g Carbohydrates 2g Protein

966. Cinnamon Butter Cookies

Preparation Time: 10 minutes
Cooking Time: 20 minutes
Servings: 24
Ingredients:
- 2 cups flour
- 1/2 cup sugar
- 5 tbsp butter
- 3 eggs
- 1 tbsp cinnamon

Directions:
1. Scourge the butter and sugar until light and fluffy. Combine the flour and the cinnamon. Beat eggs into the butter mixture. Gently add in the flour. Situate the dough onto a lightly floured surface and knead just once or twice until smooth.

2. Form a roll and divide it into 24 pieces. Grease and line baking sheets with parchment paper. Spread each piece of cookie dough into a long thin strip, then make a circle, flatten a little and set it on the prepared baking sheet. Bake cookies, in batches, in a preheated to 350 F oven, for 12 to 15 minutes. Set aside in a cooling rack.

Nutrition 111 Calories 5g Fats 3g Carbohydrates 9g Protein

967. Best French Meringues

Preparation Time: 10 minutes
Cooking Time: 2 hours and 30 minutes
Servings: 36
Ingredients:
- 4 egg whites
- 2 1/4 cups powdered sugar

Directions:
1. Ready the oven to 200 F and line a baking sheet.

2. In a glass bowl, beat egg whites with an electric mixer. Mix in sugar a little simultaneously, while continuing to beat at medium speed. When the egg white mixture becomes stiff and shiny like satin, transfer to a large pastry bag. Place the meringue onto the lined baking sheet with the use of a large round.

3. Put the meringues in the oven and leave the oven door slightly ajar. Bake until the meringues are dry.

Nutrition 110 Calories 11g Fat 6g Carbohydrates 3g Protein

968. Cinnamon Palmier

Preparation Time: 5 minutes
Cooking Time: 15 minutes
Servings: 30
Ingredients:
- 1/3 cup granulated sugar
- 2 tsp cinnamon
- 1/2 lb. puff pastry
- 1 egg, beaten (optional)

Directions:

1. Stir together the sugar and cinnamon. Spread the pastry dough into a large rectangle. Spread the cinnamon sugar in an even layer over the dough. From the long ends of the rectangle, loosely roll each side inward until they meet in the middle.
2. If needed, brush it with the egg to hold it together. Slice the pastry roll crosswise into 1/4-inch pieces and arrange them on a lined with parchment paper baking sheet. Bake cookies in a preheated to 400 F oven for 12-15 minutes, until they puff and turn golden brown. Serve warm or at room temperature.

Nutrition 114 Calories 3g Fats 8g Carbohydrates 6g Protein

969. Honey Sesame Cookies

Preparation Time: 10minutes
Cooking Time: 15 minutes
Servings: 30
Ingredients:
- 3 cups flour
- 1 cup sugar
- 1 cup butter
- 2 eggs
- 3 tbsp honey
- 1 cup pistachio nuts, roughly chopped
- 1 cup sesame seeds
- 1 tbsp vinegar
- 1 tsp vanilla
- 1 tsp baking powder
- a pinch of salt

Directions:
1. Scourge the butter and the sugar until light and fluffy. Gently add in the eggs, then the vanilla extract and the vinegar. Incorporate the flour, salt, and baking powder and stir in the butter mixture. Beat until just incorporated. Cover and refrigerate for an hour.
2. Mix the sesame seeds and the honey in a medium plate. Place the pistachios in another one. Take a teaspoonful of dough, form it into a ball, then dip it into the pistachios. Press a little and dip it into the sesame-honey mixture. Repeat with the remaining dough, arranging the cookies on a lined baking sheet.
3. Bake the cookies in a preheated to 350 F oven for 15 minutes, or until they turn light brown. Set aside in the baking sheet for 2-3 minutes then move to a wire rack.

Nutrition 117 Calories 9g Fats 7g Carbohydrates 1g Protein

970. Baked Apples

Preparation Time: 5 minutes
Cooking Time: 10 minutes
Servings: 4
Ingredients:
- 8 medium sized apples
- 1/3 cup walnuts, crushed

- 3/4 cup sugar
- 3 tbsp raisins, soaked in brandy or dark rum
- vanilla, cinnamon according to taste
- 2 oz butter

Directions:
1. Peel and carefully hollow the apples. Prepare stuffing by beating the butter, 3/4 cup of sugar, crushed walnuts, raisins and cinnamon.
2. Fill in the apples with this mixture and situate them in an oiled dish. Sprinkle the apples with 1-2 tablespoons of water and bake in a moderate oven. Serve warm and side it with vanilla ice cream.

Nutrition 107 Calories 9g Fats 7g Carbohydrates 3g Protein

971. Pumpkin Baked with Dry Fruit

Preparation Time: 10 minutes
Cooking Time: 15 minutes
Servings: 6
Ingredients:
- 1 lb. pumpkin, cut into medium pieces
- 1 cup dry fruit (apricots, plums, apples, raisins)
- 1/2 cup brown sugar

Directions:
1. Soak the dry fruit in some water, drain and discard the water. Cut the pumpkin in medium cubes. At the bottom of a pot arrange a layer of pumpkin pieces, then a layer of dry fruit and then again, some pumpkin. Add a little water.
2. Cover the pot and bring to boil. Simmer until there is no more water. When almost ready add the sugar. Serve warm or cold.

Nutrition 113 Calories 8g Fats 5g Carbohydrates 3g Protein

972. Banana Shake Bowls

Preparation Time: 5 minutes
Cooking Time: 0 minutes
Servings: 4
Ingredients:
- 4 medium bananas, peeled
- 1 avocado, peeled, pitted and mashed
- ¾ cup almond milk
- ½ teaspoon vanilla extract

Directions:
1. In a blender, meld the bananas with the avocado and the other ingredients, pulse, divide into bowls and store in the fridge until serving.

Nutrition 185 Calories 4.3g Fat 6g Carbohydrates 6.45g Protein

973. Cold Lemon Squares

Preparation time: 30 minutes
Cooking time: 0 minutes
Servings: 4

Ingredients:
- 1 cup avocado oil+ a drizzle
- 2 bananas, peeled and chopped
- 1 tablespoon honey
- ¼ cup lemon juice
- A pinch of lemon zest, grated

Directions:
1. In your food processor, mix the bananas with the rest of the ingredients, pulse well and spread on the bottom of a pan greased with a drizzle of oil. Introduce in the fridge for 30 minutes, slice into squares and serve.

Nutrition 136 Calories 11.2g Fat 7g Carbohydrates 1.1g Protein

974. Blackberry and Apples Cobbler

Preparation Time: 10 minutes
Cooking Time: 30 minutes
Servings: 6
Ingredients:
- ¾ cup stevia
- 6 cups blackberries
- ¼ cup apples, cored and cubed
- ¼ teaspoon baking powder
- 1 tablespoon lime juice
- ½ cup almond flour
- ½ cup water
- 3 and ½ tablespoon avocado oil
- Cooking spray

Directions:
1. In a bowl, combine the berries with half of the stevia and lemon juice, sprinkle some flour all over, whisk and pour into a baking dish greased with cooking spray.
2. In another bowl, mix flour with the rest of the sugar, baking powder, the water and the oil, and stir the whole thing with your hands. Spread over the berries, introduce in the oven at 375 degrees F and bake for 30 minutes.
3. Serve warm.

Nutrition 221 Calories 6.3g Fat 6g Carbohydrates 9g Protein

975. Black Tea Cake

Preparation Time: 10 minutes
Cooking Time: 35 minutes
Servings: 8
Ingredients:
- 6 tablespoons black tea powder
- 2 cups almond milk, warmed up
- 1 cup avocado oil
- 2 cups stevia
- 4 eggs
- 2 teaspoons vanilla extract

- 3 and ½ cups almond flour
- 1 teaspoon baking soda
- 3 teaspoons baking powder

Directions:
1. Stir well the almond milk with the oil, stevia and the rest of the ingredients. Pour this into a cake pan lined with parchment paper, introduce in the oven at 350 degrees F and bake for 35 minutes. Leave the cake to cool down, slice and serve.

Nutrition 200 Calories 6.4g Fat 6.5g Carbohydrates 5.4g Protein

976. Green Tea and Vanilla Cream

Preparation Time: 2 hours
Cooking Time: 0 minutes
Servings: 4
Ingredients:
- 14 ounces almond milk, hot
- 2 tablespoons green tea powder
- 14 ounces heavy cream
- 3 tablespoons stevia
- 1 teaspoon vanilla extract
- 1 teaspoon gelatin powder

Directions:
1. Incorporate well the almond milk with the green tea powder and the rest of the ingredients, cool down, divide into cups and keep in the fridge for 2 hours before serving.

Nutrition 120 Calories 3g Fat 7g Carbohydrates 4g Protein

977. Figs Pie

Preparation Time: 10 minutes
Cooking Time: 1 hour
Servings: 8
Ingredients:
- ½ cup stevia
- 6 figs, cut into quarters
- ½ teaspoon vanilla extract
- 1 cup almond flour
- 4 eggs, whisked

Directions:
1. Spread the figs on the bottom of a springform pan lined with parchment paper. In a bowl, combine the other ingredients, whisk and pour over the figs. Bake at 375 digress F for 1 hour, flip the pie upside down when it's done and serve.

Nutrition 200 Calories 4.4g Fat 7.6g Carbohydrates 8g Protein

978. Cherry Cream

Preparation Time: 2 hours
Cooking Time: 0 minutes
Servings: 4
Ingredients:

- 2 cups cherries, pitted and chopped
- 1 cup almond milk
- ½ cup whipping cream
- 3 eggs, whisked
- 1/3 cup stevia
- 1 teaspoon lemon juice
- ½ teaspoon vanilla extract

Directions:
1. In your food processor, combine the cherries with the milk and the rest of the ingredients, pulse well, divide into cups and keep in the fridge for 2 hours before serving.

Nutrition 200 Calories 4.5g Fat 5.6g Carbohydrates 3.4g Protein

979. Strawberries Cream

Preparation Time: 10 minutes
Cooking Time: 20 minutes
Servings: 4
Ingredients:
- ½ cup stevia
- 2 pounds strawberries, chopped
- 1 cup almond milk
- Zest of 1 lemon, grated
- ½ cup heavy cream
- 3 egg yolks, whisked

Directions:
1. Heat up a pan with the milk over medium-high heat, add the stevia and the rest of the ingredients, whisk well, simmer for 20 minutes, divide into cups and serve cold.

Nutrition 152 Calories 4.4g Fat 5.1g Carbohydrates 0.8g Protein

980. Apples and Plum Cake

Preparation Time: 10 minutes
Cooking Time: 40 minutes
Servings: 4
Ingredients:
- 7 ounces almond flour
- 1 egg, whisked
- 5 tablespoons stevia
- 3 ounces warm almond milk
- 2 pounds plums, pitted
- 2 apples, cored and chopped
- Zest of 1 lemon, grated
- 1 tsp baking powder

Directions:
1. Blend well the almond milk with the egg, stevia, and the rest of the ingredients except the cooking spray
2. Grease a cake pan with the oil, pour the cake mix inside, introduce in the oven at 350 degrees F for 40 minutes.
3. Cool down, slice and serve.

Nutrition 209 Calories 6.4g Fat 8g Carbohydrates 6.6g Protein

981. Cinnamon Chickpeas Cookies

Preparation Time: 10 minutes
Cooking Time: 20 minutes
Servings: 12
Ingredients:
- 1 cup canned chickpeas
- 2 cups almond flour
- 1 teaspoon cinnamon powder
- 1 teaspoon baking powder
- 1 cup avocado oil
- ½ cup stevia
- 1 egg, whisked
- 2 teaspoons almond extract
- 1 cup raisins
- 1 cup coconut, unsweetened and shredded

Directions:
1. In a bowl, combine the chickpeas with the flour, cinnamon and the other ingredients, and whisk well until you obtain a dough.
2. Scoop tablespoons of dough on a baking sheet lined with parchment paper, introduce in oven for 20 minutes at 350 degrees. Let it cool and serve.

Nutrition 200 Calories 4.5g Fat 9.5g Carbohydrates 2.4g Protein

982. Cocoa Brownies

Preparation Time: 10 minutes
Cooking Time: 20 minutes
Servings: 8
Ingredients:
- 30 ounces canned lentils, rinsed and drained
- 1 tablespoon honey
- 1 banana, peeled and chopped
- ½ teaspoon baking soda
- 4 tablespoons almond butter
- 2 tablespoons cocoa powder
- Cooking spray

Directions:
1. In a food processor, pulse well the lentils with the honey and the other ingredients except the cooking spray.
2. Transfer this into a pan greased with cooking spray, lay evenly, introduce in the oven at 375 degrees F for 20 minutes. Slice the brownies and serve cold.

Nutrition 200 Calories 4.5g Fat 8.7g Carbohydrates 4.3g Protein

983. Cardamom Almond Cream

Preparation Time: 30 minutes
Cooking Time: 0 minutes
Servings: 4

Ingredients:
- Juice of 1 lime
- ½ cup stevia
- 1 and ½ cups water
- 3 cups almond milk
- ½ cup honey
- 2 teaspoons cardamom, ground
- 1 teaspoon rose water
- 1 teaspoon vanilla extract

Directions:
1. In a blender, blend well the almond milk with the cardamom and the rest of the ingredients, divide into cups and keep in the fridge for 30 minutes before serving.

Nutrition 283 Calories 11.8g Fat 4.7g Carbohydrates 7.1g Protein

984. Banana Cinnamon Cupcakes

Preparation Time: 10 minutes
Cooking Time: 20 minutes
Servings: 4
Ingredients:
- 4 tablespoons avocado oil
- 4 eggs
- ½ cup orange juice
- 2 teaspoons cinnamon powder
- 1 teaspoon vanilla extract
- 2 bananas, peeled and chopped
- ¾ cup almond flour
- ½ teaspoon baking powder
- Cooking spray

Directions:
1. In a bowl, combine the oil with the eggs, orange juice and the other ingredients except the cooking spray, whisk well, pour in a cupcake pan greased with the cooking spray. Introduce in oven for 20 minutes, at 350 degrees F.
2. Cool the cupcakes down and serve.

Nutrition 142 Calories 5.8g Fat 5.7g Carbohydrates 1.6g Protein

985. Rhubarb and Apples Cream

Preparation Time: 10 minutes
Cooking Time: 0 minutes
Servings: 6
Ingredients:
- 3 cups rhubarb, chopped
- 1 and ½ cups stevia
- 2 eggs, whisked
- ½ teaspoon nutmeg, ground
- 1 tablespoon avocado oil
- 1/3 cup almond milk

Directions:

1. In a blender, combine the rhubarb with the stevia and the rest of the ingredients, pulse well, divide into cups and serve cold.

Nutrition 200 Calories 5.2g Fat 7.6g Carbohydrates 2.5g Protein

986. Almond Rice Dessert

Preparation Time: 10 minutes
Cooking Time: 20 minutes
Servings: 4
Ingredients:
- 1 cup white rice
- 2 cups almond milk
- 1 cup almonds, chopped
- ½ cup stevia
- 1 tablespoon cinnamon powder
- ½ cup pomegranate seeds

Directions:
1. In a pot, incorporate the rice with the milk and stevia, bring to a simmer and cook for 20 minutes, stirring often. Add the rest of the ingredients, stir, divide into bowls and serve.

Nutrition 234 Calories 9.5g Fat 12.4g Carbohydrates 6.5g Protein

987. Mediterranean Baked Apples

Preparation Time: 5 minutes
Cooking Time: 25 minutes
Serving: 4
Ingredients:
- pounds apples, peeled and sliced
- Juice from ½ lemon
- A dash of cinnamon

Directions:
1. Preheat the oven to 2500 F. Line a baking sheet with parchment paper then set aside. In a medium bowl, apples with lemon juice and cinnamon. Place the apples on the parchment paper-lined baking sheet. Bake for 25 minutes until crisp.

Nutrition 90 Calories 0.3g Fat 23.9g Carbohydrates 0.5g Protein

988. Chia Almond Butter Pudding

Preparation Time: 5 minutes
Cooking Time: 10 minutes
Serving: 1
Ingredients:
- ¼ cup chia seeds
- 1 cup unsweetened almond milk
- 1 ½ tablespoons maple syrup
- 2 ½ tablespoons almond butter

Directions:
1. Add almond milk, maple syrup, and almond butter in a bowl and stir well. Add chia seeds and stir to

mix. Pour pudding mixture into the Mason jar and place it in the refrigerator overnight. Serve and enjoy.

Nutrition 354 Calories 21.3g Fat 31.1g Carbohydrates 11.2g Protein

989. Sweet Rice Pudding

Preparation Time: 10 minutes
Cooking Time: 30 minutes
Serving: 4
Ingredients:
- 1 ¼ cup of rice
- ¼ cup dark chocolate, chopped
- 1 teaspoon vanilla
- 1/3 cup coconut butter
- 1 teaspoon liquid stevia
- 2 ½ cup almond milk

Directions:
1. Incorporate all ingredients inside the inner pot and mix well. Cover and cook on high for 20 minutes. Once done, allow to release pressure naturally. Remove lid. Stir well and serve.

Nutrition 638 Calories 39.9g Fat 63.5g Carbohydrates 8.6g Protein

990. Creamy Yogurt Banana Bowls

Preparation Time: 15 minutes
Cooking Time: 0 minute
Serving: 4
Ingredients:
- 2 bananas, sliced
- ½ teaspoon ground nutmeg
- 3 tablespoon flaxseed meal
- ¼ cup creamy peanut butter
- 4 cups Greek yogurt

Directions:
1. Divide Greek yogurt between 4 serving bowls and top with sliced bananas. Add peanut butter in microwave-safe bowl and microwave for 30 seconds.
2. Drizzle 1 tablespoon of melted peanut butter on each bowl on top of the sliced bananas. Sprinkle cinnamon and flax meal on top and serve.

Nutrition 351 Calories 13.1g Fat 35.6g Carbohydrates 19.6g Protein

991. Lemon Pear Compote

Preparation Time: 5 minutes
Cooking Time: 15 minutes
Serving: 6
Ingredients:
- 3 cups pears, cored and cut into chunks
- 1 teaspoon vanilla
- 1 teaspoon liquid stevia
- 1 tablespoon lemon zest, grated
- 2 tablespoons lemon juice

Directions:
1. Stir all ingredients into the instant pot well. Cover and cook on high for 15 minutes. Once finished, release pressure naturally for 10 minutes then releases the remaining using quick release. Remove lid. Stir and serve.

Nutrition 50 Calories 0.2g Fat 12.7g Carbohydrates 0.4g Protein

992. Healthy & Quick Energy Bites

Preparation Time: 60 minutes
Cooking Time: 0 minute
Serving: 20
Ingredients:
- 2 cups cashew nuts
- ¼ teaspoon cinnamon
- 1 teaspoon lemon zest
- 4 tablespoons dates, chopped
- 1/3 cup unsweetened shredded coconut
- ¾ cup dried apricots

Directions:
1. Put parchment paper into the baking sheet and set aside. Add all ingredients in a food processor and process until the mixture is crumbly and well combined. Make small balls from mixture and place on a prepared baking tray. Place in refrigerator for 1 hour.
2. Serve and enjoy.

Nutrition 100 Calories 7.5g Fat 7.2g Carbohydrates 2.4g Protein

993. Healthy Coconut Blueberry Balls

Preparation Time: 60 minutes
Cooking Time: 5 minutes
Serving: 12
Ingredients:
- ¼ cup flaked coconut
- ¼ cup blueberries
- ½ teaspoon vanilla
- ¼ cup honey
- ½ cup creamy almond butter
- ¼ teaspoon cinnamon
- 1 ½ tablespoon chia seeds
- ¼ cup flaxseed meal
- 1 cup rolled oats, gluten-free

Directions:
1. In a large bowl, add oats, cinnamon, chia seeds, and flaxseed meal and mix well. Add almond butter in microwave-safe bowl and microwave for 30 seconds. Stir until smooth. Add vanilla and honey in melted almond butter and stir well.

2. Incorporate almond butter mixture over oat mixture and mix. Add coconut and blueberries and stir well. Make small balls from oat mixture and place onto the baking tray and place in the refrigerator for 1 hour. Serve and enjoy.

Nutrition 129 Calories 7.4g Fat 14.1g Carbohydrates 7g Protein

994. Panna Cotta

Preparation Time: 5 minutes
Cooking Time: 10 minutes + 4 hours
Servings: 2
Ingredients:
- 1/3 cup skim milk
- 1 (0.25-ounce) envelope unflavored gelatin
- 2½ cups heavy cream
- ½ cup white sugar
- 1½ tsps. vanilla extract
- 1/3 cup red berries for decoration

Directions
1. Place milk into a small bowl and stir in the envelope of gelatin. Set aside. Add the heavy cream and sugar to a saucepan, stirring, and set over medium-low heat. Watching carefully, let it come to a full boil.
2. Pour the gelatin-milk mixture into the cream, stirring until completely dissolved. Cook for one minute, stirring. Take away from heat, stir in the vanilla extract and pour into six ramekin dishes.
3. Allow to cool to room temperature. Before serving, cover with plastic wrap and freeze for at least 4 hours, but preferably overnight. Top with red berries before serving.

Nutrition 105 Calories 9g Fat 6g Carbohydrates 1g Protein

995. Turkish Kunefe

Preparation Time: 10 minutes
Cooking Time: 55 minutes
Servings: 2
Ingredients
For syrup:
- 1 cup sugar
- 1 slice of lemon
- 1 cup water
For kunefe:
- ½ cup butter melted to room temperature
- 1 tbsp butter for pans
- 2 cups shredded raw kadaifi dough
- ½ cup unsalted melting cheese of your choice
- 1 tbsp ground pistachios

Directions
1. In a pot, add all syrup ingredients.
2. Let it boil, then adjust heat and simmer for 15 minutes until it gets a little thicker. Allow to cool.
3. Preheat the stove to 400° F. Put kadaifi dough to a bowl and coat with ½ cup melted butter. Lightly brush the bottom of four 9-inch pans with melted butter.
4. Divide the half of the dough in two pans evenly. Press it with your hand. Sprinkle noodles with cheese evenly. Press with your hand.
5. Cover with the remaining kadaifi dough and press it with your hand. Put to oven and bake for 10-15 minutes or until the top is golden-brown.
6. Turn each of two extra pans over, carefully place it above the dessert and flip the dessert into that extra pan. Now golden-brown side is on the bottom. Put it back to oven and bake for 10-15 minutes more or until the top side is golden-brown as well.
7. As soon as you remove dessert from the stove, pour syrup over them. Allow syrup to absorb and serve immediately while it's still hot, topping with ground pistachios.

Nutrition 508 Calories 25g Fat 57g Carbohydrates 19g Protein

996. Crema Catalana

Preparation Time: 3 hours
Cooking Time: 10 minutes
Servings: 2
Ingredients
- 4 large egg yolks
- 1 cup sugar
- 1 cinnamon stick
- Zest of 1 lemon
- 2 cups whole milk
- 1 Tbsp cornstarch

Directions
1. Whisk ¾ cup sugar and the egg yolks in a large saucepan until the ingredients are thoroughly mixed and the mixture becomes frothy.
2. Add the lemon zest and cinnamon stick.
3. Add the cornstarch and milk and heat the mixture slowly, stirring constantly, just until it begins to thicken. Remove the pot from the heat immediately.
4. Pull out the cinnamon stick and fill the mixture into 2 ramekins to cool.
5. Cool to room temperature, then freeze for at least 2-3 hours.
6. Before serving, heat the broiler. Sprinkle the sugar over each ramekin. Place the ramekins under the broiler and let the sugar caramelize, bubble, and turn golden brown, about 5-10 minutes. Remove and serve immediately.

Nutrition 372 Calories 10g Fat 61g Carbohydrates 12g Protein

997. Spanish Dessert Turron

Preparation Time: 15 minutes
Cooking Time: 15 minutes
Servings: 2
Ingredients
- 1 cup baked almond

- 100 g honey
- 100 g sugar
- 2 pieces egg white
- 1-piece waffles
- 1 cup hazelnut

Directions
1. Add nuts in a blender and chop for 10-15 seconds. Keep large pieces.
2. Cover baking form using a waffle paper.
3. Combine sugar and honey in a saucepan and melt on low heat.
4. Whisk egg whites. Combine nuts with egg whites and stir gently. Add nut paste to honey mix and cook for 10 minutes more on very low heat. It should have a light caramel color.
5. Spread it evenly onto the baking form. Let it chill in a cold place, and NOT IN THE FRIDGE.

Nutrition 216 Calories 14g Fat 16g Carbohydrates 6g Protein

998. Palacinke Serbian Pancake

Preparation Time: 5 minutes
Cooking Time: 15 minutes
Servings: 2
Ingredients
- 1 cup flour
- 2 eggs
- ½ cup milk
- ½ cup water
- ¼ tsp salt
- 2 tbsp butter, melted

Directions
1. Mix all components until you get a homogeneous batter. Break apart any granules.
2. Grease a crepe pan with oil or melted butter. Wait till it's hot.
3. Pour enough batter to coat the whole pan with one thin layer, swirling your wrist while you holding the pan.
4. If you lift a corner of crepe off the pan, using a knife, and it doesn't stick, then it's ready to be flipped over. Transfer to the plate when it's golden.
5. Repeat for the rest batter. Makes two portions of five thin pancakes.

Nutrition 140 Calories 8g Fat 15g Carbohydrates 4g Protein

999. Almond Tangerine Panna Cotta

Preparation Time: 15 minutes
Cooking Time: 1 hour and 15 minutes
Servings: 2
Ingredients
- 1½ tbsp sugar
- ¾ tsp unflavored gelatin
- ½ cup fat-free milk
- ½ cup plain Greek yogurt
- ¼ tsp almond extract

For sauce
- 1 tbsp sugar
- 1 tsp cornstarch
- 1/3 cup pomegranate or cranberry juice
- ½ cup tangerine sections
- 2 tbsp snipped dried tart cherries

Directions
1. Place 4 6 oz ramekins in a baking pan. Mix gelatin and sugar in a saucepan. Add in milk, and dissolve gelatin heating it and stirring over medium heat.
2. Remove from heat, add in yogurt and ¼ almond extract and whisk until smooth. Pour mixture in ramekins, cover, and chill for 4-24 hours to let it set.
3. To make sauce, mix cornstarch and sugar in a small saucepan. Add in pomegranate juice, and cook until thickened and bubbling over medium heat, stirring all the time.
4. Remove from heat, and add in tangerine, cherries, and ¼ tsp almond extract. Let it cool.
5. When ready to serve, immerse bottom half of ramekins for 10 seconds in hot water. Using a sharp knife, loosen panna cotta from the ramekin's sides. Invert a plate over each cup and turn it together. Remove cups and serve panna cotta with sauce.

Nutrition 193 Calories 13g Fat 16g Carbohydrates 3g Protein

1000. Zabaglione with Strawberries

Preparation Time: 5 minutes
Cooking Time: 10 minutes
Servings: 2
Ingredients
- 4 egg yolks, at room temperature
- ½ cup dry marsala
- ¼ cup sugar
- ½ pint strawberries, sliced

Directions
1. Add egg yolks, marsala, and sugar into a double boiler.
2. Beat mixture for 4-7 minutes with hand mixer on low until it is hot and forms a ribbon when the beaters are lifted. DO NOT cook mixture for too long, or it will start to curdle.
3. Put strawberries in the glasses. Top with the hot zabaglione and serve or refrigerate it for 1 hour.

Nutrition 205 Calories 11g Fat 30g Carbohydrates 7g Protein

1001. Muhalabieh

Preparation Time: 10 minutes
Cooking Time: 10 minutes
Servings: 2

Ingredients

- ½ cup (250 ml) milk
- 1/8 cup (50 grams) sugar
- ¾ tbsp corn flour
- ¼ tbsp rose water
- pistachios for garnish

Directions

1. Heat milk over medium in a saucepan. Add sugar, corn flour, and rose water. Whisk until milk starts to get thicker.
2. When it starts to get a cream-like consistency, remove from heat. Prepare 4 glass bowls, and divide the mixture between them. Allow to cool down, then place in the fridge and chill for 2 hours.
3. When completely chilled, flip over on a serving plate and garnish with chopped pistachios.

Nutrition 162 Calories 3g Fat 36g Carbohydrates 4g Protein

30-DAY MEAL PLAN

DAY	BREAKFAST	POULTRY AND MEAT	SIDE DISH	DESSERT
1	Avocado Egg Scramble	Chicken Shawarma	Springtime Quinoa Salad	Vanilla Cream
2	Breakfast Tostadas	Honey Balsamic Chicken	Seafood Souvlaki Bowl	Blueberries Bowls
3	Parmesan Omelet	Garlic and Lemon Chicken Dish	Spaghetti Niçoise	Brownies
4	Watermelon Pizza	Crispy Mediterranean Chicken Thighs	Mediterranean Tostadas	Strawberries Coconut Cake
5	Ham Muffins	Greek Penne and Chicken	Vegetable Ratatouille	Cocoa Almond Pudding
6	Banana Quinoa	Yogurt-Marinated Chicken Kebabs	Citrus Cups	Vanilla Avocado Cream
7	Cauliflower Fritters	Zaatar Chicken Tenders	Mediterranean Frittata	Watermelon Salad
8	Avocado Egg Scramble	Chicken Shawarma	Springtime Quinoa Salad	Vanilla Cream
9	Breakfast Tostadas	Honey Balsamic Chicken	Seafood Souvlaki Bowl	Blueberries Bowls
10	Parmesan Omelet	Garlic and Lemon Chicken Dish	Spaghetti Niçoise	Brownies
11	Watermelon Pizza	Crispy Mediterranean Chicken Thighs	Mediterranean Tostadas	Strawberries Coconut Cake
12	Ham Muffins	Greek Penne and Chicken	Vegetable Ratatouille	Cocoa Almond Pudding
13	Banana Quinoa	Yogurt-Marinated Chicken Kebabs	Citrus Cups	Vanilla Avocado Cream
14	Cauliflower Fritters	Zaatar Chicken Tenders	Mediterranean Frittata	Watermelon Salad
15	Avocado Egg Scramble	Chicken Shawarma	Springtime Quinoa Salad	Vanilla Cream
16	Breakfast Tostadas	Honey Balsamic Chicken	Seafood Souvlaki Bowl	Blueberries Bowls
17	Parmesan Omelet	Garlic and Lemon Chicken Dish	Spaghetti Niçoise	Brownies
18	Watermelon Pizza	Crispy Mediterranean Chicken Thighs	Mediterranean Tostadas	Strawberries Coconut Cake
19	Ham Muffins	Greek Penne and Chicken	Vegetable Ratatouille	Cocoa Almond Pudding
20	Banana Quinoa	Yogurt-Marinated Chicken Kebabs	Citrus Cups	Vanilla Avocado Cream
21	Cauliflower Fritters	Zaatar Chicken Tenders	Mediterranean Frittata	Watermelon Salad
22	Avocado Egg Scramble	Chicken Shawarma	Springtime Quinoa Salad	Vanilla Cream
23	Breakfast Tostadas	Honey Balsamic Chicken	Seafood Souvlaki Bowl	Blueberries Bowls
24	Parmesan Omelet	Garlic and Lemon Chicken Dish	Spaghetti Niçoise	Brownies
25	Watermelon Pizza	Crispy Mediterranean Chicken Thighs	Mediterranean Tostadas	Strawberries Coconut Cake
26	Ham Muffins	Greek Penne and Chicken	Vegetable Ratatouille	Cocoa Almond Pudding
27	Banana Quinoa	Yogurt-Marinated Chicken Kebabs	Citrus Cups	Vanilla Avocado Cream
28	Cauliflower Fritters	Zaatar Chicken Tenders	Mediterranean Frittata	Watermelon Salad
29	Avocado Egg Scramble	Chicken Shawarma	Springtime Quinoa Salad	Vanilla Cream
30	Breakfast Tostadas	Honey Balsamic Chicken	Seafood Souvlaki Bowl	Blueberries Bowls

CONCLUSION

The Mediterranean diet is straightforward, simple, and mouth-watering; your transition to the diet will be a lot smoother and easier if you do a little bit of preparation ahead of time.

The health benefit of following the Mediterranean Lifestyle is enormous. It offers well-rounded benefits that encourage optimum physical, emotional, social and mental well-being. No one is as positively charged and healthy as this. Hence, take what you have taken in and kick-start your journey to a great beginning.

No matter if you are taking your first walk down the path of the Mediterranean Lifestyle, or if you are starting to work on a new chapter in your journey, it is essential to have some basic knowledge and tools that will guide you through this process. A little preparation will make all of the difference.

The first thing to do is to clear out anything that contains any kind of unhealthy ingredient or ingredient that you know you don't like. It will be hard at first, but you will get used to it, and over time you won't even think about it.

The next thing to do is to start a food journal. You should keep track of the different ingredients that you are about to add into your diet and the way they make you feel. This way, if one of these ingredients is not good for you, you'll know it right away. That is to say, if you find that you don't feel good after eating pasta, then you will know not to eat it anymore. By doing this, you'll realize that the Mediterranean lifestyle is not only about the food, but also about what we put into our bodies.

Another thing that people usually do wrong is they skip breakfast. Breakfast is a very important meal and should start your day right.

The next thing to do is to set a small goal for you. For example, you can start with drinking a glass of extra virgin olive oil in the morning on an empty stomach. This way, you'll get used to the taste. You should keep track of your goal and how you are feeling each time you reach it.

If this is all too much for you right now, then just start with making one small change at a time until you get used to it.

As long as you do this and stick to the simple rules of a Mediterranean diet, you can attain all the benefits it offers. One of the main benefits of this diet is that it is perfectly sustainable in the long run, not to mention, it is mouth-watering and delicious.

Once you start implementing the various protocols of this diet, you will see a positive change in your overall health. Ensure that you are being patient with yourself and stick to your diet without making any excuses.

Shifting to a new diet making a lifestyle change can be tough! This cookbook will allow you gradually manage this journey and help you understand everything you need to know in this culinary tradition and finally benefit from it in the long run.